Take a trip to

NEPAL

Keith Lye

Franklin Watts

London   New York   Sydney   Toronto

Facts about Nepal

Area:
140,797 sq. km
(54,362 sq. miles)

Population:
17,422,000

Capital:
Kathmandu

Largest cities:
Kathmandu (235,000)
Biratnagar (94,000)
Patan (80,000)
Bhaktapur (48,000)

Official language:
Nepali

Religion:
Hinduism (90%),
Buddhism, Islam

Main exports:
Grains, jute, timber,
oilseeds, ghee (a kind
of butter), potatoes

Currency:
Rupee

Franklin Watts
12a Golden Square
London W1

Franklin Watts Inc.
387 Park Avenue South
New York, N.Y. 10016

ISBN: UK Edition 0 86313 718 0
ISBN: US Edition 0 531 10557–1
Library of Congress Catalog
Card No: 87-51702

Typeset by Ace Filmsetting Ltd.,
Frome, Somerset
Printed in Hong Kong

© Franklin Watts Limited 1988

Maps: Simon Roulstone

Design: Pritilata Chauhan

Stamps: Harry Allen International
Philatelic Distributors

Photographs: Neil Ardley, 3, 4, 5, 7, 10,
14, 16, 18, 24, 25, 28, 29, 30; Chris
Fairclough, 8; Hutchison Library, 11;
Keith Lye, 6, 12, 13, 15, 17, 19, 20, 21, 22,
23, 26, 27, 31

Front Cover: Neil Ardley
Back Cover: Neil Ardley

The Kingdom of Nepal is a beautiful, landlocked country in Asia. It is bordered by India and Tibet in China. The world's highest mountain range, the Himalayas, covers much of Nepal. The Himalayas are called the "Roof of the World". Nepal has eight peaks which are more than 8,000 m (26,504 ft) high.

Annapurna in Nepal is one of the world's highest mountains. It is 8,078 m (26,504 ft) high. It was first climbed in 1950. The Himalayan peaks are a challenge to the many mountaineers who visit Nepal every year.

Dhaulagiri, west of Annapurna, is
an even higher peak. It is 8,172 m
(26,810 ft) high. Few people live in
the mountainous parts of Nepal,
because the long winters are bitterly
cold and the short summers are cool.

Sheltered valleys lie in the foothills of the Himalayas. The Kathmandu valley is a fertile region. About two-thirds of Nepal's people live in this valley. The valleys have a cool climate, with heavy rain in summer.

A low-lying region, called the
Terai, is in southern Nepal. It is a
hot, wet region, with thick forests and
steamy swamps. Farmers grow such
crops as rice and sugar cane. About
a third of Nepal's people live in the
Terai.

The picture shows some stamps and money used in Nepal. The main unit of currency is the rupee, which contains 100 paisas.

WORLD
MAP
NEPAL
HIMALAYAN
MOUNTAINS
CHINA (TIBET)
Dhaulagiri
Annapurna
NEPAL
Terai
Pokhara
Everest
Kanchenjunga
Kathmandu
Chitwan
N. P.
Bhaktapur
Patan
Terai
Biratnagar
INDIA
INDIA
BANGLADESH
9

About 36 languages and dialects are spoken in Nepal. Ethnic groups include the Gurung, Newar, Tamang and Sherpa, who are great mountaineers. A Sherpa, Tenzing Norgay, and a New Zealander, Edmund Hillary, were the first to climb Mount Everest, the highest mountain in the world.

Nepalese soldiers are called
Gurkhas. Many Gurkhas have served
in the armies of Britain and India.
They are known for their bravery.
Gurkha soldiers served in both World
Wars. They also took part in the
Falkland Islands conflict in 1982.

People of Indian and Tibetan origin also live in Nepal. Many Tibetan refugees settled in Nepal in the 1950s, when Chinese troops occupied Tibet. The picture shows a Tibetan Buddhist shrine at Jawalkhel, near Patan.

Kathmandu is the capital of Nepal. It was founded by the Newars in AD 723. It became the capital in the late 18th century, after the many small kingdoms in the area had been united to form the modern country of Nepal.

The Royal Palace is in central Kathmandu. But the King of Nepal now lives in another, modern palace. King Bavendra heads the government. He can veto laws passed by the National Panchayat (or parliament).

About nine out of every ten Nepalis are Hindus, but many Hindus follow a mixture of Hindu and Buddhist beliefs. There are also some Buddhists and Muslims. Nyatapola temple in Bhaktapur is the highest in Nepal.

Durbar Square in Patan contains many temples and religious monuments. Only seven out of every hundred people live in cities. The rest live in the countryside. Many people live in cities but work on farms nearby.

Flat land is scarce in Nepal. Farmers have built step-like terraces on valley slopes to create fields. Farmland covers 16 per cent of Nepal, and grazing land covers 14 per cent. Farming employs 93 out of every 100 workers.

Grains, including millet, rice and wheat, are leading crops. This field of millet is near Pokhara. Nepal is one of the world's ten poorest countries. Because of poverty and disease, the average life of a person is only 47 years.

18

Most farming is done by hand. This picture shows farmers threshing wheat in central Bhaktapur. They have carried the sheaves of wheat into the city. Nepal exports farm products. It imports fuels and manufactured goods.

Some farmers keep livestock, including buffaloes, cattle, sheep and goats. Hindus regard cattle as sacred animals and do not kill them. Cows wander through the streets of Kathmandu and often eat the vegetables on display.

Nepal has some factories which produce goods for everyday use, such as pottery, food, cigarettes and shoes. There are also jute, sugar, cement and iron factories. But industries employ only one out of every hundred workers.

Many countries give aid to Nepal. Nepal is building roads, improving health services and starting new industries. Nepal has few resources, but several hydroelectric power stations have been built on the rivers.

Nepal does not have enough
schools and teachers for all its
children. New schools are being built,
but about four out of every five
people in Nepal cannot read or
write. This school is at Jawalkhel,
near Patan.

Nepal's population is increasing quickly and the country lacks enough services to look after its young people. Another problem facing Nepal is that only 58 per cent of the people speak the official language, Nepali.

Most houses in Nepal are made of brick or stone. The walls are thick to keep out the cold. In villages, many of the houses are small but larger houses are common in the cities.

Street markets provide fresh food for shoppers. Many stalls in the central parts of cities are set up on the steps of temples. People often use spices when cooking their food. Many Nepalese dishes are similar to Indian ones.

The Nepalis are religious people.
They have many religious festivals.
The chariot in the picture is used to
carry a depiction of a god,
Machendra, around Patan (usually
in May). Machendra is regarded as a
god of rain and plenty.

Nepal is a remote country. But it attracts tourists. In 1984, about 177,000 tourists visited Nepal. Some tourists go on treks through Nepal's spectacular mountain regions. They walk for about five to six hours a day.

Groups of people go on treks lasting several days. Sherpas and other Nepalese porters carry the equipment, tents and food. People who go on treks must be fit and prepared to sleep in simple rest houses or tents.

The Terai has plenty of wild
animals, including leopards, tigers
and rhinoceroses. The Chitwan
National Park near the Indian border
attracts many tourists. Visitors can
see the wildlife from shelters, or hides,
or from the backs of elephants.

30

One of Nepal's tourist attractions is a flight along the Himalayas to see the world's highest mountain. Mount Everest is 8,848 m (29,028 ft) high. It is on Nepal's border with Tibet. In the picture, Everest is the mountain just above the tip of the aircraft's wing.

Index

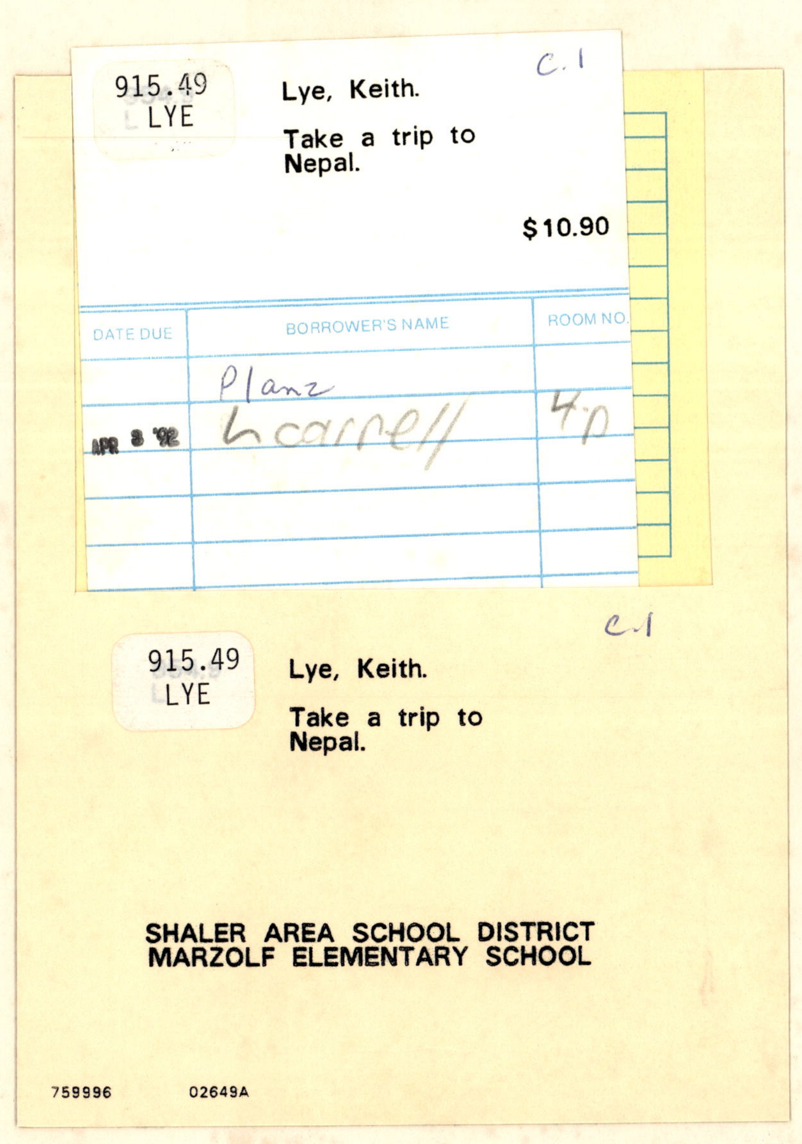

915.49
LYE
Lye, Keith.
Take a trip to Nepal.
C.1
$10.90
DATE DUE
BORROWER'S NAME
ROOM NO.
Planz
APR 3 92
Lcarrell
4p
915.49
LYE
Lye, Keith.
Take a trip to Nepal.
C.1
SHALER AREA SCHOOL DISTRICT
MARZOLF ELEMENTARY SCHOOL
759996
02649A

Autophagy in Tissue Injury and Homeostasis

Editor

Pei-Hui Lin

MDPI • Basel • Beijing • Wuhan • Barcelona • Belgrade • Manchester • Tokyo • Cluj • Tianjin

Editor
Pei-Hui Lin
The Ohio State University
USA

Editorial Office
MDPI
St. Alban-Anlage 66
4052 Basel, Switzerland

This is a reprint of articles from the Special Issue published online in the open access journal *Cells* (ISSN 2073-4409) (available at: https://www.mdpi.com/journal/cells/special_issues/tissue_injury).

For citation purposes, cite each article independently as indicated on the article page online and as indicated below:

LastName, A.A.; LastName, B.B.; LastName, C.C. Article Title. *Journal Name* **Year**, *Volume Number*, Page Range.

ISBN 978-3-03943-781-8 (Hbk)
ISBN 978-3-03943-782-5 (PDF)

Autophagy in Tissue Injury and Homeostasis

About the Editor

Pei-Hui Lin holds degrees in pharmacy (B.S.), microbiology and immunology (M.S.), and molecular and cell biology (Ph.D.), with previous appointments at Rutgers University/The University of Medicine and Dentistry of New Jersey (UMDNJ), and a current appointment at The Ohio State University Wexner Medical Center. Dr. Lin's research focuses on employing various transgenic animal models as tools to study mitochondrial homeostasis in skeletal muscle lysosomal function; the function of circulating microvesicles from muscle as myokines in organ crosstalk for tissue protection; and their roles in inflammation and immune modulation during tissue injury and viral infection. In addition, Dr. Lin's scholarly activities also focus on Ca signaling crosstalk among intracellular organelles (endoplasmic reticulum (ER), mitochondria, and nucleus) in cellular and muscle physiology.

Editorial

Advances in Autophagy, Tissue Injury, and Homeostasis: *Cells* Special Issue

Pei-Hui Lin [1,2]

[1]   Davis Heart and Lung Research Institute, The Ohio State University, Columbus, OH 43210, USA;
      Pei-Hui.Lin@osumc.edu
[2]   Department of Surgery, The Ohio State University Wexner Medical Center, Columbus, OH 43210, USA

Received: 12 July 2019; Accepted: 15 July 2019; Published: 19 July 2019

Macroautophagy (hereafter referred to as autophagy, a word derived from Greek meaning "auto-digestion") is a lysosome-dependent quality control process to degrade and turnover damaged or senescent organelles and proteins for cellular renewal. This essential process occurs in many eukaryotes to determine the cellular fitness and tissue homeostasis of organisms. Basal autophagy plays important roles during development and differentiation. Remarkably, autophagy is also a defense mechanism employed against environmental stress such as nutrient deprivation, aging, pathogen invasion, and various disease states [1]. As such, autophagy is an inducible and highly regulated process via a versatile regulatory network to intimately control several vital cellular responses, including inflammation, cell death, energy metabolism, organelles' (mitochondria and others) homeostasis, and aging. Although the role of autophagy in the maintenance of tissue homeostasis is relatively better documented, its role during tissue injury and regeneration is still emerging.

In this Special Issue, we focus on the roles of autophagy in systemic, specific tissue (organs and cells) injury or organ failure associated with sepsis, inflammation, metabolic disorder, toxic chemicals, ischemic–reperfusion, hypoxic oxidative stress, tissue fibrosis, trauma, nutrient starvation, cancer biology, and aging. This Special Issue contains 5 research papers and 10 review articles addressing the impact of autophagy on various organ injuries and homeostasis. Each of the reviews is authored by experts in their fields and our intention is to provide comprehensive updates in specific areas relating autophagy to tissue injury and homeostasis in which there has been considerable recent progress. The knowledge gained from the identification and characterization of new molecular mechanisms will shed light on biomedical applications for tissue protection through the modulation of autophagy.

Three articles focus on the role of mitochondrial ubiquitin kinase PINK1 and Parkin E3 ubiquitin ligase (PINK1/Parkin)-dependent mitophagy in organ homeostasis. Work by Zhou et al. [2] demonstrated the role of Notoginsenoside R1 (NGR1), a plant saponin extract, in ameliorating diabetic retinopathy through the PINK1-dependent activation of mitophagy and inhibition of apoptosis, oxidative stress in high glucose-stressed cultured rat retinal Müller cells (rMC-1) and retina tissue of *db/db* mice. Eid et al.'s [3] pioneering study elucidated the involvement of the PINK1/Parkin-dependent mitophagy pathway in acute ethanol intake-induced mitochondrial damage in Sertoli cells (SCs), the somatic cells of the testis which are essential for testis formation and spermatogenesis, in adult rats. This study is useful for the scientific community as it could help to define new therapeutic strategies by stimulating Parkin-mediated mitophagy in alcohol-related organ damage. Caloric restriction (or diet restriction, DR) is the best known strategy to robustly improve health, lifespan, and age-associated disease [4]. Diet restriction offers benefits against acute kidney injury (AKI) in young rats; however, such DR benefits are lost in aged animals encountering AKI due to the deterioration in the autophagy/mitophagy flux [5].

Metformin, a biguanide drug, is the most commonly prescribed drug for the treatment of type 2 diabetes as a glucose-lowering and insulin-sensitizing agent. Previous work has shown that metformin disrupts mitochondria energetics and represses the mechanistic target of rapamycin complex

1 (mTORC1) signaling in cancer cells [6]. Saladini et al. [7] demonstrated that the anti-tumoral action of metformin is due to the inhibition of glutaminase and autophagy has the potential to improve the efficacy of chemotherapy. Exosomes (and the containing paracrine factors) derived from mesenchymal stem/stromal cells (MSCs) have been demonstrated to hold great potential in regenerative medicine [8]. Ebrahim et al. [9] examined how MSC-derived exosomes attenuated diabetic nephropathy in a rat model of streptozotocin-induced diabetes through a mechanism of enhanced autophagy.

In the review articles, we included topics summarizing the current progress on the cardioprotective effects of autophagy in sepsis [10]. The specific activation of autophagy initiation factor Beclin-1 in protecting cardiac mitochondria, attenuating inflammation, and improving cardiac function in septic injury was discussed [10] (also see the comments in Reference [11]). Autophagy in various lung diseases, including acute lung injury (ALI), infectious disease, chronic obstructive pulmonary disease (COPD), idiopathic pulmonary fibrosis (IPF), pulmonary arterial hypertension (PAH), cystic fibrosis (CF), and tuberculosis are discussed [12]. Lin et al. [13] discussed the current concepts of autophagy and its molecular pathophysiologies in different kidney cell types with AKI, chronic kidney disease, drug nephrotoxicity, and aging kidneys. Some therapeutics targeting autophagy in kidney diseases are also summarized.

Two articles summarized the contribution of autophagy in the homeostasis and pathogenesis of the intestine, focusing on inflammatory bowel disease (IBD) from the aspects of intestinal innate immune cells response [14] and the clinical relevance of several autophagy-related genes (ATGs) in the pathogenesis of IBD [15]. These underscore the connection of autophagy in regulating innate immune functions such as inflammatory cytokines production and the cross-talk between various immune cells and intestine cells.

Weiskirchen and Tacke [16] excellently summarized the current knowledge on the role and mechanisms of autophagy in multiple liver cell types in health and disease. The normal hepatic functions such as gluconeogenesis, glycogenolysis, fatty acid oxidation, and disorders such as hereditary liver diseases, alcoholic liver disease, non-alcoholic fatty liver disease, hepatic fibrosis, and hepatocellular carcinoma (HCC) are discussed. Importantly, the opposing functions of autophagy in stage-specific pathogenesis in fibrosis and HCC are also discussed. The dual roles of autophagy in HCC is further supported by Yazdani et al. [17]. Both pro- and anti-tumorigenic autophagy are described for HCC. Therefore, it is critical to concisely develop autophagy-related pharmacological target therapies.

Lee et al. [18] offer a timely summarization of autophagy in skeletal muscle regeneration in aging. As the skeletal muscle is the largest organ in the body with remarkable regenerative capacity and regulation of energy metabolism and body activities, autophagy critically impacts muscle physiology. The effects of aging on autophagy, the role of myofibers, satellite (stem) cells as well as the immune system (mainly macrophages) during muscle repair/regeneration are discussed. Some rejuvenation strategies that alter autophagy to improve muscle regenerative function are also proposed. Sanchez et al. [19] reviewed the current knowledge on physical exercise's role in the regulation of cellular component turnover through multiple mechanisms involving autophagy, organelles' quality control, energy sensors, and anabolic signaling. This knowledge is critical in the design of exercise regiments and nutritional interventions and the development of countermeasures during illness.

Finally, Wu et al. [20] discussed the recent development of dual roles, both beneficial and detrimental, of autophagy to neurotrauma after spinal cord and brain injury (SCI/TBI). It is suggested that impairment of autophagic flux could serve as a secondary injury process of SCI/TBI. Moreover, modulation of the autophagy–lysosomal pathway could be with therapeutic potential in neurotrauma and neuroinflammation conditions.

The 15 publications in this Special Issue summarize the significant amount of progress that has contributed to our understanding of autophagy in normal tissue homeostasis and in disease states during dysfunction. Importantly, these publications provide future research directions for the design of therapeutic strategies targeting autophagy to combat disease and tissue injuries. I wish to thank all the authors for their contributions, the scientific communities for peer reviewing, and the staff at the *Cells* editorial office for their work on this Special Issue.

Conflicts of Interest: The author declares no conflict of interest.

References

1. Giampieri, F.; Afrin, S.; Forbes-Hernandez, T.Y.; Gasparrini, M.; Cianciosi, D.; Reboredo-Rodriguez, P.; Varela-Lopez, A.; Quiles, J.L.; Battino, M. Autophagy in Human Health and Disease: Novel Therapeutic Opportunities. *Antioxid. Redox Signal.* **2019**, *30*, 577–634. [CrossRef] [PubMed]
2. Zhou, P.; Xie, W.; Meng, X.; Zhai, Y.; Dong, X.; Zhang, X.; Sun, G.; Sun, X. Notoginsenoside R1 Ameliorates Diabetic Retinopathy through PINK1-Dependent Activation of Mitophagy. *Cells* **2019**, *8*, 213. [CrossRef] [PubMed]
3. Eid, N.; Ito, Y.; Horibe, A.; Otsuki, Y.; Kondo, Y. Ethanol-Induced Mitochondrial Damage in Sertoli Cells is Associated with Parkin Overexpression and Activation of Mitophagy. *Cells* **2019**, *8*, 283. [CrossRef]
4. Madeo, F.; Carmona-Gutierrez, D.; Hofer, S.J.; Kroemer, G. Caloric Restriction Mimetics against Age-Associated Disease: Targets, Mechanisms, and Therapeutic Potential. *Cell Metab.* **2019**, *29*, 592–610. [CrossRef]
5. Andrianova, N.V.; Jankauskas, S.S.; Zorova, L.D.; Pevzner, I.B.; Popkov, V.A.; Silachev, D.N.; Plotnikov, E.Y.; Zorov, D.B. Mechanisms of Age-Dependent Loss of Dietary Restriction Protective Effects in Acute Kidney Injury. *Cells* **2018**, *7*, 178. [CrossRef] [PubMed]
6. Wu, L.; Zhou, B.; Oshiro-Rapley, N.; Li, M.; Paulo, J.A.; Webster, C.M.; Mou, F.; Kacergis, M.C.; Talkowski, M.E.; Carr, C.E.; et al. An Ancient, Unified Mechanism for Metformin Growth Inhibition in C. elegans and Cancer. *Cell* **2016**, *167*, 1705–1718. [CrossRef] [PubMed]
7. Saladini, S.; Aventaggiato, M.; Barreca, F.; Morgante, E.; Sansone, L.; Russo, M.A.; Tafani, M. Metformin Impairs Glutamine Metabolism and Autophagy in Tumour Cells. *Cells* **2019**, *8*, 49. [CrossRef] [PubMed]
8. Zhao, T.; Sun, F.; Liu, J.; Ding, T.; She, J.; Mao, F.; Xu, W.; Qian, H.; Yan, Y. Emerging Role of Mesenchymal Stem Cell-derived Exosomes in Regenerative Medicine. *Curr. Stem Cell Res. Ther.* **2019**. [CrossRef]
9. Ebrahim, N.; Ahmed, I.A.; Hussien, N.I.; Dessouky, A.A.; Farid, A.S.; Elshazly, A.M.; Mostafa, O.; Gazzar, W.B.E.; Sorour, S.M.; Seleem, Y.; et al. Mesenchymal Stem Cell-Derived Exosomes Ameliorated Diabetic Nephropathy by Autophagy Induction through the mTOR Signaling Pathway. *Cells* **2018**, *7*, 226. [CrossRef]
10. Sun, Y.; Cai, Y.; Zang, Q.S. Cardiac Autophagy in Sepsis. *Cells* **2019**, *8*, 141. [CrossRef] [PubMed]
11. Abdellatif, M.; Sedej, S.; Madeo, F.; Kroemer, G. Cardioprotective effects of autophagy induction in sepsis. *Ann. Transl. Med.* **2018**, *6*. [CrossRef] [PubMed]
12. Wang, K.; Chen, Y.; Zhang, P.; Lin, P.; Xie, N.; Wu, M. Protective Features of Autophagy in Pulmonary Infection and Inflammatory Diseases. *Cells* **2019**, *8*, 123. [CrossRef] [PubMed]
13. Lin, T.A.; Wu, V.C.; Wang, C.Y. Autophagy in Chronic Kidney Diseases. *Cells* **2019**, *8*, 61. [CrossRef] [PubMed]
14. Iida, T.; Yokoyama, Y.; Wagatsuma, K.; Hirayama, D.; Nakase, H. Impact of Autophagy of Innate Immune Cells on Inflammatory Bowel Disease. *Cells* **2018**, *8*, 7. [CrossRef]
15. Kim, S.; Eun, H.S.; Jo, E.K. Roles of Autophagy-Related Genes in the Pathogenesis of Inflammatory Bowel Disease. *Cells* **2019**, *8*, 77. [CrossRef] [PubMed]
16. Weiskirchen, R.; Tacke, F. Relevance of Autophagy in Parenchymal and Non-Parenchymal Liver Cells for Health and Disease. *Cells* **2019**, *8*, 16. [CrossRef] [PubMed]
17. Yazdani, H.O.; Huang, H.; Tsung, A. Autophagy: Dual Response in the Development of Hepatocellular Carcinoma. *Cells* **2019**, *8*, 91. [CrossRef] [PubMed]
18. Lee, D.E.; Bareja, A.; Bartlett, D.B.; White, J.P. Autophagy as a Therapeutic Target to Enhance Aged Muscle Regeneration. *Cells* **2019**, *8*, 183. [CrossRef] [PubMed]

19. Sanchez, A.M.; Candau, R.; Bernardi, H. Recent Data on Cellular Component Turnover: Focus on Adaptations to Physical Exercise. *Cells* **2019**, *8*, 542. [CrossRef] [PubMed]
20. Wu, J.; Lipinski, M.M. Autophagy in Neurotrauma: Good, Bad, or Dysregulated. *Cells* **2019**, *8*, 693. [CrossRef] [PubMed]

Article

Ethanol-Induced Mitochondrial Damage in Sertoli Cells is Associated with Parkin Overexpression and Activation of Mitophagy

Nabil Eid [1,*], **Yuko Ito** [1], **Akio Horibe** [2], **Yoshinori Otsuki** [3] **and Yoichi Kondo** [1]

[1] Department of Anatomy and Cell Biology, Division of Life Sciences, Osaka Medical College, 2-7 Daigaku-machi, Takatsuki, Osaka 569-8686, Japan; an1006@osaka-med.ac.jp (Y.I.); konchan@osaka-med.ac.jp (Y.K.)
[2] Kubomizuki lady's clinic 3-13-8, Mikatadai, Nishi-ku, Kobe, Hyogo 651-2277, Japan; horibe@kubomizuki.or.jp
[3] Osaka Medical College, 2-7 Daigaku-machi, Takatsuki, Osaka, 569-8686, Japan; y.otsuki@osaka-med.ac.jp
* Correspondence: nabil@osaka-med.ac.jp or nabileidm@yahoo.com; Tel.: +81-72-684-7197; Fax: +81-72-684-6511

Received: 15 February 2019; Accepted: 23 March 2019; Published: 25 March 2019

Abstract: This study was conducted to elucidate the involvement of the PINK1-Parkin pathway in ethanol-induced mitophagy among Sertoli cells (SCs). In the research, adult rats were given intraperitoneal injections of ethanol (5 gm/kg) and sacrificed at various time periods within 24 h. Transmission electron microscopy was applied to reveal enhanced mitochondrial damage in SCs of the ethanol-treated rats (ETRs) in association with a significant increase in numbers of mitophagic vacuoles (mitophagosomes and autolysosomes) in contrast to very low levels in a control group treated with phosphate-buffered saline (PBS). This enhancement was ultra-structurally verified via observation of trapped mitochondria within LC3-labeled membranes, upregulation of LC3 protein levels, colocalization of LC3 and cytochrome c, and reduced expression of mitochondrial proteins. Importantly, Parkin expression was found to be upregulated in ETR SCs, specifically in mitochondria and mitophagosomes in addition to colocalization with PINK1 and pan-cathepsin, indicating augmented mitophagy. Transcription factor EB (TFEB, a transcription factor for autophagy and mitophagy proteins) was also found to be upregulated in nuclei of ETR SCs and associated with enhanced expression of iNOS. Enhanced Parkin-related mitophagy in ETR SCs may be a protective mechanism with therapeutic implications. To the authors' knowledge, this is the first report demonstrating the ultrastructural characteristics and molecular mechanisms of Parkin-related mitophagy in ETR SCs.

Keywords: ethanol; mitochondria; autophagy; LC3; apoptosis; Sertoli cell; Parkin; PINK1; TFEB; mitophagy; infertility

---

1. Introduction

Autophagy (or macroautophagy) is a catabolic pathway for lysosomal degradation of most cellular components under basal conditions and upon exposure to various stressors such as starvation, oxidative/nitrosative stress, mitochondrial damage, and lipogenic challenge [1–3]. Selective autophagic removal of damaged mitochondria, or mitophagy, is an antiapoptotic mechanism induced and specifically upregulated as a response to various damaging agents such as protonophore carbonyl cyanide m-chlorophenyl hydrazine (or CCCP; used for in vitro studies) and ethanol in animal models [4–6]. The ultrastructural characteristics of mitophagy in hepatocytes [6,7] and Sertoli cells (SCs) [8,9] of acute ethanol-treated rats (an animal model representing binge-type exposure to ethanol) were recently reported by the authors' laboratory. These include the engulfment of damaged mitochondria by microtubule-associated protein 1 light chain3 (LC3)-mediated autophagosomal membranes forming mitophagosomes that fuse with lysosomes, creating autolysosomes with perinuclear localization. The PINK1/Parkin mitophagic pathway is characterized by the interplay of two recessive Parkinson's-linked genes (PTEN-induced kinase 1 (PINK1) and Parkin (an E3 ubiquitin ligase), which maintain mitochondrial homeostasis and clear dysfunctional mitochondria via mitophagy. Mutations affecting PINK1-Parkin genes cause Parkinson's disease (PD). The specific molecular mechanisms of ethanol-induced hepatic mitophagy were recently reported to be related to the PINK1-Parkin pathway [6,7,10–13]. In these studies, ethanol-induced mitochondrial damage via mechanisms related to mitochondrial DNA (mt DNA) damage, oxidative stress, and other factors caused the stabilization of PINK1 (a sensor of mitochondrial damage) on damaged mitochondria. This results in Parkin (a specific marker of mitophagy) overexpression and translocation to damaged mitochondria, protein ubiquitination and subsequent mitochondrial fragmentation, and engulfment of mitochondria by LC3-mediated autophagosomal membranes. The pro-survival role of Parkin against ethanol toxicity has recently been reported in a few studies. In ethanol-treated Parkin knock-out (KO) mice, there was a reduction of mitophagy leading to increased hepatocyte damage and steatosis [12,13]. Parkin deficiency has been found to exacerbate ethanol-induced dopaminergic neurodegeneration in mice via the reduction of anti-apoptotic mitophagy [14]; on the other hand, Parkin overexpression protected retinal ganglion cells via mitophagy activation in an experimental glaucoma rat model [15].

Although SCs play essential roles for germ cell survival and fertility maintenance in response to toxic insults such as binge-type ethanol exposure [16], no studies investigating the mitophagy-related PINK1-Parkin pathway in SCs have yet been reported. In this study, the authors investigated the ultrastructural characteristics and specific molecular mechanisms of ethanol-induced mitophagy in SCs of acute ETRs and the involvement of the PINK1-Parkin pathway as well as associated transcription factor EB (TFEB) (a master transcription factor for autophagy and Parkin-related mitophagy) [16–18]. Light and electron microscopic techniques along with Western blot analysis showed evidences of upregulation and mitochondrial translocation of Parkin and PINK1 among ETR SCs in association with the formation of LC-3 mediated mitophagosomes and nuclear translocation of TFEB.

2. Materials and Methods

2.1. Study Approval

Twelve adult male rats (10 weeks old) with an approximate average weight of 300 g were purchased from SLC Japan Co. (Shizuoka, Japan). They were treated in keeping with the relevant Experimental Animal Research Committee of Osaka Medical College guidelines (approved by Animal Research Committee of Osaka Medical College on 10/28/2013, under code, 25090).

2.2. Antibodies and Kits

The following primary antibodies were used: Rabbit anti-LC3B antibody (PM063) from MBL, Nagoya, Japan; rabbit anti-PINK1 (BC100-494), rabbit anti-Parkin (NB100-91921), and mouse anti-p62 (H00008878-M01) antibodies from Novus Biologicals (Briarwood Avenue, Building IV Centennial, CO, USA); goat anti-pan-cathepsin (sc-6499), mouse anti-Parkin (sc-32282), mouse anti-Actin (sc-47778), and mouse anti-cytochrome c (7H8):(sc-13560) antibodies from Santa Cruz Biologicals (Dallas, TX, USA); rabbit anti-inducible nitric oxide synthase (iNOS) (ab15326) and rabbit anti-iNOS (ab15323) antibodies from Abcam Biologicals (Cambridge, MA, USA); rabbit anti-TFEB (MBS9125929) from MyBioSource Biologicals (San Diego, CA, USA); and rabbit anti-Cytochrome c oxidase (COX) IV (3E11) from cell signaling Biologicals (Danvers, MA, USA). Alexa Fluor 488- or 594-conjugated secondary antibodies (Molecular Probes, Carlsbad, CA, USA) and VectaFluor™ R.T.U. Antibody Kit DyLight® 488 were used for immunofluorescence (IF) studies (Vector, CA, USA), while 4′,6-diamidino-2-phenylindole (DAPI) (H-1200) (vector) was used for nuclear counterstaining. A TUNEL kit (Roche Diagnostics, Mannheim, Germany) was used for apoptosis detection. Vectastain ABC Standard Kit (PK-4000) and ImmPACT DAB(SK-4105) from Vector were used for immunohistochemistry (IHC). Donkey anti-rabbit IgG-HRP (sc-2077) and donkey anti-mouse IgG-HRP (SC-2096) secondary antibodies from Santa Cruz were used for Western blot. A total of 15 nm and 6 nm gold-conjugated goat anti-rabbit and anti-mouse antibodies, respectively (Aurion, Wageningen, The Netherlands), were used for immunoelectron microscopy (IEM). As a rule, we followed manufacturer's protocols and our previous publications regarding the use of antibodies and kits in Western blot, IF, IHC, and IEM.

2.3. Animals and Experimental Procedure

The animals were treated with a single 5 g/kg intraperitoneal dose of ethanol (40% v/v) consistent with animal models of binge ethanol exposure [6,16,19,20]. A control group received equal volume of phosphate buffered saline (PBS). Following ethanol administration, the rats were sacrificed by cervical dislocation at various time points (0, 3, 6, and 24 h). For paraffin embedding, the testes were divided into small pieces and fixed in 4% paraformaldehyde. Some testicular pieces were fixed in 2% paraformaldehyde and 2.5% glutaraldehyde in 0.1 M phosphate buffer for embedding in epoxy and observation under transmission electron microscopy (TEM) as we previously reported [6,8,16]. Fresh samples were frozen in liquid nitrogen for Western blot analysis consistent with our earlier study [21].

2.4. IHC for LC3, Parkin, PINK1, TFEB, and iNOS

The immunohistochemical labeling methods were performed according to the manufacturer's recommendations and our recent studies [6,18,21,22]. Paraffin-embedded sections (4-μm thickness) underwent a deparaffinization process, antigen retrieval, blocking of endogenous peroxidase activity, and non-specific antigen binding. The sections were then incubated for 1 hour at room temperature with the primary antibodies mentioned above. Immunostaining was performed by Vectastain ABC method. Then, sections were treated with DAB, counterstained with hematoxylin, and observed under Olympus BX41microscope (BX41, Olympus, Tokyo, Japan). Quantification of LC3, TFEB, and iNOS immunostaining in SCs was performed on 10–15 seminiferous tubules from ETRs and the control group. Using Adobe Photoshop, the tubules were captured and saved for computer analysis using Image J (National Institutes of Health, Bethesda, MA, USA). The intensity of protein expression in SCs was quantified as recently reported [22].

2.5. IF Single and Double Labeling of Mitophagy Proteins and Mitochondrial and Lysosomal Markers

IF labelling of TFEB was performed on paraffin sections as in IHC. In brief, after deparaffinization, antigen retrieval, and serum blocking, TFEB antibody was applied for 1 h at room temperature. The sections were incubated with Alexa Fluor 594-conjugated secondary antibody for 30 min. For double labeling of LC3 with either cytochrome c (a mitochondrial marker) or p62, we used a simultaneous application of two primary antibodies followed by Alexa Fluor 594 and 488-conjugated secondary antibodies [6,23,24]. For double labeling of pan-cathepsin (lysosomal marker) with either Parkin or LC3, we used a sequential method as previously reported [6,16,21,22]. In brief, following incubation with primary antibodies for 1 hour, Alexa Fluor 594 and VectaFluor™ R.T.U. DyLight® 488 were used as secondary reagents (30 minutes). After nuclear counterstaining with DAPI (blue reaction), the sections were observed under the BX41 fluorescence microscope.

2.6. Line Profile Plots for Co-Localization Analysis of Parkin and Pan-Cathepsin

Line profiles from the two fluorescent channels were analyzed using Image J software as reported (6,23,24). Line profile plots reflect intensity and colocalization of two different proteins as overlapped red and green peaks (vertical axis shows intensity of fluorescence while horizontal axis indicates distance).

2.7. Terminal Deoxynucleotidyl Transferase dUTP-Mediated Nick-End Labeling (TUNEL) Assay

TUNEL assay for apoptosis detection was performed as previously reported [6,16]. Deparaffinized sections were treated with TUNEL reaction mixture (TdT enzyme and fluorescent-labeled nucleotides) for 1 h at 37 °C. TUNEL positive cells showed green labeling under fluorescence microscope, while TUNEL negative nuclei appeared blue with DAPI.

2.8. TEM and Quantitative Analysis of Mitophagic Vacuoles (MVs)

Ultrathin sections at 70 nm thickness were cut with a diamond knife, double-stained with uranyl acetate and lead citrate, and examined under an H-7650 transmission electron microscope (Hitachi, Tokyo, Japan). For quantification of MVs (mitophagosomes and autolysosomes) in SCs, 15–20 lower magnification photomicrographs from the testes of controls and ETRs ($\times$2500 magnification, each image containing at least a portion of SC nucleus showing the perinuclear area) were used as described previously [6,8,16,25].

2.9. Immunogold Labeling for LC3, Parkin, and TFEB and Double Immunogold Labeling of Parkin and PINK1

The method of post embedding immune-gold labeling was based on our previous reports [6,7,26]. Ultrathin sections mounted on nickel grids were etched with either 5% sodium metaperiodate for 15 minutes [27] or 1%–2% H202 for 10 minutes [28]. The sections were then washed in filtered water and incubated in 3% BSA in PBS for 1 h. After incubation with the same primary for Parkin, LC3, and TFEB for 2 h at room temperature, the sections were incubated with 15-nm gold-conjugated goat anti-rabbit secondary antibody according to instructions of the producing company. For double immunogold labeling of Parkin and PINK1, a mixture of these antibodies was simultaneously applied for 2 h followed by a mixture of gold-conjugated goat anti-mouse (6 nm) and gold-conjugated goat anti-rabbit (15 nm) secondary antibodies for 1 h. Grids were washed and briefly stained briefly with uranyl acetate and lead citrate. For quantification of LC3 and Parkin immunogold particles (15 nm) in control and ETRs SCs, a total of 15–20 mitochondria from each group were selected and immunogold particles for each protein were counted [29]. Mitochondria with double PINK1 (15 nm) and Parkin (6 nm) immunogold labeling were identified and counted using 10–15 higher magnification photomicrographs from the testes of controls and ETRs. Quantification of nuclear TFEB immunogold particles was performed on 15–20 images from each group (each image containing at least a portion of SC nucleus). The Student *t*-test was used to assess the statistical significance of all these quantifications.

2.10. Western Blot Analysis for LC3, Cytochrome c, Parkin, TFEB, COX IV, and iNOS

After homogenization of whole testicular tissues in a modulated RIPA buffer followed by centrifugation, the supernatant was electrophoresed on 12% sodium dodecyl sulfate polyacrylamide gel and transferred onto a polyvinylidene difluoride membrane. Proteins were detected with the specific primary antibodies for LC3, cytochrome c, Parkin, TFEB, COX IV, and iNOS, and then with specific peroxidase-labeled secondary antibodies as previously reported [6,21,22]. The relative intensity of expression of various proteins against actin (43 kDa) was normalized and densitometrically measured using Image J.

2.11. Statistical Analysis

Statistical analysis was performed by GraphPad Prism 8 Software (8.0.2), San Diego, CA, USA. Differences between more than two groups were tested by analysis of variance (ANOVA) with $p < 0.05$ considered as statistically significant. The Student *t*-test was used for comparison between two groups.

3. Results

3.1. Enhanced Mitochondrial Damage and Mitophagic Vacuole (MV) Formation in ETR SCs with Predominant Localization in Perinuclear Areas

The animals were subjected to a single injection of ethanol (5 g/kg) or PBS (for the control group) and sacrificed at 0, 3, 6, and 24 h after injection (following a model of acute alcohol toxicity) [6,16,19,20]. As shown in Figure 1a–c, while SCs in the control group exhibited normal mitochondrial morphology (a smooth outer membrane and an inner membrane contiguous with a vesicular type of cristae and containing a granular, moderately electron-dense internal matrix) and distribution over the whole cytoplasm, the mitochondria in ETR SCs (Figure 1d–f) showed perinuclear aggregation with damaged or lost cristae and a dark matrix, in addition to fragmentation, along with outer-membrane irregularities. The damaged mitochondria were associated with MVs including mitophagosomes (Figure 1g–j) and autolysosomes (mitophagolysosomes) (Figure 1e,k). Multilamellar bodies (Figure 1k) were also frequently observed, indicating enhanced mitochondrial damage [6,16,26]. This juxtanuclear accumulation of MVs in ETR SCs is shown with low-power magnification (Figure S1). Importantly, based on TEM and TUNEL (Figure S2), germ cell apoptosis was frequently observed in ETR testes, but SCs nuclei appeared normal. This indicates that the enhanced mitophagic response may be anti-apoptotic in nature [6,16]. Quantitative analysis (Figure 1l) and control-group comparison revealed a significant increase in MV formation for all time periods after ethanol injection, with a peak at 24 h. With this in mind, the 24-h time point was chosen for analysis in subsequent experiments. As double-layered membranes in mitophagosomes indicate the involvement of the LC3-related autophagic mechanism [6,16,22,26], the expression of this protein was investigated.

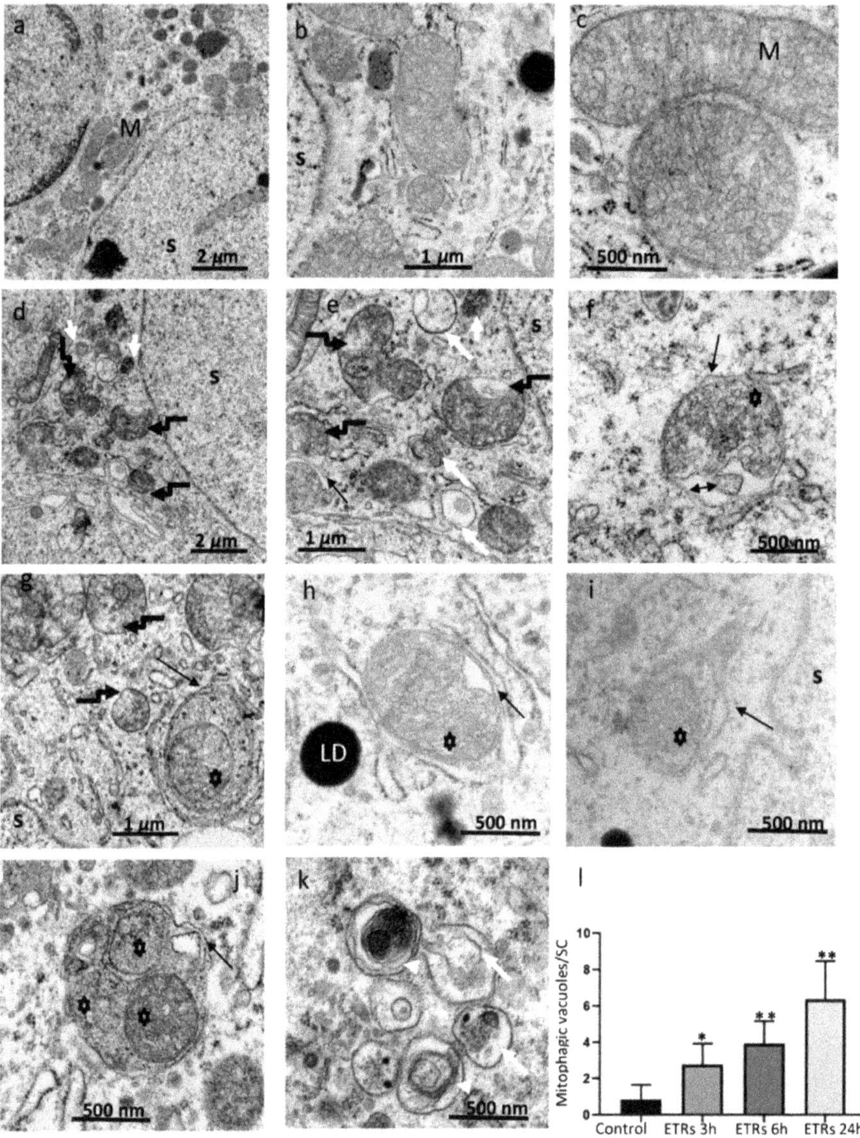

Figure 1. Ultrastructural characteristics of enhanced mitochondrial damage and mitophagy in ethanol-treated rats (ETR) Sertoli cells (SCs.) (**a–c**): control testes; (**d–k**): ETRs. Quantification of mitophagy is shown in (**l**). Note the normal mitochondria (M) in control testes with characteristic vesicular-type cristae. Broken black arrows (**d,e,g**) indicate damaged mitochondria in ETR SCs, while black arrows show autophagosomal membranes engulfing damaged mitochondria (asterisks) forming mitophagosomes. The double-head arrow indicates damaged fragmented cristae. The long and short white arrows mark autolysosomes and lysosomes, respectively. White arrow heads mark multilamellar bodies. LD: lipid droplets; S: SC nucleus. The histogram depicts quantification of mitophagic vacuoles in the control and ETRs. * $p < 0.01$ and ** $p < 0.001$ vs. control (one-way analysis of variance (ANOVA)).

3.2. Association of Ethanol-Induced Mitophagosomes in SCs with Increased LC3-II Expression and Mitochondrial Proteins Reduction

The IHC characteristic in Figure 2A clearly demonstrates enhanced formation of LC3 puncta (indicating the induction of LC3-II isoform required for maturation of autophagosomal membrane) in ETR SCs compared to very low levels in the control group, indicating elevated mitophagosome formation (mediated by LC3-II) as previously reported by other authors [6,16,22,26] and in line with the TEM findings detailed in Figure 1. Increased LC3 expression was also observed in interstitial cells of ETRs. Quantitative analysis of LC3 expression in SCs (Figure 2B) demonstrated higher LC3 intensity in ETRs SCs compared to control group, which was statistically significant. As also shown in Figure 2C,D, Western blot analysis indicated the upregulation of LC3-II (16 kDa), supporting the findings made from light-microscope observation. IF double-labeling of LC3 and P62 (an LC3 adaptor molecule) showed enhanced co-localization in ETR SCs, thereby confirming enhanced mitophagic response (Figure S3) [30]. Immunoelectron microscopy (IEM; Figure 2E) demonstrated a very low presence of LC3-II immunogold particles in control SCs. However, a significant increase in LC3-II immunogold labeling (Figure 2F) was observed within mitophagosomes on autophagosomal membranes in ETR SCs, indicating the autophagic nature of mitophagosomes [21,26]. Double-labeling with IF LC3 and cytochrome c revealed enhanced co-localization in ETR SCs (Figure 3A), indicating the formation of mitophagosomes as reported in past studies [6,10,11,23,24]. Western blot and analysis (Figure 3B,C) showed a significant reduction of cytochrome c (15 kDa), indicating mitochondrial damage within MVs [10,11,23,24,31]. Additional Western blot analysis showed that the expression level of COX IV (17 kDa) (inner mitochondrial membrane protein) was also reduced in testes of ETRs (Figure 2D,E). Against this background, Parkin expression was investigated to help identify the specific proteins potentially involved in enhanced MV formation in ETR SCs.

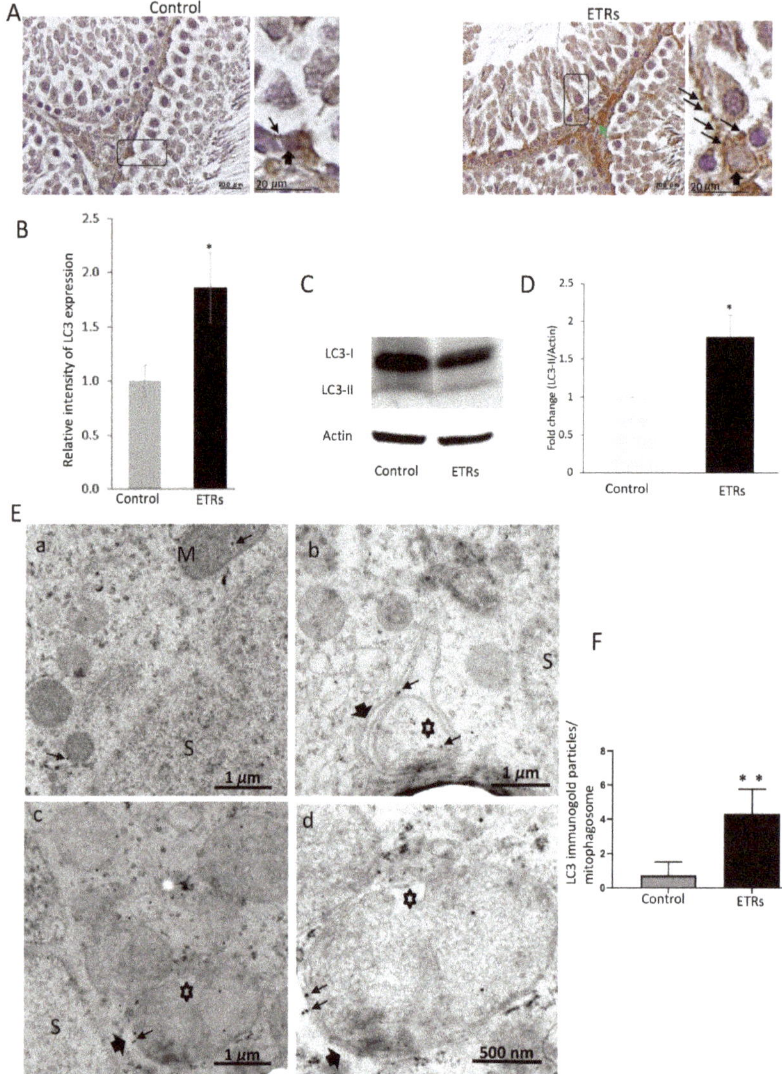

Figure 2. Enhanced light chain3 (LC3)-II expression in ETR SCs with specific localization to mitophagosomes (**A**) immunohistochemistry (IHC) of LC3. The framed areas are magnified in the insets on the right. LC3-II puncta are marked by long thin arrows, while short thick arrows indicate SCs nuclei. The green arrow marks expression in interstitial cells. (**B**) Quantification of LC3 expression in control and ETR SCs. (**C**) Western blot of LC3. The relative expression level of the protein is normalized to actin and expressed as a fold of the control ($n = 3$) (this normalization applies to blots of other proteins shown below.) (**D**) Histogram showing significant increase of LC3-II in ETRs compared to the control. $P < 0.05$ (*t*-test). (**E**) LC3 immunogold labeling in the control (**a**) and ETR SCs (**b–d**). Thin arrows indicate LC3 immunogold particles, while thick arrows mark autophagosomal membranes sequestering damaged mitochondria (asterisks) forming mitophagosomes. (**F**) Histogram demonstrating significant increase in the number of LC3-II immunogold particles in mitophagosomes of ETRs SCs compared to the control group. $P < 0.01$ (*t*-test). M: normal mitochondria; S: SC nucleus.

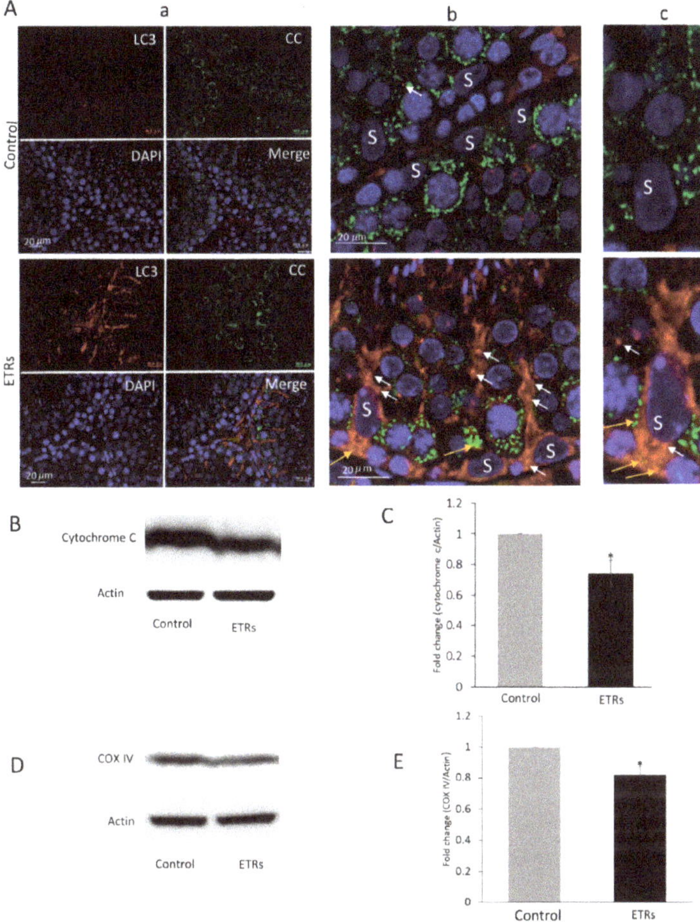

Figure 3. Enhanced colocalization of LC3 with cytochrome c in SCs of ETRs and reduced expression of mitochondrial proteins. (**A**) Immunofluorescence (IF) double-labeling of LC3 (red) and cytochrome c (CC) (green) with nuclear counterstaining using DAPI (blue). The panels in the middle (**b**) and on the right (**c**) are higher magnifications of those on the left in (**a**). Orange arrows indicate areas of colocalization for proteins (yellow-orange), while white arrows indicate LC3 puncta. S: SC nucleus. (**B**) Western blot of CC ($n = 3$). The histogram in (**C**) shows significant reduction of CC in ETRs. (**D**) Western bot of Cytochrome c oxidase (COX) IV ($n = 3$). The histogram in **E** shows significant reduction of the protein in ETRs * $p < 0.05$ (t-test).

3.3. Ethanol Increased the Expression and Mitochondrial Translocation of Parkin and PINK1 in SCs and Fusion with Lysosomal Compartment

As shown in Figure 4A–C, IHC showed enhanced expression of Parkin in SCs and Leydig cells of ETRs as compared to lower levels in control testes. A low level of expression was also observed in mature sperm (data not shown). Parkin expression was specifically perinuclear, which was consistent with TEM findings for enhanced MV formation (Figure 1). Consistent with IHC, Western blotting and analysis revealed significant upregulation of Parkin (52 kDa) in ETRs testes. As mitochondrial translocation of Parkin is essential for recognition and clearance of damaged mitochondria by LC3-II-mediated autophagic membranes [6,7,10–13], the authors studied the subcellular localization of Parkin using IEM (Figure 5). As shown in this figure and in consistency with the immunogold labeling of LC3-II in mitophagosomes (Figure 2E), Parkin-immunogold particles were observed in damaged mitochondria and mitophagosomes in ETR SCs in contrast to very low levels in the control. This supports the authors' recent liver research using the same animal mode [6,7]. As PINK1 accumulation in damaged mitochondria is required for Parkin mitochondrial translocation [6,7,10,11,26], the co-expression of PINK1 and Parkin at the ultrastructural level was investigated. As expected, PINK1 and Parkin immunogold particle presence was increased in damaged mitochondria and mitophagosomes in ETR SCs (Figure 6b–d), while signals were very weak in the control group (Figure 6a). Statistical analysis (Figure 6e) revealed significant increase in the number of mitochondria positive for both PINK1-Parkin immunogold labeling in ETRs SCs compared to control group. This accumulation of PINK1 was verified by IHC (Figure S4). To check the degradation of mitophagosomes via the lysosomal system, double-labeling of Parkin with pan-cathepsin was also performed. As shown in Figure 7, the expression levels and colocalization signals of Parkin with pan-cathepsin in ETR SCs (Figure 7D,E) were higher than control group (Figure 7A,B), indicating enhanced mitophagic activity and formation of mitophagolysosomes [10]. These findings were confirmed by plot profile analysis (Figure 7C,F) [6,7,23,24] and LC3 and pan-cathepsin double-labeling (Figure S5), thereby supporting the authors' previous findings, indicating the acceleration of autophagic flux [6,16].

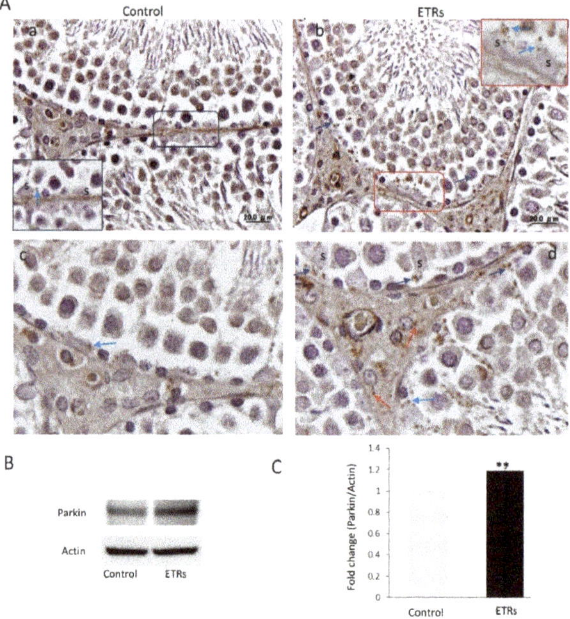

Figure 4. Ethanol-related increase in Parkin expression in SCs with predominant perinuclear localization (**A**) IHC of Parkin in the control (**a**) and ETRs (**b**). The insets are higher magnifications of the framed areas showing Parkin expression (blue arrows). The lower panels (**c,d**) are higher magnifications demonstrating Parkin expression in SCs and Leydig cells (red arrows). S: SC nuclei. (**B**) Western blot of Parkin (*n* = 3). The histogram in (**C**) shows a significant increase in Parkin expression in ETRs. ** *p* < 0.01 (*t*-test).

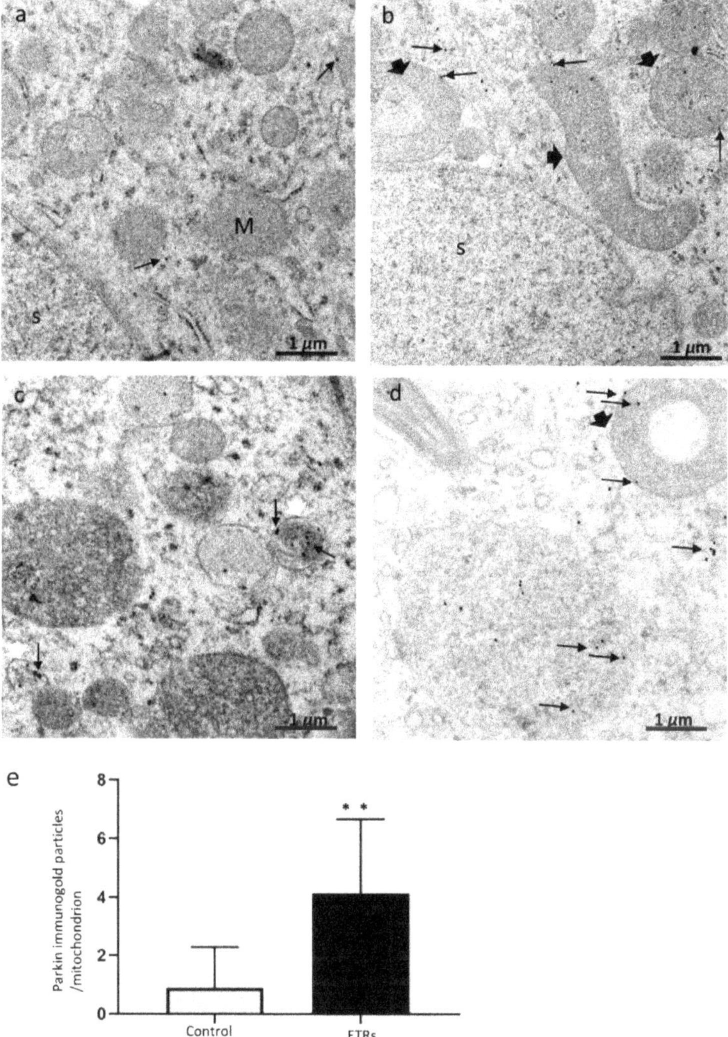

Figure 5. Ultrastructural characteristics of Parkin overexpression and mitochondrial translocation in ETR SCs. (**a**) control; (**b–d**) ETRs. The long black arrows mark Parkin immunogold particles, while the short black arrows indicate damaged mitochondria. The white arrows mark the autophagosomal membrane. S: SC nucleus; M: normal mitochondria. (**e**) Histogram demonstrating significant increase in the number of Parkin immunogold particles in the mitochondria of ETRs SCs compared to control. ** $p < 0.01$ (*t*-test).

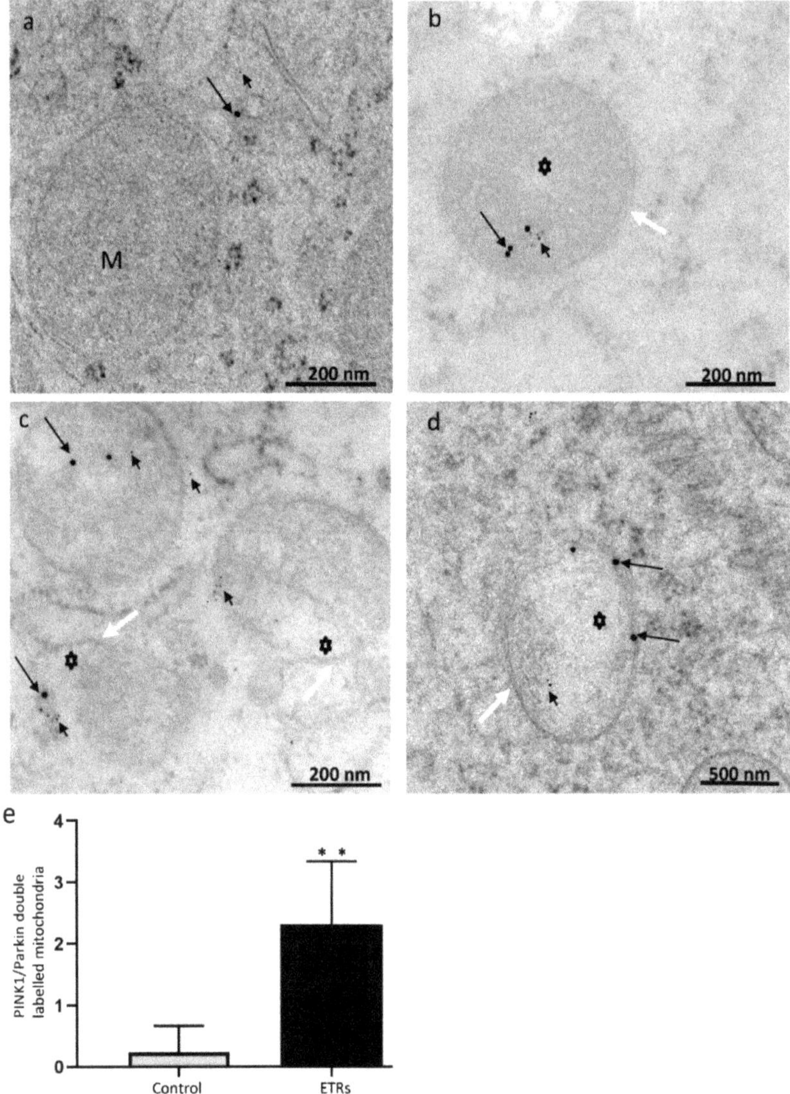

Figure 6. Immunogold double labeling of PINK1 and Parkin in control (**a**) and ETR SCs (**b–d**). The long black arrows indicate PINK1 (labeled with 15 nm gold particles), while short black arrows show Parkin (6 nm gold particles) localizations to damaged mitochondria (asterisks) of ETRs. The white arrows indicate autophagosomal membranes. M, mitochondria; S, SC nucleus. (**e**) Histogram showing quantification of mitochondria positive for both PINK1 and Parkin. ** $p < 0.01$ (*t*-test).

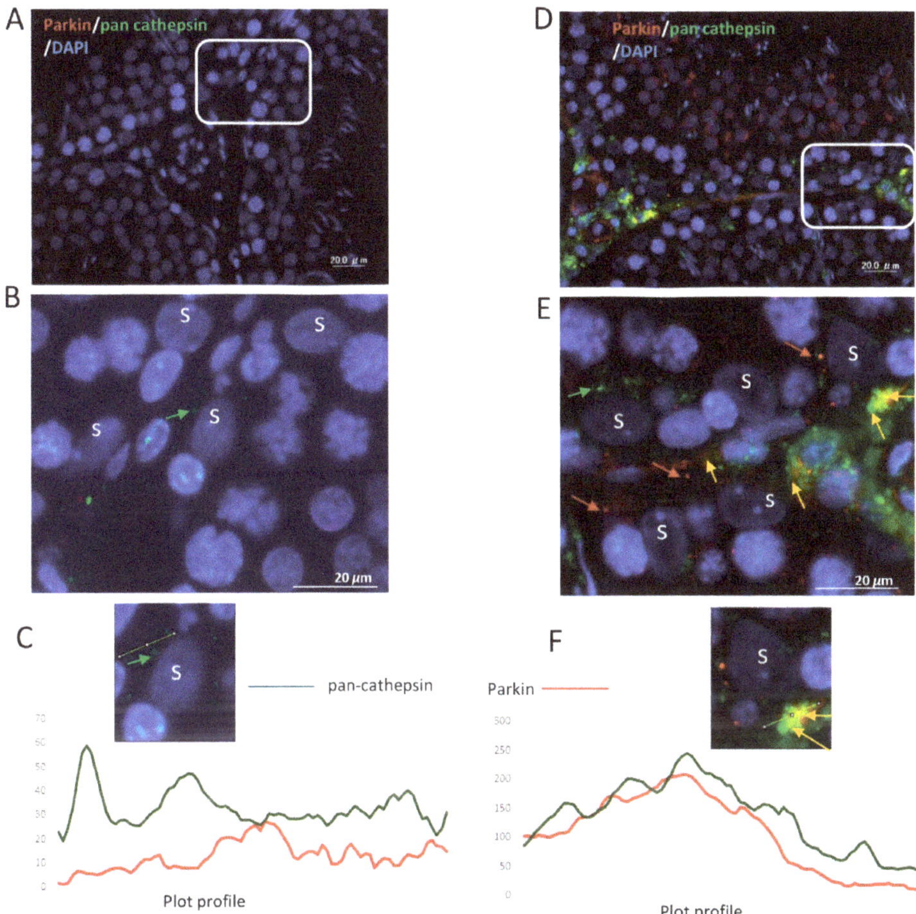

Figure 7. Elevated expression and colocalization of Parkin with pan cathepsin in ETRs SCs. (control, **A–C**), (ETRs, **D–F**). The framed areas in (**A**) and (**D**) are magnified in (**B**) and (**E**), respectively. Note the enhanced expression and colocalization of Parkin (red, red arrows) and pan-cathepsin (green, green arrows) upon merging (orange-yellow, orange arrows) in ETR SCs (**D,E**) compared to control (**A,B**). S: SC nucleus. DAPI (blue) was used for nuclear counterstaining. (**C,F**) Plot profiles demonstrating the colocalization of Parkin and pan-cathepsin defined as overlapped red and green peak at the lines positioned in images (cropped from panels **B,E**) just above the histograms.

3.4. Enhanced Mitophagy in SCs of ETRs is Associated with TFEB Nuclear Translocation and Induction of iNOS

TFEB nuclear translocation is essential for upregulation of autophagy and mitophagy proteins upon cellular exposure to acute ethanol exposure and other producers of oxidative/nitrosative stress [16–18]. The authors' investigation of this protein is shown in Figure 8. Compared to weak levels in the control group, enhanced expression and nuclear translocation of TFEB was observed in ETR SCs in IF (Figure 8A), IEM (Figure 8B), Western blot (53 kDa) (Figure 8C,D), and IHC (Figure 8E), indicating that the protein may mediate upregulated mitophagy in such cases. Quantification of nuclear TFEB expression (Figure 9A) and nuclear TFEB immunogold labeling (Figure 9B) in SCs demonstrated a significant increase in ETRs compared to control group. As nuclear translocation of this protein is related to oxidative/nitrosative stress, the expression of iNOS was investigated as shown in Figure 10. It can be seen that IHC (Figure 10A,B) and Western blot (Figure 10C,D) demonstrated the significant upregulation of iNOS (131 kDa) as observed in SCs and interstitial cells of ETR testes, compared to lower levels in the control group. This upregulation may be related to increased blood endotoxin levels and cytokines associated with ethanol toxicity [16].

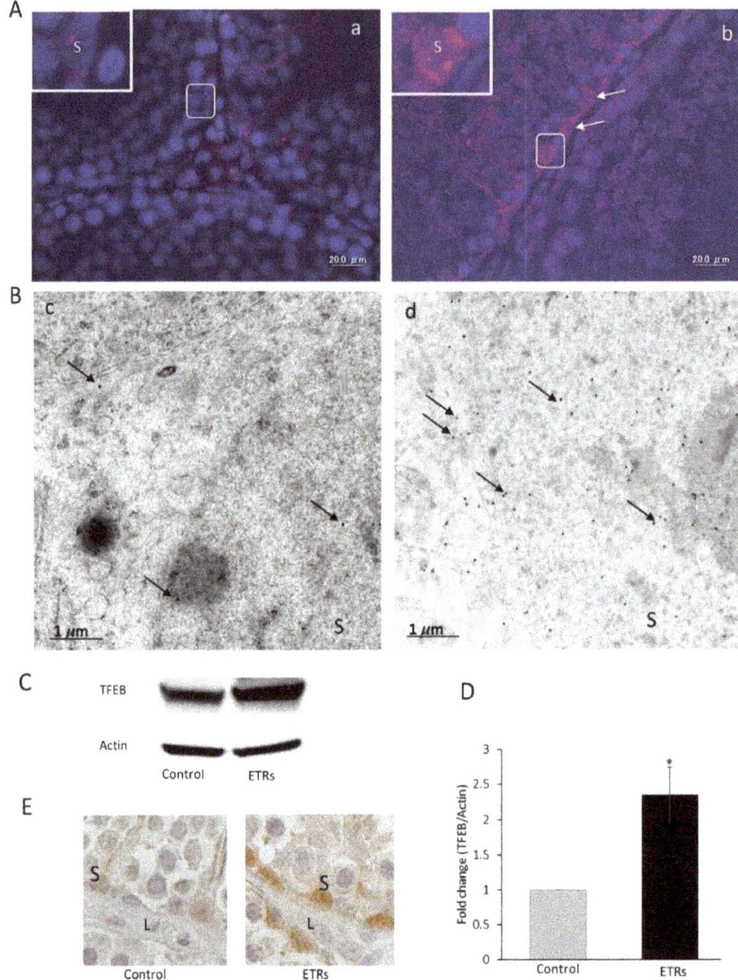

Figure 8. Elevated expression and nuclear translocation of TFEB in ETR SCs. (**A**) IF of TFEB expression in the control (**a**) and ETRs (**b**). The insets are higher magnifications of the framed areas. Note the overexpression of TFEB (white arrows) in SC nuclei of ETRs. (**B**) Immunogold labeling of TFEB (black arrows, 15 nm gold particles) in the control (**c**) and ETR SCs (**d**). (**C**) Western blot of TFEB in the control and ETR testes (*n* = 3). (**D**) Histogram showing a significant increase of TFEB expression in ETR testes. * *p* < 0.05 (*t*-test). (**E**) IHC showing TFEB nuclear translocation in ETR SCs (part of a seminiferous tubule), confirming the IF and IEM results (**A**,**B**). S: SC nucleus; L: Leydig cell.

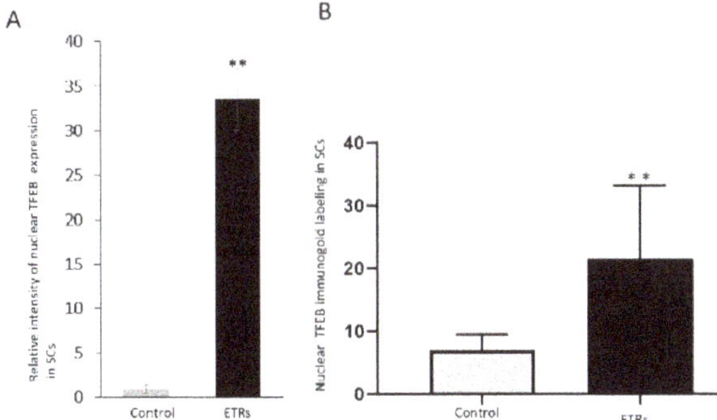

Figure 9. Quantitative analysis of nuclear TFEB expression and immunogold labeling in SCs. (**A**) Histogram showing significant increase of TFEB nuclear expression in ETRs SCs. (**B**) Quantification of nuclear TFEB immunogold particles in SCs. ** $p < 0.01$ (*t*-test).

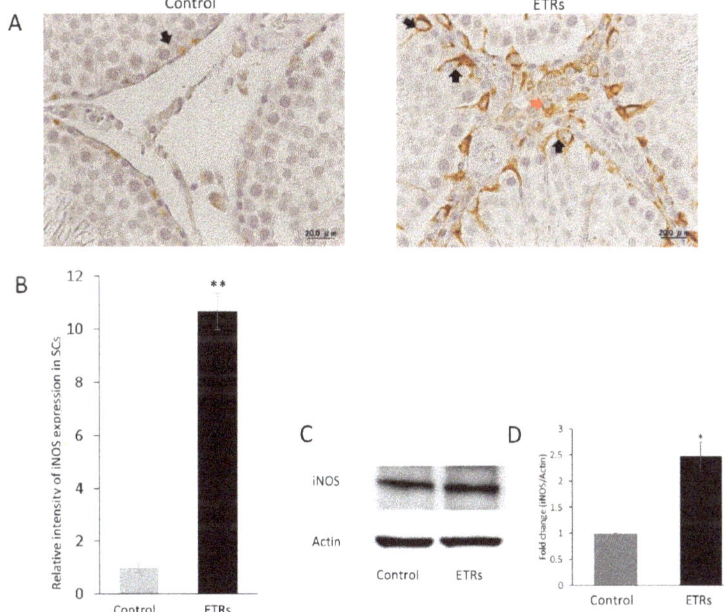

Figure 10. Upregulation of iNOS in ETR SCs. (**A**) IHC of iNOS in control and ETRs. Note the enhanced expression in SCs (black arrows) and interstitial cells (red arrows) of ETRs. (**B**) Quantification of iNOS expression in SCs. ** $p < 0.01$ (*t*-test). (**C**) Western blot of iNOS expression in control and ETR testes ($n = 3$). (**D**) Histogram demonstrating higher iNOS expression in ETR testes compared to the control. * $p < 0.05$ (t-test).

4. Discussion

An accumulating body of data indicates that Parkin-mediated mitophagy is a prosurvival mechanism for clearance of damaged mitochondria in the liver and brain in response to various stressors such as acute ethanol exposure, subsequently preventing the release of proapoptotic proteins and the generation of toxic reactive oxygen species [4,6,12–14,32]. Although SCs play a central role in germ cell survival, fertility, and maintenance of testicular homeostasis [16,33,34], no studies on the involvement of the PINK1-Parkin pathway in the enhanced mitophagic response of SCs to acute ethanol intake have yet been reported. The novel findings of the current study include enhanced mitophagic response in ETR SCs, which are associated with Parkin mitochondrial translocation and colocalization with lysosome, formation of LC3-II-decorated mitophagosomes associated with reduction of mitochondrial proteins, and nuclear translocation of TFEB. These findings are based on various methods including TEM, TUNEL, IEM, IHC, IF, and Western blot. This enhanced Parkin-related mitophagy in ETR SCs seems to be a protective mechanism and may have therapeutic implications for male fertility.

The TEM findings relating to enhanced mitochondrial damage and MV formation in ETR SCs in the current study are consistent with the authors' previous studies [6–9]. While these SCs were loaded with damaged mitochondria and MVs, they appeared normal based on TEM and TUNEL. In addition, the specific juxtanuclear accumulation of damaged mitochondria and MVs in ETR SCs indicates that the PINK1-Parkin pathway may mediate this accumulation and activate mitophagy [6,7,10,11]. Enhanced autophagic clearance of damaged mitochondria within MVs of ETR SCs in the current study is evidenced by engulfment of these mitochondria by LC3-II-decorated autophagosomal membranes [26], enhanced co-localization of LC3 with cytochrome c and p62, and reduced cytochrome c protein levels [6,10,11,23,24,31,35].

A major finding of the current study was Parkin overexpression and mitochondrial translocation in ETR SCs. This is supported by the authors' previous studies on rat liver modeling of acute ethanol exposure [6,7]. However, in the current study, IEM results demonstrated the co-overexpression of PINK1 and Parkin in damaged mitochondria and mitophagosomes of ETR SCs. This overexpression may cause a collapse in the normal tubular mitochondrial network, resulting in perinuclear mitochondrial fragmentation and MV formation as previously reported [10,11]. PINK1 and Parkin mitochondrial translocation in ETR SCs in the current study may have been induced by nitrosative/oxidative stress, mt DNA damage (as evidenced by damaged cristae and matrix elements), mitochondrial depolarization, and other mechanisms [6,7,11,12,35,36]. In addition, Parkin-labeled mitochondria within mitophagosomes in ETR SCs were targeted as lysosomes for degradation based on enhanced colocalization of pan-cathepsin with Parkin and LC3-II, indicating enhanced autolysosome or mitophagolysosome formation [6,11,16,37]. In fact, autophagy is considered essential for Parkin-mediated mitochondrial clearance, as knocking out ATG5 cells resulted in failure to eliminate damaged mitochondria even with Parkin recruitment [38].

The current study showed that the very low Parkin-related mitophagy observed in control SCs was upregulated by ethanol in SCs, indicating that this pathway is mainly activated in response to stress signals [36]. However, it is not possible to rule out the presence of PINK1-Parkin independent mitophagic mechanisms such as mitophagy with the receptors NIX, BNIP3, and FUNDC1 and prohibitins involved in enhanced mitophagy in ETR SCs [6,7,12,13,39]. In addition, Parkin upregulation in SCs of ETRs may have other functions beyond mitophagy such as mtDNA repair, selective escape of antiapoptotic proteins from mitochondria to the endoplasmic reticulum during mitophagy, and suppression of mitochondrial spheroid formation [6,7,31].

Another important finding of the current work was the detection, using light/electronic microscopic techniques and Western blot, of the overexpression and nuclear translocation of TFEB in ETR SCs. This translocation has been reported as necessary for the upregulation of autophagy and mitophagy proteins, specifically under oxidative stress [18]. The current study results indicate that such translocation may be related to ethanol-induced oxidative/nitrosative stress as evidenced by upregulation of iNOS [16–18]. A recent study revealed that mitophagy-induced translocation of TFEB to the nucleus requires both PINK1 and Parkin, in contrast with starvation-induced TFEB translocation, suggesting that mitochondria and lysosomes impact each other [40].

The enhanced mitophagic response in SCs of ETRs in the current study may be anti-apoptotic mechanism [6,12,13,16,41], and may suppress the inflammatory response related to mitochondrial damage, thus maintaining testicular homeostasis [42]. In addition, it may provide lactate for germ cells via a Warburg-like effect via catabolism of damaged mitochondria [33,34,43].

Pharmacological activation of PINK1-Parkin-related mitophagy has been reported to improve mitochondrial function in animal models of Alzheimer's disease [44,45], while overexpression of Parkin has been reported to protect retinal ganglion cells in an experimental glaucoma rat model [15] and to improve cardiac function in rats with myocardial infarction [46] via activation of mitophagy. Accordingly, Parkin-related therapy may have implications in testicular diseases and infertility associated with mitochondrial dysfunction. In addition, selective stimulation of Parkin-mediated mitophagy via the enhancement of its expression and/or mitochondrial translocation using natural or pharmaceutical products may improve mitochondrial quality as reported in relation to alcoholic liver and neurodegenerative diseases such as PD [7,45].

5. Conclusions

The results of this study showed morphological and molecular evidence for ethanol-induced mitophagy in SCs as represented by activation of the PINK1-Parkin pathway and nuclear translocation of TFEB, which may be mediated by oxidative stress.

Supplementary Materials: The following are available online at http://www.mdpi.com/2073-4409/8/3/283/s1. Figure S1: Low-power micrograph showing perinuclear accumulation of damaged mitochondria (broken arrows) and mitophagic vacuoles (arrows) in SC of ETRs. S: SC nucleus; LD: lipid droplet. Figure S2: TUNEL positive germ cells (green labeling) of ETRs with non-apoptotic. Arrows mark SCs nuclei. Figure S3: Enhanced LC3 (red) and p62 (green) colocalization in SCs of ETRs. The white arrows indicated colocalization signals upon merging (yellow-orange). Figure S4: Overexpression of PINK1 in ETR SCs. Arrows indicate SCs nuclei. Figure S5: IF double labeling of LC3 (red) and Pan cathepsin (green) in ETRs. Arrows mark enhanced colocalization signals (yellow-orange) in SCs. S, SC nucleus.

Author Contributions: Conceived and designed the experiments: N.E., A.H., Y.I., and Y.O. Performed the experiments: N.E., A.H., and Y.I. Analyzed the data: N.E., A.H. Wrote the paper: N.E. Critical revision of final draft: Y.K.

Funding: This manuscript is partially supported by Grant-in-Aid for Scientific Research (Kakenhi) (No., 16K11073) for Nabil Eid from The Ministry of Education, Culture, Sports, Science and Technology, Japan.

Acknowledgments: The authors thank Tadashi Kanayama for help in experimental work.

Conflicts of Interest: The authors declare no conflict of interest.

References

1. Kroemer, G.; Marino, G.; Levine, B. Autophagy and the integrated stress response. *Mol. Cell* **2010**, *40*, 280–293. [CrossRef] [PubMed]
2. Eid, N.; Ito, Y.; Otsuki, Y. The autophagic response to alcohol toxicity: The missing layer. *J. Hepatol.* **2013**, *59*, 398. [CrossRef]
3. Sica, V.; Galluzzi, L.; Bravo-San Pedro, J.M.; Izzo, V.; Maiuri, M.C.; Kroemer, G. Organelle-specific initiation of autophagy. *Mol. Cell* **2015**, *59*, 522–539. [CrossRef]
4. Lemasters, J.J. Variants of mitochondrial autophagy: Types 1 and2 mitophagy and micromitophagy (type 3). *Redox Biol.* **2014**, *2*, 749–754. [CrossRef]
5. Ding, W.X.; Li, M.; Chen, X.; Ni, H.M.; Lin, C.W.; Gao, W.; Lu, B.; Stolz, D.B.; Clemens, D.L.; Yin, X.M. Autophagy reduces acute ethanol-induced hepatotoxicity and steatosis in mice. *Gastroenterology* **2010**, *139*, 1740–1752. [CrossRef] [PubMed]
6. Eid, N.; Ito, Y.; Horibe, A.; Otsuki, Y. Ethanol-induced mitophagy in liver is associated with activation of the PINK1-Parkin pathway triggered by oxidative DNA damage. *Histol. Histopathol.* **2016**, *31*, 1143–1159.
7. Eid, N.; Ito, Y.; Otsuki, Y. Triggering of Parkin mitochondrial translocation in mitophagy: Implications for liver diseases. *Front. Pharmacol.* **2016**, *7*, 100. [CrossRef] [PubMed]
8. Eid, N.; Ito, Y.; Horibe, A.; Hamaoka, H.; Kondo, Y. A method for in vivo induction and ultrastructural detection of mitophagy in Sertoli cells. *Methods Mol. Biol.* **2018**, *1748*, 103–112. [PubMed]
9. Eid, N.; Kondo, Y. Ethanol-induced mitophagy in rat Sertoli cells: Implications for male fertility. *Andrologia* **2018**, *50*, e12820. [CrossRef]

10. Vives-Bauza, C.; Zhou, C.; Huang, Y.; Cui, M.; de Vries, R.L.; Kim, J.; May, J.; Tocilescu, M.A.; Liu, W.; Ko, H.S.; et al. PINK1-dependent recruitment of Parkin to mitochondria in mitophagy. *Proc. Nat. Acad. Sci. USA* **2010**, *107*, 378–383. [CrossRef]

11. Narendra, D.; Tanaka, A.; Suen, D.F.; Youle, R.J. Parkin is recruited selectively to impaired mitochondria and promotes their autophagy. *J. Cell Biol.* **2008**, *183*, 795–803. [CrossRef]

12. Williams, J.A.; Ni, H.M.; Ding, Y.; Ding, W.X. Parkin regulates mitophagy and mitochondrial function to protect against alcohol-induced liver injury and steatosis in mice. *Am. J. Physiol. Gastrointest. Liver Physiol.* **2015**, *309*, 324–340. [CrossRef]

13. Williams, J.A.; Ding, W.X. A mechanistic review of mitophagy and Its role in protection against alcoholic liver disease. *Biomolecules* **2015**, *5*, 2619–2642. [CrossRef]

14. Hwang, C.J.; Kim, Y.E.; Son, D.J.; Park, M.H.; Choi, D.Y.; Park, P.H.; Hellström, M.; Han, S.B.; Oh, K.W.; Park, E.K.; et al. Parkin deficiency exacerbate ethanol-induced dopaminergic neurodegeneration by P38 pathway dependent inhibition of autophagy and mitochondrial function. *Redox Biol.* **2017**, *11*, 456–468. [CrossRef] [PubMed]

15. Dai, Y.; Hu, X.; Sun, X. Overexpression of parkin protects retinal ganglion cells in experimental glaucoma. *Cell Death Dis.* **2018**, *9*, 88. [CrossRef]

16. Horibe, A.; Eid, N.; Ito, Y.; Hamaoka, H.; Tanaka, Y.; Kondo, Y. Upregulated autophagy in Sertoli cells of ethanol-treated rats is associated with induction of inducible nitric oxide synthase (iNOS), androgen receptor suppression and germ cell apoptosis. *Int. J. Mol. Sci.* **2017**, *18*, 1061. [CrossRef]

17. Thomes, P.G.; Trambly, C.S.; Fox, H.S.; Tuma, D.J.; Donohue, T.M., Jr. Acute and chronic ethanol administration differentially modulate hepatic autophagy and transcription factor EB. *Alcohol. Clin. Exp. Res.* **2015**, *39*, 2354–2363. [CrossRef] [PubMed]

18. Tan, S.; Wong, E. Mitophagy transcriptome: Mechanistic insights into polyphenol-mediated mitophagy. *Oxid. Med. Cell Longev.* **2017**, *2017*, 9028435. [CrossRef] [PubMed]

19. D'Souza El-Guindy, N.B.; Kovacs, E.J.; de Witte, P.; Spies, C.; Littleton, J.M.; de Villiers, W.J.; Lott, A.J.; Plackett, T.P.; Lanzke, N.; Meadows, G.G. Laboratory models available to study alcohol-induced organ damage and immune variations: Choosing the appropriate model. *Alcohol. Clin. Exp. Res.* **2010**, *3*, 1489–1511.

20. Nogales, F.; Rua, R.M.; Ojeda, M.L.; Murillo, M.L.; Carreras, O. Oral or intraperitoneal binge drinking and oxidative balance in adolescent rats. *Chem. Res. Toxicol.* **2014**, *27*, 1926–1933. [CrossRef] [PubMed]

21. Narabayashi, K.; Ito, Y.; Eid, N.; Maemura, K.; Inoue, T.; Takeuchi, T.; Otsuki, Y.; Higuchi, K. Indomethacin suppresses LAMP-2 expression and induces lipophagy and lipoapoptosis in rat enterocytes via the ER stress pathway. *J. Gastroenterol.* **2015**, *50*, 541–554. [CrossRef] [PubMed]

22. Horibe, A.; Eid, N.; Ito, Y.; Otsuki, Y.; Kondo, Y. Ethanol-induced autophagy in Sertoli cells is specifically marked at androgen-dependent stages of the spermatogenic cycle: Potential mechanisms and implications. *Int. J. Mol. Sci.* **2019**, 20. [CrossRef]

23. Amadoro, G.; Corsetti, V.; Florenzano, F.; Atlante, A.; Bobba, A.; Nicolin, V.; Nori, S.L.; Calissano, P. Morphological and bioenergetic demands underlying the mitophagy in post-mitotic neurons: The pinkparkin pathway. *Front. Aging Neurosci.* **2014**, *6*, 18. [CrossRef] [PubMed]

24. Amadoro, G.; Corsetti, V.; Florenzano, F.; Atlante, A.; Ciotti, M.T.; Mongiardi, M.P.; Bussani, R.; Nicolin, V.; Nori, S.L.; Campanella, M.; et al. AD-linked, toxic NH2 human tau affects the quality control of mitochondria in neurons. *Neurobiol. Dis.* **2014**, *62*, 489–507. [CrossRef]

25. Teckman, J.H.; An, J.K.; Blomenkamp, K.; Schmidt, B.; Perlmutter, D. Mitochondrial autophagy and injury in the liver in alpha 1-antitrypsin deficiency. *Am. J. Physiol. Gastrointest Liver Physiol.* **2004**, *286*, 851–862. [CrossRef]

26. Eid, N.; Ito, Y.; Maemura, K.; Otsuki, Y. Elevated autophagic sequestration of mitochondria and lipid droplets in steatotic hepatocytes of chronic ethanol treated rats: An immunohistochemical and electron microscopic study. *J. Mol. Histol.* **2013**, *44*, 311–326. [CrossRef] [PubMed]

27. Lobo, M.V.; Alonso, F.J.; Arenas, M.I.; Caso, E.; Fraile, B.; del Río, R.M. Ultrastructural staining with sodium metaperiodate and sodium borohydride. *J. Histochem. Cytochem.* **2002**, *50*, 11–19. [CrossRef]

28. Bergersen, L.H.; Storm-Mathisen, J.; Gundersen, V. Immunogold quantification of amino acids and proteins in complex subcellular compartments. *Nat. Protoc.* **2008**, *3*, 144–152. [CrossRef]

29. Guo, X.; Sun, X.; Hu, D.; Wang, Y.J.; Fujioka, H.; Vyas, R.; Chakrapani, S.; Joshi, A.U.; Luo, Y.; Mochly-Rosen, D.; et al. VCP recruitment to mitochondria causes mitophagy impairment and neurodegeneration in models of Huntington's disease. *Nat. Commun.* **2016**, *26*, 12646. [CrossRef] [PubMed]

30. Lim, J.; Kim, H.W.; Youdim, M.B.; Rhyu, I.J.; Choe, K.M.; Oh, Y.J. Binding preference of p62 towardsLC3-ll during dopaminergic neurotoxin-induced impairment of autophagic flux. *Autophagy* **2011**, *7*, 51–60. [CrossRef]

31. Saita, S.; Shirane, M.; Nakayama, K.I. Selective escape of proteins from the mitochondria during mitophagy. *Nat. Commun.* **2013**, *4*, 1410. [CrossRef] [PubMed]

32. Flores-Toro, J.A.; Go, K.L.; Leeuwenburgh, C.; Kim, J.S. Autophagy in the liver: Cell's cannibalism and beyond. *Arch Pharm. Res.* **2016**, *39*, 1050–1061. [CrossRef] [PubMed]

33. Oliveira, P.F.; Martins, A.D.; Moreira, A.C.; Cheng, C.Y.; Alves, M.G. The Warburg effect revisited-lesson from the Sertoli cell. *Med. Res. Rev.* **2015**, *35*, 126–151. [CrossRef] [PubMed]

34. Rato, L.; Meneses, M.J.; Silva, B.M.; Sousa, M.; Alves, M.G.; Oliveira, P.F. New insights on hormones and factors that modulate Sertoli cell metabolism. *Histol. Histopathol.* **2016**, *31*, 499–513.

35. Zhang, J. Teaching the basics of autophagy and mitophagy to redox biologists–mechanisms and experimental approaches. *Redox Biol.* **2015**, *4*, 242–459. [CrossRef]

36. Xiao, B.; Goh, J.Y.; Xiao, L.; Xian, H.; Lim, K.L.; Liou, Y.C. Reactive oxygen species trigger Parkin/PINK1 pathway-dependent mitophagy by inducing mitochondrial recruitment of Parkin. *J. Biol. Chem.* **2017**, *292*, 16697–16708. [CrossRef] [PubMed]

37. Kim, S.J.; Syed, G.H.; Siddiqui, A.; Hepatitis, C. Virus Induces the Mitochondrial Translocation of Parkin and Subsequent Mitophagy. *PLoS Pathog.* **2013**, *9*, e1003285. [CrossRef] [PubMed]

38. Yamano, K.; Matsuda, N.; Tanaka, K. The ubiquitin signal and autophagy: An orchestrated dance leading to mitochondrial degradation. *EMBO Rep.* **2016**, *3*, 300–316. [CrossRef]

39. Palikaras, K.; Lionaki, E.; Tavernarakis, N. Mechanisms of mitophagy in cellular homeostasis, physiology and pathology. *Nat. Cell Biol.* **2018**, *20*, 1013–1022. [CrossRef]

40. Raimundo, N.; Fernández-Mosquera, L.; Yambire, K.F.; Diogo, C.V. Mechanisms of communication between mitochondria and lysosomes. *Int. J. Biochem. Cell Biol.* **2016**, *79*, 345–349. [CrossRef]

41. Richburg, J.H.; Murphy, C.; Myers, J.L. The Sertoli cell as a target for toxicants. In *Comprehensive Toxicology*, 3rd ed.; McQueen, C.A., Ed.; Elsevier: Amsterdam, The Netherlands, 2014; pp. 64–82.

42. Mohanty, A.; Tiwari-Pandey, R.; Pandey, N.R. Mitochondria: The indispensable players in innate immunity and guardians of the inflammatory response. J. Cell Commun. Signal. **2019**. [CrossRef]

43. Sanchez-Alvarez, R.; Martinez-Outschoorn, U.E.; Lin, Z.; Lamb, R.; Hulit, J.; Howell, A.; Sotgia, F.; Rubin, E.; Lisanti, M.P. Ethanol exposure induces the cancer-associated fibroblast phenotype and lethal tumor metabolism: Implications for breast cancer prevention. *Cell Cycle* **2013**, *12*, 289–301. [CrossRef] [PubMed]

44. Khandelwal, P.J.; Herman, A.M.; Hoe, H.S.; Rebeck, G.W.; Moussa, C.E. Parkin mediates beclin-dependent autophagic clearance of defective mitochondria and ubiquitinated Abeta in AD models. *Hum. Mol. Genet.* **2011**, *20*, 2091–2102. [CrossRef] [PubMed]

45. Fang, E.F.; Hou, Y.; Palikaras, K.; Adriaanse, B.A.; Kerr, J.S.; Yang, B.; Lautrup, S.; Hasan-Olive, M.M.; Caponio, D.; Dan, X.; et al. Mitophagy inhibits amyloid-β and tau pathology and reverses cognitive deficits in models of Alzheimer's disease. *Nat. Neurosci.* **2019**. [Epub ahead of print]. [CrossRef] [PubMed]

46. Zhang, S.X.; Zhuang, L.L.; Liu, J.; Jing, Y.Y.; Sun, J.; Gong, L.; Liu, X.Y. The role of Parkin protein in cardiac function and ventricular remodeling in myocardial infarction rats. *Eur. Rev. Med. Pharmacol. Sci.* **2018**, *22*, 5004–5013. [PubMed]

Article

Notoginsenoside R1 Ameliorates Diabetic Retinopathy through PINK1-Dependent Activation of Mitophagy

Ping Zhou [1,2], Weijie Xie [1,2], Xiangbao Meng [1,2], Yadong Zhai [1,2], Xi Dong [1,2], Xuelian Zhang [1,2], Guibo Sun [1,2,*] and Xiaobo Sun [1,2,*]

[1] Institute of Medicinal Plant Development, Peking Union Medical College and Chinese Academy of Medical Sciences, Beijing 100193, China; zhoup0520@163.com (P.Z.); xwjginseng@126.com (W.X.); 18210482526@163.com (X.M.); shengjupan@163.com (Y.Z.); dx5212004@126.com (X.D.); xlZhang2022@163.com (X.Z.)

[2] Key Laboratory of New Drug Discovery Based on Classic Chinese Medicine Prescription, Chinese Academy of Medical Sciences, Beijing 100193, China

[*] Correspondence: ginseng123@163.com (G.S.); sunxiaobopaper@163.com (X.S.); Tel./Fax: +86-10-57833013 (X.S.)

Received: 20 January 2019; Accepted: 26 February 2019; Published: 2 March 2019

Abstract: Accumulating evidence has indicated that inflammation, oxidative stress, apoptosis, and autophagy in retinal Müller cells are involved in diabetic retinopathy (DR). Notoginsenoside R1 (NGR1), a novel saponin extracted from *Panax notoginseng*, posesses pharmacological properties, including treating diabetic encephalopathy and improving microcirculatory disorders. Nevertheless, its beneficial effects on DR and the potential mechanism remain to be elucidated. In this study, we found retinal vascular degeneration, reduced retinal thickness, and impaired retinal function in db/db mice were all dramatically attenuated by oral treatment with NGR1 (30 mg/kg) for 12 weeks. NGR1 pretreatment also significantly inhibited apoptosis, markedly suppressed the VEGF expression, markedly increased PEDF expression and markedly inhibited oxidative stress and inflammation in rat retinal Müller cells (rMC-1) subjected to high glucose (HG) and in the retinas of db/db mice. Furthermore, NGR1 pre-treatment upregulated the level of PINK1 and Parkin, increased the LC3-II/LC3-I ratio, and downregulated the level of p62/SQSTM1 in rMC-1 cells induced by HG and in the retinas of db/db mice. Moreover, NGR1 administration enhanced the co-localization of GFP-LC3 puncta and MitoTracker in rMC-1 cells. Importantly, knockdown of PINK1 abolished the protective effects of NGR1. In conclusion, these phenomena suggested that NGR1 prevented DR via PINK1-dependent enhancement of mitophagy.

Keywords: diabetic retinopathy; mitophagy; PINK1; Notoginsenoside R1

1. Introduction

Diabetic retinopathy (DR), a severe complication of diabetes, continues to be the main reason for blindness in working-age individuals on a global scale [1]. The histological features of DR include the breakdown of the blood-retinal barrier, neovascularization, capillary non-perfusion, pericyte drop out, loss of endothelial cells, and relentless abnormal fibrovascular proliferation [2]. Although extensive research has been conducted, the pathophysiology of DR has not been fully elucidated. Numerous studies have suggested the fact that the pathogenesis of DR is involved in the functional disorder of Müller cells [3,4]. Müller cells maintain the balance between angiogenic factors, including vascular endothelial growth factor (VEGF), and antiangiogenic factors, including pigment epithelium-derived factor (PEDF) [5,6].

Although strict control of glycaemia, hypertension and hyperlipidaemia is still the main strategy in the primary treatment of DR, the recommended goals are difficult to achieve in many patients [7]. Current therapies for DR, including laser photocoagulation and anti-VEGF agents, significantly reduces the incidence of severe vision loss. However, existing therapies are not uniformly successful in halting visual decline, they are associated with troublesome side effects, and potentially serious complications may occur [8]. Therefore, novel alternative pharmacological therapies based on the pathophysiological mechanisms of DR are urgently needed in the clinic. Importantly, the major overlap that has been observed between traditional Chinese medicine (especially Panax notoginseng) and DR treatment may highlight additional therapeutic options for better managing DR [9,10].

A previous study reported the use of *P. notoginseng* from traditional Chinese medicine for the treatment of DR [11,12]. However, the mechanism of the effect of *P. notoginseng* remains unclear. NGR1 is a bioactive compound separated from *P. notoginseng*. Thus, the present study was designed to evaluate the beneficial effects and mechanism of NGR1 against DR in rat retinal Müller cells (rMC-1) exposed to high glucose (HG) and in the retinas of db/db mice.

Among the various biochemical pathways implicated in the physiologic abnormalities of Müller cells in DR, studies have focused on mitochondrial homeostasis and the signal transduction pathways needed to support mitochondria [13,14]. Mitochondria play a crucial role in the regulation of inflammation, oxidative stress, autophagy and apoptosis [15–17]. Damaged and dysfunctional mitochondria accumulate in the retina of diabetic patients and diabetic rodents [18,19]. The efficient and selective elimination of damaged and dysfunctional mitochondria is critical for maintaining mitochondrial homeostasis.

Mitophagy, a specialized form of autophagy, is considered the central mechanism in mitochondrial quality and quantity control [20,21]. To initiate mitophagy, PTEN-induced putative kinase protein 1 (PINK1) expression is elevated on the outer membrane of dysfunctional mitochondria where PINK1 simultaneously raises Parkin, the E3 ubiquitin ligase [22,23]. Parkin subsequently evokes ubiquitin chain formation on mitochondrial outer membrane proteins. Then, the autophagy receptors are recruited, such as p62/SQSTM1, and link to the LC3B II autophagophore to form autophagosomes [24,25]. In this respect, PINK1 might represent an attractive novel therapeutic target for intervention in DR.

Therefore, we sought to further determine whether PINK1-mediated mitophagy involves the mechanism associated with the protective effects of NGR1.

2. Reagents and Methods

2.1. Materials

NGR1 (molecular weight = 933.15; purity > 98%) was purchased from Shanghai Winherb Medical S and T Development (Beijing, China). Dulbecco's modified Eagle's medium/F12 (DMEM/F12) and foetal bovine serum (FBS) were obtained from Gibco (Grand Island, NY, USA). 3-(4,5-Dimethylthiazol-2-yl)-2,5-diphenyltetrazolium bromide (MTT) and fluorescent dye JC-1 were acquired from Enzo Life Sciences (New York, NY, USA). ELISA kits for 4-hydroxynonenal (4-HNE), 8-hydroxy-2'-deoxyguanosine (8-OHdG) and protein carbonyl were acquired from Expandbio (Beijing, China). An Annexin V/propidium iodide (PI) kit, MitoTracker® Red CM-H2XRos and a MitoSOX™ assay kit purchased from Invitrogen (Grand Island). A terminal deoxynucleotidyl transferase biotin-dUTP nick end labelling (TUNEL) detection kit was purchased from Roche Diagnostics GmbH, Mannheim, Germany. Cell protein extraction kits, PINK1 siRNA, and control siRNA were provided by Santa Cruz Biotechnology (Dallas, TX, USA). Bicinchoninic acid assay kits were purchased from Pierce Biotechnology (Waltham, MA, USA). The pCMV-G FP-LC3 expression vector was acquired from Cell Biolabs (San Diego, CA, USA).

2.2. Cell Culture and Drug

rMC-1 cells were acquired from American Type Culture Collection (ATCC). rMC-1 cells were cultured in DMEM/F12 supplemented with 5% FBS at 37 °C in an incubator. In all experiments, rMC-1 cells in the exponential phase were used. NGR1 stock solution (1 M) was stocked in DMSO. HG (60 mM) was prepared in distilled water followed by filtering. The indicated concentrations of NGR1 and HG were prepared immediately before use.

2.3. Analysis of Cell Viability

The cell viability of rMC-1 cells was evaluated by MTT chemosensitivity testing with a microplate reader (SpectraFluor, Tecan, Sunrise, Austria). Briefly, rMC-1 cells were cultured in 96-well plates at a density of 8×10^3 cells/well followed by culturing for 24 h. The cells were pre-incubated with NGR1 and then induced by HG or co-incubated with NGR1 and HG. The control cells were incubated in DMEM/F12 that contained an equivalent concentration of DMSO (the highest concentration was less than 0.1%). The cells were treated with MTT operating fluid (1 mg/mL final concentration) at 37 °C for 4 h. Then, 100 µL of DMSO was used to replace the MTT reagent. Cell viability was reflected by absorbance, which was measured at 570 nm using a microplate reader (SpectraFluor) after 2 min of shaking. Cell viability was expressed as a percentage of the control value. Each experiment was performed in quintuplicate using three independent cultures.

2.4. Measurement of Mitochondrial Membrane Potential

JC-1 (Enzo Life Sciences International, New York, NY, USA) staining was conducted to evaluate the changes in mitochondrial membrane potential by flow cytometry analysis. rMC-1 cells $(1 \times 10^5$ cells/mL) were cultured in six-well plates and grown for 24 h. The cells were pre-treated with NGR1 (20 µM) for 24 h followed by exposure to HG (60 mM) for 48 h. Each group of cells was collected followed by incubation with JC-1 dye working fluid in the dark for 30 min at 37 °C. After rinsing twice, the stained cells were analysed using FACSCalibur (BD Biosciences, San Jose, CA, USA).

2.5. Detection of the Apoptosis Rate

We evaluated the proportions of viable and apoptotic cells in different treatment groups using the Annexin V/PI assay kits. rMC-1 cells $(1 \times 10^5$ cells/well) were planted in six-well plates. NGR1 (20 µM) was added to co-incubate with cells for 24 h followed by challenge with HG (60 mM) for 48 h. Then the cells were collected for conditioning with $1 \times$ Annexin V working solution, supplemented with PI (1 µg/mL), avoiding light for 15 min. Thereafter, 300 mL of $1\times$ binding buffer was added, and samples were mixed for analyze with a FACSCalibur flow cytometer (BD Biosciences). The results are expressed and analysed from three independent experiments.

2.6. Evaluation of DNA Fragmentation

Cell apoptosis was examined with a TUNEL staining kit in line with the recommended procedure (Roche Diagnostics GmbH, Mannheim, Germany). Briefly, after all processes, rMC-1 cells were washed with PBS, fixed in 4% buffered formaldehyde for 30 min and then incubated with a methanol solution with 0.3% H_2O_2. After rinsing with PBS, the cells were incubated with a permeabilizing solution containing 0.1% Triton X-100 for 10 min. Then, the TUNEL reaction mixture was prepared for incubation with the cells for 1 h at 37 °C in the dark. Thereafter, the rMC-1 cells were washed with PBS and counterstained with diamidino-2-phenylindole (DAPI). After washing with an equilibration buffer, photographs were acquired with a fluorescence microscope (Leica DM4000, Frankfurt, Germany).

2.7. Detection of Caspase-3 Activity

A fluorescence staining kit (BioVision, Milpitas, CA, USA) was used to detect the activation degree of caspase-3 in rMC-1 cells. Briefly, after all processes, 50 µL of precooled buffer was added to each group for 10 min; then, 50 µL of 2× reaction buffer (containing 10 mM dithiothreitol) and 5 µL of DEVD-7-amino-4-trifluoromethylcoumarin were prepared for incubation with the cells at 37 °C for 2 h. Fluorescence intensity was detected at 400 nm excitation wavelength and 505 nm emission wavelength. Three independent experiments were performed independently.

2.8. Transient Transfection

rMC-1 cells (1×10^5 cells/well) were cultured in six-well plates followed by transient transfection for 48 h with PINK1 siRNA or corresponding control siRNA or pCMV-GFP-LC3 expression vector using the GeneJammer reagent (Agilent Stratagene, Palo Alto, CA, USA) in line with the indicated procedures. PINK1 silencing was determined by RT-PCR and Western blotting.

2.9. Animals

For all experiments, principles were followed to reduce the number of animals used and to minimize their suffering. The protocol was approved by the Laboratory Animal Ethics Committee of the Institute of Medicinal Plant Development, Peking Union Medical College, and conformed to the Guide for the Care and Use of Laboratory Animals (Permit Number: SYXK 2017-0020). Five-month-old db/db mice (BKS/DB−/−) and age-matched nondiabetic littermates (BKS/DB+/+, db/m) were purchased from the Animal Laboratory Center of Nanjing University. The temperature and humidity of the breeding environment were kept within the specified ranges. The mice were fed until they were 26 weeks old and then randomly assigned to the vehicle-treated db/m (n = 12), NGR1 (30 mg/kg/day)-treated db/m (n = 12), vehicle-treated db/db mice (n = 12), and NGR1 (30 mg/kg/day)-treated db/db group (n = 12). NGR1 was freshly prepared in saline and administered by gavage for 12 weeks. The vehicle-treated db/m and db/db mice were given the same amount of saline. The general health of the mice was carefully monitored, and no significant difference was found in body weight or food and water intake between the vehicle-treated and NGR1-treated groups. After being administered by gavage for 12 weeks, retinal function was assessed by detecting OCT and ERG; two days later, the mice were sacrificed for subsequent experiments.

2.10. Electroretinogram and Visual Evoked Potential

To detect retinal function of the mice, flash electroretinography (FERG), scotopic full-field electrophysiology, and flash visual evoked potentials (FVEPs) were recorded using the Visual Electrophysiology Instrument (OPTO-III, Optoprobe, Burnaby, BC, Canada, Canada). Briefly, the mice were anaesthetized with a mixture of ketamine (100 mg/kg body weight) and xylazine (10 mg/kg body weight) after overnight adaptation to the dark. The eyes of the mice were dilated with 1% tropicamide. For ERG recordings, the loop electrode was fixed on the corneal surface of the indicated eye. Needle electrodes were inserted under the skin of the groin and leg. To detect flash VEPs, a needle electrode was inserted under the skin between the two ears to replace the loop electrode. Black plaques were used to cover unstimulated eyes during the experiment. For FERG and FVEP recordings, stimulus production and data collection were carried out with the Visual Electrophysiology Instrument (OPTO-III, Optoprobe, Canada). Signals were amplified by 10,000 bandpass filtered (0.5–100 Hz) and digitized at 300 Hz with 12-bit resolution. Mice were tested at multiple flash intensities (3.0 cd.s.m^{-2}, four times), and the stimulus interval was 15 s.

2.11. Optical Coherence Tomography

Retinal thicknesses of the mice were examined using optical coherence tomography (isOCT, 4DISOCT Microscope Imaging System, Optoprobe, Burnaby, BC, Canada). After anaesthetizing, the eyes of the mice were dilated with 1% tropicamide and coated with viscoelastic material to form a plano-concave lens. "TruTrack TM Active Eye Tracking" and "Automatic Real Time (ART)" technologies were used. The images were acquired with the optic nerve head centred on the corresponding box by altering the position and angle of the mice. Then, retinal thicknesses were analysed with software (version 2.0) from OptoProbe Research Ltd.

2.12. Transmission Electron Microscopy Analysis

The ultrastructure of retinal Müller cells was analysed by transmission electron microscopy JEOL JEM1230 (JEOL Ltd., Tokyo, Japan). Briefly, the retinas were fixed in 2.5% glutaraldehyde overnight and then the samples were processed for 60 min with 0.1 M sodium cacodylate buffer supplemented with 1% osmium tetroxide. The retinas were then treated with 2% uranyl acetate for 30 min, stimulated in different gradient concentrations of ethanol, and then embedded in PolyBed 812 resin. Sections were obtained at 70 nm thickness followed by staining with Venable's lead citrate to photograph using a transmission electron microscope (JEOL, Tokyo, Japan).

2.13. HE Staining

Cervical dislocation was used to euthanize the mice, the eyeballs were quickly removed and fixed in 4% paraformaldehyde, embedded in paraffin and sectioned (5 μm). The eye sections were stained with haematoxylin and eosin (H and E). Serial sections in close proximity (within 100 μm) to the optic nerve head were obtained to ensure the parallel comparison of different groups and digital images were captured under a light microscope (BX51, Olympus Corporation, Tokyo, Japan). The retinal thickness was determined in vertical sections by measuring the distance from the retinal pigment epithelium (RPE) layer to the top of the INL.

2.14. Determination of Mitochondrial ROS

The level of mitochondrial ROS in rMC-1 cells and the retinas were determined by the mitochondria-specific probe MitoSOX™ (Carlsbad, CA, USA) following the steps recommended. The cells were pre-incubated with NGR1 (20 μM) for 24 h and subjected to HG (60 mM) for 48 h. rMC-1 cells were trypsinized and collected. After anaesthetizing, mice were perfused transcardially followed by removing eyeballs and detached retinas. The retinal tissues were homogenized in PBS. Subsequently, the cells and the homogenates were pre-treated with MitoSOX™ (0.2 μM final concentration) at 37 °C avoiding light for 40 min. Images were obtained to evaluate fluorescence intensity using a fluorescence microplate reader. The excitation and emission wavelengths were 495 and 529 nm, respectively.

2.15. ELISA

The levels of VEGF, PEDF, 4-HNE, protein carbonyl, 8-OHdG, and the inflammatory factors (MCP-1, TNF-α, IL-6, and ICAM-1) were measured by enzyme-linked immune sorbent assay (ELISA) kits following the manufacturer's instructions. ELISA kits for 4-hydroxynonenal (4-HNE), 8-hydroxy-2′-deoxyguanosine (8-OHdG) and protein carbonyl were acquired from Expandbio (Beijing, China), and ELISA kits for VEGF, PEDF, and the inflammatory factors (MCP-1, TNF-α, IL-6 and ICAM-1) were acquired from Abcam (Cambridge, MA, USA). The equiponderant retinal tissues derived from each group were dissociated in RIPA supplemented with phosphatase and protease inhibitor. The homogenates were centrifuged at 12,000 rpm for 15 min at 4 °C, and the supernatants were collected for ELISA. The rMC-1 cells were harvested and dissociated in lysis buffer. The lysates were centrifuged at 20,000 rpm for 10 min to obtain the supernatant for ELISA.

2.16. Western Blotting

Western blotting was performed to evaluate the corresponding proteins. Briefly, proteins were obtained by cell or tissue protein extraction kits supplemented with protease inhibitor and phosphatase inhibitor (Roche, Penzberg, Upper Bavaria, Germany) and stored at 4 °C for 15 min and then centrifuged at 15,000 rpm for 20 min to acquire the supernatant containing protein. A BCA quantitative kit was used to measure the protein concentration in each sample. Thereafter, equivalent concentrations of protein samples from different groups were prepared for electrophoresis and then imprinted onto a membrane. Next, the membranes were blocked for more than 2 h in non-fat milk powder solution at approximately 25 °C followed by incubation in skimmed milk containing primary and secondary antibodies according to a certain ratio. Tris-buffered saline and Tween 20 (TBST) were used to wash the membranes for 15 min, which was repeated three times. Then, the bands were visualized using an enhanced chemiluminescence solution. Protein expression was observed using Molecular Imager Lab, and densitometric analysis was performed using Gel Pro software (version 6.3).

2.17. Statistical Analysis

All data are expressed as the mean $\pm$ standard deviation (SD). When the data were normally distributed, they were analysed by unpaired two-tailed Student's t tests, multiple groups were analysed by one-way analysis of variance (ANOVA), and multiple groups with two variables were analysed by two-way ANOVA. Data with equal variances were analysed by post hoc Bonferroni's test, and data with unequal variance were analysed by Dunnett's T3 test. When the data were not normally distributed, nonparametric tests were used. A p value < 0.05 was considered significant.

3. Results

3.1. NGR1 Pre-Treatment Exerted a Positive Effect on HG-Induced Cell Death in rMC-1 Cells

In our research, the effects of HG on rMC-1 cells were detected. rMC-1 cells treated with HG (30, 60 and 90 mM) for 12, 24, 48 and 72 h resulted in an obvious decline in cell viability in a time-dependent manner (Figure 1A). Treatment of rMC-1 cells with HG (60 mM) for 48 h reduced the cell viability to approximately 50% of the control cell viability ($p < 0.01$). Therefore, further experiments were performed using HG (60 mM) and a 48 h treatment period. In contrast, NGR1 had no effect on the cell viability of rMC-1 cells (Figure 1B; $p > 0.05$). However, NGR1 (5, 10, 20 and 40 μM) pre-treatment for 4, 8, 12 and 24 h significantly increased the cell viability of rMC-1 cells (Figure 1C; $p < 0.01$), followed by HG (60 mM) incubation. Unexpectedly, co-incubation of NGR1 (5, 10, 20 and 40 μM) with HG for 48 h led to almost no protection (Figure 1D; $p > 0.05$), which indicated that the protective function of NGR1 was conferred only when administered as a pre-treatment. In addition, to investigate whether 60 mM HG is toxic to cells due to osmotic pressure, mannitol was used as an osmotic control, and the effect of HG osmotic pressure on cells was separately investigated. No obvious toxicity was observed, and these data are provided in the Supplementary Materials (Figure S1).

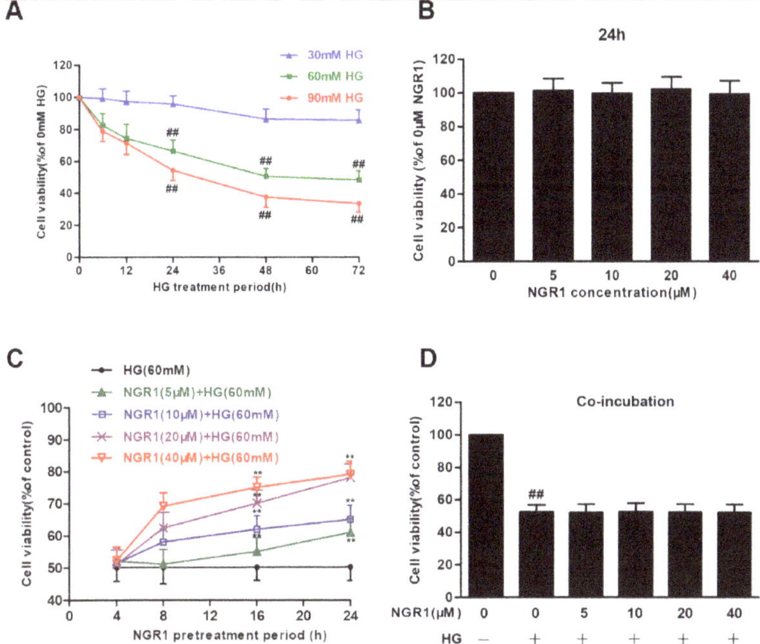

Figure 1. NGR1 preconditioning exerted a protective effect on HG-induced cell death in rMC-1 cells. Cell viability was tested by an MTT reduction assay. (**A**) HG increased cell death in rMC cells in concentration- and time-dependent manners. (**B**) NGR1 showed no effect on the cell viability of rMC cells. (**C**) NGR1 preincubation reversed HG-induced cell death in rMC cells in a dose- and time-dependent manners. (**D**) NGR1 had no protective effect when co-incubated with HG. The results were expressed as the means $\pm$ SD (n = 10). Two groups were compared by unpaired two-tailed Student's *t* tests, and multiple groups were analysed by one-way analysis of variance (ANOVA); ## indicates a significant difference vs. control cells ($p < 0.01$). ** indicates significant difference vs. HG treatment ($p < 0.01$). (+), treatment with HG; (−), treatment without HG.

3.2. NGR1 Inhibited HG-Induced Apoptosis in rMC-1 Cells

DNA fragmentation, phosphatidylserine externalization, mitochondrial membrane potential loss and caspase-3 activation are characteristic features of rMC-1 cells undergoing HG-induced apoptosis. In the present study, HG-treated rMC-1 cells exhibited marked increases in the ratio of TUNEL-positive cells (Figure 2A,D; $p < 0.01$), the rate of Annexin V/PI double-labelled cells (Figure 2B,E; $p < 0.01$) and caspase-3 activity (Figure 2G; $p < 0.01$). Moreover, HG-treated rMC-1 cells exhibited a significant decrease in the percentage of JC-1 red to green fluorescence intensity (Figure 2C,F; $p < 0.01$). However, NGR1 administration notably reduced the ratio of TUNEL-positive cells and the rate of Annexin V/PI double-labelled cells, increased the percentage of JC-1 red to green fluorescence intensity and decreased caspase-3 activity in HG-treated rMC-1 cells (Figure 2; $p < 0.01$). The above phenomena indicate that NGR1 could prevent rMC-1 cell apoptosis induced by HG. Additionally, NGR1 administration alone showed no variation compared with control cells ($p > 0.05$).

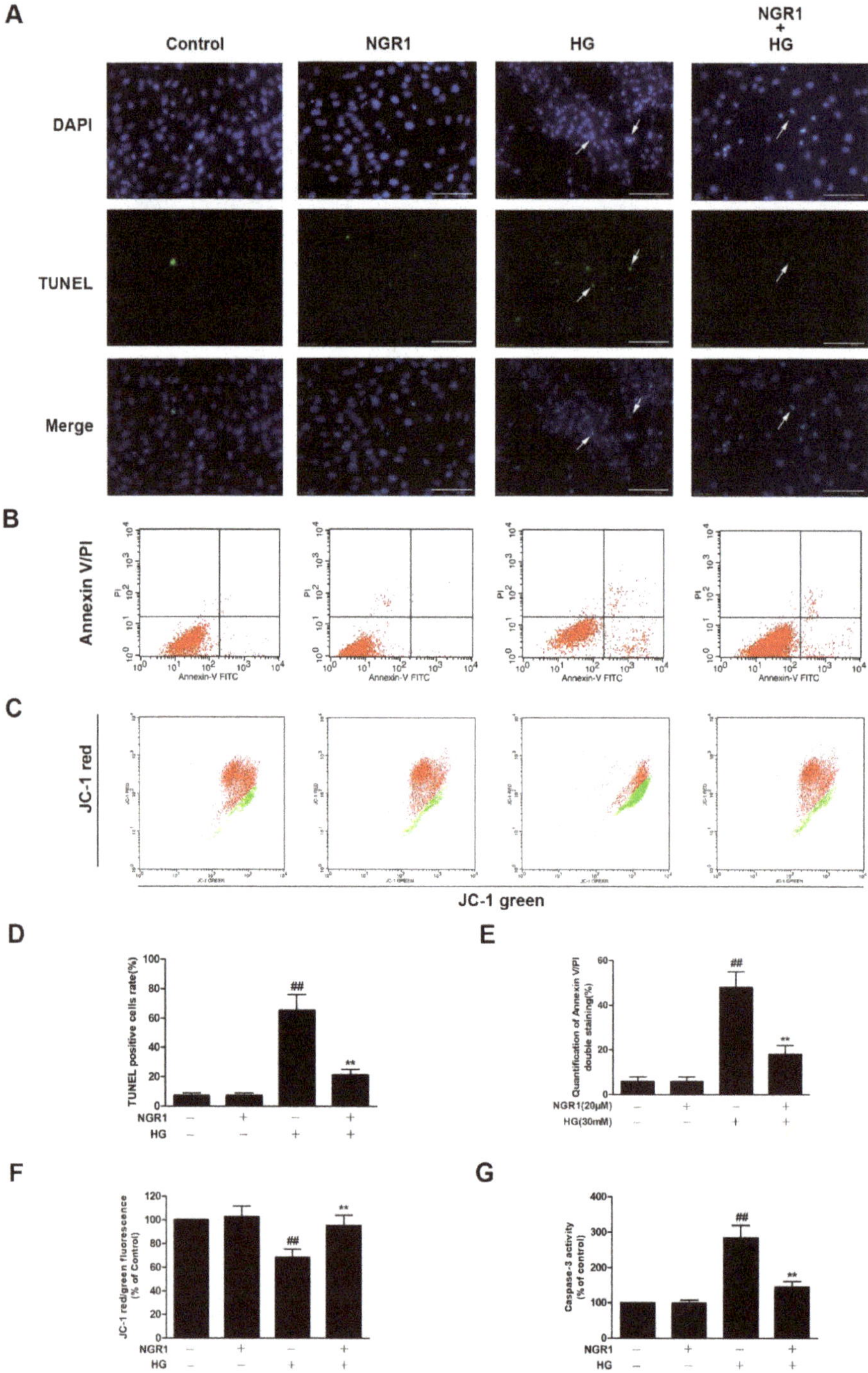

Figure 2. NGR1 preconditioning significantly inhibited HG-induced apoptosis in rMC-1 cells. NGR1 preconditioning attenuated HG-induced DNA fragmentation (**A**), Annexin V/PI double staining (**B**),

and mitochondrial membrane depolarization (**C**) in rMC-1 cells. DNA fragmentation in rMC-1 cells was determined using TUNEL staining (bar = 100 μm). Apoptosis rate was quantified with Annexin V/PI double staining followed by flow cytometry analysis. Mitochondrial membrane depolarization was detected by JC-1 staining. The rate of TUNEL-positive cells (**D**), the quantification of Annexin V/PI double staining (**E**), and the percentage of JC-1 red to green fluorescence intensity (**F**) were quantitatively analysed, and caspase 3 activity (**G**) was detected by a fluorescence staining kit. The results are expressed as the means ± SD (n = 10). ## indicates a significant difference from control cells ($p < 0.01$). Two groups were analysed by unpaired two-tailed Student's *t* tests, and multiple groups were analysed by one-way analysis of variance (ANOVA); ** indicates significant difference from HG treatment ($p < 0.01$). (+), treatment with HG or NGR1; (−), treatment without HG or NGR1.

3.3. NGR1 Significantly Attenuated DR in db/db Mice

Changes in visual functions, retinal thickness, and retinal vasculature were determined by ERG and OCT. As shown in Figure 3A, the ERG (from a wave to b wave) and VEP (P2) amplitudes were markedly decreased in db/db mice compared with db/m mice ($p < 0.01$). The amplitude of the a-wave or b-wave in db/db mice was significantly smaller than that in db/m mice, and was elevated in db/db mice by treatment with NGR1(Figure 3A, $p < 0.05$). OCT images showed that total retinal thickness, from the internal limiting membrane (ILM) to the RPE layer, was dramatically decreased in db/db mice (Figure 3B, $p < 0.05$). Treatment of db/db mice with NGR1 significantly affected the retinal thickness (Figure 3B, $p < 0.05$). Moreover, H&E staining showed that treatment of db/db mice with NGR1 for 3 months markedly increased the thickness of retinas, especially the ONL and the INL. The retinal morphology was similar between the db/m and NGR1-treated db/m groups (Figure 3C). The results of these experiments indicate that NRG1 improves retinal function and inhibits retinopathy in db/db mice.

3.4. NGR1 Reversed the Imbalance between VEGF and PEDF In Vivo and In Vitro

VEGF and PEDF play vital roles in the pathogenesis of DR. ELISA experiments demonstrated that HG treatment caused a notable upregulation in VEGF levels (Figure 4C; $p < 0.01$) and a remarkable decrease in PEDF levels (Figure 4D; $p < 0.01$) in rMC-1 cells. As expected, db/db mice showed a notable upregulation in VEGF levels (Figure 4A; $p < 0.01$) and a significant decrease in PEDF expression (Figure 4B; $p < 0.01$) in the retinas. However, NGR1 administration noticeably reduced the levels of VEGF and increased the levels of PEDF in HG-treated rMC-1 cells and in the retinas of db/db mice (Figure 4; $p < 0.01$).

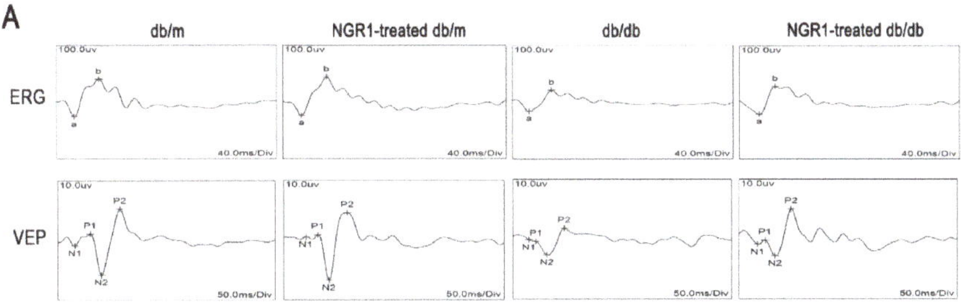

Figure 3. *Cont.*

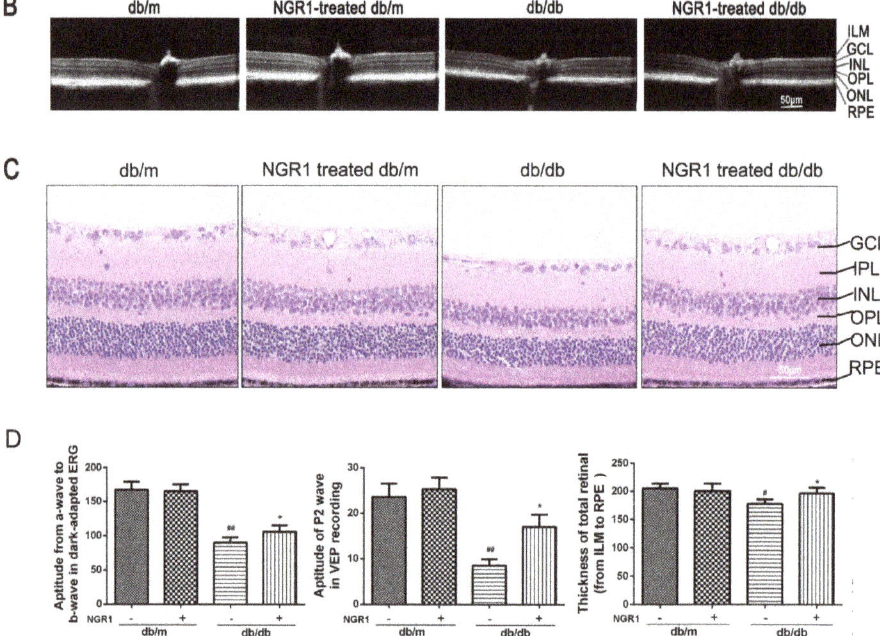

Figure 3. NGR1 pretreatment significantly attenuated DR in db/db mice. (**A**) Typical waveforms and quantitative analysis of ERG and VEPs amplitudes. (**B**) Retinal thickness was determined by OCT. (**C**) Retinal morphology was detected by HE. (**D**) Corresponding statistics of ERG, VEPs and OCT. The number of mice in this experiment was 10 (n = 10). The results are expressed as the means ± SD. Two groups were analysed by unpaired two-tailed Student's *t* tests, and multiple groups were analysed by one-way analysis of variance (ANOVA); # indicates significant difference from the control cells or db/m mice ($p < 0.05$); ## indicates a significant difference from control cells or db/m mice ($p < 0.01$). * indicates a significant difference from HG treatment or db/db mice ($p < 0.05$); ** indicates significant difference from HG treatment or db/db mice ($p < 0.01$). (+), treatment with NGR1; (−), treatment without NGR1.

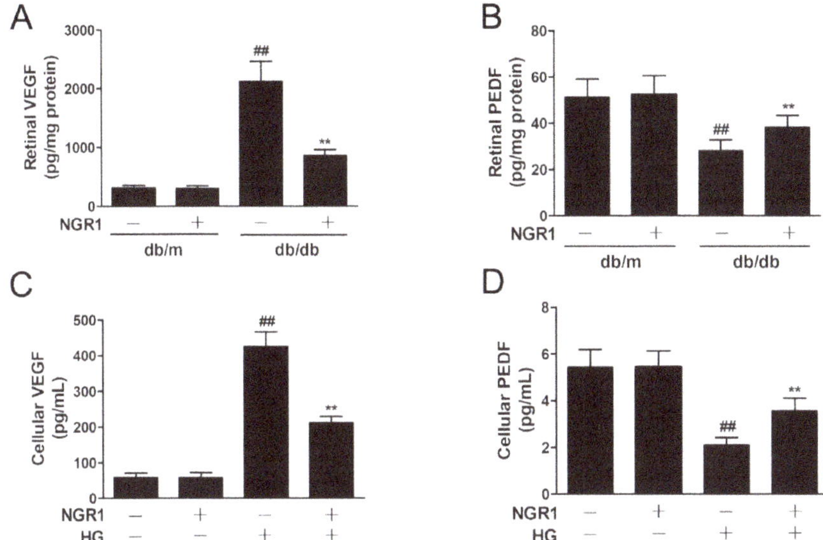

Figure 4. NGR1 pretreatment significantly attenuated the levels of VEGF and PEDF in vivo and in intro. The levels of VEGF (**A**) and PEDF (**B**) in retinas of db/db mice were determined by ELISA. The levels of VEGF (**C**) and PEDF (**D**) in HG-induced rMC cells were determined by ELISA. The results are expressed as the means $\pm$ SD (n = 10). Two groups were analysed by unpaired two-tailed Student's *t* tests, and multiple groups were analysed by one-way analysis of variance (ANOVA); ## indicates a significant difference from control cells or db/m mice ($p < 0.01$). ** indicates a significant difference from the HG treatment or db/db mice ($p < 0.01$). (+), treatment with HG or NGR1; (−), treatment without HG or NGR1.

3.5. NGR1 Inhibited Oxidative Stress In Vivo and In Vitro

Oxidative stress plays an essential role in DR progression. Compared with control cells, HG caused a notable increase in the level of mitochondrial ROS (Figure 5A; $p < 0.01$) and in the levels of 4-HNE (Figure 5B; $p < 0.01$), protein carbonyl (Figure 5C; $p < 0.01$), and 8-OHdG (Figure 5D; $p < 0.01$) in rMC-1 cells. As expected, remarkable increases in the retinal levels of mitochondrial ROS, 4-HNE, protein carbonyl and 8-OHdG were observed in the retinas of db/db mice (Figure 5E–H; $p < 0.01$). However, NGR1 treatment substantially downregulated the levels of mitochondrial ROS, 4-HNE, protein carbonyl and 8-OHdG in HG-treated rMC cells and in the retinas of db/db mice (Figure 5; $p < 0.01$).

3.6. NGR1 Inhibited Inflammation In Vivo and In Vitro

In our study, HG exposure resulted in significantly increased inflammatory factor levels (MCP-1, TNF-α, IL-6 and ICAM-1) (Figure 6A–D; $p < 0.01$) in rMC-1 cells. The levels of inflammatory factors (MCP-1, TNF-α, IL-6 and ICAM-1) were significantly increased in the retina of db/db mice compared with db/m mice (Figure 6E–H; $p < 0.01$). NGR1 treatment inhibited the expression of inflammatory cytokines in HG-treated rMC cells and in the retina of db/db mice (Figure 6; $p < 0.01$).

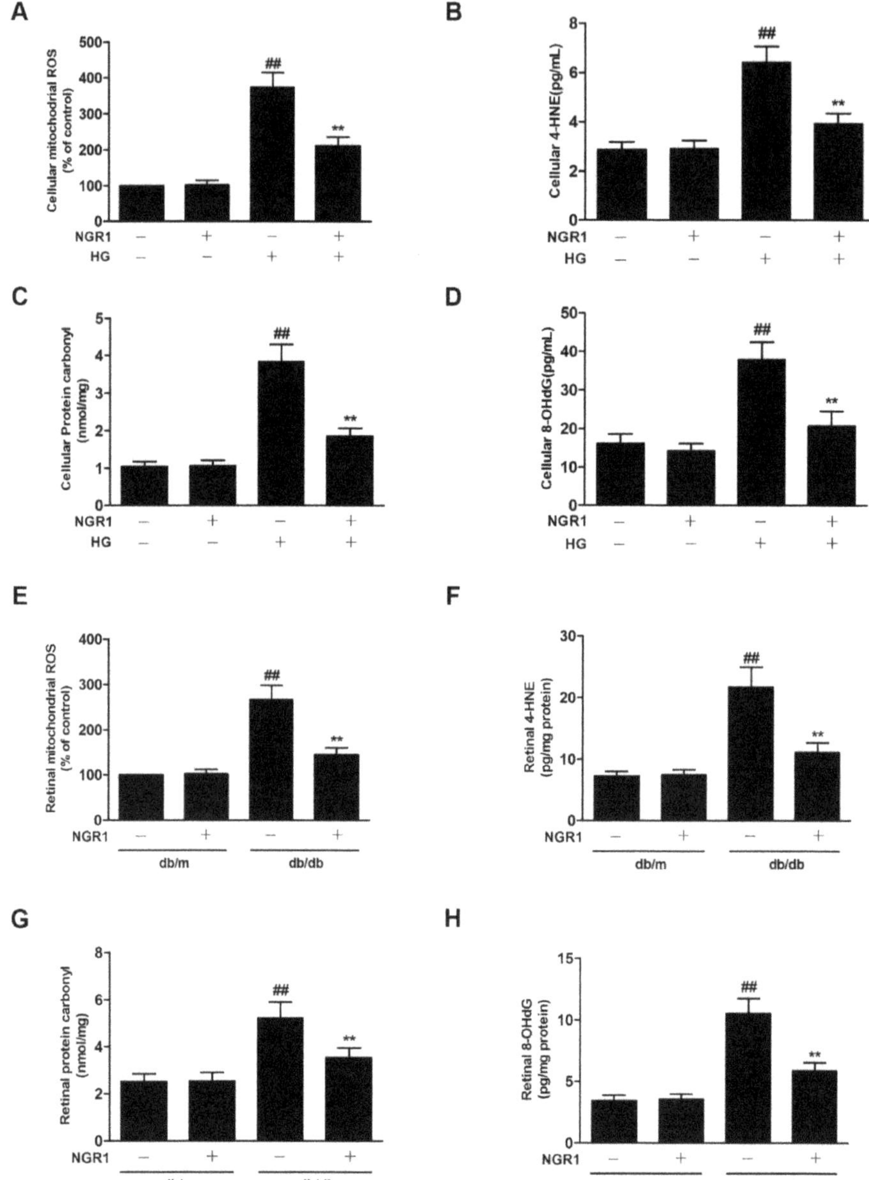

Figure 5. NGR1 pretreatment significantly suppressed oxidative stress in vivo and in intro. NGR1 preconditioning significantly suppressed HG-induced mitochondrial ROS production (**A**) and the production of 4-HNE (**B**), protein carbonyl (**C**), and 8-OHdG (**D**) in rMC cells. NGR1 pretreatment significantly decreased the level of mitochondrial ROS (**E**), 4-HNE (**F**), protein carbonyl (**G**), and 8-OHdG (**H**) in the retina of db/db mice. The level of mitochondrial ROS was determined by MitoSOX™. The production of 4-HNE, protein carbonyl, and 8-OHdG in rMC cells was detected by ELISA. The results are expressed as the means $\pm$ SD (n = 10). ## indicates a significant difference from the control cells or db/m mice ($p < 0.01$). ** indicates a significant difference from HG treatment or db/db mice ($p < 0.01$). (+), treatment with HG or NGR1; ($-$), treatment without HG or NGR1.

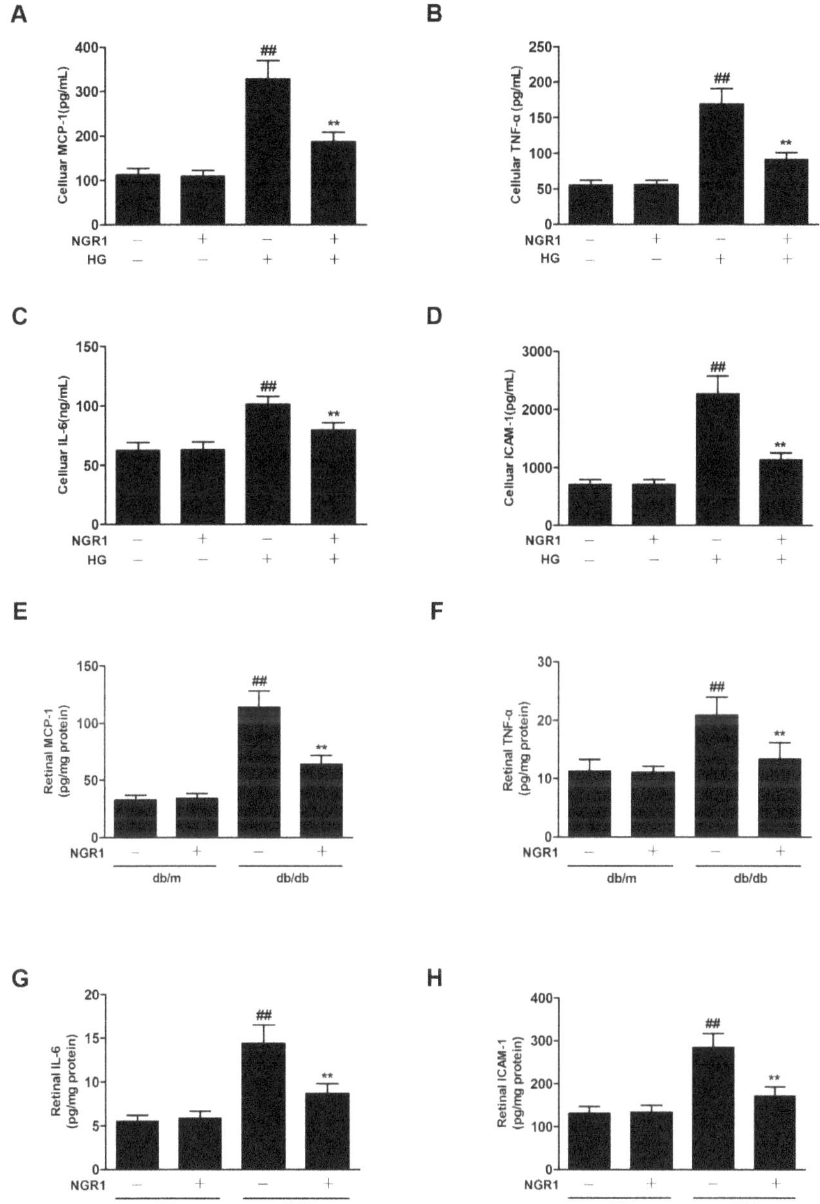

Figure 6. NGR1 pretreatment significantly inhibited inflammation in vivo and in intro. NGR1 preconditioning significantly inhibited HG-induced production of MCP-1 (**A**), TNF-α (**B**), IL-6 (**C**), and ICAM-1 (**D**) in rMC cells. NGR1 pretreatment significantly decreased the levels of MCP-1 (**E**), TNF-α (**F**), IL-6 (**G**), and ICAM-1 (**H**) in the retina of db/db mice. The levels of MCP-1, TNF-α, IL-6, and ICAM-1 were detected by ELISA. The results are expressed as the means ± SD (n = 10). ## indicates a significant difference from control cells or db/m mice ($p < 0.01$). ** indicates a significant difference from the HG treatment or db/db mice ($p < 0.01$). (+), treatment with HG or NGR1; (−), treatment without HG or NGR1.

3.7. *NGR1 Enhanced* Mitophagy *In Vivo and In Vitro*

Strategies directed at enhancing mitophagy could have far-reaching beneficial effects. Therefore, we further investigated whether NGR1 affected mitophagy. As illustrated in Figure 7, compared with db/m mice, the number of mitophagy autophagosomes was elevated in the retinas of db/db mice (Figure 7, $p < 0.01$). However, more mitophagy autophagosomes were observed in NGR1-treated db/db mice ($p < 0.01$). Moreover, NGR1 enhanced mitophagy in rMC-1 cells, as revealed by the increased co-localization of GFP-LC3 puncta and MitoTracker® Red CM-H2XRos in rMC-1 cells transiently transfected with the pCMV-GFP-LC3 expression vector (Figure 8, $p < 0.01$).

The levels of PINK1 and Parkin and the ratio of LC3-II/LC3-I were dramatically increased in the retinas of db/db mice compared with the retinas of db/m mice (Figure 9, $p < 0.01$). However, NGR1 treatment even elevated the levels of PINK1 and Parkin and the ratio of LC3-II/LC3-I in the retinas of db/db mice (Figure 9, $p < 0.01$). To evaluate whether mitophagy functioned properly in db/db mice, the p62/SQSTM1 level was examined. The expression of p62/SQSTM1 was decreased in the retinas of db/db mice (Figure 9A, $p < 0.01$). Moreover, NGR1 pre-treatment even markedly downregulated the expression of p62/SQSTM1. In accordance with these results, compared with control cells, rMC-1 cells treated with HG exhibited noticeable increases in PINK1, Parkin, and LC3-II/LC3-I expression (Figure 9B; $p < 0.01$). NGR1 pre-treatment significantly enhanced the increased PINK1, Parkin, and the ratio of LC3-II/LC3-I in rMC-1 cells exposed to HG (Figure 9; $p < 0.01$). However, the decreased SQSTM1/p62 level induced by HG was further inhibited by NGR1 pre-treatment (Figure 9, $p < 0.01$).

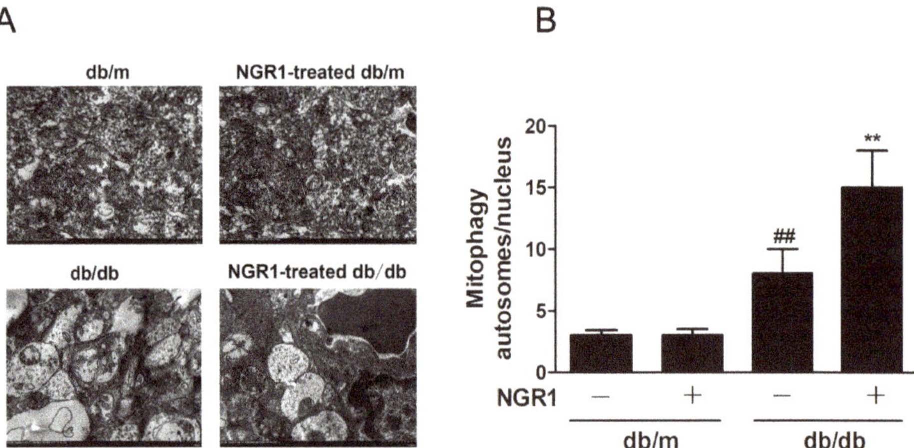

Figure 7. NGR1 pretreatment enhanced mitophagy in diabetic db/db mice with diabetic retinopathy. (**A**) The mitochondria in retinal Müller cells were analysed by transmission electron microscopy analysis. (**B**) Corresponding statistics of mitophagy autophagosomes. The results are expressed as the means ± SD (n = 5). They were analysed by unpaired two-tailed Student's *t* tests, and multiple groups were analysed by one-way analysis of variance (ANOVA); ## indicates a significant difference from db/m mice ($p < 0.01$). ** indicates a significant difference from db/db mice ($p < 0.01$). (+), treatment with NGR1; (−), treatment without NGR1.

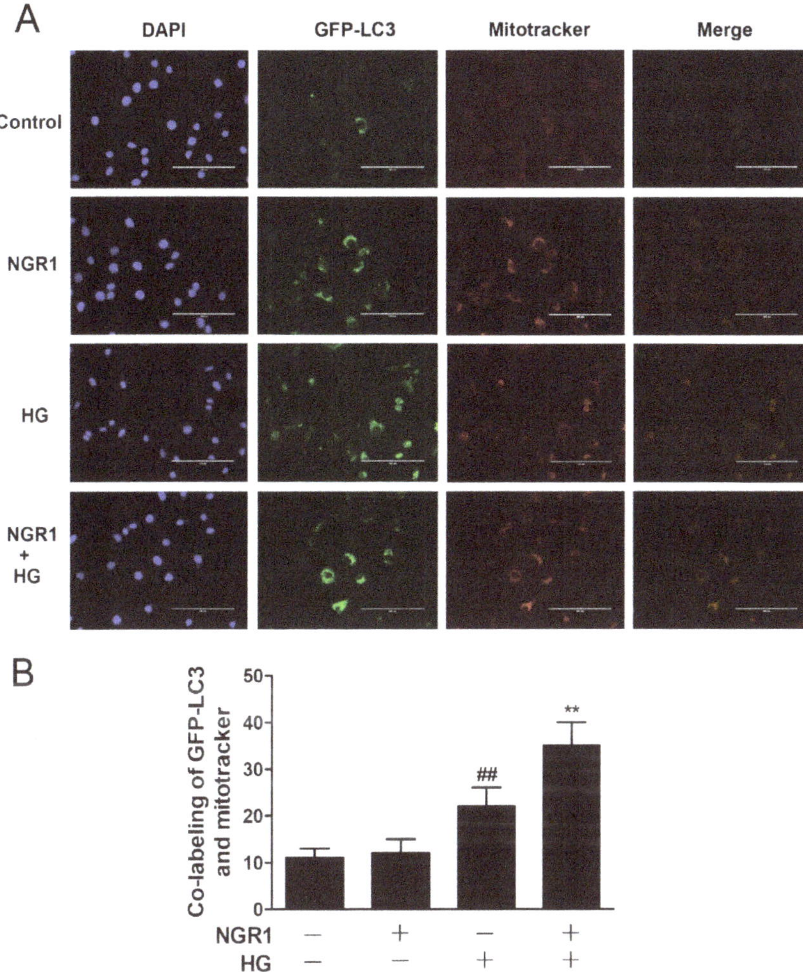

Figure 8. NGR1 pre-treatment enhanced mitophagy in HG-induced rMC1 cells. (**A**) rMC1 cells transiently transfected with the pCMV-GFP-LC3 expression vector were stained with MitoTracker® Red CM-H2XRos (Bar = 100 μm). (**B**) Corresponding statistics of the GFP-LC3 expression level. The results are expressed as the means ± SD (n = 5). Two groups were analysed by unpaired two-tailed Student's *t* tests, and multiple groups were analysed by one-way analysis of variance (ANOVA); ## indicates a significant difference from control cells ($p < 0.01$). ** indicates a significant difference from HG-treated cells ($p < 0.01$). (+), treatment with HG or NGR1; (−), treatment without HG or NGR1.

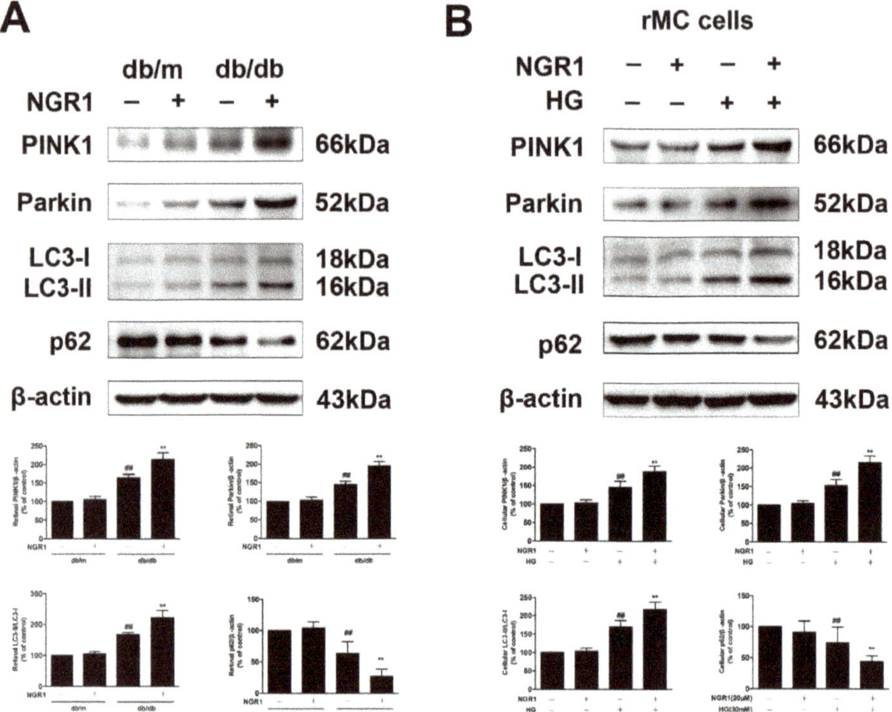

Figure 9. Effects of NGR1 pre-treatment on the expression level of mitophagy proteins in HG-induced rMC1 cells and in diabetic db/db mice with diabetic retinopathy. (**A**) PINK1, Parkin, LC3-II/LC3-I, and p62/SQSTM1 expression in the retina of db/db mice was determined by Western blotting. (**B**) The expression of PINK1, Parkin, LC3-II/LC3-I, and p62/SQSTM1 in HG-induced rMC1 cells was determined by western blotting. The results are expressed as the means $\pm$ SD (n = 10). Two groups were analysed by unpaired two-tailed Student's *t* tests, and multiple groups were analysed by one-way analysis of variance (ANOVA); ## indicates significant difference from the control cells or db/m mice ($p < 0.01$). ** indicates a significant difference from HG treatment or db/db mice ($p < 0.01$). ## indicates a significant difference from control cells or db/m mice ($p < 0.01$). ** indicates a significant difference from HG treatment or db/db mice ($p < 0.01$). (+), treatment with HG or NGR1; (−), treatment without HG or NGR1.

3.8. NGR1 Enhanced Mitophagy by Activating PINK1

To explore whether PINK1 was involved in NGR1-mediated mitophagy, rMC-1 cells were transiently transfected with PINK1 siRNA. As shown in Figure 10, PINK1 siRNA effectively reduced the expression of PINK1 and Parkin ($p < 0.01$) and abrogated the increased conversion of LC3-I to LC3-II induced by NGR1 ($p < 0.01$). Moreover, the suppression of oxidative stress (Figure 11A), the inhibition of inflammation (Figure 11B), the balance of VEGF and PEDF (Figure 12A), and the attenuation of apoptosis (Figure 12B,C) mediated by NGR1 were all abolished by PINK1 siRNA ($p < 0.01$).

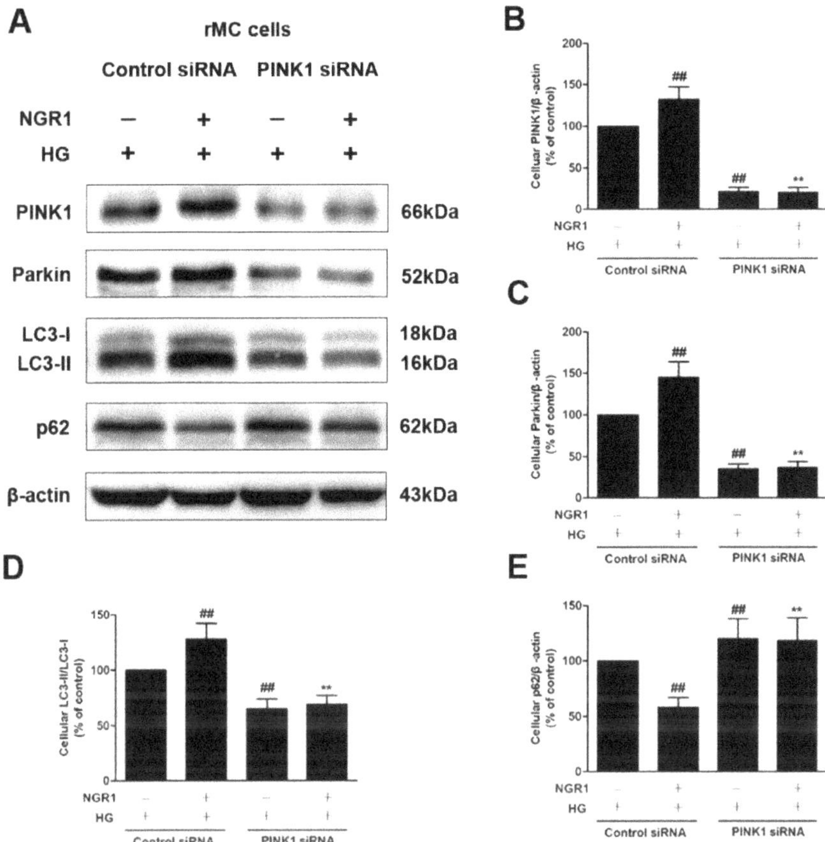

Figure 10. NGR1 enhanced mitophagy by activating PINK1. rMC cells were transiently transfected with PINK1 siRNA. (**A**) The expression of PINK1, Parkin, LC3-II/LC3-I, and p62/SQSTM1 in rMC cells was determined by Western blotting. (**B**) Quantitative densitometric analysis of PINK1 (**C**) and Parkin expression and (**D**) LC3-II/LC3-I ratio and (**E**) p62/SQSTM1 expression. The results are presented as a percentage of the control. The results are expressed as the means $\pm$ SD (n = 10). Two groups were analysed by unpaired two-tailed Student's *t* tests, and multiple groups were analysed by one-way analysis of variance (ANOVA); ## indicates a significant difference from HG-treated cells transfected with control siRNA ($p < 0.01$). ** indicates a significant difference from cells in the NGR1+HG group. (+), treatment with HG or NGR1; ($-$), treatment without HG or NGR1.

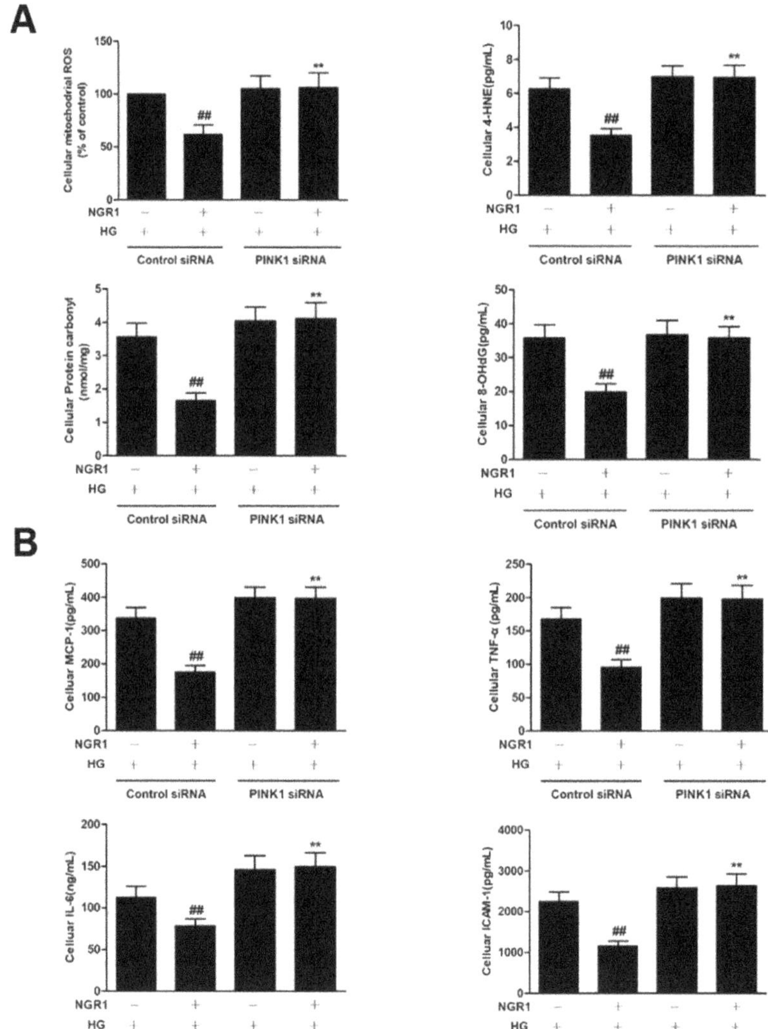

Figure 11. NGR1 suppressed oxidative stress inflammation by activating PINK1. rMC cells were transiently transfected with PINK1 siRNA. (**A**) The expression of cellular mitochondrial ROS, 4HNE, protein carbonyl and 8-OHdG. (**B**) The expression of the inflammatory factors MCP-1, TNF-α, IL-6 and ICAM-1. The results are expressed as the means $\pm$ SD (n = 10). Two groups were analysed by unpaired two-tailed Student's *t* tests, and multiple groups were analysed by one-way analysis of variance (ANOVA); ## indicates a significant difference from HG-treated cells transfected with control siRNA ($p < 0.01$). ** indicates a significant difference from cells in the NGR1+HG group. (+), treatment with HG or NGR1; ($-$), treatment without HG or NGR1.

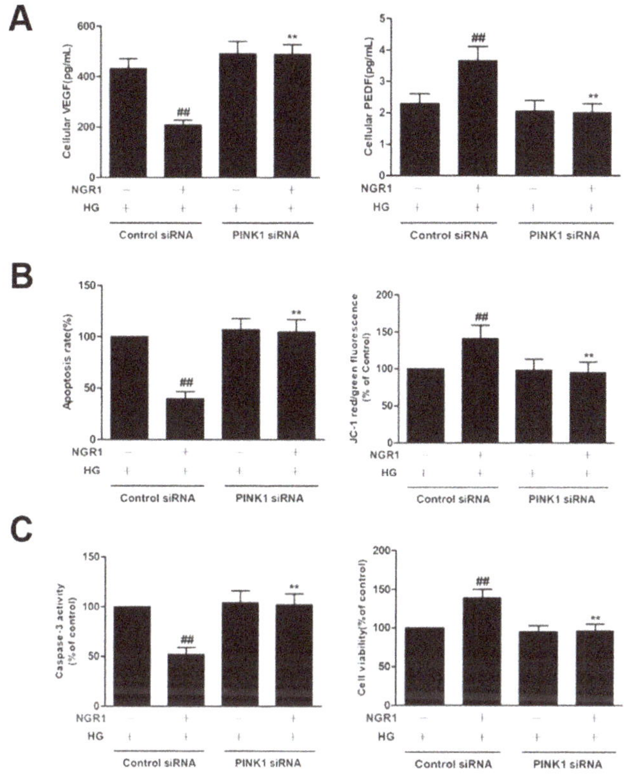

Figure 12. NGR1 attenuated apoptosis via activating PINK1. rMC cells were transiently transfected with PINK1 siRNA. (**A**) The expression of VEGF and PEDF; (**B**) the apoptosis rate and JC-1 ratio; (**C**) the caspase-3 activity and cell viability. The results are expressed as the means ± SD (n = 10). Two groups were analysed by unpaired two-tailed Student's *t* tests, and multiple groups were analysed by one-way analysis of variance (ANOVA); ## indicates a significant difference from HG-treated cells transfected with control siRNA ($p < 0.01$). ** indicates a significant difference from cells in the NGR1+HG group. (+), treatment with HG or NGR1; (−), treatment without HG or NGR1.

4. Discussion

As a serious complication of diabetes, DR is one of the most common cause of visual impairment, and its prevalence has been increasing worldwide [26]. The current treatment approach for DR based on anti-oxidative, anti-inflammatory, and anti-angiogenesis drugs and laser photocoagulation is effective but also induces adverse effects in retinal tissues. Thus, a safe and effective mode of treatment is needed to control or delay DR. Based on previous evidence, treatment with natural anti-oxidant, anti-diabetic and anti-tumoral agents may be a promising therapeutic approach for the prevention of DR. NGR1 possesses a variety of pharmacological properties, including effects of cardiac protection and neuroprotection. This study was designed to evaluate the beneficial effects of NGR1 against DR in vivo and in vitro. We further sought to determine whether PINK1-mediated mitophagy is involved in the mechanism associated with the protective effects of NGR1.

In this study, NGR1 markedly increased the amplitudes of ERG and VEP, retinal thickness and markedly decreased the retinal vascular degeneration in db/db mice, which suggests that NGR1 significantly attenuated retinal dysfunction in db/db mice. In addition, the inner blood-retinal barrier (BRB) is a gliovascular unit in which macroglial cells surround capillary endothelial cells and regulate retinal capillaries by paracrine interactions. Previous studies suggest that Müller cells play a major role in the formation of barrier properties in retinal vessels [27]. Müller cells share the ability of astrocytes to induce the formation of barrier properties by vascular endothelial cells, and modulate vascular endothelial cells by express various cytokines, which, in turn, affects the retinal microvessels [28].

Studies have shown that during the pathogenesis of DR, long-term stimulation with HG can cause damage to Müller cells and induce Müller cell apoptosis, oxidative stress, inflammatory response, overexpression of VEGF [29,30]. In this study, Müller cells were simulated with concentrations of HG (30-60-90 mM) to evaluate the "in vitro" model. Treatment of rMC-1 cells with HG (60 mM) for 48 h reduced the cell viability to approximately 50% relative to the viability of control cells, resulting in oxidative stress, an inflammatory response and excessive production of VEGF. As these mechanisms of injury are consistent with the reported literature on diabetic pathology, we chose this concentration to mimic HG injury in vivo. However, some studies have found that diabetes can induce Müller cell activation and proliferation in db/db mice [31,32].The effects of HG on Müller cells at different stages of diabetes pathogenesis require further study. In addition, it has been reported that glial cells are activated in the hippocampus of diabetic mice and sustained HG stimulation leads to glial cell apoptosis [33], suggesting that in the retina, the state of glial cells may also change over time.

Furthermore, Müller cells span the entire thickness of the retina, and contact and ensheath every type of neuronal cell body and process [34]. This morphological relationship is reflected by a multitude of functional interactions between neurons and Müller cells, including a "metabolic symbiosis" and the processing of visual information. Müller cells are also responsible for maintaining homeostasis of the retinal extracellular milieu [35]. Therefore, the thinning of the whole retina is most likely related to the morphology and function of Müller cells. Thus, in an in vitro model, we selected Müller cell damage induced by HG, and we found that NGR1 had an obvious protective effect.

In DR, retinas express low levels of PEDF and high levels of VEGF in experimental and clinical settings [36,37]. Therefore, VEGF and PEDF are now accepted as the key factors associated with DR and can constitute therapeutic targets. NGR1-treated db/db mice had a significantly elevated level of PEDF and a significantly decreased level of VEGF in retinal tissue. In parallel with these changes, NGR1 significantly increased the production of PEDF and decreased that of VEGF in HG-treated Müller cells. However, the molecular basis underlying these protective effects of NGR1 remains unknown.

Several lines of evidence raise the possibility that mitochondria dysfunction in Müller cells plays pivotal roles in oxidative stress, inflammation, and apoptosis in the retinas of patients with DR [4,15,18]. Targeting mitochondrial homeostasis may confer advantages of inhibiting angiogenesis, oxidative stress, and inflammation, thereby effectively halting the development of DR. Thus mitochondria might be a potential therapeutic target for DR treatment. In this study, we observed that HG caused mitochondrial depolarization in Müller cells, resulting in increased mitochondrial ROS generation, oxidative stress and inflammatory cytokine production. Oxidative stress and inflammation were also observed in the retinas of db/db mice. The blockade of mitochondrial damage with NGR1 caused a significant blockage of oxidative stress and inflammation in HG-treated Müller cells and in the retinas of db/db mice.

PINK1 is a recently described regulator of mitophagy [38]. Mitophagy is a conserved multistep pathway that selectively degrades and recycles damaged mitochondria [39,40]. Therefore, stimulating PINK1-mediated mitophagy may represent a novel therapeutic strategy to prevent DR. NGR1 increased GFP-LC3 puncta and MitoTracker® Red CM-H2XRos co-localization in HG-treated rMC-1 cells. To elucidate the involvement of PINK1 in NGR1-mediated mitophagy, PINK1 knockdown experiments were performed, and rMC-1 cells were transiently transfected with PINK1 siRNA. As shown in Figure 10, PINK1 siRNA abrogated the decreased p62/SQSTM1 induced by NGR1. However, the relationship between PINK and p62/SQSTM1 requires further detailed investigation. Our results show that PINK1 siRNA abolished the mitophagy mediated by NGR1. The suppression of oxidative stress, the balance of VEGF and PEDF, the inhibition of inflammation, and the attenuation of apoptosis mediated by NGR1 were all abolished by PINK1 siRNA. Based on the above results, the beneficial functions of NGR1 were PINK1-dependent.

A recent study showed that the reduced PINK and Parkin expression noted in HK-2 cells subjected to HG exposure was partially restored by MitoQ, a mitochondria-targeted antioxidant. This effect was abolished by Nrf2 siRNA and augmented by Keap1 siRNA, which suggests that PINK and Parkin expression was regulated via Nrf2/Keap1 [41]. Similar results have been confirmed in various tumour cells [42]. In addition, studies have shown that AKT signalling can selectively regulate PINK1 mitophagy [43]. Previous studies by our team have revealed that R1 pre-treatment can activate the Nrf2 signalling pathway and affect the phosphorylation level of AKT in a diabetic mouse model [44]. Therefore, whether R1 plays an anti-DR role by activating the Nrf2 signalling pathway or PI3K/AKT and, thereby, regulating the PINK1/Parkin signalling pathway is worthy of further study.

Moreover, the administration method used in this study was oral administration. Compared to the intravitreal injection, oral administration has the advantage of being non-invasive and painless, and the main disadvantage of gavage administration is the uncertainty of the active metabolite of the drug. To date, no other studies have revealed the active metabolite of NGR1. Whether the active metabolites of NGR1 are the real contributors to the protective effect of NGR1 in vivo requires further detailed investigation.

In summary, the discovery of the PINK1 activator NGR1 not only provides a potential candidate drug for DR treatment but may also increase our understanding of the functions of PINK1 in the regulation of mitophagy in DR.

Supplementary Materials: The following are available online at http://www.mdpi.com/2073-4409/8/3/213/s1, Figure S1: 60 mM HG preconditioning exerted no osmotic toxicity on rMC-1 cells.

Author Contributions: Designed and supervised the study: P.Z., G.S. and X.S. Conducted the experiments and processed the data: P.Z., W.X., Y.Z., X.D. and X.Z. Prepared the figures: P.Z., W.X. and X.M. Wrote the paper: P.Z.

Funding: This work was supported by the Major Scientific and Technological Special Project for "Significant New Drugs Formulation" (No. 2017ZX09101003-009), and the Chinese Academy of Medical Sciences (CAMS) Initiative for Innovative Medicine (No. CAMS-I2M-1-012).

Conflicts of Interest: The authors declare no conflicts of interest.

References

1. Gulshan, V.; Peng, L.; Coram, M.; Stumpe, M.C.; Wu, D.; Narayanaswamy, A.; Venugopalan, S.; Widner, K.; Madams, T.; Cuadros, J. Development and Validation of a Deep Learning Algorithm for Detection of Diabetic Retinopathy in Retinal Fundus Photographs. *JAMA* **2016**, *316*, 2402. [CrossRef] [PubMed]

2. Roy, S.; Kern, T.S.; Song, B.; Stuebe, C. Mechanistic Insights into Pathological Changes in the Diabetic Retina: Implications for Targeting Diabetic Retinopathy. *Am. J. Pathol.* **2016**, *187*, 9. [CrossRef] [PubMed]

3. Coughlin, B.A.; Feenstra, D.J.; Mohr, S. Müller cells and diabetic retinopathy. *Vis. Res.* **2017**, *139*, 93–100. [CrossRef] [PubMed]

4. Abcouwer, S.F. Müller Cell–Microglia Cross Talk Drives Neuroinflammation in Diabetic Retinopathy. *Diabetes* **2017**, *66*, 261–263. [CrossRef] [PubMed]

5. Rodrigues, M.; Xin, X.; Jee, K.; Babapoorfarrokhran, S.; Kashiwabuchi, F.; Ma, T.; Bhutto, I.; Hassan, S.J.; Daoud, Y.; Baranano, D. VEGF Secreted by Hypoxic Müller Cells Induces MMP-2 Expression and Activity in Endothelial Cells to Promote Retinal Neovascularization in Proliferative Diabetic Retinopathy. *Diabetes* **2013**, *62*, 3863–3873. [CrossRef] [PubMed]

6. Yang, X.M.; Yafai, Y.; Wiedemann, P.; Kuhrt, H.; Wang, Y.S.; Reichenbach, A.; Eichler, W. Hypoxia-induced upregulation of pigment epithelium-derived factor by retinal glial (Müller) cells. *J. Neurosci. Res.* **2012**, *90*, 257. [CrossRef] [PubMed]

7. Kang, A.Y.; Park, S.K.; Park, S.Y.; Lee, H.J.; Han, Y.; Lee, S.R.; Suh, S.H.; Kim, D.K.; Park, M.K. Therapeutic target achievement in type 2 diabetic patients after hyperglycemia, hypertension, dyslipidemia management. *Diabetes Metab. J.* **2011**, *35*, 264. [CrossRef] [PubMed]

8. Olsen, T.W. Anti-VEGF Pharmacotherapy as an Alternative to Panretinal Laser Photocoagulation for Proliferative Diabetic Retinopathy. *JAMA* **2015**, *314*, 2135–2136. [CrossRef] [PubMed]

9. Behl, T.; Kotwani, A. Chinese herbal drugs for the treatment of diabetic retinopathy. *J. Pharm. Pharmacol.* **2017**, *69*, 223. [CrossRef] [PubMed]

10. Gao, D.; Guo, Y.; Li, X.; Li, X.; Li, Z.; Xue, M.; Ou, Z.; Liu, M.; Yang, M.; Liu, S.; et al. An Aqueous Extract of Radix Astragali, Angelica sinensis, and Panax notoginseng Is Effective in Preventing Diabetic Retinopathy. *Evid.-Based Complement. Altern. Med.* **2013**, *2013*, 578165. [CrossRef] [PubMed]

11. Fengmei, L.; Lie, W.; Jiaxing, T.; Ming, J.; Shuiping, Z.; Min, Z.; Lijuan, W.; Yanlin, Z.; Yuliang, W.; Mingchang, Z. The effectiveness and safety of a danshen-containing Chinese herbal medicine for diabetic retinopathy: a randomized, double-blind, placebo-controlled multicenter clinical trial. *J. Ethnopharmacol.* **2015**, *164*, 71–77.

12. Zhang, H.W.; Zhang, H.; Grant, S.J.; Wan, X.; Li, G. Single herbal medicine for diabetic retinopathy. *Cochrane Database Syst. Rev.* **2018**, *12*, Cd007939. [CrossRef] [PubMed]

13. Tien, T.; Zhang, J.; Muto, T.; Kim, D.; Sarthy, V.P.; Roy, S. High Glucose Induces Mitochondrial Dysfunction in Retinal Müller Cells: Implications for Diabetic Retinopathy. *Investig. Ophthalmol. Vis. Sci.* **2017**, *58*, 2915–2921. [CrossRef] [PubMed]

14. Toda, C.; Kim, J.D.; Impellizzeri, D.; Cuzzocrea, S.; Liu, Z.W.; Diano, S. UCP2 Regulates Mitochondrial Fission and Ventromedial Nucleus Control of Glucose Responsiveness. *Cell* **2016**, *164*, 872–883. [CrossRef] [PubMed]

15. Dehdashtian, E.; Mehrzadi, S.; Yousefi, B.; Hosseinzadeh, A.; Reiter, R.J.; Safa, M.; Ghaznavi, H.; Naseripour, M. Diabetic retinopathy pathogenesis and the ameliorating effects of melatonin; involvement of autophagy, inflammation and oxidative stress. *Life Sci.* **2018**, *193*, 20–33. [CrossRef] [PubMed]

16. Zhenyukh, O.; Civantos, E.; Ruizortega, M.; Sánchez, M.S.; Vázquez, C.; Peiró, C.; Egido, J.; Mas, S. High concentration of branched-chain amino acids promotes oxidative stress, inflammation and migration of human peripheral blood mononuclear cells via mTORC1 activation. *Free Radic. Biol. Med.* **2017**, *104*, 165–177. [CrossRef] [PubMed]

17. Nunnari, J.; Suomalainen, A. Mitochondria: In sickness and in health. *Cell* **2012**, *148*, 1145–1159. [CrossRef] [PubMed]

18. Kowluru, R.A.; Mishra, M. Therapeutic targets for altering mitochondrial dysfunction associated with diabetic retinopathy. *Expert Opin. Targets* **2018**, *22*, 233–245. [CrossRef] [PubMed]

19. Masser, D.R.; Otalora, L.; Clark, N.W.; Kinter, M.T.; Elliott, M.H.; Freeman, W.M. Functional changes in the neural retina occur in the absence of mitochondrial dysfunction in a rodent model of diabetic retinopathy. *J. Neurochem.* **2017**, *143*, 595–608. [CrossRef] [PubMed]

20. Chen, M.; Chen, Z.; Wang, Y.; Tan, Z.; Zhu, C.; Li, Y.; Han, Z.; Chen, L.; Gao, R.; Liu, L. Mitophagy receptor FUNDC1 regulates mitochondrial dynamics and mitophagy. *Autophagy* **2016**, *12*, 689–702. [CrossRef] [PubMed]

21. Santos, J.M.D.; Tewari, S.; Goldberg, A.F.X.; Kowluru, A.R. Mitochondria biogenesis and the development of diabetic retinopathy. *Free Radic. Biol. Med.* **2011**, *51*, 1849. [CrossRef] [PubMed]

22. Lesage, S.; Drouet, V.; Majounie, E.; Deramecourt, V.; Jacoupy, M.; Nicolas, A.; Cormier-Dequaire, F.; Hassoun, S.M.; Pujol, C.; Ciura, S. Loss of VPS13C Function in Autosomal-Recessive Parkinsonism Causes Mitochondrial Dysfunction and Increases PINK1/Parkin-Dependent Mitophagy. *Am. J. Hum. Genet.* **2016**, *98*, 500–513. [CrossRef] [PubMed]

23. Devi, T.S.; Somayajulu, M.; Kowluru, R.A.; Singh, L.P. TXNIP regulates mitophagy in retinal Müller cells under high-glucose conditions: Implications for diabetic retinopathy. *Cell Death Dis.* **2017**, *8*, e2777. [CrossRef] [PubMed]

24. De, I.C.; Costa, A.C.; Celardo, I.; Tufi, R.; Dinsdale, D.; Loh, S.H.; Martins, L.M. Drosophila ref(2)P is required for the parkin-mediated suppression of mitochondrial dysfunction in pink1 mutants. *Cell Death Dis.* **2013**, *4*, e873.

25. Ashrafi, G.; Schlehe, J.S.; Lavoie, M.J.; Schwarz, T.L. Mitophagy of damaged mitochondria occurs locally in distal neuronal axons and requires PINK1 and Parkin. *J. Cell Biol.* **2014**, *206*, 655. [CrossRef] [PubMed]

26. Sabanayagam, C. Epidemiology of diabetic retinopathy, diabetic macular edema and vision loss due to diabetes. *Diabetes Res. Clin. Pract.* **2016**, *120*, S14. [CrossRef]

27. Tout, S.; Chan-Ling, T.; Holl?Nder, H.; Stone, J. The role of Müller cells in the formation of the blood-retinal barrier. *Neuroscience* **1993**, *55*, 291–301. [CrossRef]

28. Abukawa, H.; Tomi, M.; Kiyokawa, J.; Hori, S.; Kondo, T.; Terasaki, T.; Hosoya, K. Modulation of retinal capillary endothelial cells by Müller glial cell-derived factors. *Mol. Vis.* **2009**, *15*, 451–457. [PubMed]

29. Zhong, Y.; Li, J.; Chen, Y.; Wang, J.J.; Ratan, R.; Zhang, S.X. Activation of Endoplasmic Reticulum Stress by Hyperglycemia Is Essential for Müller Cell–Derived Inflammatory Cytokine Production in Diabetes. *Diabetes* **2012**, *61*, 492–504. [CrossRef] [PubMed]

30. Gardner, T.W.; Antonetti, D.A.; Barber, A.J.; LaNoue, K.F.; Levison, S.W. Diabetic Retinopathy: More than Meets the Eye. *Surv. Ophthalmol.* **2002**, *47*, S253–S262. [CrossRef]

31. Zhou, T.; Che, D.; Lan, Y.; Fang, Z.; Xie, J.; Gong, H.; Li, C.; Feng, J.; Hong, H.; Qi, W.; et al. Mesenchymal marker expression is elevated in Muller cells exposed to high glucose and in animal models of diabetic retinopathy. *Oncotarget* **2017**, *8*, 4582–4594. [PubMed]

32. Cheung, A.K.; Fung, M.K.; Lo, A.C.; Lam, T.T.; So, K.F.; Chung, S.S.; Chung, S.K. Aldose reductase deficiency prevents diabetes-induced blood-retinal barrier breakdown, apoptosis, and glial reactivation in the retina of db/db mice. *Diabetes* **2005**, *54*, 3119–3125. [CrossRef] [PubMed]

33. Na, Z.; Meng, L.; Zhang, J.; Yue, C.; Li, J.; An, J.; Zhang, J.; Pathology, D.O.; University, N.M. The activation and apoptosis of astrocytes in the hippocampus of the diabetic model rats. *Chin. J. Neuroanat.* **2016**, *32*, 13–17.

34. Bringmann, A.; Reichenbach, A. Role of Muller cells in retinal degenerations. *Front. Biosci.* **2001**, *6*, E72–E92. [CrossRef] [PubMed]

35. Reichenbach, A.; Bringmann, A. Müller Cells in the Healthy and Diseased Retina. *Prog. Retin. Eye Res.* **2006**, *25*, 397–424.

36. Xiao-Lu, L.I.; Ya-Ling, M.A. Dynamic expressions of VEGF and PEDF in retina of rats with diabetic retinopathy. *Recent Adv. Ophthalmol.* **2013**, *26*, 573–576.

37. Yang, L.; Cai-Hui, H.E.; Liu, W.X.; Guo, S.Q.; Liu, D.W.; Epidemiology, D.O.; University, H.M. Relationship between polymorphism of VEGF and PEDF with proliferative diabetic retinopathy. *Chronic Pathematol. J.* **2013**, *14*, 8–12.

38. Koyano, F.; Okatsu, K.; Kosako, H.; Tamura, Y.; Go, E.; Kimura, M.; Kimura, Y.; Tsuchiya, H.; Yoshihara, H.; Hirokawa, T.; et al. Ubiquitin is phosphorylated by PINK1 to activate parkin. *Nature* **2014**, *510*, 162–166. [CrossRef] [PubMed]

39. Egan, D.F.; Shackelford, D.B.; Mihaylova, M.M.; Gelino, S.; Kohnz, R.A.; Mair, W.; Vasquez, D.S.; Joshi, A.; Gwinn, D.M.; Taylor, R. Phosphorylation of ULK1 (hATG1) by AMP-Activated Protein Kinase Connects Energy Sensing to Mitophagy. *Science* **2011**, *331*, 456. [CrossRef] [PubMed]

40. Wei, Y.; Chiang, W.C.; Sumpter, R., Jr.; Mishra, P.; Levine, B. Prohibitin 2 Is an Inner Mitochondrial Membrane Mitophagy Receptor. *Cell* **2017**, *168*, 224. [CrossRef] [PubMed]

41. Xiao, L.; Xu, X.; Zhang, F.; Wang, M.; Xu, Y.; Tang, D.; Wang, J.; Qin, Y.; Liu, Y.; Tang, C.; et al. The mitochondria-targeted antioxidant MitoQ ameliorated tubular injury mediated by mitophagy in diabetic kidney disease via Nrf2/PINK1. *Redox Biol.* **2017**, *11*, 297–311. [CrossRef] [PubMed]

42. Murata, H.; Takamatsu, H.; Liu, S.; Kataoka, K.; Huh, N.H.; Sakaguchi, M. NRF2 Regulates PINK1 Expression under Oxidative Stress Conditions. *PLoS ONE* **2015**, *10*, e0142438. [CrossRef] [PubMed]

43. Soutar, M.P.M.; Kempthorne, L.; Miyakawa, S.; Annuario, E.; Melandri, D.; Harley, J.; O'Sullivan, G.A.; Wray, S.; Hancock, D.C.; Cookson, M.R.; et al. AKT signalling selectively regulates PINK1 mitophagy in SHSY5Y cells and human iPSC-derived neurons. *Sci. Rep.* **2018**, *8*, 8855. [CrossRef] [PubMed]

44. Zhai, Y.; Meng, X.; Luo, Y.; Wu, Y.; Ye, T.; Zhou, P.; Ding, S.; Wang, M.; Lu, S.; Zhu, L.; et al. Notoginsenoside R1 ameliorates diabetic encephalopathy by activating the Nrf2 pathway and inhibiting NLRP3 inflammasome activation. *Oncotarget* **2018**, *9*, 9344–9363. [CrossRef] [PubMed]

Correction

Correction: Zhou, P., et al. Notoginsenoside R1 Ameliorates Diabetic Retinopathy through PINK1-Dependent Activation of Mitophagy. *Cells*, 2019, *8*, 213

Ping Zhou [1,2], Weijie Xie [1,2], Xiangbao Meng [1,2], Yadong Zhai [1,2], Xi Dong [1,2], Xuelian Zhang [1,2], Guibo Sun [1,2,*] and Xiaobo Sun [1,2,*]

[1] Institute of Medicinal Plant Development, Peking Union Medical College and Chinese Academy of Medical Sciences, Beijing 100193, China; zhoup0520@163.com (P.Z.); xwjginseng@126.com (W.X.); 18210482526@163.com (X.M.); shengjupan@163.com (Y.Z.); dx5212004@126.com (X.D.); xlZhang2022@163.com (X.Z.)

[2] Key Laboratory of new drug discovery based on Classic Chinese medicine prescription, Chinese Academy of Medical Sciences, Beijing 100193, China

* Correspondence: ginseng123@163.com (G.S.); sunxiaobopaper@163.com (X.S.); Tel.: +86-10-57833013 (X.S.); Fax: +86-10-57833013 (X.S.)

Received: 30 December 2019; Accepted: 10 February 2020; Published: 17 February 2020

The authors wish to make the following corrections to this paper [1]:

In the article "Notoginsenoside R1 Ameliorates Diabetic Retinopathy through PINK1-Dependent Activation of Mitophagy", we found that not every batch of mice showed a similar FFA image in the subsequent experiment. Therefore, we decide to remove the contents (experiments and discussion) related to FFA measurement (original Figure 3D).

The corrected Figure 3 is shown as follows.

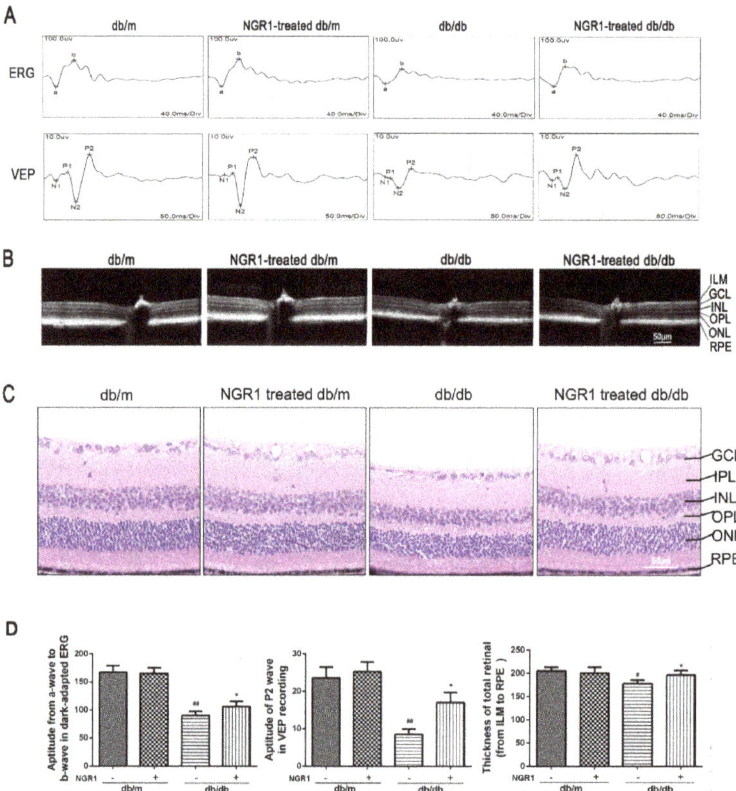

Figure 3. NGR1 pretreatment significantly attenuated DR in db/db mice. (**A**) Typical waveforms and quantitative analysis of ERG and VEPs amplitudes. (**B**) Retinal thickness was determined by OCT. (**C**) Retinal morphology was detected by HE. (**D**) Corresponding statistics of ERG, VEPs and OCT. The number of mice in this experiment was 10 (n = 10). The results are expressed as means ± SD. Two groups were analysed by unpaired two-tailed Student's *t*-tests, and multiple groups were analysed by one-way analysis of variance (ANOVA); # indicates significant difference from the control cells or db/m mice ($p < 0.05$); ## indicates a significant difference from control cells or db/m mice ($p < 0.01$). * indicates a significant difference from HG treatment or db/db mice ($p < 0.05$); ** indicates significant difference from HG treatment or db/db mice ($p < 0.01$). (+), treatment with NGR1; (−), treatment without NGR1.

Simultaneously, relevant methodologies, conclusions and discussions are deleted.

In Section 2.11, on page 5, the following text is deleted: "2.11. Fundus Fluorescein Angiography. The retinal vascular changes of the mice were detected by fundus fluorescein angiography (FFA). After anaesthetising, the eyes of the mice were dilated with 1% tropicamide, and the eyeball was coated with viscoelastic material and covered with a coverslip to form a plano-concave lens. Fundus examinations were performed 2 min after intraperitoneal injection of 0.1 mL of 2.5% fluorescein sodium (Alcon, Houston, TX, USA) using a digital fundus camera (Retinal Imaging System, OptoProbe Research Ltd., Burnaby, BC, Canada) until the fifth minute. The fluorescence intensity of the photographs obtained from each group was analysed by using ImageJ software (version 1.8.0) for statistical analysis and comparison of the groups. The specific steps performed using the software were as follows: Open the image, Image→Type→8 bit→Adjust→Threshold, Analyse→Set measurements→Measure. "

In Section 3.3, on page 9, the following text is deleted: "In addition, the FFA results showed that fluorescence leakage of microvessels and the formation of microangiomas in retinal were markedly increased in db/db mice compared with in db/m mice (Figure 3D; $p < 0.01$). However, treatment of db/db mice with NGR1 resulted in significant decreases in the leakage of retinal microvessels and the formation of microangiomas (Figure 3D, $p < 0.01$)."

In Section 4, on page 20, the following text is deleted: "Therefore, FFA was performed to observe microvessels changes under HG or R1 administration. A previous study showed no visible microvascular change by week 28 [29], our results suggested that fluorescence leakage of microvessels and the formation of microangiomas in the retinal were markedly increased in 38-week-old db/db mice compared with in db/m mice. As described by Bhatta, diabetic mice manifest significant retinal vascular degeneration at 15 months [30]. Therefore, different vascular states may be related to different time points of observation, the results of our study may further our understanding of the pathogenesis in the murine model of type 2 diabetes and provide a theoretical basis for clinical research."

In addition, references [29] and [30] on page 23 are deleted.

The authors would like to apologize for any inconvenience this has caused the readers.

References

1. Zhou, P.; Xie, W.; Meng, X.; Zhai, Y.; Dong, X.; Zhang, X.; Sun, G.; Sun, X. Notoginsenoside R1 Ameliorates Diabetic Retinopathy through PINK1-Dependent Activation of Mitophagy. *Cells* **2019**, *8*, 213. [CrossRef] [PubMed]

Article

Metformin Impairs Glutamine Metabolism and Autophagy in Tumour Cells

Serena Saladini [1]**, Michele Aventaggiato** [1]**, Federica Barreca** [1]**, Emanuela Morgante** [1]**,
Luigi Sansone** [2]**, Matteo A. Russo** [2,3] **and Marco Tafani** [1,*]

[1] Department of Experimental Medicine, Sapienza University of Rome, 00161 Rome, Italy;
    serena.saladini@live.it (S.S.); michele.aventaggiato@uniroma1.it (M.A.); federicabarreca@tiscali.it (F.B.);
    emanuela.morgante@uniroma1.it (E.M.)
[2] Department of Cellular and Molecular Pathology, IRCCS San Raffaele, 00166 Rome, Italy;
    luigi.sansone@sanraffaele.it (L.S.); matteoantonio.russo@uniroma1.it (M.A.R.)
[3] MEBIC Consortium, San Raffaele Rome Open University, 00166 Rome, Italy
*   Correspondence: marco.tafani@uniroma1.it; Tel.: +39-064-991-8234

Received: 21 December 2018; Accepted: 9 January 2019; Published: 14 January 2019

Abstract: Metformin has been shown to inhibit glutaminase (GLS) activity and ammonia accumulation thereby reducing the risk of hepatic encephalopathy in type 2 diabetic patients. Since tumour cells are addicted to glutamine and often show an overexpression of glutaminase, we hypothesize that the antitumoral mechanism of metformin could be ascribed to inhibition of GLS and reduction of ammonia and ammonia-induced autophagy. Our results show that, in different tumour cell lines, micromolar doses of metformin prevent cell growth by reducing glutamate, ammonia accumulation, autophagy markers such as MAP1LC3B-II and GABARAP as well as degradation of long-lived proteins. Reduced autophagy is then accompanied by increased BECN1/BCL2 binding and apoptotic cell death. Interestingly, GLS-silenced cells reproduce the effect of metformin treatment showing reduced MAP1LC3B-II and GABARAP as well as ammonia accumulation. Since metformin is used as adjuvant drug to increase the efficacy of cisplatin-based neoadjuvant chemotherapy, we co-treated tumour cells with micromolar doses of metformin in the presence of cisplatin observing a marked reduction of MAP1LC3B-II and an increase of caspase 3 cleavage. In conclusion, our work demonstrates that the anti-tumoral action of metformin is due to the inhibition of glutaminase and autophagy and could be used to improve the efficacy of chemotherapy.

Keywords: autophagy; cell death; glutaminase; metabolism; molecular rehabilitation.

---

1. Introduction

Autophagy is a multi-step recycling process that maintains cell and tissue homeostasis regulated by molecular components encoded by autophagy-related genes (ATGs) [1]. Three principal forms of autophagy have been identified: microautophagy, macroautophagy and chaperone-mediated autophagy [2]. In macroautophagy, hereafter referred to as "autophagy," cellular substrates or "cargo" are packed into cytosolic vesicles (autophagosomes), which are delivered to lysosomes in order to form double membrane vesicles (autolysosomes). In these structures, the autophagosomal content is digested by lysosomal hydrolases and the products are re-cycled back to cytosol in order to build up new molecules [3]. In mammals, basal autophagy removes damaged macromolecules or refills intermediate metabolites [4].

Autophagy promotes cancer resistance to radiation and chemotherapic treatments [5–7] and the abrogation of autophagic machinery renders cervical cancer cells more sensitive to cisplatin [8]. Moreover, a high basal autophagy gives a metabolic advantage to tumours sustaining their elevated energetic demand that arises from rapid proliferation and inadequate blood supply [9].

A link between autophagy and metabolism has been shown by the observation that autophagy can be stimulated also by ammonia, a by-product of glutamine metabolism. Ammonia, in fact, can act both as autocrine and paracrine modulator of autophagy [10]. Ammonia is generated by the mitochondrial glutaminolysis in which glutamine is sequentially deaminated into glutamate and then in α-ketoglutarate entering tricarboxylic acid (TCA) cycle [11]. Notably, it has been shown that under glucose starvation, tumours can survive in vitro using glutamine instead of glucose to maintain cellular ATP production [12]. Tumours show a high rate of glutaminolysis that results in high release of free ammonia. Szeliga et al. [13] observed that glutaminase and glutamate dehydrogenase enzymes, which catalyse glutamine deaminations, are often overexpressed in tumours. At the same time, elevated ammonia favours nitrogen incorporation into amino acids through reductive deamination by glutamate dehydrogenase [14]. In addition, glutaminase inhibition prevents ammonia accumulation and reduces ammonia-induced autophagy, leading to a metabolic crisis that sensitizing tumour cells to death [15].

Interestingly, a recent work has shown that metformin, the most widely prescribed drug for type 2 diabetes (T2D) therapy [16], is independently related to overt hepatic encephalopathy in patients with type 2 diabetes mellitus and high risk of hepatic encephalopathy [17]. Moreover, the same work also demonstrated that, in vitro, metformin inhibits glutaminase activity and ammonia accumulation [17].

This alternative mechanism of metformin could, as well, accompany the reduction of hepatic gluconeogenesis through mitochondrial complex I inhibition. In this case, metformin affects mitochondrial electron transport chain by modifying the AMP:ATP ratio leading to an energetic imbalance [18] that activates protein kinase AMP-activated (PRKAA2) [19]. Once activated, this enzyme, which acts as an intracellular fuel gauge, restores cellular energy balance inhibiting anabolic pathways and promoting glycolysis or fatty acid oxidation [20]. Moreover, activated PRKAA2 is able to inhibit the mechanistic target of rapamycin (MTOR) pathway which regulates cell autophagy [21]. Beyond of this glucose lowering effect, several epidemiological studies have shown that metformin reduces cancer incidence and mortality both in diabetic [22] and in not diabetic subjects [23]. Moreover, diabetic patients with breast cancer cotreated with metformin and neoadjuvant chemotherapy showed a higher pathological complete response than people with T2D on other diabetic treatments [24].

This potential application of metformin in oncology has been evaluated also in in vitro studies performed on a wide range of cancer cells [25–31]. However, cancer cells used in these studies have been treated for short times (2–3 days) with high doses of metformin (up to 10 mM), far above plasma metformin concentration of people with T2D where the drug achieves a bloody peak at 10–40 μM after 1 h of administration [32].

Starting from these considerations, we explored the effect of metformin on proliferation and autophagy in breast and cervical cancer cell lines where we observed a reduction of cellular replication rate correlated to an inhibition of glutamine metabolism, ammonia production and ammonia-induced autophagy. Moreover, these effects increased when cancer cells were co-incubated with cisplatin.

2. Materials and Methods

2.1. Cell Culture

Breast cancer cell lines, MCF7 (ATCCHTB-22) and MDA-MB-231 (ATCCHTB-26) and cervical cancer cell line Ca Ski (ATCCCRL-1550) (LGC Standards, Milan, Italy), were grown in RPMI 1640 medium (R0883; Sigma-Aldrich, Milan, Italy). Cervical cancer cell line HeLa was maintained in Dulbecco's Modified Eagle's Medium (DMEM, D5648; Sigma-Aldrich). All media were supplemented with 10% Foetal Bovine Serum (Sigma-Aldrich, F9665), 2 mM Glutamine (G7513; Sigma-Aldrich), 100 units/mL penicillin and 0.1 mg/mL streptomycin (P0781; Sigma-Aldrich). Adherent cells were detached by Trypsin-EDTA solution (TA049; Sigma-Aldrich). All cell lines were maintained at 37 °C in a humidified atmosphere of 5% CO_2 and 95% air.

2.2. Treatments Protocols and Antibodies

1,1-Dimethylbiguanide hydrochloride (metformin, D150959; Sigma-Aldrich) was dissolved in distilled water and added to cells at different concentrations (from 5 μM to 10 mM). When used at micromolar doses, metformin was added every day up to 20 days to cells without changing medium. In low-glucose and galactose medium experiments, 2 g/L sodium bicarbonate (E005761; Sigma-Aldrich) and 10 mM galactose (G0705; Sigma-Aldrich) or glucose (G8270; Sigma-Aldrich) were added to RPMI 1640 medium without glucose (R1383; Sigma-Aldrich).

Bis-2-(5-phenylacetamido-1,3,4-thiadiazol-2-yl)ethyl sulphide (BPTES, SML0601; Sigma-Aldrich) was dissolved in dimethyl sulfoxide (DMSO, D2438; Sigma-Aldrich) and added to a final concentration of 2 μM. Dimethyl-α-ketoglutarate was synthesized and provided by Prof. Mai (Sapienza University of Rome, Italy) and added to a final concentration of 1 mM. Bafilomycin A1 (B1793; Sigma-Aldrich) was dissolved in DMSO and added to a final concentration of 100 nM. NH_4Cl (A9434; Sigma-Aldrich) was dissolved in water and added to a final concentration of 20 mM. *cis*-Diamineplatinum (II) dichloride (cisplatin, 479306; Sigma-Aldrich) was dissolved in *N,N*-dimethylformamide (DMF, D4551; Sigma-Aldrich) and added to a final concentration of 0.2 μM.

The following primary antibodies were used for western blot analysis: GLS (GTX131263; Gene Tex, Milan, Italy), PHB (NB600-1292; Novus Biologicals, Abingdon, UK), BAX (sc526; Santa Cruz, Heidelberg, Germany), CYCS (Novus Biologicals, NB100-56503), BCL2 (BD, 610538), CASP3 cleaved (9661S; Cell Signalling, Milan, Italy), MAP1LC3B (NB600-1384; Novus Biologicals), GABARAP (PM037; MBL International Corporation, Heidelberg, Germany), BECN1 (9234S; Cell Signalling), SQSTM1 (sc-48402; Santa Cruz Biotechnology), phospho-PRKAA2 (Thr^{172}) (PA5-17831; Thermo Scientific, Milan, Italy), PRKAA2 (Thermo Scientific (PA5-36045), ATG5 (MBL, PM050),Phospho-AKT1 (Ser^{473}) (9271; Cell Signalling), AKT1 (9272S; Cell Signalling), phospho-RPS6KA1 (Thr^{389}) (9234S; Cell Signalling), RPS6KA1 (2708S; Cell Signalling), ACTB (A5316; Sigma-Aldrich), CDK4 (sc260; Santa Cruz). Horseradish peroxidase-linked anti-mouse (NA931V) and anti-rabbit (NA934V) were purchased from GE Healthcare (Chicago, IL, USA).

2.3. Generation of GLS-Silenced Cells

MDA-MB-231 cells were stably transfected with a pLKO.1 vector containing a shRNA insert to target human GLS (SHCLND-NM 014905; Sigma-Aldrich). Briefly, 200×10^3 cells were plated in 35 mm dishes 24 h before shRNA treatment. The following day the plasmid expressing shRNA GLS (1 μg) was introduced into cells using FuGENE® transfection reagent (E2691; Promega, Milan, Italy) according to manufacturer's protocol. The day after puromycin dihydrochloride (P9620; Sigma-Aldrich,) was added for selecting stably silenced clones at a final concentration of 1.6 μg/mL.

2.4. Viability Assays

Cell viability after prolonged metformin treatment was assessed with different protocols. In the clonogenicity assay cells (2×10^3) were plated in 100 mm dishes to allow clones formation. At the end of metformin incubation, plates were washed twice with a phosphate buffered saline solution (PBS; 79382; Sigma-Aldrich) and fixed with 4% formaldehyde solution in PBS (F8775; Sigma-Aldrich) at room temperature (rt). After 10 min, dishes were washed twice in PBS and stained for 5 min with 0.5% crystal violet (C0775; Sigma-Aldrich). Finally, cells were washed with distilled water and air-dried. The colonies were counted the following day. In trypan blue exclusion assay, cells were seeded on 6-well plates. Following treatments, cells were harvested and stained with 0.4% trypan blue (T8154; Sigma-Aldrich). The cell suspension was applied to a haemocytometer and counted with a phase contrast microscopy (NIKON EclipseTE2000U, Nikon Netherlands, Amsterdam, The Netherlands). Finally, cell viability was checked also by CellTiter96® AQueous Solution Cell Proliferation Assay (G3580; Promega). Cells were seeded in 96-well plates. Following metformin treatments, 20 μL of

CellTiter 96® Aqueous Solution was added to 100 μL of culture medium. After 2 h of incubation at 37 °C, absorbance at 490 nm was measured with the GloMax®-Multi Detection System (Promega).

2.5. Biochemical Assays

Cellular ATP and ADP levels were measured through the ADP/ATP ratio assay kit (MAK135; Sigma-Aldrich) accordingly to manufacturer's protocol. The amount of glutamate and ammonia produced by cells following metformin treatment was evaluated respectively with Glutamate Assay Kit (MAK004; Sigma-Aldrich) and Ammonia Assay Kit (AA0100; Sigma-Aldrich) as previously reported [14]. Absorbance was read through GloMax®-Multi Detection System (Promega). All the experiments were performed in triplicate and data are representative of 3–5 experiments.

2.6. Propidium Iodide Staining

To evaluate cell death, cells were analysed by flow cytometry. Cells were seeded into 10 mm dishes and treated with metformin for several days. Cells were next harvested with trypsin-EDTA, washed twice with ice cold PBS and centrifuged at $800\times g$ for 5 min at 4 °C. Samples were stained with 50 μg/mL Propidium Iodide (PI, P4864; Sigma-Aldrich) in PBS for 2 h at 4 °C cover light. Fluorescence was read by BD FACS Calibur flow cytometer (Becton Dickinson, Milan, Italy). The sub-G_1 fraction, which represents the total amount of apoptotic cells, was determined and analysed through CellQuest™ software.

2.7. Autophagic Proteolysis Assessment

Click-iT metabolic labelling for proteins (C10428; Thermo Fisher Life Technologies, Milan, Italy) was used to determine autophagic proteolysis of long-lived proteins as previously reported [15]. Cells (70% confluence) were plated on glass coverslips for confocal microscopy and in 96-well plates for fluorometric analysis. The day after, cells were washed twice with warm PBS and then incubated in L-methionine-free medium containing 10% dialyzed foetal bovine serum (26400-036; GIBCO). After 2 h, cells were pulsed for 18 h with 50 μM Click-iT AHA (L-azidohomoalanine), in L-methionine-free medium containing 10% dialyzed foetal bovine serum. At the end of this incubation, cells were washed once with PBS + 3% BSA (A2153; Sigma Aldrich) and cultured for 2 h in complete medium to chase out short-lived proteins. Cells were then treated as indicated in the figure legends. At the end of the treatments, cells were washed twice with PBS, fixed for 10 min with 4% formaldehyde solution in PBS and then washed with 3% albumin from bovine serum (BSA, A9418; Sigma-Aldrich) in PBS. Cells were permeabilized by using 0.2% Triton® X-100 (X100; Sigma-Aldrich) and 0.1 M Tris pH 7.4 (T4661; Sigma-Aldrich) in PBS for 5 min rt. After two washes in 3 % BSA in PBS, alkaline alexafluor 488 (A10267; Thermo Fisher Life Technologies) was added using Click-iT® Reaction Buffer Kit (C10269; Thermo Fisher Life Technologies). The reaction mix was finally removed and samples were washed twice with 3% BSA in PBS before fluorescence detection by LSM 510 confocal microscopy (Zeiss, Milan, Italy) or GloMax®-Multi Detection System.

2.8. Electron Microscopy

MDA-MB-231 wt and GLS shRNA cells were cultured in 10 mm dishes and treated with metformin 30 μM up to 20 days. In addition, in order to reduce autophagic flux, some samples were treated with NH₄Cl 10 mM for the last 17 h in the presence or absence of metformin. Cells were washed with warm PBS and fixed with 2% glutaraldehyde (G7651; Sigma-Aldrich) in 0.1 M sodium cacodylate buffer pH 7.3 (C0250; Sigma-Aldrich) at 4 °C overnight. The following day, samples were collected, washed three times with cacodylate buffer and fixed for 2 h rt with 2% osmium tetroxide (75632; Sigma-Aldrich) in the same buffer. After three washes in distilled water, cells were stained for 15 min at room temperature with 1% uranyl acetate. Samples were then incubated at 45 °C with 3% agarose. After solidification, agarose blocks were dehydrated with ascending acetone concentration. Blocks were embedded in Spurr medium and polymerized overnight at 65 °C. Samples were finally cut in

80-nm sections by a Reighert-Jung Ultra cut E ultramicrotome (Leica Microsystems, Wetzlar, Germany) and picked up on copper grids. The tiny pieces were post-stained in uranyl acetate and bismuth subnitrate and observed in a Philips CM-10 TEM (Fei Italia, Milan, Italy) and micrographs on Kodak 4489 sheet films (Sigma-Aldrich).

2.9. Lysosomes Labelling

Lysotracker® red DND-99 (L7528; Thermo Fisher Life Technologies) was used to track lysosomes in cells. Briefly, 300×10^3 cells were cultured on coverslips placed inside 35 mm dishes. After 20 days of incubation with 30 µM metformin, cells were washed twice with PBS ad incubated for 30 min in pre-warmed medium containing 50 nM of Lysotracker. Afterwards, fresh medium was replaced and fluorescence was observed by LSM 510 confocal microscopy (Zeiss).

2.10. JC-1 Staining

$5,5',6,6'$-tetrachloro-$1,1',3,3'$-tetrathylbenzimidazolyl-carbocyanine iodide (JC-1) dye was used as indicator of mitochondrial health (T3168; Thermo Fisher Life Technologies). In mitochondria this cationic probe can exist in a monomeric or in an aggregated form depending on mitochondrial membrane potential ($\Delta\Psi_m$). In healthy cells, $\Delta\Psi_m$ is high and JC-1 polymerizes to form J-aggregates which show a red fluorescence emission. On the contrary, in unhealthy or apoptotic cells where mitochondrial integrity is compromised, $\Delta\Psi_m$ assumes a lower value. In this condition, JC-1 remains in a monomeric form showing a green florescence emission. The fluorescence shift from red to green is an indicator of mitochondrial depolarization. Briefly, cells were grown on glass coverslips (for confocal analysis) and in 96-well plate for fluorimeter. At the end of metformin treatment, medium was discarded and 10 µg/mL of JC-1 were added to cells in pre-warmed medium. After 20 min of incubation, cells were washed in PBS and fluorescence was observed by LSM 510 confocal microscopy (Zeiss) or quantified by Epics XL-MCL flow cytometer (Beckman Coulter, Pasadena, CA, USA).

2.11. Protein Extraction and Immunoblotting

Cells (2×10^6) for whole cell lysate were centrifuged at $800\times g$ for 10 min at 4 °C and pellet were resuspended in 100 µL of a solution containing 50 mM Tris-Cl (93352; Sigma-Aldrich), 250 mM sodium chloride (NaCl, S7653; Sigma-Aldrich), 5 mM ethylenediaminetetraacetic acid (EDTA; E6758; Sigma-Aldrich), 0.1% Triton® X-100 and 0.1 mM Dithiothreitol (DTT, D9163; Sigma-Aldrich) plus 1 mM phenylmethylsulfonyl fluoride (PMSF, 93482; Sigma-Aldrich), Protease inhibitor cocktail (PI; Sigma-Aldrich, P8340), 1 mM sodium orthovanadate (NA_3VO_4, S6508; Sigma-Aldrich) and 10 mM sodium fluoride (NaF, 201154; Sigma-Aldrich) (lysis buffer). After 10 min on ice, samples were centrifuged at $14,000\times g$ for 10 min at 4 °C and the supernatants were collected. Protein concentration was determined by the Bradford assay (Bio-Rad, Milan, Italy500-0205). Clarified protein lysates (40 µg) were boiled for 5 min, electrophoresed onto denaturatingSDS-PAGE gel and transferred onto a 0.45 µM nitrocellulose membrane (162-0115, Bio-Rad). The blotting membranes were blocked with 5% non-fat dry milk (1706404, Bio-Rad) for 1 h rt and then incubated with primary antibody overnight at 4°C. The follow day, membranes were washed three-times with 0.1% Tween® 20 (P9416; Sigma-Aldrich) in PBS (PBST) for 30 min rt and incubated with the appropriate secondary antibody for 1 h rt. After other 3 washes in PBST, the detection of the relevant protein was assessed by enhanced chemiluminescence (Lite Ablot® TURBO, EMP012001; Euro Clone, Milan, Italy). Densitometric analysis of the bands, relative to ACTB, CDK4 or prohibitin (PHB,) was performed using Image J Software v1.51 (NIH, Bethesda, MD, USA).

2.12. Mitochondrial Isolation

Cells (2×10^3) were grown in 100 mm dishes. Following metformin treatment, cells were harvested and centrifuged at $700\times g$ at 4 °C for 5 min. Pellet was resuspended on ice in 200 µL of a solution containing 2 mM magnesium chloride ($MgCl_2$, M8266; Sigma-Aldrich), 10 mM potassium chloride (KCl, P9333; Sigma-Aldrich) and 10 mM Tris pH 7.4. After 10 min, each samples were mixed with 200 µL of a solution containing 400 mM sucrose (S5390; Sigma-Aldrich), 10 mM Tris pH 7.4, 2 mM EDTA, 2 mM ethylene glycol-*bis*(2-aminoethylether)-*N*, *N*, *N'*,*N'*-tetraacetic acid (EGTA, E3889; Sigma-Aldrich), 2 mM PMSF, 20 mM NaF, 2 mM Na_3VO_4 and PI. Cells were broken with 50 Dounce strokes on ice. Homogenates were transferred into 1.5 mL tubes and centrifuged at $900 \times g$ for 10 min at 4 °C. Pellet were discarded and supernatant fractions were transferred in new 1.5 mL tubes and centrifuged at $17,000 \times g$ for 30 min at 4 °C. Pellet (mitochondrial fractions) were lysed in 20 µL of lysis buffer and protein concentration determined by the Bradford assay.

2.13. Immunoprecipitation

Proteins were extracted as described above. Protein suspensions (500 µg) were pre-cleared with 20 µg of protein A/G PLUS-agarose (sc-2003; Santa Cruz) and kept in slow rotation for 1 h at 4 °C. Samples were centrifuged at $500 \times g$ for 1 min at 4 °C. Supernatants were collected and agarose pre-cleared resins were discarded. Cleared cell lysates were next incubated with 2 µg of Beclin1 antibody and kept in slow rotation overnight at 4 °C. The following day, 20 µg of protein A/G PLUS-agarose were added to each tube and kept in rotation for 4 h at 4 °C. Samples were then centrifuged at $500 \times g$ for 5 min at 4 °C. Pellet fractions, containing the protein-antibody complex, were washed 5 times with a solution containing 50 mM Tris pH 7.4, 0.5% Triton® X-100 and 150 mM NaCl and 2 times with 5 mM Tris pH 7.4. At the end of washing, pellet was mixed with 20 µL of Laemmli buffer (NP0007; Invitrogen, Milan, Italy) and heated for 5 min at 95 °C. Samples were electrophoresed on a SDS-polyacrylamide gel and immunoblotted.

2.14. Immunofluorescence Microscopy

Cells (2×10^3) were seeded onto coverslips inside 35 mm dishes and incubated for 20 days with metformin. Cells were fixed for 10 min with 4% formaldehyde in PBS, washed twice in PBS and permeabilized for 5 min in 0.1 M Tris pH 7.4 and 0.2% Triton® X-100. After two washes in PBS, samples were blocking for 1 h rt with 0.2 mg/mL BSA and incubated for 2 h rt with anti-Glutaminase C antibody at 1:1000 dilution. Cells were then washed twice with 0.05% Tween® 20 in PBS and incubated for 1 h with the secondary antibody goat anti-rabbit IgG Alexa Fluor® 555 at 1:1000 dilution (A21429; Invitrogen). Finally, samples were washed twice with PBS and mounted using ProLong® Diamond Antifade Mountant (P36961; Thermo Fisher Life Technologies). Fluorescence was observed by LSM 510 confocal microscopy (Zeiss).

2.15. Statistical Analysis

The results are expressed as means $\pm$ standard deviations (s.d.) and 95% confidence intervals (95% CI) of three independent experiments. Before using parametric tests, the assumption of normality was verified using the Shapiro-Wilk W-test. The Student paired *t*-test was used to determine any significant differences before and after treatment. Significance was set at $p < 0.05$. Statistical software package SPSS v13.0.1. (SPSS Inc., Chicago, IL, USA) was used for all statistical calculations.

3. Results

3.1. Metformin Inhibits Cancer Cell Proliferation

Metformin has demonstrated an anti-tumoral effect mainly due to the inhibition of mitochondrial function. However, the doses used in the experimental settings are in the order of mM far above the 5–30 µM measured in tissues of patients taking this drug. For this reason we aimed to unravel if and how metformin, used at micromolar concentration, still has anti-tumoral activity.

To this effect, breast cancer cell lines MDA-MB-231 and MCF7 as well as cervical cancer cell line Ca Ski were treated with 5 and 30 µM metformin for up to 20 days. Clonogenic assay showed a reduction in the number of colonies after metformin treatment (Figure 1A). Moreover, 20 days treatment with

30 µM metformin reduced cell vitality to 55% in MDA-MB-231, 58% in MCF7 and 63% in Ca Ski cells (Figure 1B). Similarly, cell titre assay showed a reduction of cell proliferation in the three cell lines used (Figure 1C). Interestingly, reducing glucose concentration below 10 mM reduced cell proliferation in both untreated and metformin treated MDA-MB-231 cells (Figure 1D).

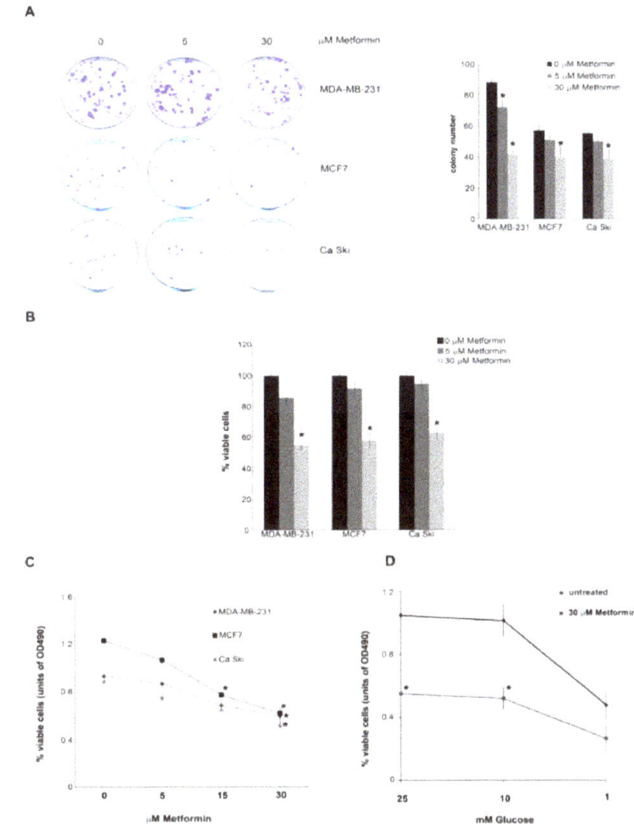

Figure 1. Low doses of metformin reduce colony formation and cell viability in tumour cell lines; (**A**) MDA-MB-231, MCF7 and Ca Ski cells were seeded at low density (2×10^3) in the presence or absence of micromolar doses of metformin. After 20 days dishes were washed in PBS and cells fixed and stained. Number of colonies were counted the following day and the results graphed in the right side of the figure; (**B**) MDA-MB-231, MCF7 and Ca Ski cells were either left untreated or treated with different doses of metformin. Cell viability was measured by trypan blue exclusion as indicated under Material and Methods; (**C**) MDA-MB-231, MCF7 and Ca Ski cells were either left untreated or treated with different doses of metformin. cell growth was measured by CellTiter 96® aqueous solution cell proliferation assay as indicated under Material and Methods; (**D**) MDA-MB-231 cells were grown in growth medium containing different glucose concentration in the presence or absence of 30 µM metformin. Cell growth was measured by CellTiter 96® aqueous solution cell proliferation assay as indicated under Material and Methods. All experiments in this figure were repeated three times. * Significantly different from control untreated cells.

3.2. Metformin Impairs Mitochondrial Function and Induces Cell Death

Metformin has been shown to have a direct impact on mitochondrial activity [33]. To test if metformin has different cellular effects if used at milli- or micromolar concentrations, we treated

MDA-MB-231 cells with high doses of metformin (mM) for 48 h and low doses (μM) up to 20 days and then we measured ATP levels. As expected, 0.1–5 mM metformin caused a 36% reduction of ATP with an increase of ADP:ATP ratio. Surprisingly, we observed an opposite effect when cells were treated with low doses of metformin for longer times (Figure 2A, lower right). Indeed, in this condition metformin led to a dose dependent increase of intracellular ATP. However, the ADP:ATP ratio did not show any change (Figure 2A, lower left). One possibility is that an energetic unbalance may alter mitochondrial membrane potential ($\Delta\Psi_m$). Therefore, MDA-MB-231 cells were stained with JC-1 [34]. As shown in Figure 2B, 15 days of metformin treatment induced an increase of depolarized mitochondria. In fact, flow cytometry analysis measured a decrease in red fluorescence in 18% of cells treated with metformin compared to the 5% of untreated cells (Figure 2B). Since $\Delta\Psi m$ reduction is critical for apoptosis, we analysed mitochondrial apoptotic markers such as BAX and cytochrome c (CYCS). BAX, a pro-apoptotic member of BCL-2 family, under an apoptotic stimulus oligomerizes to form mitochondrial pores with CYCS release from mitochondria to cytosol, followed by caspase activation and cell death [35,36]. Our results show a mitochondrial accumulation of BAX at 5 and 10 days of treatment and a decrease of mitochondrial CYCS after 10 day of metformin treatment without changes in total amount of BAX or CYCS. Similar results were obtained using MCF-7 cells where, again, 10 days of metformin treatment caused an accumulation of BAX and a release of CYCS from the mitochondria (Figure 2C, right side). The decrease in Bax observed in the mitochondrial fraction after 15 and 20 days in cells treated with 30 μM metformin, could be due to the removal of damaged mitochondria and/or cells after such a long treatment period. In fact, the accumulation of Bax in the mitochondrial membrane is a rather quick process that is followed by mitochondrial damage. Furthermore, damaged mitochondria could then be removed by mitophagy thereby diminishing Bax level. The statistical analysis of Figure 2C is reported in Supplementary Figure S1 showing a statistically significant accumulation of Bax in the mitochondrial after 5 and 10 days of metformin treatment accompanied by a decrease of cytochrome c from 10 to 20 days. The purity of mitochondrial fractions was assessed by using PHB as positive and CDK4 as negative controls as shown in Figure 2C.

Finally, we measured the percentage of MDA-MB-231 cells with sub-G_1 DNA content after 15 days of 30 μM metformin treatment. Figure 2D shows an increase of cell death from 10% of control untreated cells to 40% of metformin treated cells.

3.3. Metformin Inhibits Glutaminase Activity

Next, we measured the amount of ammonia released by MDA-MB-231 cells. As shown in Figure 3A, differences in ammonia release started after 15 days of metformin treatment and became more sustained after 20 days. Figure 3B shows that metformin strongly reduced ammonia levels in a dose-dependent manner also in MCF7 and Ca Ski cells but not in HeLa cells. Indeed, Xiao et al. [37] observed that metformin reduces proliferation of Ca Ski and Me180 but not of HeLa cells. These results suggest that metformin can, directly or indirectly, alter ammonia production in breast and cervical cancer cells. Since ammonia is generated not only by glutamine deamination but also from aminoacidic catabolism [38], we used MDA-MB-231 GLS shRNA to demonstrate that ammonia reduction depends mostly on GLS. We observed that 30 μM metformin inhibited ammonia release in wild type MDA-MB-231 cells but not in MDA-MB-231 GLS shRNA (Figure 3B). Moreover, the basal level of ammonia in untreated MDA-MB-231 GLS shRNA cells was lower than in wild type (Figure 3B). Similar results were obtained in MDA-MB-231 cells co-treated for 15 days with metformin and BPTES, a potent and selective GLS inhibitor (Figure 3C). To further evaluate the effect of metformin on GLS activity, we analysed L-glutamate concentration. Our results showed that prolonged metformin treatments reduced L-glutamate accumulation in MDA-MB-231 cells, an effect that was not observed in GLS shRNA cells (Figure 3D). Finally, we did not observe any difference in GLS expression between control and metformin treated cells (Figure 3E). There results were confirmed by immunofluorescence assay (Figure 3F).

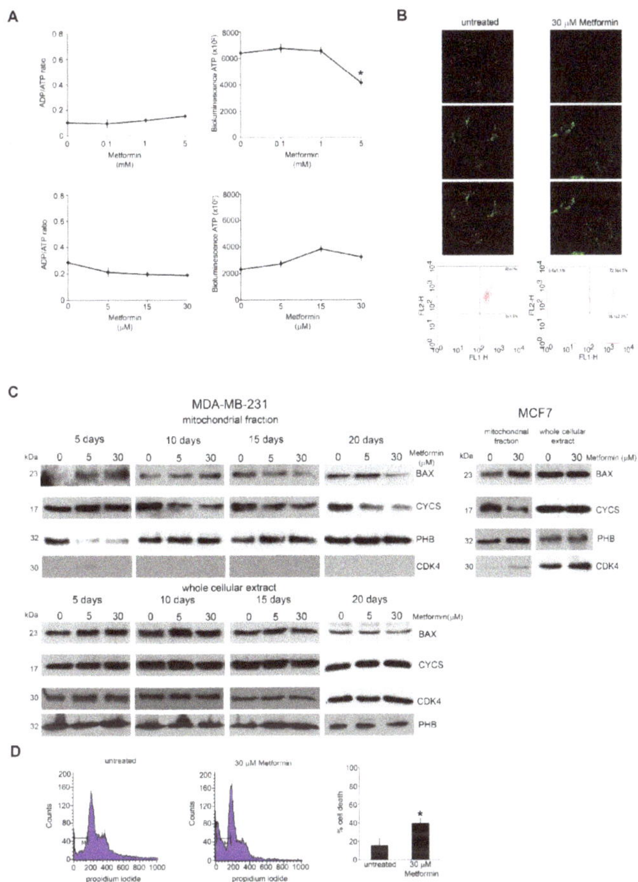

Figure 2. Metformin activates apoptotic cell death; (**A**) MDA-MB-231 cells were plated in 96 well plate and then either left untreated or treated with millimolar (upper graphs) or micromolar (lower graphs) doses of metformin. ADP/ATP ratio was determined as indicated in Material and Methods; (**B**) MDA-MB-231 cells were seeded on glass coverslip and then left untreated or treated with 30 µM metformin. At the end of the treatment, cells were stained with 10 µg/mL JC-1 as indicated under Material and Methods. Mitochondria fluorescence was observed by confocal microscopy. First row: Red fluorescence representing JC1 aggregates. Second row: Green fluorescence representing JC1 monomers. Third row: Merging of the first two rows. Alternatively, cells were treated with 30 µM metformin and stained with JC-1 as above. Red (FL2H) and green (FL1H) fluorescence intensity was quantified by Flow Cytometry; (**C**)upper panel: MDA-MB-231 cells were kept in the presence or absence of metformin for the time indicated and then processed to obtain mitochondrial fractions. BAX and CYCS expression levels were determined by Western blot as indicated under Material and Methods. Densitometric analysis of the gels was performed as indicated under Material and Methods. PHB and CDK4 were used as loading and purity control, respectively. Lower panel: MDA-MB-231 cells were kept in the presence or absence of metformin for the time indicated and then processed to obtain whole cellular extracts. BAX and CYCS expression levels were determined by Western blot as indicated under Material and Methods. Densitometric analysis of the gels was performed as indicated under Material and Methods. CDK4 and PHB were used as loading control. Right panel: MCF-7 cells were kept in the presence or absence of metformin for 20 days and then processed to obtain mitochondrial or whole cellular extracts. BAX and CYCS expression levels were determined by Western blot as indicated under Material and Methods. Densitometric analysis of the gels was performed as indicated under

Material and Methods. PHB and CDK4 were used as purity and loading controls; (**D**) MDA-MB-231 cells were kept in the presence or absence of metformin for 20 days. At the end of the treatment cells were harvested and percentage of sub-G_1 (M1) cells was determined by propidium iodide staining as described in the Material and Methods section. All experiments in this figure were repeated three times. * Significantly different from control untreated cells.

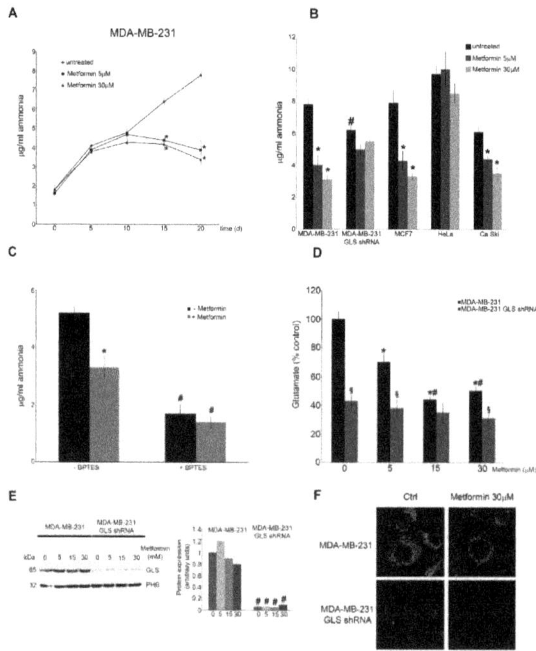

Figure 3. Metformin reduces ammonia and glutamate accumulation by inhibiting glutaminase; (**A**) MDA-MB-231 cells were either left untreated or treated with 5 or 30 µM metformin for the time indicated. Ammonia level in the culture medium was measured as indicated in the Material and Methods section; (**B**) MDA-MB-231, MDA-MB-231 GLS shRNA, MCF7, HeLa and Ca Ski cells were either left untreated or treated with 5 or 30 µM metformin for 20 days. Ammonia level in the culture medium was measured as indicated in the Material and Methods section. # Significantly different from untreated MDA-MB-231 wt cells; (**C**) MDA-MB-231 cells were either left untreated or treated with 30 µM metformin in the presence or absence of GLS inhibitor 2mM BPTES. Ammonia level in the culture medium was measured as indicated in the Material and Methods section. # Significantly different from untreated wt MDA-MB-231 cells; (**D**) MDA-MB-231 and MDA-MB-231 GLS shRNA cells were either left untreated or treated with metformin for 20 days. Glutamate level in the culture medium was measured as indicated in the Material and Methods section. # Significantly different from 5 µM treatment. § Significantly different from the corresponding treatment in MDA-MB-231 wt cells; (**E**) MDA-MB-231 and MDA-MB-231 GLS shRNA cells were either left untreated or treated with metformin for 20 days. At the end of the treatment cells were harvested to obtain mitochondria and GLS expression measured by Western blot. Data are representative of at least three separate experiments. Densitometric analysis of the gels was performed as described under Materials and Methods. PHB was used as loading control. # Significantly different from similar treatment in MDA-MB-231 wt cells; (**F**) MDA-MB-231 and MDA-MB-231 GLS shRNA cells were either left untreated or treated with 30 µM metformin for 20 days. At the end of the treatment cells were fixed and GLS expression determined by immunofluorescence. Data are representative of at least three separate experiments. GLS in red. All experiments in this figure were repeated three times. * Significantly different from control untreated cells.

3.4. Metformin alters Autophagic Flux

The effects of metformin treatment on autophagic flux were evaluated by treating wt and MDA-MB-231 GLS shRNA cells with 5–30 μM metformin for 20 days. Figure 4A shows that in wt cells, metformin reduced MAP1LC3B-II, GABARAP, BECN1 and ATG12/ATG5 expression whereas, in glutaminase-silenced cells there was a reduction of only MAP1LC3B-II. However, in GLS-silenced cells, MAP1LC3-I expression was higher than in wt cells suggesting an inhibition of autophagy. Statistical analysis of blots in Figure 4A is reported in Supplementary Figure S2. In addition, we did not observe an increase in PRKAA2 phosphorylation both in wt and silenced cells (Figure 4A). This is in accordance with the observation that low doses of metformin did not alter cellular ATP production (Figure 2A). Afterwards, we checked if the interaction between BCL2 and BECN1 could be altered after metformin treatment. The BCL2/BECN1 complex represents a molecular bridge linking autophagy to apoptosis [39,40]. Therefore, we treated MDA-MB-231 cells with 30 μM metformin for 15 days and then we measured BECN1 and BCL2 binding by immunoprecipitating BECN1 and staining for BCL2 or, on the contrary, by immunoprecipitating BCL2 and staining for BECN1. In both cases, we found that metformin increased BCL2 and BECN1 binding (Figure 4B and Figure S3).

We next inhibited GLS by co-treating cells with metformin and BPTES (Figure S4A) or with metformin and dimethyl α-ketoglutarate (DMKGB) (Figure S4B). In both cases we observed an almost complete inhibition of MAP1LC3B-II. To confirm that the reduction of autophagic markers induced by metformin was due to an inhibition and not to an increase of the autophagic flux, we added bafilomycin A1 (BafA1), which inhibits autophagic vacuoles maturation causing autophagy markers accumulation [41]. As shown in Figure 4C, MAP1LC3B-II levels in MDA-MB-231 cells cotreated with 30 μM metformin and BafA1 were lower compared to BafA1 alone. Similar results were obtained in MCF7 cells (Figure S5). On the contrary, in MDA-MB-231 GLS shRNA cells we observed a weaker MAP1LC3B-II accumulation in the presence of BafA1 (Figure 4C and Figure S3).

To further prove this result, we either left untreated or treated daily MDA-MB-231 cells for 20 days with different metformin concentrations without medium replacement (CAM, cell-aged medium). At the end of treatments, we applied medium from CAM-cells to a secondary fresh-plated untreated MDA-MB-231 cultures for 48 h (CCM, cell-conditioned medium). Afterward, we monitored the autophagic markers in CAM and CCM-cells. As control we used cells where metformin containing medium was changed every two days for 20 days (fresh CAM). Again, medium from fresh CAM cells was applied to fresh seeded MDA-MB-231 cells for 48 h (fresh CCM cells). As shown in Figure 4D, untreated CAM cells presented a higher basal level of autophagy than untreated fresh CAM cells, an effect that was reduced upon metformin treatment. Interestingly, in CCM cells autophagy induction followed the trend seen in CAM cells (Figure 4D). In fact, autophagy markers were increased when using conditioned medium (CM) from control cells and decreased when using CM from metformin-treated cells (Figure 4D). Statistical analysis is reported in Supplementary Figure S3. Metformin inhibition of autophagy was MTOR independent as shown in Figure S6 where we did not observe any significant increase in RPS6KA1^{Thr389} or AKT1^{Ser473} phosphorylation neither in CAM nor in CCM cells.

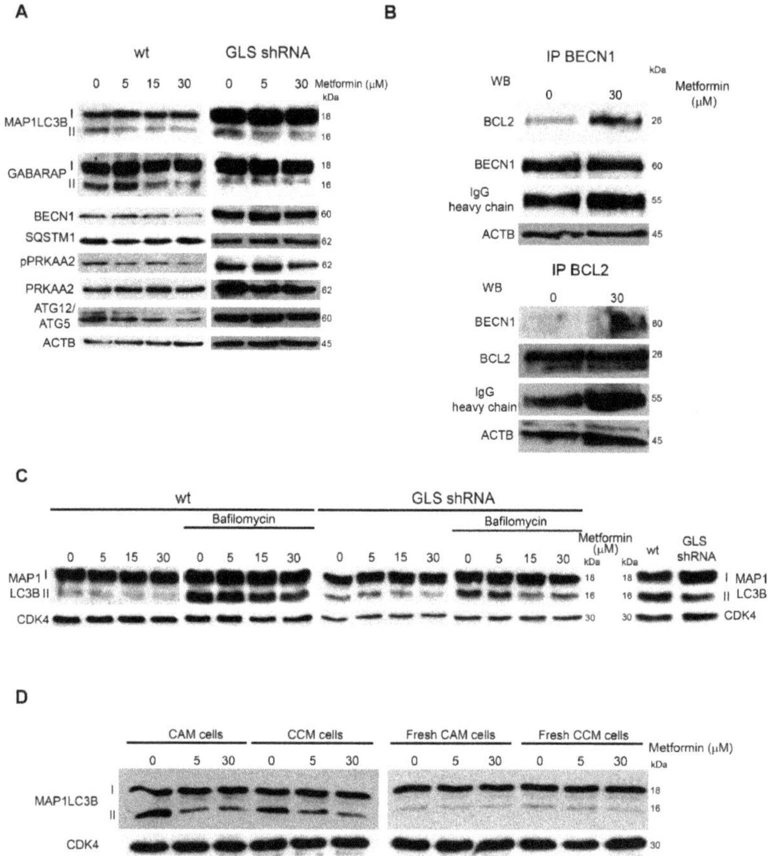

Figure 4. Metformin alters autophagy response; (**A**) MDA-MB-231 and MDA-MB-231 GLS shRNA cells were either left untreated or treated with metformin for 20 days. At the end of the treatment, cells were processed to obtain whole cellular extracts. Expression level of autophagy markers MAP1LC3B, GABARAP, BECN1, SQSTM1, pPRKAA2, PRKAA2 and ATG12/ATG5 was determined by Western blot. ACTB was used as loading control; (**B**) MDA-MB-231 cells were either left untreated or treated with 30 μM metformin for 20 days. At the end of the treatment, cells were processed. Cellular extracts were immunoprecipitated with an anti-BECN1 antibody, electrophoresed on a SDS-polyacrylamide gel and immunoblotted with and anti-BCL2 or anti-BECN1 antibody as described under Materials and Methods (upper panel). Alternatively, cellular extracts were immunoprecipitated with an anti-BLC2 and immunoblotted with an anti-BECN1 or anti-BCL2 antibody (lower panel). Densitometric analysis of the gels was performed as described under Materials and Methods. Data are representative of three separate experiments. ACTB and IgG heavy chains were used as loading controls; (**C**) MDA-MB-231 and MDA-MB-231 GLS shRNA cells were either left untreated or treated with metformin for 20 days. Where indicated in the figure, bafilomycin 100 nM was added for 17 h to the cells. At the end of the treatment cells were processed to obtain whole cellular extracts. MAP1LC3B expression was determined by Western blot. CDK4 was used as loading control. densitometric analysis of the gels was performed as described under Materials and Methods. Data are representative of three separate experiments; (**D**) left side: MDA-MB-231 cells were either left untreated or treated with metformin for 20 days (CAM cells). At the end of the treatment, medium from CAM cells was applied to fresh-seeded MDA-MB-231 cells (CCM cells) for 48 h. Both CAM and CCM cells were processed to obtain whole

cellular extracts. MAP1LC3B expression was determined by Western blot. CDK4 was used as loading control. densitometric analysis of the gels was performed as described under Materials and Methods; right side: MDA-MB-231 cells were either left untreated or treated with metformin for 20 days changing medium every 2 days (fresh CAM cells). At the end of the treatment, medium from fresh CAM cells was added to fresh plated cell (fresh CCM cells). CAM cells was applied to fresh-seeded MDA-MB-231 cells (fresh CCM cells) for 48 h. Both fresh CAM and fresh CCM cells were processed to obtain whole cellular extracts. MAP1LC3B expression was determined by Western blot. CDK4 was used as loading control. Densitometric analysis of the gels was performed as described under Materials and Methods. All experiments in this figure were repeated three times.

Autophagy inhibition induced by metformin was also quantified by measuring degradation of long-lived protein through the Click-it AHA technique [42]. Again, we made use of CCM cells, that is, MDA-MB-231 cells incubated with 20-days old conditioned medium from the same cell line kept in the presence or absence of 30 µM metformin. After 2 days, CCM cells were plated in L-methionine free medium in the presence of L-azidohomoalanine (AHA). After 2 h we measured the changes of AHA fluorescence intensity, which is representative of autophagy-mediated proteolysis. We observed a decrease of AHA fluorescence in cells incubated with CCM compared to CCM plus metformin (Figure 5A, left side). Quantification of AHA fluorescence revealed a decrease of about 30% in CCM cells compared to control cells in fresh medium (Figure 5A, right side). Metformin treatment maintained AHA fluorescence to levels similar to that of Ctrl cells (Figure 5A, right side). To further confirm these data, we investigated metformin-mediated autophagy reduction by Transmission Electron Microscopy (TEM). Figure 5B shows that MDA-MB-231 cells treated with metformin had a lower number of autophagosomes than untreated cells. This reduction of autophagosomes and autophagolysosomes was clearer following ammonium chloride treatment, as evidenced in the right panels of Figure 5B. Importantly, glutaminase-silenced cells showed a reduced basal accumulation of autophagosomes and autophagolysosomes than wt cells, reproducing results obtained upon metformin treatment. These results were quantified in the graph on the right side of Figure 5B showing the reduction of autophagy due to either metformin treatment or glutaminase silencing.

Autophagy was also monitored by labelling MDA-MB-231 wt and GLS-silenced cells with lysotracker red. At first we observed a reduction of autophagy-associated lysosomes in wt cells after metformin treatment (Figure 5C, upper right). On the contrary, in GLS-silenced cells we observed a lower basal level of red fluorescence than wt cells (Figure 5C, lower left) that was not affected by metformin treatment (Figure 5C, lower right).

We also investigated the effects of high doses of metformin on MDA-MB-231 cells. In fact, when used at millimolar doses, metformin has been shown to trigger autophagy through PRKAA2/MTOR axis modulation [21]. For this reason, we analysed PRKAA2^{Thr172} phosphorylation which is representative of its activation status, the phosphorylation of RPS6KA1, which is a marker of *MTOR complex I activity (mTORC1)*, negatively regulated by PRKAA2 [43] as well as MAP1LC3B-II accumulation. Upon 48 h of metformin treatment, MAP1LC3B and PRKAA2^{Thr172} increased in a dose-dependent manner (Figure 5D). Statistical analysis of the blots in Figure 5D is reported in Supplementary Figure S7. Importantly, we did not observe a reduction of ammonia in the medium of MDA-MB-231 cells treated with millimolar concentration of metformin (Figure 5E). These findings are in line with the present literature data [44] and confirm our ATP assay results (Figure 2A). Together, these results suggest that, millimolar doses of metformin induce an energetic unbalance with ATP reduction leading to PRKAA2 activation and autophagy without altering ammonia levels.

Finally, some studies have shown that in MDA-MB-231 cells metformin is able to impair the activity of hexokinase HK1 and HK2 [45]. Therefore, we replaced high glucose medium with galactose medium before adding metformin. In this case, we treated MDA-MB-231 cells up to 10 days because the removal of glucose in association with metformin treatment strongly influenced cell proliferation, as shown in clonogenicity assay in Figure S8A. Again, we observed that metformin inhibited autophagy as evidenced by MAP1LC3B, GABARAP and ATG5/ATG12 reduction (Figure S8B) without altering PRKAA2 phosphorylation.

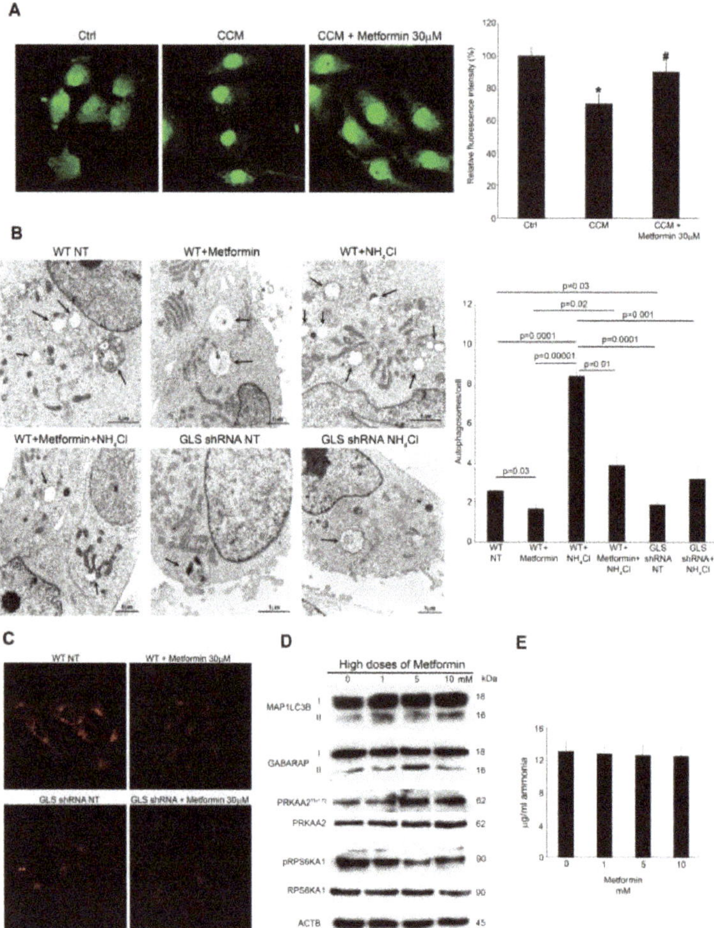

Figure 5. Metformin or GLS silencing reduces autophagosomes formation; (**A**) MDA-MB-231 cells (CCM) were plated in conditioned medium from CAM cells as described in Figure 4D for 48 h to stimulate autophagy in the presence or absence of metformin. At the same time MDA-MB-231 control cells (Ctrl) were plated in fresh medium for 48 h. At the end of the treatments, both Ctrl and CCM cells were labelled with AHA as described under Material and Methods. Cells were then fixed, permeabilized and stained for 2 h with alkine-Alexa Fluor 488. Fluorescence from long-lived proteins was observed using aLSM 510 confocal microscopy (Zeiss). MDA-MB-231 cells were placed in a 96 well plate, treated and labelled as described above. Right side: Fluorescence from long-lived protein was measured using a GloMax®-Multi Detection System (Promega). # Significantly different from CCM treated cells.; (**B**) MDA-MB-231 cells were either left untreated or treated with metformin 30 µM, NH₄Cl 10 mM or a combination of the two. Alternatively, MDA-MB-231 GLS shRNA cells were left untreated or treated with NH₄Cl 10 mM. The cells were then processed for electron microscopy as described under Materials and Methods. Upper left: WT cells showing autophagosomes, (Magnification 15,500×). Upper middle: WT + metformin cells showing a lower number of autophagosomes (magnification 11,500×). Upper right: WT + NH₄Cl cells showing an increase in autophagosomes (magnification

11,500×). Lower left: WT + metformin + NH$_4$Cl cells showing a reduction in autophagosomes (magnification 11,500×). Lower middle: GLS shRNA cells showing a low number of autophagosomes (magnification 15,000×). Lower right: GLS shRNA + NH$_4$Cl cells showing a large autophagosome (magnification 11,500×). Black arrows point to autophagosomes and autophagolysosomes. Results were quantified on the graph reported on the right side showing reduction of autophagosomes following metformin treatment or GLS silencing. Number of autophagosomes were obtained by counting three different fields for each image from two separate experiments; (**C**) MDA-MB-231 WT and GLS shRNA cells were either left untreated or treated with metformin 30 μM for 20 days. At the end of the treatment, 50 nM Lysotracker red was added to the cells for 30 min followed by a wash in PBS before confocal analysis of lysosome staining as described under materials and methods. Upper left: WT untreated cells showing lysosomes accumulation. Upper right: reduced lysosomes in metformin treated cells. Lower left: GLS shRNA cells showing reduced lysosome staining. Lower right: Metformin treatment did not reduce lysosomes accumulation in GLS shRNA cells; (**D**) MDA-MB-231 cells were treated with high doses of metformin from 1 to 10 mM for 48 h. At the end of the treatment, cells were processed to obtain whole cell lysates. MAP1LC3B, GABARAP, pPRKAA2^{Thr172}, PRKAA2, pRPS6KA1 and RPS6KA1 expression was determined by Western blot. ACTB was used as loading control. Densitometric analysis of the gels was performed as described under Materials and Methods; (**E**) MDA-MB-231 cells were treated with high doses of metformin from 1 to 10 mM for 48 h. Ammonia level in the culture medium was measured as indicated in the Material and Methods section. All experiments in this figure were repeated three times. * Significantly different from control untreated cells.

3.5. Effects of a Combined Metformin and Cisplatin Treatment

Metformin is often used in gynaecological oncology as adjuvant drug to increase the efficacy of cisplatin-based neoadjuvant (NACT) chemotherapy [24], in neck and cervix cancer [46] and earlier-stage operable breast cancer [47]. For this reason, we treated cervical and breast cancer cell lines with low doses of metformin and cisplatin for 15 days. Figure 6A shows that, in MDA-MB-231 cells, the combined metformin/cisplatin treatment did not alter PRKAA2^{Thr172} phosphorylation. On the contrary MAP1LC3B-II accumulation was strongly reduced as also evidenced in Supplementary Figure S9. This trend was less relevant in Ca Ski cell line probably because breast cancer cells are more sensitive to metformin action than cervical cancer cell lines (Figure 3B). In addition, we observed that reduction of ammonia levels induced by metformin was intensified when cells were co-treated with a nontoxic concentration of cisplatin. Once again, this reduction was clearer in MDA-MB-231 cells than in Ca Ski (Figure 6B). Metformin increased the level of cleaved-CASP3 in both cell lines, an effect that was also present in cisplatin-treated cells and that was enhanced by the combined metformin and cisplatin treatment (Figure 6A). This is probably due to the reduced ammonia accumulation and inhibition of autophagy by metformin as shown in Figure 6B.

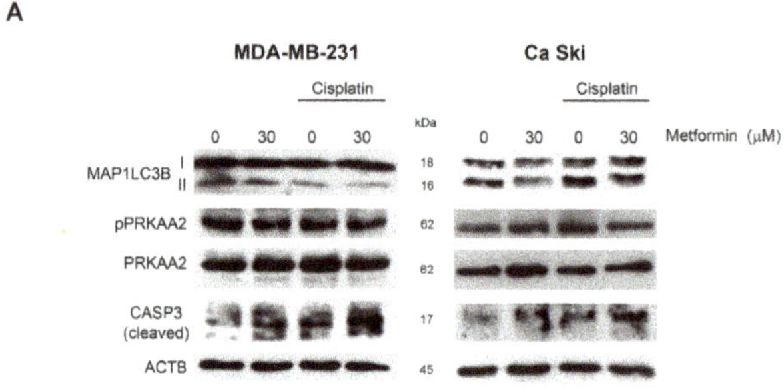

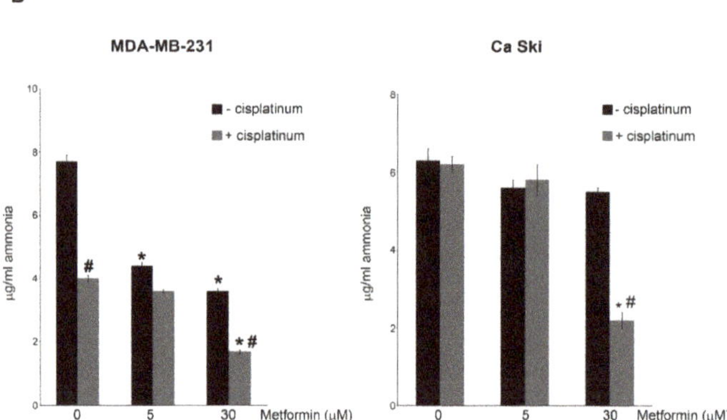

Figure 6. Metformin treatment increases cisplatin effects; (**A**) MDA-MB-231 and Ca Ski cells were either left untreated or treated with metformin or cisplatin alone or metformin in combination with cisplatin for 15 days. At the end of the treatment, cells were processed to obtain whole cell lysates. MAP1LC3B, pPRKAA2^{Thr172}, PRKAA2 and CASP3 (cleaved) expression was determined by Western blot. ACTB was used as loading control. Densitometric analysis of the gels was performed as described under Materials and Methods; (**B**) MDA-MB-231 and Ca Ski cells were either left untreated or treated with metformin or cisplatin alone or metformin in combination with cisplatin for 15 days. Ammonia level in the culture medium was measured as indicated in the Material and Methods section. [#] Significantly different from treatment with metformin alone. All experiments in this figure were repeated three times. * Significantly different from control untreated cells.

4. Discussion

Metformin, a biguanide commonly used for T2D therapy, can reduce the risk of cancer in diabetic patients compared to other anti-diabetic treatments [48]. Therefore, we aimed to investigate the molecular mechanism behind the anti-tumoral action of metformin. Our results demonstrate that low doses (5–30 µM) of metformin have two major effects: i) autophagy inhibition by decreasing glutamine metabolism and ammonia accumulation, ii) apoptosis induction by altering mitochondrial energization. Moreover, we also demonstrate that, along this pathway, mitochondrial GLS, involved in the first step of glutamine metabolism and often overexpressed in tumour cells, is a target of metformin.

We are aware that several groups showed that millimolar doses of metformin can inhibit Mitochondrial Complex 1, ATP production and tumour cell growth [49]. However, these in vitro concentrations are far above those measured in tissues from T2D patients assuming metformin. In fact, this drug rapidly reaches its peak (2 h) with a tissue concentration around 5–30 µM [50].

Therefore, we decided to incubate cancer cells with micromolar doses of metformin for a longer time. Surprisingly, we discovered that these doses of metformin still showed an antitumoral effect (Figure 1) increasing cell death in different tumour cell lines. Moreover, also in our hands, high doses of metformin reduce ATP levels and activate autophagy, an effect that, then, increases cell death [49]. In fact, a drop in ATP was observed when treating tumour cells with a dose of 5 mM metformin (Figure 1A) similarly to what reported using 10 mM metformin [49]. As expected this drop in ATP was accompanied by AMPK activation (Figure 5D) and autophagy induction with LC3-II and GABARAP-II accumulation (Figure 5D). By contrast, using low doses of metformin we inhibited autophagy increasing mitochondrial depolarization and apoptosis (Figure 2). At present, we do not know the precise mechanisms underneath such divergent effects of low and high metformin dosage on autophagy. We can speculate that they may be due to off-target effects obtained when using high doses, that is, above 30 μM, of metformin. Moreover, it is important to consider that these divergent effects are not a peculiarity of metformin. In fact, many anti-oxidant compounds becomes pro-oxidant if used at high concentration such as, for example, resveratrol and vitamin C [51,52] depending on the presence of transition metals or on the fact that they can be oxidized. However, in the case of metformin, it is interesting to consider that both low and high doses causes cell death by de-regulating a basic survival process such as autophagy.

However, in light of our observations, herewith, we suggest that low doses of metformin (5–30 μM) and long times of treatment (up to 20 days) may be the best in vitroconditions necessary to investigate the molecular mechanism behind the anti-tumoral effect of this drug.

A large number of cancer cells are addicted to glutamine [53] showing a high rate of glutaminolysis. Glutamine is sequentially deaminated in glutamate and then in α-ketoglutarate, an intermediate of TCA cycle. Supporting and extending the work by Ampuero et al. [17], we observed that metformin drastically reduces GLS activity in breast and cervical cancer cells without altering its cellular expression (Figure 3).

The biological relevancies of the GLS impairment induced by metformin are mainly two. On one hand, it reduces the support of α-ketoglutarate to TCA cycle leading to a deregulation of tumour cell metabolism. On the other hand, GLS inhibition reduces cellular ammonia amount. This molecule normally stimulates cellular catabolism through autophagy activation. Moreover, it can also act in a paracrine way diffusing in the intercellular space where it triggers autophagy also in neighbouring cancer cells [10]. GLS is overexpressed in cancer cells [54] and consequently ammonia levels are higher in tumours than normal tissue [55]. Our study shows that metformin can reduce cellular ammonia accumulation leading to an impairment of autophagy. In fact, when we daily added metformin to MDA-MB-231 cells for 20 days, we observed a strong reduction of some autophagic markers such as MAP1LC3B-II, GABARAP, SQSTM1 (Figure 4). Such a reduction was not due to an accelerated autophagic flux because blocking autophagosome degradation with BafA1 did not increase MAP1LC3B-II levels in metformin treated cells (Figure 4C). In fact, metformin treatment, is accompanied by the reduction of both cellular accumulation of autophagosomes and autophagic proteolysis of long-lived proteins (Figure 5A,B). to demonstrate the central role of *gls*in the autophagy impairment induced by metformin, we silenced the expression of this enzyme through shRNA. We documented that, compared to wild type cells, GLS silenced cells show reduced ammonia levels and reduced autophagy. Moreover, to confirm the involvement of the ammonia-induced autophagy in metformin action, we transferred cellular media of MDA-MB-231 cells treated for 20 days with metformin (CAM cells) to a secondary culture (CCM cells). Again, in CCM cells we observed the same autophagy reduction seen in CAM cells treated with metformin. We suppose that this is due to the reduction of ammonia accumulation impairing autophagy induction. This result is similar to the one obtained by Eng et al. [10] demonstrating that ammonia accumulating in a conditioned medium of a culture cell line induces autophagy in a secondary culture [56]. Moreover, such ammonia-induced autophagy is MTOR-independent [10]. Indeed, RPS6KA1, a marker of MTORC1 activity [57], or AKT, a marker of MTORC2 activity, [58] were not phosphorylated in CCM cells (Figure S6). Instead, in CAM cells we observed that metformin did not induce a phosphorylation of RPS6KA1 but surprisingly AKT1 seems to be progressively dephosphorylated at Ser 473. AKT1 activity is often increased in breast cancer and its activation is essential to protect cells against death insults [59]. We supposed that such AKT1 dephosphorylation is due to the activation of the apoptotic cascade that we observed after 10 days of metformin treatment (Figure 3). In fact, autophagy inhibition observed with low doses of metformin is accompanied by an increase of apoptosis. In particular, we demonstrated an increase in BECN1/BCL2 complex formation (Figure 4B) that frees BAX to bind to mitochondria membrane to induce depolarization and CYCS release (Figure 2). However, we still do not know if the effect of metformin on BECN1/BCL2 complex are direct or indirect. This is due to the fact that metformin interferes with both the apoptotic and autophagic mechanisms by impinging on mitochondria function and ammonia production, respectively. Interestingly, when we added cisplatin to metformin treatment we observed an additive decrease of ammonia accumulation and autophagy and increase of CASP3 cleavage (Figure 6A). Cisplatin is an anti-neoplastic agent used together with other drugs during the platinum-based neoadjuvant chemotherapy (NACT) to reduce gynaecological tumours [60]. However, NACT efficacy is limited by its high toxicity due to serious effects such as renal and liver dysfunctions. To this effect, metformin could be used in these patients in association with NACT therapy, to lower the dosage of anti-neoplastic drugs in NACT cocktail without altering its efficacy.

In conclusion, our results suggest that the documented anti-tumoral effect of metformin is due to its effect on GLS with inhibition of glutamine metabolism and reduction of ammonia-induced autophagy.

Supplementary Materials: The following are available online at http://www.mdpi.com/2073-4409/8/1/49/s1, Figure S1. Densitometric analysis of Western Blots of Figure 2C. Figure S2. Densitometric analysis of Western Blots of Figure 4A. Figure S3. Densitometric analysis of Western Blots of Figure 4B–D. Figure S4. Inhibition of GLS reduces autophagy. Figure S5. Metformin inhibits autophagy in MCF7 cells. Figure S6. Autophagy inhibition by metformin is MTOR -independent. Figure S7. Densitometric analysis of Western Blots of Figure 5D. Figure S8. Metformin inhibits autophagy in galactose supplemented medium. Figure S9. Densitometric analysis of Western Blots of Figure 6A.

Author Contributions: Conceptualization: S.S., M.T.; Methodology: S.S., M.A., F.B.; Investigation: E.M., L.S.; Writing-original draft preparation: M.T., S.S., M.A.R.; Supervision: M.T.

Funding: This research was funded by the Sapienza University, Ricerca Scientifica Ateneo 2017.

Acknowledgments: We would like to thank Antonello Mai for providing α-ketoglutarate and for the scientific support and Claudia Marchetti for the helpful discussion about the use of metformin in NACT therapy.

Conflicts of Interest: The authors declare that they have no conflicts of interest.

Abbreviations

ACTB	Actin, b
AHA	L-azidohomoalanine
AKT1	Thymoma viral proto-oncogene homolog 1
ATG	Autophagy-related
BAX	BCL2-associated X protein
BCL2	B-cell CLL/lymphoma 2
BECN1	Beclin 1
BPTES	*Bis*-2-(5-phenylacetamido-1, 3, 4-thiadiazol-2-yl)ethylsulfide
CAM	Cell-aged medium
CASP3	Caspase 3
CCM	Cell-conditioned medium
CDK4	Cyclin dependent kinase 4
CYCS	Cytochrome c
GABARAP	GABA(A) receptor-associated protein
GLS	Glutaminase
HK	Hexokinase
MAP1LC3B	Microtubule-associated protein 1 light chain 3 b
MAPK	Mitogen-activated protein kinases

IGF	Insulin growth factor
JC-1	5,5′,6,6′-tetrachloro-1,1′3,3′-tetrathylbenzimidazolyl-carbocyanine iodide
mTOR	Mechanistic target of rapamycin
mTORC	mTOR complex
PHB	Prohibitin
PI3K	Phosphatidylinositol 3-kinase;
NACT	Neoadjuvant chemotherapy
PRKAA2	Protein kinase AMP-activated
RPS6KA1	Ribosomal protein S6 kinase A1
SQSTM1	Sequestosome 1
T2D	Type 2 diabetes
TCA	Tricarboxylic acid cycle
TEM	Transmission electron microscopy

References

1. Mizushima, N.; Levine, B.; Cuervo, A.M.; Klionsky, D.J. Autophagy fights disease through cellular self-digestion. *Nature* **2008**, *451*, 1069–1075. [CrossRef]
2. Galluzzi, L.; Baehrecke, E.H.; Ballabio, A.; Boya, P.; Bravo-San Pedro, J.M.; Cecconi, F.; Choi, A.M.; Chu, C.T.; Codogno, P.; Colombo, M.I.; et al. Molecular definitions of autophagy and related processes. *EMBO J.* **2017**, *36*, 1811–1836. [CrossRef]
3. Gozuacik, D.; Akkoc, Y.; Ozturk, D.G.; Kocak, M. Autophagy-Regulating microRNAs and Cancer. *Front. Oncol.* **2017**, *7*, 65. [CrossRef]
4. Levine, B.; Klionsky, D.J. Development by self-digestion: Molecular mechanisms and biological functions of autophagy. *Dev. Cell* **2004**, *6*, 463–477. [CrossRef]
5. Kroemer, G.; Mariño, G.; Levine, B. Autophagy and the integrated stress response. *Mol. Cell* **2010**, *40*, 280–293. [CrossRef]
6. Lin, M.G.; Hurley, J.H. Structure and function of the ULK1 complex in autophagy. *Curr. Opin. Cell Biol.* **2016**, *39*, 61–68. [CrossRef]
7. Chen, S.; Rehman, S.K.; Zhang, W.; Wen, A.; Yao, L.; Zhang, J. Autophagy is a therapeutic target in anticancer drug resistance. *Biochim. Biophys. Acta* **2010**, *1806*, 220–229. [CrossRef]
8. Leisching, G.; Loos, B.; Botha, M.; Engelbrecht, A.M. A nontoxic concentration of cisplatin induces autophagy in cervical cancer: Selective cancer cell death with autophagy inhibition as an adjuvant treatment. *Int. J. Gynecol. Cancer* **2015**, *25*, 380–388. [CrossRef]
9. Mathew, R.; Karantza-Wadsworth, V.; White, E. Role of autophagy in cancer. *Nat. Rev. Cancer* **2007**, *7*, 961–967. [CrossRef]
10. Eng, C.H.; Abraham, R.T. Glutaminolysis yields a metabolic by-product that stimulates autophagy. *Autophagy* **2010**, *6*, 968–970. [CrossRef]
11. Yuneva, M.; Zamboni, N.; Oefner, P.; Sachidanandam, R.; Lazebnik, Y. Deficiency in glutamine but not glucose induces MYC-dependent apoptosis in human cells. *J. Cell Biol.* **2007**, *178*, 93–105. [CrossRef]
12. Reitzer, L.J.; Wice, B.M.; Kennell, D. Evidence that glutamine, not sugar, is the major energy source for cultured HeLa cells. *J. Biol. Chem.* **1979**, *254*, 2669–2676.
13. Szeliga, M.; Obara-Michlewska, M. Glutamine in neoplastic cells: Focus on the expression and roles of glutaminases. *Neurochem. Int.* **2009**, *55*, 71–75. [CrossRef]
14. Spinelli, J.B.; Yoon, H.; Ringel, A.E.; Jeanfavre, S.; Clish, C.B.; Haigis, M.C. Metabolic recycling of ammonia via glutamate dehydrogenase supports breast cancer biomass. *Science* **2017**, *358*, 941–946. [CrossRef]
15. Polletta, L.; Vernucci, E.; Carnevale, I.; Arcangeli, T.; Rotili, D.; Palmerio, S.; Steegborn, C.; Nowak, T.; Schutkowski, M.; Pellegrini, L.; et al. SIRT5 regulation of ammonia-induced autophagy and mitophagy. *Autophagy* **2015**, *11*, 253–270. [CrossRef]
16. Sterne, J. Treatment of diabetes mellitus with *N,N*-dimethylguanylguanidine (LA. 6023, glucophage). *Therapie* **1959**, *14*, 625–630.

17. Ampuero, J.; Ranchal, R.; Nuñez, D.; Díaz-HerreroMdel, M.; Maraver, M.; del Campo, J.A.; Rojas, Á.; Camacho, I.; Figueruela, B.; Bautista, J.D.; et al. Metformin inhibits glutaminase activity and protects against hepatic encephalopathy. *PLoS ONE* **2012**, *7*, e49279. [CrossRef]

18. El-Mir, M.Y.; Nogueira, V.; Fontaine, E.; Avéret, N.; Rigoulet, M.; Leverve, X. Dimethylbiguanide inhibits cell respiration via an indirect effect targeted on the respiratory chain complex I. *J. Biol. Chem.* **2000**, *275*, 223–228. [CrossRef]

19. Cazzaniga, M.; Bonanni, B. Breast Cancer Metabolism and Mitochondrial Activity: The Possibility of Chemoprevention with metformin. *Biomed. Res. Int.* **2015**, *2015*, 972193. [CrossRef]

20. Musi, N.; Hirshman, M.F.; Nygren, J.; Svanfeldt, M.; Bavenholm, P.; Rooyackers, O.; Zhou, G.; Williamson, J.M.; Ljunqvist, O.; Efendic, S.; et al. Metformin increases AMP-activated protein kinase activity in skeletal muscle of subjects with type 2 diabetes. *Diabetes* **2002**, *51*, 2074–2081. [CrossRef]

21. Wang, Y.; Xu, W.; Yan, Z.; Zhao, W.; Mi, J.; Li, J.; Yan, H. Metformin induces autophagy and G_0/G_1 phase cell cycle arrest in myeloma by targeting the AMPK/mTORC1 and mTORC2 pathways. *J. Exp. Clin. Cancer Res.* **2018**, *37*, 63. [CrossRef]

22. Libby, G.; Donnelly, L.A.; Donnan, P.T.; Alessi, D.R.; Morris, A.D.; Evans, J.M. New users of metformin are at low risk of incident cancer: A cohort study among people with type 2 diabetes. *Diabetes Care* **2009**, *32*, 1620–1625. [CrossRef]

23. Hosono, K.; Endo, H.; Takahashi, H.; Sugiyama, M.; Sakai, E.; Uchiyama, T.; Suzuki, K.; Iida, H.; Sakamoto, Y.; Yoneda, K.; et al. Metformin suppresses colorectal aberrant crypt foci in a short-term clinical trial. *Cancer Prev. Res.* **2010**, *3*, 1077–1083. [CrossRef]

24. Jiralerspong, S.; Palla, S.L.; Giordano, S.H.; Meric-Bernstam, F.; Liedtke, C.; Barnett, C.M.; Hsu, L.; Hung, M.C.; Hortobagyi, G.N.; Gonzalez-Angulo, A.M. Metformin and pathologic complete responses to neoadjuvant chemotherapy in diabetic patients with breast cancer. *J. Clin. Oncol.* **2009**, *27*, 3297–3302. [CrossRef]

25. Ben Sahra, I.; Le Marchand-Brustel, Y.; Tanti, J.F.; Bost, F. Metformin in cancer therapy: A new perspective for an old antidiabetic drug? *Mol. Cancer Ther.* **2010**, *9*, 1092–1099. [CrossRef]

26. Rattan, R.; Graham, R.P.; Maguire, J.L.; Giri, S.; Shridhar, V. Metformin suppresses ovarian cancer growth and metastasis with enhancement of cisplatin cytotoxicity in vivo. *Neoplasia* **2011**, *13*, 483–491. [CrossRef]

27. Tsai, M.J.; Yang, C.J.; Kung, Y.T.; Sheu, C.C.; Shen, Y.T.; Chang, P.Y.; Huang, M.S.; Chiu, H.C. Metformin decreases lung cancer risk in diabetic patients in a dose-dependent manner. *Lung Cancer* **2014**, *86*, 137–143. [CrossRef]

28. Sarfstein, R.; Friedman, Y.; Attias-Geva, Z.; Fishman, A.; Bruchim, I.; Werner, H. Metformin downregulates the insulin/IGF-I signaling pathway and inhibits different uterine serous carcinoma (USC) cells proliferation and migration in p53-dependent or –independent manners. *PLoS ONE* **2013**, *8*, e61537. [CrossRef]

29. Adamek, A.; Kasprzak, A. Insulin-Like Growth Factor (IGF) System in Liver Diseases. *Int. J. Mol. Sci.* **2018**, *19*, 1308. [CrossRef]

30. Zhao, Y.; Sun, H.; Feng, M.; Zhao, J.; Zhao, X.; Wan, Q.; Cai, D. Metformin is associated with reduced cell proliferation in human endometrial cancer by inhibiting PI3K/AKT/mTOR signaling. *Gynecol. Endocrinol.* **2018**, *34*, 428–432. [CrossRef]

31. Kennedy, B.K.; Pennypacker, J.K. Mammalian Target of Rapamycin: A Target for (Lung) Diseases and Aging. *Ann. Am. Thorac. Soc.* **2016**, *13*, S398–S401. [CrossRef] [PubMed]

32. Stocker, S.L.; Morrissey, K.M.; Yee, S.W.; Castro, R.A.; Xu, L.; Dahlin, A.; Ramirez, A.H.; Roden, D.M.; Wilke, R.A.; McCarty, C.A.; et al. The effect of novel promoter variants in MATE1 and MATE2 on the pharmacokinetics and pharmacodynamics of metformin. *Clin. Pharmacol. Ther.* **2013**, *93*, 186–194. [CrossRef] [PubMed]

33. Andrzejewski, S.; Gravel, S.P.; Pollak, M.; St-Pierre, J. Metformin directly acts on mitochondria to alter cellular bioenergetics. *Cancer Metab.* **2014**, *2*, 12. [CrossRef] [PubMed]

34. Perry, S.W.; Norman, J.P.; Barbieri, J.; Brown, E.B.; Gelbard, H.A. Mitochondrial membrane potential probes and the proton gradient: A practical usage guide. *Biotechniques* **2011**, *50*, 98–115. [CrossRef] [PubMed]

35. Marchetti, P.; Castedo, M.; Susin, S.A.; Zamzami, N.; Hirsch, T.; Macho, A.; Haeffner, A.; Hirsch, F.; Geuskens, M.; Kroemer, G. Mitochondrial permeability transition is a central coordinating event of apoptosis. *J. Exp. Med.* **1996**, *184*, 1155–1160. [CrossRef] [PubMed]

36. Van Loo, G.; Saelens, X.; van Gurp, M.; MacFarlane, M.; Martin, S.J.; Vandenabeele, P. The role of mitochondrial factors in apoptosis: A Russian roulette with more than one bullet. *Cell Death Differ.* **2002**, *9*, 1031–1042. [CrossRef] [PubMed]

37. Xiao, X.; He, Q.; Lu, C.; Werle, K.D.; Zhao, R.X.; Chen, J.; Davis, B.C.; Cui, R.; Liang, J.; Xu, Z.X. Metformin impairs the growth of liver kinase B1-intact cervical cancer cells. *Gynecol. Oncol.* **2012**, *127*, 249–255. [CrossRef] [PubMed]

38. Goldstein, L. Regulation of renal glutamine deamination. *Med. Clin. N. Am.* **1975**, *59*, 667–680. [CrossRef]

39. Pattingre, S.; Tassa, A.; Qu, X.; Garuti, R.; Liang, X.H.; Mizushima, N.; Packer, M.; Schneider, M.D.; Levine, B. Bcl-2 antiapoptotic proteins inhibit Beclin 1-dependent autophagy. *Cell* **2005**, *122*, 927–939. [CrossRef] [PubMed]

40. Wei, Y.; Pattingre, S.; Sinha, S.; Bassik, M.; Levine, B. JNK1-mediated phosphorylation of Bcl-2 regulates starvation-induced autophagy. *Mol. Cell* **2008**, *30*, 678–688. [CrossRef]

41. Yamamoto, A.; Tagawa, Y.; Yoshimori, T.; Moriyama, Y.; Masaki, R.; Tashiro, Y. Bafilomycin A1 prevents maturation of autophagic vacuoles by inhibiting fusion between autophagosomes and lysosomes in rat hepatoma cell line, H-4-II-E cells. *Cell Struct. Funct.* **1998**, *23*, 33–42. [CrossRef] [PubMed]

42. Zhang, J.; Wang, J.; Ng, S.; Lin, Q.; Shen, H.M. Development of a novel method for quantification of autophagic protein degradation by AHA labeling. *Autophagy* **2014**, *10*, 901–912. [CrossRef] [PubMed]

43. Carling, D.; Mayer, F.V.; Sanders, M.J.; Gamblin, S.J. AMP-activated protein kinase: nature's energy sensor. *Nat. Chem. Biol.* **2011**, *7*, 512–518. [CrossRef] [PubMed]

44. Gil-Gomez, A.; Gómez-Sotelo, A.I.; Ranchal, I.; Rojas, Á.; García-Valdecasas, M.; Muñoz-Hernández, R.; Gallego-Durán, R.; Ampuero, J.; Romero Gómez, M. Metformin modifies glutamine metabolism in an in vitro and in vivo model of hepatic encephalopathy. *Rev. Esp. Enferm. Dig.* **2018**, *110*, 427–433. [CrossRef] [PubMed]

45. Marini, C.; Salani, B.; Massollo, M.; Amaro, A.; Esposito, A.I.; Orengo, A.M.; Capitanio, S.; Emionite, L.; Riondato, M.; Bottoni, G.; et al. Direct inhibition of hexokinase activity by metformin at least partially impairs glucose metabolism and tumor growth in experimental breast cancer. *Cell Cycle* **2013**, *12*, 3490–3499. [CrossRef] [PubMed]

46. Glynne-Jones, R.; Hoskin, P. Neoadjuvant cisplatin chemotherapy before chemoradiation: A flawed paradigm? *J. Clin. Oncol.* **2007**, *25*, 5281–5286. [CrossRef]

47. King, T.A.; Morrow, M. Surgical issues in patients with breast cancer receiving neoadjuvant chemotherapy. *Nat. Rev. Clin. Oncol.* **2015**, *12*, 335–343. [CrossRef]

48. Pfeffer, C.M.; Singh, A.T.K. Apoptosis: A Target for Anticancer Therapy. *Int. J. Mol. Sci.* **2018**, *19*, 448. [CrossRef]

49. Mayer, M.J.; Klotz, L.H.; Venkateswaran, V. Metformin and prostate cancer stem cells: A novel therapeutic target. *Prostate Cancer Prostatic Dis.* **2015**, *18*, 303–309. [CrossRef]

50. Sun, L.; Kwok, E.; Gopaluni, B.; Vahidi, O. Pharmacokinetic-Pharmacodynamic Modeling of metformin for the Treatment of Type II Diabetes Mellitus. *Open Biomed. Eng. J.* **2011**, *5*, 1–7. [CrossRef]

51. Martins, L.A.; Coelho, B.P.; Behr, G.; Pettenuzzo, L.F.; Souza, I.C.; Moreira, J.C.; Borojevic, R.; Gottfried, C.; Guma, F.C. Resveratrol induces pro-oxidant effects and time-dependent resistance to cytotoxicity in activated hepatic stellate cells. *Cell Biochem. Biophys.* **2014**, *68*, 247–257. [CrossRef] [PubMed]

52. Poljsak, B.; Raspor, P. The antioxidant and pro-oxidant activity of vitamin C and trolox in vitro: A comparative study. *J. Appl. Toxicol.* **2008**, *28*, 183–188. [CrossRef] [PubMed]

53. Wise, D.R.; Thompson, C.B. Glutamine addiction: A new therapeutic target in cancer. *Trends Biochem. Sci.* **2010**, *35*, 427–433. [CrossRef] [PubMed]

54. Hudson, C.D.; Savadelis, A.; Nagaraj, A.B.; Joseph, P.; Avril, S.; DiFeo, A.; Avril, N. Altered glutamine metabolism in platinum resistant ovarian cancer. *Oncotarget* **2016**, *7*, 41637–41649. [CrossRef] [PubMed]

55. Luo, C.; Shen, G.; Liu, N.; Gong, F.; Wei, X.; Yao, S.; Liu, D.; Teng, X.; Ye, N.; Zhang, N.; et al. Ammonia drives dendritic cells into dysfunction. *J. Immunol.* **2014**, *193*, 1080–1089. [CrossRef] [PubMed]

56. Cheong, H.; Lindsten, T.; Thompson, C.B. Autophagy and ammonia. *Autophagy* **2012**, *8*, 122–123. [CrossRef] [PubMed]

57. Isotani, S.; Hara, K.; Tokunaga, C.; Inoue, H.; Avruch, J.; Yonezawa, K. Immunopurified mammalian target of rapamycin phosphorylates and activates p70 S6 kinase alpha in vitro. *J. Biol. Chem.* **1999**, *274*, 34493–34498. [CrossRef] [PubMed]

58. Sarbassov, D.D.; Guertin, D.A.; Ali, S.M.; Sabatini, D.M. Phosphorylation and regulation of Akt/PKB by the rictor-mTOR complex. *Science* **2005**, *307*, 1098–1101. [CrossRef]
59. Nicholson, K.M.; Anderson, N.G. The protein kinase B/Akt signalling pathway in human malignancy. *Cell Signal.* **2002**, *14*, 381–395. [CrossRef]
60. Lapresa, M.; Parma, G.; Portuesi, R.; Colombo, N. Neoadjuvant chemotherapy in cervical cancer: An update. *Expert Rev. Anticancer Ther.* **2015**, *15*, 1171–1181. [CrossRef]

Article

Mesenchymal Stem Cell-Derived Exosomes Ameliorated Diabetic Nephropathy by Autophagy Induction through the mTOR Signaling Pathway

Nesrine Ebrahim [1,2], Inas A. Ahmed [3,4], Noha I. Hussien [5], Arigue A. Dessouky [6], Ayman Samir Farid [7,*], Amal M. Elshazly [8], Ola Mostafa [1], Walaa Bayoumie El Gazzar [3], Safwa M. Sorour [9], Yasmin Seleem [9], Ahmed M. Hussein [10] and Dina Sabry [11,12]

1   Department of Histology and Cell Biology, Faculty of Medicine, Benha University, Benha 13518, QG, Egypt; nesrien.salem@fmed.bu.edu.eg (N.E.); ola.mostafa.moez@gmail.com (O.M.)
2   Stem Cell Unit, Faculty of Medicine, Benha University, Benha 13518, QG, Egypt
3   Department of Medical Biochemistry, Faculty of Medicine, Benha University, Benha 13518, QG, Egypt; inas.ahmed@fmed.bu.edu.eg (I.A.A.); bioch_2004@yahoo.com (W.B.E.G.)
4   Molecular Biology and Biotechnology Unit, Faculty of Medicine, Benha University, Benha 13518, QG, Egypt
5   Department of Physiology, Faculty of Medicine, Benha University, Benha 13518, QG, Egypt; drnohaibrahim79@gmail.com
6   Department of Histology and Cell Biology, Faculty of Medicine, Zagazig University, Zagazig 44519, Egypt; arigueamir@yahoo.com
7   Department of Clinical Pathology, Faculty of Veterinary Medicine, Benha University, Moshtohor, Toukh 13736, QG, Egypt
8   Department of Anatomy, Faculty of Medicine, Benha University, Benha 13518, QG, Egypt; Amal.elshazly79@yahoo.com
9   Department of Clinical Pharmacology, Faculty of Medicine, Benha University, Benha 13518, QG, Egypt; safwa.sorour@fmed.bu.edu.eg (S.M.S.); yasmeen.seleem@fmed.bu.edu.eg (Y.S.)
10   Department of Internal Medicine, Faculty of Medicine, Benha University, Benha 13518, QG, Egypt; drdabour@yahoo.com
11   Department of Medical Biochemistry, Faculty of Medicine, Cairo University, Cairo 11562, Egypt; dinasabry@kasralainy.edu.eg
12   Molecular Biology and Stem Cell Unit, Faculty of Medicine, Cairo University, Cairo 11562, Egypt
*   Correspondence: ayman.samir@fvtm.bu.edu.eg; Tel.: +20-122-666-1174

Received: 11 October 2018; Accepted: 21 November 2018; Published: 22 November 2018

Abstract: Background: Diabetic nephropathy (DN) is a serious complication of diabetes mellitus and a common cause of end-stage renal disease. Autophagy has a defensive role against kidney damage caused by hyperglycemia. Mesenchymal stem cell (MSC)-derived exosomes are currently considered as a new promising therapy for chronic renal injury. However, the renal-protective mechanism of exosomes on DN is not completely understood. We examined the potential role of MSC-derived exosomes for enhancement of autophagy activity and their effect on DN. In our study, we used five groups of rats: control; DN; DN treated with exosomes; DN treated with 3-methyladenine (3-MA) and chloroquine (inhibitors of autophagy); and DN treated with 3-methyladenine (3-MA), chloroquine, and exosome groups. We assessed renal function, morphology, and fibrosis. Moreover, ratios of the autophagy markers mechanistic target of rapamycin (mTOR), Beclin-1, light chain-3 (LC3-II), and LC3-II/LC3-I were detected. Additionally, electron microscopy was used for detection of autophagosomes. Results: Exosomes markedly improved renal function and showed histological restoration of renal tissues, with significant increase of LC3 and Beclin-1, and significant decrease of mTOR and fibrotic marker expression in renal tissue. All previous effects were partially abolished by the autophagy inhibitors chloroquine and 3-MA. Conclusion: We conclude that autophagy induction by exosomes could attenuate DN in a rat model of streptozotocin-induced diabetes mellitus.

Keywords: diabetic nephropathy; exosomes; autophagy; mTOR

---

1. Introduction

Diabetic nephropathy (DN) is a devastating complication of diabetes mellitus and a leading cause of end-stage renal disease (ESRD) worldwide [1]. According to statistics, nearly 347 million people worldwide have diabetes, and this number is expected to increase to 430 million by 2030. DN is becoming more prevalent and, to some extent, reaching epidemic proportions [1,2]. Various functional and structural changes are involved in the pathogenesis of DN, including hemodynamic changes, oxidative stress, mesangial cell expansion, glomerulosclerosis, and the development of fibrosis [3]. However, despite conventional therapies, such as those that ameliorate hyperglycemia and hypertension, effective therapeutic strategies to counteract and reverse the progression of DN are lacking [4–6].

Current therapeutic modalities for DN are directed at controlling the diabetes-associated metabolic and hemodynamic changes to slow disease progression, while no therapy exists to repair the imminent renal damage [7]. Nevertheless, over the past decade, mesenchymal stem cells (MSCs) have gained increasing interest as a novel regenerative therapy against renal damage [8]. MSCs have the ability to differentiate into a number of different lineages [9]. The therapeutic impact of applied MSCs largely relies on released factors, including exosomes [10]. Recently, cell-derived exosomes were demonstrated to be a unique mechanism of cell-to-cell communication [11]. Exosomes are cell-derived vesicles, 30–100 nm in diameter, and discharged in the microenvironment by several cell types, including stem cells and their progenitors [12]. Exosomes contain mRNAs, microRNAs (miRNA), and proteins that could be transferred to target cells inducing genetic and epigenetic changes in target cells [13]. In addition, horizontal transfer of vesicular mRNAs and miRNAs can lead to an angiogenic program in endothelial cells or regulate the phenotypes of injured cells [14].

Macroautophagy (hereafter referred to as autophagy) is an evolutionarily conserved homeostatic process that mainly plays a role in damaged organelle degradation and intracellular content digestion [15]. Autophagy is a tightly regulated process that eliminates cytotoxic protein aggregates and damaged organelles through lysosomal degradation and allows cells to recycle mitochondrial energy sources and maintain survival [15]. Impairment of autophagy in renal cells, particularly podocytes and tubular cells, has been implicated in the pathogenesis of various kidney diseases, including DN [16]. Therefore, improvement and restoration of autophagy are considered as promising therapeutic targets for DN [17].

Impairment of autophagy is implicated in the pathogenesis of DN via activation of the mechanistic target of rapamycin (mTOR) pathway [18]. mTOR exists as two separate signaling complexes, mTOR complex 1 (mTORC1) and mTORC2, which are regulating autophagic activity. In general, mTORC1 inhibits autophagy via phosphorylation of ULK1. Nutrient starvation induces autophagy primarily through the inhibition of mTORC1 [19]. Enhanced mTORC1 activity is seen in human and experimental type 1 and type 2 DN [20–22]. Thus, in the present study, we evaluated the effects of MSC-derived exosomes in ameliorating histological alterations in DN in order to clarify their role in inducing autophagy by modulating the mTOR signaling pathway.

2. Materials and Methods

2.1. Experimental Animals

Inbred adult male albino rats (250–270 g), eight weeks of age, were obtained from the Experimental Animal Unit, Faculty of Veterinary Medicine, Benha University, Egypt. All animals were housed in clean cages and given a standard diet and clean water ad libitum. Their environment was controlled in terms of light (12 h cycle starting at 8:00 AM) and room temperature (23 $\pm$ 3 °C). This study was carried

out in strict accordance with the recommendations in the Guide for the Care and Use of Laboratory
Animals of the National Institutes of Health (NIH publication 85–23, revised 2011). All protocols were
approved by the institutional review board for animal experiments of the Faculty of Medicine, Benha
University, Egypt.

2.2. Preparation of MSC-Derived Exosomes

MSC-derived exosomes were obtained from the supernatant of MSCs, representing conditioned
media. First, rat bone marrow-derived MSCs (BM-MSCs) were prepared in the Central Lab, Faculty
of Medicine, Benha University [23]. The MSCs were cultured in Dulbecco's Modified Eagle Medium
(DMEM) without fetal bovine serum (FBS), but with 0.5% human serum albumin (HSA) (Sigma-Aldrich,
St. Louis, MO, USA), overnight. The viability of the cells cultured overnight was more than 99%, as
detected by trypan blue exclusion. Cells were plated at 4000 cells/cm^2 for 7 days. On day 7, cells were
trypsinized, counted, and replated in expansion medium at a density of 2000 cells/cm^2 for another
seven days (end of passage 1). The expansion was performed until the third passage.

The conditioned medium was collected and stored at –80 °C. The medium was centrifuged at
2000g for 20 min to remove debris, and then ultracentrifuged at 100,000× g in a SW41 swing rotor
(Beckman Coulter, Fullerton, CA, USA) for 1 hour at 4 °C. Exosomes were washed once with serum-free
M199 (Sigma-Aldrich) containing 25 mM 4-(2-hydroxyethyl)-1-piperazineethanesulfonic acid (HEPES)
(pH = 7.4), and submitted to a second ultracentrifugation in the same conditions. Exosomes were
labeled with PKH26 fluorescent linker dye to trace them in vivo. Exosomes were stored at –80 °C for
the experiment.

2.3. Characterization of MSC-Derived Exosomes

Exosome Labeling with PKH-26

Exosomes were isolated from the supernatant of the first, second, and third passages of MSCs
cultured in α-MEM deprived of FBS. The MSC-derived exosomes were fixed with 2.5% glutaraldehyde
in HSA for 2 h. After they were washed, exosomes were ultracentrifuged and suspended in 100 μL
HSA. A total of 20 μL of exosomes was loaded onto a formvar/carbon-coated grid, negatively stained
with 3% aqueous phosphor-tungstic acid for 1 min, and observed by transmission electron microscopy
(Hitachi H-7650, Hitachi, Tokyo, Japan) [24]. The protein content of the exosome pellet was quantified
by the Bradford method (BioRad, Hercules, CA, USA) [24]. The dose of injected exosomes was adjusted
to 100 μg protein/suspended in 0.2 ml PBS [25]. Additionally, PKH26 (Sigma-Aldrich, St. Louis, MO,
USA) was used to confirm the exosome localization within the renal tissue. The exosome pellet was
diluted with PKH-26 kit solution to 1 mL, and 2 μL of fluorochrome was added to this suspension
and incubated at 38.5 °C for 15 min. After that, 7 mL of serum-free HG-DMEM was added to the
suspension, then it was ultracentrifuged for second time at 100,000× g for 1 h at 4 °C. The final pellet
was resuspended rapidly in HG-DMEM and stored at −80 °C for future injection in experimentally
induced rats [26].

2.4. Western Blot for Characterization of Exosomes

The antibody used was antigen affinity-purified polyclonal sheep IgG anti-rabbit CD81 (Biolegend,
Cat No.: 0349509) and CD63 (Biolegend, cat no.: 0353007). Protein was isolated from isolated exosomes
using RIPA buffer. A total of 20 ng of protein was loaded and separated by SDS-PAGE on 4–20%
polyacrylamide gradient gels. After incubation in 5% nonfat dry milk, Tris-HCL, and 0.1% Tween 20
for 1 h, primary antibodies (CD81 and CD63 polyclonal antibodies, and β-actin antibody) were added
to one of the membranes containing specimen samples and incubated at 4 °C overnight with β-actin as
a loading control. After washing the membrane twice with 1× TBST, appropriate secondary antibodies
were then added and incubated for 2 h at room temperature. After being washed twice with 1× TBST,
densitometric analysis of the immunoblots was performed to quantify the amounts of CD81, CD63

and β-actin against control sample by total protein normalization using image analysis software on the ChemiDoc MP imaging system (version 3) produced by BioRad (Hercules, CA, USA).

2.5. Experimental Chemicals

Streptozotocin powder was obtained from Sigma-Aldrich Chemical Co. (St. Louis, MO, USA). The powder was stored at −20 °C, and the amount needed was dissolved in 0.1 mol/L citrate buffer, pH 4.5, immediately before use.

3-Methyladenine was purchased from Sigma-Aldrich in powder form. The powder was dissolved in distilled water, and then placed in 50 °C bath water.

Chloroquine diphosphate salt was purchased from Sigma-Aldrich in powder form. The powder was dissolved in distilled water.

2.6. Induction of DN

Type I diabetes was induced in overnight fasted rats by a single intraperitoneal (IP) injection of freshly prepared STZ (60 mg/kg, dissolved in 0.1 M cold citrate buffer, pH 4.5). After STZ injection, rats acquired drinking water containing sucrose (15 g/L) for 48 h, to lessen the early death due to insulin discharge from partially injured pancreatic islets. Seventy-two hours later, rats were checked for hyperglycemia, and those with fasting blood sugar more than 250 mg/dL were included in the study. Diabetic rats received long-acting insulin (2–4 U/rat) via subcutaneous injection to maintain blood glucose levels in a desirable range (350 mg/dL) and to avoid subsequent development of ketonuria [27].

2.7. Experimental Design and Treatment Protocol

The experimental design is shown in Figure 1. Fifty-six male rats were randomly divided into five groups as follows:

Group I (control group; $n = 21$): Rats were fed a regular chow diet for 12 weeks. The rats were divided equally into three subgroups of 7 rats each:

Subgroup IA: The rats were left without intervention.

Subgroup IB: The rats were injected intraperitoneally with a single dose of 0.25 mL/kg body weight sodium citrate buffer (vehicle for STZ).

Subgroup IC: The rats were injected intraperitoneally with distilled water for four weeks (vehicle for chloroquine diphosphate). Simultaneously, they were intravenously injected with 0.2 mL phosphate-buffered saline (PBS), one injection at the 8th week. and the other injection at the 10th week of the experiment (vehicle for exosomes).

Group II (DN group; $n = 14$): DN was induced and the rats were subdivided equally into two subgroups:

Group IIA: DN was induced and rats were scarified at the end of the 8th week of the experiment to confirm histological changes of DN.

Group IIB: DN was induced and rats were scarified at the end of the experiment at the 12th week.

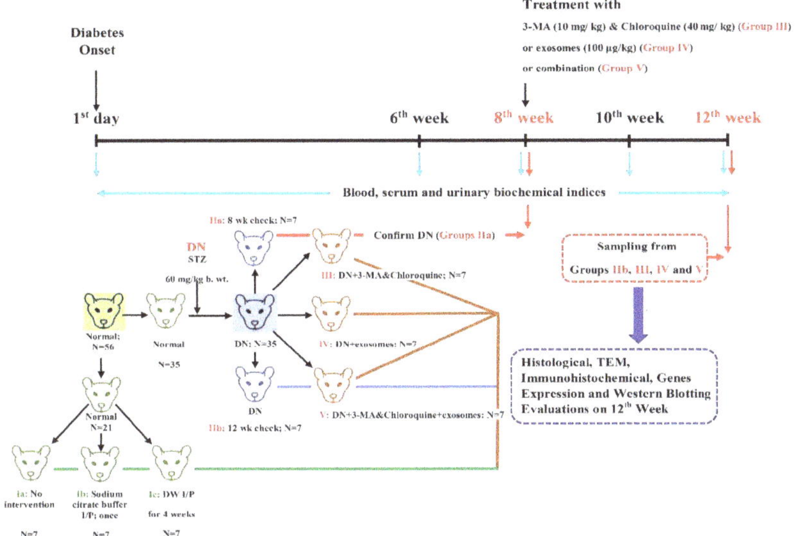

Figure 1. Experimental design and treatment procedure. Rats were divided into five groups: Group I (control group; n = 21 subdivided into three subgroups, seven rats each), Group II (DN group; n = 14 subdivided into two groups, seven rats each), Group III (DN + 3-MA and chloroquine; n = 7), Group IV (DN + exosomes; n = 7), and Group V (DN + 3-MA and chloroquine + exosomes; n = 7). Rats of DN groups were injected with streptozotocin (STZ) without/with treatment by 3-MA and chloroquine, exosome, or both. On the first day, and at weeks 6, 8, 10, and 12, blood samples were collected from all rats for biochemical assays, and at weeks 8 and 12, and renal tissues were collected for histological and molecular biological examinations.

Group III (DN + 3-MA and chloroquine; n = 7): DN was induced and rats were intraperitoneally injected with 3-MA (10 mg/kg) and chloroquine (40 mg/kg) [28], once per day for four weeks, from the 8th week until the end of the experiment.

Group IV (DN + exosomes; n = 7): DN was induced and rats were treated with two injections of exosomes (100 µg/kg/dose suspended in 0.2 ml PBS) through the tail tail vein [25]. once per day for four weeks, from the 8th week until the end of the experiment.

Group IV (DN + exosomes; n = 7): DN was induced and rats were treated with two injections of exosomes (100 µg/kg/dose suspended in 0.2 mL PBS) through the tail vein [25]. The first injection was at the 8th week of the experiment, and the second at the end of the 10th week.

Group V (DN + 3-MA and chloroquine + exosomes; n = 7): DN was induced and rats were intraperitoneally injected with 3-MA (10 mg/kg) and chloroquine (40 mg/kg), once per day for four weeks, from the 8th week until the end of the experiment. Simultaneously, exosomes were injected at the 8th and 10th weeks of the experiment.

2.8. Sampling

Blood samples were obtained from retro-orbital venous plexus on the first day, then the 6th, 8th, 10th, and 12th weeks, to measure blood glucose, serum creatinine, and blood urea nitrogen (BUN). Serum levels of creatinine and BUN were determined using an auto-analyzer (Hitachi 912 Auto-Analyzer, Hitachi, Tokyo, Japan). Fasting blood glucose was estimated by the glucose oxidase-peroxidase method (GOD-POD kit from Biodiagnostic, Giza, Egypt). Additionally, rats were located in metabolic cages for collection of 24 h urine, to measure urinary proteins at the same intervals. Urinary protein excretion was determined using (Fortress Diagnostics Ltd., Antrim, UK).

Nephropathy was confirmed in rats at the end of the 6th week by significant increases in protein in the urine, serum creatinine, and BUN, when compared with controls. Rats having these significant values were enrolled in the study.

At the end of the 12th week, the rats were anesthetized by sodium thiopental anesthesia (40 mg/kg IP) after 12 h of fasting. The rats were fixed on an operating table and blood samples were obtained from retro-orbital venous plexus using a fine-walled Pasteur pipette. Then, vascular perfusion fixation through the left ventricle with 1% glutaraldehyde was performed. The kidneys were collected from the rats of all groups for histological and immunohistochemical analysis, transmission electron microscopy, qPCR study, and Western blot

2.9. Histological Analysis

2.9.1. Light Microscopy Study

The specimens were excised, and paraffin sections of 4–6 μm thickness were created and then mounted on glass slides for H and E and Masson's trichrome stains [29]. Immunohistochemistry staining was done for detection of transforming growth factor β (TGF-β). The primary monoclonal antibody used was rabbit monoclonal antibody to TGF-β (Lab Vision/NeoMarkers, Fremont, CA, USA). Positive reaction was detected as a brown color in the cytoplasm [30].

2.9.2. Transmission Electron Microscopy Study

Vascular perfusion fixation through the left ventricle with 1% glutaraldehyde was performed, then the kidneys were dissected and 1 mm^3 kidney samples were taken in 0.1 M phosphate-buffered solution (PBS), pH 7.4, at 4 °C for 2 h, then washed three times with PBS (10 min each). Samples were post fixed in 1% osmic acid for 30 min, then washed three times with PBS (10 min each). Samples were dehydrated with an ascending series of ethyl alcohol (30, 50, 70, 90%, and absolute alcohol) for 30 min at each concentration. Samples were infiltrated with acetone for 1 h, and then embedded in Araldite 502 resin. The plastic molds were cut using a Leica UCT ultramicrotome, then stained with 1% toluidine blue. After examination of semithin sections, ultrathin sections (50–60 nm thick) were cut, stained with uranyl acetate, then counterstained with lead citrate, examined, and photographed using a JEOL-JEM-100 SX electron microscope (Japan), electron microscope unit, Tanta University [31].

2.10. Morphometric Study

The mean area percentage of collagen fiber deposition by Masson's trichrome and of TGF-β expression were quantified in five images from five nonoverlapping fields from each rat of each group using Image-Pro Plus version 6.0 (Media Cybernetics Inc., Bethesda, MD, USA).

2.10.1. Determination of the Expressions of *LC3*, *mTOR*, and *Beclin-1* Genes by qPCR

Total RNA Extraction and Reverse Transcription

Total RNA was extracted from frozen kidney tissue samples by TRIzol method (Invitrogen, USA) using RNeasy Mini Kit (Qiagen, Germany) as previously described [32]. Samples were quantified using a NanoDrop One spectrophotometer (Thermo Fisher Scientific, USA). RNA (1 μg) was reverse transcribed using a T100 Thermal Cycler (BioRad, USA) and the Maxima First Strand cDNA Synthesis Kit (Thermo Fisher Scientific, USA), following the manufacturer's guidelines [33].

Quantitative Real-Time PCR

Real-time PCR was performed according to the manufacturer's instructions, using Maxima SYBR Green/ROX qPCR Master Mix (Thermo Fisher, USA), by Step One Plus Real-Time PCR System (Life Technologies, USA) [34]. The primer sequences were as follows: *GAPDH* forward, TGATTCTACCCACGGCAAGTT; *GAPDH* reverse, TGATGGGTTTCCCATTGATGA;

LC3-II forward, ACTGCCGCCCTAAAGGTTAC; *LC3-II* reverse, CGAGGTCCAACCCACAAAGA; Beclin-1 forward, CGGCTCCTATTCCATCAAAA; Beclin-1 reverse, AACTGTGAGGACAC CCAAGC [35]; *mTOR* forward, TTGAGGTTGCTATGACCAGAGAGAA; and *mTOR* reverse, TTACCAGAAAGGACACCAGCCAATG [34]. The mRNA expression of each sample was determined after correction by *GAPDH* expression. The relative expression was calculated using the $2^{-\Delta\Delta CT}$ method. The results are expressed as the n-fold difference relative to the control group. Each sample was assayed three times.

2.11. Western Blot

The mTOR, LC3-I, LC3-II, S6K1, p62, fibronectin, TGF-β, and β-actin antibodies used were purchased from Abcam (anti-fibronectin antibody (ab23750), rabbit polyclonal antibody [36], anti-TGF beta 1 antibody (ab92486), rabbit polyclonal antibody [37], anti-LC3-I/II antibody (ABC929, Sigma-Aldrich), rabbit polyclonal antibody [38], anti-S6K1 antibody (ab9366), rabbit polyclonal antibody [39], anti-SQSTM1/p62 antibody (ab155686), rabbit polyclonal antibody [40] and anti-mTOR antibody (ab2732), rabbit polyclonal antibody [41]). The proteins of renal tissues were extracted by RIPA lysis buffer, which was delivered by Bio Basic Inc. (Markham, ON, Canada). Extracted proteins were separated by SDS-PAGE on 4–20% polyacrylamide gradient gels. After incubation in 5% nonfat dry milk, Tris-HCL, and 0.1% Tween 20 for 1 h, primary antibodies (fibronectin, TGF-β, mTOR, LC3 II polyclonal antibodies, and β-actin antibody) were added to one of the membranes containing specimen samples and incubated at 4 °C overnight with β-actin as a loading control. After washing the membrane twice with 1× TBST, appropriate secondary antibodies were then added and incubated for 2 h at room temperature. After being washed twice with 1× TBST, densitometric analysis of the immunoblots was performed to quantify the amounts of collagen-I and β-actin against control sample by total protein normalization using image analysis software on the ChemiDoc MP imaging system (version 3) produced by BioRad (Hercules, CA, USA).

A statistical analysis was performed using the statistical software package SPSS for Windows (Version 18.0; SPSS Inc., Chicago, IL, USA). Differences between groups were evaluated using a one-way ANOVA followed by a Duncan post-hoc test. For each test, all the data are expressed as the mean ± standard error of mean (SE), and a *p* value <0.05 was considered significant.

3. Results

3.1. Exosome Characterization

A transmission electron microscopy examination of purified exosomes demonstrated their characteristic spheroid double-membrane bound morphology with a diameter of 40–100 nm (Figure 2A). Also, the exosomes were detected in renal tissues by PKH26 dye tracing (Figure 2B). The amount of purified exosome was significantly ($p < 0.05$) increased over the passages, and reached maximum concentration in the third passage, which was used for administration to rats (Figure 2 C,D).

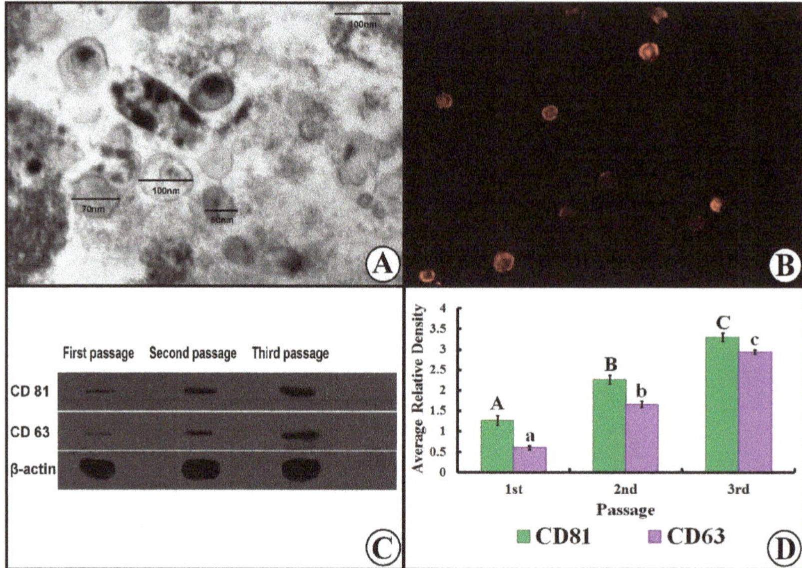

Figure 2. (**A**) TEM of exosomes showed spheroid double-membrane bound morphology (arrows) with a diameter of 40–100 nm. (**B**) Exosomes were also detected in renal tissues by PKH26. (**C**) Western blot for exosome characterization. (**D**) Histogram of exosome characterization. For CD81 panel, means with uppercase letters (A, B, and C) indicate significant differences at $p < 0.05$. For CD63 panel, means with lowercase letters (a, b, and c) indicate significant differences at $p < 0.05$. Data are shown as mean $\pm$ SEM, $n = 5$.

3.2. Biochemical Analysis

Examination of all subgroups of the control group showed similar results regarding biochemical examinations; therefore, results of subgroup Ia were used to represent this group. Injection of streptozotocin (STZ) resulted in significant increases in blood glucose, serum creatinine, blood urea nitrogen (BUN), and urinary proteins excretion at the end of weeks 6, 8, 10, and 12, compared to the control group ($p < 0.05$) (Figure 3). Injection of exosomes caused significant decreases ($p < 0.05$) in blood glucose, serum creatinine, BUN, and urinary proteins excretion at weeks 10 and 12, compared with the DN group. On the other hand, treatment of DN with 3-MA and chloroquine aggravated the effects of injected STZ and reduced the protective effects of exosome, indicated by significant ($p < 0.05$) increases in blood glucose, serum creatinine, BUN, and urinary proteins excretion at weeks 10 and 12, when compared with the DN and exosome-treated groups. Similarly, the DN group treated with 3-MA and chloroquine and exosome showed significant ($p < 0.05$) increases in blood glucose, serum creatinine, BUN, and urinary proteins excretion at weeks 10 and 12 when compared with the exosome-treated group.

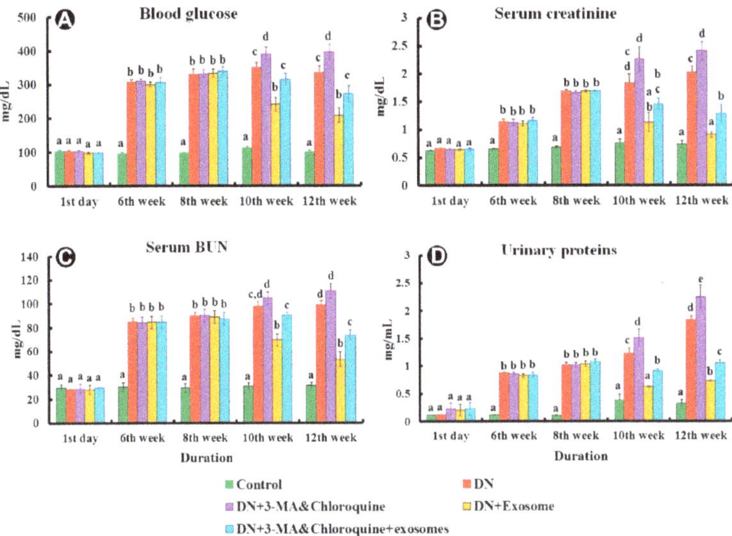

Figure 3. (**A**) Blood glucose, (**B**) serum creatinine, (**C**) blood urea nitrogen (BUN), and (**D**) urinary proteins from different experimental groups. Subgroup Ic was used as a control. Different superscripts (a, b, c, d, and e) at the same checkpoint indicate significant differences at $p < 0.05$. Data are shown as mean $\pm$ SEM, $n = 7$.

3.3. Histological Examination

Histological examination of the different subgroups of Group I (control group) showed similar results; therefore, results of subgroup Ia were used to represent this group.

3.3.1. Light Microscope Examination

Hematoxylin and Eosin

Sections of Group I (control group) revealed renal corpuscles consisting of glomeruli surrounded by narrow Bowman's space and Bowman's capsule. The corpuscles were surrounded by proximal and distal convoluted tubules (Figure 4A). Group IIa (DN group at the end of week 8): The renal tissues showed numerous glomeruli with mesangial expansion and glomerular nodular sclerosis (Kimmelstien–Wilson nodules), which appeared as acidophilic nodules with palisading nuclei at the periphery of glomeruli. Many tubules demonstrated darkly stained nuclei (Figure 4B). Also, sections of Group IIb (DN group at the end of week 12) demonstrated shrunken glomeruli with wide Bowman's spaces (glomerulosclerosis). The tubules showed swollen epithelial lining obliterating their lumens, in addition to darkly staining nuclei. Some nuclei were basal, while others were apical (Figure 4C). The renal corpuscles of Group III (DN + 3-MA and chloroquine) showed marked shrinkage of glomeruli with obvious widening of the Bowman's spaces (glomerulosclerosis). The tubules showed swollen tubular epithelium obliterating the lumen and darkly stained nuclei with loss of their polarity (some nuclei were basal, while others were apical) (Figure 4D). Glomeruli of Group IV (DN + exosomes) exhibited decreased mesangial expansion. The tubules showed open lumens and normal nuclear polarity (basal nuclei) of their lining epithelium (Figure 4E). Group V (DN + 3-MA and chloroquine + exosomes) demonstrated persistent mesangial expansion with swollen tubular epithelial lining, obliterated lumens, and darkly staining nuclei with loss of nuclear polarity (Figure 4F).

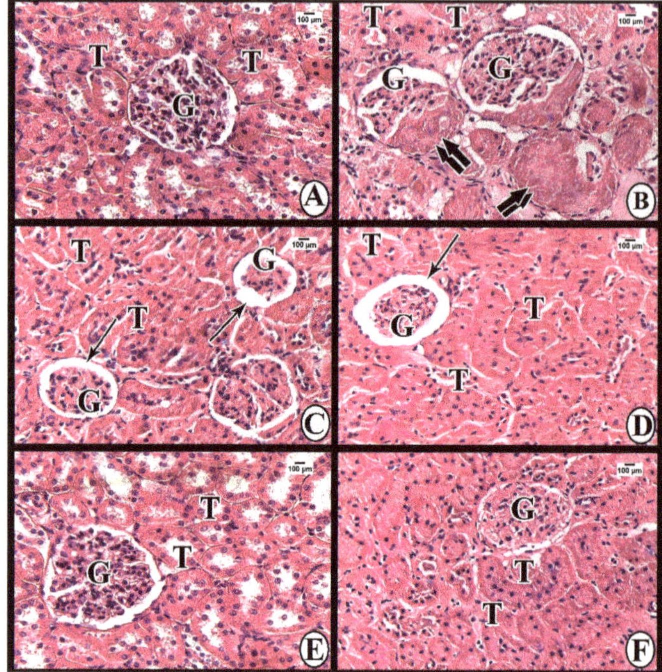

Figure 4. (**A**) Hematoxylin and eosin (H&E) stained sections of renal tissue of Group I show normal glomerulus (G) and tubules (T). (**B**) Group IIa shows mesangial expansion in the glomeruli (G) and glomerular nodular sclerosis (double arrows). Tubules (T) show obliterated lumens and darkly stained nuclei with loss of nuclear polarity. (**C, D**) Groups IIb and III demonstrate shrunken glomeruli (G) with wide Bowman's spaces (thin arrows). The tubules (T) show swollen epithelial lining obliterating the lumens in addition to darkly staining nuclei with loss of polarity. (**E**) Group IV shows decreased mesangial expansion in the glomeruli (G). Tubules (T) have open lumens and normal nuclear polarity. (**F**) Group V shows persistent mesangial expansion in the glomeruli (G), swollen tubular epithelia (T) obliterating the lumens, and darkly stained nuclei with loss of polarity.

Masson's Trichrome Stain

Masson's trichrome stained sections of Group I (control group) demonstrated minimal amounts of collagen fibers among the glomerular capillaries and surrounding the renal corpuscles and tubules (Figure 5A). Groups IIa and IIb (DN groups) and Group III (DN + 3-MA and chloroquine) showed an obvious increase in the amount of collagen fiber deposition among the glomerular capillaries and between the tubules, with a greater increase observed in Group III (Figure 5B–D). On the other hand, Group IV (DN + exosomes) revealed decreased amounts of collagen fibers among the glomerular capillaries and surrounding the renal corpuscles and tubules (Figure 5E), while Group V (DN + 3-MA and chloroquine + exosomes) demonstrated a persistent increase in collagen fibers among the glomerular capillaries and surrounding the renal corpuscles and tubules (Figure 5F).

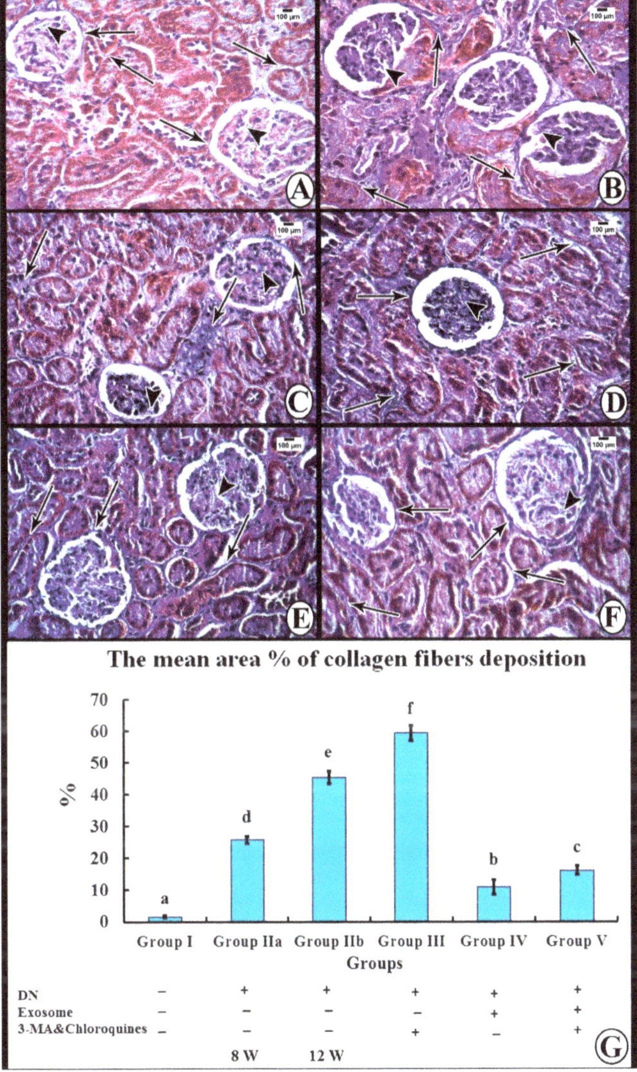

Figure 5. (**A**) Masson's trichrome stained sections of renal cortex of Group I show minimal collagen fibers among the glomerular capillaries (arrowhead) and surrounding the renal corpuscles and tubules (thin arrows). (**B**) Group IIa demonstrates accumulation of collagen fibers among the glomerular capillaries (arrowheads) and surrounding the renal corpuscles and tubules (thin arrows). (**C**) Group IIb shows marked accumulations of collagen fibers among the glomerular capillaries (arrowheads) and surrounding the renal corpuscles and tubules (thin arrows). (**D**) Group III shows extensive accumulation of collagen fibers among the glomerular capillaries (arrowhead) and surrounding the renal corpuscles and tubules (thin arrows). (**E**) Group IV has few collagen fibers among the glomerular capillaries (arrowhead) and around the renal corpuscles and tubules (thin arrows). (**F**) Group V demonstrates persistent accumulation of collagen fibers among the glomerular capillaries (arrowhead) and surrounding the renal corpuscles and tubules (thin arrows). (**G**) A histogram represents the mean area percentage of collagen fiber deposition in all experimental groups. Different superscripts (a, b, c, d, e, and f) indicate significant differences among the experimental groups at $p < 0.05$. Data are shown as mean $\pm$ SEM, $n = 6$.

3.4. Immunohistochemical Study

The immunohistochemical reaction for transforming growth factor β (TGF-β) in Group I showed a minimal positive cytoplasmic reaction in the tubular epithelial cells (Figure 6A). In Group IIa, the tubular cells showed a moderate positive cytoplasmic reaction (Figure 6B), while the reaction was strongly positive in tubular cells of Group IIb (Figure 6C). Tubular epithelial cells of Group III showed an intensely positive cytoplasmic reaction (Figure 6D). On the other hand, Group IV revealed a mildly positive cytoplasmic reaction (Figure 6E), while Group V showed a moderately positive cytoplasmic reaction (Figure 6F).

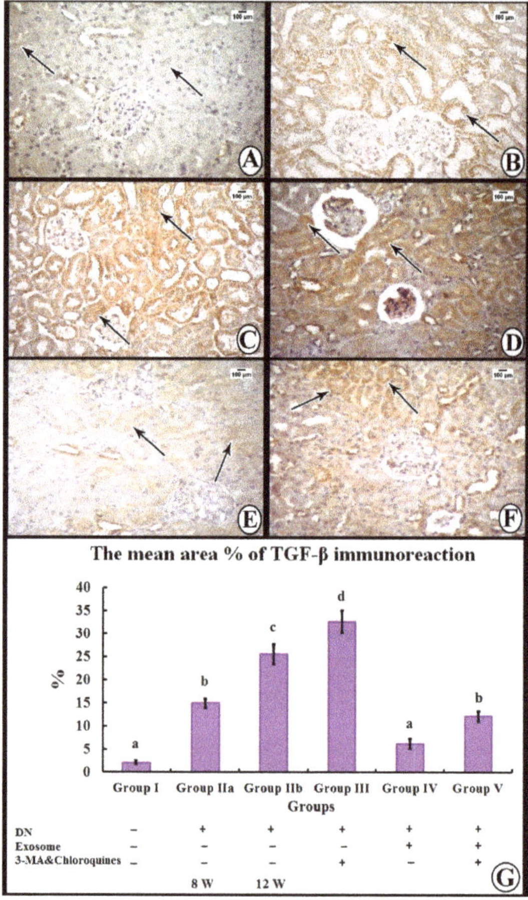

Figure 6. Immunohistochemical reaction for transforming growth factor β (TGF-β) in sections of the renal cortex. (**A**) Group I shows mild positive cytoplasmic reaction in the tubular epithelial cells (thin arrows). (**B**) Group IIa shows tubular cells with a moderate positive cytoplasmic reaction (thin arrows). (**C**) Group IIb shows a strong positive reaction in the cytoplasm of the tubular cells (thin arrows). (**D**) Group III shows intense positive reactions in the cytoplasm of the tubular cells (thin arrows). (**E**) Group IV shows a mild positive cytoplasmic reaction (thin arrows). (**F**) Group V tubular cells show a moderate positive cytoplasmic reaction (thin arrows). (**G**) Histogram representing the mean area percentage of TGF-β immunoreaction in all experimental groups. Different superscripts (a, b, c, and d) indicate significant differences among the experimental groups at $p < 0.05$. Data are shown as mean $\pm$ SEM, $n = 6$.

3.5. Morphometric Analysis

The mean area percentage of collagen fiber deposition and TGF-β immunoexpression for all groups is presented in Figures 4 and 6. The diabetic nephropathy groups (Group IIa and IIb) and Group III showed a significant increase in the mean area percentage of collagen fiber deposition and TGF-β immunoexpression compared to the control group. Furthermore, administration of exosomes caused a significant decrease in the mean area percentage of collagen fiber deposition and TGF-β immunoexpression compared to both DN groups. On the contrary, administration of 3-MA and chloroquine caused a significant decrease in the antifibrotic effect of exosomes, as evidenced by a significant increase in the mean area percentage of collagen fiber deposition and TGF-β immunoexpression compared to the exosome-treated group.

3.6. Transmission Electron Microscopy Study

The ultrastructure of glomerular filtration barriers of Group I (control group) consisted of thin fenestrated endothelial cells and thin regular glomerular basement membranes, in addition to the foot processes of the podocytes (Figure 7A). Groups IIa and IIb (DN groups) demonstrated extensive fusion and effacement of the foot processes in addition to diffuse thickening of the glomerular basement membrane (Figure 7B,C). Group III (DN + 3-MA and chloroquine) showed that glomerular basement membranes had extensive areas of irregular thickening with areas of thickening, fusion, and effacement of the foot processes (Figure 7D). Group IV (DN + exosomes) revealed thin regular glomerular basement membranes in addition to the foot processes of the podocytes (Figure 7E). On the other hand, Group V (DN + 3-MA and chloroquine + exosomes) revealed persistent thickening of the glomerular basement membranes, and fusion and effacement of podocytes in many areas (Figure 7F).

The proximal tubular epithelial cells of Group I (control group) were seen resting on thin regular basement membranes. They possessed numerous tightly packed apical microvilli, round euchromatic nuclei, and numerous mitochondria in the cytoplasm (Figure 8A). Tubular cells of Group IIa (DN group after 8 weeks) rested on slightly thickened basement membranes. Their apical microvilli appeared swollen and disrupted, and the nuclei were shrunken. The cytoplasm contained areas of rarefaction in addition to numerous swollen mitochondria and scattered dense bodies (Figure 8B). Group IIb (DN group after 12 weeks) revealed increased thickening of the tubular basement membranes with disrupted apical microvilli and pyknotic nuclei. The cytoplasm contained multiple variably sized vacuoles, variably sized mitochondria, and few scattered electron-dense bodies (Figure 8C). Group III (DN + 3-MA and chloroquine) showed tubular epithelial cells resting on a thickened basement membrane with swollen and disrupted apical microvilli. The cytoplasm contained numerous swollen mitochondria of various sizes and shapes with few electron-dense bodies. The nuclei contained peripheral clumps of heterochromatin. Also, the interstitium revealed abundant collagen fibrils (Figure 8D). Group IV (DN + exosomes) showed the tubular cells resting on thin basement membranes. The apical microvilli were numerous and tightly packed, and the nuclei appeared round and euchromatic. The cytoplasm contained numerous autophagosomes containing cellular debris, numerous scattered electron-dense bodies, and elongated mitochondria (Figure 8E). In Group V (DN + 3-MA and chloroquine + exosomes), tubular cells showed persistent thickening of the tubular basement membranes in many areas, swollen apical microvilli, and slightly shrunken nuclei. The cytoplasm showed areas of rarefication in addition to variably sized mitochondria and scattered electron-dense bodies (Figure 8F).

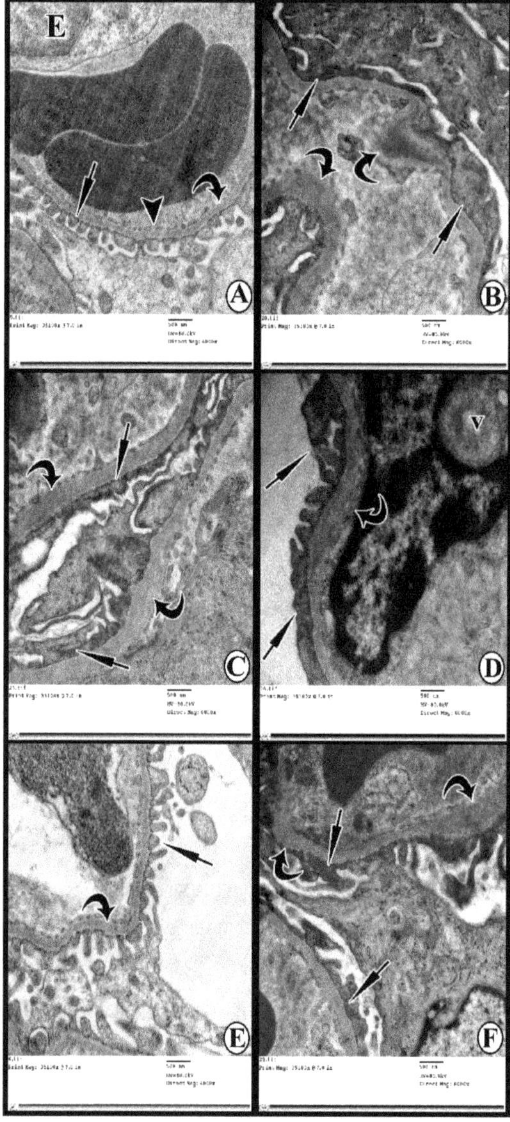

Figure 7. Ultrathin sections showing glomerular filtration barriers of (**A**) Group I, consisting of thin fenestrated endothelial cell (E; arrowhead), thin regular glomerular basement membrane (curved arrow), and the foot processes of the podocytes (short arrow). (**B**) Group IIa shows extensive fusion and effacement of the foot processes (short arrows) and diffuse thickening of the glomerular basement membrane (curved arrows). (**C**) Group IIb shows complete fusion and effacement of the foot processes (short arrows) and thickened glomerular basement membrane (curved arrows). (**D**) Group III shows areas of fusion and effacement of the podocytes (thin arrows) and diffuse thickening of the glomerular basement membrane (curved arrow). A vacuole (v) is seen compressing the nucleus of the endothelial cell. (**E**) Group IV shows thin regular glomerular basement membrane (curved arrow) and foot processes of podocytes (thin arrow). (**F**) Group V shows persistent fusion and effacement of the foot processes (short arrows) and thickening of the glomerular basement membrane (curved arrows) in some areas.

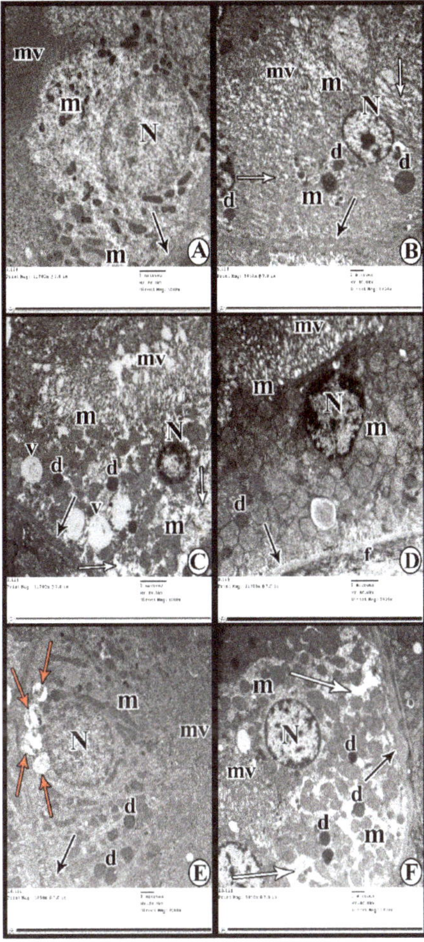

Figure 8. Ultrathin sections showing proximal tubular cells of (**A**) Group I resting on a thin regular basement membrane (thin arrow). Apical microvilli (mv) are numerous and tightly packed. The nucleus (N) appears oval and euchromatic, and the cytoplasm contains numerous mitochondria (m). (**B**) Group IIa shows a slightly thickened tubular basement membrane (thin arrow), swollen disrupted apical microvilli (mv), and a shrunken nucleus (N). The cytoplasm shows areas of rarefaction (white arrows), numerous swollen mitochondria (m), and scattered electron-dense bodies (d). (**C**) Group IIb shows increased thickening of the tubular basement membrane (thin arrow), disrupted apical microvilli (mv), and a shrunken heterochromatic nucleus (N). The cytoplasm shows multiple variably sized vacuoles (v), variably sized mitochondria (m), and few scattered electron-dense bodies (d). (**D**) Group III shows a tubular cell resting on thickened basement membrane (thin arrow). Apical microvilli (mv) appear swollen and distorted. The nucleus (N) shows clumps of heterochromatin. The cytoplasm contains numerous swollen mitochondria (m) of various shapes and sizes. A small electron-dense body (d) is also observed. Thin collagen fibrils (f) are seen in the interstitium. (**E**) Group IV shows proximal tubular cells resting on a thin basement membrane (thin arrow). The apical microvilli (mv) appear numerous and tightly packed, and the nucleus (N) is round and euchromatic. The cytoplasm contains numerous autophagosomes (red arrows) containing cellular debris, numerous scattered electron-dense bodies (d), and elongated mitochondria (m). (**F**) Group V shows persistent thickening of the tubular basement membrane in some areas (thin arrow), swollen apical microvilli (mv), and slightly shrunken nucleus (N). The cytoplasm shows areas of rarefication (white arrows), variably sized mitochondria (m), and scattered electron-dense bodies (d).

3.7. Gene Expression Results of LC3-II, mTOR, and Beclin-1 Genes in All Experimental Groups

Gene expressions of LC3-II, mTOR, and Beclin-1 genes are presented in Figure 9. The DN group showed significant ($p < 0.05$) downregulation of LC3 and Beclin-1 with significant ($p < 0.05$) upregulation in mTOR gene expression in renal tissues compared to the control group. Furthermore, treatment of DN with exosomes caused significant ($p < 0.05$) upregulation of Beclin-1 and LC3-II, as well as significant ($p < 0.05$) downregulation of mTOR gene expression in renal tissues when compared with the DN group. On the other hand, injection of both 3-MA and chloroquine caused significant ($p < 0.05$) downregulation of autophagy markers Beclin-1 and LC3-II, with significant ($p < 0.05$) upregulation of mTOR mRNA in renal tissues compared to the exosome-treated group.

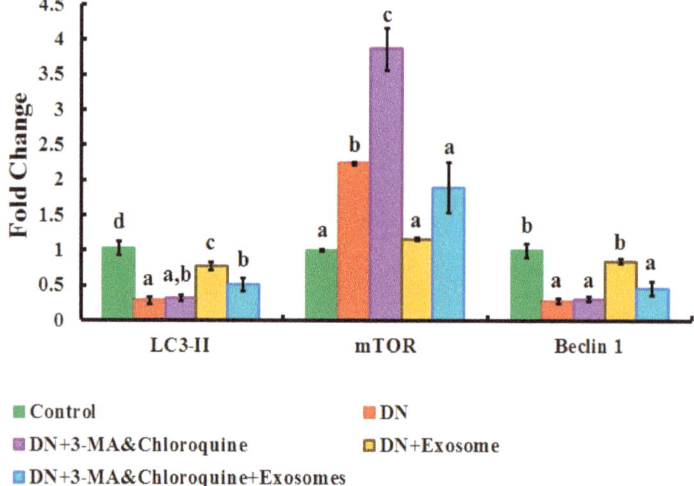

Figure 9. Quantitative analysis of relative light chain-3 (LC3-II), mechanistic target of rapamycin (mTOR), and Beclin-1 gene expression after treatment with 3-methyladenine (3-MA) and chloroquine and/or exosomes. Subgroup Ic was used as a control. Different superscript letters (a, b, and c) within each parameter panel indicate significant differences at $p < 0.05$. Data are shown as mean ± SEM, $n = 5$.

3.8. mTOR, LC3-I, LC3-II, S6K1, p62, Fibronectin, TGF-β, and β-Actin Detection by Western Blotting

As shown in Figure 10, protein expressions of mTOR, fibronectin, S6K1 and TGF-β in the DN group were significantly ($p < 0.05$) higher than in the control group, and exosome treatment significantly ($p < 0.05$) reduced their levels. On the other hand, the ratio of LC3-II and LC3-I as well as p62 protein expression (Figure 10B) in the DN group decreased significantly when compared with the control group, while exosome treatment significantly enhanced LC3-II/LC3-I and p62 protein expression compared to the DN group ($p < 0.05$). Furthermore, injection of both 3-MA and chloroquine resulted in significant increases in fibronectin, TGF-β, S6K1, and mTOR protein expression, and a significant decrease in LC3-II and p62 protein expression compared with the exosome-treated group.

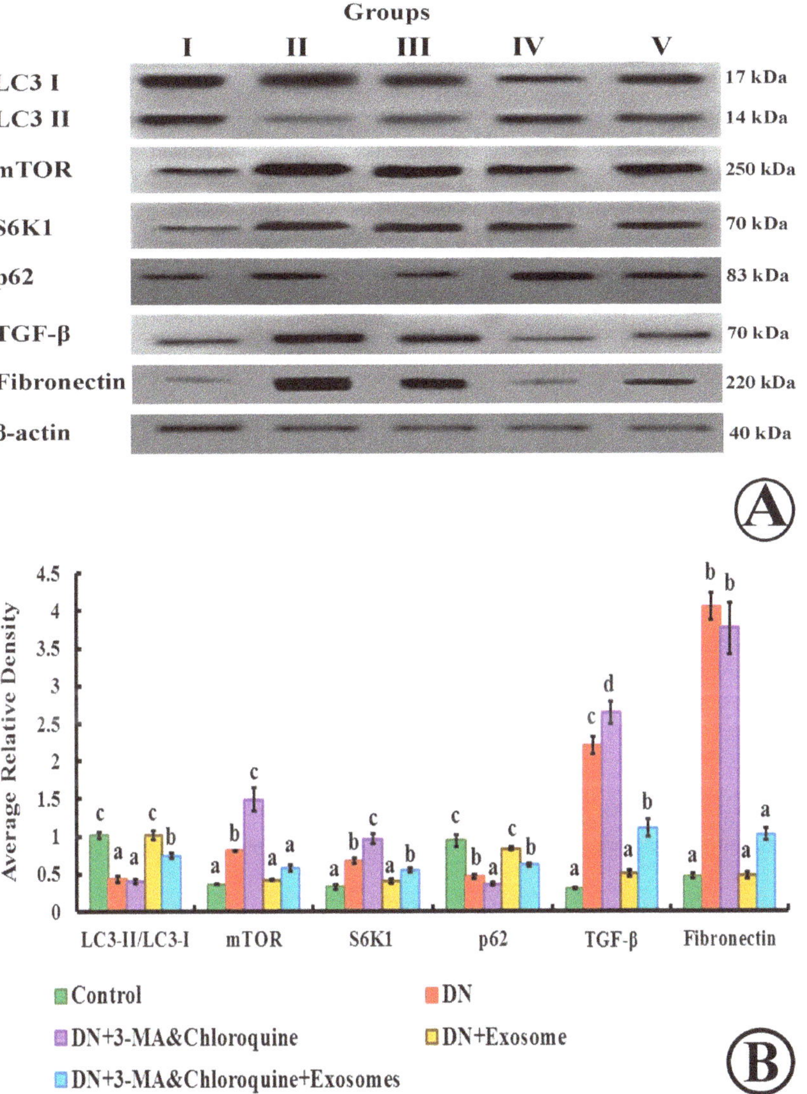

Figure 10. (**A**) Western blot assay and downstream target proteins for mTOR, LC3-I, LC3-II, S6K1, p62 fibronectin, TGF-β, and β-actin expression after treatment with 3-MA, chloroquine, and/or exosomes, and quantified using image analysis software on the ChemiDoc MP imaging system. (**B**) Histogram of blotting intensity in different groups Group I (control), Group II (DN), Group III (DN + 3-MA and chloroquine), Group IV (DN + exosomes), and Group V (DN + 3-MA and chloroquine + exosomes). Subgroup Ic was used as a control. Different superscript letters (a, b, c, and d) within each parameter panel indicate significant differences at $p < 0.05$. Data are shown as mean ± SEM, $n = 5$

4. Discussion

The rapidly increasing prevalence of diabetes is resulting in a concomitant increase in the prevalence of DN [42]. Given the large worldwide healthcare burden associated with DN, there has been much interest in the search for novel treatment targets. Therefore, in recent decades, many researchers have been making a great deal of effort to recognize the molecular mechanisms in initiation and progression of diabetic nephropathy, in order to develop novel therapeutic approaches. However, end-stage kidney disease, due to DN, is still increasing worldwide. There is an urgent need to find additional novel therapeutic agents for the prevention of DN [43,44]. The present study demonstrates, for the first time, that MSC-derived exosomes could ameliorate DN by autophagy regulation through the mTOR signaling pathway in vivo in kidneys of diabetic rats.

The current study shows marked deterioration of renal function in DN rats, indicated by significant increases in serum creatinine, BUN, and urinary proteins excretion (Figure 3), supported by the histological lesions of classical DN, which were demonstrated by light (Figures 4–6) and electron (Figures 7 and 8) microscopy, in the form of thickening of the glomerular basement membrane and mesangial expansion, deformity of the filtration barrier, and interstitial fibrosis with diffuse glomerular sclerosis. These findings coincide with previous reports on patients with DN [45,46]. Glomerular cell loss is considered to be a result of diabetes-induced nephrotoxicity [47]. Furthermore, diabetes-induced nephrotoxicity affects the diameter of blood vessels; a vasodilatation effect [48]. Glomerular vasodilatation could induce podocyte mechanical stretch, leading to foot process effacement and, after that, cellular detachment. In agreement with what has been published [49,50], podocyte stretch induces decreased expression of podocyte nephrin, the main slit diaphragm protein, leading to disturbances in glomerular filtration function and proteinuria. Furthermore, accumulation of edematous fluids in diabetic patients induces an increase in Bowman's space. The two main causes of glomerular edema are increased movement of renal fluid from the glomerular pool to the urinary pool and blockade of the renal tubular system. As described before [51,52], dilated glomerular vessels could increase the vascular endothelium fenestrae, leading to increased fluid movement from the glomerular pool to the urinary pool, inducing edema formation. Additionally, Lenoir et al. [53] showed mesangial expansion and glomerulosclerosis by histological analysis and glomerular basement membrane thickening, podocyte foot process broadening, and effacement by TEM in endothelial cell-specific Atg5-deficient diabetic glomeruli.

Autophagy generated by various harmful factors contributes to the maintenance of cell homeostasis. Autophagy principally serves an adaptive or "programmed cell survival" mechanism to protect organisms during periods of enhanced cellular distress [54]. In our study, the deterioration of renal function in the DN group was possibly caused by defect(s) in the autophagy process. We evaluated LC3, Beclin-1, and mTOR, and conducted TEM examination of autophagosomes as proper procedures for monitoring autophagy [55]. The present study demonstrated significant downregulation of autophagy markers LC3II and Beclin-1 in renal tissue, as well as a significant upregulation of mTOR expression in the DN rats compared with the controls (Figure 9). These outcomes are in concurrence with those of Fang et al. [56], who found that the renal expression of autophagy-related proteins, including Beclin-1 and LC3II, was markedly suppressed in rats with DN. Also, the findings of the present study support the findings of Gödel et al. [22], who reported significant upregulation of mTOR itself and mTORC1 target genes in human patients with progressive DN, as compared to the controls. Gödel and colleagues also demonstrated that activation of mTORC1 inhibits diabetes-related autophagy in renal tissues of diabetic mice and patients. Nowadays, the gold standard for autophagy monitoring is TEM, the only technique able to elucidate the real presence of subcellular autophagic structures like autophagosome, lysosome, and autophagolysosome [55,57]. In the current study, TEM showed rare autophagic vacuoles in the tubular cells of the DN group compared to the control group (Figures 7 and 8). In line with these results, Lenoir et al. [53] evaluated the role of autophagy in the endothelial cells of diabetic kidneys using endothelial cell-specific Atg5-deficient mice. Lenoir explained that the ultrastructural analysis exhibited glomerular endothelial cell cytoplasmic disorganization and vacuolization, as well as detached cells—most likely endothelial cells—in the lumen of the capillaries of the glomeruli of endothelial cell-specific Atg5-deficient diabetic mice.

As a central element for signaling cell growth and enhancing protein translation, mammalian target of rapamycin (mTOR), when inhibited, induces autophagy. Likewise, as a critical feedback mechanism, reactivation of mTOR terminates autophagy and initiates lysosome reformation [54]. In our study, we found that rats with DN showed significant upregulation of mTOR mRNA, as well as protein expression. This upregulation is aggravated by 3-MA and chloroquine administration, and alleviated by exosome treatment (Figures 9 and 10). Numerous studies have revealed that hyperactivation of the mTOR pathway in DN has an essential role in glomerular and tubular cell hypertrophy [58,59], and is related to injury of podocytes and decline of glomerular filtration rates. A growing number of studies have suggested that mTORC1 pathway inhibition with rapamycin has renoprotective effects on DN progression in models of type 1 [60] and type 2 [61] diabetes. Overactivation of mTOR resulted from prolonged exposure to hyperglycemia, which is a crucial factor in diabetic kidney injury [62,63]. These studies demonstrated that overactivation of mTOR in the podocytes results in albuminuria, due to the widening of glomerular basement membrane, mesangial expansion, and collagen deposition. Also, they showed that mTORC1 hyperactivity in podocytes disrupts localization of the proteins constructing the filtration slits, with eventual increased glomerular permeability to macromolecules. Additionally, other studies attributed progressive renal tissue injury to activation of mTORC1 and suppression of autophagy, and explained this issue by different mechanisms. First, defective autophagy impairs clearance of advanced glycation end products (AGEs) [64] and damages mitochondria in podocytes [17]. Second, autophagic insufficiency further increases hypoxia and endoplasmic reticulum (ER) stress, thus increasing the vulnerability of tubular cells [44,64]. Third, suppressed autophagy leads to collagen accumulation due to defective degradation [17].

More importantly, suppression of autophagy due to mTOR activation was studied by Fang et al. [56], who reported that autophagy initiation is triggered by the action of unc-51-like kinase 1 (ULK1) (mammalian ortholog of the yeast Atg1), which binds to and phosphorylates other autophagy essential proteins such as ribosome protein subunit 6 kinase 1 (S6K1) and eIF4E-binding protein 1 (4EBP-1), to inhibit autophagy through affecting the transcription and translation of related proteins [65]. However, exposure to hyperglycemia leads to activation of mTORC1 which, in turn, phosphorylates and inactivates ULK1, thus preventing initiation of autophagosome formation [66]. Of note, mTORC1 activation not only inhibits autophagy, but also is implicated in the synthesis of proteins and other macromolecules. It has been reported that activated mTOR enhances interstitial fibrosis in diabetic kidneys [20]. These findings are parallel to those of the present study, as we demonstrated a significant increase in TGF-β1 and fibronectin protein expression (Figure 10), and collagen fiber deposition among the glomerular capillaries and surrounding the renal corpuscles and tubules in renal specimens stained by Masson's trichrome in DN rats, as compared to controls (Figure 5). It has been suggested that hyperglycemia-activated mTORC1 stimulates fibroblast proliferation and collagen synthesis. Furthermore, it enhances the expression of profibrotic cytokines, such as TGF-β1 and connective tissue growth factor, resulting in progressive fibrosis and tubulointerstitial changes in DN [20]. Fibrosis considered as a noteworthy step of the pathogenesis of DN. Myofibroblasts assume an imperative job in the initiation of fibrosis in both the glomerulus and renal tubulointerstitium. Epithelial-to-mesenchymal transition (EMT) is a main source of myofibroblasts in podocytes and proximal tubular cells in DN. TGF-β has directly targeted several signaling pathways involving not only EMT induction, but also the synthesis of extracellular matrix molecules, such as fibronectin, collagen type I, and laminin, causing renal fibrosis. Therefore, regulation of TGF-β is a potential therapeutic target for DN cells [67].

The results of the present study also demonstrate that multiple injections of exosomes in Group IV significantly improved renal function in the DN group, indicated by significant decreases in serum creatinine, BUN, and urinary proteins (Figure 3). Moreover, renal histological changes improved in the form of decreased mesangial expansion and open-walled tubules (Figure 4), with a significant decrease in collagen expression by Masson's trichrome staining and TGF-β immunoexpression (Figure 5). These results were supported by TEM, which demonstrated multiple autophagic vacuoles, euchromatic nuclei, scattered mitochondria, and closely packed apical microvilli, in proximal tubule epithelial cells (PTECs). Also, there were nearly normal glomerular basement membranes with nearly normal podocytes, and more thinning of the glomerular filtration barrier (Figures 6 and 7).

These results were in accordance with Nassar et al. [68], who demonstrated that MSC administration could reverse DN through paracrine mechanisms, rather than by MSC transdifferentiation. MSC-derived exosomes might be such a paracrine mechanism for cell-to-cell communication. Evidence from previous studies indicate that MSCs mediate their paracrine effects via release of exosomes that deliver their cargo of various mRNAs, miRNAs, and proteins to recipient cells [23]. Additionally, Nagaishi et al. [67] proved that kidney that received exosome injection exhibited improvement in the histological picture of DN in the form of decreased degeneration, vacuolation, atrophic changes, and inflammatory cell infiltration of PTEC, confirmed by H and E staining, with decreased fibrous components, as confirmed by Azan staining.

The nephroprotective effect of exosomes was explained by Bruno et al. [23], who found that the exosomes got from MSCs exhibit defensive impacts in acute renal damage through the transportation of a particular subset of cell mRNAs, which are associated with the mesenchymal phenotype and with the control of transcription, proliferation, and immunoregulation. Furthermore, Bruno et al. revealed that exosomes initiated a proliferative program of PTEC and hindered apoptosis through inducing the synthesis of hepatocyte growth factor and macrophage-stimulating protein by the horizontal transfer of mRNAs packed in the exosomes.

However, the accumulation of autophagic vacuoles did not always mean increased autophagosome formation and may denote inhibited autolysosome maturation, so LC3-II detection via Western blotting was valuable in monitoring the autophagosome number [44]; therefore, we detected the autophagosome formation-related proteins (LC3 conversion and Beclin-1). We also detected the autophagic flux by measuring the protein expression of p62 that serves as a connection between LC3 and ubiquitinated substrates [69]. We found that the DN group showed significant decreases in the expression level of LC3 and Beclin-1 compared with control. Additionally, accumulation of p62 protein has been observed DN group, indicating a deficiency in autophagy. Exosome-treated DN rats significantly increased the expression of Beclin-1 mRNA as well as the LC3-II/LC3-I and p62 protein expression ratio, indicating increased autophagosome formation (Figure 10). Accordingly, our results revealed that injections of exosomes upregulated the expression of the autophagy markers LC3 and Beclin-1, and downregulated mTOR and S6K1 in Group IV as compared to rats of the DN group, suggesting that exosomes may activate autophagy by decreasing mTOR. These results run parallel to an earlier study that reported that genetic reduction of mTOR levels in mTORC1 knockout mice significantly reduced the effects of mTOR hyperactivation in renal tissues and suppressed the progression of DN in diabetic animals [61]. As a limitation of our study, the expression of phosphorylated products of mTOR and S6K1 were not included during monitoring of autophagic activity in various study groups, however; therefore, it is recommended to be addressed in further studies.

In this context, our data were in accordance with earlier results of Liu and colleagues [70], who showed that MSC-derived exosomes significantly reduced the expression of phosphorylated mTOR/mTOR in rat cardiomyocytes after ischemia reperfusion injury. They attributed the enhanced autophagic activities in exosome-treated cells partly to inhibition of the mTOR pathway. These results provide a possible explanation for the improved biochemical and histological features of DN in Group IV.

Regarding the effects of exosomes on renal fibrosis induced by diabetes, repeated injection of MSC-derived exosomes in Group IV caused a significant decrease in the immunoexpression of TGF-β1 and collagen fiber deposition between glomeruli and tubules of renal samples stained by Masson's trichrome, and these findings were confirmed by a significant decrease in protein expression of TGF-β and fibronectin by Western blot. Such results suggest that multiple injections of exosomes exhibit a potent antifibrotic effect and, therefore, may improve renal function indirectly by reducing disease-associated fibrosis. These outcomes run parallel to former reports [65]. suggesting that barricading the mTOR pathway decreased TGF-β1 in kidney. Previous studies showed that exosomes with selective microRNA patterns improved renal function and reversed TGF-β1 morphological changes in renal cells [67]. Thus, MSC-derived exosomes provide a new, potentially effective therapeutic approach to slow down the progression of renal disease and improve renal function, by modulating autophagy.

To confirm the role of autophagy in mediating the protective impact of exosomes on DN, we used both 3-MA and chloroquine, autophagy inhibitors, in Groups III and V. Our study demonstrated that both 3-MA and chloroquine (CQ) are beneficial in inhibiting the process of autophagy (Group III). 3-MA is an early autophagy inhibitor, which could suppress the activity of type III of phosphoinositide-3-kinase (PI3K) and the formation of autophagosome to inhibit autophagy [71], while chloroquine reverses autophagy by inhibiting lysosomal acidification, resulting in lysosome accumulation and autophagy blockade [28]. We used both 3-MA and chloroquine to be sure of autophagy inhibition, because a previous study revealed that, in nutrient-rich conditions such as ours, 3-MA may even stimulate autophagy flux instead of blocking it [72].

Treatment of DN rats with chloroquine and 3-MA (Group III) resulted in significant downregulation of LC3 and Beclin-1 (Figure 9). In addition, there was a reduction in the number of autophagic vacuoles, confirmed by TEM, when compared to the exosome-treated group (Figures 7 and 8), indicating that autophagy was inhibited by 3-MA and chloroquine. Furthermore, pretreatment with chloroquine and 3-MA exacerbated renal insult, manifested by significant increases in serum creatinine, BUN, and urinary proteins (Figure 3), in parallel with deterioration of renal histology (Figures 4 and 5). Such deterioration was evidenced by persistent mesangial expansion, swollen tubular epithelial lining with obliteration of their lumens, and darkly staining nuclei with loss of their polarity. Inhibition of autophagy by chloroquine not only decreased the protective effect of exosomes on renal function (Group V), but also decreased their antifibrotic effect, indicated by a significant increase in the protein expression of TGF-β (Figure 6) and fibronectin (Figure 10) with collagen fiber deposition (Figure 5), leading to persistent thickening of the glomerular basement membranes in many areas when compared to the exosome-treated group. In this context, our data were in accordance with earlier results of Verschooten and colleagues, who showed that chloroquine is an autophagy inhibitor enhancing the cell death-inducing effect of the flavonoid luteolin in metastatic squamous cell carcinoma cells. In our study, combined treatment of chloroquine and 3-MA with exosomes in Group V alleviated what was found in Group III [73].

5. Conclusions

In conclusion, the potential nephroprotective effects of MSC-derived exosomes in a diabetic nephropathy model are based on their ability to upregulate autophagy associated with suppression of mTOR pathway, and by their antifibrotic effect. These findings provide a basis for the future use of exosomes as a new biological therapeutic approach for DN.

Authors Contributions

Conceptualization: N.E., I.A.A., N.I.H., A.A.D., and A.S.F.; methodology: A.S.F., N.E., I.A.A., N.I.H., A.A.D., and D.S.; validation: O.M. and W.B.E.G.; investigation: N.E., D.S., I.A.A., N.I.H., O.M., and A.S.F.; resources: N.E., A.A.D., O.M., A.M.H., N.I.H., A.M.E., W.B.E.G., S.M.S., and Y.S.; formal analysis: A.A.D., A.S.F., N.I.H., and N.E.; data curation: A.A.D., O.M., N.I.H., and A.S.F.; writing—original draft preparation: N.E., N.I.H., I.A.A., and A.S.F.; writing—review and editing: A.S.F., N.E., N.I.H,. I.A.A., and A.A.D.; supervision, paper writing, and final editing: A.S.F., A.A.D., N.E., Y.S., and S.M.S.

Funding: This research received no external funding.

Acknowledgments: We would like to represent our acknowledgments for the research team of the Central Lab at Faculty of Medicine, Benha University and Molecular Biology Unit, Faculty of Medicine, Cairo University.

Conflicts of Interest: The authors declare no conflict of interest.

Abbreviations

3-MA: 3-methyladenine; BUN: blood urea nitrogen; DN: diabetic nephropathy; ESRD: end-stage renal disease; LC3: Microtubule-associated protein 1A/1B-light chain 3; MSCs: mesenchymal stem cells; mTOR: mechanistic target of rapamycin; STZ: Streptozotocin; TGF: Transforming growth factor; ULK1: Unc-51 like autophagy activating kinase.

References

1. Martínez-Castelao, A.; Navarro-González, J.F.; Górriz, J.L.; de Alvaro, F. The concept and the epidemiology of diabetic nephropathy have changed in recent years. *J. Clin. Med.* **2015**, *4*, 1207–1216. [CrossRef] [PubMed]
2. Saran, R.; Robinson, B.; Abbott, K.C.; Agodoa, L.Y.; Albertus, P.; Ayanian, J.; Balkrishnan, R.; Bragg-Gresham, J.; Cao, J.; Chen, J.L.; et al. US renal data system 2016 annual data report: Epidemiology of kidney disease in the United States. *Am. J. Kidney Dis.* **2017**, *69*, A7–A8. [CrossRef] [PubMed]
3. Forbes, J.M.; Coughlan, M.T.; Cooper, M.E. Oxidative stress as a major culprit in kidney disease in diabetes. *Diabetes* **2008**, *57*, 1446–1454. [CrossRef] [PubMed]
4. Lorenzen, J.M.; Haller, H.; Thum, T. MicroRNAs as mediators and therapeutic targets in chronic kidney disease. *Nat. Rev. Nephrol.* **2011**, *7*, 286. [CrossRef] [PubMed]
5. Fernandez-Fernandez, B.; Ortiz, A.; Gomez-Guerrero, C.; Egido, J. Therapeutic approaches to diabetic nephropathy—Beyond the RAS. *Nat. Rev. Nephrol.* **2014**, *10*, 325. [CrossRef] [PubMed]
6. Ahmad, J. Management of diabetic nephropathy: Recent progress and future perspective. *Diabetes Metab. Syndrome* **2015**, *9*, 343–358. [CrossRef] [PubMed]
7. Satirapoj, B.; Adler, S.G. Comprehensive approach to diabetic nephropathy. *Kidney Res. Clin. Pract.* **2014**, *33*, 121–131. [CrossRef] [PubMed]
8. Tögel, F.; Weiss, K.; Yang, Y.; Hu, Z.; Zhang, P.; Westenfelder, C. Vasculotropic, paracrine actions of infused mesenchymal stem cells are important to the recovery from acute kidney injury. *Am. J. Physiol.* **2007**, *292*, F1626–F1635. [CrossRef] [PubMed]
9. Ullah, I.; Subbarao, R.B.; Rho, G.J. Human mesenchymal stem cells-current trends and future prospective. *Biosci. Rep.* **2015**, *35*, e00191. [CrossRef] [PubMed]
10. Katsuda, T.; Kosaka, N.; Takeshita, F.; Ochiya, T. The therapeutic potential of mesenchymal stem cell-derived extracellular vesicles. *Proteomics* **2013**, *13*, 1637–1653. [CrossRef] [PubMed]
11. Roy, S.; Hochberg, F.H.; Jones, P.S. Extracellular vesicles: the growth as diagnostics and therapeutics; a survey. *J. Extracell. Vesicles* **2018**, *7*. [CrossRef] [PubMed]
12. Yeagy, B.A.; Cherqui, S. Kidney repair and stem cells: a complex and controversial process. *Pediatric Nephrol.* **2011**, *26*, 1427–1434. [CrossRef] [PubMed]
13. Zarjou, A.; Kim, J.; Traylor, A.M.; Sanders, P.W.; Balla, J.; Agarwal, A.; Curtis, L.M. Paracrine effects of mesenchymal stem cells in cisplatin-induced renal injury require heme oxygenase-1. *Am. J. Physiol.* **2011**, *300*, F254–F262. [CrossRef] [PubMed]
14. Chen, Y.; Qian, H.; Zhu, W.; Zhang, X.; Yan, Y.; Ye, S.; Peng, X.; Li, W.; Xu, W. Hepatocyte growth factor modification promotes the amelioration effects of human umbilical cord mesenchymal stem cells on rat acute kidney injury. *Stem Cells Dev.* **2010**, *20*, 103–113. [CrossRef] [PubMed]
15. Johansen, T.; Lamark, T. Selective autophagy mediated by autophagic adapter proteins. *Autophagy* **2011**, *7*, 279–296. [CrossRef] [PubMed]
16. De Rechter, S.; Decuypere, J.-P.; Ivanova, E.; van den Heuvel, L.P.; De Smedt, H.; Levtchenko, E.; Mekahli, D. Autophagy in renal diseases. *Pediatric Nephrol.* **2016**, *31*, 737–752. [CrossRef] [PubMed]
17. Ding, Y.; Choi, M.E. Autophagy in diabetic nephropathy. *J. Endocrinol.* **2014**, *224*, R15–R30. [CrossRef] [PubMed]
18. Deng, X.; Xie, Y.; Zhang, A. Advance of autophagy in chronic kidney diseases. *Renal Fail.* **2017**, *39*, 306–313. [CrossRef] [PubMed]
19. Zoncu, R.; Efeyan, A.; Sabatini, D.M. mTOR: From growth signal integration to cancer, diabetes and ageing. *Nat. Rev. Mol. Cell Biol.* **2011**, *12*, 21. [CrossRef] [PubMed]

20. Lloberas, N.; Cruzado, J.M.; Franquesa, M.; Herrero-Fresneda, I.; Torras, J.; Alperovich, G.; Rama, I.; Vidal, A.; Grinyó, J.M. Mammalian target of rapamycin pathway blockade slows progression of diabetic kidney disease in rats. *J. Am. Soc. Nephrol.* **2006**, *17*, 1395–1404. [CrossRef] [PubMed]

21. Mori, H.; Inoki, K.; Masutani, K.; Wakabayashi, Y.; Komai, K.; Nakagawa, R.; Guan, K.-L.; Yoshimura, A. The mTOR pathway is highly activated in diabetic nephropathy and rapamycin has a strong therapeutic potential. *Biochem. Biophys. Res. Commun.* **2009**, *384*, 471–475. [CrossRef] [PubMed]

22. Gödel, M.; Hartleben, B.; Herbach, N.; Liu, S.; Zschiedrich, S.; Lu, S.; Debreczeni-Mór, A.; Lindenmeyer, M.T.; Rastaldi, M.-P.; Hartleben, G.; et al. Role of mTOR in podocyte function and diabetic nephropathy in humans and mice. *J. Clin. Invest.* **2011**, *121*, 2197–2209.

23. Bruno, S.; Grange, C.; Collino, F.; Deregibus, M.C.; Cantaluppi, V.; Biancone, L.; Tetta, C.; Camussi, G. Microvesicles derived from mesenchymal stem cells enhance survival in a lethal model of acute kidney injury. *PLoS ONE* **2012**, *7*, e33115. [CrossRef] [PubMed]

24. Gatti, S.; Bruno, S.; Deregibus, M.C.; Sordi, A.; Cantaluppi, V.; Tetta, C.; Camussi, G. Microvesicles derived from human adult mesenchymal stem cells protect against ischaemia–Reperfusion-induced acute and chronic kidney injury. *Nephrol. Dialysis Transplantation* **2011**, *26*, 1474–1483. [CrossRef] [PubMed]

25. Yang, J.; Liu, X.-X.; Fan, H.; Tang, Q.; Shou, Z.-X.; Zuo, D.-M.; Zou, Z.; Xu, M.; Chen, Q.-Y.; Peng, Y.; et al. Extracellular vesicles derived from bone marrow mesenchymal stem cells protect against experimental colitis via attenuating colon inflammation, oxidative stress and apoptosis. *PLoS ONE* **2015**, *10*, e0140551. [CrossRef] [PubMed]

26. Lange-Consiglio, A.; Perrini, C.; Albini, G.; Modina, S.; Lodde, V.; Orsini, E.; Esposti, P.; Cremonesi, F. Oviductal microvesicles and their effect on in vitro maturation of canine oocytes. *Reproduction* **2017**, *154*, 167–180. [CrossRef] [PubMed]

27. Tesch, G.H.; Allen, T.J. Rodent models of streptozotocin-induced diabetic nephropathy (Methods in Renal Research). *Nephrology* **2007**, *12*, 261–266. [CrossRef] [PubMed]

28. Tang, Y.; Cai, Q.-H.; Wang, Y.-J.; Fan, S.-H.; Zhang, Z.-F.; Xiao, M.-Q.; Zhu, J.-Y.; Wu, D.-M.; Lu, J.; Zheng, Y.-L. Protective effect of autophagy on endoplasmic reticulum stress-induced apoptosis of alveolar epithelial cells in rat models of COPD. *Biosci. Rep.* **2017**. [CrossRef] [PubMed]

29. Hayat, M.A. Principles and techniques of electron microscopy. In *Biological Applications*; Edward Arnold: London, UK, 1981; Volume I, p. 412.

30. Yang, B.; El Nahas, A.M.; Thomas, G.L.; Haylor, J.L.; Watson, P.F.; Wagner, B.; Johnson, T.S. Caspase-3 and apoptosis in experimental chronic renal scarring. *Kidney Int.* **2001**, *60*, 1765–1776. [CrossRef] [PubMed]

31. Wiame, I.; Remy, S.; Swennen, R.; Sagi, L. Irreversible heat inactivation of DNase I without RNA degradation. *BioTechniques* **2000**, *29*, 252–256. [CrossRef] [PubMed]

32. Helming, L.; Winter, J.; Gordon, S. The scavenger receptor CD36 plays a role in cytokine-induced macrophage fusion. *J. Cell Sci.* **2009**, *122*, 453–459. [CrossRef] [PubMed]

33. Fleige, S.; Pfaffl, M.W. RNA integrity and the effect on the real-time qRT-PCR performance. *Mol. Aspects Med.* **2006**, *27*, 126–139. [CrossRef] [PubMed]

34. Xu, J.T.; Zhao, X.; Yaster, M.; Tao, Y.X. Expression and distribution of mTOR, p70S6K, 4E-BP1, and their phosphorylated counterparts in rat dorsal root ganglion and spinal cord dorsal horn. *Brain Res.* **2010**, *1336*, 46–57. [CrossRef] [PubMed]

35. Wang, X.; Zhou, G.; Liu, C.; Wei, R.; Zhu, S.; Xu, Y.; Wu, M.; Miao, Q. Acanthopanax versus 3-methyladenine ameliorates sodium taurocholate-induced severe acute pancreatitis by inhibiting the autophagic pathway in rats. *Mediators Inflammation* **2016**, *2016*, 12. [CrossRef] [PubMed]

36. Cao, X.; Wang, Y.; Wu, C.; Li, X.; Fu, Z.; Yang, M.; Bian, W.; Wang, S.; Song, Y.; Tang, J.; et al. Cathelicidin-OA1, a novel antioxidant peptide identified from an amphibian, accelerates skin wound healing. *Sci. Rep.* **2018**, *8*, 943. [CrossRef] [PubMed]

37. Magalhaes, J.; Gegg, M.; Migdalska-Richards, A.; Schapira, A. Effects of ambroxol on the autophagy-lysosome pathway and mitochondria in primary cortical neurons. *Sci. Rep.* **2018**, *8*, 1385. [CrossRef] [PubMed]

38. Qian, G.; Liu, D.; Hu, J.; Gan, F.; Hou, L.; Zhai, N.; Chen, X.; Huang, K. SeMet attenuates OTA-induced PCV2 replication promotion by inhibiting autophagy by activating the AKT/mTOR signaling pathway. *Veterinary Res.* **2018**, *49*, 15. [CrossRef] [PubMed]

39. Liu, F.; Bu, Z.; Zhao, F.; Xiao, D. Increased T-helper 17 cell differentiation mediated by exosome-mediated micro RNA-451 redistribution in gastric cancer infiltrated T cells. *Cancer Sci.* **2018**, *109*, 65–73. [CrossRef] [PubMed]

40. Yuan, J.; Zhao, X.; Hu, Y.; Sun, H.; Gong, G.; Huang, X.; Chen, X.; Xia, M.; Sun, C.; Huang, Q.; et al. Autophagy regulates the degeneration of the auditory cortex through the AMPK-mTOR-ULK1 signaling pathway. *Int. J. Mol. Sci.* **2018**, *41*, 2086–2098. [CrossRef] [PubMed]

41. Kitada, M.; Takeda, A.; Nagai, T.; Ito, H.; Kanasaki, K.; Koya, D. Dietary restriction ameliorates diabetic nephropathy through anti-inflammatory effects and regulation of the autophagy via restoration of Sirt1 in diabetic Wistar fatty (*fa/fa*) rats: a model of type 2 diabetes. *Exp. Diabetes Res.* **2011**, *2011*. [CrossRef] [PubMed]

42. Thomas, M.C.; Cooper, M.E.; Zimmet, P. Changing epidemiology of type 2 diabetes mellitus and associated chronic kidney disease. *Nat. Rev. Nephrol.* **2016**, *12*, 73. [CrossRef] [PubMed]

43. Mokdad, A.H.; Ford, E.S.; Bowman, B.A.; Dietz, W.H.; Vinicor, F.; Bales, V.S.; Marks, J.S. Prevalence of obesity, diabetes, and obesity-related health risk factors, 2001. *Jama* **2003**, *289*, 76–79. [CrossRef] [PubMed]

44. Tanaka, Y.; Kume, S.; Kitada, M.; Kanasaki, K.; Uzu, T.; Maegawa, H.; Koya, D. Autophagy as a therapeutic target in diabetic nephropathy. *Exp. Diabetes Res.* **2011**. [CrossRef] [PubMed]

45. Matboli, M.; Eissa, S.; Ibrahim, D.; Hegazy, M.G.; Imam, S.S.; Habib, E.K. Caffeic acid attenuates diabetic kidney disease via modulation of autophagy in a high-fat diet/streptozotocin-induced diabetic rat. *Sci. Rep.* **2017**, *7*, 2263. [CrossRef] [PubMed]

46. Abou-Hany, H.O.; Atef, H.; Said, E.; Elkashef, H.A.; Salem, H.A. Crocin mediated amelioration of oxidative burden and inflammatory cascade suppresses diabetic nephropathy progression in diabetic rats. *Chem. Biol. Interact.* **2018**, *284*, 90–100. [CrossRef] [PubMed]

47. Duan, P.; Hu, C.; Quan, C.; Yu, T.; Huang, W.; Chen, W.; Tang, S.; Shi, Y.; Martin, F.L.; Yang, K. 4-Nonylphenol induces autophagy and attenuates mTOR-p70S6K/4EBP1 signaling by modulating AMPK activation in Sertoli cells. *Toxicol. Lett.* **2017**, *267*, 21–31. [CrossRef] [PubMed]

48. Hsieh, C.-Y.; Miaw, C.-L.; Hsieh, C.-C.; Tseng, H.-C.; Yang, Y.-H.; Yen, C.-H. Effects of chronic 4-n-nonylphenol treatment on aortic vasoconstriction and vasorelaxation in rats. *Arch. Toxicol.* **2009**, *83*, 941–946. [CrossRef] [PubMed]

49. Malik, A.; Mehmood, M.H.; Channa, H.; Akhtar, M.S.; Gilani, A.-H. Pharmacological basis for the medicinal use of polyherbal formulation and its ingredients in cardiovascular disorders using rodents. *BMC Complementary Altern. Med.* **2017**, *17*, 142. [CrossRef] [PubMed]

50. Kriz, W.; LemLey, K.V. Mechanical challenges to the glomerular filtration barrier: adaptations and pathway to sclerosis. *Pediatric Nephrol.* **2017**, *32*, 405–417. [CrossRef] [PubMed]

51. Swiatecka-Urban, A. Endocytic trafficking at the mature podocyte slit diaphragm. *Front. Pediatrics* **2017**, *5*, 32. [CrossRef] [PubMed]

52. Cara-Fuentes, G.; Clapp, W.L.; Johnson, R.J.; Garin, E.H. Pathogenesis of proteinuria in idiopathic minimal change disease: Molecular mechanisms. *Pediatric Nephrol.* **2016**, *31*, 2179–2189. [CrossRef] [PubMed]

53. Lenoir, O.; Jasiek, M.; Hénique, C.; Guyonnet, L.; Hartleben, B.; Bork, T.; Chipont, A.; Flosseau, K.; Bensaada, I.; Schmitt, A. Endothelial cell and podocyte autophagy synergistically protect from diabetes-induced glomerulosclerosis. *Autophagy* **2015**, *11*, 1130–1145. [CrossRef] [PubMed]

54. Kang, R.; Zeh, H.; Lotze, M.; Tang, D. The Beclin 1 network regulates autophagy and apoptosis. *Cell Death Differ.* **2011**, *18*, 571. [CrossRef] [PubMed]

55. Klionsky, D.J.; Abdelmohsen, K.; Abe, A.; Abedin, M.J.; Abeliovich, H.; Arozena, A.A.; Adachi, H.; Adams, C.M.; Adams, P.D.; Adeli, K.; et al. Guidelines for the use and interpretation of assays for monitoring autophagy. *Autophagy* **2016**, *12*, 1–222. [CrossRef] [PubMed]

56. Fang, L.; Zhou, Y.; Cao, H.; Wen, P.; Jiang, L.; He, W.; Dai, C.; Yang, J. Autophagy attenuates diabetic glomerular damage through protection of hyperglycemia-induced podocyte injury. *PLoS ONE* **2013**, *8*, e60546. [CrossRef] [PubMed]

57. Liu, W.J.; Huang, W.F.; Ye, L.; Chen, R.H.; Yang, C.; Wu, H.L.; Pan, Q.J.; Liu, H.F. The activity and role of autophagy in the pathogenesis of diabetic nephropathy. *Eur. Rev. Med. Pharmacol. Sci.* **2018**, *22*, 3182–3189. [PubMed]

58. Lee, C.-H.; Inoki, K.; Guan, K.-L. mTOR pathway as a target in tissue hypertrophy. *Annu. Rev. Pharmacol. Toxicol.* **2007**, *47*, 443–467. [CrossRef] [PubMed]

59. Chen, J.-K.; Chen, J.; Neilson, E.G.; Harris, R.C. Role of mammalian target of rapamycin signaling in compensatory renal hypertrophy. *J. Am. Soc. Nephrol.* **2005**, *16*, 1384–1391. [CrossRef] [PubMed]

60. Yang, Y.; Wang, J.; Qin, L.; Shou, Z.; Zhao, J.; Wang, H.; Chen, Y.; Chen, J. Rapamycin prevents early steps of the development of diabetic nephropathy in rats. *Am. J. Nephrol.* **2007**, *27*, 495–502. [CrossRef] [PubMed]

61. Inoki, K.; Mori, H.; Wang, J.; Suzuki, T.; Hong, S.; Yoshida, S.; Blattner, S.M.; Ikenoue, T.; Rüegg, M.A.; Hall, M.N.; et al. mTORC1 activation in podocytes is a critical step in the development of diabetic nephropathy in mice. *J. Clin. Invest.* **2011**, *121*, 2181–2196. [CrossRef] [PubMed]

62. Gonzalez, C.D.; Lee, M.-S.; Marchetti, P.; Pietropaolo, M.; Towns, R.; Vaccaro, M.I.; Watada, H.; Wiley, J.W. The emerging role of autophagy in the pathophysiology of diabetes mellitus. *Autophagy* **2011**, *7*, 2–11. [CrossRef] [PubMed]

63. Yamahara, K.; Kume, S.; Koya, D.; Tanaka, Y.; Morita, Y.; Chin-Kanasaki, M.; Araki, H.; Isshiki, K.; Araki, S.-I.; Haneda, M.; et al. Obesity-mediated autophagy insufficiency exacerbates proteinuria-induced tubulointerstitial lesions. *J. Am. Soc. Nephrol.* **2013**, *24*, 1769–1781. [CrossRef] [PubMed]

64. Peng, K.Y.; Horng, L.Y.; Sung, H.C.; Huang, H.C.; Wu, R.T. Hepatocyte growth factor has a role in the amelioration of diabetic vascular complications via autophagic clearance of advanced glycation end products: Dispo85E, an HGF inducer, as a potential botanical drug. *Metabolism* **2011**, *60*, 888–892. [CrossRef] [PubMed]

65. Hosokawa, N.; Hara, T.; Kaizuka, T.; Kishi, C.; Takamura, A.; Miura, Y.; Iemura, S.-I.; Natsume, T.; Takehana, K.; Yamada, N.; et al. Nutrient-dependent mTORC1 association with the ULK1–Atg13–FIP200 complex required for autophagy. *Mol. Biol. Cell* **2009**, *20*, 1981–1991. [CrossRef] [PubMed]

66. Mizushima, N. The role of the Atg1/ULK1 complex in autophagy regulation. *Curr. Opin. Cell Biol.* **2010**, *22*, 132–139. [CrossRef] [PubMed]

67. Nagaishi, K.; Mizue, Y.; Chikenji, T.; Otani, M.; Nakano, M.; Konari, N.; Fujimiya, M. Mesenchymal stem cell therapy ameliorates diabetic nephropathy via the paracrine effect of renal trophic factors including exosomes. *Sci. Rep.* **2016**, *6*, 34842. [CrossRef] [PubMed]

68. Nassar, W.; El-Ansary, M.; Sabry, D.; Mostafa, M.A.; Fayad, T.; Kotb, E.; Temraz, M.; Saad, A.N.; Essa, W.; Adel, H. Umbilical cord mesenchymal stem cells derived extracellular vesicles can safely ameliorate the progression of chronic kidney diseases. *Biomater. Res.* **2016**, *20*, 21. [CrossRef] [PubMed]

69. Komatsu, M.; Ichimura, Y. Physiological significance of selective degradation of p62 by autophagy. *FEBS Lett.* **2010**, *584*, 1374–1378. [CrossRef] [PubMed]

70. Liu, L.; Jin, X.; Hu, C.F.; Li, R.; Zhou, Z.; Shen, C.X. Exosomes derived from mesenchymal stem cells rescue myocardial ischaemia/reperfusion injury by inducing cardiomyocyte autophagy via AMPK and Akt pathways. *Cell. Physiol. Biochem.* **2017**, *43*, 52–68. [CrossRef] [PubMed]

71. Mu, Y.; Yan, W.J.; Yin, T.L.; Zhang, Y.; Li, J.; Yang, J. Diet-induced obesity impairs spermatogenesis: A potential role for autophagy. *Sci. Rep.* **2017**, *7*, 43475. [CrossRef] [PubMed]

72. Wu, Y.T.; Tan, H.L.; Shui, G.; Bauvy, C.; Huang, Q.; Wenk, M.R.; Ong, C.N.; Codogno, P.; Shen, H.M. Dual role of 3-methyladenine in modulation of autophagy via different temporal patterns of inhibition on class I and III phosphoinositide 3-kinase. *J. Biol. Chem.* **2010**, *285*, 10850–10861. [CrossRef] [PubMed]

73. Verschooten, L.; Barrette, K.; Van Kelst, S.; Rubio Romero, N.; Proby, C.; De Vos, R.; Agostinis, P.; Garmyn, M. Autophagy inhibitor chloroquine enhanced the cell death inducing effect of the flavonoid luteolin in metastatic squamous cell carcinoma cells. *PLoS ONE* **2012**, *7*, e48264. [CrossRef] [PubMed]

Article

Mechanisms of Age-Dependent Loss of Dietary Restriction Protective Effects in Acute Kidney Injury

Nadezda V. Andrianova [1], Stanislovas S. Jankauskas [2], Ljubava D. Zorova [2], Irina B. Pevzner [2], Vasily A. Popkov [1,2], Denis N. Silachev [2], Egor Y. Plotnikov [2,*] and Dmitry B. Zorov [2,*]

[1] Faculty of Bioengineering and Bioinformatics, Lomonosov Moscow State University, 119992 Moscow, Russia; andnadya12@yandex.ru (N.V.A.); popkov.vas@gmail.com (V.A.P.)

[2] A.N. Belozersky Institute of Physico-Chemical Biology, Lomonosov Moscow State University, 119992 Moscow, Russia; jankauskas.ss@gmail.com (S.S.J.); lju_2003@list.ru (L.D.Z.); irinapevzner@mail.ru (I.B.P.); silachevdn@belozersky.msu.ru (D.N.S.)

* Correspondence: plotnikov@belozersky.msu.ru (E.Y.P.), zorov@belozersky.msu.ru (D.B.Z.); Tel.: +7-495-939-5944 (E.Y.P.)

Received: 1 October 2018; Accepted: 19 October 2018; Published: 22 October 2018

Abstract: Dietary restriction (DR) is one of the most efficient approaches ameliorating the severity of different pathological conditions including aging. We investigated the protective potential of short-term DR in the model of acute kidney injury (AKI) in young and old rats. In kidney tissue, the levels of autophagy and mitophagy were examined, and proliferative properties of renal cells obtained from rats of different age were compared. DR afforded a significant nephroprotection to ischemic kidneys of young rats. However, in old rats, DR did not provide such beneficial effect. On the assessment of the autophagy marker, the LC3 II/LC3 I ratio, and after staining the tissue with LysoTracker Green, we concluded that in old rats activity of the autophagic-lysosomal system decreased. Mitophagy, as assessed by the levels of PINK-1, was also deteriorated in old animals. Renal cells from old rats showed impaired proliferative capacity, a worse rate of recovery after ischemic injury, increased levels of oxidative stress, accumulation of lipofuscin granules and lower mitochondria membrane potential. The results suggest that the loss of DR benefits in old animals could be due to deterioration in the autophagy/mitophagy flux.

Keywords: aging; dietary restriction; acute kidney injury; mitochondria; autophagy; mitophagy; ischemia; renal tubular cells

1. Introduction

Caloric or dietary restriction (DR), defined as a reduced food intake without evident signs of malnutrition, is an approach which for many organisms has shown an increase in lifespan and a slowdown in the manifestation of age-associated diseases [1]. DR improves the functioning of organs and tissues including those of old animals. For instance, even a short-term DR postpones the onset of age-dependent changes in the heart, brain, liver, and kidneys [2–5]. Moreover, DR affords increased tolerance to such harmful challenges as myocardial infarction [6], brain diseases [7], hypertension [8], and diabetes mellitus [9]. Recently, several studies have been initiated to verify the beneficial effects of DR on longevity and the attenuation of pathologies in humans [10,11].

A broad study of the mechanisms underlying the beneficial effects of DR pointed to autophagy as a key element of the protective mechanism [12]. In particular, due to the activation of autophagy mechanisms, one can expect a decrease in the levels of damaged macromolecules and organelles, for example, mitochondria. However, with age, the processes of autophagy gradually deteriorate, which leads to a disruption in the quality control of macromolecules and organelles [13]. DR at least partially can restore the ability of the aging organism's cells to eliminate damaged components and to improve tolerance to various damaging factors, which results in the "rejuvenation" of tissues [1].

Even though the protective effect of DR has been revealed quite a long time ago and has been intensively studying [1,14], there is too little data covering its beneficial effects in the kidney tissue. Nevertheless, previous studies have shown that DR exhibits a protective effect in acute cisplatin and cadmium nephrotoxicity [15–17], as well as in the model of chronic kidney disease and diabetic nephropathy [18,19], i.e., DR affects both acute and chronic kidney injuries.

Acute kidney injury (AKI) is a widespread pathology affecting more than 20% of hospitalized patients in developed countries [20]. Approximately 90% of patients with this disease are individuals of 64+ years of age [21]. Since the majority of patients with AKI are elderly, it is essential to study the tolerance of the kidneys specifically in old organisms. It should be considered that with age, the kidney tissue becomes more sensitive to various damaging factors due to progressive molecular, structural and functional deleterious rearrangements [22].

Since available methods for the treatment of AKI are scarce and applied strategies are mostly symptomatic and mostly limited by the use of hemodialysis, the development of alternative specific approaches for therapy is needed [23]. However, the effectiveness of these elaborated approaches should be tested both in young and old animals, since approaches that have been shown to be efficient in young organisms, not always retained their protective effects in the elderly [24]. In particular, ischemic pre- and postconditioning, demonstrating a significant reduction of the severity of ischemic injury in the renal tissue of young animals, had no effect in old animals [25,26].

Since the proven ability of DR to reduce the severity of AKI after ischemia/reperfusion (I/R) has been obtained in rodents of a young age [27–29], the goal of our study was to compare the therapeutic potential of DR in animals of different age and to assess the mechanisms of ischemic tolerance underlying the beneficial effects of DR, particularly the autophagic pathway.

2. Materials and Methods

2.1. Animals

Experiments were performed on male outbred rats of different ages: young (3–4 month old, 300–400 g), adult (12 months old, 500–600 g) and old rats (20–23 months old, 550–700 g). The animal protocols were evaluated and approved by the animal ethics committee of A.N. Belozersky Institute of Physico-Chemical Biology (Protocol 2/13 from 8 April 2013). They were in accordance with the Federation of Laboratory Animal Science Associations (FELASA) guidelines.

2.2. Dietary Protocol

The amount of food consumed ad libitum (AL) was approximately 25 g/day for young rats and 30–33 g/day for adult and old rats, as measured by weighing the remaining food for two weeks. DR was performed for 4 weeks by limiting the amount of food by 35% (35% DR) or by 25% (25% DR) of the daily intake. Food was administered once daily at 2:00 pm. Fasting (100% DR) lasted for 3 days without any access to food. After kidney I/R, ad libitum administration of food was restored. For all groups, the free access to water was implemented.

2.3. Kidney I/R Protocol

Rats were anesthetized with chloralhydrate (300 mg/kg, i.p.) and subjected to 40-min warm ischemia of the left kidney as previously described [30]. Briefly, the renal vascular bundle was occluded with a microvascular clip for 40 min. Circulation was restored by removing the clip. The lack of blood flow during ischemia and its restoration during reperfusion were assessed visually. Nephrectomy of the right kidney was performed simultaneously with the ischemia of the left one. During operation, the body temperature of the rats maintained at $37 \pm 0.5\,^{\circ}\text{C}$. Blood samples were taken 48 h after I/R from the carotid artery to determine the blood urea nitrogen (BUN) and serum creatinine (SCr) using AU480 Chemistry System (Beckman Coulter, Brea, CA, USA).

2.4. Western Blotting

Rats were sacrificed and kidneys were taken 48 h after I/R. Kidney tissue was homogenized with a glass-Teflon homogenizer in a PBS buffer, containing 10 mM phenylmethylsulfonylfluoride at 4 °C. Kidney samples were loaded onto 15% Tris–glycine polyacrylamide gels (10 μg protein/lane). After electrophoresis, gels were blotted onto PVDF membranes (Sigma-Aldrich, St. Louis, MO, USA). Membranes were blocked with 5% non-fat milk in PBS with 0.05% Tween-20 and subsequently incubated with primary antibodies: anti-LC3 A/B monoclonal rabbit 1:1000 (Cell Signaling, Danvers, MA, USA), anti-ubiquitin polyclonal rabbit 1:1000 (Abcam, Cambridge, MA, USA), anti-PINK1 polyclonal rabbit 1:1000 (Abcam, Cambridge, MA, USA), anti-SIRT-3 monoclonal rabbit 1:2000 (Cell Signaling, Danvers, MA, USA), anti-β-actin monoclonal mouse 1:1500 (Sigma-Aldrich, St. Louis, MO, USA), and anti-COX IV monoclonal mouse 1:1500 (Abcam, Cambridge, MA, USA). Membranes were stained with secondary antibodies: anti-rabbit IgG or anti-mouse IgG conjugated with horseradish peroxidase 1:7500 (Jackson ImmunoResearch, Ely, UKUSA). Detection was performed by a Chemidoc MP (BioRad, Hercules, CA, USA). Protein concentration was measured by bicinchoninic acid assay (Sigma-Aldrich, St. Louis, MO, USA).

Since on western blots LC3 is represented by several bands, some of the young rats were subjected to chloroquine (20 mg/kg/day, i.p.) for 3 days to localize the position of the LC3 II band, which increases after chloroquine inhibition of its lysosomal degradation.

The rat kidney mitochondria for western blotting were isolated by differential centrifugation in the medium containing 0.25 M sucrose, 10 mM HEPES, 1 mM EDTA, 0.1% BSA, with a pH 7.4.

2.5. Lysosomes Imaging

Kidneys were excised 24 h after I/R and placed in the incubation medium (DMEM/F12 without sodium bicarbonate) to wash the blood out. Then, 100–150 μm thick sections through the cortical zone of the kidneys were made. Vital tissue slices were washed using the incubation medium (all procedures and incubation were done at 25 °C) and loaded for 30 min with 1 μM LysoTracker Green (Invitrogen, Thermo Fisher Scientific, Waltham, MA, USA). Kidney slices were imaged with an LSM510 inverted confocal microscope (Carl Zeiss, Jena, Germany). Images were processed using ImageJ software (NIH, Bethesda, MD, USA).

2.6. Primary Culture of Renal Tubular Cells (RTCs)

Kidneys from young and old intact rats were excised under aseptic conditions. The cortex of the kidneys was ground, carefully washed from blood, and dissociated by type II collagenase (0.25%, 30 min at 37 °C; Gibco, Thermo Fisher Scientific, Waltham, MA, USA). Pieces of tissue were removed, and the suspension was centrifuged for 5 min at $100 \times g$ after which the renal tubules were pelleted and the dissociated cells remaining in the suspension were discarded. The pellet was resuspended in a complete culture medium (DMEM/F12 with 10% FCS and 10 ng/mL EGF (Invitrogen, USA)) and seeded onto 6-well plates, or special iCelligence 8-well plates, or 35-mm glass-bottom Petri dishes (FluoroDish, WPI, Sarasota, Florida, USA). Cultures were kept at 37 °C under 5% CO_2 in a humidified atmosphere. The culture medium was changed after 48 h in order to eliminate non-adherent cells and residual cellular fragments. RTCs formed confluent monolayers 5 days after plating, therefore, all procedures were carried out on 2–4 days in vitro.

Cultures of RTCs were loaded with 1 μM MitoTracker Red (Invitrogen, Thermo Fisher Scientific, Waltham, MA, USA). Incubation was conducted in DMEM/F12 without sodium bicarbonate for 30 min at 37 °C. Then, RTCs were washed with saline and dissociated with 0.05% Trypsin-EDTA. Cells were resuspended in 1.5 mL DMEM/F12. The fluorescence intensity was evaluated by flow cytometry as described below.

To evaluate the autophagy activation, RTCs were incubated with 500 nM rapamycin (Sigma-Aldrich, St. Louis, MO, USA) and 30 µM chloroquine (Sigma-Aldrich, St. Louis, MO, USA). Rapamycin and chloroquine were dissolved in a complete medium (DMEM/F12 with 10% FCS). Incubation was performed for 3 h, after which RTCs were washed with saline and loaded with 2 µM Cyto-ID (Enzo Life Sciences, New York, NY, USA). Further steps were the same as for MitoTracker Red staining.

2.7. Non-Cultured Renal Tubular Cells (NC-RTCs) from the Kidneys of Young and Old Rats

In addition to primary cell cultures of RTCs, we also used NC-RTCs, which were in situ isolated from kidneys of young and old rats. Cell suspensions were analyzed in situ without any growth in the culture medium, i.e., immediately after isolation.

Similar to RTCs preparation, pieces of cortex were ground and dissociated by type II collagenase (0.25%, 30 min at 37 °C). The pieces of tissue were repeatedly resuspended and kept for 2 min to pellet large pieces. The supernatant was centrifuged for 5 min at $100\times g$ after which the renal tubules were precipitated. The supernatant was discarded and tubules were again incubated with type II collagenase (0.25%, 10 min at 37 °C) one more time, after which the suspension was intensively pipetted. Then, the suspension was centrifuged for 5 min at $100\times g$ for sedimentation of undissociated tubules, the resulting supernatant was centrifuged for 5 min at $600\times g$ to pellet the cells. The resulted suspensions of NC-RTCs were diluted to concentration 1×10^6 cells/mL and incubated for 30 min with 1 µM MitoTracker Green (Invitrogen, Thermo Fisher Scientific, Waltham, MA, USA), 1 µM MitoTracker Red (Invitrogen, Thermo Fisher Scientific, Waltham, MA, USA), or 10 µM DCF-H2 (Invitrogen, Thermo Fisher Scientific, Waltham, MA, USA) at 37 °C. The fluorescence intensity in cells was analyzed by flow cytometry.

2.8. Flow Cytometry

Flow cytometry was performed by using Cytomics FC500 (Beckman Coulter, Brea, CA, USA). Primary cultures of RTCs and NC-RTCs were obtained and stained as described above. Cyto-ID, MitoTracker Green and DCF-mediated fluorescence were measured on the FL1 channel, while MitoTracker Red-mediated fluorescence was evaluated on the FL3 channel. Argon laser with λ_{ex} = 488 nm was used to excite the fluorescence.

2.9. Real-Time Cell Proliferation Monitoring

Analysis of cells growth kinetics was performed using an RTCA iCELLigence™ instrument (ACEA, San Diego, CA, USA). This method is based on using electrical impedance of cell-covered electrodes [31] and may be used in particular for studies of RTCs proliferation and death [32]. The iCELLigence RTCA instrument was placed in a humidified incubator at 37 °C and 5% CO_2. RTCs from young and old rats were seeded on 8-well plates with microelectrodes; 48 h after, the medium was changed to dispose of unattached and dead cells. After the next 24 h, cells were subjected to 17 h of oxygen-glucose deprivation (OGD): the medium was changed to DPBS (Dulbecco's phosphate-buffered saline) and oxygen was replaced with N_2 in multi-gas incubator Galaxy 170R (Eppendorf/NewBrunswick, Hamburg, Germany). After OGD, the DPBS was changed back to the culture medium with a normoxic O_2 content. Proliferation rates were detected during 48 h after OGD.

2.10. Lipofuscin Detection

RTCs from young and old rats were obtained and cultured as described above. A neonatal culture of RTCs was prepared from kidneys of 7-days-old rats by the same protocol as for young and old rats, but with a less prolonged incubation with collagenase type II (0.125%, 15 min at 37 °C). On the 2nd day in vitro, cells were washed with saline and fixed in a 10% neutral buffered formalin solution for 15 min, washed out, and lipofuscin red autofluorescence was analyzed by an LSM510 inverted confocal microscope (Carl Zeiss, Jena, Germany). Analysis of fluorescence was performed in glass-bottom dishes with the excitation at 488 nm and 543 nm and emission collected beyond 585 nm.

Lipofuscin red autofluorescence was also measured by flow cytometry using Cytomics FC500 (Beckman Coulter, Brea, CA, USA). On the 3rd day in vitro, RTCs were washed, dissociated with 0.05% Trypsin-EDTA and suspension was centrifuged for 5 min at $600\times g$. The pellet was resuspended in 2 mL of DMEM/F12 without sodium bicarbonate. The autofluorescence of unstained RTCs was detected on FL5 channel with $\lambda_{ex} = 635$ nm.

2.11. Statistics

Values are presented as mean $\pm$ SEM. Comparisons between groups were made using the Mann–Whitney U-test. Data were analyzed in Microsoft Excel.

3. Results

3.1. Effect of DR on the Severity of AKI in Young and Old Rats

Since ischemic injury is the most common factor leading to AKI [23], we used kidney I/R as a model, evaluating AKI severity by BUN and SCr measuring. There was about an 8-fold increase of BUN 48 h after I/R in young AL rats (55.1 mM $\pm$ 5.4 mM of BUN vs. 7.1 mM $\pm$ 0.2 mM in intact young rats) (Figure 1A). In adult and old rats, BUN increased up to 71.3 mM $\pm$ 3.6 mM and n, correspondingly (Figure 1B,C).

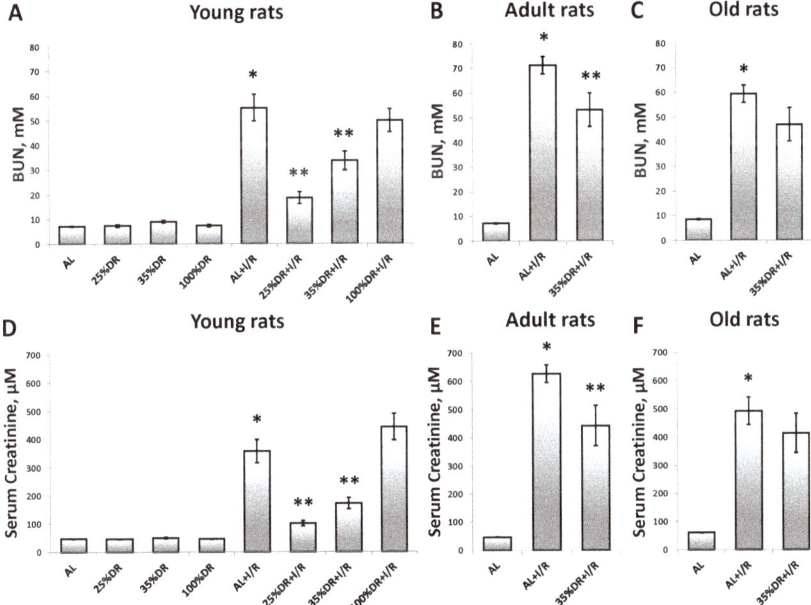

Figure 1. The evaluation of kidney function by the blood urea nitrogen (BUN) and serum creatinine (SCr) in young, adult, and old rats kept on an ad libitum (AL) diet or using different protocols of dietary restriction (DR). (**A**) Assessment of renal function in young (3–4 months) control days (100% DR). Evaluation of the severity of acute kidney injury (AKI) in these groups of rats 48 hours after I/R; (**B**) Assessment of kidney function and severity of AKI 48 hours after I/R in adult (12 months) rats; (**C**) Assessment of kidney function and severity of AKI 48 hours after I/R in old (20–23 months) rats; (**D–F**) Evaluation of SCr concentration in young, adult, and old rats on AL or DR 48 hours after I/R. Control groups contained more than 3 rats, while groups with I/R included more than 6 rats. * $p < 0.05$ compared to AL, ** $p < 0.05$ compared to AL + I/R.

In young rats, we tried different protocols of DR; 25% DR and 35% DR significantly reduced BUN 48 h after I/R compared to the AL group. However, 35% DR decreased BUN twice more effective than 25% DR which resulted in a drop of BUN by 39% against the AL group (33.6 mM ± 3.8 mM and 55.1 mM ± 5.4 mM, respectively), whereas 35% DR reduced BUN to 18.6 mM ± 2.4 mM compared to 55.1 mM ± 5.4 mM in the AL group. Fasting for 3 days (100% DR) did not cause a significant change in the severity of AKI in young rats.

In adult and old rats, we only tested 35% DR since it showed a higher efficiency in young rats. Some decrease of the BUN level in the 35% DR group was found in adult rats (aged 12 months) 48 h after I/R: 53.2 mM ± 6.7 mM as compared to 71.3 mM ± 3.6 mM in the AL group (Figure 1B). In contrast to young and adult animals, in old rats, 35% DR did not result in any significant nephroprotective effect (Figure 1C). Of note, no morbidity or mortality was observed as a result of different DR protocols.

Changes in renal functions were proven by detecting SCr concentrations. We evaluated SCr levels in all experimental groups of rats and observed the same tendencies as when we measured the BUN (Figure 1D–F).

3.2. Autophagy in Renal Tissue of Young and Old Rats

It is well known that DR is a strong factor that stimulates the processes of autophagy [33]. Indeed, we found an increase in the LC3 II/LC3 I ratio in the kidneys of young rats after 4 weeks of 35% DR. On the other hand, 25% DR did not result in a significant increase of the LC3 II/LC3 I ratio (Figure 2A). In contrast to the young rats, in old rats, 35% DR did not cause an augmentation of the LC3 II/LC3 I ratio compared to the AL old rats (Figure 2B).

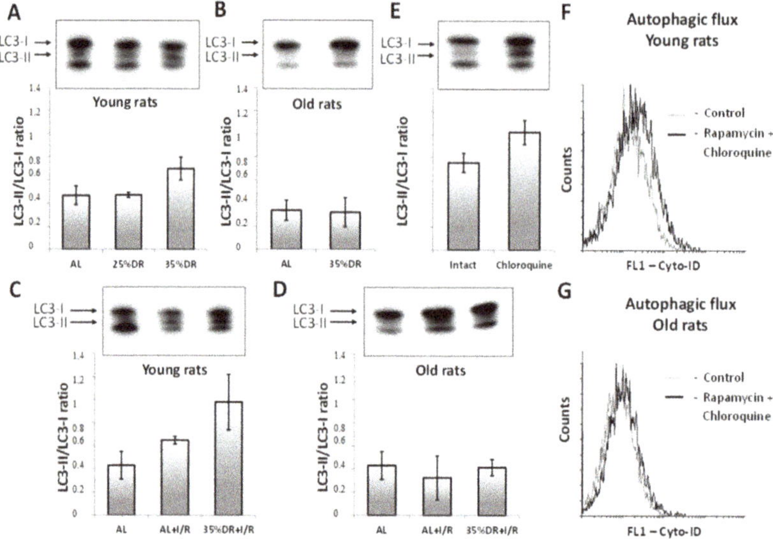

Figure 2. The assessment of autophagic activity in young and old rats. (**A,B**) LC3 II/LC3 I ratio in kidney homogenates of young and old control rats on AL or DR; (**C,D**) LC3 II/LC3 I ratio in kidney homogenates of young and old rats on AL or DR 48 hours after I/R; (**E**) LC3 II/LC3 I ratio in kidney homogenates of young rats after the injections of chloroquine (20 mg/kg/day) for 3 days; (**F,G**) Autophagic flux in primary cultures of renal tubular cells (RTCs) obtained from the kidneys of young and old rats, after incubation with rapamycin and chloroquine.

I/R is also able to activate autophagic signaling pathways [34]. In the kidneys of young rats taken 48 h after I/R, we observed an increased LC3 II/LC3 I ratio (Figure 2C). The ratio increased even more in the group of rats that underwent 35% DR before exposure to I/R (Figure 2C). In old rats, such changes of LC3 II/LC3 I were not revealed: in these animals, the ratio remained the same in all groups (Figure 2D).

Since on western blots LC3 is represented by several bands, some of the young rats were subjected to chloroquine for 3 days to localize the position of the LC3 II band. A relatively low concentration of chloroquine was chosen because higher doses of chloroquine caused a decrease in rats' food intake. The band that appeared after chloroquine treatment was assumed as LC3 II (Figure 2E).

A stronger activation of autophagy in young rats than in old ones was confirmed by examination of primary RTCs cultures with Cyto-ID which is selectively accumulated in autophagosomes and autophagolysosomes [35]. The aggregate effect of the autophagy activator, rapamycin, and the inhibitor of the late stages of autophagy, chloroquine, resulted in a great increase in the fluorescence intensity of Cyto-ID in RTCs from young rats (Figure 2F). RTCs from old rats did not show any increase in Cyto-ID fluorescence in response to rapamycin and chloroquine (Figure 2G). Moreover, RTCs from old rats at the baseline showed a weaker intensity of Cyto-ID fluorescence than RTCs from young rats (Figure 2F,G).

For the analysis of lysosomal function, vital slices that were obtained from the kidneys of AL and 35% DR rats were loaded with LysoTracker Green. We observed an increase in LysoTracker Green fluorescence intensity in kidney slices from young rats exposed to 35% DR compared to AL rats (Figure 3A). The levels of fluorescence in young AL group were the same as in old AL rats. However, the kidney slices from old rats did not demonstrate any increase in fluorescence intensity of LysoTracker Green after 35% DR (Figure 3B). Besides the estimation of average intensity, we also analyzed the coefficient of kurtosis, which measures the sharpness of the peak of dye distribution and can indirectly characterize the heterogeneity of the tubules regarding the lysosomes' function. In young rats, the degree of kurtosis was low which could indicate that the fluorescence intensity of the tubules on the slices was distributed evenly. In old rats, the degree of kurtosis was higher, especially in the 35% DR group, indicating an increase in the heterogeneity of lysosomal activity among the tubules (Figure 3C).

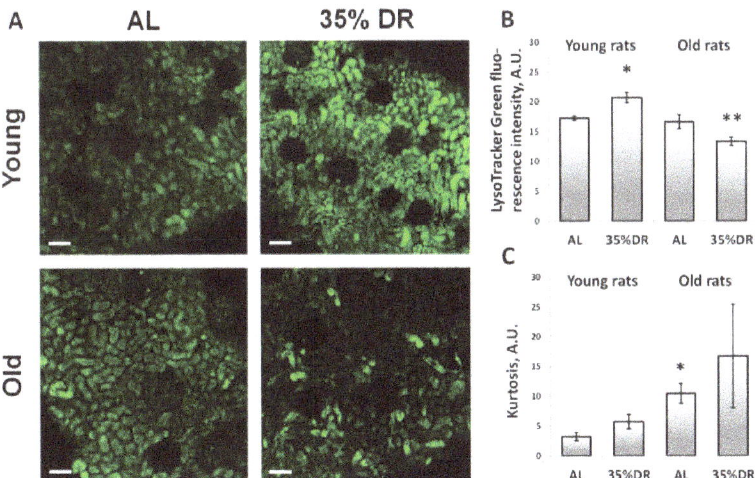

Figure 3. The staining of vital renal cortex slices of young and old rats fed AL or subjected to 35% DR with LysoTracker Green. (**A**) Confocal microscopy after LysoTracker Green staining. The scale bar indicates 100 μm. (**B**) Quantification of LysoTracker Green fluorescence intensity on the vital renal slices of young and old rats; (**C**) Quantification of the coefficient of kurtosis of LysoTracker Green distribution on the vital renal slices of young and old rats. * $p < 0.05$ compared to the AL group of young rats, ** $p < 0.05$ compared to the AL group of old rats.

3.3. Deterioration of Mitophagy and Mitochondrial Functions in the Kidneys of Old Rats

We assessed the function of mitochondria and the intensity of mitophagy in the kidneys of young and old rats. One of the proteins responsible for mitophagy is PTEN-induced putative kinase 1 (PINK-1). PINK-1 binds to mitochondria carrying a low membrane potential and such mitochondria become labeled by ubiquitin ligase Parkin and further eliminated in autophagolysosomes [36].

In our experiments, we isolated mitochondria from the kidneys of rats kept on normal or restricted diets and evaluated the amount of bound PINK-1 by western blotting. We found that the level of PINK-1 dropped in the mitochondria of the young 35% DR group (Figure 4A), which might indicate the elimination of a population of poorly functioning mitochondria during 4 weeks of DR. Mitochondria in kidneys of old rats from AL group contained lower levels of PINK-1 than mitochondria from young rats. Moreover, the levels of PINK-1 did not decrease in old rats kept on 35% DR (Figure 4A), which might be a consequence of impairments in the autophagic signaling pathways in the kidneys of old rats.

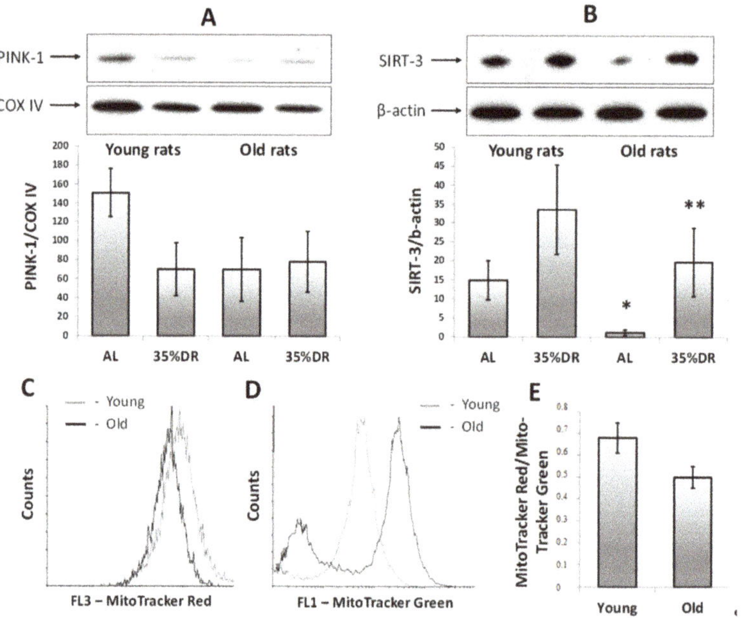

Figure 4. The comparison of the mitophagic activity, the level of SIRT-3, and the mitochondrial membrane potential in the kidneys of young and old rats fed AL or subjected to 35% DR. (**A**) Level of PTEN-induced kinase 1 (PINK-1) in isolated mitochondria from the kidneys of young and old rats; (**B**) Levels of SIRT-3 in kidney homogenates of young and old rats; (**C**) Flow cytometry of primary cultures of RTCs obtained from the kidneys of young and old rats, which were loaded with MitoTracker Red; (**D**) Flow cytometry of non-cultured renal tubular cells (NC-RTCs) obtained from the kidneys of young and old rats and in situ stained with MitoTracker Green; (**E**) Quantification of MitoTracker Red/MitoTracker Green ratio in NC-RTCs from the kidneys of young and old rats. * $p < 0.05$ compared to the AL group of young rats, ** $p < 0.05$ compared to the AL group of old rats.

We analyzed the levels of mitochondrial deacetylase SIRT-3 in the kidneys of young and old rats. In young rats, 35% DR induced an increase in the amount of SIRT-3 compared to the AL group. Old AL-rats were initially characterized by a significantly lower SIRT-3 level than in young animals. However, after 4 weeks of maintenance on 35% DR, the levels of SIRT-3 increased (Figure 4B).

We used flow cytometry to estimate the number of mitochondria and the mitochondrial potential as measured by the accumulation of MitoTracker Green and MitoTracker Red probes. The primary cultures of RTCs obtained from young animals demonstrated a higher MitoTracker Red intensity meaning that their mitochondria had higher mitochondrial potential, compared to RTCs from old animals (Figure 4C). NC-RTCs obtained directly from the kidneys of old rats and loaded with MitoTracker Green demonstrated two populations (Figure 4D), indicating the presence of cells with a small number of mitochondria. In young rats, such a segregation into two populations was not observed. Nevertheless, the MitoTracker Red/MitoTracker Green ratio revealed that NC-RTCs from the old kidneys had a lower mitochondrial membrane potential than NC-RTCs from young rats.

3.4. Proliferative Capacity of Primary Cultures of RTCs Obtained from Young and Old Rats

We assessed the proliferative capacity of primary cultures of RTCs obtained from young and old kidneys by the real-time monitoring of the cell growth rate (Figure 5A). The analysis was performed by using iCELLigence, which has already been used for studying proliferation and the death of RTCs [32]. We found that RTCs isolated from the kidneys of young rats characterized by a more rapid growth rate exceeding the growth of old cells by more than 4 fold (Figure 5B). After 2 days in vitro, RTCs were subjected to OGD. This method simulates I/R by depriving cells of both oxygen and nutrients. During OGD, some cells died, which could be observed by the decrease of the cell index in those wells (Figure 5A). The proliferation of RTCs resumed after restoration normoxic conditions, but RTCs from old kidneys proliferated about 3 times slower after OGD than RTCs from young animals (Figure 5C).

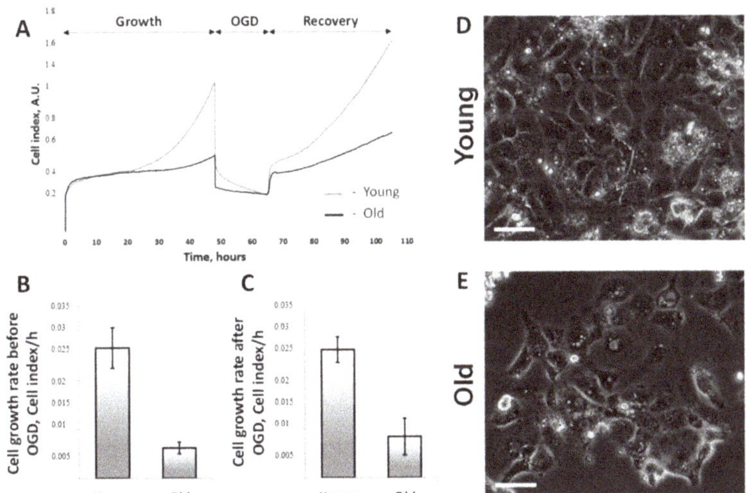

Figure 5. The proliferation of primary cultures of RTCs obtained from kidneys of young and old rats, and the rate of recovery after oxygen-glucose deprivation (OGD). (**A**) Kinetics of proliferation of primary cultures of RTCs evaluated by iCelligence, including growth under normoxic conditions, death during OGD, and the recovery of RTCs after the restoration of oxygen supply and complete culture medium; (**B**) Growth rate of RTCs under standard conditions; (**C**) Growth rate after OGD; (**D,E**) Phase-contrast microscopy images of the primary cultures of RTCs obtained from kidneys of young and old rats. The scale bar indicates 100 μm. * $p < 0.05$ compared to young rats.

Data from iCELLigence was visually confirmed by phase-contrast microscopy. RTC cultures were monitored every day and we verified that RTCs obtained from the kidneys of young rats proliferated more intensively and reached a higher density in a shorter time (Figure 5D,E).

3.5. Oxidative Stress and the Accumulation of Lipofuscin

It is well known that aging is associated with the accumulation of lipofuscin granules in all tissues including renal tissue [37], so we analyzed the content of lipofuscin in RTCs taken from animals of different ages. Indeed, analysis of RTCs by flow cytometry revealed that primary cell cultures isolated from old kidneys exhibited a higher red autofluorescence (Figure 6A,B), which might indicate a greater content of lipofuscin. These data were confirmed by comparison of the confocal images of RTCs. We observed that the number of lipofuscin granules was significantly higher in RTCs from old rats rather than in RTCs of neonatal cells (Figure 6C,D).

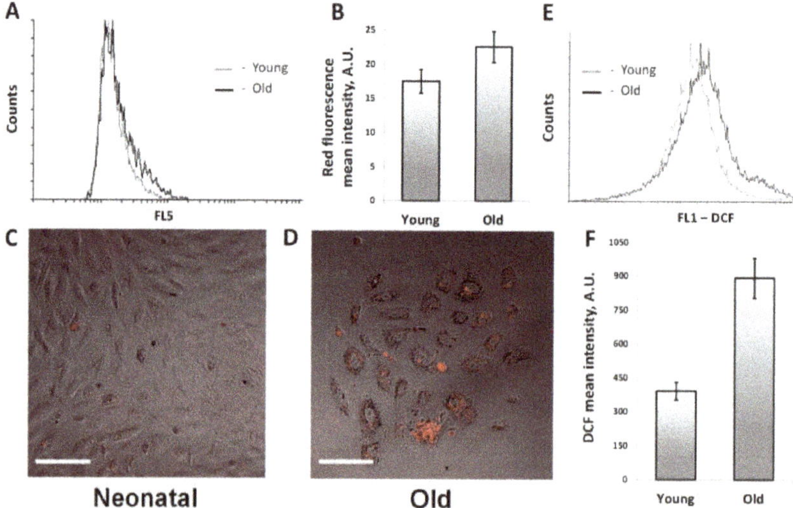

Figure 6. The comparison of lipofuscin content and the level of oxidative stress in cells obtained from the kidneys of young and old rats. (**A,B**) Flow cytometry of primary cultures of RTCs for the assessment of red autofluorescence, and its quantification for young and old rats; (**C,D**) Confocal images of RTCs from neonatal and old rats, and red autofluorescence emission analysis. The scale bar indicates 100 μm; (**E,F**) Flow cytometry of non-cultured renal tubular cells (NC-RTCs) of young and old rats and stained with DCF-H2.

Cells from the kidneys of different ages were also compared by the levels of oxidative stress. Staining with DCF, a reactive oxygen species (ROS)-sensitive probe showed that in old kidneys cells DCF fluorescence is more than 2 times higher than in cells from young kidneys (Figure 6E,F).

4. Discussion

Beneficial properties of DR were discovered as early as in 1935 and since then the mechanisms of DR have been intensively studied [1]. In 2010, for the first time, a protective effect of a short-term DR was demonstrated against the deleterious action of renal I/R in young mice [27]. In our study, DR maintained for 4 weeks had a significant nephroprotective effect against renal I/R in young rats, however, it did not afford protection in the old rats.

The loss of protective effects of DR with age is gradual: in the adult, but not old, rats some beneficial effect of the DR was still observed. Probably, the manifestation of a nephroprotective effect of DR correlates with the percentage of weight loss during DR. Old rats might need longer exposure to DR to achieve a nephroprotective effect from I/R. Recent work revealed that old rats needed to be exposed to 40% DR for 8 weeks to provide a protective effect from cisplatin nephrotoxicity [15], while young animals were afforded protection after exposure to DR for 4 weeks [16]. It should be noted that in the study on mice, 100% DR for 3 days was almost as effective as 40% DR for 4 weeks [27]. However, in another study, 100% DR for 1 day did not cause any activation of the autophagic system in old mice, although in young mice even such a short period of fasting increased the amount of LC3 II in the kidney tissue [38]. We were also unable to find any nephroprotection under conditions of 100% DR both in young and old mice.

Previously, a similar loss of protective effects in old animals was reported when attempted to apply ischemic pre- and postconditioning to aged kidneys and hearts [25,26,39,40]. Such loss of effectiveness can partly be explained by the fact that during aging tissue accumulate various age-dependent alterations affecting the functioning of organs [41]. Additionally, in the kidney, structural changes ultimately expressed in the lower number of functional nephrons, degenerative changes in proximal tubules, glomerulosclerosis, as well as changes at the molecular level, are observed [42]. The aging of the kidney modulates the expression of various genes, e.g., the levels of mRNA of claudin-7, KIM-1, and metalloproteinase MMP-7, which are good markers associated with renal injury and various kidney pathologies. Prolonged DR normalizes the expression of these genes [43] and prevents the accumulation of age-dependent changes in the kidney [44]. However, even shorter periods of DR were reported to reduce age-dependent changes in the kidney [45].

Besides the disturbances in expression patterns of several genes, deterioration in the work of the autophagic system has been well documented [13]. In our experiments, we did not detect the decrease in the LC3 II/LC3 I ratio in the kidneys of old intact rats, compared to the young rats, as well as found no changes in lysosomal activity. Similar results were obtained earlier in mice [44]. This data suggests that lysosomal dysfunction rather than a decrease in autophagosome biogenesis occurs within advanced age [24]. However, we evaluated some abnormality in the biogenesis of autophagosomes in the primary culture of RTCs from old kidneys while treating cells with rapamycin and chloroquine. We subjected RTCs from young and old kidneys to incubation with rapamycin, the activator of biogenesis of autophagosomes, and chloroquine, the inhibitor of the late stages of autophagy, leading to the maximal accumulation of autophagosomes in cells. Probably, there were some changes at the biogenesis level while such treatment did not provide a significant increase in Cyto-ID fluorescence intensity in the culture of RTCs from old rats.

The pivotal role of autophagy in the normal functioning of the kidney was recently evidenced by the experiments with the knockouts of autophagy-associated genes. For instance, the deletion of *Atg5* in the podocytes led to glomerulosclerosis, proteinuria, and other abnormalities typical for the aging kidney, e.g., lipofuscin accumulation, the presence of damaged mitochondria, and oxidize or ubiquitinated proteins [46]. Genetically modified mice with tamoxifen-induced inhibition of *Atg5* in the proximal tubules demonstrated renal failure, the atrophy of kidney tissue, mitochondrial dysfunction, and an increase in oxidative stress products in the kidney [47].

It is believed that I/R stimulates autophagic cascades which provide the elimination of intracellular proteinaceous aggregates and damaged organelles formed during I/R [34]. These processes play an important role after renal I/R since the knockout of *Atg5* and *Atg7* leads to a more severe AKI [48]. Relying on the LC3 II/LC3 I ratio, we may assume that, in old rats, autophagy is activated not as effectively as it takes place in young animals. Earlier, we demonstrated impaired autophagy in response to the damaging effect of I/R in premature senescent OXYS rats [25]; that could be another argument in favor of the dysfunction of the autophagic system caused by aging. In our experiments, even a preliminary exposure to DR, which is one of the most powerful autophagy-stimulating factors, did not restore the effective work of that system in old rats after I/R. On the contrary, in young animals, DR increased the LC3 II/LC3 I ratio and the amount of lysosomes that correlated with a decrease in the severity of AKI.

The deterioration of autophagy with aging also worsens the functioning of mitophagy, which is the only mechanism for mitochondrial degradation [49]. The elimination of mitochondria with low membrane potential is very important for the cells since dysfunctional mitochondria may be the source of pathological ROS [50]. For instance, in mice with a knockout of *Atg5*, an elevated accumulation of damaged mitochondria after I/R was shown, which correlated with an increased AKI [48]. It is also suggested that the accumulation of damaged mitochondria as a result of the ineffective work of mitophagy leads to the progression of tissue aging [51]. In many organisms, aging is associated with the morphological alterations and the increased size of mitochondria [52], as well as with the accumulation of age-associated proteins [53].

In this study, we evaluated the intensity of mitophagy by the levels of PINK1 in isolated mitochondria. This protein is considered to be the marker of damaged mitochondria and the initiator of mitophagy. PINK1 carries a mitochondrial address and is delivered into mitochondria. When the mitochondrial membrane potential decreases, this protein is unable to penetrate into the mitochondria and cannot be cleaved by presenilin-associated rhomboid-like protein (PARL). Consequently, PINK1 remains located on the outer membrane of the mitochondria with a low potential, where it is marked by the ubiquitin ligase Parkin, which serves as a signal for the onset of mitophagy [54].

An increase in the levels of PINK1 is usually associated with the accumulation of damaged mitochondria in the cell. For instance, a high-calorie diet causes the rise in the levels of PINK1 whereas DR decreases the amount of this protein in mitochondria [55]. In our experiments, we observed a two-fold decrease in PINK1 levels in the mitochondrial fraction after 4 weeks of 35% DR in young rats, which shows the result of the effective elimination of low functional mitochondria. In old rats, the PINK1 levels were initially lower than in young animals, and DR did not affect the levels of PINK1. We speculate that the lower content of PINK1 in older rats may indicate a deficiency in this protein and the malfunctioning of the mechanism of mitophagy. A similar decrease of the PINK1 levels was observed in lung tissue with aging [56] and was accompanied by a pulmonary pathology. Moreover, the decrease in PINK1 activity was described in many pathological conditions, for example, in cells of patients with Parkinson's disease [57]. It was shown that decreased PINK1 synthesis led to the fragmentation of mitochondria, decrease of the mitochondrial membrane potential [58], the development of fibrosis [59], which indicates the importance of the PINK1 protein in the normal functioning of mitochondria.

Since mitophagy is the only way to eliminate poorly functioning mitochondria, deterioration in the work of this system must inevitably lead to the accumulation of mitochondria with low membrane potentials [60]. Indeed, a large number of studies have demonstrated that mitochondria isolated from the tissues of old organisms had lower membrane potentials than mitochondria from young [52,61]. Taken together with higher levels of ROS in the tissues of old animals, it is assumed that age impacts either on the functioning of mitochondria or on the process of their quality control [50]. Our findings fit this assumption as we showed a lower mitochondrial membrane potential in kidney cells isolated from old rats, as well as a higher heterogeneity in mitochondria of cells obtained from old rats' kidneys revealed by flow cytometry. A similar heterogeneity of mitochondrial membrane potential was observed in hepatocytes from old rats [62]. Earlier, the phenomenon of the augmentation of the mitochondrial membrane potential heterogeneity in the kidney tissue after I/R was reported [63]. We also revealed an increase in LysoTracker Green distribution heterogeneity in the tubules of old rats. Probably, the increase in heterogeneity is a process that accompanies the aging of tissues.

Another important factor reflecting the state of mitochondria is the activity of deacetylase SIRT-3. This NAD$^+$-dependent deacetylase is localized predominantly in mitochondria and is considered to be a mitochondrial stress sensor that can modulate the activity of several mitochondrial proteins involved in metabolism and oxidative stress regulatory pathways [64]. SIRT-3 is suggested to be one of the mediators of the protective effect of DR [65]. In this study, DR increased the levels of SIRT-3 more than 2 times in the kidneys of young rats. In kidneys of old rats, the levels of SIRT-3 were significantly lower than in young, while DR significantly increased the content of this deacetylase. An age-associated drop of mitochondrial SIRT-3 was previously reported for some tissues of old people and old animals [66,67]. Contrarily, some variants of the *SIRT-3* gene were associated with longevity in humans [68], proving the key role of this deacetylase in the aging process.

Recent studies have demonstrated that increased levels of SIRT-3 protect the kidney from cisplatin nephrotoxicity [69], whereas the knockout of *SIRT-3* led to more severe damage after myocardial infarction [70]. The levels of SIRT-3 depended on physical activity and diet, e.g., the levels of the deacetylase rose in muscles after exercise [71] and in cells exposed to decreased glucose concentration in culture medium [72]. In addition, the knockout of *SIRT-3* in the kidneys of mice caused fibrosis, increased in the TGF-β1 level and the hyperacetylation of the kinase of glycogen synthase 3β (GSK3β) that adversely affected its phosphorylating activity [73]. Similarly, another deacetylase, SIRT-1, was detected to be lower in old animals, while 12-month-long DR increased the levels of this enzyme [44].

Our experiments with cell cultures showed that primary RTCs obtained from kidneys of old rats proliferated 4 times slower compared to cells from the kidneys of young rats. Such a dependence of proliferation rate on the age of the donor was demonstrated for various cells. For instance, hematopoietic stem cells derived from neonatal rats proliferated much better, and, unlike stem cells derived from adult rats, they were able to exhibit protective properties under myocardial I/R [74]. Although cardiomyocytes obtained from adult animals are thought to represent processes in the tissue better than neonatal cardiomyocytes, they proliferate much more slowly in culture [75].

Furthermore, primary kidney cells from old rats not only proliferated worse than those of young rats, but we also observed their less pronounced recovering ability after OGD. We believe that this impairment could be explained by deterioration in the functioning of the autophagy system, which could lead to the accumulation of lipofuscin, as well as to more pronounced oxidative stress.

5. Conclusions

In this study, we showed that a short-term 35% DR for 4 weeks has a significant nephroprotective effect against renal I/R in young rats, but DR does not provide such a beneficial effect in old rats. The lack of effectiveness in old animals can be explained by the deterioration in the work of both autophagy and mitophagy. Impairment in these recycling mechanisms results in accumulation of poorly functioning mitochondria, lipofuscin granules, and increased levels of oxidative stress. All these processes affect the normal functioning of the kidney and lead to a decrease in the ischemic tolerance of renal tissue. Molecular and structural alterations occurring in aging renal tissue make the manifestation of beneficial effects of DR in aged kidneys not as pronounced. Thus, an important problem is to develop approaches that would be helpful in the therapy of elderly patients.

Author Contributions: Conceptualization, S.S.J., E.Y.P. and N.V.A.; Methodology, S.S.J., I.B.P. and L.D.Z.; Software, V.A.P.; Validation, I.B.P. and L.D.Z.; Formal Analysis, N.V.A., L.D.Z. and I.B.P.; Investigation, N.V.A., L.D.Z. and E.Y.P.; Resources, D.N.S.; Data Curation, N.V.A. and S.S.J.; Writing-Original Draft Preparation, N.V.A.; Writing-Review & Editing, E.Y.P., D.N.S. and D.B.Z.; Visualization, A.N.V. and V.A.P.; Supervision, E.Y.P. and D.B.Z.; Project Administration, E.Y.P. and D.B.Z.

Funding: This research was funded by Russian science foundation grant number 18-15-00058.

Conflicts of Interest: The authors declare no conflict of interest.

References

1. Speakman, J.R.; Mitchell, S.E. Caloric restriction. *Mol. Asp. Med.* **2011**, *32*, 159–221. [CrossRef] [PubMed]
2. Shinmura, K.; Tamaki, K.; Sano, M.; Murata, M.; Yamakawa, H.; Ishida, H.; Fukuda, K. Impact of long-term caloric restriction on cardiac senescence: Caloric restriction ameliorates cardiac diastolic dysfunction associated with aging. *J. Mol. Cell. Cardiol.* **2011**, *50*, 117–127. [CrossRef] [PubMed]
3. Van Cauwenberghe, C.; Vandendriessche, C.; Libert, C.; Vandenbroucke, R.E. Caloric restriction: Beneficial effects on brain aging and Alzheimer's disease. *Mamm. Genome* **2016**, *27*, 300–319. [CrossRef] [PubMed]
4. Jové, M.; Naudí, A.; Ramírez-Núñez, O.; Portero-Otín, M.; Selman, C.; Withers, D.J.; Pamplona, R. Caloric restriction reveals a metabolomic and lipidomic signature in liver of male mice. *Aging Cell* **2014**, *13*, 828–837. [CrossRef] [PubMed]

5. Wiggins, J.E.; Goyal, M.; Sanden, S.K.; Wharram, B.L.; Shedden, K.A.; Misek, D.E.; Kuick, R.D.; Wiggins, R.C. Podocyte hypertrophy, "adaptation," and "decompensation" associated with glomerular enlargement and glomerulosclerosis in the aging rat: Prevention by calorie restriction. *J. Am. Soc. Nephrol.* **2005**, *16*, 2953–2966. [CrossRef] [PubMed]

6. Rohrbach, S.; Aslam, M.; Niemann, B.; Schulz, R. Impact of caloric restriction on myocardial ischaemia/reperfusion injury and new therapeutic options to mimic its effects. *Br. J. Pharmacol.* **2014**, *171*, 2964–2992. [CrossRef] [PubMed]

7. Fusco, S.; Pani, G. Brain response to calorie restriction. *Cell. Mol. Life Sci.* **2013**, *70*, 3157–3170. [CrossRef] [PubMed]

8. Han, X.; Ren, J. Caloric restriction and heart function: Is there a sensible link? *Acta Pharmacol. Sin.* **2010**, *31*, 1111–1117. [CrossRef] [PubMed]

9. Sathananthan, M.; Shah, M.; Edens, K.L.; Grothe, K.B.; Piccinini, F.; Farrugia, L.P.; Micheletto, F.; Man, C.D.; Cobelli, C.; Rizza, R.A.; et al. Six and 12 Weeks of Caloric Restriction Increases β Cell Function and Lowers Fasting and Postprandial Glucose Concentrations in People with Type 2 Diabetes. *J. Nutr.* **2015**, *145*, 2046–2051. [CrossRef] [PubMed]

10. Ravussin, E.; Redman, L.M.; Rochon, J.; Das, S.K.; Fontana, L.; Kraus, W.E.; Romashkan, S.; Williamson, D.A.; Meydani, S.N.; Villareal, D.T.; et al. A 2-Year Randomized Controlled Trial of Human Caloric Restriction: Feasibility and Effects on Predictors of Health Span and Longevity. *J. Gerontol. Ser. A Biol. Sci. Med. Sci.* **2015**, *70*, 1097–1104. [CrossRef] [PubMed]

11. Picca, A.; Pesce, V.; Lezza, A. Does eating less make you live longer and better? An update on calorie restriction. *Clin. Interv. Aging* **2017**, *12*, 1887–1902. [CrossRef] [PubMed]

12. Lee, S.-H.; Min, K.-J. Caloric restriction and its mimetics. *BMB Rep.* **2013**, *46*, 181–187. [CrossRef] [PubMed]

13. Cuervo, A.M. Autophagy and aging: Keeping that old broom working. *Trends Genet.* **2008**, *24*, 604–612. [CrossRef] [PubMed]

14. Masoro, E.J. Overview of caloric restriction and ageing. *Mech. Ageing Dev.* **2005**, *126*, 913–922. [CrossRef] [PubMed]

15. Ning, Y.-C.; Cai, G.-Y.; Zhuo, L.; Gao, J.-J.; Dong, D.; Cui, S.-Y.; Shi, S.-Z.; Feng, Z.; Zhang, L.; Sun, X.-F.; et al. Beneficial Effects of Short-Term Calorie Restriction against Cisplatin-Induced Acute Renal Injury in Aged Rats. *Nephron Exp. Nephrol.* **2014**, *124*, 19–27. [CrossRef] [PubMed]

16. Estrela, G.R.; Wasinski, F.; Batista, R.O.; Hiyane, M.I.; Felizardo, R.J.F.; Cunha, F.; de Almeida, D.C.; Malheiros, D.M.A.C.; Câmara, N.O.S.; Barros, C.C.; et al. Caloric Restriction Is More Efficient than Physical Exercise to Protect from Cisplatin Nephrotoxicity via PPAR-Alpha Activation. *Front. Physiol.* **2017**, *8*, 116. [CrossRef] [PubMed]

17. Shaikh, Z.A.; Jordan, S.A.; Tang, W. Protection against chronic cadmium toxicity by caloric restriction. *Toxicology* **1999**, *133*, 93–103. [CrossRef]

18. Gumprecht, L.A.; Long, C.Y.R.; Soper, K.A.; Smith, P.F.; Haschek-Hock, W.M.; Keenan, K.P. The Early Effects of Dietary Restriction on the Pathogenesis of Chronic Renal Disease in Sprague-Dawley Rats at 12 Months. *Toxicol. Pathol.* **1993**, *21*, 528–537. [CrossRef] [PubMed]

19. Kume, S.; Koya, D. Autophagy: A Novel Therapeutic Target for Diabetic Nephropathy. *Diabetes Metab. J.* **2015**, *39*, 451–460. [CrossRef] [PubMed]

20. Susantitaphong, P.; Cruz, D.N.; Cerda, J.; Abulfaraj, M.; Alqahtani, F.; Koulouridis, I.; Jaber, B.L. Acute Kidney Injury Advisory Group of the American Society of Nephrology World Incidence of AKI: A Meta-Analysis. *Clin. J. Am. Soc. Nephrol.* **2013**, *8*, 1482–1493. [CrossRef] [PubMed]

21. Xue, J.L.; Daniels, F.; Star, R.A.; Kimmel, P.L.; Eggers, P.W.; Molitoris, B.A.; Himmelfarb, J.; Collins, A.J. Incidence and mortality of acute renal failure in Medicare beneficiaries, 1992 to 2001. *J. Am. Soc. Nephrol.* **2006**, *17*, 1135–1142. [CrossRef] [PubMed]

22. Rosner, M.H. Acute Kidney Injury in the Elderly. *Clin. Geriatr. Med.* **2013**, *29*, 565–578. [CrossRef] [PubMed]

23. Lameire, N.H.; Bagga, A.; Cruz, D.; De Maeseneer, J.; Endre, Z.; Kellum, J.A.; Liu, K.D.; Mehta, R.L.; Pannu, N.; Van Biesen, W.; et al. Acute kidney injury: An increasing global concern. *Lancet* **2013**, *382*, 170–179. [CrossRef]

24. Jankauskas, S.S.; Silachev, D.N.; Andrianova, N.V.; Pevzner, I.B.; Zorova, L.D.; Popkov, V.A.; Plotnikov, E.Y.; Zorov, D.B. Aged kidney: Can we protect it? Autophagy, mitochondria and mechanisms of ischemic preconditioning. *Cell Cycle* **2018**, *17*, 1291–1309. [CrossRef] [PubMed]

25. Jankauskas, S.S.; Pevzner, I.B.; Andrianova, N.V.; Zorova, L.D.; Popkov, V.A.; Silachev, D.N.; Kolosova, N.G.; Plotnikov, E.Y.; Zorov, D.B. The age-associated loss of ischemic preconditioning in the kidney is accompanied by mitochondrial dysfunction, increased protein acetylation and decreased autophagy. *Sci. Rep.* **2017**, *7*, 44430. [CrossRef] [PubMed]

26. Chen, H.; Xing, B.; Wang, L.; Weng, X.; Chen, Z.; Liu, X. Aged kidneys are refractory to ischemic postconditioning in a rat model. *Ren. Fail.* **2014**, *36*, 1575–1580. [CrossRef] [PubMed]

27. Mitchell, J.R.; Verweij, M.; Brand, K.; van de Ven, M.; Goemaere, N.; van den Engel, S.; Chu, T.; Forrer, F.; Müller, C.; de Jong, M.; et al. Short-term dietary restriction and fasting precondition against ischemia reperfusion injury in mice. *Aging Cell* **2010**, *9*, 40–53. [CrossRef] [PubMed]

28. Robertson, L.T.; Trevino-Villarreal, J.H.; Mejia, P.; Grondin, Y.; Harputlugil, E.; Hine, C.; Vargas, D.; Zheng, H.; Ozaki, C.K.; Kristal, B.S.; et al. Protein and Calorie Restriction Contribute Additively to Protection from Renal Ischemia Reperfusion Injury Partly via Leptin Reduction in Male Mice. *J. Nutr.* **2015**, *145*, 1717–1727. [CrossRef] [PubMed]

29. Jongbloed, F.; Saat, T.C.; Verweij, M.; Payan-Gomez, C.; Hoeijmakers, J.H.J.; van den Engel, S.; van Oostrom, C.T.; Ambagtsheer, G.; Imholz, S.; Pennings, J.L.A.; et al. A signature of renal stress resistance induced by short-term dietary restriction, fasting, and protein restriction. *Sci. Rep.* **2017**, *7*, 40901. [CrossRef] [PubMed]

30. Plotnikov, E.Y.; Kazachenko, A.V.; Vyssokikh, M.Y.; Vasileva, A.K.; Tcvirkun, D.V.; Isaev, N.K.; Kirpatovsky, V.I.; Zorov, D.B. The role of mitochondria in oxidative and nitrosative stress during ischemia/reperfusion in the rat kidney. *Kidney Int.* **2007**, *72*, 1493–1502. [CrossRef] [PubMed]

31. Giaever, I.; Keese, C.R. Monitoring fibroblast behavior in tissue culture with an applied electric field. *Proc. Natl. Acad. Sci. USA* **1984**, *81*, 3761–3764. [CrossRef] [PubMed]

32. Popkov, V.A.; Andrianova, N.V.; Manskikh, V.N.; Silachev, D.N.; Pevzner, I.B.; Zorova, L.D.; Sukhikh, G.T.; Plotnikov, E.Y.; Zorov, D.B. Pregnancy protects the kidney from acute ischemic injury. *Sci. Rep.* **2018**, *8*, 14534. [CrossRef] [PubMed]

33. Robertson, L.T.; Mitchell, J.R. Benefits of short-term dietary restriction in mammals. *Exp. Gerontol.* **2013**, *48*, 1043–1048. [CrossRef] [PubMed]

34. Kaushal, G.P.; Shah, S.V. Autophagy in acute kidney injury. *Kidney Int.* **2016**, *89*, 779–791. [CrossRef] [PubMed]

35. Stankov, M.; Panayotova-Dimitrova, D.; Leverkus, M.; Klusmann, J.-H.; Behrens, G. Flow Cytometric Analysis of Autophagic Activity with Cyto-ID Staining in Primary Cells. *Bio-Protocol* **2014**, *4*. [CrossRef]

36. Vives-Bauza, C.; Zhou, C.; Huang, Y.; Cui, M.; de Vries, R.L.A.; Kim, J.; May, J.; Tocilescu, M.A.; Liu, W.; Ko, H.S.; et al. PINK1-dependent recruitment of Parkin to mitochondria in mitophagy. *Proc. Natl. Acad. Sci. USA* **2010**, *107*, 378–383. [CrossRef] [PubMed]

37. Melk, A.; Schmidt, B.M.W.; Takeuchi, O.; Sawitzki, B.; Rayner, D.C.; Halloran, P.F. Expression of p16INK4a and other cell cycle regulator and senescence associated genes in aging human kidney. *Kidney Int.* **2004**, *65*, 510–520. [CrossRef] [PubMed]

38. Yamamoto, T.; Takabatake, Y.; Kimura, T.; Takahashi, A.; Namba, T.; Matsuda, J.; Minami, S.; Kaimori, J.; Matsui, I.; Kitamura, H.; et al. Time-dependent dysregulation of autophagy: Implications in aging and mitochondrial homeostasis in the kidney proximal tubule. *Autophagy* **2016**, *12*, 801–813. [CrossRef] [PubMed]

39. Abete, P.; Testa, G.; Ferrara, N.; De Santis, D.; Capaccio, P.; Viati, L.; Calabrese, C.; Cacciatore, F.; Longobardi, G.; Condorelli, M.; et al. Cardioprotective effect of ischemic preconditioning is preserved in food-restricted senescent rats. *Am. J. Physiol. Heart Circ. Physiol.* **2002**, *282*, H1978–H1987. [CrossRef] [PubMed]

40. Boengler, K.; Buechert, A.; Heinen, Y.; Roeskes, C.; Hilfiker-Kleiner, D.; Heusch, G.; Schulz, R. Cardioprotection by Ischemic Postconditioning Is Lost in Aged and STAT3-Deficient Mice. *Circ. Res.* **2008**, *102*, 131–135. [CrossRef] [PubMed]

41. Rezzani, R.; Stacchiotti, A.; Rodella, L.F. Morphological and biochemical studies on aging and autophagy. *Ageing Res. Rev.* **2012**, *11*, 10–31. [CrossRef] [PubMed]

42. Bolignano, D.; Mattace-Raso, F.; Sijbrands, E.J.G.; Zoccali, C. The aging kidney revisited: A systematic review. *Ageing Res. Rev.* **2014**, *14*, 65–80. [CrossRef] [PubMed]

43. Chen, G.; Bridenbaugh, E.A.; Akintola, A.D.; Catania, J.M.; Vaidya, V.S.; Bonventre, J.V.; Dearman, A.C.; Sampson, H.W.; Zawieja, D.C.; Burghardt, R.C.; et al. Increased susceptibility of aging kidney to ischemic injury: Identification of candidate genes changed during aging, but corrected by caloric restriction. *Am. J. Physiol. Ren. Physiol.* **2007**, *293*, F1272–F1281. [CrossRef] [PubMed]

44. Kume, S.; Uzu, T.; Horiike, K.; Chin-Kanasaki, M.; Isshiki, K.; Araki, S.-I.; Sugimoto, T.; Haneda, M.; Kashiwagi, A.; Koya, D. Calorie restriction enhances cell adaptation to hypoxia through Sirt1-dependent mitochondrial autophagy in mouse aged kidney. *J. Clin. Investig.* **2010**, *120*, 1043–1055. [CrossRef] [PubMed]

45. Ning, Y.-C.; Cai, G.-Y.; Zhuo, L.; Gao, J.-J.; Dong, D.; Cui, S.; Feng, Z.; Shi, S.-Z.; Bai, X.-Y.; Sun, X.-F.; et al. Short-term calorie restriction protects against renal senescence of aged rats by increasing autophagic activity and reducing oxidative damage. *Mech. Ageing Dev.* **2013**, *134*, 570–579. [CrossRef] [PubMed]

46. Hartleben, B.; Gödel, M.; Meyer-Schwesinger, C.; Liu, S.; Ulrich, T.; Köbler, S.; Wiech, T.; Grahammer, F.; Arnold, S.J.; Lindenmeyer, M.T.; et al. Autophagy influences glomerular disease susceptibility and maintains podocyte homeostasis in aging mice. *J. Clin. Investig.* **2010**, *120*, 1084–1096. [CrossRef] [PubMed]

47. Baisantry, A.; Bhayana, S.; Rong, S.; Ermeling, E.; Wrede, C.; Hegermann, J.; Pennekamp, P.; So rensen-Zender, I.; Haller, H.; Melk, A.; et al. Autophagy Induces Prosenescent Changes in Proximal Tubular S3 Segments. *J. Am. Soc. Nephrol.* **2016**, *27*, 1609–1616. [CrossRef] [PubMed]

48. Kimura, T.; Takabatake, Y.; Takahashi, A.; Kaimori, J.; Matsui, I.; Namba, T.; Kitamura, H.; Niimura, F.; Matsusaka, T.; Soga, T.; et al. Autophagy protects the proximal tubule from degeneration and acute ischemic injury. *J. Am. Soc. Nephrol.* **2011**, *22*, 902–913. [CrossRef] [PubMed]

49. Weber, T.A.; Reichert, A.S. Impaired quality control of mitochondria: Aging from a new perspective. *Exp. Gerontol.* **2010**, *45*, 503–511. [CrossRef] [PubMed]

50. Gomez-Cabrera, M.C.; Sanchis-Gomar, F.; Garcia-Valles, R.; Pareja-Galeano, H.; Gambini, J.; Borras, C.; Viña, J. Mitochondria as sources and targets of damage in cellular aging. *Clin. Chem. Lab. Med.* **2012**, *50*, 1287–1295. [CrossRef] [PubMed]

51. Cuervo, A.M.; Bergamini, E.; Brunk, U.T.; Dröge, W.; Ffrench, M.; Terman, A. Autophagy and aging: The importance of maintaining "clean" cells. *Autophagy* **2005**, *1*, 131–140. [CrossRef] [PubMed]

52. Sastre, J.; Pallardó, F.V.; Plá, R.; Pellín, A.; Juan, G.; O'Connor, J.E.; Estrela, J.M.; Miquel, J.; Viña, J. Aging of the liver: Age-associated mitochondrial damage in intact hepatocytes. *Hepatology* **1996**, *24*, 1199–1205. [CrossRef] [PubMed]

53. Cui, J.; Bai, X.-Y.; Shi, S.; Cui, S.; Hong, Q.; Cai, G.; Chen, X. Age-related changes in the function of autophagy in rat kidneys. *Age* **2012**, *34*, 329–339. [CrossRef] [PubMed]

54. Jin, S.M.; Lazarou, M.; Wang, C.; Kane, L.A.; Narendra, D.P.; Youle, R.J. Mitochondrial membrane potential regulates PINK1 import and proteolytic destabilization by PARL. *J. Cell Biol.* **2010**, *191*, 933–942. [CrossRef] [PubMed]

55. Cui, J.; Shi, S.; Sun, X.; Cai, G.; Cui, S.; Hong, Q.; Chen, X.; Bai, X.-Y. Mitochondrial autophagy involving renal injury and aging is modulated by caloric intake in aged rat kidneys. *PLoS ONE* **2013**, *8*, e69720. [CrossRef] [PubMed]

56. Sosulski, M.L.; Gongora, R.; Danchuk, S.; Dong, C.; Luo, F.; Sanchez, C.G. Deregulation of selective autophagy during aging and pulmonary fibrosis: The role of TGFβ1. *Aging Cell* **2015**, *14*, 774–783. [CrossRef] [PubMed]

57. Rogaeva, E.; Johnson, J.; Lang, A.E.; Gulick, C.; Gwinn-Hardy, K.; Kawarai, T.; Sato, C.; Morgan, A.; Werner, J.; Nussbaum, R.; et al. Analysis of the PINK1 gene in a large cohort of cases with Parkinson disease. *Arch. Neurol.* **2004**, *61*, 1898–1904. [CrossRef] [PubMed]

58. Exner, N.; Treske, B.; Paquet, D.; Holmström, K.; Schiesling, C.; Gispert, S.; Carballo-Carbajal, I.; Berg, D.; Hoepken, H.-H.; Gasser, T.; et al. Loss-of-function of human PINK1 results in mitochondrial pathology and can be rescued by parkin. *J. Neurosci.* **2007**, *27*, 12413–12418. [CrossRef] [PubMed]

59. Bueno, M.; Lai, Y.-C.; Romero, Y.; Brands, J.; Croix, C.M.S.; Kamga, C.; Corey, C.; Herazo-Maya, J.D.; Sembrat, J.; Lee, J.S.; et al. PINK1 deficiency impairs mitochondrial homeostasis and promotes lung fibrosis. *J. Clin. Investig.* **2015**, *125*, 521–538. [CrossRef] [PubMed]

60. Chistiakov, D.A.; Sobenin, I.A.; Revin, V.V.; Orekhov, A.N.; Bobryshev, Y.V. Mitochondrial aging and age-related dysfunction of mitochondria. *BioMed Res. Int.* **2014**, *2014*, 238463. [CrossRef] [PubMed]

61. Serviddio, G.; Bellanti, F.; Romano, A.D.; Tamborra, R.; Rollo, T.; Altomare, E.; Vendemiale, G. Bioenergetics in aging: Mitochondrial proton leak in aging rat liver, kidney and heart. *Redox Rep.* **2007**, *12*, 91–95. [CrossRef] [PubMed]

62. Hagen, T.M.; Yowe, D.L.; Bartholomew, J.C.; Wehr, C.M.; Do, K.L.; Park, J.Y.; Ames, B.N. Mitochondrial decay in hepatocytes from old rats: Membrane potential declines, heterogeneity and oxidants increase. *Proc. Natl. Acad. Sci. USA* **1997**, *94*, 3064–3069. [CrossRef] [PubMed]

63. Popkov, V.A.; Plotnikov, E.Y.; Lyamzaev, K.G.; Silachev, D.N.; Zorova, L.D.; Pevzner, I.B.; Jankauskas, S.S.; Zorov, S.D.; Babenko, V.A.; Zorov, D.B. Mitodiversity. *Biochemistry* **2015**, *80*, 532–541. [CrossRef] [PubMed]

64. Ahn, B.-H.; Kim, H.-S.; Song, S.; Lee, I.H.; Liu, J.; Vassilopoulos, A.; Deng, C.-X.; Finkel, T. A role for the mitochondrial deacetylase Sirt3 in regulating energy homeostasis. *Proc. Natl. Acad. Sci. USA* **2008**, *105*, 14447–14452. [CrossRef] [PubMed]

65. Guarente, L.; Picard, F. Calorie restriction–the SIR2 connection. *Cell* **2005**, *120*, 473–482. [CrossRef] [PubMed]

66. Lanza, I.R.; Short, D.K.; Short, K.R.; Raghavakaimal, S.; Basu, R.; Joyner, M.J.; McConnell, J.P.; Nair, K.S. Endurance exercise as a countermeasure for aging. *Diabetes* **2008**, *57*, 2933–2942. [CrossRef] [PubMed]

67. Kwon, Y.; Kim, J.; Lee, C.-Y.; Kim, H. Expression of SIRT1 and SIRT3 varies according to age in mice. *Anat. Cell Biol.* **2015**, *48*, 54–61. [CrossRef] [PubMed]

68. Rose, G.; Dato, S.; Altomare, K.; Bellizzi, D.; Garasto, S.; Greco, V.; Passarino, G.; Feraco, E.; Mari, V.; Barbi, C.; et al. Variability of the SIRT3 gene, human silent information regulator Sir2 homologue, and survivorship in the elderly. *Exp. Gerontol.* **2003**, *38*, 1065–1070. [CrossRef]

69. Morigi, M.; Perico, L.; Rota, C.; Longaretti, L.; Conti, S.; Rottoli, D.; Novelli, R.; Remuzzi, G.; Benigni, A. Sirtuin 3-dependent mitochondrial dynamic improvements protect against acute kidney injury. *J. Clin. Investig.* **2015**, *125*, 715–726. [CrossRef] [PubMed]

70. Porter, G.A.; Urciuoli, W.R.; Brookes, P.S.; Nadtochiy, S.M. SIRT3 deficiency exacerbates ischemia-reperfusion injury: Implication for aged hearts. *AJP Heart Circ. Physiol.* **2014**, *306*, H1602–H1609. [CrossRef] [PubMed]

71. Palacios, O.M.; Carmona, J.J.; Michan, S.; Chen, K.Y.; Manabe, Y.; Ward, J.L.W., III; Goodyear, L.J.; Tong, Q. Diet and exercise signals regulate SIRT3 and activate AMPK and PGC-1α in skeletal muscle. *Aging* **2009**, *1*, 771–783. [CrossRef] [PubMed]

72. Zhang, B.; Cui, S.; Bai, X.; Zhuo, L.; Sun, X.; Hong, Q.; Fu, B.; Wang, J.; Chen, X.; Cai, G. SIRT3 overexpression antagonizes high glucose accelerated cellular senescence in human diploid fibroblasts via the SIRT3–FOXO1 signaling pathway. *Age* **2013**, *35*, 2237–2253. [CrossRef] [PubMed]

73. Sundaresan, N.R.; Bindu, S.; Pillai, V.B.; Samant, S.; Pan, Y.; Huang, J.-Y.; Gupta, M.; Nagalingam, R.S.; Wolfgeher, D.; Verdin, E.; et al. SIRT3 Blocks Aging-Associated Tissue Fibrosis in Mice by Deacetylating and Activating Glycogen Synthase Kinase 3β. *Mol. Cell. Biol.* **2016**, *36*, 678–692. [CrossRef] [PubMed]

74. Markel, T.A.; Crisostomo, P.R.; Manukyan, M.C.; Al-Azzawi, D.; Herring, C.M.; Lahm, T.; Novotny, N.M.; Meldrum, D.R. Are Neonatal Stem Cells as Effective as Adult Stem Cells in Providing Ischemic Protection? *J. Surg. Res.* **2009**, *152*, 325–330. [CrossRef] [PubMed]

75. Graham, E.L.; Balla, C.; Franchino, H.; Melman, Y.; del Monte, F.; Das, S. Isolation, Culture, and Functional Characterization of Adult Mouse Cardiomyoctyes. *J. Vis. Exp.* **2013**, e50289. [CrossRef] [PubMed]

Review

Autophagy in Chronic Kidney Diseases

Tien-An Lin [1], Victor Chien-Chia Wu [2] and Chao-Yung Wang [2,3,*]

[1] Department of General Surgery, Chang Gung Memorial Hospital, Taoyuan City 333, Taiwan; doroz1119@gmail.com

[2] Department of Cardiology, Chang Gung Memorial Hospital and Chang Gung University College of Medicine, Taoyuan City 333, Taiwan; victorcwu@hotmail.com

[3] Institute of Cellular and System Medicine, National Health Research Institutes, Zhunan 350, Taiwan

* Correspondence: cwang@ocean.ag; Tel.: +886-3-328-1200 (ext. 8750); Fax: +886-3-328-9134

Received: 8 December 2018; Accepted: 9 January 2019; Published: 16 January 2019

Abstract: Autophagy is a cellular recycling process involving self-degradation and reconstruction of damaged organelles and proteins. Current evidence suggests that autophagy is critical in kidney physiology and homeostasis. In clinical studies, autophagy activations and inhibitions are linked to acute kidney injuries, chronic kidney diseases, diabetic nephropathies, and polycystic kidney diseases. Oxidative stress, inflammation, and mitochondrial dysfunction, which are implicated as important mechanisms underlying many kidney diseases, modulate the autophagy activation and inhibition and lead to cellular recycling dysfunction. Abnormal autophagy function can induce loss of podocytes, damage proximal tubular cells, and glomerulosclerosis. After acute kidney injuries, activated autophagy protects tubular cells from apoptosis and enhances cellular regeneration. Patients with chronic kidney diseases have impaired autophagy that cannot be reversed by hemodialysis. Multiple nephrotoxic medications also alter the autophagy signaling, by which the mechanistic insights of the drugs are revealed, thus providing the unique opportunity to manage the nephrotoxicity of these drugs. In this review, we summarize the current concepts of autophagy and its molecular aspects in different kidney cells pathophysiology. We also discuss the current evidence of autophagy in acute kidney injury, chronic kidney disease, toxic effects of drugs, and aging kidneys. In addition, we examine therapeutic possibilities targeting the autophagy system in kidney diseases.

Keywords: autophagy; kidney diseases; oxidative stress; inflammation; mitochondria

---

1. Introduction

Autophagy is a dynamic cellular balancing mechanism for energy and resource. The word autophagy is derived from the Greek word, where *auto* means "self" and *phagy* means "eating". This "self-eating" process helps cells recycle their endogenous materials and build essential macromolecules to maintain cellular homeostasis and reutilize energy [1,2]. Autophagy was initially referred to the catabolic process that could provide nutrition and energy to cells during starvation. Recently, more evidence has shown that autophagy plays a critical role in synthesis and degradation and has complex cross-talks to apoptosis and cell cycle regulations [3]. Thus, autophagy acts as a protective mechanism in living organisms and can interfere in pathogenesis [4,5].

In 1963, Christian de Duve first described the autophagy as the degradation process that occurred after cytoplasmic materials were delivered to the lysosome. In the 1990's the autophagy research bloomed after the team of Dr. Yoshinori Ohsumi identified the important genes related to the autophagy-defective mutants in yeasts called the autophagy-related gene (Atg) and its related protein [6]. Soon after, the research advances that focused on the genetic aspects and several Atg proteins were discovered [4,5], providing a better understanding of the function and mechanisms of autophagy. Recently, autophagy has been widely implicated not only in yeasts and animal models but also in human pathophysiological processes [5,7]. In 2016, Yoshinori Ohsumi was awarded the Nobel Prize in Physiology or Medicine in recognition for his work on laying the foundation for a better understanding of the ability of cells to manage starvation, stress, and diseases [4].

Autophagy works through intracellular lysosomal degradation and recycling, and in turn, helps to maintain cellular integrity more efficiently by regenerating metabolic precursors and clearing subcellular debris [5]. Autophagy is a series of catabolic processes, starting with a small membrane phagophore in the cytoplasm and elongating to form a cup-shaped structure. It then matures and becomes a double-membrane structure called autophagosome that engulfs the damaged components. The autophagosome then fuses with lysosomes to form autophagolysosome [4,8] (Figure 1). After forming the autophagolysosome, the mTOR (mammalian target of rapamycin) signaling is activated to degenerate the intercellular components and transport back to the cytoplasm to reuse the macromolecule [9].

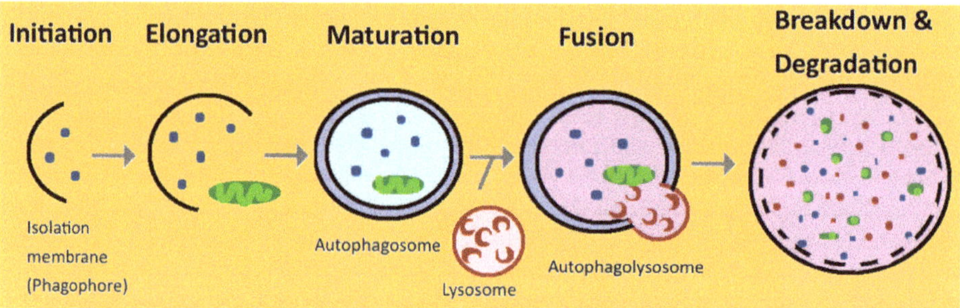

Figure 1. Schematic overview of the normal autophagy function in the kidney. Multiple steps in autophagy are modulated in kidney diseases, including autophagy initiation, elongation, maturation, fusion, and final degradation and recycling.

Defective autophagy signaling is now found in multiple diseases, such as autoimmune diseases, infectious diseases, metabolic diseases, muscular disorders, neurodegenerative diseases, cardiovascular and pulmonary diseases [5,7,10]. Many pathophysiologic mechanisms, including ischemic, toxic, infection, oxidative stress, circadian rhythm, and aging, are also confirmed to have close interactions with autophagy. In certain stressed situations, selective autophagy occurs in order to remove toxic materials within cells and organs [1,11]. Currently, only a few studies review the relationship between kidney diseases and autophagy. Therefore, our aim is to summarize the recent advances in understanding the role of autophagy in acute and chronic kidney disease patients [12].

2. Autophagy in Normal Kidney

Previous studies from human and animals provide the evidence that autophagy has a great impact on the maintenance of renal functions and homeostasis [13]. However, autophagy is nonessential for embryonic renal development. The embryonic *Atg5* knockout mice show no significant impairment of glomerular development, no change in podocyte maturation, normal tubular function, and normal nephrons development [3,14]. In terms of kidney physiology in adult animals, the autophagy affects different renal cell types and helps maintain kidney pathophysiology and homeostasis [13].

2.1. Autophagy in Glomerular Mesangial Cells

Glomerular mesangial cells are located in the mesangium of the glomerulus, in the centrilobular region of the kidneys. Mesangial cells are specialized pericytes with contractile activities. They regulate glomerular filtration and act as primary producers of the extracellular matrix that constitutes the mesangium, thus playing a vital role in maintaining mesangial matrix homeostasis [3]. Autophagy plays dual roles in modulating mesangial cell survival. After mesangial cells are exposed to stress, autophagy is activated and directed to type II programmed cell death. At the same time, autophagy can also serve as a protective role through transforming growth factor-β1 (TGF-β1) activation and inhibit mesangial cells from apoptosis and necrosis [3].

The advanced glycation end-products (AGEs) induced mesangial cells injury is one of the leading causes of glomerular dysfunction in diabetic nephropathy [15]. Autophagy could serve as a protective manner through increased LC3 cleavage (LC3-II/LC3-I ratio), enhanced Atg5 protein expression, and decreased p62 level in mesangial cells in dose- and time-dependent manners after exposed to AGEs. Also, inhibition of Atg5 expression could aggravate AGEs related mesangial cells injury [16]. This indicates that autophagy may protect mesangial cells from apoptosis. Previous studies suggest that the AGEs could induce autophagy through a RAGE/PI3K/AKT/mTOR signaling pathway in cardiomyocytes [17].

After the environmental toxin cadmium exposure, the reactive oxygen species (ROS) increases and activates glycogen synthase kinase-3β (GSK-3β) to trigger autophagy that promotes mesangial cells death [3,18]. Cadmium exposure can also increase autophagy through Ca^{2+} signaling and mitochondrial depolarization pathway and serve as a housekeeping process to protect the kidney and an early biomarker for cadmium toxicity [18] (Figure 2A).

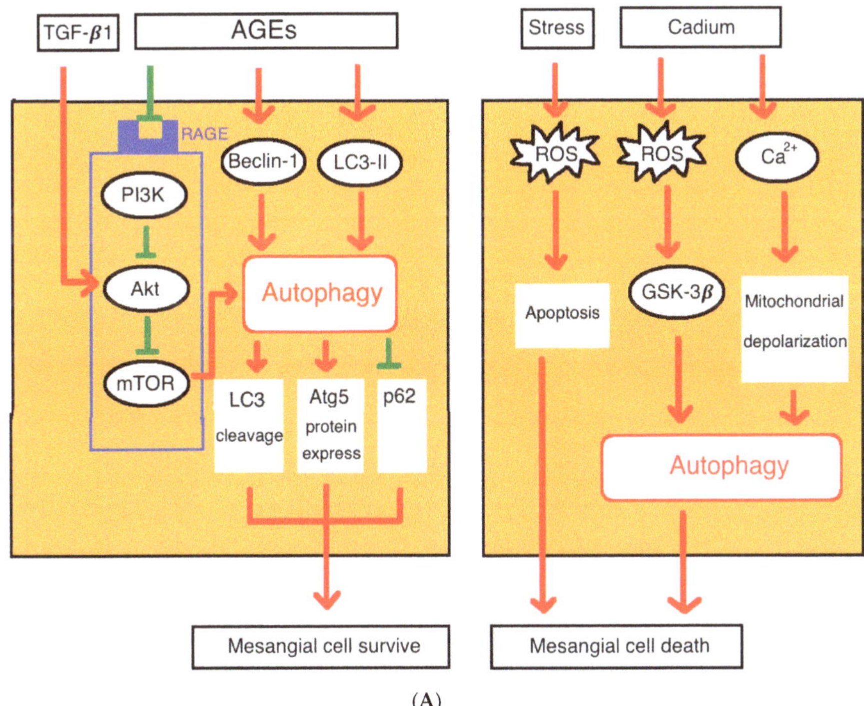

(**A**)

Figure 2. *Cont.*

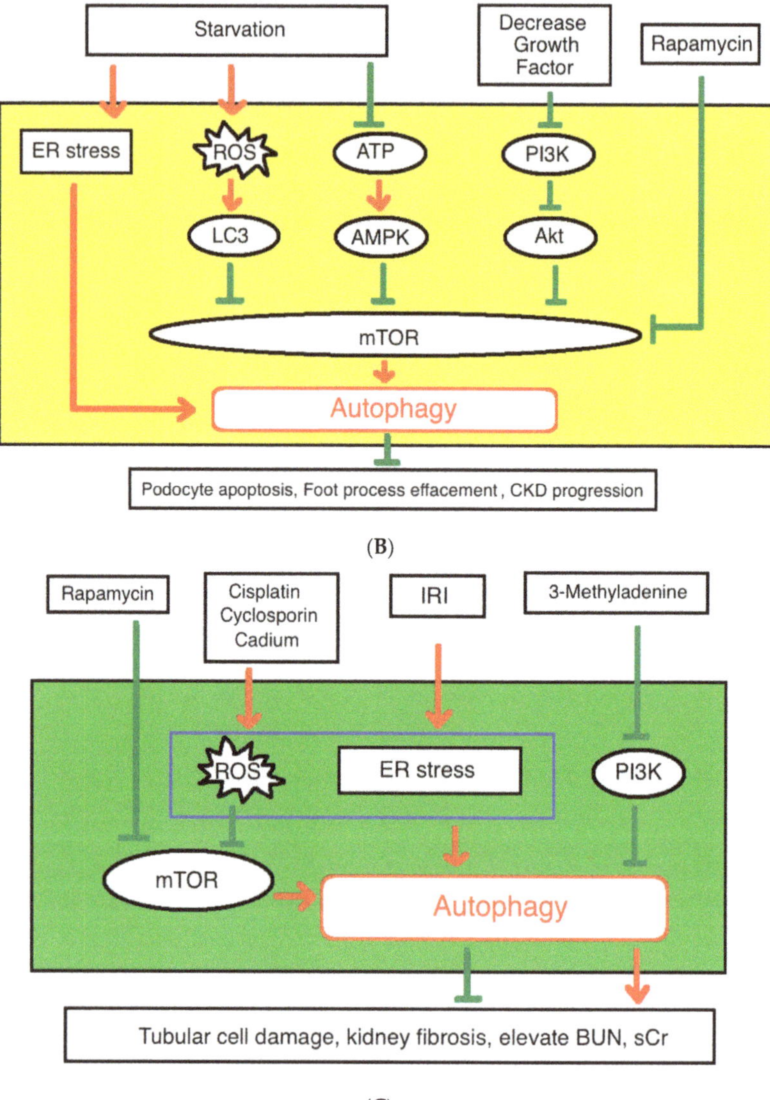

Figure 2. (**A**). Autophagy in glomerular mesangial cells. AGEs: advanced glycation end-products; Akt: also stand for PKB (Protein kinase B); GSK-3β: glycogen synthase kinase-3β; PI3K: Phosphoinositide 3-kinase; ROS: reactive oxygen species; TGF-β1: transforming growth factor-β1; ER stress: endoplasmic reticulum stress; (**B**). Autophagy in podocytes. PI3K: Phosphoinositide 3-kinase; AMPK: AMP-activated protein kinase Akt: also stand for PKB (Protein kinase B); ROS: reactive oxygen species; ER stress: endoplasmic reticulum stress; (**C**). Autophagy in proximal tubular cells. IRI: ischemic reperfusion injury; ROS: reactive oxygen species; ER stress: endoplasmic reticulum stress; PI3K: Phosphoinositide 3-kinase; BUN, blood urea nitrogen; sCr, serum creatinine.

2.2. Autophagy in Podocytes

Autophagy is vital in post-mitotic cells, such as neuron cells and podocytes. [19]. Podocytes are highly differentiated epithelial cells located in the visceral site of the Bowman's capsule and surrounding capillaries of the glomerulus. Podocytes have characteristic foot processes called pedicles that wrap around the capillaries and extend into them to form a filtration slit diaphragm. The podocyte foot processes and slit diaphragm control the selective permeability of the glomerular filtration barrier that filters circulating blood to form urine [20]. Podocytes can also act as glomerular filtration rate regulators through contraction and filtration slit closure [21]. Podocyte injuries are typical hallmarks of acute kidney injury and can cause proteinuria and nutrient loss [19,20]. The degree of podocytes damages parallels the severity of glomerulosclerosis, proteinuria, and kidney injury [22].

Studies in mice suggested that podocytes exhibit a high basal level of autophagy with abundant autophagosomes [3]. Nine-week-old mice with podocyte-specific deletion of Class III PI3K vacuolar protein sorting 34 (Vps34), which helps to maintain autophagic regulation, develop early proteinuria, progressive glomerulosclerosis, and renal failure [3]. The podocyte-specific depletion of the Atg5 gene leads to glomerulopathy in aging mice, whose oxidative and ubiquitinated protein accumulation and podocyte endoplasmic reticulum stress eventually lead to loss of podocytes, increased proteinuria, and glomerulosclerosis [20,22]. Moreover, the inadvertently increased autophagosomes in podocytes can be found in different glomerular diseases such as IgA nephropathy, membranous glomerulonephritis, and focal segmental glomerulosclerosis [20,23].

The autophagy activated by mTOR pathway protects podocytes from apoptosis, foot process effacement, and chronic kidney diseases progression [24]. In podocyte-specific mTor knockout mice, the proteinuria and end-stage renal diseases (ESRD) occur in 3–5 weeks. Their podocytes accumulate with autophagosomes, microtubule-associated protein 1A/1B-light chain 3 (LC3), and damaged mitochondria [25]. The evidence suggest that autophagy could be regulated through the mTOR pathway in podocytes in both rat models and human. The physiologic level of mTOR activity inhibits autophagy and maintains autophagosomes at a basal level to remove damaged organelles, excessive lipids, and long-lived or misfolded proteins in podocytes. The decrease of growth factor signal or exogenous stimulation such as starvation or rapamycin could inhibit mTOR pathway and upregulate autophagy function (Figure 2B). The activation of autophagy as demonstrated by increase LC3 and Lysotracker markers enhanced autophagosome and autophagolysosomes formation [25]. The renal biopsy study demonstrates that podocyte markers such as synaptopodin, podocin, CD2AP, and nephrin were also decreased after being treated with sirolimus in podocytes [26]. Although the mechanism is not completely understood, the evidence indicates that autophagy plays a major role in maintaining podocyte homeostasis and renal function.

2.3. Autophagy in Renal Tubular Cells

Autophagy is important in proximal tubular cells. Proximal tubular cells consume much energy during electrolyte reabsorption, which requires high lysosomal activity and mitochondrial turnover [27]. The Atg5 deletion in both proximal and distal tubules results in severe tubular damage and renal dysfunction. However, distal tubules only-specific Atg5 knockout mice show no tubular damage and have normal renal functions [20,28,29]. This indicates that autophagy is critical and integral in proximal tubule function while distal tubular cells rely less on autophagy for their homeostasis due to its function being more passive and less energy dependent [30]. The tubular cells are vulnerable to renal toxic agents, such as cisplatin, cyclosporin, and cadmium [3,31]. Autophagy activation protects renal tubular cells from these renal toxic agents and eliminates the damaged proteins and DNA [3,11]. Selective tubular cell *Atg5* and *Atg7* knockout mice develop more severe tubular cells damages and acute kidney injury (AKI) after ischemia-reperfusion injury [30]. Another study that applied PI3K inhibitor 3-MA to reduced autophagosome sequestration, revealed that it can significantly reduce autophagy function and cause more severe elevation of BUN and serum Cr while rapamycin treatments showed the opposite effect after ischemia-reperfusion injury in vivo and in vitro [8] (Figure 2C). Moreover, constant autophagy activations lead to tubular cells atrophy and promote kidney fibrosis. A delicate balance of the autophagy effects will be required to protect the renal proximal tubular cells from nephrotoxicity drugs and ischemic-reperfusion injury [13].

3. Autophagy in Acute Kidney Injury

AKI is a common clinical condition in critical care units. It presents as an abrupt decline of kidney function and imbalance of water, electrolytes, and protein homeostasis [9]. Patients with AKI are associated with higher morbidity and mortality. Major causes of AKI are infections, nephrotoxins, and ischemia-reperfusion injury all inducing inflammation. These diseases will result in direct tubular cell damage, accumulation of oxidative stress (ROS), and endothelium microvasculature dysfunction [9]. Among all, the ischemia-reperfusion injury is considered the most frequent and important etiology that usually causes severe injury to the renal tubular cells [32,33].

3.1. The Kidney Ischemia-Reperfusion Injury and Autophagy

The ischemia-reperfusion injury occurs when an organ is exposed to a prolonged duration of blood flow restriction with subsequent restoration of perfusion. The reoxygenation after ischemia will exacerbate the tissue injury and inflammation response [34]. This pathophysiological process is common in many diseases, such as myocardial infarction [35], ischemic stroke, acute kidney injury, trauma, sleep apnea, hypovolemic shock, surgery, and organ dysfunction after transplantation [34]. After ischemia-reperfusion occurs, reactive oxygen species (ROS) in mitochondria will increase and alter cell cycle, damage DNA, and lead to cell dysfunction and death [36]. These ROS and damaged mitochondria are the major upstream cellular signals for the autophagy during renal injury [37,38]. Previous data suggested that ischemia-reperfusion injury to the renal tubular cells results in upregulating the autophagic activity [20,28]. The accumulation of apoptotic cells also activates the autophagy. The activation of autophagy after ischemia is rapid and proceeds to tissue damages or tubular apoptosis [39]. However, newer evidence suggested that prolonged autophagy activations may have adverse effects after ischemic injury in mice. The persistent autophagy activation may trigger renal cell death pathways and exaggerate the kidney damage [9,20]. Although the exact mechanism responsible for the autophagy activation after AKI is still controversial, the autophagy activation after AKI is crucial for the renal protections after AKI.

3.2. Autophagy Protects the Renal Cells from Acute Injury

Many studies have proven that the autophagy has renoprotective effects on the proximal tubular cells during AKI [37,39]. Deletion of global Atg5 in mice results in a more vulnerable tubular cell phenotype after exposure to hypoxemia and ROS [27]. Mice with the proximal tubules-specific Atg5 knockout exhibits an accumulation of the damaged organelles and proteins in the proximal tubules and irreversible kidney injury [30,40]. The proximal tubule-specific Atg7 knockout mice also have increased renal injuries [31]. Renal protective role of autophagy has also been shown in cisplatin-induced AKI and sepsis-induced AKI. During the resolution phase of the AKI, modulation of autophagy can promote tubular cell regeneration and repair [8,27]. Moreover, the severity of AKI is associated with the possibility to progress to chronic kidney disease (CKD). Around 15% to 20% of patients with AKI advance to end-stage renal disease [41]. It is important to study the role of autophagy affecting the transition from AKI to CKD.

4. Autophagy in Chronic Kidney Disease

The incidence and prevalence of the CKD are increasing in the past two decades [32,42,43]. The CKD is a multifactorial disease with two major causes of CKD being diabetes and hypertension [43]. Other common causes of CKD include glomerulonephritis, polycystic kidney disease, kidney stones, urinary infections, drugs, and nephrotoxins [44]. The increasing prevalence of CKD has become a great burden to the healthcare system worldwide [32,44].

4.1. Pathophysiology

Currently, the exact mechanism of CKD is still unknown. The final common pathway of CKD involves glomerulosclerosis, vascular sclerosis, and tubulointerstitial fibrosis. The progression of the CKD involves complex mechanisms, including glomerular hypertension, renin-angiotensin-aldosterone signaling, podocyte homeostasis, dyslipidemia, tubulointerstitial fibrosis, and genetic factors. Recent advances also show that autophagy has an important role in CKD [45–47]. CKD patients have elevated oxidative stress and increased ROS production in mitochondria in addition to altered body homeostasis, protein aggregation, and inflammation. Autophagy is essential in keeping the balance of body homeostasis and protein recycling. Autophagy activation is critical in inflammatory responses. Moreover, oxidative stress and ROS are both important regulators of autophagy. Clinical data also show that patients with CKD have altered autophagy responses [48].

4.2. Our Previous Research

According to the 2016 guideline for autophagy monitoring, there is no absolute criteria that are applicable in every clinical or experimental context for determining autophagic status. Although some autophagy markers have been used to estimate the autophagic activity in patients, such as increase synthesis or lipidation of LC3 and increase autophagosomes formation [49]. However, it is difficult to measure the exact autophagy flux in clinical settings.

In 2013, we have designed a method to measure the autophagic function in leukocytes from patients. LC3 proteins are involved in phagophore formation and characterized as autophagosome markers. A cytosolic form of LC3 (LC3-I) is conjugated to phosphatidylethanolamine to form LC3-II, which usually reflects the formation of autophagosomes. Previous studies showed that the LC3-I level is very stable during starvation and that the LC3-II level is reflective of changes in the autophagic function and flow. We, therefore, postulated that LC3-I can serve as an ideal control in human leukocytes. The ratio of the 14 kDa LC3-II versus the 16 kDa LC3-I (LC3-II/LC3-I) in leukocytes can serve as an indicator of autophagy flux. The ratio of LC3-II/LC3-I after fasting for 12 h (LC3-II/LC3-I-AC) versus LC3-II/LC3-I 2 h after breakfast (LC3-II/LC3-I-PC) in the same subject can be calculated as γLC3 and regarded as an indicator of autophagy flux or activation. We enrolled 60 patients diagnosed with stages 4–5 CKD (30 with hemodialysis and 30 without hemodialysis), and 30 healthy volunteers as the control group who were sex- and age-matched. In the CKD with hemodialysis group, the blood sample was collected one day after hemodialysis. Using γLC3 as the marker, we have measured the autophagy flux in CKD patients. The isolated LC3-I or LC3-II after fasting or feeding showed no significant associations with healthy subjects and CKD patients with or without hemodialysis. Overnight fasting increased autophagy flux and γLC3 in healthy subjects, which were nearly absent in CKD patients. Moreover, hemodialysis could not correct the autophagy flux deficiency in CKD patients. The *Atg5* and *Beclin-1* transcript levels also increased after starvation in the healthy group, while there were no significant changes in the CKD group. Our data thus provided the direct evidence supporting that CKD patients have impaired autophagy activation and could not be reversed by hemodialysis. The γLC3 was a better autophagic activity indicator then the isolated LC3-I or LC3-II [48].

We also highlighted the relationship between cardiovascular diseases in CKD patients using echocardiography to measure the cardiac functions and structures. The γLC3 was negatively associated with left atrial sizes; changes of the *Atg5* transcript were negatively associated with LVEDD, and; changes of the *Beclin-1* transcript were negatively associated with diastolic mitral inflow E- and A-wave values. The different autophagy markers are associated with different echocardiographic parameters [48]. Because the increased LA size correlates with the increased incidence of atrial fibrillation, stroke, acute myocardial infarction, and congestive heart failure [50], our observation suggested a close relationship of autophagy and CKD-related cardiovascular diseases. The exact mechanism of how CKD has autophagy deficiency is still unclear and will require further studies.

4.3. Diabetic Nephropathy

Diabetic nephropathy is a major cause of CKD and end-stage renal disease worldwide [51,52]. Olivia Lenoir and colleagues have reported that high glucose concentration environs activated autophagy in podocytes and protected the podocytes from hyperglycemia-related apoptosis [47]. Deficiency of autophagy activation by knockout Atg5 in diabetic mice resulted in more severe proteinuria and impaired renal function [52,53]. Impaired autophagy in the kidney also resulted in podocyte loss and massive proteinuria in diabetic nephropathy [54]. Decreased mTORC1 activation in diabetic mice could stimulate autophagy and decrease glomerulosclerosis, proteinuria, and podocyte loss to slow down progression to diabetic nephropathy [55].

However, there were some studies suggesting the opposite effect of high glucose on podocyte. Through CASP3 activation, high glucose lead to podocyte apoptosis [56]. With the high glucose stimulation, human podocytes exhibited a dramatically reduced LC3-II and Beclin-1 and decreased autophagy activation [57]. The controversies are still unsolved, and more evidence is needed for making the conclusion.

Currently, only a few studies have described the relationship between autophagic markers and podocyte-specific proteins. The podocin protein is a key protein of the slit diaphragm of podocytes. In patients with diabetic nephropathy and severe proteinuria, their kidney biopsy samples express podocin with a granular and irregularly scattered pattern under immunofluorescent study, whereas intense accumulation of p62 proteins is presented in glomeruli. In the 50-week-old diabetic nephropathy rats model with massive proteinuria, the podocytes showed a reduction in podocin-positive areas, p62 accumulation, a decrease of LC3-II, and alteration of foot processes. These suggest that the insufficient autophagic function could cause podocytes injury in diabetic nephropathy with severe proteinuria [58].

Autophagy also protects mesangial cells from undergoing apoptosis in diabetic nephropathy after induced by TGF-β1 via TAK1 and PI3K–AKT-dependent pathways [55]. In proximal tubular cells, autophagy activation is reduced by hyperglycemia while p62 is increased in both type 1 and type 2 diabetes animal models [59,60]. Studies indicated that diabetic nephropathy is associated with decreased autophagy activity and increased apoptosis [54,55,61]. These evidence support that autophagy can be a therapeutic target for diabetic nephropathy [60].

4.4. Autoimmune Kidney Disease

Autophagy may regulate autoimmune responses by modulating innate immunity and lymphocyte homeostasis [62]. Several studies have manifested the relationship between autoimmune diseases and autophagy in both animal models and human studies. Autophagy helps to understand the mechanism of autoimmune diseases and open the possible therapeutic strategies in systemic lupus erythematosus (SLE), Sjögren's syndrome, Crohn's disease, rheumatoid arthritis, multiple sclerosis, and type 1 diabetes mellitus. [63,64]. The Lupus nephritis is the most common of all and manifested as severe complications of the SLE. Severe lupus nephritis can lead to end-stage renal disease and is an important predictor of mortality in SLE patients [65]. The lupus nephritis results from complement activation, autoantibody formation, immune complexes formation, and dysfunctional adaptive immune responses. The autophagy interacts with these processes and preserves renal function [66]. Some SLE patients have activated autophagic genes, such as *Atg5* and *Atg7*. They also have increased autophagic vacuoles in B cells, T cells, and macrophage in peripheral blood mononuclear cells [64,67]. Current evidence suggest that lupus nephritis may be associated with renal Epstein–Barr virus infection, which can induce autophagy in B cells in a dose-dependent manner [68,69]. In the mice lupus nephritis model, podocytes exhibit autophagy activation that protects renal function from deterioration. The mice podocytes from lupus nephritis have increased autophagosomes, increased LC3-II/LC3-I ratios, and decreased p62 [70]. The aggregated lupus autoantibodies can assist injured podocytes being degraded by autophagy activation [71]. Several drugs given to SLE patients are mTOR inhibitors which can induce the autophagy activity, suggesting autoimmune diseases are related to autophagy dysfunction and therefore give rise to future possible therapeutic intervention options [64].

4.5. Infection

Severe systemic infection and sepsis induce a cytokine storm and influence multiple tissues and organs including the kidney. Autophagy is up-regulated early after sepsis and protects organs from pathogen by modulating the immune systems and regulating macrophage, dendritic cells, B cells, CD4[+], and CD8[+] T cells functions. [63,72]. Autophagy has been suggested to protect kidneys against septic kidney injury [41,66,73]. In the cecal ligation and puncture mice model, the sepsis induced by the peritoneal infections activates the autophagy. The activated autophagy protects the kidney function by decreasing circulating cytokines and endothelial activation [41]. In a sepsis rat model, the decline of autophagy response is associated with the development of kidney injury. Knockdown of *Atg7* decreases tumor necrosis factor α-related proximal tubular cell death, which can be reversed with rapamycin [73]. Autophagy harbors the capacity to both pro- and anti-inflammatory responses to suppress sepsis-induced kidney injury through regulation of infection and through targeting inflammasome and type I interferon responses [66]. These observations suggest that autophagy may be a therapeutic target to protect kidney injury from sepsis.

4.6. Renal Tubulointerstitial Diseases and Ureter Obstruction

On 2010, Li and colleagues demonstrated that autophagy was significantly activated in a unilateral ureteral obstruction mice model. The conversion of LC3-I to LC3-II, activation of Beclin-1, and accumulation of autophagosomes with massive autophagic vesicles were observed in atrophic tubules with tubulointerstitial injury [74]. Mice with LC3B knockout exhibited a deficit in autophagy activation and severe tubulointerstitial fibrosis after ureter obstruction [75]. The development of tubular atrophy and nephron loss correlated with autophagy in a time-dependent manner [13]. However, persistent activation of autophagy in kidney tubular cells would promote renal interstitial fibrosis through fibroblast growth factor 2 [76]. These studies suggested that the balance of autophagy activation is important in regulating the tubulointerstitial function and renal fibrosis in obstructive kidney disease [27].

4.7. Toxic Effects of Drugs

Nephrotoxicity of many therapeutic medications can cause acute kidney injuries and worsening renal function in patients with CKD. The non-steroidal anti-inflammatory drugs, iodinated contrast medium, and cisplatin are important drugs causing nephrotoxicity related acute kidney injuries. Recently, in vitro studies have shown that iodinated contrast leads to enhancement of mitophagy, and may protect kidneys from iodinated contrast related renal tubular epithelial injury. The mitophagy is one type of the autophagy that can selectively remove the damaged mitochondria [77]. Cisplatin-induced AKI involves multiple mechanisms, including proximal tubular injury, oxidative stress, inflammation, and vascular injury. The injury is predominantly acute tubular necrosis in the proximal tubules [78–80]. Previous studies suggest that the autophagic responses to cisplatin treatment may protect many types of cancer cells and result in cisplatin resistance [78]. Cisplatin also activated autophagy in the proximal tubules with massive autophagosome formation and LC3-II accumulation for protection purpose [79,81]. Also, in proximal tubule-specific Atg5-knockout mice, cisplatin prompted more severe DNA damage and p53 activation, as well as accumulated more protein aggregates in proximal tubules [79,82]. Furthermore, rapamycin, an mTOR inhibitor, could treat the cisplatin-induced AKI in mice to improve renal function [78,79]. Oral anti-diabetic agents, metformin, also activated the autophagy and protected against cisplatin-induced tubular injury by activating autophagy cascades and slowing down the apoptosis of tubular cells [83]. These data indicated that autophagy can protect renal tubule injury against cisplatin [29].

The Adriamycin- and Puromycin aminonucleoside-induced podocyte apoptosis is widely used for studying the pathophysiology of glomerular diseases in vitro and in vivo. The activation of autophagy with rapamycin could suppress the Adriamycin-induced apoptosis while inhibiting autophagy with chloroquine enhanced apoptosis. The podocyte-specific Atg7 knockout mouse model described the aggravated podocyte injury, glomerulopathy, and proteinuria after adriamycin treatment [84]. The upregulation of LC3-positive autophagosomes protects puromycin aminonucleoside-induced nephrosis in rats in vivo and immortalized mouse podocytes in vitro [85]. Puromycin aminonucleoside reduces the autophagy in human podocytes with the activation of mTORC1. When inhibiting autophagy with the 3-methyladenine or chloroquine, the podocyte apoptosis increased significantly along with the elevation of active caspase-3 [86]. The rapamycin activated autophagy led to decreased proteinuria and less severe foot-process effacement [87] (Figure 3). Collectively, this evidence supports autophagy may be an early adaptive cytoprotective mechanism for podocytes under Adriamycin and puromycin aminonucleoside-induced apoptosis intervention.

Although evidence has explicated the relationship between toxin/drug and the autophagy in the kidney, future studies are still necessary to investigate the mechanism of autophagy in many other nephrotoxic agents.

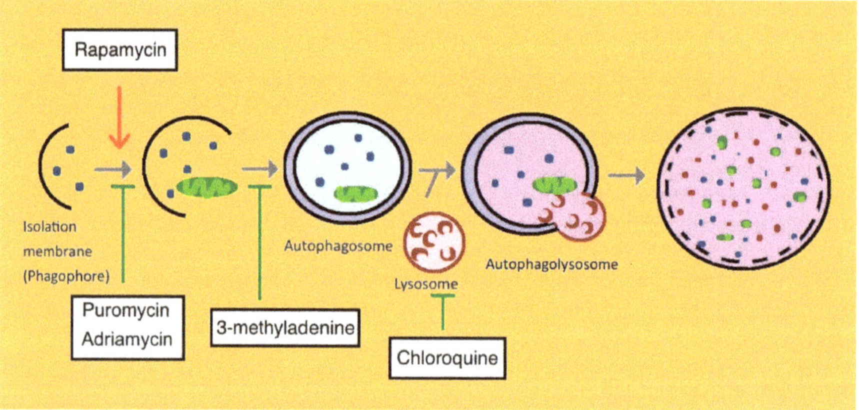

Figure 3. Overview of the different medications that regulate autophagy in different steps, including Rapamycin, Adriamycin, Puromycin, 3-methyladenine and Chloroquine.

4.8. Cystic Disease (Polycystic Kidney Disease)

Autosomal dominant polycystic kidney disease (ADPKD) is one of the most prevalent inherited renal cyst diseases and frequently leads to end-stage renal disease. The main cause of this disease is gene mutation. Approximately 85% of the mutations in ADPKD occur in the *pkd1* gene encoding for polycystin-1, and 10–15% in its interaction partner *pkd2*, encoding for polycystin-2. These ciliary proteins are involved in cellular repair and growth mechanisms [88].

Both in vitro and in vivo studies have shown that multiple autophagic molecular parameters and signaling pathways are involved in ADPKD, including mTOR, cyclic adenosine monophosphate, and several growth factors [89]. The current evidence suggests that autophagy processes may relate to the cystic formation and size growth by activating the mTOR signaling pathway [89,90]. ADPKD is a cilia-related disease and autophagy activation is essential in ciliogenesis [12]. Studies revealed that autophagy regulates cilia length by modulating protein synthesis and degradation. Through modulating autophagy activation, the primary cilium controls epithelial cell volume in a fluid flow dependent manner [91]. The ADPKD exhibiting autophagosome increases with LC3-II and Beclin-1 overexpression in tubular cyst-lining cells, suggesting autophagic flux dysregulation [1]. In a mice model with mutated PKD1 and patients with ADPKD, autophagy activation is impaired [92].

Polycystin-1 negatively regulates polycystin-2 via the autophagosomes-dependent pathway. Failure of pathogenic polycystin-1 mutants to induce this function may lead to ADPKD [93]. All this evidence suggests that the ADPKD may be present with dysfunctional autophagy [1,94]. Currently, the regulation of autophagy in ADPKD is incompletely understood. Autophagy may be one of the therapeutic targets in the future.

4.9. Autophagy in Aging-Associated CKD

Aging is associated with a deterioration and imbalance of the general homeostasis ability, which results in loss of the compensation mechanism in the kidneys. In the elderly population, the prevalence of non-dialysis CKD is markedly higher. The normal aging kidneys exhibit decreases in renal mass, increases in parenchymal tissue fibrosis and fat deposition, and accumulation of glomerular sclerosis [95,96]. Development of CKD is a major risk factor of ESRD in the elderly population. The mortality among the age of 75 with CKD is double compared to the healthy population [97,98].

The podocyte-specific *Atg5* knockout mice develop glomerulopathy gradually during aging. The podocytes without *Atg5* have decreased organelles turnover with the accumulation of ubiquitinated and oxidative protein. The deficiency of autophagy and proteasome pathways leads to proteinuria, loss of podocytes, and development of glomerulosclerosis in aging mice [22]. In aging mice, podocyte-specific autophagy-deficient mice have mild forms of glomerulosclerosis compared with tubular cell-specific autophagy-deficient mice [66]. Yamamoto and colleagues demonstrated that proximal tubule-specific deletion of Atg5 in mice resulted in significant deteriorations of kidney function and fibrosis at 24 months of age [99]. These results indicate that tubular cells play an important role in aging-related autophagy regulation of kidney function. The inability of older mice to recover from AKI has been attributed to an age-dependent loss of autophagy resulting in CKD [41]. These results suggest that autophagy is vital for maintaining kidney tissue homeostasis and aging-associated injury [3].

Caloric restriction has been shown to strongly induce autophagy in kidneys and slow down the process of interstitial fibrosis and tubular atrophy [100]. Moreover, caloric restriction prolongs lifespan in animals and decreases the age-related mitochondrial oxidative damage and the kidney tissue injury by enhancing autophagy [101,102]. Caloric restriction in AKI with rats of different ages suggests that the caloric restriction can significantly increase autophagy activation by increasing LC3-I/LC3-II ratio and improving renal function. The nephroprotection effects gradually decline with the age due to deteriorations of the autophagic system [103]. The mTOR pathway acts as a two-way regulator during starvation and caloric restriction in rat. At first, the mTOR inhibition activates autophagy to form autophagolysosome and breakdown the cellular content for regeneration to further protect the kidney function. However, prolonged starvation will reactivate the mTOR pathway and inhibit autophagy by negative feedback and accumulation of autophagolysosome degradation content. [104]. Therefore, a balanced caloric restriction strategy taking into consideration of the autophagy activation is one of the therapeutic options to delay the progression of CKD among elderly patients [100].

5. Autophagy in Dialysis and Renal Transplantation

The end-stage renal disease is the most severe outcome of CKD and can only be treated with dialysis or renal transplantation. Patients with end-stage renal disease have increased risks of cardiovascular disease, cerebrovascular accident, infection, and cognitive impairment [44].

Until recently, very few studies have investigated the relationship between dialysis and autophagy. Our previous study indicated that autophagy flux could not be rescued by hemodialysis in patients with end-stage renal disease, suggesting that hemodialysis has no role of modulating autophagy [48]. When it comes to peritoneal dialysis (PD), one study suggests that autophagy stimulates the fibrosis and apoptosis in peritoneal mesothelium cells due to long-term exposure to the high-glucose peritoneal dialysis solution. The activation of Beclin 1-dependent autophagy results in decreases of the viability of peritoneal mesothelium cells and finally PD failure [105]. Another study, however, suggests that the PD solution promotes autophagosome formation and decreases cells death to maintain the PD function [106]. Therefore, future studies are required to understand the exact relationship of dialysis and autophagy regulation.

Renal transplantation is considered as the definitive treatment to ESRD. Currently, some evidence supports the connections between autophagy and renal transplantation. The mTOR inhibitor is frequently used in renal transplantation as an immunosuppressant, including rapamycin, sirolimus, and everolimus. Rapamycin inhibits T cell proliferation and activates autophagy to maintain the renal homeostasis [107,108]. Cyclosporine is another immunosuppressive drug commonly used in renal transplantation patients [109]. Cyclosporine induces autophagy in primary cultured renal tubular cells. After treatment of cyclosporine in mice, the kidney proximal tubule cells exhibit an increase in numbers and sizes of autophagosomes and autophagy flow [110]. Deficiency in autophagy function will lead to an exacerbation of cyclosporine-related endoplasmic reticulum stress and renal injury [110,111]. Another indirect clue is that a kidney from elderly donors is now considered to have a higher risk of post-transplant ischemic injury, which may be due to the decline of autophagy activation with aging [107,112].

6. Therapeutic Consideration and Conclusion

Autophagy defects can occur at different stages of the pathway in CKD, and this may influence treatment strategies. Early studies examine the rapamycin through upregulating autophagy to enable the clearance of intracytoplasmic aggregation-prone proteins. Rapamycin is currently the only drug that could be used to target autophagy in CKD treatments. However, the long-term side effects of rapamycin should be taken into consideration [7]. Some studies have used the rapamycin under intermittent dosing protocols in mice that could create pulsatile upregulation of autophagosome formations. This gives us a possible therapeutic regimen to reduce rapamycin side effects in patients.

6.1. Future Therapeutic Considerations

Several candidate drugs targeting autophagy have been shown to inhibit or activate the autophagy function. However, many of them are still under animal trials or early phase clinical trials and are not ready to be used clinically. Some drugs that are used clinically for other diseases also are found to have the potential to regulate autophagy through different autophagic pathways. The psychotropic drug lithium, carbamazepine, and valproic acid can activate autophagy through the phosphatidylinositol signaling pathway. The clonidine and rilmenidine act as the imidazoline receptor agonists to enhance autophagy. Verapamil targets L-type Ca^{2+} channels to modulate autophagic flux. Metformin upregulates AMPK signaling and induces autophagy function. In contrary, chloroquine is a lysosomotropic agent that inhibits autophagosome-lysosome fusion and lead to autophagy downregulation [113]. Ultimately, whether autophagy represents a useful target in CKD prevention or treatment will need to be addressed by conducting clinical trials in patients in the future.

6.2. Conclusions

We summarize the autophagy pathophysiology in chronic kidney disease (Figure 4). The exposure of normal kidneys to selective stresses, such as ischemic-reperfusion injury, toxin, and sepsis, will result in acute kidney injury, ROS accumulation, and autophagy activation. The protective mechanisms of autophagy take place in podocytes, mesangial cells, and tubular cells, help repair and regenerate the damaged kidneys. After several episodes of stresses, the balancing by the autophagic repair mechanism cannot keep up and CKD ensues. Different CKDs also modulate autophagy in diverse pathways and help to slow down the progression to ESRD as in Table 1.

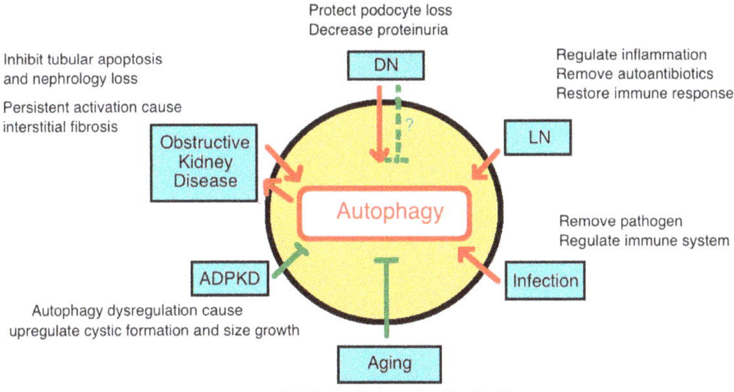

Figure 4. Diagram depicting the roles of autophagy in various chronic kidney disease. DN: diabetic nephropathy; LN: lupus nephropathy; APCKD: adult polycystic kidney disease.

Table 1. Overview of the autophagy in chronic kidney diseases (CKD).

CKD Categories		Reference
	Increase	
Diabetes Nephropathy (DN)	• High glucose environment activates autophagy in podocytes	[47]
	• *Atg5* knockout mice with DM result in more severe proteinuria and renal failure	[52,53]
	• Reduced mTORC1 activation stimulates autophagy and protects DN progression	[55]
	• DN activates TGF-β1 via TAK1 and PI3K–AKT-dependent pathways and protects mesangial cells from apoptosis	[55]
	Decrease	
	• High glucose activates CASP3 and leads to podocyte apoptosis	[56]
	• High glucose reduces LC3-II and Beclin-1 in podocytes and decreases autophagy activity	[57]
	• High glucose reduces autophagy activity in proximal tubular cells	[59,60]
	• DN decreases autophagy activity and increase apoptosis	[54,55,61]
	Increase	
Lupus nephritis (LN)	• SLE activates autophagic genes (*Atg5* and *Atg7*) and increases autophagic vacuoles in B cells, T cells and macrophage in peripheral blood mononuclear cells	[64,67]
	• EBV related LN induces autophagy in B cells in a dose-dependent manner	[68,69]
	• Podocytes increase autophagosomes, increase LC3-II/LC3-I ratios, and decrease p62 to protect renal function	[70]
	• mTOR inhibitor improves LN by inducing autophagy activity	[64]
	Increase	
Infection	• Early autophagy up-regulation after infection modulates the immune system and regulates immune cells function including macrophage, dendritic cells, B cells and CD4+, and CD8+ T cells.	[63,72]
	• Cecal ligation and puncture mice model activates autophagy to protect renal function	[41]
	• *Atg7* knockout mice increase tumor necrosis factor-α promote tubular cells death. Rapamycin may reverse the effect.	[73]
	• Autophagy regulates infection through targeting inflammasome and type I interferon responses	[66]

Table 1. *Cont.*

CKD Categories		Reference
	Protect	
Tubulointerstitial injury	• UUO increases conversion of LC3-I to LC3-II, activation of Beclin-1, and accumulation of autophagosomes	[74]
	• LC3B knockout mice have more severe tubulointerstitial injury	[75]
	• Tubular atrophy and nephron loss correlate with autophagy in a time-dependent manner	[13]
	Damage	
	• Persistent activation of autophagy promotes interstitial fibrosis through fibroblast growth factor 2	[75]
	Iodinated contrast	
	• Enhance mitophagy protects kidneys from tubular epithelial injury	[77]
	Cisplatin	
Toxic/Drugs	• Autophagic activation protects some cancer cells and results in cisplatin resistance	[78]
	• Cisplatin activates autophagy in the proximal tubules with autophagosome formation and LC3-II accumulation	[79,81]
	• *Atg5* deficiency results in more severe tubular damage and can be reversed by rapamycin	[78,79,82]
	• Metformin increases autophagy and protects renal from cisplatin-induced tubular injury	[83]
	• Adriamycin/Puromycin aminonucleoside	
	• Adriamycin and Puromycin aminonucleoside activate mTOR pathway to inhibit autophagy causing podocyte apoptosis	[84,85]
Autosomal dominant polycystic kidney disease (ADPKD)	**Dysregulation**	
	• Autophagy is related to the cystic formation and size growth by activating the mTOR signaling pathway. Autophagy regulates cilia length by modulating protein synthesis and degradation	[89–91]
	• Increased autophagosome formation and LC3-II/Beclin-1 overexpression in tubular cyst-lining cells;ADPKD may present with dysfunctional autophagy	[1,94]
Aging-Associated CKD	**Deficiency**	
	• Autophagy deficiency leads to proteinuria, loss of podocytes, and development of glomerulosclerosis in aging mice	[22]
	• Proximal tubule-specific *Atg5* deletion mice result in significant deteriorations of kidney function and fibrosis at 24 months of age	[99]
	• Inability of older mice to recover from AKI in an age-dependent manner	[41]
	• Caloric restriction prolongs lifespan and decreases kidney tissue injury by enhancing autophagy	[101,102]

At the turning point of autophagy research in the early 1990s with the identification of the autophagy-related gene, many researchers have devoted their efforts to finding the potential therapeutic use of autophagy in human diseases. The relationships between autophagy and kidney diseases are well-founded, but there is still no clinically useable agent targeting the autophagic pathway for patients with CKD or AKI. The complex nature of CKD or AKI further complicates the development of therapeutic advancement. The evidence from mice or cells have provided us with comprehensive mechanistic insights into the etiology and pathophysiology of the disease. Since autophagic machinery has a vital role in controlling immunity, it will be crucial for clinicians to monitor the occurrence of infection and autoimmune diseases with autophagy inducers or inhibitors [104]. Besides, inhibition or activation of the autophagy will impact multiple aspects of organism physiology with various effects [114–116]. Therefore, it is necessary to take these diverse interactions into consideration when developing autophagy-targeting drugs. In the end, medications developed by tackling these mechanistic pathways still require prospective and randomized trials to verify their therapeutic potentials and adverse events when administered in humans.

Author Contributions: T.-A.L. and C.-Y.W. construct the manuscript structure and wrote the manuscript. V.C.-C.W. proofread and polished the manuscript.

Funding: C.Y.W. received support from the National Health Research Institute (NHRI-EX106-10617SI), National Science Council (105-2628-B-182-009-MY4), and Chang Gung Memorial Hospital (CMRPG3H0131, CMRPG3H0271, CMRPG3I0321, and CMRPG3H0841).

Conflicts of Interest: The authors declare no conflict of interest.

References

1. De Rechter, S.; Decuypere, J.P.; Ivanova, E.; van den Heuvel, L.P.; De Smedt, H.; Levtchenko, E.; Mekahli, D. Autophagy in renal diseases. *Pediatr. Nephrol.* **2016**, *31*, 737–752. [CrossRef] [PubMed]
2. Parzych, K.R.; Klionsky, D.J. An overview of autophagy: Morphology, mechanism, and regulation. *Antioxid. Redox Signal.* **2014**, *20*, 460–473. [CrossRef] [PubMed]
3. Wang, Z.; Choi, M.E. Autophagy in kidney health and disease. *Antioxid. Redox Signal.* **2014**, *20*, 519–537. [CrossRef] [PubMed]
4. Ohsumi, Y. Historical landmarks of autophagy research. *Cell. Res.* **2014**, *24*, 9–23. [CrossRef]
5. Choi, A.M.; Ryter, S.W.; Levine, B. Autophagy in human health and disease. *N. Engl. J. Med.* **2013**, *368*, 651–662. [CrossRef]
6. Takeshige, K.; Baba, M.; Tsuboi, S.; Noda, T.; Ohsumi, Y. Autophagy in Yeast Demonstrated with Proteinase-deficient Mutants and Conditions for its Induction. *J. Cell Biol.* **1992**, *119*, 301–311. [CrossRef]
7. Cheng, Y.; Ren, X.; Hait, W.N.; Yang, J.M. Therapeutic targeting of autophagy in disease: Biology and pharmacology. *Pharmacol. Rev.* **2013**, *65*, 1162–1197. [CrossRef] [PubMed]
8. Guan, X.; Qian, Y.; Shen, Y.; Zhang, L.; Du, Y.; Dai, H.; Qian, J.; Yan, Y. Autophagy protects renal tubular cells against ischemia/reperfusion injury in a time-dependent manner. *Cell. Physiol. Biochem.* **2015**, *36*, 285–298. [CrossRef]
9. Duann, P.; Lianos, E.A.; Ma, J.; Lin, P.H. Autophagy, Innate Immunity and Tissue Repair in Acute Kidney Injury. *Int. J. Mol. Sci.* **2016**, *17*, 662. [CrossRef] [PubMed]
10. Shintani, T.; Klionsky, D.J. Autophagy in health and disease: A double-edged sword. *Science* **2004**, *306*, 990–995. [CrossRef] [PubMed]
11. Mehrpour, M.; Esclatine, A.; Beau, I.; Codogno, P. Autophagy in health and disease. 1. Regulation and significance of autophagy: An overview. *Am. J. Physiol. Cell Physiol.* **2010**, *298*, C776–C785. [CrossRef] [PubMed]
12. Lenoir, O.; Tharaux, P.L.; Huber, T.B. Autophagy in kidney disease and aging: Lessons from rodent models. *Kidney Int.* **2016**, *90*, 950–964. [CrossRef]
13. He, L.; Livingston, M.J.; Dong, Z. Autophagy in acute kidney injury and repair. *Nephron Clin. Pract.* **2014**, *127*, 56–60. [CrossRef]
14. Hartleben, B.; Godel, M.; Meyer-Schwesinger, C.; Liu, S.; Ulrich, T.; Kobler, S.; Wiech, T.; Grahammer, F.; Arnold, S.J.; Lindenmeyer, M.T.; et al. Autophagy influences glomerular disease susceptibility and maintains podocyte homeostasis in aging mice. *J. Clin. Investig.* **2010**, *120*, 1084–1096. [CrossRef] [PubMed]
15. Angoorani, P.; Ejtahed, H.S.; Mirmiran, P.; Mirzaei, S.; Azizi, F. Dietary consumption of advanced glycation end products and risk of metabolic syndrome. *Int. J. Food Sci. Nutr.* **2016**, *67*, 170–176. [CrossRef] [PubMed]
16. Chiang, C.K.; Wang, C.C.; Lu, T.F.; Huang, K.H.; Sheu, M.L.; Liu, S.H.; Hung, K.Y. Involvement of Endoplasmic Reticulum Stress, Autophagy, and Apoptosis in Advanced Glycation End Products-Induced Glomerular Mesangial Cell Injury. *Sci. Rep.* **2016**, *6*, 34167. [CrossRef]
17. Hou, X.; Hu, Z.; Xu, H.; Xu, J.; Zhang, S.; Zhong, Y.; He, X.; Wang, N. Advanced glycation endproducts trigger autophagy in cadiomyocyte via RAGE/PI3K/AKT/mTOR pathway. *Cardiovasc. Diabetol.* **2014**, *13*, 78. [CrossRef] [PubMed]
18. Wang, S.H.; Shih, Y.L.; Ko, W.C.; Wei, Y.H.; Shih, C.M. Cadmium-induced autophagy and apoptosis are mediated by a calcium signaling pathway. *Cell. Mol. Life Sci.* **2008**, *65*, 3640–3652. [CrossRef]
19. Nagata, M. Podocyte injury and its consequences. *Kidney Int.* **2016**, *89*, 1221–1230. [CrossRef]

20. Decuypere, J.P.; Ceulemans, L.J.; Agostinis, P.; Monbaliu, D.; Naesens, M.; Pirenne, J.; Jochmans, I. Autophagy and the Kidney: Implications for Ischemia-Reperfusion Injury and Therapy. *Am. J. Kidney Dis.* **2015**, *66*, 699–709. [CrossRef]

21. Kreidberg, J.A. Podocyte Differentiation and Glomerulogenesis. *J. Am. Soc. Nephrol.* **2013**, *14*, 806–814. [CrossRef]

22. Wharram, B.L.; Goyal, M.; Wiggins, J.E.; Sanden, S.K.; Hussain, S.; Filipiak, W.E.; Saunders, T.L.; Dysko, R.C.; Kohno, K.; Holzman, L.B.; et al. Podocyte depletion causes glomerulosclerosis: Diphtheria toxin-induced podocyte depletion in rats expressing human diphtheria toxin receptor transgene. *J. Am. Soc. Nephrol.* **2005**, *16*, 2941–2952. [CrossRef] [PubMed]

23. Sato, S.; Yanagihara, T.; Ghazizadeh, M.; Ishizaki, M.; Adachi, A.; Sasaki, Y.; Igarashi, T.; Fukunaga, Y. Correlation of Autophagy Type in Podocytes with Histopathological Diagnosis of IgA Nephropathy. *Pathobiology* **2009**, *76*, 221–226. [CrossRef] [PubMed]

24. Andrade, L.; Rodrigues, C.E.; Gomes, S.A.; Noronha, I.L. Acute Kidney Injury as a Condition of Renal Senescence. *Cell Transplant.* **2018**, *27*, 739–753. [CrossRef] [PubMed]

25. Cina, D.P.; Onay, T.; Paltoo, A.; Li, C.; Maezawa, Y.; De Arteaga, J.; Jurisicova, A.; Quaggin, S.E. Inhibition of MTOR disrupts autophagic flux in podocytes. *J. Am. Soc. Nephrol.* **2012**, *23*, 412–420. [CrossRef]

26. Stallone, G.; Infante, B.; Pontrelli, P.; Gigante, M.; Montemurno, E.; Loverre, A.; Rossini, M.; Schena, F.P.; Grandaliano, G.; Gesualdo, L. Sirolimus and proteinuria in renal transplant patients: Evidence for a dose-dependent effect on slit diaphragm-associated proteins. *Transplantation* **2011**, *91*, 997–1004. [CrossRef]

27. Lin, F. Autophagy in renal tubular injury and repair. *Acta Physiol.* **2017**, *220*, 229–237. [CrossRef]

28. Liu, S.; Hartleben, B.; Kretz, O.; Wiech, T.; Igarashi, P.; Mizushima, N.; Walz, G.; Huber, T.B. Autophagy plays a critical role in kidney tubule maintenance, aging and ischemia-reperfusion injury. *Autophagy* **2012**, *8*, 826–837. [CrossRef]

29. Li, L.; Wang, Z.V.; Hill, J.A.; Lin, F. New Autophagy Reporter Mice Reveal Dynamics of Proximal Tubular Autophagy. *J. Am. Soc. Nephrol.* **2013**, *25*, 305–315. [CrossRef]

30. Kimura, T.; Takabatake, Y.; Takahashi, A.; Kaimori, J.Y.; Matsui, I.; Namba, T.; Kitamura, H.; Niimura, F.; Matsusaka, T.; Soga, T.; et al. Autophagy protects the proximal tubule from degeneration and acute ischemic injury. *J. Am. Soc. Nephrol.* **2011**, *22*, 902–913. [CrossRef]

31. Jiang, M.; Wei, Q.; Dong, G.; Komatsu, M.; Su, Y.; Dong, Z. Autophagy in proximal tubules protects against acute kidney injury. *Kidney Int.* **2012**, *82*, 1271–1283. [CrossRef] [PubMed]

32. He, L.; Wei, Q.; Liu, J.; Yi, M.; Liu, Y.; Liu, H.; Sun, L.; Peng, Y.; Liu, F.; Venkatachalam, M.A.; et al. AKI on CKD: Heightened injury, suppressed repair, and the underlying mechanisms. *Kidney Int.* **2017**, *92*, 1071–1083. [CrossRef] [PubMed]

33. Sureshbabu, A.; Ryter, S.W.; Choi, M.E. Oxidative stress and autophagy: Crucial modulators of kidney injury. *Redox Biol.* **2015**, *4*, 208–214. [CrossRef]

34. Eltzschig, H.K.; Eckle, T. Ischemia and reperfusion—from mechanism to translation. *Nat. Med.* **2011**, *17*, 1391–1401. [CrossRef]

35. Raedschelders, K.; Ansley, D.M.; Chen, D.D. The cellular and molecular origin of reactive oxygen species generation during myocardial ischemia and reperfusion. *Pharmacol. Ther.* **2012**, *133*, 230–255. [CrossRef]

36. Martin, J.L.; Gruszczyk, A.V.; Beach, T.E.; Murphy, M.P.; Saeb-Parsy, K. Mitochondrial mechanisms and therapeutics in ischaemia reperfusion injury. *Pediatr. Nephrol.* **2018**, 1–8. [CrossRef]

37. Melk, A.; Baisantry, A.; Schmitt, R. The yin and yang of autophagy in acute kidney injury. *Autophagy* **2016**, *12*, 596–597. [CrossRef]

38. Wang, Y.; Nartiss, Y.; Steipe, B.; McQuibban, G.A.; Kim, P.K. ROS-induced mitochondrial depolarization initiates PARK2/PARKIN-dependent mitochondrial degradation by autophagy. *Autophagy* **2012**, *8*, 1462–1476. [CrossRef]

39. Jiang, M.; Liu, K.; Luo, J.; Dong, Z. Autophagy is a renoprotective mechanism during in vitro hypoxia and in vivo ischemia-reperfusion injury. *Am. J. Pathol.* **2010**, *176*, 1181–1192. [CrossRef] [PubMed]

40. Kimura, T.; Takahashi, A.; Takabatake, Y.; Namba, T.; Yamamoto, T.; Kaimori, J.Y.; Matsui, I.; Kitamura, H.; Niimura, F.; Matsusaka, T.; et al. Autophagy protects kidney proximal tubule epithelial cells from mitochondrial metabolic stress. *Autophagy* **2013**, *9*, 1876–1886. [CrossRef] [PubMed]

41. Kaushal, G.P.; Shah, S.V. Autophagy in acute kidney injury. *Kidney Int.* **2016**, *89*, 779–791. [CrossRef] [PubMed]

42. Coresh, J.; Byrd-Holt, D.; Astor, B.C.; Briggs, J.P.; Eggers, P.W.; Lacher, D.A.; Hostetter, T.H. Chronic kidney disease awareness, prevalence, and trends among U.S. adults, 1999 to 2000. *J. Am. Soc. Nephrol.* **2005**, *16*, 180–188. [CrossRef] [PubMed]

43. Hill, N.R.; Fatoba, S.T.; Oke, J.L.; Hirst, J.A.; O'Callaghan, C.A.; Lasserson, D.S.; Hobbs, F.D. Global Prevalence of Chronic Kidney Disease—A Systematic Review and Meta-Analysis. *PLoS ONE* **2016**, *11*, e0158765. [CrossRef]

44. Levey, A.S.; Coresh, J. Chronic kidney disease. *Lancet* **2012**, *379*, 165–180. [CrossRef]

45. Song, Y.; Tao, Q.; Yu, L.; Li, L.; Bai, T.; Song, X.; Hu, H.; Li, Y.; Tan, X. Activation of autophagy contributes to the renoprotective effect of postconditioning on acute kidney injury and renal fibrosis. *Biochem. Biophys. Res. Commun.* **2018**, *504*, 641–646. [CrossRef] [PubMed]

46. Leventhal, J.S.; Wyatt, C.M.; Ross, M.J. Recycling to discover something new: The role of autophagy in kidney disease. *Kidney Int.* **2017**, *91*, 4–6. [CrossRef] [PubMed]

47. Lenoir, O.; Jasiek, M.; Henique, C.; Guyonnet, L.; Hartleben, B.; Bork, T.; Chipont, A.; Flosseau, K.; Bensaada, I.; Schmitt, A.; et al. Endothelial cell and podocyte autophagy synergistically protect from diabetes-induced glomerulosclerosis. *Autophagy* **2015**, *11*, 1130–1145. [CrossRef]

48. Chen, W.T.; Hung, K.C.; Wen, M.S.; Hsu, P.Y.; Chen, T.H.; Wang, H.D.; Fang, J.T.; Shie, S.S.; Wang, C.Y. Impaired leukocytes autophagy in chronic kidney disease patients. *Cardiorenal Med.* **2013**, *3*, 254–264. [CrossRef] [PubMed]

49. Klionsky, D.J.; Abdelmohsen, K.; Abe, A.; Abedin, M.J.; Abeliovich, H.; Acevedo Arozena, A.; Adachi, H.; Adams, C.M.; Adams, P.D.; Adeli, K.; et al. Guidelines for the use and interpretation of assays for monitoring autophagy (3rd edition). *Autophagy* **2016**, *12*, 1–222. [CrossRef]

50. Blume, G.G.; Mcleod, C.J.; Barnes, M.E.; Seward, J.B.; Pellikka, P.A.; Bastiansen, P.M.; Tsang, T.S. Left atrial function: Physiology, assessment, and clinical implications. *Eur. J. Echocardiogr.* **2011**, *12*, 421–430. [CrossRef]

51. Dai, H.; Liu, Q.; Liu, B. Research Progress on Mechanism of Podocyte Depletion in Diabetic Nephropathy. *J. Diabetes Res.* **2017**, *2017*, 2615286. [CrossRef]

52. Liu, N.; Xu, L.; Shi, Y.; Zhuang, S. Podocyte Autophagy: A Potential Therapeutic Target to Prevent the Progression of Diabetic Nephropathy. *J. Diabetes Res.* **2017**, *2017*, 3560238. [CrossRef] [PubMed]

53. Ma, T.; Zhu, J.; Chen, X.; Zha, D.; Singhal, P.C.; Ding, G. High glucose induces autophagy in podocytes. *Exp. Cell. Res.* **2013**, *319*, 779–789. [CrossRef] [PubMed]

54. Yasuda-Yamahara, M.; Kume, S.; Tagawa, A.; Maegawa, H.; Uzu, T. Emerging role of podocyte autophagy in the progression of diabetic nephropathy. *Autophagy* **2015**, *11*, 2385–2386. [CrossRef] [PubMed]

55. Ding, Y.; Choi, M.E. Autophagy in diabetic nephropathy. *J. Endocrinol.* **2015**, *224*, R15–R30. [CrossRef]

56. Susztak, K.; Raff, A.C.; Schiffer, M.; Böttinger, E.P. Glucose-Induced Reactive Oxygen Species Cause Apoptosis of Podocytes and Podocyte Depletion at the Onset of Diabetic Nephropathy. *Diabetes* **2006**, *55*, 225–233. [CrossRef]

57. Xin, W.; Li, Z.; Xu, Y.; Yu, Y.; Zhou, Q.; Chen, L.; Wan, Q. Autophagy protects human podocytes from high glucose-induced injury by preventing insulin resistance. *Metabolism* **2016**, *65*, 1307–1315. [CrossRef]

58. Tagawa, A.; Yasuda, M.; Kume, S.; Yamahara, K.; Nakazawa, J.; Chin-Kanasaki, M.; Araki, H.; Araki, S.; Koya, D.; Asanuma, K.; et al. Impaired Podocyte Autophagy Exacerbates Proteinuria in Diabetic Nephropathy. *Diabetes* **2016**, *65*, 755–767. [CrossRef]

59. Kitada, M.; Takeda, A.; Nagai, T.; Ito, H.; Kanasaki, K.; Koya, D. Dietary restriction ameliorates diabetic nephropathy through anti-inflammatory effects and regulation of the autophagy via restoration of Sirt1 in diabetic Wistar fatty (fa/fa) rats: A model of type 2 diabetes. *Exp. Diabetes Res.* **2011**, *2011*, 908185. [CrossRef]

60. Kitada, M.; Ogura, Y.; Monno, I.; Koya, D. Regulating Autophagy as a Therapeutic Target for Diabetic Nephropathy. *Curr. Diabetes Rep.* **2017**, *17*, 53. [CrossRef]

61. Yamahara, K.; Kume, S.; Koya, D.; Tanaka, Y.; Morita, Y.; Chin-Kanasaki, M.; Araki, H.; Isshiki, K.; Araki, S.; Haneda, M.; et al. Obesity-mediated autophagy insufficiency exacerbates proteinuria-induced tubulointerstitial lesions. *J. Am. Soc. Nephrol.* **2013**, *24*, 1769–1781. [CrossRef]

62. Martinez, J.; Cunha, L.D.; Park, S.; Yang, M.; Lu, Q.; Orchard, R.; Li, Q.Z.; Yan, M.; Janke, L.; Guy, C.; et al. Noncanonical autophagy inhibits the autoinflammatory, lupus-like response to dying cells. *Nature* **2016**, *533*, 115–119. [CrossRef] [PubMed]

63. Zhou, X.J.; Zhang, H. Autophagy in immunity: Implications in etiology of autoimmune/autoinflammatory diseases. *Autophagy* **2012**, *8*, 1286–1299. [CrossRef] [PubMed]

64. Bonam, S.R.; Wang, F.; Muller, S. Autophagy: A new concept in autoimmunity regulation and a novel therapeutic option. *J. Autoimmun.* **2018**, *94*, 16–32. [CrossRef] [PubMed]

65. Maroz, N.; Segal, M.S. Lupus Nephritis and End-stage Kidney Disease. *Am. J. Med. Sci.* **2013**, *346*, 319–323. [CrossRef]

66. Kimura, T.; Isaka, Y.; Yoshimori, T. Autophagy and kidney inflammation. *Autophagy* **2017**, *13*, 997–1003. [CrossRef]

67. Leung, C.S.; Haigh, T.A.; Mackay, L.K.; Rickinson, A.B.; Taylor, G.S. Nuclear location of an endogenously expressed antigen, EBNA1, restricts access to macroautophagy and the range of CD4 epitope display. *Proc. Natl. Acad. Sci. USA* **2010**, *107*, 2165–2170. [CrossRef]

68. Lee, D.Y.; Sugden, B. The latent membrane protein 1 oncogene modifies B-cell physiology by regulating autophagy. *Oncogene* **2008**, *27*, 2833–2842. [CrossRef]

69. Leventhal, J.S.; Ross, M.J. LAPping up dead cells to prevent lupus nephritis: A novel role for noncanonical autophagy in autoimmunity. *Kidney Int.* **2016**, *90*, 238–239. [CrossRef] [PubMed]

70. Jin, J.; Ye, M.; Zhao, L.; Zou, W.; Shen, W.; Zhang, H.; Gong, J.; He, Q. The novel involvement of podocyte autophagic activity in the pathogenesis of lupus nephritis. *Histol. Histopathol.* **2018**, *33*, 803–814.

71. Wang, L.; Law, H.K. The Role of Autophagy in Lupus Nephritis. *Int. J. Mol. Sci.* **2015**, *16*, 25154–25167. [CrossRef] [PubMed]

72. Ren, C.; Zhang, H.; Wu, T.T.; Yao, Y.M. Autophagy: A Potential Therapeutic Target for Reversing Sepsis-Induced Immunosuppression. *Front. Immunol.* **2017**, *8*, 1832. [CrossRef] [PubMed]

73. Hsiao, H.W.; Tsai, K.L.; Wang, L.F.; Chen, Y.H.; Chiang, P.C.; Chuang, S.M.; Hsu, C. The decline of autophagy contributes to proximal tubular dysfunction during sepsis. *Shock* **2012**, *37*, 289–296. [CrossRef]

74. Li, L.; Zepeda-Orozco, D.; Black, R.; Lin, F. Autophagy is a component of epithelial cell fate in obstructive uropathy. *Am. J. Pathol.* **2010**, *176*, 1767–1778. [CrossRef]

75. Ding, Y.; Kim, S.L.; Lee, S.Y.; Koo, J.K.; Wang, Z.; Choi, M.E. Autophagy Regulates TGF- Expression and Suppresses Kidney Fibrosis Induced by Unilateral Ureteral Obstruction. *J. Am. Soc. Nephrol.* **2014**, *25*, 2835–2846. [CrossRef] [PubMed]

76. Livingston, M.J.; Ding, H.F.; Huang, S.; Hill, J.A.; Yin, X.M.; Dong, Z. Persistent activation of autophagy in kidney tubular cells promotes renal interstitial fibrosis during unilateral ureteral obstruction. *Autophagy* **2016**, *12*, 976–998. [CrossRef] [PubMed]

77. Lei, R.; Zhao, F.; Tang, C.Y.; Luo, M.; Yang, S.K.; Cheng, W.; Li, X.W.; Duan, S.B. Mitophagy Plays a Protective Role in Iodinated Contrast-Induced Acute Renal Tubular Epithelial Cells Injury. *Cell. Physiol. Biochem.* **2018**, *46*, 975–985. [CrossRef] [PubMed]

78. Yang, C.; Kaushal, V.; Shah, S.V.; Kaushal, G.P. Autophagy is associated with apoptosis in cisplatin injury to renal tubular epithelial cells. *Am. J. Physiol. Renal Physiol.* **2008**, *294*, F777–F787. [CrossRef]

79. Inoue, K.; Kuwana, H.; Shimamura, Y.; Ogata, K.; Taniguchi, Y.; Kagawa, T.; Horino, T.; Takao, T.; Morita, T.; Sasaki, S.; et al. Cisplatin-induced macroautophagy occurs prior to apoptosis in proximal tubules in vivo. *Clin. Exp. Nephrol.* **2010**, *14*, 112–122. [CrossRef]

80. Ning, Y.; Shi, Y.; Chen, J.; Song, N.; Cai, J.; Fang, Y.; Yu, X.; Ji, J.; Ding, X. Necrostatin-1 Attenuates Cisplatin-Induced Nephrotoxicity Through Suppression of Apoptosis and Oxidative Stress and Retains Klotho Expression. *Front. Pharmacol.* **2018**, *9*, 384. [CrossRef]

81. Liu, J.; Livingston, M.J.; Dong, G.; Tang, C.; Su, Y.; Wu, G.; Yin, X.M.; Dong, Z. Histone deacetylase inhibitors protect against cisplatin-induced acute kidney injury by activating autophagy in proximal tubular cells. *Cell Death Dis.* **2018**, *9*, 322. [CrossRef] [PubMed]

82. Takahashi, A.; Kimura, T.; Takabatake, Y.; Namba, T.; Kaimori, J.; Kitamura, H.; Matsui, I.; Niimura, F.; Matsusaka, T.; Fujita, N.; et al. Autophagy guards against cisplatin-induced acute kidney injury. *Am. J. Pathol.* **2012**, *180*, 517–525. [CrossRef] [PubMed]

83. Li, J.; Gui, Y.; Ren, J.; Liu, X.; Feng, Y.; Zeng, Z.; He, W.; Yang, J.; Dai, C. Metformin Protects Against Cisplatin-Induced Tubular Cell Apoptosis and Acute Kidney Injury via AMPKalpha-regulated Autophagy Induction. *Sci. Rep.* **2016**, *6*, 23975. [CrossRef] [PubMed]

84. Yi, M.; Zhang, L.; Liu, Y.; Livingston, MJ.; Chen, JK.; Nahman NS, Jr.; Liu, F.; Dong, Z. Autophagy is activated to protect against podocyte injury in adriamycin-induced nephropathy. *Am. J. Physiol. Renal Physiol.* **2017**, *313*, F74–F84. [CrossRef]

85. Asanuma, K.; Tanida, I.; Shirato, I.; Ueno, T.; Takahara, H.; Nishitani, T.; Kominami, E.; Tomino, Y. MAP-LC3, a promising autophagosomal marker, is processed during the differentiation and recovery of podocytes from PAN nephrosis. *FASEB J.* **2003**, *17*, 1165–1167. [CrossRef] [PubMed]

86. Kang, Y.L.; Saleem, M.A.; Chan, K.W.; Yung, B.Y.; Law, H.K. The cytoprotective role of autophagy in puromycin aminonucleoside treated human podocytes. *Biochem. Biophys. Res. Commun.* **2014**, *443*, 628–634. [CrossRef] [PubMed]

87. Zeng, C.; Fan, Y.; Wu, J.; Shi, S.; Chen, Z.; Zhong, Y.; Zhang, C.; Zen, K.; Liu, Z. Podocyte autophagic activity plays a protective role in renal injury and delays the progression of podocytopathies. *J. Pathol.* **2014**, *234*, 203–213. [CrossRef] [PubMed]

88. Peintner, L.; Borner, C. Role of apoptosis in the development of autosomal dominant polycystic kidney disease (ADPKD). *Cell Tissue Res.* **2017**, *369*, 27–39. [CrossRef]

89. Ravichandran, K.; Edelstein, C.L. Polycystic kidney disease: A case of suppressed autophagy? *Semin. Nephrol.* **2014**, *34*, 27–33. [CrossRef]

90. Distefano, G.; Boca, M.; Rowe, I.; Wodarczyk, C.; Ma, L.; Piontek, K.B.; Germino, G.G.; Pandolfi, P.P.; Boletta, A. Polycystin-1 regulates extracellular signal-regulated kinase-dependent phosphorylation of tuberin to control cell size through mTOR and its downstream effectors S6K and 4EBP1. *Mol. Cell. Biol.* **2009**, *29*, 2359–2371. [CrossRef]

91. Chang, M.Y.; Ong, A.C.M. Targeting new cellular disease pathways in autosomal dominant polycystic kidney disease. *Nephrol. Dial. Transplant.* **2017**, *33*, 1310–1316. [CrossRef] [PubMed]

92. Rowe, I.; Chiaravalli, M.; Mannella, V.; Ulisse, V.; Quilici, G.; Pema, M.; Song, X.W.; Xu, H.; Mari, S.; Qian, F.; et al. Defective glucose metabolism in polycystic kidney disease identifies a new therapeutic strategy. *Nat. Med.* **2013**, *19*, 488–493. [CrossRef]

93. Cebotaru, V.; Cebotaru, L.; Kim, H.; Chiaravalli, M.; Boletta, A.; Qian, F.; Guggino, W.B. Polycystin-1 Negatively Regulates Polycystin-2 Expression via the Aggresome/Autophagosome Pathway. *J. Biol. Chem.* **2014**, *289*, 6404–6414. [CrossRef] [PubMed]

94. Zhu, P.; Sieben, C.J.; Xu, X.; Harris, P.C.; Lin, X. Autophagy activators suppress cystogenesis in an autosomal dominant polycystic kidney disease model. *Hum. Mol. Genet.* **2017**, *26*, 158–172. [CrossRef] [PubMed]

95. Nyengaard, J.R.; Bendtsen, T.F. Glomerular number and size in relation to age, kidney weight, and body surface in normal man. *Anat. Rec.* **1992**, *232*, 194–201. [CrossRef]

96. Wang, X.; Bonventre, J.V.; Parrish, A.R. The aging kidney: Increased susceptibility to nephrotoxicity. *Int. J. Mol. Sci.* **2014**, *15*, 15358–15376. [CrossRef] [PubMed]

97. De Nicola, L.; Minutolo, R.; Chiodini, P.; Borrelli, S.; Zoccali, C.; Postorino, M.; Iodice, C.; Nappi, F.; Fuiano, G.; Gallo, C.; et al. The effect of increasing age on the prognosis of non-dialysis patients with chronic kidney disease receiving stable nephrology care. *Kidney Int.* **2012**, *82*, 482–488. [CrossRef]

98. Nitta, K.; Okada, K.; Yanai, M.; Takahashi, S. Aging and chronic kidney disease. *Kidney Blood Press Res.* **2013**, *38*, 109–120. [CrossRef] [PubMed]

99. Yamamoto, T.; Takabatake, Y.; Kimura, T.; Takahashi, A.; Namba, T.; Matsuda, J.; Minami, S.; Kaimori, J.Y.; Matsui, I.; Kitamura, H.; et al. Time-dependent dysregulation of autophagy: Implications in aging and mitochondrial homeostasis in the kidney proximal tubule. *Autophagy* **2016**, *12*, 801–813. [CrossRef]

100. Schmitt, R.; Melk, A. Molecular mechanisms of renal aging. *Kidney Int.* **2017**, *92*, 569–579. [CrossRef]

101. Boutouja, F.; Stiehm, C.M.; Platta, H.W. mTOR: A cellular regulator interface in health and disease. *Cells* **2019**, *8*, 18. [CrossRef]

102. Jankauskas, S.S.; Silachev, D.N.; Andrianova, N.V.; Pevzner, I.B.; Zorova, L.D.; Popkov, V.A.; Plotnikov, E.Y.; Zorov, D.B. Aged kidney: Can we protect it? Autophagy, mitochondria and mechanisms of ischemic preconditioning. *Cell Cycle* **2018**, *17*, 1291–1309. [CrossRef]

103. Andrianova, N.V.; Jankauskas, S.S.; Zorova, L.D.; Pevzner, I.B.; Popkov, V.A.; Silachev, D.N.; Plotnikov, E.Y.; Zorov, D.B. Mechanisms of Age-Dependent Loss of Dietary Restriction Protective Effects in Acute Kidney Injury. *Cells* **2018**, *7*, 178. [CrossRef] [PubMed]

104. Yu, L.; McPhee, C.K.; Zheng, L.; Mardones, G.A.; Rong, Y.; Peng, J.; Mi, N.; Zhao, Y.; Liu, Z.; Wan, F.; et al. Termination of autophagy and reformation of lysosomes regulated by mTOR. *Nature* **2010**, *465*, 942–946. [CrossRef] [PubMed]

105. Wu, J.; Xing, C.; Zhang, L.; Mao, H.; Chen, X.; Liang, M.; Wang, F.; Ren, H.; Cui, H.; Jiang, A.; et al. Autophagy promotes fibrosis and apoptosis in the peritoneum during long-term peritoneal dialysis. *J. Cell. Mol. Med.* **2018**, *22*, 1190–1201. [CrossRef] [PubMed]

106. Wang, H.H.; Lin, C.Y.; Su, S.H.; Chuang, C.T.; Chang, Y.L.; Lee, T.Y.; Lee, S.C.; Chang, C.J. Activation of salt-inducible kinase 2 promotes the viability of peritoneal mesothelial cells exposed to stress of peritoneal dialysis. *Cell Death Dis.* **2016**, *7*, 2290–2298. [CrossRef]

107. Bizargity, P.; Schroppel, B. Autophagy: Basic principles and relevance to transplant immunity. *Am. J. Transplant.* **2014**, *14*, 1731–1739. [CrossRef]

108. Nakagawa, S.; Nishihara, K.; Inui, K.; Masuda, S. Involvement of autophagy in the pharmacological effects of the mTOR inhibitor everolimus in acute kidney injury. *Eur. J. Pharmacol* **2012**, *696*, 143–154. [CrossRef]

109. da Silva, J.B.; de Melo Lima, M.H.; Secoli, S.R. Influence of cyclosporine on the occurrence of nephrotoxicity after allogeneic hematopoietic stem cell transplantation: A systematic review. *Revista Brasileira de Hematologia e Hemoterapia* **2014**, *36*, 363–368. [CrossRef]

110. Lim, S.W.; Hyoung, B.J.; Piao, S.G.; Doh, K.C.; Chung, B.H.; Yang, C.W. Chronic cyclosporine nephropathy is characterized by excessive autophagosome formation and decreased autophagic clearance. *Transplantation* **2012**, *94*, 218–225. [CrossRef]

111. Wu, Q.; Wang, X.; Nepovimova, E.; Wang, Y.; Yang, H.; Kuca, K. Mechanism of cyclosporine A nephrotoxicity: Oxidative stress, autophagy, and signalings. *Food Chem. Toxicol.* **2018**, *118*, 889–907. [CrossRef]

112. Schroppel, B.; Legendre, C. Delayed kidney graft function: From mechanism to translation. *Kidney Int.* **2014**, *86*, 251–258. [CrossRef]

113. Rubinsztein, D.C.; Codogno, P.; Levine, B. Autophagy modulation as a potential therapeutic target for diverse diseases. *Nat. Rev. Drug Discov.* **2012**, *11*, 709–730. [CrossRef] [PubMed]

114. Giampieri, F.; Afrin, S.; Forbes-Hernandez, T.Y.; Gasparrini, M.; Cianciosi, D.; Reboredo-Rodriguez, P.; Varela-Lopez, A.; Quiles, J.L.; Battino, M. Autophagy in Human Health and Disease: Novel Therapeutic Opportunities. *Antioxid. Redox Signal.* **2019**, *30*, 577–634. [CrossRef] [PubMed]

115. Shivakumar, S.; Panigrahi, T.; Shetty, R.; Subramani, M.; Ghosh, A.; Jeyabalan, N. Chloroquine Protects Human Corneal Epithelial Cells from Desiccation Stress Induced Inflammation without Altering the Autophagy Flux. *Biomed. Res. Int.* **2018**, *2018*, 7627329. [CrossRef]

116. Bullon, P.; Cordero, M.D.; Quiles, J.L.; Ramirez-Tortosa, M.D.C.; Gonzalez-Alonso, A.; Alfonsi, S.; García-Marín, R.; de Miguel, M.; Battino, M. Autophagy in periodontitis patients and gingival fibroblasts: Unraveling the link between chronic diseases and inflammation. *BMC Med.* **2012**, *10*, 122. [CrossRef]

Review

Autophagy in Neurotrauma: Good, Bad, or Dysregulated

Junfang Wu [1,2,3,*] and Marta M. Lipinski [1,2]

[1] Department of Anesthesiology and Center for Shock, Trauma and Anesthesiology Research (STAR), University of Maryland School of Medicine, Baltimore, MD 21201, USA

[2] Department of Anatomy and Neurobiology, University of Maryland School of Medicine, Baltimore, MD 21201, USA

[3] Center to Advance Chronic Pain Research, University of Maryland, Baltimore, MD 21201, USA

* Correspondence: junfang.wu@som.umaryland.edu; Tel.: +1-410-706-5189

Received: 31 May 2019; Accepted: 9 July 2019; Published: 10 July 2019

Abstract: Autophagy is a physiological process that helps maintain a balance between the manufacture of cellular components and breakdown of damaged organelles and other toxic cellular constituents. Changes in autophagic markers are readily detectable in the spinal cord and brain following neurotrauma, including traumatic spinal cord and brain injury (SCI/TBI). However, the role of autophagy in neurotrauma remains less clear. Whether autophagy is good or bad is under debate, with strong support for both a beneficial and detrimental role for autophagy in experimental models of neurotrauma. Emerging data suggest that autophagic flux, a measure of autophagic degradation activity, is impaired in injured central nervous systems (CNS), and interventions that stimulate autophagic flux may provide neuroprotection in SCI/TBI models. Recent data demonstrating that neurotrauma can cause lysosomal membrane damage resulting in pathological autophagosome accumulation in the spinal cord and brain further supports the idea that the impairment of the autophagy–lysosome pathway may be a part of secondary injury processes of SCI/TBI. Here, we review experimental work on the complex and varied responses of autophagy in terms of both the beneficial and detrimental effects in SCI and TBI models. We also discuss the existing and developing therapeutic options aimed at reducing the disruption of autophagy to protect the CNS after injuries.

Keywords: spinal cord injury; traumatic brain injury; autophagy; autophagic flux; neuronal cell death; lysosomal damage

1. Introduction

The role of autophagy after the central nervous system (CNS) insults is under perusal, as investigation has begun to determine how autophagy and related pathways contribute to secondary injury and functional recovery following neurotrauma [1–5], including spinal cord injury (SCI) and traumatic brain injury (TBI). Whether detected autophagic responses to injury are protective or detrimental remains controversial, with experimental reports revealing protective effects of both enhancing and hindering autophagy [1,6].

Autophagy is a vital intracellular degradation pathway that delivers cytoplasmic constituents to the lysosomes for degradation [7]. There are three different types of autophagy that have been described so far, including macroautophagy, microautophagy, and chaperone-mediated autophagy [8–10]. In addition, several types of targeted autophagy have been described, including mitophagy, which is a selective form of macroautophagy that specifically targets and degrades damaged mitochondria. Macroautophagy involves the formation of a cytoplasmic membrane that engulfs cargo and eventually elongates to form double-membrane vesicles termed autophagosomes. It culminates in the fusion of cargo-containing autophagosomes to the lysosomes and the degradation of the cargo by lysosomal hydrolases [11]. As macroautophagy is the best characterized form of autophagy, hereafter, the term autophagy refers to macroautophagy unless otherwise specified. Under normal conditions, autophagy is an essential physiological process that maintains a balance between the manufacture of cellular components and breakdown of damaged organelles and other toxic cellular constituents. Its processing is strictly regulated under physiological conditions [12]. Recent considerable progress has demonstrated that autophagy is dysregulated in injured CNS following trauma, and may play either beneficial or detrimental functions after injury, depending on the context and the mechanisms leading to its perturbation [1,6,13,14]. Emerging data also suggest that the restoration and/or augmentation of proper autophagy function, for example by inducing lysosomal biogenesis, may be a potential therapeutic target for TBI and SCI.

This review explores the current research on the function and mechanisms of autophagy in two models of CNS injury: SCI and TBI. Cell-type specific responses of autophagy are discussed according to different locations, severity, and time windows of traumatic injury. We discuss recent findings suggesting that impairment of the autophagy–lysosomal pathway may be part of the secondary injury processes of SCI/TBI. We also review recent studies and novel mechanistic discoveries on cytosolic phospholipase A2 (cPLA2) participation in lysosomal damage, and provide therapeutic options, with an emphasis on the pharmacological modulation of autophagy and lysosomal biogenesis for neuroprotection and the prevention of neuroinflammation after CNS trauma.

2. Traumatic Spinal Cord and Brain Injury and Their Injury Mechanisms

According to the National Spinal Cord Injury Statistical Center [NSCISC, 2018], in the United States (U.S.), there are approximately 288,000 people living with SCI, and 17,000 new SCI cases occur each year. The impact of these injuries is devastating for individuals, and the health care costs associated with the injury are some of the highest in the U.S. [15,16]. Experimental and clinical studies [17–21] have indicated that acute SCI is a two-step process involving primary and secondary mechanisms. Primary injury of the spinal cord refers to the initial mechanical tissue damage. It also includes ruptured microvessels in the spinal cord, and subsequent hemorrhage and edema that are associated with secondary injury. SCI-mediated secondary injury processes include a cascade of biochemical and cellular events [22], such as free-radical formation, excitatory amino acid release, axonal damage, neuronal and oligodendroglial cell death, the infiltration of macrophages and peripheral immune cells, microglia, and astrocyte activation/glial scar formation. These delayed secondary injury processes can occur over hours, days, and months after initial impact [23,24], contributing to progressive neuronal degeneration and neurological dysfunction. Despite considerable research over the past 30 years, there is still no established effective treatment to improve recovery following SCI. In part, this reflects an incomplete understanding of the complex secondary pathobiological mechanisms involved.

TBI represents a major public health problem, with more than 1.7 million new cases annually in the United States [25] and accounting for 60% of all trauma deaths in the U.S. [26]. Similar to SCI, TBI causes cell loss and neurological functional deficits through both the direct physical damage of tissue (primary injury), and through subsequent biochemical changes (secondary injury). The latter reflects delayed and potentially reversible molecular and cellular pathophysiological mechanisms [27,28], which begin within seconds to minutes after the primary insult, and may continue for months to years [29,30]. Such secondary injury processes, similar in SCI, lead to cellular changes that include neuronal and oligodendroglial cell death, as well as microglia and astrocyte activation and glial scar formation. Although most of the research to date has been directed at early cellular and molecular events, both experimental and clinical evidence suggests that CNS trauma-mediated pathophysiological changes may continue for years [30–33], leading to chronic post-mitotic cell loss and microglial/astrocytes activation, and contributing to chronic functional deficits.

Cell death after neurotrauma is a major cause of neurological deficits and mortality. Although CNS injury induces changes in multiple cell types such as neurons and oligodendrocytes, the mechanisms of neuronal cell death have been the predominant focus. There are multiple cell death mechanisms in injured CNS following trauma [34,35]. Three main morphological types of cell death include apoptosis, autophagic cell death, and necrosis. Molecular and biochemical pathways that are involved in cell death after both TBI and SCI include, among others, caspases-dependent apoptosis (the Bcl-2 family), cell cycle activation-dependent pathways, the autophagy-related (ATG) protein family-mediated cell death (autophagy), caspase-independent programmed cell death [including extracellular-signal-regulated kinase 2 (ERK2), poly[Adenosine diphosphate (ADP)-ribose] polymerase (PARP)-1, apoptosis-inducing factor (AIF)], calpains and cathepsis-mediated calcium-dependent cell death, and the c-Jun N-terminal kinase-mediated non-apoptotic cell death (oncosis) [34,36,37]. Interestingly, apoptosis and autophagy share many regulatory factors, including the Bcl-2 family proteins [38]. The pro-apoptotic B-cell lymphoma 2 (Bcl-2) proteins Bim, Bid, and Bax, are known mediators of lysosomal membrane permeabilization (LMP) [39–42], while the anti-apoptotic Bcl-1 and Mcl-1 negatively regulate autophagy through interaction with Beclin 1. Additionally, necroptosis, the regulated receptor interacting protein kinase (RIPK)-dependent necrosis pathway, may also contribute to secondary neuronal cell death after CNS insults [3,43,44]. Obstacles to successful therapy against neurotrauma-induced neuronal cell death include the diversity of cell death pathways, which have both overlapping and distinct molecular mechanisms, and the narrow therapeutic windows for some types of neuronal cell death [34,45]. Thus, we emphasize that the effective neuroprotective strategies will need to concurrently modulate multiple signaling pathways to reflect the spatial and temporal changes underlying the diversity of neuronal cell death.

Stimulation by pro-inflammatory cytokines, chemokines, or alterations in the CNS environment induces microglial activation and the attraction of macrophages to the injury site [46,47]. Activated microglia undergo a transition from a resting, ramified phenotype to a phagocytosis-capable, 'macrophage-like' phenotype that is virtually indistinguishable from blood-borne macrophages [48–50]. Microglia and macrophages are found in the injured CNS within 12 to 24 h post-injury, with maximal concentration at four to eight days post-injury [49,51]. These cells produce free radicals, nitric oxide, and arachidonic acid derivatives, as well as a number of cytokines and chemokines in an effort to remove debris and dysfunctional cells. However, excessive inflammation may also result in the death of neighboring undamaged cells [52–56]. It is reported [57] that the activation of microglia-associated inflammatory factors may continue indefinitely after CNS trauma: certainly, it lasts for many months in rodents.

3. Autophagy, Autophagy Flux, and the Lysosomal Functions in Neurotrauma

3.1. Autophagy and Autophagy Flux

The process of autophagy includes several essential steps, including the induction, sequestration of cargo within the autophagosomal membrane, maturation of the autophagosomes, and degradation [12,58]. While baseline autophagy proceeds at all times, in adverse conditions such as environmental stress, nutrient starvation, or acute cellular injury, it is further activated. Cytoplasmic components including damaged organelles and toxic protein aggregates are sequestered by a unique membrane called the phagophore or isolation membrane. Complete sequestration by the elongating phagophore results in the formation of the autophagosome, which is typically a double-membraned vesicle. Then, autophagosomes are transported within the cell and fuse with lysosomes. Then, the inner membrane of the autophagosome and the cytoplasm-derived materials contained in the autophagosome are degraded by lysosomal hydrolases. The whole process of autophagy is referred to autophagic flux [7], which represents the dynamic process of autophagy from cargo sequestration to its degradation.

Completion of the autophagic flux requires the coordinated activity of various members of the autophagy-related (ATG) protein family [59,60]. For example, ATG13, ATG101, and FIP200 (homolog of yeast ATG17) are part of the ULK1 kinase complex that initiates autophagy. ATG9 also mediates an essential function in early autophagosome formation. Expansion of the autophagosomal membrane depends on two ubiquitin-like conjugating systems: the ATG12–ATG5–ATG16L system and the phosphatidylethanolamine (PE)–LC3 system. LC3 is the commonly used name for microtubule-associated protein 1 light chain 3β (MAP1LC3B). Upon activation of the autophagic pathway, the cytosolic, proteolytically processed form of LC3 (termed LC3-I) is lipidated to form LC3–PE (termed LC3-II), which is specifically recruited to the phagophore membrane. LC3-II accumulates on autophagosomal membranes and—through interaction with adaptor proteins—helps recruit substrates that are tagged for autophagic degradation. Thus, LC-II levels correlate well with autophagosome numbers. In addition, rapamycin complex 1 (MTORC1) operates as a central suppressor of autophagy. Conversely, beclin 1 (BECN1), a regulatory subunit of the type III phosphatidylinositol (PI) 3 kinase, promotes autophagy by promoting the formation of phosphatidylinositol 3 phosphate, which is necessary for autophagosome formation [60]. Moreover, ubiquitylated structures, including protein aggregated and in some cases mitochondria, are bound by the autophagic adaptor sequestosome 1 (SQSTM1; also known as p62), which enables their uptake by autophagosomes through LC3-II [61]. p62/SQSTM1 is one of several factors that target specific cargoes for autophagy, also including NBR1 [neighbor of breast cancer type 1 (BRCA1) gene], NDP52 (nuclear domain 10 protein 52), and OPTN (optineurin).

A number of methods are currently utilized to assess autophagic flux [62]. Transmission electron microscopy can be used for the partial analysis of the autophagosome pool size in vitro and in vivo without a time dimension. One of the most common ways to monitor autophagy is by measuring LC3-II protein turnover, which is incorporated into autophagosomes and then degraded in the lysosome. There are many different ways to measure LC3-II protein levels, including Western blot and immunofluorescent microscopy. However, these methods are complicated by the LC3-II levels increasing with autophagy induction due to increased autophagosomal formation, but also decreasing as these autophagosomes are turned over. Thus, a more reliable way to accurately monitor LC3-II levels is with a flux assay that uncouples autophagosome formation from its degradation by using lysosomal inhibitors such as bafilomycin-A1 (V-ATPase inhibitor) or chloroquine (a lysosomotropic compound that neutralizes lysosomal pH). As the flux is a rate, an analysis of both LC3-II and p62 levels over time in the presence and absence of lysosomal inhibitor is required. Another possibility in vitro is monitoring the half-life of labeled long-lived proteins that are known to be degraded via autophagy [63]. Fluorescence microscopy is an extremely valuable tool for the assessment of autophagic flux and the autophagosome pool size per cell. Use of the green fluorescent protein (GFP)–LC3 reporter allowing direct visualization of autophagosomes has been especially valuable. It is widely used for the evaluation of autophagy flux in vitro via image-based flux assay and live cell microscopy, and of the autophagosome pool in vivo using transgenic *GFP-LC3* reporter mice. Recent developments of the dual RFP-GFP-LC3 reporter further improved the evaluation of autophagy flux. It takes advantage of differential pH sensitivity of GFP (acid labile) and RFP (acid stable) to directly assess the fusion of autophagosomes (red and green) with lysosomes to form autolysosomes (red only) [62]. However, it remains challenging to employ these techniques in vivo in a manner that uniformly expresses autophagic flux quantitatively and assesses the magnitude of change in flux.

3.2. Impairment of Autophagy Flux in SCI and TBI

Increased markers of autophagy have been observed in different experimental SCI models [64–68]. Several reports indicate that the accumulation of autophagosomes is initiated very early during secondary injury, in some cases within hours after the initial impact. In SCI, depending on the injury models and severities as well as different species and sex, some reported significant increases in expression levels of the autophagosome marker LC3-II during the first 24 h after SCI [3,4,67,69,70], whereas others have only detected a delayed increase of this marker three to seven days after injury [64,65,68,71–73]. In some cases, the expression of Beclin 1, a key protein in the initiation of autophagy [74], has been reported to increase after SCI, supporting the hypothesis that SCI may lead to an increase of autophagy initiation [64,65,73,75,76]. However, other works have reported unaltered levels of Beclin 1 and other upstream mediators and regulators of autophagy [4,68], suggesting that increased autophagy initiation is unlikely to account for an increase in the number of autophagosomes. The p62/SQSTM1 protein, similar to all autophagy cargo adaptors, is degraded by autophagy along with its cargo. Therefore, provided no changes in transcription/synthesis are observed, p62 levels can be often used to approximate the autophagy-dependent degradation rate, with low levels of p62 protein associated with high autophagy flux (high degradation) and high p62 levels associated with low autophagy flux (inhibited degradation). Most reports describe the accumulation of both LC3 and p62 in the damaged spinal cord tissues [3,4,68]. Since p62/*Sqstm1* mRNA expression is not changed after SCI, this suggests that an accumulation of autophagosomes after SCI is likely a result of inhibited autophagy flux rather than its increased initiation [1]. This includes diverse injury models such as acute contusion SCI in male rat [4] and male mouse [3] and chronic spinal cord compression in both sexes [66,77]. The inhibition of autophagy flux was also recently reported following moderate contusion SCI in *GFP–LC3* male mice [3], and demonstrated the accumulation of both GFP–LC3 positive autophagosomes and p62 in the same cells near the injury site. Although autophagic changes in response to SCI show some discrepancies observed among studies, species, injury models, and injury severities, the vast majority of data support the inhibition of autophagic flux in the damaged spinal cord.

Increased markers of autophagy, including LC3-II, beclin1, p62, and autophagosomes, have been reported in human TBI autopsy samples [78,79], as well as in cerebrospinal fluid (CSF) [80]. TBI-mediated accumulation of p62 in both brain autopsy samples [78] and CSF [80] is associated with injury severity and worse recovery [80], and likely reflects an impairment of autophagic flux. Similarly, in experimental models of TBI, LC3-II expression levels as well as the accumulation of autophagosomes observed by electron microscope [81] has been demonstrated in the injured brain [79,82–84]. However, autophagy flux has not been directly assessed until more recently [62]. Interestingly, these data indicate that unlike in the spinal cord, in the brain, the autophagic flux capacity may be dependent on injury severity [14]. Supporting this possibility, the accumulation of p62 appears most pronounced at or near the lesion area after moderate to severe injury in both rodent TBI models [5,85] and human TBI brain samples [78]. The initiation of autophagy is not changed after moderate/severe injury in a controlled cortical impact (CCI) model [85]. Recently, an inhibition of autophagy flux was also reported in *GFP–LC3* mice after moderate CCI [5], and further confirmed by ex vivo flux assay in organotypic brain slices in the presence or absence of a lysosomal inhibitor (chloroquine). Conversely, in a mild CCI model [85], p62 was reduced in the ipsilateral cortex accompanied by increased beclin 1, ATG5, and ATG12, suggesting the enhancement of autophagy initiation. Increased autophagy has also been reported in rat models of TBI following a fluid percussion injury [83] and CCI [86,87]. Bayir et al. [88] reported that increased LC3-II after moderate CCI injury on postnatal day 17 rats is more prominent in male versus female rats, suggesting that trauma-induced autophagy is not limited to the mature mammalian brain, and that similar to nutrient deprivation studies in vitro [89], there are sex-dependent differences in the autophagic response. The divergent findings in autophagy flux following TBI may be explained by the different lesion paradigms and tissue sampling or time windows after injury. Nonetheless, autophagy flux is impaired in most models of moderate to severe brain injury.

3.3. Lysosomal Functions In Neurotrauma

Lysosomes are membrane-enclosed organelles that contain an array of enzymes that are capable of breaking down all types of biological polymers: proteins, nucleic acids, carbohydrates, and lipids [90–93]. Lysosomes function as the digestive system of the cell, serving both to degrade material taken up from outside the cell and the obsolete or superfluous components of the cell itself. Autophagic degradation is dependent on lysosomal proteases. Defects in the lysosomal function have been demonstrated in various neurodegenerative diseases and aging. In many of these disease paradigms, lysosomal dysfunction can be caused by the increase in lysosomal membrane permeability (LMP) [94–99]. We and others [3–5,100] demonstrated that decreased protein levels and activity of lysosomal enzymes accompanied the inhibition of autophagy flux in both TBI and SCI. The altered intracellular localization of soluble lysosomal enzymes including cathepsin D (CTSD) diffuse rather than discrete punctate, which further suggests the possibility that LMP allows the leakage of CTSD into cytosol, resulting in decreased lysosomal activity and the inhibition of autophagy flux after neurotrauma. In addition to its detrimental effect on autophagy, the leakage of the highly degradative lysosomal enzymes into the cytosol could lead to significant damage to other cellular components.

Similar to most cellular organelles, lysosomes are surrounded by a single-layer phospholipid membrane. Therefore, they are vulnerable to the activation of phospholipases. There are three major phospholipases present in the CNS: namely, calcium-dependent secretory phospholipase A2 (sPLA2), calcium-dependent cytosolic phospholipase A2 (cPLA2), and calcium-independent phospholipase A2 (iPLA2) [101,102]. Among these, cPLA2 is considered to be the most important PLA2 isoform, because it exhibits a strong preference for the deacylation of arachidonic acid (AA) over other fatty acids, and has been implicated as an effector in the receptor-mediated release of AA [103,104]. Both the expression levels and activity of cPLA2 are increased in several neurodegenerative diseases [101,105–108] as well as following SCI [109,110] and TBI [111]. cPLA2 cleaves the fatty acyl linkage of glycerophospholipids at the sn-2 position, releasing AA and leaving lysophospholipids remaining in the membrane [101,102,112–115]. Then, AA is oxygenated and further transformed into a variety of products such as prostaglandins, leukotrienes, and thromboxanes, which mediate or modulate inflammatory reactions. The accumulation of lysophospholids can affect the membrane properties, including its fluidity and permeability [112,113,115]. Although the signaling function of cPLA2 metabolites has been widely studied, the consequences of its action on the properties of the affected membranes and organelles are less well understood.

We recently used mass spectrometry (MS)-based in vivo lysosomal lipidomics to demonstrate an increase in several classes of lysosophospholipids, which are the products of phospholipases A (PLAs), as well as the accumulation of PLA activators and ceramides in lysosomes purified from the injured brain [111] and spinal cord [110]. Further in vitro and in vivo data indicated that cPLA2-mediated LMP leads to release of lysosomal enzymes into the cytosol, the inhibition of autophagy flux, and neuronal cell death. Taken together, our data implicate cPLA2 in the mediation of the lysosomal defects observed in the pathophysiology of neurotrauma. cPLA2-mediated lysosomal damage in turn causes the inhibition of autophagy flux and autophagosome accumulation, which are associated with neuronal cell death (Figure 1). Interestingly, our in vitro results indicate that the inhibition of cPLA2 can also limit amyloid-β-induced LMP and the inhibition of autophagy [111], suggesting that similar mechanisms may also contribute to Alzheimer's and potentially other neurodegenerative diseases.

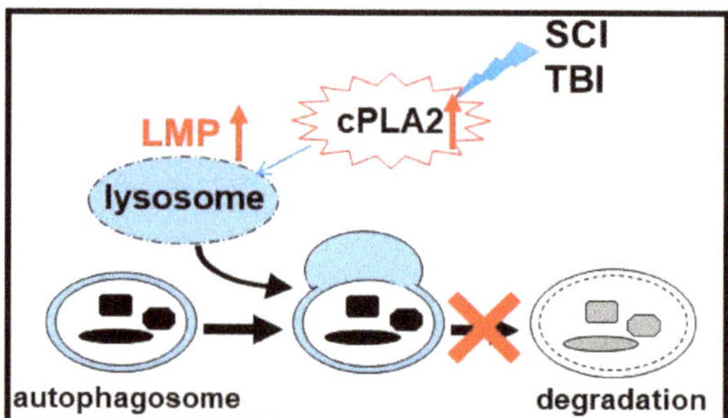

Figure 1. Spinal cord injury (SCI) and traumatic brain injury (TBI) activate cytosolic phospholipase A2 (cPLA2), mediating increased lysosomal membrane permeability (LMP), and leading to lysosomal damage and the inhibition of autophagy after SCI and TBI.

4. Beneficial or Detrimental Effects of Autophagy in CNS Cells After Trauma

4.1. Function of Autophagy in Neurons after Neurotrauma

Neurons, the fundamental units of the CNS, are post-mitotic cells, and most neurons have a cell body, an axon, and dendrites. CNS trauma causes progressive secondary injury processes including neuronal cell death and axonal damage, contributing to neurological dysfunction. Neurons are also the cell type that are most commonly associated with dysregulated autophagy after both TBI and SCI [1]. Afterwards, TBI markers of autophagy are predominantly reported in the neurons of the ipsilateral cortex and hippocampus, and appear within 24 h after injury [5,79,83]. In a mouse closed head injury model, Diskin et al. [82] reported that 17–37% of Beclin-1+ neurons were also terminal deoxynucleotidyl transferase dUTP (2′-deoxyuridine 5′-triphosphate) nick end labeling (TUNEL) positive, suggesting that cell death was associated with autophagy. In agreement with this observation, we observed significant numbers of GFP-LC3+ and p62+ neurons expressing cleaved caspase-3 in the injured cortex at day (d) 1 and 3 after injury in a mouse controlled cortical impact CCI model [5]. In addition, neuronal GFP-LC3 and p62 also co-localized with markers of caspase-independent cell death (such as AIF), indicating that impaired autophagy flux may contribute to both apoptotic and non-apoptotic neuronal cell death.

In SCI, changes in neuronal autophagy appear to be dependent on both the injury model and neuronal subtype. In rat and mouse contusion SCI models, the accumulation of both LC3 and p62 was greater in the ventral horn motor neurons as compared to the dorsal horn sensory neurons, despite the latter being located closer to the impact site [3,4,68]. This suggests that motor neurons may be relatively more vulnerable to the disruption of autophagy flux. Moreover, in these models, motor neurons with impaired autophagy also expressed higher levels of caspase12 and cleaved caspase 3 [4], supporting a role for impaired autophagy in mediating neuronal apoptosis. However, the inhibition of autophagy flux in the dorsal horn neurons was observed in spinal nerve ligation, which is a model of neuropathic pain [116,117], suggesting that neuronal subclasses may respond differentially to specific types of injury. That autophagy flux was inhibited even in this mild injury model also suggests that overall, spinal cord neurons may be more prone to the inhibition of autophagy flux as compared to brain neurons.

Endoplasmic reticulum (ER) stress induces a variety of neuronal cell death pathways, and has been implicated in the secondary injury processes after CNS trauma [118,119], but its mechanisms remain unclear. The induction of ER stress and activation of caspase 12 following TBI and SCI have been previously reported [4,5,118]. ER stress is a potent inducer of autophagy [120,121], and autophagy can protect cells from ER stress-mediated cell death [122]. Consistently, several studies indicate that markers of inhibited autophagy flux after injury correlate with the exacerbation of ER stress, suggesting a connection between the inhibition of autophagy and induction of ER stress-mediated neuronal cell death after neurotrauma [4,5] (Figure 2).

Necroptosis is a programmed form of necrosis, or inflammatory cell death, mediated by the RIPK1/RIPK3 complex [123]. The inhibition of necroptosis can improve functional recovery after both SCI and TBI, suggesting that it is involved in the mediation of the secondary injury [43,44]. A recent study [3] demonstrated the accumulation of markers of necroptosis specifically in neurons displaying signs of autophagy flux inhibition and lysosomal damage, pointing to a previously unexplored link between the inhibition of the autophagy-lysosomal pathway and the induction of neuronal necroptosis after SCI. Additionally, the inhibition of lysosomal function in vitro resulted in the accumulation of necroptosis mediators RIPK1 and RIPK3. Therefore, the inhibition of lysosomal function and autophagy in CNS trauma could also contribute to neuronal necroptosis (Figure 2).

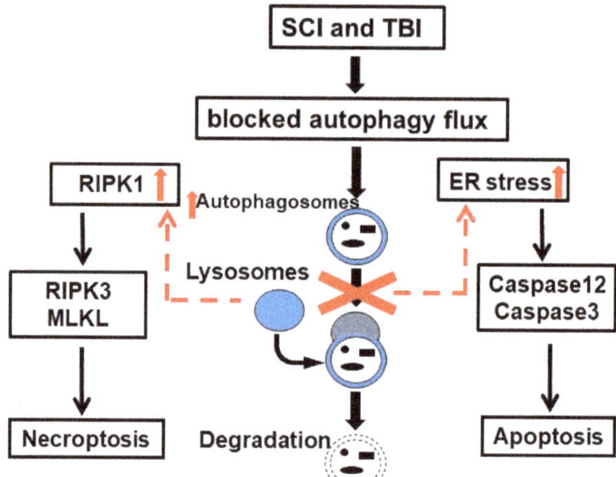

Figure 2. Lysosomal damage after spinal cord injury (SCI) and traumatic brain injury (TBI) cause endoplasmic reticulum (ER) stress and the accumulation of receptor interacting protein kinases (RIPK1/RIPK3), leading to neuronal apoptosis and necroptosis.

Recent findings have identified another type of cell death called 'autosis', which is an autophagy-dependent non-apoptotic form of cell death with unique features. It is characterized by enhanced cell-substrate adhesion, focal ballooning of the perinuclear space, and the dilation and fragmentation of ER. Autosis is mediated by the Na^+, K^+-ATPase pump in the mitochondria, and it is triggered by autophagy-inducing peptides, starvation, and neonatal cerebral hypoxia–ischemia. Whether or not autophagy-dependent autosis participates in neuronal cell death in injured CNS is unknown. While it's known that autophagy can mediate the execution of cell death in the absence of other death pathways, it is difficult to determine in vivo whether cell death is caused by high autophagy or if it is the by-product of other processes that happen alongside autophagy.

In addition to neuronal cell bodies, autophagosome accumulation has been reported to occur in damaged axons after both TBI and SCI [68,79,124]. While autophagy has been proposed to participate in the process of axonal degeneration in vitro, it is currently not known whether it is involved in axonal damage after neurotrauma. Another possibility is that axonal accumulation of autophagosomes could reflect the inhibition of autophagy flux due to lysosomal defects and cytoskeletal collapse, similar to what is observed in neurodegenerative diseases.

4.2. Role of Autophagy in Oligodendrocyte Survival after Neurotrauma

Oligodendrocytes (OLs), also called oligodendroglia, are a type of neuroglia whose main functions are to provide support and insulation to axons, and are the myelinating cells of the CNS [125]. Mature OLs are the end product of oligodendrocyte precursor cells (OPCs), which have to undergo a complex and precisely timed program of proliferation, migration, differentiation, and myelination to finally produce the insulating sheath of axons. Due to this complex differentiation program, and due to their unique metabolism and physiology, OLs count among the most vulnerable cells of the CNS. It is known that OLs undergo apoptosis following CNS trauma, thus the loss and demyelination of OLs contribute as major pathological processes to secondary damages after injury [126]. Increased numbers of autophagosomes have been reported in OLs after both TBI and SCI [4,5,65,66,68,127]. The accumulation of phagophores and autophagosomes in OLs was observed at three to seven days post-injury [4,5,68], which is later than in neurons in most reports. In a mouse contusion SCI model [127], myelin fractions purified from injured spinal cord tissues at eight days post-injury showed enrichment in autophagic proteins, including LC3-II, Atg5, and beclin 1. This study [127] has also demonstrated the increased co-localization of p62 with Olig2 at 3 days post-SCI, indicating impaired autophagic flux in OLs. Additionally, after TBI, increased LC3+ cells have been observed not only in mature OLs, but also in NG2+ OPCs [5].

While the current data strongly support changes in autophagy in OLs during functional recovery after CNS trauma, much less is known about either the mechanisms or the function of autophagy in OL and OPC cells. It has been previously demonstrated in a rat model of demyelination that autophagy is necessary to support oligodendrocyte precursor survival and myelin development [128]. Thus, it is possible that autophagy in OPCs/OLs may play a similar function after CNS trauma. Using transgenic mice with OL-specific loss of the essential autophagy gene *Atg5*, Saraswat et al. reported [127] that the loss of autophagy in OLs exacerbates the inhibition of the autophagic flux in OLs and correlates with worse functional recovery after SCI and greater myelin loss.

ER stress is also a potent inducer of autophagy in OLs [127]. In vitro, a pharmacological blockade of ER stress-induced autophagy in OPCs increases survival. *Atg5* deletion specifically in OLs increased ER stress and reduced cell viability in vitro and in vivo after SCI, indicating a critical regulation of ER stress by autophagy in OLs. This is consistent with the beneficial contribution of *Atg5* and autophagy to OPC/OL health after SCI. Whether or not *Atg5* and ER stress in OLs/OPCs play a similar function following TBI needs to be determined.

4.3. Function of Autophagy in Microglia and Astrocytes after CNS Trauma

Microglia are a type of glial cell that is located throughout the CNS. They account for 10–15% of all cells found within the brain. As the resident macrophage cells, microglia act as the first and main form of active immune defense in the CNS. Microglia are activated in response to injury and are one of the main drivers of inflammatory responses after both TBI and SCI [129]. An increase in markers of autophagy has been reported in microglia after both TBI and SCI [4,5,66]. Interestingly, only the most activated CD68-expressing microglia with amoeboid morphology were reported to accumulate autophagosomes and p62 after TBI in a mouse CCI model [5]. This is consistent with the recently discovered function for autophagy in the regulation of inflammatory responses in macrophages and other immune cells [130,131], including microglia [132]. In general, high levels of autophagy flux are associated with anti-inflammatory properties and the inhibition of flux, with pro-inflammatory phenotypes [133]. Several autophagy genes are also linked to inflammatory and autoimmune diseases [133,134]. On the mechanistic level, autophagy is thought to control the activity of the inflammasomes, both directly by degrading components of activated NLRP3 (nucleotide-binding oligomerization domain, leucine rich repeat and pyrin domain containing 3) and AIM2 (absent in melanoma 2) inflammasomes, and indirectly by limiting mitochondrial damage and reactive oxygen species (ROS) production [135–137]. Additionally, autophagy can modulate inflammatory polarization through its influence on NFκB (nuclear factor kappa B subunit) activity by directly targeting the RELA/p65 protein and by affecting the availability of the p62 protein, which is needed for NFκB activation [138–140]. Conversely, a pro-inflammatory environment may also regulate levels of autophagy, as in primary cultured mouse microglia, where interleukin 1 Beta (IL-1β) induced the accumulation of many acidic vesicles loaded with autophagic markers (p62 and LC3) [141]. It is possible that autophagy may similarly be regulated by and contribute to the regulation of inflammatory responses in microglia and/or infiltrating macrophages after CNS injury.

Astrocytes are the largest and most numerous types of glial cells in the CNS, and are known to have a wide variety of physiological functions, including the maintenance of neurons, formation of the blood–brain barrier, and regulation of synaptic function. Similarly, to microglia, in response to injury, astrocytes are activated and become hypertrophic. Several groups reported that glial fibrillary acid protein (GFAP)-positive astrocytes accumulate autophagosomes after neurotrauma [65,66,82,84]. In mouse contusion SCI, reactive astrocytes accumulated phagophores and autophagosomes at seven d post-injury. Unlike other cell types, this was associated with increased autophagy initiation rather than its inhibition [68]. Much less is known about either the mechanisms or the function of autophagy in astrocytes. Autophagy has been implicated in protective cellular responses in astrocytes [142–144]; however, further work will be necessary to determine how it may affect astrocyte survival and function after CNS trauma.

4.4. Beneficial or Detrimental Effects of Autophagy Activation in Neurotrauma

Defects in autophagy are thought to contribute to Parkinson's disease [145], Alzheimer's disease [146], and other age-related dementias. The accumulated evidence suggests that autophagy deficiency contributes to neurodegenerative diseases by perturbing protein homeostasis, as well as by directly contributing to neuronal cell death, axonal degeneration, and synaptic dysfunction. Conversely, the upregulation of autophagy has been proposed as a potential therapeutic strategy and shows considerable promise in both pre-clinical and clinical studies. However, the function of autophagy in neurodegeneration after traumatic CNS injury has been more controversial [1], with both beneficial and detrimental roles proposed. This may reflect that, as discussed above, either the induction or inhibition of autophagy flux may occur after acute CNS injury, especially in the brain. Since the function of autophagy is dependent on its flux, in cases where flux is inhibited, such as moderate to severe TBI or most cases of SCI, it would be expected to contribute to neuronal cell death and exacerbate other pathological phenotypes. Conversely, in cases where autophagy flux is increased, such as mild TBI, it would be expected to promote cell survival and improve outcomes. Thus, in each neurotrauma model, it is pertinent to ascertain whether observed changes in autophagy are the result of its induction or the inhibition of flux.

5. Therapeutic Potential of Autophagy–Lysosomal Pathway Modulation in Neurotrauma

5.1. Neuroprotection

The most common drugs used to manipulate autophagy in vivo are the mTOR (mechanistic target of Rapamycin kinase) inhibitor rapamycin, which is used to stimulate autophagy, and the type III PI3 kinase inhibitor 3-methyladenine (3-MA), which inhibits autophagosome formation. In general, pharmacological modulations that promote autophagy flux have been shown to provide neuroprotection in both TBI and SCI. However, in addition to autophagy, rapamycin is known to affect other cellular functions such protein synthesis, cell proliferation, and immune responses. Therefore, it is important to confirm that the neuroprotective effects of rapamycin are mediated via the restoration of the autophagy–lysosomal pathway. In a neonatal hypoxia–ischemia injury model, the protective effects of rapamycin were attenuated in animals treated with 3-MA [147]. Rapamycin-induced neuroprotection was also attenuated by AKT1 inhibition, suggesting that both autophagy and AKT1 signaling may be involved downstream of mTOR. Involvement of this pathway in TBI and SCI remains to be confirmed. However, as an improvement in functional recovery was reported after both pharmacologically enhancing [64,148] or blocking autophagy [149,150] after a thoracic SCI, further studies are warranted.

Another complicated factor is that activity of the target of rapamycin, mTOR, plays a vital role in oligodendrocyte differentiation [151] and myelination, and is also involved in axonal sprouting [152], which are both necessary for functional recovery after CNS injury, especially in the spinal cord. Therefore, the inhibition of mTOR may not be optimal as a treatment for CNS injury in general, and SCI in particular. In agreement with this, some [127,149] reported no effects of rapamycin on functional recovery after SCI. This suggests that drugs that are able to promote autophagy flux without inhibiting mTOR function may offer the best therapeutic benefits after neurotrauma. Trehalose is a naturally occurring sugar containing two glucose molecules, and has been reported as a novel mTOR-independent autophagy enhancer [153,154]. Trehalose has been shown to improve outcomes in rodent models of neurodegenerative diseases [155,156] and in a rabbit model of spinal cord ischemia [157]. However, trehalose is known to also act as a chemical chaperone [153], which could attenuate injury and improve recovery independently of autophagy. A specific mTOR inhibitor, Torin 1 [158,159], has been reported to increase autophagy flux. Both trehalose and Torin 1 induce lysosomal biogenesis via activation of the transcriptional factor E-box (TFEB) [160] and increase autophagy flux but are known to act through different molecular pathways (mTOR-independent and mTOR-dependent, respectively). However, whether or not a combination of trehalose and Torin 1 is able to overcome the block of autophagy flux after neurotrauma and lead to improved functional outcomes needs to be investigated.

As lysosomal function is necessary to support autophagy flux, increasing lysosomal biogenesis has been shown to augment autophagy flux and improve outcomes in animal models of neurodegenerative diseases [161]. Enhancing lysosomal function by reducing lysosomal damage or promoting lysosomal biogenesis may also provide an attractive approach for therapy after neurotrauma. In both contusion TBI and SCI mice models, we recently demonstrated that the early administration of cPLA2 inhibitor arachidonyl trifluoromethyl ketone (AACOCF3) reduced lysosomal damage, improved autophagy flux, limited neuronal cell death, and improved functional outcomes [110,111]. Another possibility is the enhancing activity of the transcription factor EB (TFEB). TFEB is the master regulator of lysosomal biogenesis and is negatively regulated by mTOR [162]. The enhancement of autophagic flux by activating TFEB is protective in experimental brain injuries produced by cadmium [163]. This supports the notion that enhancing autophagy flux by stimulating lysosomal biogenesis may represent a potential treatment strategy after neurotrauma.

There are also other autophagy inducers reported in the context of neurotruama. Baicalin (7-D-glucuronic acid-5,6-dihydroxyflavone) is a major flavonoid in traditional Chinese medicinal herb isolated from the radix of Scutellaria baicalensis that was found to increase expression levels of LC3, Beclin 1, and p62 at 24 h following the weight-drop TBI model in mice [164]. Salubrinal is the selective phosphatase inhibitor of p-eIF2α. Wang et al. reported [165] that salubrinal reduced the expression of the ER stress marker as well as the number of CHOP+/TUNEL+ and CHOP+/LC3+ cells at 48 h after mouse TBI, which was associated with neuroprotection and improved recovery. Omega-3 polyunsaturated fatty acids (ω-3 PUFA) are known to have anti-oxidative and anti-inflammatory effects. ω-3 PUFA supplementation increased Beclin-1 deacetylation and its nuclear export, and induced direct interactions between cytoplasmic Beclin-1 and Bcl-2 by increasing the sirtuin family of proteins (SIRT1) activity following a weight-drop TBI model in rat [166]. Valproic acid (VPA), a class I/II histone deacetylase inhibitor, is able to significantly increase expression levels of the autophagic markers (LC3-II, Beclin, ATG-3, and ATG-7) at one day after TBI in rat [167]. These data are consistent with the notion that enhancing autophagy may be beneficial after neurotrauma. However, while the treatments affected the expression of autophagy markers after neurotrauma, their influence on autophagy flux remains to be assessed. Additionally, none of the compounds used are specific for autophagy, and have many additional cellular and organismal effects. Therefore, it remains to be determined if their beneficial effects are in fact dependent on autophagy.

5.2. Neuroinflammation

The crosstalk between autophagy and inflammation has been reported [168] in diseases associated with inflammation, such as inflammatory bowel diseases [169], type 2 diabetes [170], cardiac disorders [171], and cystic fibrosis [172]. Autophagy is known to be involved in the development, homeostasis, and survival of all inflammatory cells, including macrophages, neutrophils, and lymphocytes, thus playing critical roles in the development and pathogenesis of inflammation. In a mouse Alzheimer's disease model, a recent study [173] demonstrated positive correlation between Beclin-1, IL-1β, and TNF-α (tumor necrosis factor alpha) in the cortex and/or hippocampus, suggesting a relationship between inflammatory responses and autophagy. It remains to be determined whether a similar relationship exists after neurotrauma, and whether enhancing autophagy can be used to manipulate neuroinflammatory responses in this context. Conversely, as inflammation can affect cellular autophagy [1], the anti-inflammatory treatments could also improve autophagy flux.

Neurotrauma-induced neuroinflammation can cause the excessive generation of reactive oxygen species (ROS), which non-selectively damages neurons and glia, and thus participates in pathophysiology [174]. ROS can also regulate autophagy in both a positive and negative manner, depending on the levels and context [175,176]. Excessive ROS as well as reactive nitrogen species (RNS) can inhibit autophagy through the S-nitrosylation of proteins in the JNK (c-Jun N-terminal kinase) and mTOR pathways, which are important for the regulation of autophagy [177]. Lysosomal membranes can also be directly subjected to oxidative damage, leading to LMP. This suggests that ROS could be an important factor contributing to alterations in autophagy levels after neurotrauma. Conversely, autophagy can also be stimulated by ROS through its influence on ATG4 activity. Therefore, depending on the injury severity and mechanism, CNS injury-mediated ROS and RNS could either stimulate or inhibit autophagy flux.

6. Conclusions and Perspectives

When the CNS is injured, many cellular processes are activated that attempt to heal the damage. The activation of other cellular responses can increase damage over time. In case of autophagy, both protective and pathological functions are possible. Although we need to more thoroughly understand the complex and heterogeneous autophagic response triggered by the CNS trauma, in general, the enhancement of autophagy is considered protective in many injury paradigms, and helps restore homeostasis. Autophagy-enhancing drugs could positively affect multiple cell types, promoting neuron and oligodendrocyte survival, oligodendrocyte differentiation, and decreasing neuroinflammation. So, while we need to understand the mechanisms in more detail, the enhancement of autophagy after TBI and SCI carries a promise of a potential pleiotropic treatment that could target multiple cell types and pathways.

Author Contributions: Writing—original draft preparation, J.W.; figure drawing, J.W.; writing—review and editing, M.M.L. and J.W.

Funding: This research was funded by the National Institutes of Health (NIH), R01NS094527, R01NR013601, R01 NS110635, and R01 NS110567 to J.W., and R01NS091218 to M.M.L. and the APC was funded by R01NS094527.

Conflicts of Interest: The authors declare no conflict of interest.

References

1. Lipinski, M.M.; Wu, J.; Faden, A.I.; Sarkar, C. Function and Mechanisms of Autophagy in Brain and Spinal Cord Trauma. *Antioxid. Redox Signal.* **2015**, *23*, 565–577. [CrossRef] [PubMed]

2. Lipinski, M.M.; Wu, J. Modification of autophagy-lysosomal pathway as a neuroprotective treatment for spinal cord injury. *Neural Regen. Res.* **2015**, *10*, 892–893. [CrossRef] [PubMed]

3. Liu, S.; Li, Y.; Choi, H.M.C.; Sarkar, C.; Koh, E.Y.; Wu, J.; Lipinski, M.M. Lysosomal damage after spinal cord injury causes accumulation of RIPK1 and RIPK3 proteins and potentiation of necroptosis. *Cell Death Dis.* **2018**, *9*, 476. [CrossRef] [PubMed]

4. Liu, S.; Sarkar, C.; Dinizo, M.; Faden, A.I.; Koh, E.Y.; Lipinski, M.M.; Wu, J. Disrupted autophagy after spinal cord injury is associated with ER stress and neuronal cell death. *Cell Death Dis.* **2015**, *6*, e1582. [CrossRef] [PubMed]

5. Sarkar, C.; Zhao, Z.; Aungst, S.; Sabirzhanov, B.; Faden, A.I.; Lipinski, M.M. Impaired autophagy flux is associated with neuronal cell death after traumatic brain injury. *Autophagy* **2014**, *10*, 2208–2222. [CrossRef]

6. Galluzzi, L.; Bravo-San Pedro, J.M.; Blomgren, K.; Kroemer, G. Autophagy in acute brain injury. *Nat. Rev. Neurosci.* **2016**, *17*, 467–484. [CrossRef] [PubMed]

7. Mizushima, N.; Levine, B.; Cuervo, A.M.; Klionsky, D.J. Autophagy fights disease through cellular self-digestion. *Nature* **2008**, *451*, 1069–1075. [CrossRef]

8. Cuervo, A.M.; Wong, E. Chaperone-mediated autophagy: Roles in disease and aging. *Cell Res.* **2014**, *24*, 92–104. [CrossRef]

9. Li, W.W.; Li, J.; Bao, J.K. Microautophagy: Lesser-known self-eating. *Cell. Mol. Life Sci.* **2012**, *69*, 1125–1136. [CrossRef]

10. Levine, B.; Klionsky, D.J. Development by self-digestion: Molecular mechanisms and biological functions of autophagy. *Dev. Cell* **2004**, *6*, 463–477. [CrossRef]

11. Lamb, C.A.; Yoshimori, T.; Tooze, S.A. The autophagosome: Origins unknown, biogenesis complex. *Nat. Rev. Mol. Cell Biol.* **2013**, *14*, 759–774. [CrossRef] [PubMed]

12. Mizushima, N. Autophagy: Process and function. *Genes Dev.* **2007**, *21*, 2861–2873. [CrossRef]

13. Smith, C.M.; Chen, Y.; Sullivan, M.L.; Kochanek, P.M.; Clark, R.S. Autophagy in acute brain injury: Feast, famine, or folly? *Neurobiol. Dis.* **2011**, *43*, 52–59. [CrossRef] [PubMed]

14. Wolf, M.S.; Bayir, H.; Kochanek, P.M.; Clark, R.S.B. The role of autophagy in acute brain injury: A state of flux? *Neurobiol. Dis.* **2019**, *122*, 9–15. [CrossRef] [PubMed]

15. Ackery, A.; Tator, C.; Krassioukov, A. A global perspective on spinal cord injury epidemiology. *J. Neurotrauma* **2004**, *21*, 1355–1370. [CrossRef] [PubMed]

16. Wood-Dauphinee, S.; Exner, G.; Bostanci, B.; Exner, G.; Glass, C.; Jochheim, K.A.; Kluger, P.; Koller, M.; Krishnan, K.R.; Post, M.W.; et al. Quality of life in patients with spinal cord injury–basic issues, assessment, and recommendations. *Restor. Neurol. Neurosci.* **2002**, *20*, 135–149. [PubMed]

17. Tator, C.H. Experimental and clinical studies of the pathophysiology and management of acute spinal cord injury. *J. Spinal Cord Med.* **1996**, *19*, 206–214. [CrossRef]

18. Tator, C.H.; Fehlings, M.G. Review of the secondary injury theory of acute spinal cord trauma with emphasis on vascular mechanisms. *J. Neurosurg.* **1991**, *75*, 15–26. [CrossRef]

19. Beattie, M.S.; Farooqui, A.A.; Bresnahan, J.C. Review of current evidence for apoptosis after spinal cord injury. *J. Neurotrauma* **2000**, *17*, 915–925. [CrossRef]

20. Osterholm, J.L. The pathophysiological response to spinal cord injury. The current status of related research. *J. Neurosurg.* **1974**, *40*, 5–33. [CrossRef]

21. Mautes, A.E.; Weinzierl, M.R.; Donovan, F.; Noble, L.J. Vascular events after spinal cord injury: Contribution to secondary pathogenesis. *Phys. Ther.* **2000**, *80*, 673–687. [PubMed]

22. Zhang, B.; Gensel, J.C. Is neuroinflammation in the injured spinal cord different than in the brain? Examining intrinsic differences between the brain and spinal cord. *Exp. Neurol.* **2014**, *258*, 112–120. [CrossRef] [PubMed]

23. Beck, K.D.; Nguyen, H.X.; Galvan, M.D.; Salazar, D.L.; Woodruff, T.M.; Anderson, A.J. Quantitative analysis of cellular inflammation after traumatic spinal cord injury: Evidence for a multiphasic inflammatory response in the acute to chronic environment. *Brain* **2010**, *133*, 433–447. [CrossRef] [PubMed]

24. Wu, J.; Pajoohesh-Ganji, A.; Stoica, B.A.; Dinizo, M.; Guanciale, K.; Faden, A.I. Delayed expression of cell cycle proteins contributes to astroglial scar formation and chronic inflammation after rat spinal cord contusion. *J. Neuroinflammation* **2012**, *9*, 169. [CrossRef] [PubMed]

25. Faul, M.X.L.; Wald, M.M.; Coronado, V.G. *Traumatic Brain Injury in the United States: Emergency Department Visits, Hospitalizations, and Deaths*; Centers for Disease Control and Prevention NcfIPaC: Atlanta, GA, USA, 2010.

26. Dutton, R.P.; Stansbury, L.G.; Leone, S.; Kramer, E.; Hess, J.R.; Scalea, T.M. Trauma mortality in mature trauma systems: Are we doing better? An analysis of trauma mortality patterns, 1997-2008. *J. Trauma* **2010**, *69*, 620–626. [CrossRef] [PubMed]

27. Panter, S.S.; Faden, A.I. Biochemical changes and secondary injury from stroke and trauma, Chapter 4. In *Principles and Practice of Restorative Neurology*; Butterworth's: New York, NY, USA, 1992; pp. 32–52.

28. Keane, R.W.; Davis, A.R.; Dietrich, W.D. Inflammatory and apoptotic signaling after spinal cord injury. *J. Neurotrauma* **2006**, *23*, 335–344. [CrossRef] [PubMed]

29. Hall, E.D.; Springer, J.E. Neuroprotection and acute spinal cord injury: A reappraisal. *NeuroRx* **2004**, *1*, 80–100. [CrossRef]

30. Bramlett, H.M.; Dietrich, W.D. Progressive damage after brain and spinal cord injury: Pathomechanisms and treatment strategies. *Prog. Brain Res.* **2007**, *161*, 125–141.

31. Sidaros, A.; Engberg, A.W.; Sidaros, K.; Liptrot, M.G.; Herning, M.; Petersen, P.; Paulson, O.B.; Jernigan, T.L.; Rostrup, E. Diffusion tensor imaging during recovery from severe traumatic brain injury and relation to clinical outcome: A longitudinal study. *Brain* **2008**, *131*, 559–572. [CrossRef]

32. Ramlackhansingh, A.F.; Brooks, D.J.; Greenwood, R.J.; Bose, S.K.; Turkheimer, F.E.; Kinnunen, K.M.; Gentleman, S.; Heckemann, R.A.; Gunanayagam, K.; Gelosa, G.; et al. Inflammation after trauma: Microglial activation and traumatic brain injury. *Ann. Neurol.* **2011**, *70*, 374–383. [CrossRef]

33. Faden, A.I. Microglial activation and traumatic brain injury. *Ann. Neurol.* **2011**, *70*, 345–346. [CrossRef] [PubMed]

34. Stoica, B.A.; Faden, A.I. Cell death mechanisms and modulation in traumatic brain injury. *Neurotherapeutics* **2010**, *7*, 3–12. [CrossRef] [PubMed]

35. Schoch, K.M.; Madathil, S.K.; Saatman, K.E. Genetic manipulation of cell death and neuroplasticity pathways in traumatic brain injury. *Neurotherapeutics* **2012**, *9*, 323–337. [CrossRef] [PubMed]

36. Bredesen, D.E. Key note lecture: Toward a mechanistic taxonomy for cell death programs. *Stroke* **2007**, *38*, 652–660. [CrossRef] [PubMed]

37. Bredesen, D.E. Programmed cell death mechanisms in neurological disease. *Curr. Mol. Med.* **2008**, *8*, 173–186. [CrossRef] [PubMed]

38. Pattingre, S.; Tassa, A.; Qu, X.; Garuti, R.; Liang, X.H.; Mizushima, N.; Packer, M.; Schneider, M.D.; Levine, B. Bcl-2 antiapoptotic proteins inhibit Beclin 1-dependent autophagy. *Cell* **2005**, *122*, 927–939. [CrossRef]

39. Frankel, L.B.; Lund, A.H. MicroRNA regulation of autophagy. *Carcinogenesis* **2012**, *33*, 2018–2025. [CrossRef]

40. Xu, J.; Wang, Y.; Tan, X.; Jing, H. MicroRNAs in autophagy and their emerging roles in crosstalk with apoptosis. *Autophagy* **2012**, *8*, 873–882. [CrossRef]

41. Alqurashi, N.; Hashimi, S.M.; Wei, M.Q. Chemical Inhibitors and microRNAs (miRNA) Targeting the Mammalian Target of Rapamycin (mTOR) Pathway: Potential for Novel Anticancer Therapeutics. *Int. J. Mol. Sci.* **2013**, *14*, 3874–3900. [CrossRef]

42. Johansson, A.C.; Appelqvist, H.; Nilsson, C.; Kagedal, K.; Roberg, K.; Ollinger, K. Regulation of apoptosis-associated lysosomal membrane permeabilization. *Apoptosis* **2010**, *15*, 527–540. [CrossRef]

43. You, Z.; Savitz, S.I.; Yang, J.; Degterev, A.; Yuan, J.; Cuny, G.D.; Moskowitz, M.A.; Whalen, M.J. Necrostatin-1 reduces histopathology and improves functional outcome after controlled cortical impact in mice. *J. Cereb. Blood Flow Metab.* **2008**, *28*, 1564–1573. [CrossRef] [PubMed]

44. Wang, Y.; Wang, H.; Tao, Y.; Zhang, S.; Wang, J.; Feng, X. Necroptosis inhibitor necrostatin-1 promotes cell protection and physiological function in traumatic spinal cord injury. *Neuroscience* **2014**, *266*, 91–101. [CrossRef] [PubMed]

45. Faden, A.I. Neuroprotection and traumatic brain injury: Theoretical option or realistic proposition. *Curr. Opin. Neurol.* **2002**, *15*, 707–712. [CrossRef] [PubMed]

46. Gomes-Leal, W.; Corkill, D.J.; Freire, M.A.; Picanco-Diniz, C.W.; Perry, V.H. Astrocytosis, microglia activation, oligodendrocyte degeneration, and pyknosis following acute spinal cord injury. *Exp. Neurol.* **2004**, *190*, 456–467. [CrossRef] [PubMed]

47. Smith, M.E.; van der Maesen, K.; Somera, F.P. Macrophage and microglial responses to cytokines in vitro: Phagocytic activity, proteolytic enzyme release, and free radical production. *J. Neurosci. Res.* **1998**, *54*, 68–78. [CrossRef]

48. Suh, H.S.; Kim, M.O.; Lee, S.C. Inhibition of Granulocyte-Macrophage Colony-Stimulating Factor Signaling and Microglial Proliferation by Anti-CD45RO: Role of Hck Tyrosine Kinase and Phosphatidylinositol 3-Kinase/Akt. *J. Immunol.* **2005**, *174*, 2712–2719. [CrossRef] [PubMed]

49. Popovich, P.G.; Wei, P.; Stokes, B.T. Cellular inflammatory response after spinal cord injury in Sprague-Dawley and Lewis rats. *J. Comp. Neurol.* **1997**, *377*, 443–464. [CrossRef]

50. Watanabe, T.; Yamamoto, T.; Abe, Y.; Saito, N.; Kumagai, T.; Kayama, H. Differential activation of microglia after experimental spinal cord injury. *J. Neurotrauma* **1999**, *16*, 255–265. [CrossRef] [PubMed]

51. Carlson, S.L.; Parrish, M.E.; Springer, J.E.; Doty, K.; Dossett, L. Acute inflammatory response in spinal cord following impact injury. *Exp. Neurol.* **1998**, *151*, 77–88. [CrossRef] [PubMed]

52. Dehghani, F.; Conrad, A.; Kohl, A.; Korf, H.W.; Hailer, N.P. Clodronate inhibits the secretion of proinflammatory cytokines and NO by isolated microglial cells and reduces the number of proliferating glial cells in excitotoxically injured organotypic hippocampal slice cultures. *Exp. Neurol.* **2004**, *189*, 241–251. [CrossRef]

53. Delves, P.J.; Roitt, I.M. The immune system. First of two parts. *N. Engl. J. Med.* **2000**, *343*, 37–49. [CrossRef] [PubMed]

54. McTigue, D.M.; Tani, M.; Krivacic, K.; Chernosky, A.; Kelner, G.S.; Maciejewski, D.; Maki, R.; Ransohoff, R.M.; Stokes, B.T. Selective chemokine mRNA accumulation in the rat spinal cord after contusion injury. *J. Neurosci. Res.* **1998**, *53*, 368–376. [CrossRef]

55. Pan, J.Z.; Ni, L.; Sodhi, A.; Aguanno, A.; Young, W.; Hart, R.P. Cytokine activity contributes to induction of inflammatory cytokine mRNAs in spinal cord following contusion. *J. Neurosci. Res.* **2002**, *68*, 315–322. [CrossRef] [PubMed]

56. Wang, C.X.; Olschowka, J.A.; Wrathall, J.R. Increase of interleukin-1beta mRNA and protein in the spinal cord following experimental traumatic injury in the rat. *Brain Res.* **1997**, *759*, 190–196. [CrossRef]

57. Byrnes, K.R.; Garay, J.; Di Giovanni, S.; De Biase, A.; Knoblach, S.M.; Hoffman, E.P.; Movsesyan, V.; Faden, A.I. Expression of two temporally distinct microglia-related gene clusters after spinal cord injury. *Glia* **2006**, *53*, 420–433. [CrossRef] [PubMed]

58. Nikoletopoulou, V.; Papandreou, M.E.; Tavernarakis, N. Autophagy in the physiology and pathology of the central nervous system. *Cell Death Differ.* **2015**, *22*, 398–407. [CrossRef] [PubMed]

59. Lee, J.A. Neuronal autophagy: A housekeeper or a fighter in neuronal cell survival? *Exp. Neurobiol.* **2012**, *21*, 1–8. [CrossRef]

60. Noda, N.N.; Inagaki, F. Mechanisms of Autophagy. *Annu. Rev. Biophys.* **2015**, *44*, 101–122. [CrossRef]

61. Narendra, D.; Kane, L.A.; Hauser, D.N.; Fearnley, I.M.; Youle, R.J. P62/SQSTM1 is required for Parkin-induced mitochondrial clustering but not mitophagy; VDAC1 is dispensable for both. *Autophagy* **2010**, *6*, 1090–1106. [CrossRef]

62. Klionsky, D.J.; Abdelmohsen, K.; Abe, A.; Abedin, M.J.; Abeliovich, H.; Acevedo Arozena, A.; Adachi, H.; Adams, C.M.; Adams, P.D.; Adeli, K.; et al. Guidelines for the use and interpretation of assays for monitoring autophagy (3rd edition). *Autophagy* **2016**, *12*, 1–222. [CrossRef]

63. Zhao, J.; Brault, J.J.; Schild, A.; Cao, P.; Sandri, M.; Schiaffino, S.; Lecker, S.H.; Goldberg, A.L. FoxO3 coordinately activates protein degradation by the autophagic/lysosomal and proteasomal pathways in atrophying muscle cells. *Cell Metab.* **2007**, *6*, 472–483. [CrossRef] [PubMed]

64. Sekiguchi, A.; Kanno, H.; Ozawa, H.; Yamaya, S.; Itoi, E. Rapamycin promotes autophagy and reduces neural tissue damage and locomotor impairment after spinal cord injury in mice. *J. Neurotrauma* **2012**, *29*, 946–956. [CrossRef] [PubMed]

65. Kanno, H.; Ozawa, H.; Sekiguchi, A.; Yamaya, S.; Itoi, E. Induction of autophagy and autophagic cell death in damaged neural tissue after acute spinal cord injury in mice. *Spine* **2011**, *36*, E1427–E1434. [CrossRef] [PubMed]

66. Tanabe, F.; Yone, K.; Kawabata, N.; Sakakima, H.; Matsuda, F.; Ishidou, Y.; Maeda, S.; Abematsu, M.; Komiya, S.; Setoguchi, T. Accumulation of p62 in degenerated spinal cord under chronic mechanical compression: Functional analysis of p62 and autophagy in hypoxic neuronal cells. *Autophagy* **2011**, *7*, 1462–1471. [CrossRef] [PubMed]

67. Hao, H.H.; Wang, L.; Guo, Z.J.; Bai, L.; Zhang, R.P.; Shuang, W.B.; Jia, Y.J.; Wang, J.; Li, X.Y.; Liu, Q. Valproic acid reduces autophagy and promotes functional recovery after spinal cord injury in rats. *Neurosci. Bull.* **2013**, *29*, 484–492. [CrossRef]

68. Munoz-Galdeano, T.; Reigada, D.; Del Aguila, A.; Velez, I.; Caballero-Lopez, M.J.; Maza, R.M.; Nieto-Diaz, M. Cell Specific Changes of Autophagy in a Mouse Model of Contusive Spinal Cord Injury. *Front. Cell. Neurosci.* **2018**, *12*, 164. [CrossRef]

69. Chen, H.C.; Fong, T.H.; Lee, A.W.; Chiu, W.T. Autophagy is activated in injured neurons and inhibited by methylprednisolone after experimental spinal cord injury. *Spine* **2012**, *37*, 470–475. [CrossRef]

70. Hou, H.; Zhang, L.; Zhang, L.; Tang, P. Acute spinal cord injury in rats should target activated autophagy. *J. Neurosurg. Spine* **2014**, *20*, 568–577. [CrossRef] [PubMed]

71. Zhang, H.Y.; Wang, Z.G.; Wu, F.Z.; Kong, X.X.; Yang, J.; Lin, B.B.; Zhu, S.P.; Lin, L.; Gan, C.S.; Fu, X.B. Regulation of autophagy and ubiquitinated protein accumulation by bFGF promotes functional recovery and neural protection in a rat model of spinal cord injury. *Mol. Neurobiol.* **2013**, *48*, 452–464. [CrossRef]

72. Zhang, Q.; Huang, C.; Meng, B.; Tang, T.S.; Yang, H.L. Changes in autophagy proteins in a rat model of spinal cord injury. *Chin. J. Traumatol.* **2014**, *17*, 193–197.

73. Berliocchi, L.; Maiaru, M.; Varano, G.P.; Russo, R.; Corasaniti, M.T.; Bagetta, G.; Tassorelli, C. Spinal autophagy is differently modulated in distinct mouse models of neuropathic pain. *Mol. Pain* **2015**, *11*, 3. [CrossRef] [PubMed]

74. He, C.; Levine, B. The Beclin 1 interactome. *Curr. Opin. Cell Biol.* **2010**, *22*, 140–149. [CrossRef] [PubMed]

75. Wang, Z.Y.; Lin, J.H.; Muharram, A.; Liu, W.G. Beclin-1-mediated autophagy protects spinal cord neurons against mechanical injury-induced apoptosis. *Apoptosis* **2014**, *19*, 933–945. [CrossRef] [PubMed]

76. Kanno, H.; Ozawa, H.; Sekiguchi, A.; Itoi, E. Spinal cord injury induces upregulation of Beclin 1 and promotes autophagic cell death. *Neurobiol. Dis.* **2009**, *33*, 143–148. [CrossRef] [PubMed]

77. Chen, Z.; Fu, Q.; Shen, B.; Huang, X.; Wang, K.; He, P.; Li, F.; Zhang, F.; Shen, H. Enhanced p62 expression triggers concomitant autophagy and apoptosis in a rat chronic spinal cord compression model. *Mol. Med. Rep.* **2014**, *9*, 2091–2096. [CrossRef] [PubMed]

78. Sakai, K.; Fukuda, T.; Iwadate, K. Immunohistochemical analysis of the ubiquitin proteasome system and autophagy lysosome system induced after traumatic intracranial injury: Association with time between the injury and death. *Am. J. Forensic. Med. Pathol.* **2014**, *35*, 38–44. [CrossRef]

79. Clark, R.S.; Bayir, H.; Chu, C.T.; Alber, S.M.; Kochanek, P.M.; Watkins, S.C. Autophagy is increased in mice after traumatic brain injury and is detectable in human brain after trauma and critical illness. *Autophagy* **2008**, *4*, 88–90. [CrossRef]

80. Au, A.K.; Aneja, R.K.; Bayir, H.; Bell, M.J.; Janesko-Feldman, K.; Kochanek, P.M.; Clark, R.S.B. Autophagy Biomarkers Beclin 1 and p62 are Increased in Cerebrospinal Fluid after Traumatic Brain Injury. *Neurocrit. Care* **2017**, *26*, 348–355. [CrossRef]

81. Lai, Y.; Hickey, R.W.; Chen, Y.; Bayir, H.; Sullivan, M.L.; Chu, C.T.; Kochanek, P.M.; Dixon, C.E.; Jenkins, L.W.; Graham, S.H.; et al. Autophagy is increased after traumatic brain injury in mice and is partially inhibited by the antioxidant gamma-glutamylcysteinyl ethyl ester. *J. Cereb. Blood Flow Metab.* **2008**, *28*, 540–550. [CrossRef]

82. Diskin, T.; Tal-Or, P.; Erlich, S.; Mizrachy, L.; Alexandrovich, A.; Shohami, E.; Pinkas-Kramarski, R. Closed head injury induces upregulation of Beclin 1 at the cortical site of injury. *J. Neurotrauma* **2005**, *22*, 750–762. [CrossRef]

83. Liu, C.L.; Chen, S.; Dietrich, D.; Hu, B.R. Changes in autophagy after traumatic brain injury. *J. Cereb. Blood Flow Metab.* **2008**, *28*, 674–683. [CrossRef] [PubMed]

84. Erlich, S.; Alexandrovich, A.; Shohami, E.; Pinkas-Kramarski, R. Rapamycin is a neuroprotective treatment for traumatic brain injury. *Neurobiol. Dis.* **2007**, *26*, 86–93. [CrossRef] [PubMed]

85. Zeng, X.J.; Li, P.; Ning, Y.L.; Zhao, Y.; Peng, Y.; Yang, N.; Zhao, Z.A.; Chen, J.F.; Zhou, Y.G. Impaired autophagic flux is associated with the severity of trauma and the role of A2AR in brain cells after traumatic brain injury. *Cell Death Dis.* **2018**, *9*, 252. [CrossRef] [PubMed]

86. Zhang, Y.B.; Li, S.X.; Chen, X.P.; Yang, L.; Zhang, Y.G.; Liu, R.; Tao, L.Y. Autophagy is activated and might protect neurons from degeneration after traumatic brain injury. *Neurosci. Bull.* **2008**, *24*, 143–149. [CrossRef] [PubMed]

87. Sadasivan, S.; Dunn, W.A.; Jr Hayes, R.L.; Wang, K.K. Changes in autophagy proteins in a rat model of controlled cortical impact induced brain injury. *Biochem. Biophys. Res. Commun.* **2008**, *373*, 478–481. [CrossRef] [PubMed]

88. Bayir, H.; Tyurin, V.A.; Tyurina, Y.Y.; Viner, R.; Ritov, V.; Amoscato, A.A.; Zhao, Q.; Zhang, X.J.; Janesko-Feldman, K.L.; Alexander, H.; et al. Selective early cardiolipin peroxidation after traumatic brain injury: An oxidative lipidomics analysis. *Ann. Neurol.* **2007**, *62*, 154–169. [CrossRef] [PubMed]

89. Du, L.; Hickey, R.W.; Bayir, H.; Watkins, S.C.; Tyurin, V.A.; Guo, F.; Kochanek, P.M.; Jenkins, L.W.; Ren, J.; Gibson, G.; et al. Starving neurons show sex difference in autophagy. *J. Biol. Chem.* **2009**, *284*, 2383–2396. [CrossRef] [PubMed]

90. Xu, H.; Ren, D. Lysosomal physiology. *Annu. Rev. Physiol.* **2015**, *77*, 57–80. [CrossRef]

91. Kilpatrick, B.S.; Eden, E.R.; Hockey, L.N.; Futter, C.E.; Patel, S. Methods for monitoring lysosomal morphology. *Methods. Cell Biol.* **2015**, *126*, 1–19.

92. de Duve, D. The peroxisome: A new cytoplasmic organelle. *Proc. R. Soc. Lond.Ser. B Biol. Sci.* **1969**, *173*, 71–83.

93. Luzio, J.P.; Pryor, P.R.; Bright, N.A. Lysosomes: Fusion and function. *Nat. Rev. Mol. Cell Biol.* **2007**, *8*, 622–632. [CrossRef]

94. Gomez-Sintes, R.; Ledesma, M.D.; Boya, P. Lysosomal cell death mechanisms in aging. *Ageing Res. Rev.* **2016**, *32*, 150–168. [CrossRef] [PubMed]

95. Rodriguez-Muela, N.; Hernandez-Pinto, A.M.; Serrano-Puebla, A.; Garcia-Ledo, L.; Latorre, S.H.; de la Rosa, E.J.; Boya, P. Lysosomal membrane permeabilization and autophagy blockade contribute to photoreceptor cell death in a mouse model of retinitis pigmentosa. *Cell Death Differ.* **2015**, *22*, 476–487. [CrossRef] [PubMed]

96. Aits, S.; Jaattela, M. Lysosomal cell death at a glance. *J. Cell Sci.* **2013**, *126*, 1905–1912. [CrossRef] [PubMed]

97. Boya, P.; Kroemer, G. Lysosomal membrane permeabilization in cell death. *Oncogene* **2008**, *27*, 6434–6451. [CrossRef] [PubMed]

98. Yamashima, T.; Oikawa, S. The role of lysosomal rupture in neuronal death. *Prog. Neurobiol.* **2009**, *89*, 343–358. [CrossRef] [PubMed]

99. Cuervo, A.M.; Dice, J.F. When lysosomes get old. *Exp. Gerontol.* **2000**, *35*, 119–131. [CrossRef]

100. Yin, Y.; Li, E.; Sun, G.; Yan, H.Q.; Foley, L.M.; Andrzejczuk, L.A.; Attarwala, I.Y.; Hitchens, T.K.; Kiselyov, K.; Dixon, C.E.; et al. Effects of DHA on Hippocampal Autophagy and Lysosome Function After Traumatic Brain Injury. *Mol. Neurobiol.* **2018**, *55*, 2454–2470. [CrossRef] [PubMed]

101. Lee, J.C.; Simonyi, A.; Sun, A.Y.; Sun, G.Y. Phospholipases A2 and neural membrane dynamics: Implications for Alzheimer's disease. *J. Neurochem.* **2011**, *116*, 813–819. [CrossRef]

102. Burke, J.E.; Dennis, E.A. Phospholipase A2 structure/function, mechanism, and signaling. *J. Lipid Res.* **2009**, *50*, S237–S242. [CrossRef]

103. Farooqui, A.A.; Yang, H.C.; Rosenberger, T.A.; Horrocks, L.A. Phospholipase A2 and its role in brain tissue. *J. Neurochem.* **1997**, *69*, 889–901. [CrossRef] [PubMed]

104. Clark, J.D.; Schievella, A.R.; Nalefski, E.A.; Lin, L.L. Cytosolic phospholipase A2. *J. Lipid Mediat. Cell Signal.* **1995**, *12*, 83–117. [CrossRef]

105. Sanchez-Mejia, R.O.; Newman, J.W.; Toh, S.; Yu, G.Q.; Zhou, Y.; Halabisky, B.; Cisse, M.; Scearce-Levie, K.; Cheng, I.H.; Gan, L.; et al. Phospholipase A2 reduction ameliorates cognitive deficits in a mouse model of Alzheimer's disease. *Nat. Neurosci.* **2008**, *11*, 1311–1318. [CrossRef] [PubMed]

106. Leslie, C.C. Cytosolic phospholipase A(2): Physiological function and role in disease. *J. Lipid Res.* **2015**, *56*, 1386–1402. [CrossRef] [PubMed]

107. Phillis, J.W.; O'Regan, M.H. A potentially critical role of phospholipases in central nervous system ischemic, traumatic, and neurodegenerative disorders. *Brain Res. Rev.* **2004**, *44*, 13–47. [CrossRef] [PubMed]

108. Zhang, Z.; Lee, Y.C.; Kim, S.J.; Choi, M.S.; Tsai, P.C.; Saha, A.; Wei, H.; Xu, Y.; Xiao, Y.J.; Zhang, P.; et al. Production of lysophosphatidylcholine by cPLA2 in the brain of mice lacking PPT1 is a signal for phagocyte infiltration. *Hum. Mol. Genet.* **2007**, *16*, 837–847. [CrossRef] [PubMed]

109. Liu, N.K.; Deng, L.X.; Zhang, Y.P.; Lu, Q.B.; Wang, X.F.; Hu, J.G.; Oakes, E.; Bonventre, J.V.; Shields, C.B.; Xu, X.M. Cytosolic phospholipase A2 protein as a novel therapeutic target for spinal cord injury. *Ann. Neurol.* **2014**, *75*, 644–658. [CrossRef]

110. Li, Y.; Jones, J.W.; Choi, H.M.C.; Sarkar, C.; Kane, M.A.; Koh, E.Y.; Lipinski, M.M.; Wu, J. cPLA2 activation contributes to lysosomal defects leading to impairment of autophagy after spinal cord injury. *Cell Death Dis.* **2019**, in press.

111. Sarkar, C.; Jones, J.W.; Hegdekar, N.; Thayer, J.A.; Kumar, A.; Faden, A.I.; Kane, M.A.; Lipinski, M.M. PLA2G4A/cPLA2-mediated lysosomal membrane damage leads to inhibition of autophagy and neurodegeneration after brain trauma. *Autophagy* **2019**, 1–20. [CrossRef]

112. Farooqui, A.A.; Horrocks, L.A. Brain phospholipases A2: A perspective on the history. *Prostaglandin. Leukot. Essent. Fatty Acids* **2004**, *71*, 161–169. [CrossRef]

113. Gijon, M.A.; Leslie, C.C. Regulation of arachidonic acid release and cytosolic phospholipase A2 activation. *J. Leukoc. Biol.* **1999**, *65*, 330–336. [CrossRef] [PubMed]

114. Murakami, M.; Taketomi, Y.; Miki, Y.; Sato, H.; Hirabayashi, T.; Yamamoto, K. Recent progress in phospholipase A(2) research: From cells to animals to humans. *Prog. Lipid Res.* **2011**, *50*, 152–192. [CrossRef]

115. Farooqui, A.A.; Ong, W.Y.; Horrocks, L.A. Inhibitors of brain phospholipase A2 activity: Their neuropharmacological effects and therapeutic importance for the treatment of neurologic disorders. *Pharmacol. Rev.* **2006**, *58*, 591–620. [CrossRef]

116. Berliocchi, L.; Russo, R.; Maiaru, M.; Levato, A.; Bagetta, G.; Corasaniti, M.T. Autophagy impairment in a mouse model of neuropathic pain. *Mol. Pain* **2011**, *7*, 83. [CrossRef]

117. Zhang, E.; Yi, M.H.; Ko, Y.; Kim, H.W.; Seo, J.H.; Lee, Y.H.; Lee, W.; Kim, D.W. Expression of LC3 and Beclin 1 in the spinal dorsal horn following spinal nerve ligation-induced neuropathic pain. *Brain Res.* **2013**, *1519*, 31–39. [CrossRef] [PubMed]
118. Larner, S.F.; Hayes, R.L.; McKinsey, D.M.; Pike, B.R.; Wang, K.K. Increased expression and processing of caspase-12 after traumatic brain injury in rats. *J. Neurochem.* **2004**, *88*, 78–90. [CrossRef] [PubMed]
119. Ohri, S.S.; Hetman, M.; Whittemore, S.R. Restoring endoplasmic reticulum homeostasis improves functional recovery after spinal cord injury. *Neurobiol. Dis.* **2013**, *58*, 29–37. [CrossRef]
120. Yorimitsu, T.; Nair, U.; Yang, Z.; Klionsky, D.J. Endoplasmic reticulum stress triggers autophagy. *J. Biol. Chem.* **2006**, *281*, 30299–30304. [CrossRef] [PubMed]
121. Kouroku, Y.; Fujita, E.; Tanida, I.; Ueno, T.; Isoai, A.; Kumagai, H.; Ogawa, S.; Kaufman, R.J.; Kominami, E.; Momoi, T. ER stress (PERK/eIF2alpha phosphorylation) mediates the polyglutamine-induced LC3 conversion, an essential step for autophagy formation. *Cell Death Differ.* **2007**, *14*, 230–239. [CrossRef] [PubMed]
122. Boyce, M.; Lipinski, M.M.; Py, B.F.; Yuan, J. Endoplasmic reticulum stress response in cell death and cell survival. In *Apoptosis: Physiology and Pathology*, 1st ed.; Reed, J.C., Green, D.R., Eds.; Cambridge University Press: Cambridge, UK, 2011; pp. 51–62.
123. Vandenabeele, P.; Galluzzi, L.; Vanden Berghe, T.; Kroemer, G. Molecular mechanisms of necroptosis: An ordered cellular explosion. *Nat. Rev. Mol. Cell Biol.* **2010**, *11*, 700–714. [CrossRef]
124. Ribas, V.T.; Schnepf, B.; Challagundla, M.; Koch, J.C.; Bahr, M.; Lingor, P. Early and sustained activation of autophagy in degenerating axons after spinal cord injury. *Brain Pathol.* **2015**, *25*, 157–170. [CrossRef] [PubMed]
125. Bradl, M.; Lassmann, H. Oligodendrocytes: Biology and pathology. *Acta Neuropathol.* **2010**, *119*, 37–53. [CrossRef]
126. Beattie, M.S.; Hermann, G.E.; Rogers, R.C.; Bresnahan, J.C. Cell death in models of spinal cord injury. *Prog. Brain Res.* **2002**, *137*, 37–47. [PubMed]
127. Saraswat Ohri, S.; Bankston, A.N.; Mullins, S.A.; Liu, Y.; Andres, K.R.; Beare, J.E.; Howard, R.M.; Burke, D.A.; Riegler, A.S.; Smith, A.E.; et al. Blocking Autophagy in Oligodendrocytes Limits Functional Recovery after Spinal Cord Injury. *J. Neurosci.* **2018**, *38*, 5900–5912. [CrossRef]
128. Smith, C.M.; Mayer, J.A.; Duncan, I.D. Autophagy promotes oligodendrocyte survival and function following dysmyelination in a long-lived myelin mutant. *J. Neurosci.* **2013**, *33*, 8088–8100. [CrossRef] [PubMed]
129. Loane, D.J.; Byrnes, K.R. Role of microglia in neurotrauma. *Neurotherapeutics* **2010**, *7*, 366–377. [CrossRef] [PubMed]
130. Messer, J.S. The cellular autophagy/apoptosis checkpoint during inflammation. *Cell. Mol. Life Sci.* **2017**, *74*, 1281–1296. [CrossRef]
131. Zhong, Z.; Sanchez-Lopez, E.; Karin, M. Autophagy, Inflammation, and Immunity: A Troika Governing Cancer and Its Treatment. *Cell* **2016**, *166*, 288–298. [CrossRef]
132. Su, P.; Zhang, J.; Wang, D.; Zhao, F.; Cao, Z.; Aschner, M.; Luo, W. The role of autophagy in modulation of neuroinflammation in microglia. *Neuroscience* **2016**, *319*, 155–167. [CrossRef]
133. Sil, P.; Muse, G.; Martinez, J. A ravenous defense: Canonical and non-canonical autophagy in immunity. *Curr. Opin. Immunol.* **2018**, *50*, 21–31. [CrossRef]
134. Cadwell, K.; Liu, J.Y.; Brown, S.L.; Miyoshi, H.; Loh, J.; Lennerz, J.K.; Kishi, C.; Kc, W.; Carrero, J.A.; Hunt, S.; et al. A key role for autophagy and the autophagy gene Atg16l1 in mouse and human intestinal Paneth cells. *Nature* **2008**, *456*, 259–263. [CrossRef] [PubMed]
135. Cho, M.H.; Cho, K.; Kang, H.J.; Jeon, E.Y.; Kim, H.S.; Kwon, H.J.; Kim, H.M.; Kim, D.H.; Yoon, S.Y. Autophagy in microglia degrades extracellular beta-amyloid fibrils and regulates the NLRP3 inflammasome. *Autophagy* **2014**, *10*, 1761–1775. [CrossRef] [PubMed]
136. Nakahira, K.; Haspel, J.A.; Rathinam, V.A.; Lee, S.J.; Dolinay, T.; Lam, H.C.; Englert, J.A.; Rabinovitch, M.; Cernadas, M.; Kim, H.P.; et al. Autophagy proteins regulate innate immune responses by inhibiting the release of mitochondrial DNA mediated by the NALP3 inflammasome. *Nat. Immunol.* **2011**, *12*, 222–230. [CrossRef] [PubMed]
137. Shi, C.S.; Shenderov, K.; Huang, N.N.; Kabat, J.; Abu-Asab, M.; Fitzgerald, K.A.; Sher, A.; Kehrl, J.H. Activation of autophagy by inflammatory signals limits IL-1beta production by targeting ubiquitinated inflammasomes for destruction. *Nat. Immunol.* **2012**, *13*, 255–263. [CrossRef] [PubMed]

138. Duran, A.; Linares, J.F.; Galvez, A.S.; Wikenheiser, K.; Flores, J.M.; Diaz-Meco, M.T.; Moscat, J. The signaling adaptor p62 is an important NF-kappaB mediator in tumorigenesis. *Cancer Cell* **2008**, *13*, 343–354. [CrossRef] [PubMed]

139. Lee, H.M.; Shin, D.M.; Yuk, J.M.; Shi, G.; Choi, D.K.; Lee, S.H.; Huang, S.M.; Kim, J.M.; Kim, C.D.; Lee, J.H.; et al. Autophagy negatively regulates keratinocyte inflammatory responses via scaffolding protein p62/SQSTM1. *J. Immunol.* **2011**, *186*, 1248–1258. [CrossRef] [PubMed]

140. Chang, C.P.; Su, Y.C.; Hu, C.W.; Lei, H.Y. TLR2-dependent selective autophagy regulates NF-kappaB lysosomal degradation in hepatoma-derived M2 macrophage differentiation. *Cell Death Differ.* **2013**, *20*, 515–523. [CrossRef] [PubMed]

141. Francois, A.; Terro, F.; Janet, T.; Rioux Bilan, A.; Paccalin, M.; Page, G. Involvement of interleukin-1beta in the autophagic process of microglia: Relevance to Alzheimer's disease. *J. Neuroinflammation* **2013**, *10*, 151. [CrossRef] [PubMed]

142. Shen, C.; Xian, W.; Zhou, H.; Chen, L.; Pei, Z. Potential protective effects of autophagy activated in MPP+ treated astrocytes. *Exp. Ther. Med.* **2016**, *12*, 2803–2810. [CrossRef] [PubMed]

143. Pla, A.; Pascual, M.; Guerri, C. Autophagy Constitutes a Protective Mechanism against Ethanol Toxicity in Mouse Astrocytes and Neurons. *PLoS ONE* **2016**, *11*, e0153097. [CrossRef]

144. Cao, L.; Fu, M.; Kumar, S.; Kumar, A. Methamphetamine potentiates HIV-1 gp120-mediated autophagy via Beclin-1 and Atg5/7 as a pro-survival response in astrocytes. *Cell Death Dis.* **2016**, *7*, e2425. [CrossRef] [PubMed]

145. Lynch-Day, M.A.; Mao, K.; Wang, K.; Zhao, M.; Klionsky, D.J. The role of autophagy in Parkinson's disease. *Cold Spring Harb. Perspect. Med.* **2012**, *2*, a009357.

146. Bordi, M.; Berg, M.J.; Mohan, P.S.; Peterhoff, C.M.; Alldred, M.J.; Che, S.; Ginsberg, S.D.; Nixon, R.A. Autophagy flux in CA1 neurons of Alzheimer hippocampus: Increased induction overburdens failing lysosomes to propel neuritic dystrophy. *Autophagy* **2016**, *12*, 2467–2483. [CrossRef] [PubMed]

147. Carloni, S.; Girelli, S.; Scopa, C.; Buonocore, G.; Longini, M.; Balduini, W. Activation of autophagy and Akt/CREB signaling play an equivalent role in the neuroprotective effect of rapamycin in neonatal hypoxia-ischemia. *Autophagy* **2010**, *6*, 366–377. [CrossRef] [PubMed]

148. Chen, H.C.; Fong, T.H.; Hsu, P.W.; Chiu, W.T. Multifaceted effects of rapamycin on functional recovery after spinal cord injury in rats through autophagy promotion, anti-inflammation, and neuroprotection. *J. Surg. Res.* **2013**, *179*, e203–e210. [CrossRef]

149. Hu, L.Y.; Sun, Z.G.; Wen, Y.M.; Cheng, G.Z.; Wang, S.L.; Zhao, H.B.; Zhang, X.R. ATP-mediated protein kinase B Akt/mammalian target of rapamycin mTOR/p70 ribosomal S6 protein p70S6 kinase signaling pathway activation promotes improvement of locomotor function after spinal cord injury in rats. *Neuroscience* **2010**, *169*, 1046–1062. [CrossRef]

150. Walker, C.L.; Walker, M.J.; Liu, N.K.; Risberg, E.C.; Gao, X.; Chen, J.; Xu, X.M. Systemic bisperoxovanadium activates Akt/mTOR, reduces autophagy, and enhances recovery following cervical spinal cord injury. *PLoS ONE* **2012**, *7*, e30012. [CrossRef]

151. Wahl, S.E.; McLane, L.E.; Bercury, K.K.; Macklin, W.B.; Wood, T.L. Mammalian target of rapamycin promotes oligodendrocyte differentiation, initiation and extent of CNS myelination. *J.Neurosci.* **2014**, *34*, 4453–4465. [CrossRef]

152. Lee, D.H.; Luo, X.; Yungher, B.J.; Bray, E.; Lee, J.K.; Park, K.K. Mammalian target of rapamycin's distinct roles and effectiveness in promoting compensatory axonal sprouting in the injured CNS. *J. Neurosci.* **2014**, *34*, 15347–15355. [CrossRef]

153. Sarkar, S.; Davies, J.E.; Huang, Z.; Tunnacliffe, A.; Rubinsztein, D.C. Trehalose, a novel mTOR-independent autophagy enhancer, accelerates the clearance of mutant huntingtin and alpha-synuclein. *J. Biol. Chem.* **2007**, *282*, 5641–5652. [CrossRef]

154. Dehay, B.; Bove, J.; Rodriguez-Muela, N.; Perier, C.; Recasens, A.; Boya, P.; Vila, M. Pathogenic lysosomal depletion in Parkinson's disease. *J Neurosci.* **2010**, *30*, 12535–12544. [CrossRef] [PubMed]

155. Schaeffer, V.; Lavenir, I.; Ozcelik, S.; Tolnay, M.; Winkler, D.T.; Goedert, M. Stimulation of autophagy reduces neurodegeneration in a mouse model of human tauopathy. *Brain* **2012**, *135*, 2169–2177. [CrossRef] [PubMed]

156. Zhang, X.; Chen, S.; Song, L.; Tang, Y.; Shen, Y.; Jia, L.; Le, W. MTOR-independent, autophagic enhancer trehalose prolongs motor neuron survival and ameliorates the autophagic flux defect in a mouse model of amyotrophic lateral sclerosis. *Autophagy* **2014**, *10*, 588–602. [CrossRef] [PubMed]

157. Takahashi, S.; Isaka, M.; Hamaishi, M.; Imai, K.; Orihashi, K.; Sueda, T. Trehalose protects against spinal cord ischemia in rabbits. *J. Vasc. Surg.* **2014**, *60*, 490–496. [CrossRef] [PubMed]

158. Thoreen, C.C.; Kang, S.A.; Chang, J.W.; Liu, Q.; Zhang, J.; Gao, Y.; Reichling, L.J.; Sim, T.; Sabatini, D.M.; Gray, N.S. An ATP-competitive mammalian target of rapamycin inhibitor reveals rapamycin-resistant functions of mTORC1. *J. Biol. Chem.* **2009**, *284*, 8023–8032. [CrossRef]

159. Liu, Q.; Chang, J.W.; Wang, J.; Kang, S.A.; Thoreen, C.C.; Markhard, A.; Hur, W.; Zhang, J.; Sim, T.; Sabatini, D.M.; et al. Discovery of 1-(4-(4-propionylpiperazin-1-yl)-3-(trifluoromethyl)phenyl)-9-(quinolin-3-yl)benzo[h][1,6]naphthyridin-2(1H)-one as a highly potent, selective mammalian target of rapamycin (mTOR) inhibitor for the treatment of cancer. *J. Med. Chem.* **2010**, *53*, 7146–7155. [CrossRef]

160. Sardiello, M.; Palmieri, M.; di Ronza, A.; Medina, D.L.; Valenza, M.; Gennarino, V.A.; Di Malta, C.; Donaudy, F.; Embrione, V.; Polishchuk, R.S.; et al. A gene network regulating lysosomal biogenesis and function. *Science* **2009**, *325*, 473–477. [CrossRef]

161. Bove, J.; Martinez-Vicente, M.; Vila, M. Fighting neurodegeneration with rapamycin: Mechanistic insights. *Nat. Rev. Neurosci.* **2011**, *12*, 437–452. [CrossRef]

162. Pena-Llopis, S.; Vega-Rubin-de-Celis, S.; Schwartz, J.C.; Wolff, N.C.; Tran, T.A.; Zou, L.; Xie, X.J.; Corey, D.R.; Brugarolas, J. Regulation of TFEB and V-ATPases by mTORC1. *EMBO J.* **2011**, *30*, 3242–3258. [CrossRef]

163. Pi, H.; Li, M.; Tian, L.; Yang, Z.; Yu, Z.; Zhou, Z. Enhancing lysosomal biogenesis and autophagic flux by activating the transcription factor EB protects against cadmium-induced neurotoxicity. *Sci. Rep.* **2017**, *7*, 43466. [CrossRef]

164. Fang, J.; Zhu, Y.; Wang, H.; Cao, B.; Fei, M.; Niu, W.; Zhou, Y.; Wang, X.; Li, X.; Zhou, M. Baicalin Protects Mice Brain From Apoptosis in Traumatic Brain Injury Model Through Activation of Autophagy. *Front. Neurosci.* **2018**, *12*, 1006. [CrossRef]

165. Wang, Z.F.; Gao, C.; Chen, W.; Gao, Y.; Wang, H.C.; Meng, Y.; Luo, C.L.; Zhang, M.Y.; Chen, G.; Chen, X.P.; et al. Salubrinal offers neuroprotection through suppressing endoplasmic reticulum stress, autophagy and apoptosis in a mouse traumatic brain injury model. *Neurobiol. Learn. Mem.* **2019**, *161*, 12–25. [CrossRef] [PubMed]

166. Chen, X.; Pan, Z.; Fang, Z.; Lin, W.; Wu, S.; Yang, F.; Li, Y.; Fu, H.; Gao, H.; Li, S. Omega-3 polyunsaturated fatty acid attenuates traumatic brain injury-induced neuronal apoptosis by inducing autophagy through the upregulation of SIRT1-mediated deacetylation of Beclin-1. *J. Neuroinflammation* **2018**, *15*, 310. [CrossRef]

167. Chen, X.; Wang, H.; Zhou, M.; Li, X.; Fang, Z.; Gao, H.; Li, Y.; Hu, W. Valproic Acid Attenuates Traumatic Brain Injury-Induced Inflammation in Vivo: Involvement of Autophagy and the Nrf2/ARE Signaling Pathway. *Front. Mol. Neurosci.* **2018**, *11*, 117. [CrossRef]

168. Qian, M.; Fang, X.; Wang, X. Autophagy and inflammation. *Clin. Transl. Med.* **2017**, *6*, 24. [CrossRef]

169. Randall-Demllo, S.; Chieppa, M.; Eri, R. Intestinal epithelium and autophagy: Partners in gut homeostasis. *Front. Immunol.* **2013**, *4*, 301. [CrossRef] [PubMed]

170. Marselli, L.; Bugliani, M.; Suleiman, M.; Olimpico, F.; Masini, M.; Petrini, M.; Boggi, U.; Filipponi, F.; Syed, F.; Marchetti, P. Beta-Cell inflammation in human type 2 diabetes and the role of autophagy. *Diabetes Obes. Metab.* **2013**, *15* (Suppl. 3), 130–136. [CrossRef]

171. Pan, L.; Li, Y.; Jia, L.; Qin, Y.; Qi, G.; Cheng, J.; Qi, Y.; Li, H.; Du, J. Cathepsin S deficiency results in abnormal accumulation of autophagosomes in macrophages and enhances Ang II-induced cardiac inflammation. *PLoS ONE* **2012**, *7*, e35315. [CrossRef] [PubMed]

172. Junkins, R.D.; McCormick, C.; Lin, T.J. The emerging potential of autophagy-based therapies in the treatment of cystic fibrosis lung infections. *Autophagy* **2014**, *10*, 538–547. [CrossRef]

173. Francois, A.; Rioux Bilan, A.; Quellard, N.; Fernandez, B.; Janet, T.; Chassaing, D.; Paccalin, M.; Terro, F.; Page, G. Longitudinal follow-up of autophagy and inflammation in brain of APPswePS1dE9 transgenic mice. *J. Neuroinflammation* **2014**, *11*, 139. [CrossRef]

174. von Leden, R.E.; Yauger, Y.J.; Khayrullina, G.; Byrnes, K.R. Central Nervous System Injury and Nicotinamide Adenine Dinucleotide Phosphate Oxidase: Oxidative Stress and Therapeutic Targets. *J. Neurotrauma* **2016**, *34*, 755–764. [CrossRef] [PubMed]

175. Filomeni, G.; De Zio, D.; Cecconi, F. Oxidative stress and autophagy: The clash between damage and metabolic needs. *Cell Death Differ.* **2014**, *22*, 377. [CrossRef] [PubMed]

176. Lipinski, M.M.; Zheng, B.; Lu, T.; Yan, Z.; Py, B.F.; Ng, A.; Xavier, R.J.; Li, C.; Yankner, B.A.; Scherzer, C.R.; et al. A genome-wide analysis reveals differential regulation of autophagy in normal brain aging and in Alzheimer's disease. *Proc. Natl. Acad. Sci. USA* **2010**, *107*, 14164–14169. [CrossRef] [PubMed]

177. Sarkar, S.; Korolchuk, V.I.; Renna, M.; Imarisio, S.; Fleming, A.; Williams, A.; Garcia-Arencibia, M.; Rose, C.; Luo, S.; Underwood, B.R.; et al. Complex inhibitory effects of nitric oxide on autophagy. *Mol. Cell* **2011**, *43*, 19–32. [CrossRef] [PubMed]

Review

Recent Data on Cellular Component Turnover: Focus on Adaptations to Physical Exercise

Anthony MJ Sanchez [1,*], Robin Candau [2] and Henri Bernardi [3]

[1]   Laboratoire Européen Performance Santé Altitude, EA4604, University of Perpignan Via Domitia, Faculty of Sports Sciences, F-66120 Font-Romeu, France

[2]   Université de Montpellier, INRA, UMR866 Dynamique Musculaire et Métabolisme, F-34060 Montpellier, France; robin.candau@umontpellier.fr

[3]   INRA, UMR866 Dynamique Musculaire et Métabolisme, F-34060 Montpellier, France; henri.bernardi@inra.fr

*   Correspondence: anthony.sanchez@univ-perp.fr; Tel.: +33-(04)-6830-2955

Received: 15 May 2019; Accepted: 2 June 2019; Published: 5 June 2019

Abstract: Significant progress has expanded our knowledge of the signaling pathways coordinating muscle protein turnover during various conditions including exercise. In this manuscript, the multiple mechanisms that govern the turnover of cellular components are reviewed, and their overall roles in adaptations to exercise training are discussed. Recent studies have highlighted the central role of the energy sensor (AMP)-activated protein kinase (AMPK), forkhead box class O subfamily protein (FOXO) transcription factors and the kinase mechanistic (or mammalian) target of rapamycin complex (MTOR) in the regulation of autophagy for organelle maintenance during exercise. A new cellular trafficking involving the lysosome was also revealed for full activation of MTOR and protein synthesis during recovery. Other emerging candidates have been found to be relevant in organelle turnover, especially Parkin and the mitochondrial E3 ubiquitin protein ligase (Mul1) pathways for mitochondrial turnover, and the glycerolipids diacylglycerol (DAG) for protein translation and FOXO regulation. Recent experiments with autophagy and mitophagy flux assessment have also provided important insights concerning mitochondrial turnover during ageing and chronic exercise. However, data in humans are often controversial and further investigations are needed to clarify the involvement of autophagy in exercise performed with additional stresses, such as hypoxia, and to understand the influence of exercise modality. Improving our knowledge of these pathways should help develop therapeutic ways to counteract muscle disorders in pathological conditions.

Keywords: autophagy; mitophagy; mitochondria; exercise; AMPK; FOXO; MTOR; parkin

1. Introduction

Skeletal muscles are fundamental to the body's maintenance, and disorders in their function or metabolism are related to numerous diseases. Improved skeletal muscle activity has a significant effect on major processes in the body, such as the regulation of glucose homeostasis, contributing to enhanced health. Importantly, our capacity to recover from illness also depends on skeletal muscle oxidative capacity. Hence, skeletal muscle displays noteworthy adaptive responses from several stimuli, such as contractile activity, nutritional interventions, and environmental factors like hypoxia. These conditions may induce a transitory cellular stress leading to numerous adaptations, such as modifications in fiber composition, improvements of cell ability to renew cellular proteins and organelles, and modifications of muscle size [1–3].

Among the molecular sensors involved in adaptations to training, the adenosine monophosphate (AMP)-activated protein kinase (AMPK) is an enzyme composed of two regulatory domains (i.e., AMPK-ß, AMPK-γ) and a catalytic domain (i.e., AMPK-α). AMPK is a critical enzyme for preserving cellular homeostasis under conditions of low energy [4,5]. AMPK activity is increased by several energy stresses, including hypoxia/ischemia [6,7], electrical-stimulated muscle contraction [8,9], starvation [10], and physical exercise [11–13]. When cellular ATP is depleted, AMP modulates AMPK activity in an allosteric way, thereby promoting the phosphorylation of a threonine residue (Thr-172) within the α subunit by other enzymes called the "AMPK kinases" (AMPKK) [14]. There are three AMPKK proposed to date, the Ca^{2+}/calmodulin- dependent protein kinase ß (CaMKKß) [15,16], the liver kinase B1 (LKB1) [17,18], and the transforming growth factor ß-activated kinase 1 (TAK-1) [19]. Of note, the binding of ADP, like AMP, prevents AMPK Thr-172 dephosphorylation [20]. On the contrary, AMPK is inhibited by ATP and glycogen [21,22]. AMPK is involved in cell metabolism and several data have highlighted the physiological relevance of its activation in skeletal muscle [4,23]. Thus, AMPK promotes energy production through the anaerobic and aerobic systems (i.e., glycolysis and oxidation of fatty acids) and, conversely, inhibits glycogenesis and cholesterol synthesis [5,24–28]. AMPK enhances mitochondrial biogenesis by stimulating PGC-1α (peroxisome proliferator-activated receptor gamma coactivator 1 alpha) expression [29]. A study by Jager et al. also showed that AMPK phosphorylates PGC-1α on two residues (Thr-117 and Ser-538) in vitro and in cells [30]. PGC-1α consecutively regulates the activity of PPARs (peroxisome proliferator-activated receptors) and NRFs (nuclear respiratory factors), leading to mitochondrial adaptations [30–32].

AMPK's biological functions are not limited to energy metabolism. In the last decade, AMPK was found to coordinate cell component turnover. AMPK decreases protein translation by reducing the activity of the mechanistic (or mammalian) target of rapamycin complex 1 (MTORC1) signaling, and promotes protein breakdown by regulating several component of the ubiquitin-proteasome and autophagosome-lysosome systems [5]. Major targets of AMPK are the forkhead box class O subfamily proteins 1 and 3 (FOXO1 and FOXO3, respectively). FOXO proteins are important transcription factors highly conserved through evolution and their various functions in skeletal muscle (i.e., cell cycle, DNA damage repair, apoptosis, energy metabolism, and oxidative stress resistance) have been recently reviewed [33]. In recent years, the AMPK-FOXO3 axis has been extensively studied with an important focus on processes regulating organelle turnover, especially mitophagy.

In this review, recent discoveries on AMPK-MTORC1 and AMPK-FOXO axes in the coordination of muscle organelle renewal and the importance of physical exercise on both acute and chronic adaptations are discussed. The multiple modes of regulation of these sensors are detailed, as their implication in the regulation of skeletal muscle protein and organelle turnover, especially mitophagy. Apparent discrepancies between the data are discussed in regard to the methodology used to access autophagy or mitophagy activity. The functions of newly identified actors in protein and organelle quality control, specifically the diacylglycerol kinase ζ (DGKζ), Parkin (RING-between-RING E3 ligase), and Mul1 (mitochondrial E3 ubiquitin protein ligase), are also presented. We finally discuss the impact of exercise modality, hypoxia, and examine the current limitations in the literature to suggest other perspectives.

2. AMPK and MTORC1 Pathways

2.1. AMPK/MTORC1 Axis in Organelle Quality Control during Exercise

Protein synthesis machinery is globally decreased during exercise. The MTORC1 pathway is a central regulator of protein turnover under conditions of increased external loading by the regulation of ribosomal translation. Thus, the kinase MTOR modulates mRNA translation and protein synthesis by regulating major regulators of ribosomal activity, 4E-BP1 (eukaryotic translation initiation factor 4E-binding protein 1) and S6K1 (ribosomal protein S6 kinase 1). MTOR phosphorylates S6K1 at Thr-389 (its hydrophobic motif), which, in turn, phosphorylates translational effectors such as rpS6 (ribosomal protein S6) and eIF4B (eukaryotic translation initiation factor 4B) [34,35]. In addition, PDK1 (phosphoinositide-dependent kinase-1) phosphorylates S6K1 at Thr-229 provides its full activation [36,37]. 4E-BP1 phosphorylation by MTOR on Thr-37/46 provides its disconnection from the preinitiation complex (PIC) promoting the transcription of protein-coding genes [38,39]. In a study conducted in mice, moderate endurance exercise decreased the phosphorylation state of MTORC1 signaling (i.e., MTOR, S6K1, rpS6, and 4E-BP1) from 90 min [40]. These modulations were concomitant with a raise of the phosphorylation state of eiF2α (Ser-51), an indicator of endoplasmic reticulum stress and AMPK activation. The AMPK mediates inhibition of MTORC1 through phosphorylation of MTOR at Thr-2446 [41], of the tuberous sclerosis complex 2 (TSC2) at Thr-1227 and Ser-1345 [42] and the associated regulatory protein of MTOR complex-1 (RPTOR) on two well-conserved serine residues (Ser-722/792) [43,44] leads to the sequestration of the raptor by 14-3-3 proteins [44]. These events promote the inhibition of Rheb (Ras homolog enriched in brain) and overall MTORC1 inhibition (Figure 1). However, data on the involvement of AMPK/RPTOR axis for MTORC1 inhibition during endurance exercise are lacking.

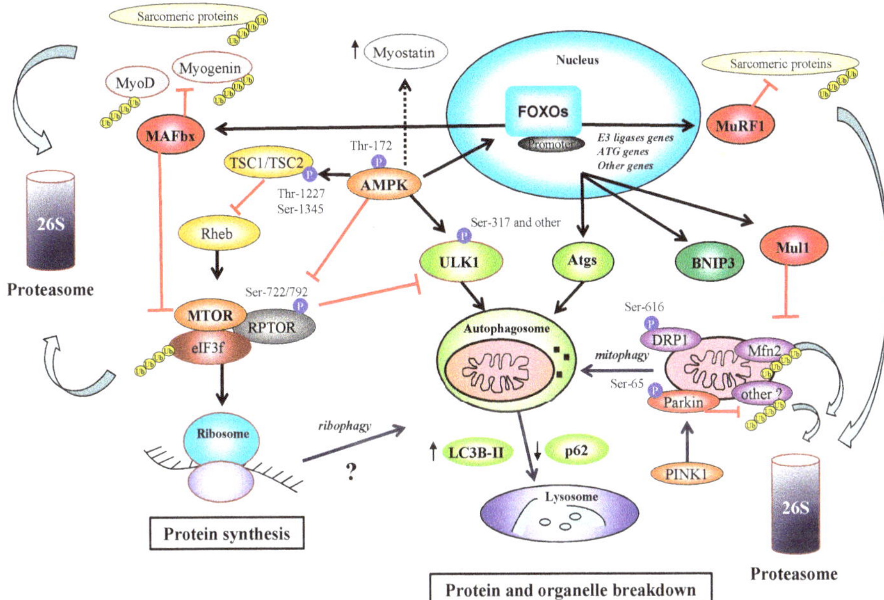

Figure 1. (AMP)-activated protein kinase (AMPK), forkhead box class O subfamily protein (FOXO), and mechanistic (or mammalian) target of rapamycin complex 1 (MTORC1) in the regulation of protein and organelle turnover. FOXO proteins increase the transcription of the E3 ubiquitin protein ligases muscle atrophy F-box (MAFbx)/atrogin-1, muscle RING finger 1 (MuRF1), mitochondrial E3 ubiquitin protein ligase (Mul1), several autophagic genes (Atgs), and BCL2/adenovirus E1B 19 kDa protein-interacting protein 3 (BNIP3) in muscle cells. MTOR and AMPK differentially modulate autophagy initiation by phosphorylation of the Unc-51-like kinase (ULK1). AMPK also activates FOXO1 and FOXO3 and tuberous sclerosis complex 2 (TSC)1/TSC2 complex, and inhibits MTORC1 complex through phosphorylation of the associated regulatory protein of MTOR complex-1 (RPTOR). MAFbx/atrogin-1 and MuRF1 target sarcomeric proteins. MAFbx/atrogin-1 also targets factors involved in cell growth including the transcription factors Myogenin and MyoD, and the eukaryotic initiation factor 3f (eIF3f). PTEN-induced putative kinase protein 1 (PINK1)/Parkin and Mul1 axes enhance mitophagy through ubiquitination of mitochondrial proteins.

A single bout of exercise may lead to a strong stimulation of muscle protein synthesis during the recovery period. Synthesis of myofibrillar proteins is elevated after resistance exercise [45–47] and seems to become more pronounced in trained athletes compared to untrained individuals [48]. Endurance training also increases protein synthesis during the recovery since the MTORC1 pathway is altered in response to this type of exercise. Indeed, increased phosphorylation of several MTOR targets occur in both mice and humans after moderate and exhaustive endurance exercises [40,49,50]. However, selective activation of MTORC1 by specific intracellular signaling pathways is involved according to the exercise modality. Acute sprint exercise or electrical stimulation at high frequency increases PKB (protein kinase B or Akt) and MTOR phosphorylation during recovery [51,52]. Importantly, a recent study conducted in rats compared different resistance exercise models and suggested that hypertrophic response is correlated with the phosphorylation level of MTOR and its regulators or targets (i.e., Akt, the extracellular signal-regulated kinases ERKs, p38, the mitogen-activated protein kinases MAPKs, 4E-BP1) [53]. Finally, the study by Ogasawara highlighted that both rapamycin-sensitive and rapamycin-insensitive MTOR signaling regulate MTOR-dependent muscle protein synthesis during resistance exercise [54]. Concerning endurance exercise, several studies failed to observe modulation of Akt during recovery, whatever exercise intensity [52,55]. Thus, it has been proposed that an AMPK-Akt switch may be involved in the occurrence of specific adaptations to resistance and endurance training [55], with a more specific contribution of Akt/TSC1/TSC2 cascade for resistance, strength, and sprint exercises. This also means that Akt is not essential for MTORC1 activation and protein synthesis during endurance exercise. AMPK activation also contributes to decrease the rate of protein production during resistance exercise. However, protein translation augments from 1 h post-exercise even if AMPK activity becomes less pronounced from 2 h [56]. Finally, in individuals accustomed to training, MTORC1 signaling appears preferably involved for hypertrophy-inducing exercises and the AMPK axis seems to be more specific to endurance training adaptations [57]. It is interesting to note that a combination of endurance and resistance training may affect protein synthesis differentially. Indeed, AMPK activation via endurance exercise may negatively affect MTORC1 activation induced by resistance training. This effect is increased when the endurance exercise is carried-out after a bout of resistance exercise [58].

2.2. MTORC1 Regulators and Exercise: Recent Data on DGKs, FOXO, eIF3f and Cellular Trafficking

Among MTORC1 regulators, the PI3K (phosphoinositide 3-kinase)/Akt axis is notably modulated by exogenous nutrients and the release of growth factors [59–62]. MTOR phosphorylation during mechanical overload, and at the early phase of recovery, is related to MEK/ERK signaling through phosphorylation of TSC2 at Ser-664 but not to PI3K/Akt signaling [63]. ERK1/2 also regulates nuclear transcriptional factors, such as Elk-1 (E-26-like protein 1), c-Myc, c-Jun, and c-Fos that play a role in muscle growth [64]. Activation of ERK1/2 and MTORC1 seems to be required for full stimulation of protein synthesis in humans [65]. However, none of these MTORC1 regulators are recognized as critical actors for fiber hypertrophy during resistance exercise [59–61].

It is also recognized that mechanical stimulus enhances the activation of PLD (phospholipase D) and production of PA (phosphatidic acid), promoting activation of MTORC1. PA is a lipid messenger that binds to MTOR's FKBP12- rapamycin binding domain, favoring its activation [61,66–68]. Nonetheless, PLD activity modulation does not seem only implicated in PA production or MTORC1 activation [69]. Thus, studies from Hornberger's lab investigated the role of diacylglycerol (DAG) and DAG kinases (DGKs) in PA production during mechanical stimulation. DGKζ (DAG zeta) is known to be involved in PA accumulation via DAG phosphorylation and was strongly suggested to be essential for PA production and enhanced MTORC1 activity during mechanical stimulation. More recently, the same group explored the importance of DGKζ in muscle adaptations in vivo with a hypertrophic model of mechanical loading [70]. Thus, the authors reported that DGKζ isoform is the most highly raised and is of importance for muscle growth and hypertrophy. Studies on the mechanisms underlying these adaptations highlighted that DGKζ also suppresses FOXO3 activity, leading to a decline of MAFbx (muscle atrophy F-box)/atrogin-1 and MuRF1 (muscle RING finger 1) induction. Conversely, the expression of these E3 ligases during exercise was increased in DGKζ knock-out muscles, confirming the role of DGKζ in limiting protein breakdown during mechanical overload. Even if the precise mechanism needs to be identified, DGKζ relocation in the nucleus seems to be essential for inhibiting FOXO3 transcriptional activity during mechanical overload. Interestingly, the authors also found that mechanical overload increases expression of the eukaryotic initiation factor 3 subunit f (eIF3f), and this increase is totally blunted in DGKζ knock-out muscles. Given the importance of eIF3f in protein translation process, it can be hypothesized that DGKζ-dependent alteration of FOXO pathway during mechanical overload may also have effects on the translational machinery. Indeed, the FOXO-dependent E3 ligase MAFbx/atrogin-1 is well known to target eIF3f leading to its proteasomal degradation [71].

The role of eIF3f and MTORC1 intracellular trafficking in adaptation to exercise has been also recently investigated. eIF3f belongs to the translation initiation factor complex eIF3f among its 13 subunits involved in mRNA translation initiation. In the last two decades, studies from Leibovitch's lab highlighted eIF3f's involvement in skeletal muscle protein synthesis and hypertrophy [72]. It was demonstrated that a TOS (TOR signaling) motif in eIF3f operates as a scaffold to connect MTORC1 with its translational substrates and to support the initiation of cap-dependent translation [73]. Starvation muscle atrophy is suppressed when an eIF3f mutant insensitive to polyubiquitination by MAFbx is overexpressed, showing its critical role in muscle homeostasis during such a stress [74]. More recently, eIF3f was found to be essential for mouse embryonic development and its partial depletion reduces adult skeletal mass and amplifies muscle loss during disuse by mainly modulating protein synthesis [75]. Concerning exercise, an increase of eIF3f expression was evidenced during overload [70], suggesting a role in adaptations to exercise. Studies in human tissue model that used immunofluorescence approaches identified a type of cellular trafficking involving eIF3f that occurs during a single bout of resistance exercise [76]. Thus, the complex composed of MTORC1/eIF3f was found to co-localize with the lysosome, where the GTPase Rheb is known to trigger the kinase activity of MTOR enhancing MTORC1 substrates phosphorylation [77]. In accordance, studies in vitro and in animals highlighted that MTORC1 recruitment to the lysosome surface is critical to raise MTOR kinase activity [78,79]. After resistance exercise, the MTORC1/LAMP2 complex was found to rapidly translocate at the cell membrane in close proximity to capillaries [76]. Importantly, TSC2 abundance at the cell membrane was also reduced with a dissociation from Rheb, suggesting a decrease of MTOR inhibition favorable to its full activation. These innovative results suggest that, at least in humans, MTORC1 is recruited and activated at the cell periphery following resistance exercise. Interestingly, a protein–carbohydrate beverage post-exercise does not alter MTORC1/eIF3f translocation but increases the interaction between MTOR and eIF3f [76], an association well recognized to drive MTORC1 activation and enhance MTOR target activity [72]. Thus, a bout of resistance exercise may enhance mRNA translational capacity through the association and the translocation to the cell periphery of MTOR and its positive regulators eIF3f and Rheb.

Interestingly, nonprotein dietary factors also influence post-exercise myofibrillar protein synthesis. In humans, it was recently reported that the ingestion of egg whites alone results in lower myofibrillar protein synthesis activation than the ingestion of whole eggs during the recovery from resistance exercise [80]. In accordance, whole egg ingestion increases the phosphorylation level of MTOR, 4E-BP1, rpS6 to a greater extent than egg white ingestion. Whole egg ingestion was also found to increase MTORC1 co-localization with the lysosome after resistance exercise, and this result was correlated with higher rates of myofibrillar protein synthesis [81]. This observation suggests a better mRNA translational capacity after whole egg consumption than after egg white consumption. The underlying mechanisms have been partially studied and PA was proposed to have a role among the potential factors involved in MTORC1 recruitment to the lysosome. Egg yolk contains phosphatidylcholine and oleic acid that can be converted to PA via de novo synthesis, and DAG [82–84]. In addition, the egg yolk is enriched in low-density lipoprotein (LDL)-derived cholesterol that was shown to play a role in MTORC1 recruitment to the lysosome in a SLC38A9-Niemann-Pick C1 (a sterol transport system) signaling complex fashion [85]. In summary, these results highlighted the importance of a new intracellular trafficking mechanism and nonprotein dietary factors that drive optimal myofibrillar protein synthesis after resistance exercise (Figure 2).

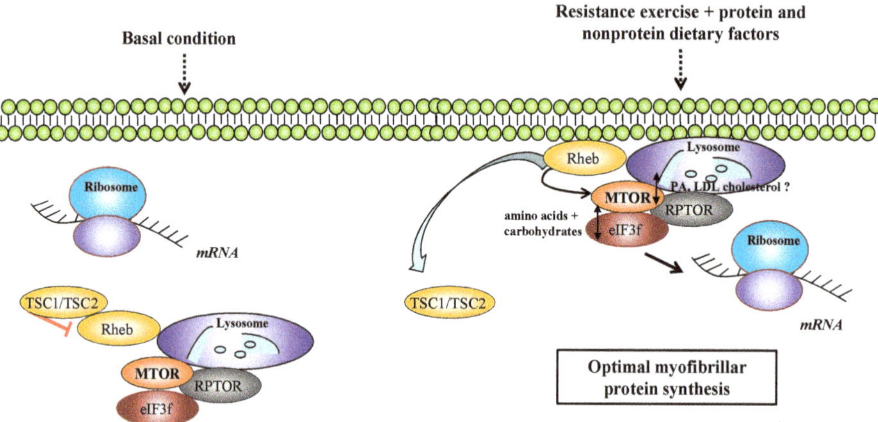

Figure 2. Cellular trafficking of mechanistic (or mammalian) target of rapamycin complex 1 (MTORC1) and lysosome after resistance exercise. In response to resistance exercise, MTORC1 co-localizes with the lysosome and translocates at the cell membrane. MTORC1 recruitment to the lysosome surface is critical to increase MTOR kinase activity. Contractions lead to a decrease of tuberous sclerosis complex 2 (TSC2) abundance and, conversely, to the activation of MTOR by the GTPase Ras homolog enriched in brain (Rheb). A protein-carbohydrate beverage post-exercise increases the interaction between MTOR and eukaryotic initiation factor 3f (eIF3f) without altering MTORC1/eIF3f translocation. Whole eggs ingestion enhances MTORC1 co-localization to the lysosome after resistance exercise.

3. AMPK and FOXO Transcription Factors

3.1. FOXO Homologues in Energy Metabolism and Post-Translational Modifications

Four FOXO members (FOXO1/3/4/6) are expressed in muscle. FOXO6 represses PGC-1α expression and low intensity exercise reduces FOXO6 induction [86], suggesting that exercise-induced PGC-1α may be partially dependent on FOXO6. Nonetheless, data concerning this factor remain limited in this tissue. FOXO1, 3, and 4 have been more extensively investigated, notably due to their important roles in cell cycle, apoptosis, muscle growth, and muscle regeneration [33]. FOXO3 regulates MyoD (an essential myogenic differentiation factor) transcription [87]. FOXO1 and FOXO3 play critical roles in energy homeostasis by favoring mitochondrial metabolism, inhibiting glycolysis, and enhancing lipolytic flux [88–91]. FOXO3 plays a role in the regulation of mitochondrial genome through AMPK and the mitochondrial Sirtuin 3 (SIRT3) [92,93]. FOXO1 and FOXO3 also regulate exercise-induced angiogenesis. FOXOs contribute to the repression of muscle angiogenic response through the induction of thrombospondin 1 (THBS1) during the first days of chronic exercise. Importantly, FOXO repression is critical for long term adaptations to endurance training, especially for angiogenesis [94,95].

FOXO proteins are regulated by several post-translational mechanisms, and numerous enzymes have been identified as kinases of FOXO, including AMPK, Akt, and, more recently, DGKζ. In muscle cells, AMPK activates FOXO3 by phosphorylation at Ser413/588 [23,96]. We recently found that AMPK activation by 5-aminoimidazole-4-carboxamide-1-ß-D-ribofuranoside (AICAR) extends the FOXO3 protein half-life in skeletal muscle primary cells [97]. AMPK also increases the cellular NAD$^+$ level, thus enhancing the activity of histone deacetylase Sirtuin 1 (SIRT1) [98]. This process induces the deacetylation of FOXO1 and 3 leading to their activation [98]. Conversely, Akt, when inhibited by the phosphatidylinositol 3-kinase (PI3K), is responsible for FOXO1 protein translocation from the nucleus to the cytoplasm, leading to its inactivation [99]. Akt phosphorylates FOXO3 on several residues (Thr-32, Ser-253/315), and the phosphorylation of residues Thr-32 and Ser-253 promotes its cytoplasmic retention by a mechanism involving the 14-3-3 chaperone protein [100]. FOXO regulation by Akt induces a decrease in the binding between FOXO and its DNA sequences targets and, consequently, decreases

FOXO transcriptional activity [101,102]. In addition, FOXO3 is targeted by the histone acetyl-transferase p300 for its ubiquitination by Mdm2 (E3 ligase murine double minute 2) and subsequent degradation by the proteasome [103]. In muscle, p300 alters differentially the expression of FOXO 1 and 4 without affecting the expression of FOXO3 [104]. Furthermore, p300 alters FOXO3 and FOXO4 activity but increases the nuclear localization of FOXO1 and the transcription of FOXO1-dependant genes underlining the differential regulation of the FOXO homologues [104]. Finally, DGKζ has been recently found to suppress FOXO3 activity in skeletal muscle [70], extending the role of the DGK to the regulation of catabolism (Figure 3).

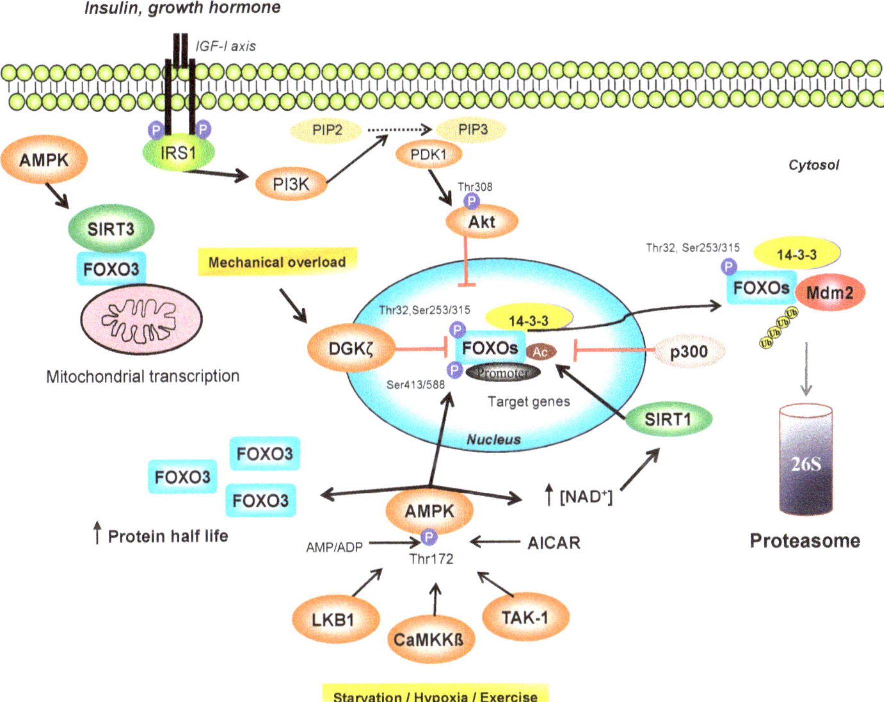

Figure 3. (AMP)-activated protein kinase AMPK and forkhead box class O subfamily protein FOXO regulation in skeletal muscle. FOXO proteins are phosphorylated and inhibited by protein kinase B (PKB or Akt) in response to insulin or growth factor. Under the condition of energy stress, AMPK, which is activated by the AMPK kinases (AMPKK) Ca^{2+}/calmodulin- dependent protein kinase ß (CaMKKß), liver kinase B1 (LKB1), and transforming growth factor ß-activated kinase 1 (TAK-1), phosphorylates and increases FOXO3 activity. AMPK is also involved in FOXO deacetylation through Sirtuin 1 (SIRT1) and Sirtuin 3 (SIRT3). AMPK activation by 5-aminoimidazole-4-carboxamide-1-ß-D-ribofuranoside (AICAR) stabilizes FOXO3 by increasing its protein half-life. Moreover, AMPK favors the association between FOXO3 and mitochondrial DNA through SIRT3, mediating the transcription of mitochondrial genes. During mechanical overload, FOXO3 transcriptional activity is inhibited by diacylglycerol kinase ζ (DGKζ) by a mechanism independent of DGKζ kinase activity within the nucleus. Cytosolic FOXO3 is targeted by E3 ligase murine double minute 2 (Mdm2) for degradation via the ubiquitin-proteasome system. FOXO3 and FOXO4 are acetylated by the histone acetyltransferase p300. Abbreviations undefined in the main text: IRS1, insulin receptor substrate 1; PIP2, phosphatidylinositol 4,5-bisphosphate; PIP3, phosphatidylinositol 3,4,5-triphosphate.

3.2. AMPK/FOXO Axis in Organelle Quality Control during Exercise

In addition to its role in muscle metabolism, AMPK/FOXO axis represents a major actor in cellular components turnover via the ubiquitin-proteasome and autophagosome-lysosome proteolytic systems. The ubiquitin-proteasome pathway involves E3 ubiquitin-ligases that target substrates to the 26S proteasome for degradation after poly-ubiquitination. FOXO1 and FOXO3 regulate the transcription of crucial ubiquitin ligases, including MuRF1, Trim32 (tripartite motif-containing protein 32), and MAFbx/atrogin-1, implicated in myofibrillar protein removal (i.e., myosin light chain 1 and 2, myosin heavy chain protein, myosin-binding protein C, actin, tropomyosin, troponins, alpha-actinin, desmin, Z-bands, thin filaments), and myogenic/growth factors (i.e., MyoD, myogenin, eIF3f) [71,89,99,105–116]. Autophagy is a critical stress response that allows the replacement of protein, organelles, and other cellular components. In the first stage, proteins or other cellular constituents (e.g., mitochondria, ribosomes, peroxisomes, endoplasmic reticulum, lipids, polysaccharides) are incorporated in a double-membrane vesicle called the autophagosome. Then, the content of the autophagosome is removed by another vesicle named the lysosome that contents acid hydrolases. FOXO3 promotes the transcription of a plethora of autophagy genes (ATGs) involved in autophagosome biogenesis and maturation, including ATG4B, ATG12L, Beclin, BNIP3 (BCL2/adenovirus E1B 19 kDa protein-interacting protein 3), GABARAPL1 (GABA Type A Receptor Associated Protein Like 1), LC3 (microtubule-associated protein light chain 3), PI3KIII, ULK2 (Unc-51-like kinase) [106,117]. Of note, BNIP3/BNIP3L are involved in mitophagy since BNIP3 is a mitochondrial receptor that directly connects to the Atg8 homolog LC3 and GABARAP, leading to the recruitment of autophagosome to damaged mitochondria [118–120]. FOXO1 also activates the lysosomal protease cathepsin L in skeletal muscle [121]. In mice, several autophagy markers are more expressed in slow-twitch muscles but basal autophagy flux appears to be higher in glycolytic muscles, suggesting that autophagy in glycolytic muscle might be more tightly regulated [122]. Importantly, AMPK and MTOR differentially regulate the initiator of autophagy ULK1 (Atg1) through phosphorylation [123–125], noticeably in skeletal muscle [5,23,126]. AMPK phosphorylates ULK1 at several residues (Ser-317/467/555/777) leading to autophagy initiation in condition of energy stress. Conversely, MTOR inhibits ULK1 by phosphorylating Ser-757 when nutrients are plentiful.

In the last decade, studies have revealed that acute endurance exercise affect the expression and phosphorylation level of markers involved in protein and organelle removal. FOXO1 and FOXO3 level increases after exhaustive exercises [33], and it was found that several proteolytic actors (i.e., MAFbx/atrogin-1, MuRF1, LC3B-II, and Atg12 expression, etc.) and proteasome β2 subunit activity may be enhanced after marathon or ultra-endurance exercise [127,128]. Some of these modulations were also reported in response to exercise performed at moderate intensity [129–131]. Increases in protein breakdown may be useful to favor cell component turnover during recovery, or, alternatively, amino acids can serve as substrates when exercise is prolonged. Interestingly, the enhanced muscle protein anabolic response with ingestion of essential amino acids and carbohydrates during the recovery of resistance exercise seems primarily due to an increase in protein translation compared to modulation of protein degradation [132]. More conventional endurance exercise may augment the expression of autophagy markers according to exercise intensity and the nutritional state. When performed in a fasted state, exercise promotes more important increases of autophagy markers (LC3B, GABARAPL1 lipidation, cATG12 protein level, p62 mRNA level) and more specific inductions of actors involved in mitophagy (BNIP3 and Parkin expression) compared to exercise conducted in a fed state [133]. Consistently, rises in DRP1 (dynamin related protein 1) phosphorylation, a GTPase involved in fission of mitochondria, quickly occurs during exercise, including endurance exercise conducted at moderate intensity (40–50% of $\dot{V}O_2max$) in sedentary rodents [40]. Exercise at moderate intensity quickly increases phosphorylation of AMPK and induces initiation of the autophagy pathway through ULK1 [40]. An increase in autophagy markers (i.e., LC3 lipidation and p62 expression) can be observed near to exhaustion [40]. Importantly, the modulation of autophagy markers during endurance exercise differs between rodent and human muscles. Indeed, regarding LC3 lipidation or p62 expression, acute endurance exercise seems to promote enhanced autophagosome content in mice, while the opposite can be found in humans [134,135]. However, 60 min of cycling exercise at moderate intensity increases ULK1 phosphorylation concomitantly to a decrease in LC3 lipidation in human skeletal muscle, suggesting an initiation of autophagy [129]. It will be necessary to define if these contradictive results found in humans can be explained by a decrease in autophagy or alternatively by a fast degradation of the autophagosome by the lysosome because of an abrupt induction of overall system. Development of valid markers of autophagic flux in humans should contribute to a better understanding of this pathway.

Autophagy is an essential system for muscle maintenance since chronic autophagy deficiency leads to increased proportion of centralized nuclei and pro-apoptotic markers, reduced force, altered twitch kinetics in glycolytic muscle, as well as enhanced calpain and proteasomal enzymatic activity [122]. In cardiac and skeletal muscles, autophagy plays a role in the exercise-related metabolic effects [130,131]. Disruption in autophagy decreases endurance performance and alters glucose metabolism. In addition, autophagy failure results in mitochondria degeneration, sarcoplasmic reticulum distension and disorganization of sarcomere [136], confirming the critical role of autophagy in mitochondria and myofiber homeostasis. In response to chronic exercise, autophagy appears to be needed for exercise training-induced mitochondrial remodeling and fiber-type transition [137].

3.3. Exercise and Autophagy/Mitophagy Flux

The majority of the aforementioned studies investigated autophagy at the transcriptional or translational level. However, these approaches are not suitable for the interpretation of autophagy activity. The "autophagic flux assay", an accurate method to access autophagy activity, is based on the turnover of LC3 and p62. Inhibitors of autophagy (colchicine, chloroquine, NH_4Cl, or bafilomycin A1) are used to block the incorporation of the autophagosomes into the lysosome or to reduce the activity of lysosomal enzymes. This method avoids incorrect analysis of LC3-II or p62 protein level. For example, LC3-II content can be increased when autophagy activity is enhanced but also when the latter stages of the process (e.g., fusion between autophagosome and lysosome) is altered. Per contra, a decrease of LC3-II levels could mean either a decrease or, when lysosomal degradation is fast, an elevation in autophagy activity. Experiments with autophagy flux are lacking, especially in the evaluation of the responses to chronic exercise in vivo. However, in a recent investigation [138], the authors used colchicine treatment to establish a link between autophagy modulation during endurance training and mitochondrial biogenesis in mice skeletal muscle. Thus, autophagy suppression by colchicine abrogated mitochondrial adaptations linked to training. More recently, studies from Hood's lab examined the impact of ageing and chronic contractile activity on basal muscle autophagy and mitophagy flux. In these experiments, mitophagy flux was assessed on isolated mitochondria. The authors found that aged muscles present accelerated basal mitophagy flux, especially in intermyofibrillar mitochondria [139,140]. This result indicates that, during ageing, autophagy activity is increased to promote the targeting of damaged organelles, especially mitochondria. Importantly, chronic contractile activity decreases mitophagy flux in both aged and young muscles [139,140]. Hence, one might hypothesize that, in this context, chronic contractile activity improves mitochondria quality and decreases the necessity to recycle them through the autophagosome-lysosome pathway. Additional investigation using mitophagy flux experiments is needed to examine the effect of exercise training on basal mitochondria turnover in vivo. Importantly, the same group also reported that contractile activity may normalize autophagy flux and reverse mitochondrial abnormalities during autophagy suppression [141]. In that respect, exercise may represent an effective therapeutic issue to counterbalance diseases with defects in organelle replacement. However, to date, no data have been made available on the effect of exercise on the turnover of other organelles such as ribosomes or endoplasmic reticulum that represent crucial components in muscle protein homeostasis.

4. The Emerging Roles of Parkin and FOXO3-Dependant Mul1 Pathway in Organelle Turnover and Adaptations to Exercise

In the last decades, the E3-ubiquitin ligase Parkin has been implicated in the control of mitophagy with a particular focus on neuronal degeneration, especially during Parkinson disease (PD) [142–144]. PINK1 (PTEN- induced putative kinase protein 1) is a mitochondrial serine/threonine protein kinase that is activated by the depolarization of mitochondrial membrane. PINK1 phosphorylates and enhances Parkin activity [144]. Data highlighted that Parkin phosphorylation at Ser-65 is necessary for its mitochondrial translocation, leading to the degradation of several actors involved in mitochondrial dynamics and motility [142,145]. Parkin is known to ubiquitinate TOMM20 (translocase of outer mitochondrial membrane 20), the mitochondrial fusion protein Mitofusin 1/2 (Mfn2 1/2), DRP1, Fis1, Miro, and VDAC (voltage-dependent anion channel) [146–151], leading to the translocation of autophagy receptors to mitochondria (i.e., LC3, SQSTM1/p62 and NBR1/autophagy cargo receptor) [152] (Figure 1). In addition to its roles in mitophagy and mitochondrial dynamics, Parkin targets the transcriptional repressor of PGC-1α PARIS (ZNF746, zinc finger protein 746), favoring mitochondrial biogenesis [153]. Finally, a role of Parkin in the production of mitochondrial-derived vesicles playing a role in mitochondrial quality control has also been revealed [154–158].

A recent study investigated the involvement of Parkin in the muscle phenotype of PD [159]. The authors reported that the mitochondrial uncoupler carbonyl cyanide m-chlorophenylhydrazone (CCCP) promotes PINK1/Parkin-mediated mitophagy in C2C12 cells, and myotube atrophy. Ablation of Parkin resulted in accumulation of dysfunctional mitochondria and myotubular atrophy, suggesting that Parkin plays a role in skeletal muscle mitochondrial removal. More recently, Gouspillou and co-workers highlighted, for the first time, the critical role of Parkin in contractile and mitochondrial properties of healthy muscle [160]. The authors found that Parkin ablation causes muscle contractile dysfunction associated with higher cross-sectional area of type-IIb fibers. Importantly, Parkin ablation results in mitochondrial dysfunction with reduced maximal mitochondrial respiration and mitochondrial uncoupling but without alteration of mitochondrial content. This study has also suggested that Parkin ablation favors oxidative stress, decreases mitochondrial fusion, and increases mitochondrial fission. Even if specific mitophagy flux has not been assessed, the authors also found an increase of autophagy markers in Parkin$^{-/-}$ muscles. Thus, these data are consistent with global mitochondria alteration and Parkin appears to be a critical actor in maintaining contractile properties efficiency in normal skeletal muscle. In addition, a recent study from Hood's lab [161] revealed that Parkin and mitophagy are of importance for training-induced mitochondrial adaptations. However, in this study, the authors showed that Parkin ablation does not significantly affect basal mitophagy flux. In response to a single bout of endurance exercise, enhanced mitophagy flux and alterations of PGC-1α signaling were observed in Parkin deficient mice, but mitochondrial content was increased in a similar extension to the wild-type population. This result indicates that Parkin/PGC-1α axis seems unessential for mitochondrial biogenesis during exercise. Importantly, the authors demonstrated that acute endurance exercise elevates mitophagy flux and training attenuates this elevation in wild-type but not in Parkin deficient animals. However, training does not alter basal mitophagy flux, even if the presence of Parkin to mitochondrial membrane is enhanced in the basal state. These data seem to indicate that a lower rate of mitophagy may occur thanks to training adaptations that may lead to a better mitochondria quality. In agreement, the authors also found that training increased mitochondrial content in Parkin knock-out mice, but these mitochondria showed several dysfunctions.

The E3-ligase Mul1 (or MULAN/GIDE/MAPL) was recently proposed to be associated to the AMPK-FOXO3 signaling pathway in muscle [97]. Mul1 plays a role in the control of mitochondrial quality by coordinating mitochondrial removal and dynamics but also apoptosis [162–164]. Mul1 is upregulated by AMPK activation in primary myotubes [97] and AMPK could block the preservative effects of IGF-1 on contractility of sensory-innervated muscle cells through Mul1 enhancement [165]. In skeletal muscle, changes in Mul1 expression lead to the degradation of Mfn2 and mitochondrial fission, inducing mitochondrial elimination [166]. Mul1 also favors the fragmentation of mitochondria through DRP1 stabilization [167]. Interestingly, Mul1 was also found to stabilize ULK1 in HeLa cells [163]. However, these recent findings have not yet been evaluated in muscle cells. Even if these data highlight a role of Mul1 in mitochondrial turnover and muscle atrophy, data on exercise are still limited and there is a need to examine the implication of Mul1 in adaptations to training. A recent study revealed that Mul1 and the mitophagy pathway seems not to be involved in adaptations to training in muscle of patients with type 2 diabetes [168]. However, an increase of Mul1 protein expression, but not mRNA level, has been observed during acute endurance exercise in the muscles of healthy rodents [40], indicating a potential role for Mul1 during such a stress.

5. Exercise in Hypoxia

Athletes currently use training under hypoxia as a method to enhance performance at sea level or to prepare competitions at altitude. The addition of hypoxia during training elicits higher metabolic stress and can promote selective adaptive responses for aerobic performance [169,170]. Recently, it was found that repeated-sprint training in hypoxia also enhances repeated sprint ability in swimming and team-sports [171–173]. Another protocol in which high-intensity exercises were conducted under hypoxia and recoveries in normoxia, was also proposed for highly-trained athletes to provide additional effects on endurance performance [174]. The most recognized effects of training under hypoxia on skeletal muscle are related to oxidative capacity, capillary density, mitochondrial density, and enhanced blood glucose utilization [170,175,176]. However, occurrence of adaptations depends on several factors (e.g., hypoxic dose and duration) [177], and studies also reported no further positive effect on performance at sea level [178–180].

Acute exposition to normobaric hypoxia was found to modulate basal protein turnover markers. However, the majority of the works on hypoxia mainly focused on the modulation of protein translation markers [181–184] and data on the effect of exercise conducted under hypoxia on protein balance are lacking. Nevertheless, studies from Deldique's lab recently suggested that acute exposition to hypoxia increases or does not have effect on the MTORC1 pathway [185,186]. This discrepancy between studies could be explained by differences in the nutritional pattern that affect insulin (or catecholamines) concentration. Indeed, high plasma insulin concentration may upregulate the MTORC1 pathway during exposure to hypoxia [185]. Concerning autophagy, recent studies from Masschlelein and co-workers investigated its regulation during acute normobaric hypoxia in humans [186]. The authors observed a raise in the LC3-II/I ratio and a reduction of p62 expression at rest, suggesting enhanced autophagy. In addition, moderate cycling exercise increased the BNIP3 mRNA level, a marker of mitophagy [186]. However, no study has performed autophagy flux measurement in response to both acute and chronic hypoxia, limiting possible interpretations. Finally, concerning resistance training in humans, a recent study from Deldique's lab [187] highlighted that hypoxia (FiO$_2$: 14%) blunts the activation of protein synthesis and down-regulates the transcriptional program of autophagy. Importantly, resistance exercise performed in hypoxia seems to initiate the transcription of genes involved in satellite cell incorporation that potentially participate in gains of force production observed in the long term [187]. Additional studies are also required to evaluate the gains in muscle mass and force production compared to normoxia.

Although studies on the acute effects of hypoxia on protein turnover are emerging, chronic adaptations to altitude or normobaric hypoxic training remain largely unexplored. It is documented that chronic hypoxia can cause skeletal muscle atrophy in rodent through a downregulation of protein translation and enhanced proteolysis, as well as alterations in oxidative metabolism [188–190]. In humans, high altitude hypoxia exposure (4559 m) for 7–9 days induces a decline of iron transport-related protein expression, tricarboxylic acid cycle, oxidative phosphorylation, and oxidative stress [191]. Moreover, MTOR level may be reduced in such a condition [191], suggesting alteration in protein translation. However, the effects of ambient hypoxia on both others proteins synthesis markers (i.e., translational initiation markers) and catabolic signaling pathways (i.e., autophagy) remain to be clarified in humans, especially in combination with exercise training and nutritional strategies [185,192].

6. Muscle Contraction Regimens and Cell Component Turnover

Numerous investigations have shown that resistance training with eccentric actions performed at high intensities may have higher benefits for muscle strength and hypertrophy compared to concentric or isometric contraction modes [193]. In addition, early adaptations have been reported with eccentric overload training [194]. Protein turnover pathways can be affected by different modes of contraction and the higher effects of eccentric mode on muscle growth seems to be associated with a greater activation of MTORC1 pathway [195]. However, contraction mode appears less influential on muscle hypertrophy with prolonged high-volume resistance training and protein and carbohydrate supplementation becomes more critical factors to further increase muscle mass [195]. Furthermore, when the magnitude of the force–time integral is normalized, studies in both rodents and humans found that eccentric mode induces similar anabolic responses to concentric mode [196,197]. From a molecular viewpoint, MTORC1 activation after eccentric contractions seems more related to PA synthesis than the PI3K/Akt signaling pathway [198]. Even if muscular hypertrophy involves the MTORC1 pathway during the post-exercise period [199], many weeks of training do not necessarily induce major changes on the basal MTORC1 pathway [195]. Under the same force–time integral, with regard to proteolytic markers (i.e., FOXO3 and ULK1 phosphorylation, LC3B-II/I ratio, and MAFbx/atrogin-1, MuRF1 and p62 expression), the study from Ato and co-workers suggests that the contraction mode does not appear as a factor that may differentially regulate proteolytic pathways in the early phase of muscle contractions [200]. During exercise, a study from Sandri's lab highlighted that autophagy seems important to preserve mitochondrial function during damaging muscle eccentric contractions [201]. Altogether, these data still suggest that the magnitude of force–time integral should be the main factor to explain differences in anabolic or catabolic response. The energy cost of eccentric actions is lower compared with concentric contractions, and eccentric exercise allows one to develop higher loads during a training session. In addition, autophagy flux experiments remain to be performed to avoid misinterpretation of the modulation of autophagy or mitophagy according to contraction mode. Thus, from our point of view, further studies have to consider these features.

Some studies explored the response to the combination of eccentric endurance exercise and hypoxia in skeletal muscle. Thus, the study from Klarod and co-workers suggests that downhill walking performed at a low altitude may present some advantages for physical fitness in pre-diabetic men [202]. In this study, eccentric endurance exercise training at a low altitude (from 850 to 1360 m) was shown to improve aerobic performance. At a moderate altitude (from 2000 to 2447 m), the same exercise training program increased the biological antioxidant activity of plasma. In rodents, the study from Rizo-Roca investigated if intermittent hypobaric hypoxia combined with aerobic exercise may be beneficial for recovery from eccentric-damaging exercises. The authors found that this strategy may reverse the signs of muscle damages and reinforce or preserve the fiber oxidative phenotype in response to several weeks of training [203]. The same group reported that this strategy may improve important mitochondrial aspects (i.e., fission/fusion markers and the expression of actors involved in mitochondrial biogenesis) during recovery from eccentric exercises [204]. These results open important perspectives on the use of hypoxia combined with aerobic exercise as a recovery method from damaging exercises in both athletes and patients. However, to provide further recommendations and better understand cellular adaptations, more studies have to be developed, especially studies on myofibrillar protein synthesis and mitochondria remodeling, in response to the eccentric exercise performed in hypoxia.

7. Conclusions and Perspectives

The preservation of muscle mass and oxidative capacity are essential for maintaining quality of life. In the past few years, advances have expanded our understanding on the impact of exercise on the events that govern organelle turnover and the role played by crucial factors, especially AMPK, MTORC1, and FOXO. Concerning protein synthesis, a major discovery of this last decade is that DGKζ appears as a key regulator of MTORC1 during overload. Importantly, the modulation and trafficking of eIF3f and its potential regulation through DGKζ/FOXO3 axis has been, for the first time, pointed out in the context of exercise. In addition, our knowledge on the physiological significance of MTORC1 recruitment to the lysosome and to the cell periphery has been significantly improved by using immunofluorescence approaches. Concerning protein breakdown during exercise, Parkin and Mul1 have been recognized as critical E3-ligases for normal skeletal muscle and mitochondria maintenance. Parkin appears essential for mitochondrial adaptations to endurance training and the maintenance of functioning mitochondria. However, the potential role of Mul1 in mitochondrial adaptations to chronic exercise has to be addressed. Furthermore, studies on hypoxia highlighted that hypoxic stress may blunt the MTORC1 pathway after resistance training but compensative mechanisms (i.e., transcription of satellite cells regulators) are potentially involved in hypertrophy and strength gains. Studies have to be initiated, in particular, with measurements of autophagy/mitophagy flux to reinforce our knowledge on the effects of training in hypoxia on organelle quality control. Regarding the mode of contraction, eccentric exercises lead to a greater activation of the MTORC1 pathway, probably through a PA-dependent mechanism. Finally, further studies on this topic and the impact of nutritional interventions have to be developed, to better understand skeletal muscle adaptations to training, thanks to organelle quality, and to develop countermeasures during illness.

Funding: This research received no external funding.

Acknowledgments: The authors thank S. Hamborgesa for helpful discussion.

Conflicts of Interest: The authors declare no conflict of interest.

References

1. Hood, D.A.; Memme, J.M.; Oliveira, A.N.; Triolo, M. Maintenance of Skeletal Muscle Mitochondria in Health, Exercise, and Aging. *Annu. Rev. Physiol.* **2018**, *81*, 19–41. [CrossRef] [PubMed]

2. McGlory, C.; van Vliet, S.; Stokes, T.; Mittendorfer, B.; Phillips, S.M. The impact of exercise and nutrition on the regulation of skeletal muscle mass. *J. Physiol.* **2018**, *597*, 1251–1258. [CrossRef] [PubMed]

3. Sanchez, A.M.J.; Bernardi, H.; Py, G.; Candau, R.B. Autophagy is essential to support skeletal muscle plasticity in response to endurance exercise. *Am. J. Physiol. Regul. Integr. Comp. Physiol.* **2014**, *307*, R956–R969. [CrossRef] [PubMed]

4. Kjøbsted, R.; Hingst, J.R.; Fentz, J.; Foretz, M.; Sanz, M.-N.; Pehmøller, C.; Shum, M.; Marette, A.; Mounier, R.; Treebak, J.T.; et al. AMPK in skeletal muscle function and metabolism. *FASEB J. Off. Publ. Fed. Am. Soc. Exp. Biol.* **2018**, *32*, 1741–1777. [CrossRef] [PubMed]

5. Sanchez, A.M.J.; Candau, R.B.; Csibi, A.; Pagano, A.F.; Raibon, A.; Bernardi, H. The role of AMP-activated protein kinase in the coordination of skeletal muscle turnover and energy homeostasis. *Am. J. Physiol. Cell Physiol.* **2012**, *303*, C475–C485. [CrossRef]

6. Marsin, A.-S.; Bouzin, C.; Bertrand, L.; Hue, L. The stimulation of glycolysis by hypoxia in activated monocytes is mediated by AMP-activated protein kinase and inducible 6-phosphofructo-2-kinase. *J. Biol. Chem.* **2002**, *277*, 30778–30783. [CrossRef]

7. Kudo, N.; Barr, A.J.; Barr, R.L.; Desai, S.; Lopaschuk, G.D. High rates of fatty acid oxidation during reperfusion of ischemic hearts are associated with a decrease in malonyl-CoA levels due to an increase in 5′-AMP-activated protein kinase inhibition of acetyl-CoA carboxylase. *J. Biol. Chem.* **1995**, *270*, 17513–17520. [CrossRef]

8. Vavvas, D.; Apazidis, A.; Saha, A.K.; Gamble, J.; Patel, A.; Kemp, B.E.; Witters, L.A.; Ruderman, N.B. Contraction-induced changes in acetyl-CoA carboxylase and 5′-AMP-activated kinase in skeletal muscle. *J. Biol. Chem.* **1997**, *272*, 13255–13261. [CrossRef]

9. Derave, W.; Ai, H.; Ihlemann, J.; Witters, L.A.; Kristiansen, S.; Richter, E.A.; Ploug, T. Dissociation of AMP-activated protein kinase activation and glucose transport in contracting slow-twitch muscle. *Diabetes* **2000**, *49*, 1281–1287. [CrossRef]

10. Salt, I.P.; Connell, J.M.; Gould, G.W. 5-aminoimidazole-4-carboxamide ribonucleoside (AICAR) inhibits insulin-stimulated glucose transport in 3T3-L1 adipocytes. *Diabetes* **2000**, *49*, 1649–1656. [CrossRef]

11. Park, H.; Kaushik, V.K.; Constant, S.; Prentki, M.; Przybytkowski, E.; Ruderman, N.B.; Saha, A.K. Coordinate regulation of malonyl-CoA decarboxylase, sn-glycerol-3-phosphate acyltransferase, and acetyl-CoA carboxylase by AMP-activated protein kinase in rat tissues in response to exercise. *J. Biol. Chem.* **2002**, *277*, 32571–32577. [CrossRef] [PubMed]

12. Winder, W.W.; Hardie, D.G. Inactivation of acetyl-CoA carboxylase and activation of AMP-activated protein kinase in muscle during exercise. *Am. J. Physiol.* **1996**, *270*, E299–E304. [CrossRef] [PubMed]

13. Wojtaszewski, J.F.; Nielsen, P.; Hansen, B.F.; Richter, E.A.; Kiens, B. Isoform-specific and exercise intensity-dependent activation of 5'-AMP-activated protein kinase in human skeletal muscle. *J. Physiol.* **2000**, *528 Pt 1*, 221–226. [CrossRef]

14. Stein, S.C.; Woods, A.; Jones, N.A.; Davison, M.D.; Carling, D. The regulation of AMP-activated protein kinase by phosphorylation. *Biochem. J.* **2000**, *345 Pt 3*, 437–443. [CrossRef]

15. Hawley, S.A.; Selbert, M.A.; Goldstein, E.G.; Edelman, A.M.; Carling, D.; Hardie, D.G. 5'-AMP activates the AMP-activated protein kinase cascade, and Ca2+/calmodulin activates the calmodulin-dependent protein kinase I cascade, via three independent mechanisms. *J. Biol. Chem.* **1995**, *270*, 27186–27191. [CrossRef] [PubMed]

16. Hawley, S.A.; Pan, D.A.; Mustard, K.J.; Ross, L.; Bain, J.; Edelman, A.M.; Frenguelli, B.G.; Hardie, D.G. Calmodulin-dependent protein kinase kinase-beta is an alternative upstream kinase for AMP-activated protein kinase. *Cell Metab.* **2005**, *2*, 9–19. [CrossRef] [PubMed]

17. Hong, S.-P.; Leiper, F.C.; Woods, A.; Carling, D.; Carlson, M. Activation of yeast Snf1 and mammalian AMP-activated protein kinase by upstream kinases. *Proc. Natl. Acad. Sci. USA* **2003**, *100*, 8839–8843. [CrossRef]

18. Woods, A.; Johnstone, S.R.; Dickerson, K.; Leiper, F.C.; Fryer, L.G.D.; Neumann, D.; Schlattner, U.; Wallimann, T.; Carlson, M.; Carling, D. LKB1 is the upstream kinase in the AMP-activated protein kinase cascade. *Curr. Biol.* **2003**, *13*, 2004–2008. [CrossRef]

19. Herrero-Martín, G.; Høyer-Hansen, M.; García-García, C.; Fumarola, C.; Farkas, T.; López-Rivas, A.; Jäättelä, M. TAK1 activates AMPK-dependent cytoprotective autophagy in TRAIL-treated epithelial cells. *EMBO J.* **2009**, *28*, 677–685. [CrossRef] [PubMed]

20. Xiao, B.; Sanders, M.J.; Underwood, E.; Heath, R.; Mayer, F.V.; Carmena, D.; Jing, C.; Walker, P.A.; Eccleston, J.F.; Haire, L.F.; et al. Structure of mammalian AMPK and its regulation by ADP. *Nature* **2011**, *472*, 230–233. [CrossRef] [PubMed]

21. Davies, S.P.; Helps, N.R.; Cohen, P.T.; Hardie, D.G. 5'-AMP inhibits dephosphorylation, as well as promoting phosphorylation, of the AMP-activated protein kinase. Studies using bacterially expressed human protein phosphatase-2C alpha and native bovine protein phosphatase-2AC. *FEBS Lett.* **1995**, *377*, 421–425. [PubMed]

22. McBride, A.; Ghilagaber, S.; Nikolaev, A.; Hardie, D.G. The glycogen-binding domain on the AMPK beta subunit allows the kinase to act as a glycogen sensor. *Cell Metab.* **2009**, *9*, 23–34. [CrossRef] [PubMed]

23. Sanchez, A.M.J.; Csibi, A.; Raibon, A.; Cornille, K.; Gay, S.; Bernardi, H.; Candau, R. AMPK promotes skeletal muscle autophagy through activation of forkhead FoxO3a and interaction with Ulk1. *J. Cell. Biochem.* **2012**, *113*, 695–710. [CrossRef] [PubMed]

24. Holmes, B.F.; Kurth-Kraczek, E.J.; Winder, W.W. Chronic activation of 5'-AMP-activated protein kinase increases GLUT-4, hexokinase, and glycogen in muscle. *J. Appl. Physiol. Bethesda MD 1985* **1999**, *87*, 1990–1995. [CrossRef] [PubMed]

25. Marsin, A.S.; Bertrand, L.; Rider, M.H.; Deprez, J.; Beauloye, C.; Vincent, M.F.; Van den Berghe, G.; Carling, D.; Hue, L. Phosphorylation and activation of heart PFK-2 by AMPK has a role in the stimulation of glycolysis during ischaemia. *Curr. Biol.* **2000**, *10*, 1247–1255. [CrossRef]

26. Thomson, D.M.; Herway, S.T.; Fillmore, N.; Kim, H.; Brown, J.D.; Barrow, J.R.; Winder, W.W. AMP-activated protein kinase phosphorylates transcription factors of the CREB family. *J. Appl. Physiol. Bethesda MD 1985* **2008**, *104*, 429–438. [CrossRef]

27. Stoppani, J.; Hildebrandt, A.L.; Sakamoto, K.; Cameron-Smith, D.; Goodyear, L.J.; Neufer, P.D. AMP-activated protein kinase activates transcription of the UCP3 and HKII genes in rat skeletal muscle. *Am. J. Physiol. Endocrinol. Metab.* **2002**, *283*, E1239–E1248. [CrossRef]

28. Barnes, T.; Di Sebastiano, K.M.; Vlavcheski, F.; Quadrilatero, J.; Tsiani, E.; Mourtzakis, M. Glutamate increases glucose uptake in L6 myotubes in a concentration- and time-dependent manner that is mediated by AMPK. *Appl. Physiol. Nutr. Metab. Physiol. Appl. Nutr. Metab.* **2018**, *43*, 1307–1313. [CrossRef]

29. Jørgensen, S.B.; Viollet, B.; Andreelli, F.; Frøsig, C.; Birk, J.B.; Schjerling, P.; Vaulont, S.; Richter, E.A.; Wojtaszewski, J.F.P. Knockout of the alpha2 but not alpha1 5′-AMP-activated protein kinase isoform abolishes 5-aminoimidazole-4-carboxamide-1-beta-4-ribofuranosidebut not contraction-induced glucose uptake in skeletal muscle. *J. Biol. Chem.* **2004**, *279*, 1070–1079. [CrossRef]

30. Jäger, S.; Handschin, C.; St-Pierre, J.; Spiegelman, B.M. AMP-activated protein kinase (AMPK) action in skeletal muscle via direct phosphorylation of PGC-1alpha. *Proc. Natl. Acad. Sci. USA* **2007**, *104*, 12017–12022. [CrossRef]

31. Wu, Z.; Puigserver, P.; Andersson, U.; Zhang, C.; Adelmant, G.; Mootha, V.; Troy, A.; Cinti, S.; Lowell, B.; Scarpulla, R.C.; et al. Mechanisms controlling mitochondrial biogenesis and respiration through the thermogenic coactivator PGC-1. *Cell* **1999**, *98*, 115–124. [CrossRef]

32. Puigserver, P.; Wu, Z.; Park, C.W.; Graves, R.; Wright, M.; Spiegelman, B.M. A cold-inducible coactivator of nuclear receptors linked to adaptive thermogenesis. *Cell* **1998**, *92*, 829–839. [CrossRef]

33. Sanchez, A.M.J.; Candau, R.B.; Bernardi, H. FoxO transcription factors: Their roles in the maintenance of skeletal muscle homeostasis. *Cell. Mol. Life Sci. CMLS* **2014**, *71*, 1657–1671. [CrossRef] [PubMed]

34. Holz, M.K.; Ballif, B.A.; Gygi, S.P.; Blenis, J. mTOR and S6K1 mediate assembly of the translation preinitiation complex through dynamic protein interchange and ordered phosphorylation events. *Cell* **2005**, *123*, 569–580. [CrossRef] [PubMed]

35. Holz, M.K.; Blenis, J. Identification of S6 kinase 1 as a novel mammalian target of rapamycin (mTOR)-phosphorylating kinase. *J. Biol. Chem.* **2005**, *280*, 26089–26093. [CrossRef] [PubMed]

36. Thomas, G. The S6 kinase signaling pathway in the control of development and growth. *Biol. Res.* **2002**, *35*, 305–313. [CrossRef] [PubMed]

37. Pullen, N.; Dennis, P.B.; Andjelkovic, M.; Dufner, A.; Kozma, S.C.; Hemmings, B.A.; Thomas, G. Phosphorylation and activation of p70s6k by PDK1. *Science* **1998**, *279*, 707–710. [CrossRef] [PubMed]

38. Youtani, T.; Tomoo, K.; Ishida, T.; Miyoshi, H.; Miura, K. Regulation of human eIF4E by 4E-BP1: Binding analysis using surface plasmon resonance. *IUBMB Life* **2000**, *49*, 27–31. [CrossRef] [PubMed]

39. Miyoshi, H.; Youtani, T.; Ide, H.; Hori, H.; Okamoto, K.; Ishikawa, M.; Wakiyama, M.; Nishino, T.; Ishida, T.; Miura, K. Binding analysis of Xenopus laevis translation initiation factor 4E (eIF4E) in initiation complex formation. *J. Biochem. (Tokyo)* **1999**, *126*, 897–904. [CrossRef]

40. Pagano, A.F.; Py, G.; Bernardi, H.; Candau, R.B.; Sanchez, A.M.J. Autophagy and protein turnover signaling in slow-twitch muscle during exercise. *Med. Sci. Sports Exerc.* **2014**, *46*, 1314–1325. [CrossRef]

41. Cheng, S.W.Y.; Fryer, L.G.D.; Carling, D.; Shepherd, P.R. Thr2446 is a novel mammalian target of rapamycin (mTOR) phosphorylation site regulated by nutrient status. *J. Biol. Chem.* **2004**, *279*, 15719–15722. [CrossRef] [PubMed]

42. Inoki, K.; Zhu, T.; Guan, K.-L. TSC2 mediates cellular energy response to control cell growth and survival. *Cell* **2003**, *115*, 577–590. [CrossRef]

43. Hardie, D.G. AMPK and Raptor: Matching cell growth to energy supply. *Mol. Cell* **2008**, *30*, 263–265. [CrossRef] [PubMed]

44. Gwinn, D.M.; Shackelford, D.B.; Egan, D.F.; Mihaylova, M.M.; Mery, A.; Vasquez, D.S.; Turk, B.E.; Shaw, R.J. AMPK phosphorylation of raptor mediates a metabolic checkpoint. *Mol. Cell* **2008**, *30*, 214–226. [CrossRef] [PubMed]

45. Phillips, S.M.; Tipton, K.D.; Aarsland, A.; Wolf, S.E.; Wolfe, R.R. Mixed muscle protein synthesis and breakdown after resistance exercise in humans. *Am. J. Physiol.* **1997**, *273*, E99–E107. [CrossRef] [PubMed]

46. Phillips, S.M. Protein requirements and supplementation in strength sports. *Nutrition* **2004**, *20*, 689–695. [CrossRef] [PubMed]

47. Moore, D.R.; Phillips, S.M.; Babraj, J.A.; Smith, K.; Rennie, M.J. Myofibrillar and collagen protein synthesis in human skeletal muscle in young men after maximal shortening and lengthening contractions. *Am. J. Physiol. Endocrinol. Metab.* **2005**, *288*, E1153–E1159. [CrossRef] [PubMed]

48. Lysenko, E.A.; Popov, D.V.; Vepkhvadze, T.F.; Sharova, A.P.; Vinogradova, O.L. Moderate-Intensity Strength Exercise to Exhaustion Results in More Pronounced Signaling Changes in Skeletal Muscles of Strength-Trained Compared with Untrained Individuals. *J. Strength Cond. Res.* **2018**. [CrossRef] [PubMed]

49. Mascher, H.; Andersson, H.; Nilsson, P.-A.; Ekblom, B.; Blomstrand, E. Changes in signalling pathways regulating protein synthesis in human muscle in the recovery period after endurance exercise. *Acta Physiol. Oxf. Engl.* **2007**, *191*, 67–75. [CrossRef] [PubMed]

50. Mascher, H.; Ekblom, B.; Rooyackers, O.; Blomstrand, E. Enhanced rates of muscle protein synthesis and elevated mTOR signalling following endurance exercise in human subjects. *Acta Physiol. Oxf. Engl.* **2011**, *202*, 175–184. [CrossRef] [PubMed]

51. Esbjörnsson, M.; Rundqvist, H.C.; Mascher, H.; Österlund, T.; Rooyackers, O.; Blomstrand, E.; Jansson, E. Sprint exercise enhances skeletal muscle p70S6k phosphorylation and more so in women than in men. *Acta Physiol. Oxf. Engl.* **2012**, *205*, 411–422. [CrossRef] [PubMed]

52. Nader, G.A.; Esser, K.A. Intracellular signaling specificity in skeletal muscle in response to different modes of exercise. *J. Appl. Physiol. Bethesda Md 1985* **2001**, *90*, 1936–1942. [CrossRef] [PubMed]

53. Luciano, T.F.; Marques, S.O.; Pieri, B.L.; de Souza, D.R.; Araújo, L.V.; Nesi, R.T.; Scheffer, D.L.; Comin, V.H.; Pinho, R.A.; Muller, A.P.; et al. Responses of skeletal muscle hypertrophy in Wistar rats to different resistance exercise models. *Physiol. Res.* **2017**, *66*, 317–323. [PubMed]

54. Ogasawara, R.; Suginohara, T. Rapamycin-insensitive mechanistic target of rapamycin regulates basal and resistance exercise-induced muscle protein synthesis. *FASEB J. Off. Publ. Fed. Am. Soc. Exp. Biol.* **2018**. [CrossRef] [PubMed]

55. Atherton, P.J.; Babraj, J.; Smith, K.; Singh, J.; Rennie, M.J.; Wackerhage, H. Selective activation of AMPK-PGC-1alpha or PKB-TSC2-mTOR signaling can explain specific adaptive responses to endurance or resistance training-like electrical muscle stimulation. *FASEB J. Off. Publ. Fed. Am. Soc. Exp. Biol.* **2005**, *19*, 786–788.

56. Dreyer, H.C.; Fujita, S.; Cadenas, J.G.; Chinkes, D.L.; Volpi, E.; Rasmussen, B.B. Resistance exercise increases AMPK activity and reduces 4E-BP1 phosphorylation and protein synthesis in human skeletal muscle. *J. Physiol.* **2006**, *576*, 613–624. [CrossRef] [PubMed]

57. Vissing, K.; McGee, S.L.; Farup, J.; Kjølhede, T.; Vendelbo, M.H.; Jessen, N. Differentiated mTOR but not AMPK signaling after strength vs endurance exercise in training-accustomed individuals. *Scand. J. Med. Sci. Sports* **2013**, *23*, 355–366. [CrossRef]

58. Ogasawara, R.; Sato, K.; Matsutani, K.; Nakazato, K.; Fujita, S. The order of concurrent endurance and resistance exercise modifies mTOR signaling and protein synthesis in rat skeletal muscle. *Am. J. Physiol. Endocrinol. Metab.* **2014**, *306*, E1155–E1162. [CrossRef]

59. Hornberger, T.A.; Chien, S. Mechanical stimuli and nutrients regulate rapamycin-sensitive signaling through distinct mechanisms in skeletal muscle. *J. Cell. Biochem.* **2006**, *97*, 1207–1216. [CrossRef]

60. Hornberger, T.A.; Stuppard, R.; Conley, K.E.; Fedele, M.J.; Fiorotto, M.L.; Chin, E.R.; Esser, K.A. Mechanical stimuli regulate rapamycin-sensitive signalling by a phosphoinositide 3-kinase-, protein kinase B- and growth factor-independent mechanism. *Biochem. J.* **2004**, *380*, 795–804. [CrossRef]

61. Hornberger, T.A.; Chu, W.K.; Mak, Y.W.; Hsiung, J.W.; Huang, S.A.; Chien, S. The role of phospholipase D and phosphatidic acid in the mechanical activation of mTOR signaling in skeletal muscle. *Proc. Natl. Acad. Sci. USA* **2006**, *103*, 4741–4746. [CrossRef] [PubMed]

62. West, D.W.D.; Kujbida, G.W.; Moore, D.R.; Atherton, P.; Burd, N.A.; Padzik, J.P.; De Lisio, M.; Tang, J.E.; Parise, G.; Rennie, M.J.; et al. Resistance exercise-induced increases in putative anabolic hormones do not enhance muscle protein synthesis or intracellular signalling in young men. *J. Physiol.* **2009**, *587*, 5239–5247. [CrossRef] [PubMed]

63. Miyazaki, M.; McCarthy, J.J.; Fedele, M.J.; Esser, K.A. Early activation of mTORC1 signalling in response to mechanical overload is independent of phosphoinositide 3-kinase/Akt signalling. *J. Physiol.* **2011**, *589*, 1831–1846. [CrossRef] [PubMed]

64. Davis, R.J. The mitogen-activated protein kinase signal transduction pathway. *J. Biol. Chem.* **1993**, *268*, 14553–14556. [PubMed]

65. Drummond, M.J.; Fry, C.S.; Glynn, E.L.; Dreyer, H.C.; Dhanani, S.; Timmerman, K.L.; Volpi, E.; Rasmussen, B.B. Rapamycin administration in humans blocks the contraction-induced increase in skeletal muscle protein synthesis. *J. Physiol.* **2009**, *587*, 1535–1546. [CrossRef] [PubMed]

66. You, J.S.; Frey, J.W.; Hornberger, T.A. Mechanical stimulation induces mTOR signaling via an ERK-independent mechanism: Implications for a direct activation of mTOR by phosphatidic acid. *PLoS ONE* **2012**, *7*, e47258. [CrossRef] [PubMed]

67. Veverka, V.; Crabbe, T.; Bird, I.; Lennie, G.; Muskett, F.W.; Taylor, R.J.; Carr, M.D. Structural characterization of the interaction of mTOR with phosphatidic acid and a novel class of inhibitor: Compelling evidence for a central role of the FRB domain in small molecule-mediated regulation of mTOR. *Oncogene* **2008**, *27*, 585–595. [CrossRef] [PubMed]

68. Yoon, M.-S.; Sun, Y.; Arauz, E.; Jiang, Y.; Chen, J. Phosphatidic acid activates mammalian target of rapamycin complex 1 (mTORC1) kinase by displacing FK506 binding protein 38 (FKBP38) and exerting an allosteric effect. *J. Biol. Chem.* **2011**, *286*, 29568–29574. [CrossRef] [PubMed]

69. You, J.-S.; Lincoln, H.C.; Kim, C.-R.; Frey, J.W.; Goodman, C.A.; Zhong, X.-P.; Hornberger, T.A. The role of diacylglycerol kinase ζ and phosphatidic acid in the mechanical activation of mammalian target of rapamycin (mTOR) signaling and skeletal muscle hypertrophy. *J. Biol. Chem.* **2014**, *289*, 1551–1563. [CrossRef]

70. You, J.-S.; Dooley, M.S.; Kim, C.-R.; Kim, E.-J.; Xu, W.; Goodman, C.A.; Hornberger, T.A. A DGKζ-FoxO-ubiquitin proteolytic axis controls fiber size during skeletal muscle remodeling. *Sci. Signal.* **2018**, *11*, eaao6847. [CrossRef]

71. Lagirand-Cantaloube, J.; Offner, N.; Csibi, A.; Leibovitch, M.P.; Batonnet-Pichon, S.; Tintignac, L.A.; Segura, C.T.; Leibovitch, S.A. The initiation factor eIF3-f is a major target for Atrogin1/MAFbx function in skeletal muscle atrophy. *EMBO J.* **2008**, *27*, 1266–1276. [CrossRef] [PubMed]

72. Sanchez, A.M.J.; Csibi, A.; Raibon, A.; Docquier, A.; Lagirand-Cantaloube, J.; Leibovitch, M.-P.; Leibovitch, S.A.; Bernardi, H. eIF3f: A central regulator of the antagonism atrophy/hypertrophy in skeletal muscle. *Int. J. Biochem. Cell Biol.* **2013**, *45*, 2158–2162. [CrossRef] [PubMed]

73. Csibi, A.; Cornille, K.; Leibovitch, M.-P.; Poupon, A.; Tintignac, L.A.; Sanchez, A.M.J.; Leibovitch, S.A. The translation regulatory subunit eIF3f controls the kinase-dependent mTOR signaling required for muscle differentiation and hypertrophy in mouse. *PLoS ONE* **2010**, *5*, e8994. [CrossRef] [PubMed]

74. Csibi, A.; Leibovitch, M.P.; Cornille, K.; Tintignac, L.A.; Leibovitch, S.A. MAFbx/Atrogin-1 controls the activity of the initiation factor eIF3-f in skeletal muscle atrophy by targeting multiple C-terminal lysines. *J. Biol. Chem.* **2009**, *284*, 4413–4421. [CrossRef] [PubMed]

75. Docquier, A.; Pavlin, L.; Raibon, A.; Bertrand-Gaday, C.; Sar, C.; Leibovitch, S.; Candau, R.; Bernardi, H. eIF3f depletion impedes mouse embryonic development, reduces adult skeletal muscle mass and amplifies muscle loss during disuse. *J. Physiol.* **2019**. [CrossRef] [PubMed]

76. Song, Z.; Moore, D.R.; Hodson, N.; Ward, C.; Dent, J.R.; O'Leary, M.F.; Shaw, A.M.; Hamilton, D.L.; Sarkar, S.; Gangloff, Y.-G.; et al. Resistance exercise initiates mechanistic target of rapamycin (mTOR) translocation and protein complex co-localisation in human skeletal muscle. *Sci. Rep.* **2017**, *7*, 5028. [CrossRef]

77. Groenewoud, M.J.; Zwartkruis, F.J.T. Rheb and Rags come together at the lysosome to activate mTORC1. *Biochem. Soc. Trans.* **2013**, *41*, 951–955. [CrossRef]

78. Sancak, Y.; Bar-Peled, L.; Zoncu, R.; Markhard, A.L.; Nada, S.; Sabatini, D.M. Ragulator-Rag complex targets mTORC1 to the lysosomal surface and is necessary for its activation by amino acids. *Cell* **2010**, *141*, 290–303. [CrossRef]

79. Jacobs, B.L.; You, J.-S.; Frey, J.W.; Goodman, C.A.; Gundermann, D.M.; Hornberger, T.A. Eccentric contractions increase the phosphorylation of tuberous sclerosis complex-2 (TSC2) and alter the targeting of TSC2 and the mechanistic target of rapamycin to the lysosome. *J. Physiol.* **2013**, *591*, 4611–4620. [CrossRef]

80. Van Vliet, S.; Shy, E.L.; Abou Sawan, S.; Beals, J.W.; West, D.W.; Skinner, S.K.; Ulanov, A.V.; Li, Z.; Paluska, S.A.; Parsons, C.M.; et al. Consumption of whole eggs promotes greater stimulation of postexercise muscle protein synthesis than consumption of isonitrogenous amounts of egg whites in young men. *Am. J. Clin. Nutr.* **2017**, *106*, 1401–1412. [CrossRef]

81. Abou Sawan, S.; van Vliet, S.; West, D.W.D.; Beals, J.W.; Paluska, S.A.; Burd, N.A.; Moore, D.R. Whole egg, but not egg white ingestion, induces mTOR co-localization with the lysosome after resistance exercise in trained young men. *Am. J. Physiol. Cell Physiol.* **2018**, *315*, C537–C543. [CrossRef] [PubMed]

82. Yamamoto, I.; Mazumi, T.; Handa, T.; Miyajima, K. Effects of 1,2-diacylglycerol and cholesterol on the hydrolysis activity of phospholipase D in egg-yolk phosphatidylcholine bilayers. *Biochim. Biophys. Acta* **1993**, *1145*, 293–297. [CrossRef]

83. Yamamoto, I.; Konto, A.; Handa, T.; Miyajima, K. Regulation of phospholipase D activity by neutral lipids in egg-yolk phosphatidylcholine small unilamellar vesicles and by calcium ion in aqueous medium. *Biochim. Biophys. Acta* **1995**, *1233*, 21–26. [CrossRef]

84. Menon, D.; Salloum, D.; Bernfeld, E.; Gorodetsky, E.; Akselrod, A.; Frias, M.A.; Sudderth, J.; Chen, P.-H.; DeBerardinis, R.; Foster, D.A. Lipid sensing by mTOR complexes via de novo synthesis of phosphatidic acid. *J. Biol. Chem.* **2017**, *292*, 6303–6311. [CrossRef] [PubMed]

85. Castellano, B.M.; Thelen, A.M.; Moldavski, O.; Feltes, M.; van der Welle, R.E.N.; Mydock-McGrane, L.; Jiang, X.; van Eijkeren, R.J.; Davis, O.B.; Louie, S.M.; et al. Lysosomal cholesterol activates mTORC1 via an SLC38A9-Niemann-Pick C1 signaling complex. *Science* **2017**, *355*, 1306–1311. [CrossRef] [PubMed]

86. Chung, S.Y.; Huang, W.C.; Su, C.W.; Lee, K.W.; Chi, H.C.; Lin, C.T.; Chen, S.-T.; Huang, K.M.; Tsai, M.S.; Yu, H.P.; et al. FoxO6 and PGC-1α form a regulatory loop in myogenic cells. *Biosci. Rep.* **2013**, *33*, e00045. [CrossRef] [PubMed]

87. Hu, P.; Geles, K.G.; Paik, J.-H.; DePinho, R.A.; Tjian, R. Codependent activators direct myoblast-specific MyoD transcription. *Dev. Cell* **2008**, *15*, 534–546. [CrossRef]

88. Furuyama, T.; Kitayama, K.; Yamashita, H.; Mori, N. Forkhead transcription factor FOXO1 (FKHR)-dependent induction of PDK4 gene expression in skeletal muscle during energy deprivation. *Biochem. J.* **2003**, *375*, 365–371. [CrossRef]

89. Kamei, Y.; Mizukami, J.; Miura, S.; Suzuki, M.; Takahashi, N.; Kawada, T.; Taniguchi, T.; Ezaki, O. A forkhead transcription factor FKHR up-regulates lipoprotein lipase expression in skeletal muscle. *FEBS Lett.* **2003**, *536*, 232–236. [CrossRef]

90. Tsuchida, A.; Yamauchi, T.; Ito, Y.; Hada, Y.; Maki, T.; Takekawa, S.; Kamon, J.; Kobayashi, M.; Suzuki, R.; Hara, K.; et al. Insulin/Foxo1 pathway regulates expression levels of adiponectin receptors and adiponectin sensitivity. *J. Biol. Chem.* **2004**, *279*, 30817–30822. [CrossRef]

91. Bastie, C.C.; Nahlé, Z.; McLoughlin, T.; Esser, K.; Zhang, W.; Unterman, T.; Abumrad, N.A. FoxO1 stimulates fatty acid uptake and oxidation in muscle cells through CD36-dependent and -independent mechanisms. *J. Biol. Chem.* **2005**, *280*, 14222–14229. [CrossRef] [PubMed]

92. Peserico, A.; Chiacchiera, F.; Grossi, V.; Matrone, A.; Latorre, D.; Simonatto, M.; Fusella, A.; Ryall, J.G.; Finley, L.W.S.; Haigis, M.C.; et al. A novel AMPK-dependent FoxO3A-SIRT3 intramitochondrial complex sensing glucose levels. *Cell. Mol. Life Sci. CMLS* **2013**, *70*, 2015–2029. [CrossRef] [PubMed]

93. Lombard, D.B.; Alt, F.W.; Cheng, H.-L.; Bunkenborg, J.; Streeper, R.S.; Mostoslavsky, R.; Kim, J.; Yancopoulos, G.; Valenzuela, D.; Murphy, A.; et al. Mammalian Sir2 homolog SIRT3 regulates global mitochondrial lysine acetylation. *Mol. Cell. Biol.* **2007**, *27*, 8807–8814. [CrossRef] [PubMed]

94. Slopack, D.; Roudier, E.; Liu, S.T.K.; Nwadozi, E.; Birot, O.; Haas, T.L. Forkhead BoxO transcription factors restrain exercise-induced angiogenesis. *J. Physiol.* **2014**, *592*, 4069–4082. [CrossRef]

95. Sanchez, A.M.J. FoxO transcription factors and endurance training: A role for FoxO1 and FoxO3 in exercise-induced angiogenesis. *J. Physiol.* **2015**, *593*, 363–364. [CrossRef] [PubMed]

96. Tong, J.F.; Yan, X.; Zhu, M.J.; Du, M. AMP-activated protein kinase enhances the expression of muscle-specific ubiquitin ligases despite its activation of IGF-1/Akt signaling in C2C12 myotubes. *J. Cell. Biochem.* **2009**, *108*, 458–468. [CrossRef] [PubMed]

97. Sanchez, A.M.J.; Candau, R.; Bernardi, H. AMP-activated protein kinase stabilizes FOXO3 in primary myotubes. *Biochem. Biophys. Res. Commun.* **2018**, *499*, 493–498. [CrossRef]

98. Cantó, C.; Gerhart-Hines, Z.; Feige, J.N.; Lagouge, M.; Noriega, L.; Milne, J.C.; Elliott, P.J.; Puigserver, P.; Auwerx, J. AMPK regulates energy expenditure by modulating NAD+ metabolism and SIRT1 activity. *Nature* **2009**, *458*, 1056–1060. [CrossRef]

99. Stitt, T.N.; Drujan, D.; Clarke, B.A.; Panaro, F.; Timofeyva, Y.; Kline, W.O.; Gonzalez, M.; Yancopoulos, G.D.; Glass, D.J. The IGF-1/PI3K/Akt pathway prevents expression of muscle atrophy-induced ubiquitin ligases by inhibiting FOXO transcription factors. *Mol. Cell* **2004**, *14*, 395–403. [CrossRef]

100. Brunet, A.; Bonni, A.; Zigmond, M.J.; Lin, M.Z.; Juo, P.; Hu, L.S.; Anderson, M.J.; Arden, K.C.; Blenis, J.; Greenberg, M.E. Akt promotes cell survival by phosphorylating and inhibiting a Forkhead transcription factor. *Cell* **1999**, *96*, 857–868. [CrossRef]

101. Kops, G.J.; de Ruiter, N.D.; De Vries-Smits, A.M.; Powell, D.R.; Bos, J.L.; Burgering, B.M. Direct control of the Forkhead transcription factor AFX by protein kinase B. *Nature* **1999**, *398*, 630–634. [CrossRef] [PubMed]

102. Zhang, B.H.; Tang, E.D.; Zhu, T.; Greenberg, M.E.; Vojtek, A.B.; Guan, K.L. Serum- and glucocorticoid-inducible kinase SGK phosphorylates and negatively regulates B-Raf. *J. Biol. Chem.* **2001**, *276*, 31620–31626. [CrossRef] [PubMed]

103. Bertaggia, E.; Coletto, L.; Sandri, M. Posttranslational modifications control FoxO3 activity during denervation. *Am. J. Physiol. Cell Physiol.* **2012**, *302*, C587–C596. [CrossRef] [PubMed]

104. Senf, S.M.; Sandesara, P.B.; Reed, S.A.; Judge, A.R. p300 Acetyltransferase activity differentially regulates the localization and activity of the FOXO homologues in skeletal muscle. *Am. J. Physiol. Cell Physiol.* **2011**, *300*, C1490–C1501. [CrossRef] [PubMed]

105. Sandri, M.; Sandri, C.; Gilbert, A.; Skurk, C.; Calabria, E.; Picard, A.; Walsh, K.; Schiaffino, S.; Lecker, S.H.; Goldberg, A.L. Foxo transcription factors induce the atrophy-related ubiquitin ligase atrogin-1 and cause skeletal muscle atrophy. *Cell* **2004**, *117*, 399–412. [CrossRef]

106. Mammucari, C.; Milan, G.; Romanello, V.; Masiero, E.; Rudolf, R.; Del Piccolo, P.; Burden, S.J.; Di Lisi, R.; Sandri, C.; Zhao, J.; et al. FoxO3 controls autophagy in skeletal muscle in vivo. *Cell Metab.* **2007**, *6*, 458–471. [CrossRef] [PubMed]

107. Bodine, S.C.; Latres, E.; Baumhueter, S.; Lai, V.K.; Nunez, L.; Clarke, B.A.; Poueymirou, W.T.; Panaro, F.J.; Na, E.; Dharmarajan, K.; et al. Identification of ubiquitin ligases required for skeletal muscle atrophy. *Science* **2001**, *294*, 1704–1708. [CrossRef] [PubMed]

108. Gomes, M.D.; Lecker, S.H.; Jagoe, R.T.; Navon, A.; Goldberg, A.L. Atrogin-1, a muscle-specific F-box protein highly expressed during muscle atrophy. *Proc. Natl. Acad. Sci. USA* **2001**, *98*, 14440–14445. [CrossRef]

109. Lagirand-Cantaloube, J.; Cornille, K.; Csibi, A.; Batonnet-Pichon, S.; Leibovitch, M.P.; Leibovitch, S.A. Inhibition of atrogin-1/MAFbx mediated MyoD proteolysis prevents skeletal muscle atrophy in vivo. *PLoS ONE* **2009**, *4*, e4973. [CrossRef]

110. Tintignac, L.A.; Lagirand, J.; Batonnet, S.; Sirri, V.; Leibovitch, M.P.; Leibovitch, S.A. Degradation of MyoD mediated by the SCF (MAFbx) ubiquitin ligase. *J. Biol. Chem.* **2005**, *280*, 2847–2856. [CrossRef]

111. Jogo, M.; Shiraishi, S.; Tamura, T. Identification of MAFbx as a myogenin-engaged F-box protein in SCF ubiquitin ligase. *FEBS Lett.* **2009**, *583*, 2715–2719. [CrossRef] [PubMed]

112. Lokireddy, S.; Wijesoma, I.W.; Sze, S.K.; McFarlane, C.; Kambadur, R.; Sharma, M. Identification of atrogin-1-targeted proteins during the myostatin-induced skeletal muscle wasting. *Am. J. Physiol. Cell Physiol.* **2012**, *303*, C512–C529. [CrossRef] [PubMed]

113. Clarke, B.A.; Drujan, D.; Willis, M.S.; Murphy, L.O.; Corpina, R.A.; Burova, E.; Rakhilin, S.V.; Stitt, T.N.; Patterson, C.; Latres, E.; et al. The E3 Ligase MuRF1 degrades myosin heavy chain protein in dexamethasone-treated skeletal muscle. *Cell Metab.* **2007**, *6*, 376–385. [CrossRef] [PubMed]

114. Cohen, S.; Brault, J.J.; Gygi, S.P.; Glass, D.J.; Valenzuela, D.M.; Gartner, C.; Latres, E.; Goldberg, A.L. During muscle atrophy, thick, but not thin, filament components are degraded by MuRF1-dependent ubiquitylation. *J. Cell Biol.* **2009**, *185*, 1083–1095. [CrossRef] [PubMed]

115. Cohen, S.; Zhai, B.; Gygi, S.P.; Goldberg, A.L. Ubiquitylation by Trim32 causes coupled loss of desmin, Z-bands, and thin filaments in muscle atrophy. *J. Cell Biol.* **2012**, *198*, 575–589. [CrossRef] [PubMed]

116. Kudryashova, E.; Kudryashov, D.; Kramerova, I.; Spencer, M.J. Trim32 is a ubiquitin ligase mutated in limb girdle muscular dystrophy type 2H that binds to skeletal muscle myosin and ubiquitinates actin. *J. Mol. Biol.* **2005**, *354*, 413–424. [CrossRef]

117. Zhao, J.; Brault, J.J.; Schild, A.; Cao, P.; Sandri, M.; Schiaffino, S.; Lecker, S.H.; Goldberg, A.L. FoxO3 coordinately activates protein degradation by the autophagic/lysosomal and proteasomal pathways in atrophying muscle cells. *Cell Metab.* **2007**, *6*, 472–483. [CrossRef]

118. Novak, I.; Kirkin, V.; McEwan, D.G.; Zhang, J.; Wild, P.; Rozenknop, A.; Rogov, V.; Löhr, F.; Popovic, D.; Occhipinti, A.; et al. Nix is a selective autophagy receptor for mitochondrial clearance. *EMBO Rep.* **2010**, *11*, 45–51. [CrossRef]

119. Kanki, T. Nix, a receptor protein for mitophagy in mammals. *Autophagy* **2010**, *6*, 433–435. [CrossRef]

120. Novak, I. Mitophagy: A complex mechanism of mitochondrial removal. *Antioxid. Redox Signal.* **2012**, *17*, 794–802. [CrossRef]

121. Yamazaki, Y.; Kamei, Y.; Sugita, S.; Akaike, F.; Kanai, S.; Miura, S.; Hirata, Y.; Troen, B.R.; Kitamura, T.; Nishino, I.; et al. The cathepsin L gene is a direct target of FOXO1 in skeletal muscle. *Biochem. J.* **2010**, *427*, 171–178. [CrossRef] [PubMed]

122. Paré, M.F.; Baechler, B.L.; Fajardo, V.A.; Earl, E.; Wong, E.; Campbell, T.L.; Tupling, A.R.; Quadrilatero, J. Effect of acute and chronic autophagy deficiency on skeletal muscle apoptotic signaling, morphology, and function. *Biochim. Biophys. Acta Mol. Cell Res.* **2017**, *1864*, 708–718. [CrossRef] [PubMed]

123. Kim, J.; Guan, K.-L. Regulation of the autophagy initiating kinase ULK1 by nutrients: Roles of mTORC1 and AMPK. *Cell Cycle Georget. Tex* **2011**, *10*, 1337–1338. [CrossRef] [PubMed]

124. Kim, J.; Kundu, M.; Viollet, B.; Guan, K.-L. AMPK and mTOR regulate autophagy through direct phosphorylation of Ulk1. *Nat. Cell Biol.* **2011**, *13*, 132–141. [CrossRef] [PubMed]

125. Egan, D.; Kim, J.; Shaw, R.J.; Guan, K.-L. The autophagy initiating kinase ULK1 is regulated via opposing phosphorylation by AMPK and mTOR. *Autophagy* **2011**, *7*, 643–644. [CrossRef] [PubMed]

126. Sanchez, A.M.J.; Candau, R.; Raibon, A.; Bernardi, H. Autophagy, a Highly Regulated Intracellular System Essential to Skeletal Muscle Homeostasis—Role in Disease, Exercise and Altitude Exposure. *Muscle Cell Tissue* **2015**. [CrossRef]

127. Mahoney, D.J.; Parise, G.; Melov, S.; Safdar, A.; Tarnopolsky, M.A. Analysis of global mRNA expression in human skeletal muscle during recovery from endurance exercise. *FASEB J. Off. Publ. Fed. Am. Soc. Exp. Biol.* **2005**, *19*, 1498–1500. [CrossRef] [PubMed]

128. Jamart, C.; Francaux, M.; Millet, G.Y.; Deldicque, L.; Frère, D.; Féasson, L. Modulation of autophagy and ubiquitin-proteasome pathways during ultra-endurance running. *J. Appl. Physiol. Bethesda MD 1985* **2012**, *112*, 1529–1537. [CrossRef]

129. Møller, A.B.; Vendelbo, M.H.; Christensen, B.; Clasen, B.F.; Bak, A.M.; Jørgensen, J.O.L.; Møller, N.; Jessen, N. Physical exercise increases autophagic signaling through ULK1 in human skeletal muscle. *J. Appl. Physiol. Bethesda MD 1985* **2015**, *118*, 971–979. [CrossRef]

130. He, C.; Sumpter, R.; Levine, B. Exercise induces autophagy in peripheral tissues and in the brain. *Autophagy* **2012**, *8*, 1548–1551. [CrossRef]

131. He, C.; Bassik, M.C.; Moresi, V.; Sun, K.; Wei, Y.; Zou, Z.; An, Z.; Loh, J.; Fisher, J.; Sun, Q.; et al. Exercise-induced BCL2-regulated autophagy is required for muscle glucose homeostasis. *Nature* **2012**, *481*, 511–515. [CrossRef] [PubMed]

132. Glynn, E.L.; Fry, C.S.; Drummond, M.J.; Dreyer, H.C.; Dhanani, S.; Volpi, E.; Rasmussen, B.B. Muscle protein breakdown has a minor role in the protein anabolic response to essential amino acid and carbohydrate intake following resistance exercise. *Am. J. Physiol. Regul. Integr. Comp. Physiol.* **2010**, *299*, R533–R540. [CrossRef] [PubMed]

133. Jamart, C.; Naslain, D.; Gilson, H.; Francaux, M. Higher activation of autophagy in skeletal muscle of mice during endurance exercise in the fasted state. *Am. J. Physiol. Endocrinol. Metab.* **2013**, *305*, E964–E974. [CrossRef] [PubMed]

134. Sanchez, A.M.J. Autophagy regulation in human skeletal muscle during exercise. *J. Physiol.* **2016**, *594*, 5053–5054. [CrossRef] [PubMed]

135. Fritzen, A.M.; Madsen, A.B.; Kleinert, M.; Treebak, J.T.; Lundsgaard, A.-M.; Jensen, T.E.; Richter, E.A.; Wojtaszewski, J.; Kiens, B.; Frøsig, C. Regulation of autophagy in human skeletal muscle: Effects of exercise, exercise training and insulin stimulation. *J. Physiol.* **2016**, *594*, 745–761. [CrossRef] [PubMed]

136. Masiero, E.; Agatea, L.; Mammucari, C.; Blaauw, B.; Loro, E.; Komatsu, M.; Metzger, D.; Reggiani, C.; Schiaffino, S.; Sandri, M. Autophagy is required to maintain muscle mass. *Cell Metab.* **2009**, *10*, 507–515. [CrossRef]

137. Lira, V.A.; Okutsu, M.; Zhang, M.; Greene, N.P.; Laker, R.C.; Breen, D.S.; Hoehn, K.L.; Yan, Z. Autophagy is required for exercise training-induced skeletal muscle adaptation and improvement of physical performance. *FASEB J. Off. Publ. Fed. Am. Soc. Exp. Biol.* **2013**, *27*, 4184–4193. [CrossRef]

138. Ju, J.-S.; Jeon, S.-I.; Park, J.-Y.; Lee, J.-Y.; Lee, S.-C.; Cho, K.-J.; Jeong, J.-M. Autophagy plays a role in skeletal muscle mitochondrial biogenesis in an endurance exercise-trained condition. *J. Physiol. Sci. JPS* **2016**, *66*, 417–430. [CrossRef]

139. Carter, H.N.; Kim, Y.; Erlich, A.T.; Zarrin-Khat, D.; Hood, D.A. Autophagy and mitophagy flux in young and aged skeletal muscle following chronic contractile activity. *J. Physiol.* **2018**, *596*, 3567–3584. [CrossRef]

140. Sanchez, A.M.J. Mitophagy flux in skeletal muscle during chronic contractile activity and ageing. *J. Physiol.* **2018**, *596*, 3461–3462. [CrossRef]

141. Parousis, A.; Carter, H.N.; Tran, C.; Erlich, A.T.; Mesbah Moosavi, Z.S.; Pauly, M.; Hood, D.A. Contractile activity attenuates autophagy suppression and reverses mitochondrial defects in skeletal muscle cells. *Autophagy* **2018**, *14*, 1886–1897. [CrossRef] [PubMed]

142. Vives-Bauza, C.; Zhou, C.; Huang, Y.; Cui, M.; de Vries, R.L.A.; Kim, J.; May, J.; Tocilescu, M.A.; Liu, W.; Ko, H.S.; et al. PINK1-dependent recruitment of Parkin to mitochondria in mitophagy. *Proc. Natl. Acad. Sci. USA* **2010**, *107*, 378–383. [CrossRef] [PubMed]

143. Matsuda, N.; Sato, S.; Shiba, K.; Okatsu, K.; Saisho, K.; Gautier, C.A.; Sou, Y.-S.; Saiki, S.; Kawajiri, S.; Sato, F.; et al. PINK1 stabilized by mitochondrial depolarization recruits Parkin to damaged mitochondria and activates latent Parkin for mitophagy. *J. Cell Biol.* **2010**, *189*, 211–221. [CrossRef] [PubMed]

144. Kondapalli, C.; Kazlauskaite, A.; Zhang, N.; Woodroof, H.I.; Campbell, D.G.; Gourlay, R.; Burchell, L.; Walden, H.; Macartney, T.J.; Deak, M.; et al. PINK1 is activated by mitochondrial membrane potential depolarization and stimulates Parkin E3 ligase activity by phosphorylating Serine 65. *Open Biol.* **2012**, *2*, 120080. [CrossRef] [PubMed]

145. Kim, Y.; Park, J.; Kim, S.; Song, S.; Kwon, S.-K.; Lee, S.-H.; Kitada, T.; Kim, J.-M.; Chung, J. PINK1 controls mitochondrial localization of Parkin through direct phosphorylation. *Biochem. Biophys. Res. Commun.* **2008**, *377*, 975–980. [CrossRef]

146. Tanaka, A.; Cleland, M.M.; Xu, S.; Narendra, D.P.; Suen, D.-F.; Karbowski, M.; Youle, R.J. Proteasome and p97 mediate mitophagy and degradation of mitofusins induced by Parkin. *J. Cell Biol.* **2010**, *191*, 1367–1380. [CrossRef]

147. Chan, N.C.; Salazar, A.M.; Pham, A.H.; Sweredoski, M.J.; Kolawa, N.J.; Graham, R.L.J.; Hess, S.; Chan, D.C. Broad activation of the ubiquitin-proteasome system by Parkin is critical for mitophagy. *Hum. Mol. Genet.* **2011**, *20*, 1726–1737. [CrossRef]

148. Glauser, L.; Sonnay, S.; Stafa, K.; Moore, D.J. Parkin promotes the ubiquitination and degradation of the mitochondrial fusion factor mitofusin 1. *J. Neurochem.* **2011**, *118*, 636–645. [CrossRef]

149. Wang, X.; Winter, D.; Ashrafi, G.; Schlehe, J.; Wong, Y.L.; Selkoe, D.; Rice, S.; Steen, J.; LaVoie, M.J.; Schwarz, T.L. PINK1 and Parkin target Miro for phosphorylation and degradation to arrest mitochondrial motility. *Cell* **2011**, *147*, 893–906. [CrossRef]

150. Sarraf, S.A.; Raman, M.; Guarani-Pereira, V.; Sowa, M.E.; Huttlin, E.L.; Gygi, S.P.; Harper, J.W. Landscape of the PARKIN-dependent ubiquitylome in response to mitochondrial depolarization. *Nature* **2013**, *496*, 372–376. [CrossRef]

151. Nardin, A.; Schrepfer, E.; Ziviani, E. Counteracting PINK/Parkin Deficiency in the Activation of Mitophagy: A Potential Therapeutic Intervention for Parkinson's Disease. *Curr. Neuropharmacol.* **2016**, *14*, 250–259. [CrossRef] [PubMed]

152. Heo, J.-M.; Ordureau, A.; Paulo, J.A.; Rinehart, J.; Harper, J.W. The PINK1-PARKIN Mitochondrial Ubiquitylation Pathway Drives a Program of OPTN/NDP52 Recruitment and TBK1 Activation to Promote Mitophagy. *Mol. Cell* **2015**, *60*, 7–20. [CrossRef] [PubMed]

153. Shin, J.-H.; Ko, H.S.; Kang, H.; Lee, Y.; Lee, Y.-I.; Pletinkova, O.; Troconso, J.C.; Dawson, V.L.; Dawson, T.M. PARIS (ZNF746) repression of PGC-1α contributes to neurodegeneration in Parkinson's disease. *Cell* **2011**, *144*, 689–702. [CrossRef] [PubMed]

154. Roberts, R.F.; Fon, E.A. Presenting mitochondrial antigens: PINK1, Parkin and MDVs steal the show. *Cell Res.* **2016**, *26*, 1180–1181. [CrossRef] [PubMed]

155. Sugiura, A.; McLelland, G.-L.; Fon, E.A.; McBride, H.M. A new pathway for mitochondrial quality control: Mitochondrial-derived vesicles. *EMBO J.* **2014**, *33*, 2142–2156. [CrossRef] [PubMed]

156. Matheoud, D.; Sugiura, A.; Bellemare-Pelletier, A.; Laplante, A.; Rondeau, C.; Chemali, M.; Fazel, A.; Bergeron, J.J.; Trudeau, L.-E.; Burelle, Y.; et al. Parkinson's Disease-Related Proteins PINK1 and Parkin Repress Mitochondrial Antigen Presentation. *Cell* **2016**, *166*, 314–327. [CrossRef] [PubMed]

157. Roberts, R.F.; Tang, M.Y.; Fon, E.A.; Durcan, T.M. Defending the mitochondria: The pathways of mitophagy and mitochondrial-derived vesicles. *Int. J. Biochem. Cell Biol.* **2016**, *79*, 427–436. [CrossRef] [PubMed]

158. McLelland, G.-L.; Lee, S.A.; McBride, H.M.; Fon, E.A. Syntaxin-17 delivers PINK1/parkin-dependent mitochondrial vesicles to the endolysosomal system. *J. Cell Biol.* **2016**, *214*, 275–291. [CrossRef]

159. Peker, N.; Donipadi, V.; Sharma, M.; McFarlane, C.; Kambadur, R. Loss of Parkin Impairs Mitochondrial Function and Leads to Muscle Atrophy. *Am. J. Physiol. Cell Physiol.* **2018**, *315*, C164–C185. [CrossRef]

160. Gouspillou, G.; Godin, R.; Piquereau, J.; Picard, M.; Mofarrahi, M.; Mathew, J.; Purves-Smith, F.M.; Sgarioto, N.; Hepple, R.T.; Burelle, Y.; et al. Protective role of Parkin in skeletal muscle contractile and mitochondrial function. *J. Physiol.* **2018**, *596*, 2565–2579. [CrossRef]

161. Chen, C.C.W.; Erlich, A.T.; Hood, D.A. Role of Parkin and endurance training on mitochondrial turnover in skeletal muscle. *Skelet. Muscle* **2018**, *8*, 10. [CrossRef] [PubMed]

162. Neuspiel, M.; Schauss, A.C.; Braschi, E.; Zunino, R.; Rippstein, P.; Rachubinski, R.A.; Andrade-Navarro, M.A.; McBride, H.M. Cargo-selected transport from the mitochondria to peroxisomes is mediated by vesicular carriers. *Curr. Biol.* **2008**, *18*, 102–108. [CrossRef] [PubMed]

163. Li, J.; Qi, W.; Chen, G.; Feng, D.; Liu, J.; Ma, B.; Zhou, C.; Mu, C.; Zhang, W.; Chen, Q.; et al. Mitochondrial outer-membrane E3 ligase MUL1 ubiquitinates ULK1 and regulates selenite-induced mitophagy. *Autophagy* **2015**, *11*, 1216–1229. [CrossRef] [PubMed]

164. Peng, J.; Ren, K.-D.; Yang, J.; Luo, X.-J. Mitochondrial E3 ubiquitin ligase 1: A key enzyme in regulation of mitochondrial dynamics and functions. *Mitochondrion* **2016**, *28*, 49–53. [CrossRef] [PubMed]

165. Ding, Y.; Li, J.; Liu, Z.; Liu, H.; Li, H.; Li, Z. IGF-1 potentiates sensory innervation signalling by modulating the mitochondrial fission/fusion balance. *Sci. Rep.* **2017**, *7*, 43949. [CrossRef]

166. Lokireddy, S.; Wijesoma, I.W.; Teng, S.; Bonala, S.; Gluckman, P.D.; McFarlane, C.; Sharma, M.; Kambadur, R. The ubiquitin ligase Mul1 induces mitophagy in skeletal muscle in response to muscle-wasting stimuli. *Cell Metab.* **2012**, *16*, 613–624. [CrossRef] [PubMed]

167. Braschi, E.; Zunino, R.; McBride, H.M. MAPL is a new mitochondrial SUMO E3 ligase that regulates mitochondrial fission. *EMBO Rep.* **2009**, *10*, 748–754. [CrossRef] [PubMed]

168. Brinkmann, C.; Przyklenk, A.; Metten, A.; Schiffer, T.; Bloch, W.; Brixius, K.; Gehlert, S. Influence of endurance training on skeletal muscle mitophagy regulatory proteins in type 2 diabetic men. *Endocr. Res.* **2017**, *42*, 325–330. [CrossRef]

169. Katayama, K.; Matsuo, H.; Ishida, K.; Mori, S.; Miyamura, M. Intermittent hypoxia improves endurance performance and submaximal exercise efficiency. *High Alt. Med. Biol.* **2003**, *4*, 291–304. [CrossRef]

170. Flaherty, G.; O'Connor, R.; Johnston, N. Altitude training for elite endurance athletes: A review for the travel medicine practitioner. *Travel Med. Infect. Dis.* **2016**, *14*, 200–211. [CrossRef] [PubMed]

171. Brocherie, F.; Girard, O.; Faiss, R.; Millet, G.P. Effects of Repeated-Sprint Training in Hypoxia on Sea-Level Performance: A Meta-Analysis. *Sports Med.* **2017**, *47*, 1651–1660. [CrossRef] [PubMed]

172. Girard, O.; Brocherie, F.; Millet, G.P. Effects of Altitude/Hypoxia on Single- and Multiple-Sprint Performance: A Comprehensive Review. *Sports Med.* **2017**, *47*, 1931–1949. [CrossRef] [PubMed]

173. Van der Zwaard, S.; Brocherie, F.; Kom, B.L.G.; Millet, G.P.; Deldicque, L.; van der Laarse, W.J.; Girard, O.; Jaspers, R.T. Adaptations in muscle oxidative capacity, fiber size, and oxygen supply capacity after repeated-sprint training in hypoxia combined with chronic hypoxic exposure. *J. Appl. Physiol. Bethesda MD 1985* **2018**, *124*, 1403–1412. [CrossRef] [PubMed]

174. Sanchez, A.M.J.; Borrani, F. Effects of intermittent hypoxic training performed at high hypoxia level on exercise performance in highly trained runners. *J. Sports Sci.* **2018**, *36*, 2045–2052. [CrossRef] [PubMed]

175. Bailey, D.M.; Davies, B. Physiological implications of altitude training for endurance performance at sea level: A review. *Br. J. Sports Med.* **1997**, *31*, 183–190. [CrossRef] [PubMed]

176. Böning, D. Altitude and hypoxia training—A short review. *Int. J. Sports Med.* **1997**, *18*, 565–570. [CrossRef] [PubMed]

177. Park, H.-Y.; Hwang, H.; Park, J.; Lee, S.; Lim, K. The effects of altitude/hypoxic training on oxygen delivery capacity of the blood and aerobic exercise capacity in elite athletes—A meta-analysis. *J. Exerc. Nutr. Biochem.* **2016**, *20*, 15–22. [CrossRef]

178. Roels, B.; Millet, G.P.; Marcoux, C.J.L.; Coste, O.; Bentley, D.J.; Candau, R.B. Effects of hypoxic interval training on cycling performance. *Med. Sci. Sports Exerc.* **2005**, *37*, 138–146. [CrossRef]

179. Czuba, M.; Waskiewicz, Z.; Zajac, A.; Poprzecki, S.; Cholewa, J.; Roczniok, R. The effects of intermittent hypoxic training on aerobic capacity and endurance performance in cyclists. *J. Sports Sci. Med.* **2011**, *10*, 175–183. [PubMed]

180. Nakamoto, F.P.; Ivamoto, R.K.; Andrade, M.D.S.; de Lira, C.A.B.; Silva, B.M.; da Silva, A.C. Effect of Intermittent Hypoxic Training Followed by Intermittent Hypoxic Exposure on Aerobic Capacity of Long Distance Runners. *J. Strength Cond. Res.* **2016**, *30*, 1708–1720. [CrossRef]

181. Hoppeler, H.; Kleinert, E.; Schlegel, C.; Claassen, H.; Howald, H.; Kayar, S.R.; Cerretelli, P. Morphological adaptations of human skeletal muscle to chronic hypoxia. *Int. J. Sports Med.* **1990**, *11* (Suppl. 1), S3–S9. [CrossRef]

182. MacDougall, J.D.; Green, H.J.; Sutton, J.R.; Coates, G.; Cymerman, A.; Young, P.; Houston, C.S. Operation Everest II: Structural adaptations in skeletal muscle in response to extreme simulated altitude. *Acta Physiol. Scand.* **1991**, *142*, 421–427. [CrossRef] [PubMed]

183. Mizuno, M.; Savard, G.K.; Areskog, N.-H.; Lundby, C.; Saltin, B. Skeletal muscle adaptations to prolonged exposure to extreme altitude: A role of physical activity? *High Alt. Med. Biol.* **2008**, *9*, 311–317. [CrossRef] [PubMed]

184. Watier, T.; Sanchez, A.M. Micro-RNAs, Exercise and Cellular Plasticity in Humans: The Impact of Dietary Factors and Hypoxia. *MicroRNA* **2017**, *6*, 110–124. [CrossRef] [PubMed]

185. D'Hulst, G.; Jamart, C.; Van Thienen, R.; Hespel, P.; Francaux, M.; Deldicque, L. Effect of acute environmental hypoxia on protein metabolism in human skeletal muscle. *Acta Physiol.* **2013**, *208*, 251–264. [CrossRef] [PubMed]

186. Masschelein, E.; Van Thienen, R.; D'Hulst, G.; Hespel, P.; Thomis, M.; Deldicque, L. Acute environmental hypoxia induces LC3 lipidation in a genotype-dependent manner. *FASEB J. Off. Publ. Fed. Am. Soc. Exp. Biol.* **2014**, *28*, 1022–1034. [CrossRef] [PubMed]

187. Gnimassou, O.; Fernández-Verdejo, R.; Brook, M.; Naslain, D.; Balan, E.; Sayda, M.; Cegielski, J.; Nielens, H.; Decottignies, A.; Demoulin, J.-B.; et al. Environmental hypoxia favors myoblast differentiation and fast phenotype but blunts activation of protein synthesis after resistance exercise in human skeletal muscle. *FASEB J. Off. Publ. Fed. Am. Soc. Exp. Biol.* **2018**, *32*, 5272–5284. [CrossRef] [PubMed]

188. Aragonés, J.; Schneider, M.; Van Geyte, K.; Fraisl, P.; Dresselaers, T.; Mazzone, M.; Dirkx, R.; Zacchigna, S.; Lemieux, H.; Jeoung, N.H.; et al. Deficiency or inhibition of oxygen sensor Phd1 induces hypoxia tolerance by reprogramming basal metabolism. *Nat. Genet.* **2008**, *40*, 170–180. [CrossRef]

189. Kelly, D.P. Hypoxic reprogramming. *Nat. Genet.* **2008**, *40*, 132–134. [CrossRef]

190. Chaillou, T.; Koulmann, N.; Simler, N.; Meunier, A.; Serrurier, B.; Chapot, R.; Peinnequin, A.; Beaudry, M.; Bigard, X. Hypoxia transiently affects skeletal muscle hypertrophy in a functional overload model. *Am. J. Physiol. Regul. Integr. Comp. Physiol.* **2012**, *302*, R643–R654. [CrossRef]

191. Viganò, A.; Ripamonti, M.; De Palma, S.; Capitanio, D.; Vasso, M.; Wait, R.; Lundby, C.; Cerretelli, P.; Gelfi, C. Proteins modulation in human skeletal muscle in the early phase of adaptation to hypobaric hypoxia. *Proteomics* **2008**, *8*, 4668–4679. [CrossRef] [PubMed]

192. Bigard, X. Molecular factors involved in the control of muscle mass during hypoxia-exposure: The main hypotheses are revisited. *Acta Physiol.* **2013**, *208*, 222–223. [CrossRef] [PubMed]

193. Roig, M.; O'Brien, K.; Kirk, G.; Murray, R.; McKinnon, P.; Shadgan, B.; Reid, W.D. The effects of eccentric versus concentric resistance training on muscle strength and mass in healthy adults: A systematic review with meta-analysis. *Br. J. Sports Med.* **2009**, *43*, 556–568. [CrossRef] [PubMed]

194. Norrbrand, L.; Fluckey, J.D.; Pozzo, M.; Tesch, P.A. Resistance training using eccentric overload induces early adaptations in skeletal muscle size. *Eur. J. Appl. Physiol.* **2008**, *102*, 271–281. [CrossRef] [PubMed]

195. Rahbek, S.K.; Farup, J.; Møller, A.B.; Vendelbo, M.H.; Holm, L.; Jessen, N.; Vissing, K. Effects of divergent resistance exercise contraction mode and dietary supplementation type on anabolic signalling, muscle protein synthesis and muscle hypertrophy. *Amino Acids* **2014**, *46*, 2377–2392. [CrossRef] [PubMed]

196. Ato, S.; Makanae, Y.; Kido, K.; Fujita, S. Contraction mode itself does not determine the level of mTORC1 activity in rat skeletal muscle. *Physiol. Rep.* **2016**, *4*, e12976. [CrossRef] [PubMed]

197. Garma, T.; Kobayashi, C.; Haddad, F.; Adams, G.R.; Bodell, P.W.; Baldwin, K.M. Similar acute molecular responses to equivalent volumes of isometric, lengthening, or shortening mode resistance exercise. *J. Appl. Physiol. Bethesda MD 1985* **2007**, *102*, 135–143. [CrossRef] [PubMed]

198. O'Neil, T.K.; Duffy, L.R.; Frey, J.W.; Hornberger, T.A. The role of phosphoinositide 3-kinase and phosphatidic acid in the regulation of mammalian target of rapamycin following eccentric contractions. *J. Physiol.* **2009**, *587*, 3691–3701. [CrossRef] [PubMed]

199. Ochi, E.; Ishii, N.; Nakazato, K. Time Course Change of IGF1/Akt/mTOR/p70s6k Pathway Activation in Rat Gastrocnemius Muscle During Repeated Bouts of Eccentric Exercise. *J. Sports Sci. Med.* **2010**, *9*, 170–175. [PubMed]

200. Ato, S.; Makanae, Y.; Kido, K.; Sase, K.; Yoshii, N.; Fujita, S. The effect of different acute muscle contraction regimens on the expression of muscle proteolytic signaling proteins and genes. *Physiol. Rep.* **2017**, *5*, e13364. [CrossRef] [PubMed]

201. Lo Verso, F.; Carnio, S.; Vainshtein, A.; Sandri, M. Autophagy is not required to sustain exercise and PRKAA1/AMPK activity but is important to prevent mitochondrial damage during physical activity. *Autophagy* **2014**, *10*, 1883–1894. [CrossRef] [PubMed]

202. Klarod, K.; Philippe, M.; Gatterer, H.; Burtscher, M. Different training responses to eccentric endurance exercise at low and moderate altitudes in pre-diabetic men: A pilot study. *Sport Sci. Health* **2017**, *13*, 615–623. [CrossRef] [PubMed]

203. Rizo-Roca, D.; Ríos-Kristjánsson, J.G.; Núñez-Espinosa, C.; Santos-Alves, E.; Gonçalves, I.O.; Magalhães, J.; Ascensão, A.; Pagès, T.; Viscor, G.; Torrella, J.R. Intermittent hypobaric hypoxia combined with aerobic exercise improves muscle morphofunctional recovery after eccentric exercise to exhaustion in trained rats. *J. Appl. Physiol. Bethesda MD 1985* **2017**, *122*, 580–592. [CrossRef] [PubMed]

204. Rizo-Roca, D.; Ríos-Kristjánsson, J.G.; Núñez-Espinosa, C.; Santos-Alves, E.; Magalhães, J.; Ascensão, A.; Pagès, T.; Viscor, G.; Torrella, J.R. Modulation of mitochondrial biomarkers by intermittent hypobaric hypoxia and aerobic exercise after eccentric exercise in trained rats. *Appl. Physiol. Nutr. Metab. Physiol. Appl. Nutr. Metab.* **2017**, *42*, 683–693. [CrossRef] [PubMed]

Review

Autophagy as a Therapeutic Target to Enhance Aged Muscle Regeneration

David E. Lee [1], Akshay Bareja [1], David B. Bartlett [1,2,3] and James P. White [1,3,4,*]

[1] Duke Molecular Physiology Institute, Duke University School of Medicine, Durham, NC 27701, USA; david.e.lee@duke.edu (D.E.L.); Akshay.bareja@duke.edu (A.B.); david.bartlett@duke.edu (D.B.B.)

[2] Division of Medical Oncology, Department of Medicine, Duke University School of Medicine, Durham, NC 27701, USA

[3] Duke Center for the Study of Aging and Human Development, Duke University School of Medicine, Durham, NC 27701, USA

[4] Division of Hematology, Department of Medicine, Duke University School of Medicine, Durham, NC 27701, USA

* Correspondence: James.white@dm.duke.edu; Tel.: +1-919-681-6931

Received: 31 December 2018; Accepted: 14 February 2019; Published: 20 February 2019

Abstract: Skeletal muscle has remarkable regenerative capacity, relying on precise coordination between resident muscle stem cells (satellite cells) and the immune system. The age-related decline in skeletal muscle regenerative capacity contributes to the onset of sarcopenia, prolonged hospitalization, and loss of autonomy. Although several age-sensitive pathways have been identified, further investigation is needed to define targets of cellular dysfunction. Autophagy, a process of cellular catabolism, is emerging as a key regulator of muscle regeneration affecting stem cell, immune cell, and myofiber function. Muscle stem cell senescence is associated with a suppression of autophagy during key phases of the regenerative program. Macrophages, a key immune cell involved in muscle repair, also rely on autophagy to aid in tissue repair. This review will focus on the role of autophagy in various aspects of the regenerative program, including adult skeletal muscle stem cells, monocytes/macrophages, and corresponding age-associated dysfunction. Furthermore, we will highlight rejuvenation strategies that alter autophagy to improve muscle regenerative function.

Keywords: muscle regeneration; aging; stem cell; immune; macrophage; senescence; exercise; caloric restriction

---

1. Introduction

The physiological process of aging consists of diverse cellular changes including proliferation, metabolism, inflammation, and apoptosis. To identify and provide new therapeutic targets and approaches to counteract the physiological decline of advanced age, a thorough understanding of cellular processes involved is paramount. Autophagy has emerged over the years as an important regulator of age-related changes in various tissues including skeletal muscle. Aging is directly associated with adverse changes to skeletal muscle including a decline in functional capacity which contributes to lower quality of life, reduced independence, and greater mortality in the elderly. The capacity of skeletal muscle to regenerate following injury is, likewise, negatively affected by aging and appears to be associated with alterations in cellular autophagy [1,2]. The regenerative properties of muscle are dictated by the efficient removal and clearance of damaged tissue and the myogenic ability of resident, adult muscle stem cells to replace mature myofibers. Not only does regeneration require autophagy to resolve properly, but in leveraging autophagy, it appears possible to attenuate the age-related decline in skeletal muscle regenerative function.

2. Molecular Process of Autophagy

Macroautophagy (hereafter referred to as autophagy and distinct from micro- and chaperone-mediated autophagy as reviewed in [3]) was originally characterized as the apparent self-consumption of mitochondria by the lysosome in mouse kidney cells [4]. Currently, autophagy is understood as a broad process that regulates the delivery of a wide range of proteins and organelles into the lysosome for catabolic degradation. Under pathophysiological conditions, autophagy dysfunction is generally characterized by its insufficiency to remove damaged organelles or debris. Autophagy activation was originally identified as a response to nutrient deprivation in eukaryotic systems [5,6]. We now know that autophagy is activated during various cellular stressors including exercise, endoplasmic reticulum stress, infection, and hypoxia [7]. A functional role of autophagy is expanding to include energy production, cellular remodeling/differentiation and influence over apoptosis [8–12]. Numerous preclinical and clinical efforts target autophagy to treat pathologies such as cardiovascular disease, cancer, and neurodegeneration among others [13]. The process is regulated by a highly-conserved family of proteins referred to as autophagy-related genes (*Atgs*). *Atgs* facilitate specific stages in the autophagic process such as initiation, formation, elongation, and fusion [14].

A number of molecular signals are involved in the coordination and control of the process (readers are referred to a previous review [14]). Transcriptional regulation of autophagy includes the transcription factors JNK [15], NFKappaB [16], HIF-1 [17], and FOXOs [18]. Of key interest is autophagy regulation by the mTOR complexes (mTORC1 and mTORC2) [19]. At high nutrient concentrations, mTOR phosphorylates and inactivates UNC-51-like kinase 1 (ULK1) and Atg13 to prevent the initiation of autophagosome formation [20]. Under starvation conditions, or when autophagy is favored for proteostatic maintenance [21], mTOR dissociation allows the formation of the ULK1:Atg13:FIP200 to initiate autophagy [20]. Subsequent formation and maturation of autophagosomes involves the Beclin1:Vps34 complex, which is negatively regulated by interactions involving the apoptosis promoting members of the Bcl-2 family of proteins [15]. Elongation of the autophagosome membrane utilizes Atg5:Atg12 conjugation and the conversion of cytosolic LC3 (LC3-I) into a membrane-associated PE-conjugated LC3 (LC3-II) facing the interior and exterior of the autophagosome [22]. A summary of the molecular events involved in the autophagy process is illustrated in Figure 1. Once the autophagosome fuses with the lysosome, the contents are broken down into constituent macromolecular precursors that can be reused as raw "bio" material or, alternatively, metabolized. Biochemical markers suggesting this process has been resolved include protein expression patterns of LC3 isoforms and the autophagosome targeting molecule p62.

Aging is a complex process associated with diminished ability for tissues to maintain biological homeostasis. This is especially relevant in tissues that exhibit age-related changes in autophagic function. In numerous cell types tested, autophagy upregulation is capable of mitigating aging-induced apoptosis and necrosis [23]. Proliferating cells (including stem cells) tend to utilize autophagy for metabolite generation, improved genomic stability and limit oncogenic transformations while postmitotic cells (such as myocytes) rely on autophagy to remove dysfunctional or mutated mitochondria and protein aggregates formed over time [23]. Even in simple eukaryotic models such as *Saccharomyces cerevisiae*, screens for short-lived mutants include various autophagy loss-of-function *Atg* mutants [24]. Similar findings were extended to Unc-51 mutant *Ceanorhabditis elegans* [25] and Beclin mutant *Drosophila melanogaster* [26]. In humans, autophagy downregulation is coincident with numerous pathologies associated with advanced age. Chronic diseases often display reductions in autophagy as demonstrated in brain tissue [27], circulating mononuclear cells [28], connective tissue [29], and cardiac muscle [30]. Wound repair is another relatively unexplored area where age-related changes in autophagy may play an important role [31]. Taken together, these lines of evidence show how autophagy is intricately related to biological aging and senescence.

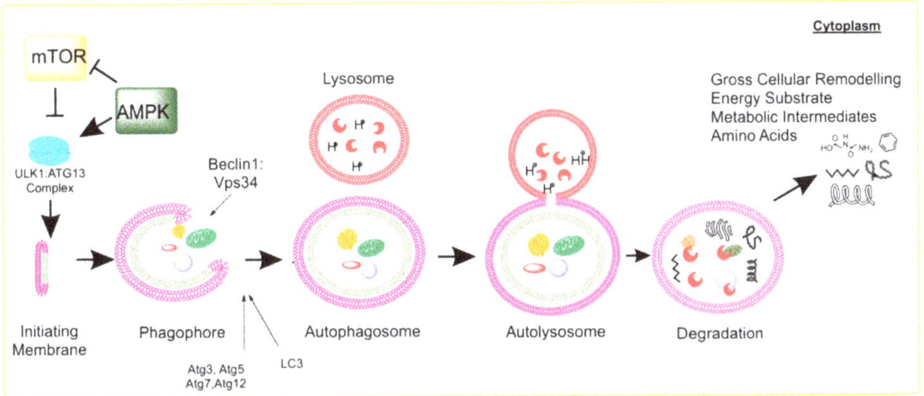

Figure 1. Molecular Events of Autophagy and related Signaling Pathways. Autophagy is a highly-conserved cellular process across eukaryotes from yeast to human. The initiation membrane matures and develops into a phagophore around cytoplasmic compartments containing a variety of macromolecules, organelles, and other cytoplasmic contents. Once fully enclosed, the autophagosome will fuse with the lysosome exposing the contents of the autophagosome to an acidic pH and various digestive enzymes of the lysosome. Following degradation of the contents of the autolysosome, the resulting molecules become available for cytoplasmic utilization (including amino acids, carbon fuel substrates, nucleotides, and reducing cofactors). This process simultaneously allows the cell to undergo drastic and rapid remodeling. Previous research has specifically shown the interaction of mTOR and AMPK in the initial steps of the autophagy process through phosphorylation interaction with the ULK1:Atg13:FIP200 complex.

3. Autophagy Effects on Skeletal Muscle Homeostasis, Regeneration, and Aging

Skeletal muscle is a dynamic tissue that is constantly adapting and changing to physical and metabolic demands. As such, autophagy seems to be a key step in healthy muscle homeostasis and physiology [32]. Pathophysiological conditions of muscle that implicate maladaptive autophagy including Duchenne's muscular dystrophy [33], type II diabetes mellitus/insulin resistance [34], sarcopenia [35], cancer-induced wasting [36], and myotube regeneration [37]; however, the origin of signals inducing autophagy for each scenario seems to differ. In the case of sarcopenia and cachexia, autophagy seems to be an outcome of systemic inflammation signals and dietary hypophagia that contributes to a skeletal muscle phenotype [35,36,38,39]. In other instances, cellular remodeling or tissue repair is seen in dystrophic muscle, and autophagy helps to clear damaged cellular components including myofibrillar components and sequestered cytoplasm [33,37]. These claims are supported when muscle-specific Atg7 knockout in mice resulted in abnormal mitochondrial morphology, oxidative stress, and sarcomeric alterations [32]. Moreover, high-fat diets alter vesicle membrane composition which can also impact rates of autophagy implicating obesity as a modulator of muscle autophagy [40].

In addition to maintaining muscle homeostasis, the activation of autophagy becomes an important factor for skeletal muscle remodeling after stimuli like contractile activity/exercise [41,42]. Not only is autophagy required for skeletal muscle adaptations to physical activity, but autophagy also contributes to improvements in whole body insulin sensitivity [42]. Conversely, mice that maintain basal autophagy rates but lack BCL2-inducible autophagy do not show insulin resistance or alterations in muscle size compared to littermates that are able to activate autophagy above basal levels [34]. The molecular signals responsible include the BCL2-dependent upregulation of Beclin1 as well as AMPK phosphorylation of ULK1 [34,41]. These studies help to define an important role for autophagy signaling in skeletal muscle metabolism and chronic diseases; however, less is known about the function autophagy plays in regeneration.

Skeletal muscle has extensive regenerative capabilities due to resident stem cell functions and a highly coordinated interaction with hematopoietic/immune cells during the repair process. This complex, yet efficient process results in complete return of morphology and function in healthy muscle. Blocking autophagy by genetic (Atg5, Beclin1) or pharmacological (chloroquine) methods causes accumulation of sarcomeric and nuclear debris following muscle damage in zebrafish showing the key role autophagy plays in the repair process [37]. In the mouse, treatment with a pharmacological inhibitor of global autophagy such as 3-methyladenine (3-MA) after injury slows functional recovery 14 days postinjury [43]. Similarly, mice treated with hydroxy chloroquine (CQ), another chemical inhibitor of autophagy, perturbs muscle regeneration and exacerbates the pathology of *mdx* mice [44]. Genetic inhibition of autophagy through whole body knockdown of Atg16 results in impaired regeneration following cardiotoxin-induced injury [45]. While the importance of autophagy in the regenerative programs have been shown largely using whole body blockage of autophagy, limited investigation has focused on myofiber-specific manipulation of autophagy. Knockout of ULK1 under a myogenin promoter (muscle cell specific) in mice prevents the initiation of autophagy, which impairs the recovery of force production following both cardiotoxin and ischemia/reperfusion-induced damage [46]. These data suggest a possible role for autophagy to clear damaged proteins and organelles to allow myofiber regeneration. Moreover, work in C2C12 cells show autophagy is required for successful differentiation of C2C12 myoblasts, in part by protecting differentiating myoblasts from apoptosis [47]. Together, autophagy may regulate various processes in the regenerating myofiber including proteostasis and survival mechanisms.

Successful muscle regeneration requires a coordinated effort from various other cell types including mast cells, neutrophils, T regulatory cells, eosinophils, and CD8+ T cells [48]. While each of these cell types contributes specifically to muscle recovery, two cell types that have been studied extensively related to autophagy mechanisms are the muscle satellite cell and the macrophage. The following sections will discuss how autophagy regulates their function and direct or theoretical contributions to muscle regeneration.

4. Muscle Satellite Cells

Adult skeletal muscle maintains a relatively remarkable ability to regenerate and recover following mild damage or insult throughout much of the lifespan [49]. The functional adult stem cell of skeletal muscle is the satellite cell [50]. Termed this way based on its appearance at the periphery of muscle fibers, the satellite cell is the source of replenishment of myonuclei following damage and is called upon to meet the transient demands of myofiber hypertrophy and repair [51–54]. Quiescent satellite cells are identified as $Pax7^+/Myod^-$ cells that are capable of asymmetric cell division and forming mature myonuclei when transplanted into injured muscle. Successful regeneration requires two stages of satellite cell function: proliferation and fusion/myogenesis. Both phases of repair show evidence of dysfunction with advanced age. The function of satellite cells is measured by their ability to activate from quiescence and undergo asymmetric proliferation into (1) daughter cells that are capable of further proliferation and differentiation into mature muscle fibers and (2) daughter cells that are capable of reentering quiescence. Therefore, we refer to satellite cell function as their ability to proliferate and/or undergo myogenesis. A summary of the general mechanism of myogenesis and myofibrillar regeneration is shown in Figure 2.

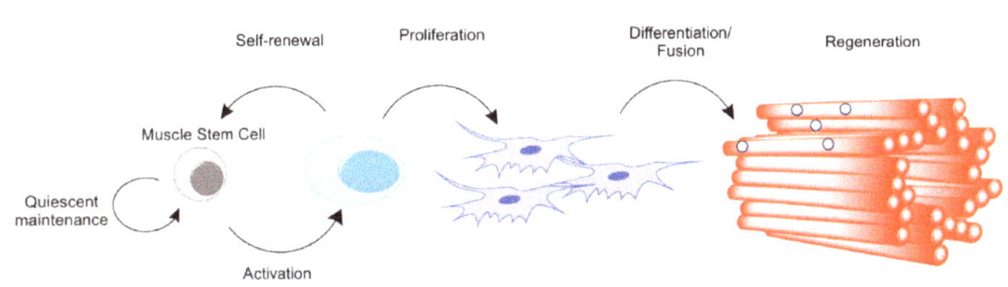

Figure 2. Activation of the Muscle Stem Cell. Adult, resident skeletal muscle stem cells—termed satellite cells—were originally identified in the hind limb muscle of frogs and rats by electron microscopy by 1961 [55]. These cells lie in a quiescent state; dormant with low metabolic flux and little cytoplasm (low energy demand/low energy storage). Following damage by mechanical or chemical stimuli, an activated satellite cell will hypertrophy to accommodate cytosolic machinery and organelle requirements for proliferation. This key functional step leaves the (recently quiescent and still relatively small) satellite cell with little in the way of energy stores or metabolic machinery (i.e., mitochondria) but an extremely high demand for energy substrates, metabolic intermediates, and amino acids. This state of high energy demand/low energy storage in accompanied by a simultaneous remodeling of the cell architecture. By using autophagy as a process to remove aged, unnecessary, or damaged components, the young/healthy activated satellite cell is capable of recycling those components into the building blocks needed to further proliferate. The proliferated satellite cells will asymmetrically divide allowing the self-renewal of the activated stem cell into the quiescent state; likewise requiring significant cytoplasmic reorganization and remodeling. The satellite cell progeny will undergo subsequent differentiation into mature myogenic cells that are able to fuse with the damaged myofibers accomplishing successful and complete regeneration.

4.1. Satellite Cells in Health and Aging

Aging has long been known to be inversely related to the proliferative potential of satellite cells [56–58]. Depletion of satellite cells drastically inhibits proper muscle regeneration in response to damaging stimuli in old and young mice [59]. Early investigation used eccentric contraction-induced injury in animals combined with irradiation (a method to prevent satellite cell proliferation) to demonstrate a contribution of satellite cells to hypertrophy and recovery. In irradiated mice, isometric torque recovery was reduced by ~25% in mice that were irradiated and damaged compared to nonirradiated controls [60]. Similarly, stretch-induced damage was able to upregulate key myogenic regulatory factors, including Mrf4, MyoD, and myogenein in quail muscle; however, myogenin gene expression was reduced if the muscle had been irradiated prior to stretch overload [61]. These studies suggest that satellite cells contribute to recovery from physiological forms of injury such as contraction and overload, which are translatable to injuries observed in the elderly or sarcopenic [62]. Conditional ablation of *Pax7*-expressing satellite cells suggests a minimal role in the development of sarcopenia (under sedentary conditions) as measured by specific force and muscle morphology comparing young (~5 months) and aged (~22 months) mice [63]. Similarly, the *Pax7*-dependent contribution of BrdU to myofiber nuclei was also shown to be minimal in unchallenged muscle [63]. While these studies demonstrate a role for *Pax7* positive satellite cells in regeneration, several groups have reported age-associated decrements in the number of satellite cells [64–66]. Not only is the number of satellite cells reduced in aged muscle but the ability of the cell to exit quiescence and activate is negatively impacted [67]. The mechanism(s) directing the age-related impairments in satellite cell function are uncertain; however, there is evidence for systemic, intercellular, and niche-associated contributors [68–70].

Satellite cells isolated from aged mice can be transplanted into injured muscles of young recipients and contribute to regeneration but fail to repair myofibers and replenish the quiescent resident stem cell pool to a similar extent of young donor cells [2,71]. This model has repeatedly shown the limited ability of satellite cells from aged donors to expand, self-renew, and fuse into myofibers regardless of host age supporting some intrinsic change in the satellite cell that cannot be reversed by engraftment into a youthful environment [71,72]. Several reports have elucidated cellular mechanisms responsible for age-associated dysfunction which include p38α/β mitogen-activated protein kinase (MAPK) signaling axis, FGFR-Sprouty1 signaling axis, JAK2-STAT3 signaling axis, and p16^{Ink4a} [56,67,70,71]. Recently published evidence further highlights a function for the tumor suppressor gene p53 in regulating cell cycle progression in activated muscle stem cells which is decreased in aged mice and leads to reduced proliferative and regenerative function [73]. Alterations in the satellite cell niche of older mice alters Notch signals [57] which, in turn, upregulates Mdm2 and limits p53 protein. This results in a propensity for impaired satellite cell proliferation and regenerative decline [73]. Age-related intrinsic changes can activate and/or repress many of the pathways mentioned, resulting in a limited ability to self-renew, and successfully differentiate into mature myofibers.

4.2. Autophagy and Muscle Satellite Cells

The importance of skeletal muscle autophagy is evident as impairments in autophagy in muscle tissue cause myopathy [32], altered regeneration [46], and accelerated aging [74]. The role of autophagy in satellite cell biology is less clear but several studies have helped to elucidate a better understanding in this area. Reports from our group [2] and others [1,75] have demonstrated that autophagy plays a crucial regulatory role in satellite cell quiescence, activation, differentiation and apoptosis. Advanced aged demonstrates a clear reduction in autophagy markers in isolated MuSCs [1,2]. Tang and Rando [76] show that autophagy is critical for activation and proliferation by acting as a temporary energy source to fuel initiation of proliferation. This is necessary because the relatively sparse cytoplasm and mitochondria of the satellite cell provide meager energy substrate when exiting quiescence; therefore, relying on autophagy to produce new biomass [77]. Conversely, aging muscle stem cells have a reduction in autophagy which, when rescued, has a rejuvenating effect and suppresses senescence [1]. In addition, impairment of autophagy in young satellite cells leads to a reduction in proliferation and myogenesis similar to what is observed in aged cells [1]. Aged satellite cells are inherently susceptible to apoptosis following cellular stress compared to healthy cells demonstrating a shift from autophagy to apoptosis with aging [78]. Recently published work by our group shows advanced age drives muscle stem cell dysfunction, in part through impairments in the AMPK/p27^{Kip1} pathway [2]. MuSC activation requires the induction of AMPK/p27^{Kip1} signaling to promote autophagy and subsequent proliferative/myogenic function. Aged MuSCs had suppressed AMPK/p27^{Kip1} signaling associated with reductions in autophagy and proliferation with increased apoptosis and senescence. Genetic or pharmacological activation of AMPK or p27^{Kip1} was effective in inducing autophagy and returning myogenic potential of aged MuSCs in addition to blocking the induction of senescence markers [2]. A summary of autophagy associated mechanisms in the satellite cell and approaches used to manipulate autophagy are shown in Figure 3. Although these studies suggest a key role for autophagy in satellite cell activation and regeneration, further investigation is warranted. Specifically, if autophagy is required to meet the energetic demands of satellite cell activation, then which autophagy-derived substrates are necessary for successful activation and how are these substrate concentrations affected in aged MuSCs? Furthermore, does the age-related reduction in MuSC autophagy contribute to the loss in satellite cell number with age?

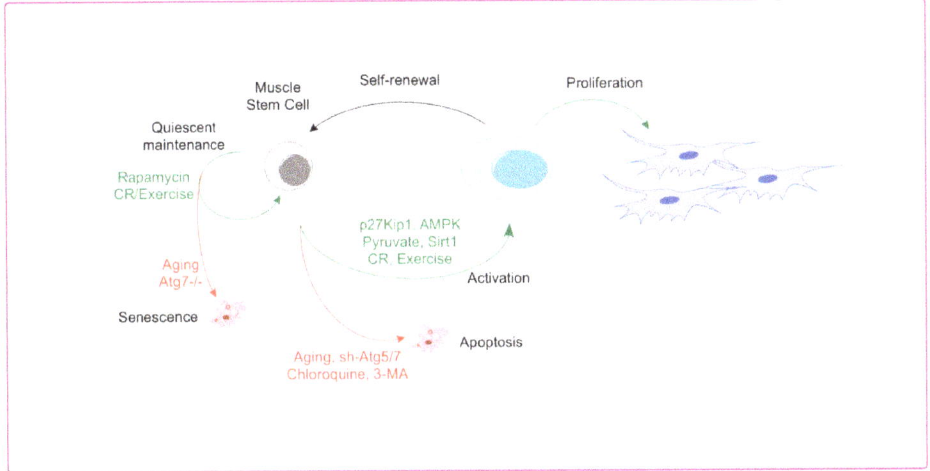

Figure 3. Aging and Autophagy Directly Impact Muscle Stem Cell Activation. Autophagy in the muscle stem cell can directly affect cell fate decisions including the maintenance of quiescence or entering into senescence. These can be controlled by aging, exercise, and caloric restriction or by direct manipulators of autophagy such as rapamycin and genetic ablation of the Atg system. Similarly, muscle stem cell activation requires sufficient energy substrate that can be limiting when autophagy is reduced (i.e., aging or with the autophagy inhibitiors chloroquine or 3-MA). Restoring the energetic signaling through AMPK activation (AICAR) or by supplementing the energy stores through pyruvate can help to replenish stem cell activation.

5. Monocytes and Macrophages

Alongside satellite cells, the innate immune system, specifically myeloid cells, plays a principal role in development, homeostasis, and regeneration of skeletal muscle [79–82]. Following damage, muscle exhibits traditional inflammatory responses including rapid and dramatic infiltration of monocytes and macrophages. Monocytes are derived from a hematopoietic stem cell (HSC) lineage and are activated and recruited to tissues where they differentiate into macrophages [83]. Recently, the importance of monocytes throughout the muscle repair process has become clear from early migration and removal of damaged tissue, inflammatory vs. anti-inflammatory macrophage roles, and physiological impacts of aging on regenerative potential [84,85]. Monocytes are key intermediaries between the innate and adaptive immunity and the role of autophagy is pertinent to all functions of the monocyte. Monocytes are critical in directing immune responses and the repair and maintenance of tissues throughout the body. This is done by chemotaxis towards inflammation such as tissue damage and infection where they can aid and orchestrate the repair process. Monocytes are a short-lived ($t_{1/2}$ = 3 days) and highly mobile cell residing in the blood and spleen which respond to inflammation by differentiation into macrophages and dendritic cells as well as tissue specific cells such as the Kupffer cells of the liver. The process of differentiating from a monocyte to a macrophage dictates the extent and duration of both immune responses and tissue remodeling. Without appropriate stimulation to differentiate, monocytes undergo apoptotic cell death and are cleared from the system. Here we will focus on the role autophagy plays on monocyte differentiation with age and the impact this has on macrophage function during regeneration. In order to fully appreciate the regenerative function of these immune cells, one must appreciate the phenotypic spectrum and heterogeneity of the macrophage population recruited during the regenerative process.

5.1. Autophagy in Monocyte Development and Macrophage Differentiation

Monocytes are derived from quiescent HSCs found in the hypoxic bone marrow environment. This environment limits oxidative metabolism and nutrient availability to HSCs which are typical activators of the autophagic process [86–88]. In fact, evidence shows that basal autophagy is elevated in human HSCs [89]. The importance of autophagy in quiescent of HSCs is partly due to a greater need for catabolism to remove damaged cellular components/organelles that are not actively removed by cell division [90]. Others have shown the value of autophagy as a source for ATP and to mitigate production of ROS through mitochondrial clearance by mitophagy [91,92]. FOXO3A and Atg7 are specific mechanistic pathways that have each been shown to contribute to quiescent maintenance through autophagy in HSCs [93,94]. Furthermore, evidence implicates an age-related decline in HSC autophagy [95] and function which can be rejuvenated by rapamycin treatment in mice [96]. This is highlighted through use of Tsc1-deficient HSC mice with constitutive activation of mTOR which show upregulated mitochondrial biogenesis, ROS production, and HSC activation that can be reversed by rapamycin treatment [97]. Additionally, Akt activation results in loss of HSC populations and increased cycling leading to leukemia in mice [98]. These studies have helped to establish a key role for autophagy in the maintenance of HSC quiescence as well as activation through an mTOR dependent route. However, the importance of autophagy extends beyond the HSC to the monocyte–macrophage differentiation process.

Monocytes are short-lived in circulation and undergo apoptosis unless stimulated by inflammatory factors such as TNF to upregulate survival pathways. Upon activation by inflammatory signals, monocytes use autophagy as a means to differentiate into macrophages or dendritic cells [99]. The specific signals stimulating the monocyte–macrophage transition have been shown to require autophagy in an ULK1- and Atg7-dependent manner in human and mouse primary cells [100,101]. Using both pharmacological inhibition of Atg7-/- mouse cells, monocytes were unable to differentiate when stimulated by CSF1 [100]. CSF2 stimulation of monocyte differentiation also appears to depend on autophagy through a Beclin1/Bcl2 interaction mechanism [99]. In addition to monocytes triggering towards a macrophage fate, autophagy can impact the polarization of the subsequent cell.

5.2. Monocyte and Macrophage Heterogeneity

During the early stages of the recovery process (roughly 0–48 h post injury), neutrophils help to condition the tissue environment at the site of injury helping to direct subsequent regenerative immune events. Monocyte extravasation in to the muscle is controlled by chemotaxis towards pro-inflammatory cytokines such as interferon-γ (IFNγ) and tumor necrosis factor (TNF). Following classical activation and recruitment to the damaged muscle, monocyte differentiation will lean towards a pro-inflammatory macrophage (M1) designed to ingest cellular debris and necrotic tissue to combat the initial insult and direct the subsequent immune response. Following the initial M1 response, monocytes will begin to differentiate towards alternatively activated, anti-inflammatory macrophages (M2), which reduces local inflammation and tampers the immune response to promote tissue remodeling (see Figure 4). The characterization of macrophages as M1 versus M2 phenotypes is an approach which fails to account for the diverse continuum of macrophage phenotypes [102]. In some scenarios, macrophages isolated from damaged muscle can express transcripts associated with either/both M1 and M2 phenotypes and the change in expression of these transcripts can be highly transient [103–105]. NF-κB transcriptional control of selective autophagy appears to be responsible for some aspects of M2 polarization [106]. Through inhibition of autophagy, NF-κB activity can force M2-polarized macrophages to secrete relevant levels of M1-cytokines [107]. Others have found that autophagy activation through rapamycin treatment leads to the classical M1 phenotype in macrophages from human blood [108]. These studies suggest that greater autophagy activation is directly related to the differential polarization of macrophages in response to stimuli [109]; however, a knowledge gap still exists in the field supporting autophagy as a direct contributor to either macrophage phenotype. Many of these studies rely on transcriptional control of NF-κB on autophagy or pharmaceutical modulators of autophagy each of which could have many confounding effects in the cell. Further evidence is needed to solidify a causative relationship between cellular autophagy and remodeling in macrophages, especially in the context of muscle regeneration and aging.

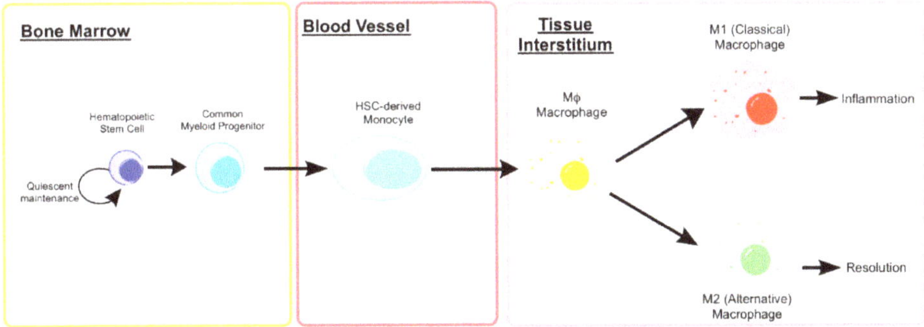

Figure 4. Development of Bone Marrow-derived Macrophages. Hematopoietic stem cells (HSCs) reside in their hypoxic niche within the bone marrow and maintain a quiescent state. When activated, the HSC can generate daughter cells of the common myeloid progenitor lineage and subsequently, into circulating monocytes. When stimulated by inflammatory cytokines (i.e., IL-6 or TNF, such as following muscle damage), monocytes undergo transcriptional changes that prevent apoptosis and enhance autophagy machinery during the differentiation into a macrophage. Mature macrophages (both classical and alterative) rely heavily on autophagy to aid in their function of clearing the damaged tissue and cellular debris that is the result of muscle injury.

5.3. Autophagy and Macrophage Function and Phenotype

It is clear that autophagy is a critical component to the efficient function of immune cells to clear pathogens or cellular debris. This is highlighted by macrophage function during skeletal muscle repair [110,111]. We refer to macrophage function as the ability of the cell to ingest and eliminate debris from a site of injury while aiding in the coordination of inflammation/resolution through cytokine production and excretion. In mature macrophages lacking ATG7, fewer autophagosomes are formed; there is a reduction in functional surface receptors, increased glycolytic flux, and greater basal inflammation [112]. ATG7 is essential to the elongation of the phagosomal membrane and lysosome function so this alters the inherent function of macrophages to use lysosomal means to degrade phagocytosed cellular debris. This implies macrophage autophagy is needed to clear away damaged muscle tissue and when this is prolonged, inflammatory cytokine production will persist. Others have used similar *Atg*-deficient mouse models to show that there is a need for effective autophagy to promote an anti-inflammatory environment through LC3-associated phagocytosis and appropriate cytokine signal release [113,114].

In addition to regulating macrophage function, autophagy appears to play a role in phenotype as well. By using a LysM-Cre recombinase system with *Atg7$^{fl/fl}$* mice, macrophage-specific autophagy was shown to play a role in M1/M2 polarization potential. When differentiated macrophages are unable to use autophagy, the macrophage population shifts towards a proinflammatory M1 phenotype along with greater glycolytic metabolism [115]. Conversely, the proportion of M2 macrophages was reduced by limiting fatty acid oxidation through lysosomal acid lipase—a portion of the autophagic degradation system [116]. The interaction between autophagy and macrophage polarization is unsurprising because of the initial ULK1 signal in monocytes initiating the differentiation response. ULK1 directly interacts with mTOR and autophagy is inhibited when nutrient stimulation of mTOR is high [117]. When mTOR is constitutively active, IL-4-stimulated macrophage polarization is tilted towards an inflammatory M1 phenotype [118,119].

5.4. Age-Associated Suppression of Monocyte/Macrophage Function

Immune cells are subjected to an age-associated decline in effective response, termed immunesenescence [120]. Although all aspects of immunity are affected by age, the impact to the innate system is particularly significant [121]. Aging of the innate immune system is accompanied by an increased number of circulating monocytes which have reduced effector functions (i.e., chemotaxis, phagocytosis, and antigen presentation) [121]. Evidence demonstrates age-related deterioration of NO burst, fewer toll-like receptor antigen recognition particles, and greater inflammatory cytokine release by macrophages [122–125]. Accompanying this is an increased level of chronic systemic inflammation that is in part associated with innate immunesenescence [126]. The complex mechanisms responsible for immunesenescence are unclear but the reduced immune effector function and increased low level inflammation contribute to reduced tissue homeostasis and repair after damaging insult. These deficiencies of innate immunity can result in age-related frailty and greater mortality for the elderly [127,128]. Interestingly, many of the key roles for autophagy in macrophages become dysregulated with advanced age unveiling a key link between aging and macrophage function [127–129].

Evidence supports age-associated changes in macrophage function across the lifespan. Early studies showed altered response and expression of toll-like receptors in aged mice compared to young [123]. Monocytes isolated from young and old mice that are then stimulated ex vivo with LPS show an age-related reduction in the secretion of pro-inflammatory (M1) cytokines including IL-6, IL-1β, and TNF-α [130]. Similarly, when stimulated with IFN-γ and IL-4, aged monocytes expressed the markers Arg1, Ym1, and FIZZ1 to a lesser extent than young counterparts [130]. This series of experiments indicates that macrophages from old mice (>2 years) produce fewer cytokines than young mice both under situations of pro-inflammatory and anti-inflammatory stimuli. Moreover, some investigations into human inflammatory markers have shown an imbalance in the circulating IFNγ- and IL-4-related markers in elderly humans (81–100 years) compared to young [131]. Age-associated changes to macrophage function and related effects of autophagy manipulation are summarized in Figure 5.

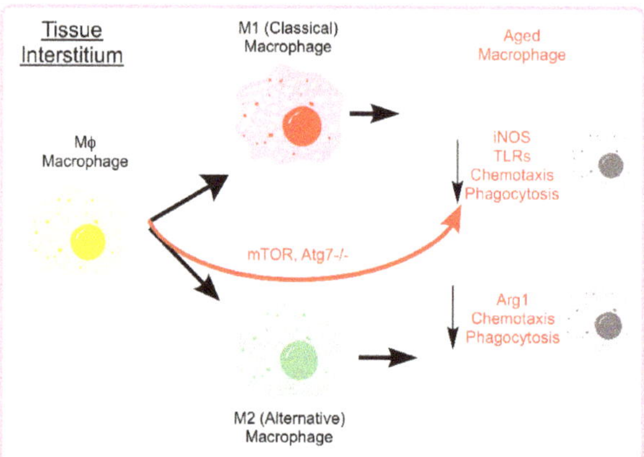

Figure 5. Aging Negatively Effects Macrophage Autophagy and Associated Phenotype/Function. The mature macrophage uses autophagy as part of the cell's inherent function to phagocytose and eliminate pathogens or debris. The aged macrophages tend to have impairments in the autophagic functions, phagocytosis, and chemotaxis. While aged individuals tend to have elevated circulating inflammatory markers, aged M1 and M2 macrophages show reductions in iNOS and Arg1, respectively. By limiting autophagy through Atg7 genetic ablation or constitutive mTOR activation, M2 macrophages show a shift towards M1 cytokine secretion.

6. Rejuvenation of Autophagy for Muscle Regeneration

After having established the importance of autophagy in various aspects of skeletal muscle repair, autophagy, and related pathways present an obvious therapeutic target to enhance muscle function and regenerative capacity. Exercise and caloric restriction (CR) are two established methods shown to induce autophagy in several tissues [42,132–135]. In addition, exercise and CR enhance cellular function of both MuSCs and macrophages [136–140]. The following sections will discuss how autophagy may play a role for each approach.

6.1. Rejuvenation of Satellite Cells through Exercise and CR

6.1.1. Exercise

Exercise is an established method to prevent the onset of sarcopenia. In addition, exercise may also aid to enhance regenerative capacity in aged muscle. Moderate intensity treadmill running is capable of increasing the number of MuSCs isolated from hindlimb muscles in young and old mice while increasing aged MuSC proliferative function [64,141]. In regard to signaling, voluntary wheel running upregulated Wnt/β-catenin activity, irrespective of structural damage [142]. Thus, suggesting a possible mechanism to explain why exercise can increase satellite cells numbers of young and old muscle. To the best of our knowledge, the effects of physical activity on satellite cell autophagy have not been investigated in satellite cells/MuSCs. Considering exercise is able to induce autophagy in peripheral tissues that are not actively performing contraction [133], satellite cells may receive some exercise-induced signals to increase autophagy similar to what was observed in nonmuscle tissue [133]. Well-controlled studies directly linking exercise with enhanced satellite cell autophagy are needed. An increase in satellite cell autophagy could help to explain a mechanism for enhanced satellite cell number and function with exercise.

6.1.2. Caloric Restriction

An additional intervention shown to induce global autophagy and related extension in health/lifespan is caloric restriction [143]. The benefits of longevity through moderate reductions in caloric intake have been shown in numerous models [136,137,143,144]. Moreover, CR has shown beneficial effects on adult stem cell function across various tissues [145]. Even short term (12 weeks) CR improves the number and proliferative function of satellite cells in young mice (eight weeks) with the benefits extending to aged mice (21 months old) [146]. In addition to improved regenerative capacity, CR also enhances engraftment capability of MuSCs isolated from ad libitum fed donors [146]. The contribution of autophagy to the pro-regenerative effects of CR is unclear as yet; however, Cerletti et al. [146] show improvements in oxidative characteristics and mitochondrial markers suggesting altered energy status of the MuSC [147]. Extending upon these results, a similar CR regiment in aged mice resulted in a greater phosphorylation of AMPK and p27^{Kip1} in activating aged MuSCs [2]. These data suggest CR may "prime" the aged MuSC to initiate autophagy upon activation. Further investigation is certainly warranted to understand CR-sensitive pathways in quiescent and activated satellite cells/MuSCs.

6.2. Rejuvenation of Macrophages through Exercise and CR

6.2.1. Exercise

Little has been shown on how exercise training might improve immune function in the elderly or mitigate the immunosenescent phenotype. Early studies have shown a connection between exercise and macrophage phagocytic function in athletes [148]. A 10-week exercise program with varying exercise intensities improves immune function compared to pre-exercise measurements [149]. In addition, exercise increased neutrophil migratory function in old adults [150]. In the mouse, aging reduced the cytokine production and function of both M1 and M2 macrophages; exercise training appears to sensitize macrophages to LPS-induced cytokine production [151]. Long-term treadmill running in mice has been shown to elevate markers on M2 macrophages (higher CD163 and lower TLR4) in high-fat diet-fed mice adipose tissue suggesting an exercise-induced alternative macrophage promoting phenotype. While these data showed a correction of high-fat diet-induced M1 markers by exercise (Cd11c and ICAM-1), exercise training in healthy mice did not have any effect on the macrophage phenotype [152]. To date, no study has investigated the association between immune cell autophagy and exercise. However, autophagy regulates macrophage differentiation and therefore exercise could enhance muscle regeneration by promoting the transition between pro and anti-inflammatory macrophages.

6.2.2. Caloric Restriction

Similar to the MuSC, macrophage polarization and function seems to be sensitive to caloric restriction [153]. Greater M2 macrophage-related cytokine production and cellular markers were measured in the adipose tissue of caloric restricted mice [153]. It remains unclear if these changes are associated with alterations in cellular autophagy. Caloric restriction has been shown to enhance the anti-inflammatory characteristics of macrophages, but it remains unclear how this might relate to autophagy function in the context of muscle regeneration.

6.3. Pharmacological Inducers of Autophagy

As has been alluded to, the pharmacological induction of autophagy represents a promising strategy to improve stress resistance and regeneration of skeletal muscle. Spermidine and rapamycin are two examples of drugs that have been studied for their autophagy-inducing effects and lifespan extension in rodent models [154,155]. While rapamycin acts directly on mTOR, spermidine's polyamine effects on histone acetylation status upregulates various autophagy-related transcripts and suppresses necrosis [156]. The positive benefits of spermidine in muscle tissues of mice and rats have been shown by mitigating age-related muscular atrophy as well as functional myopathies that originate from autophagy failure [157,158]. The autophagy-inducing effects of spermidine and rapamycin have also been detailed specifically within the muscle stem cell [1,159,160]. Satellite cells were isolated from aged mice and treated ex vivo with either rapamycin or spermidine and a dramatic increase in autophagy was measured by immunofluorescence of LC3 puncta. Gracia-Prat et al. further demonstrated that the pharmacological induction of autophagy reverses age-related declines in mitochondrial morphology and regenerative function [1]. Spermidine also modulates macrophage polarization in mice towards reduced inflammation, though some evidence suggests the autophagy inducing effects of rapamycin more directly target T lymphocytes [161,162]. Taken together, these agents act as "caloric restriction mimetics" to induce autophagy and contribute to improvements in lifespan of mice. Specifically, the effects of autophagy induction show promise as it related to therapies targeting muscle stem cell myogenic capacity. Figure 6 illustrates general age-related differences across various components of the regenerative process in addition to known lifespan/healthspan approaches and their common effects to enhance tissue regeneration.

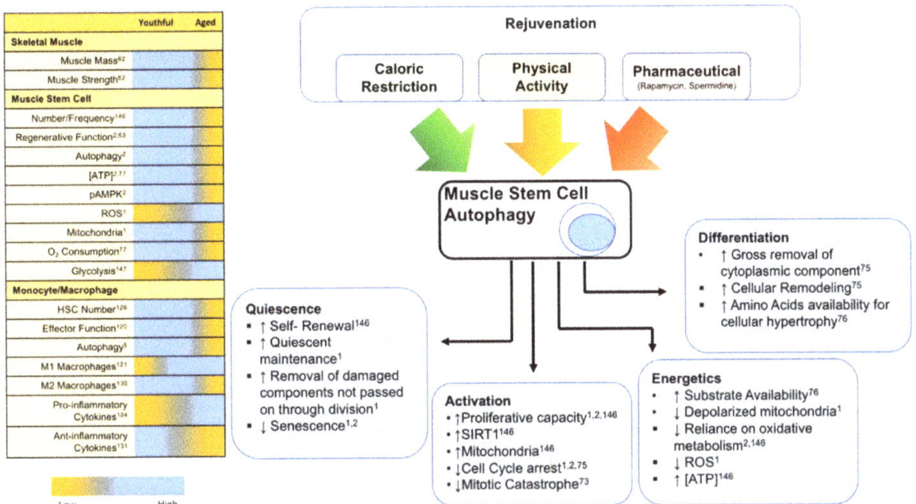

Figure 6. Rejuvenation of Muscle Stem cell autophagy. **Left**: Chart summarizing various physiological and functional parameters involved in skeletal muscle regeneration and how they are susceptible to age-related alterations. **Right**: Conceptualization of the rejuvenation potential targeting stem cell autophagy and how various cellular functions are affected. Caloric restriction, physical activity, and certain pharmaceuticals are known to affect stem cell autophagy. The role of autophagy in the stem cell is multifaceted with implications in quiescence vs. senescence, activation/proliferation vs. apoptosis, and differentiation outcomes. A substantial contribution of autophagy in the function of a muscle stem cell is alterations in the cellular metabolic landscape or energetics.

7. Conclusions and Future Perspectives

The ability to repair damaged tissue and continuously respond to stressful stimuli is essential to preserve whole body function throughout life. Muscle stem cells and macrophages are an integral part of this process and their loss of function with age contributes to degenerative diseases. This review highlights how muscle stem cells and monocytes/macrophages are essential for skeletal muscle homeostasis and regeneration. A common theme among these cell populations is the idea that autophagy is a key process that is altered in aged cells leading to functional decline. Autophagy is no longer an emerging regulator of cellular function but has consistently been shown to play a central and important role, especially in the context of aging. Stem cells, in particular, show dysfunctional autophagy during initial stages of activation while caloric restriction and physical activity allow a sensitization to autophagy with beneficial outcomes in cellular activation and function. The exact role for autophagy in muscle regeneration will be complex considering the temporal nature and diverse cell types contributing to the regenerative program. However, global induction of autophagy appears beneficial to the regenerative capacity in the aged muscle. Continuing to uncover the molecular events responsible for age-related perturbations in these pathways is critical for exposing pharmaceutical targets to combat the aging process and improve tissue regeneration in aged individuals.

Funding: J.P.W. was supported by NIH/NIA K01AG056664, NIH/NIA Pepper Center grant AG028716 and the Borden Scholar Award through Duke University. D.B.B. was supported by NIH/NIA Pepper Center grant AG028716.

Conflicts of Interest: The authors declare no conflict of interest.

References

1. Garcia-Prat, L.; Martinez-Vicente, M.; Perdiguero, E.; Ortet, L.; Rodriguez-Ubreva, J.; Rebollo, E.; Ruiz-Bonilla, V.; Gutarra, S.; Ballestar, E.; Serrano, A.L.; et al. Autophagy maintains stemness by preventing senescence. *Nature* **2016**, *529*, 37–42. [CrossRef] [PubMed]
2. White, J.P.; Billin, A.N.; Campbell, M.E.; Russell, A.J.; Huffman, K.M.; Kraus, W.E. The AMPK/p27(Kip1) Axis Regulates Autophagy/Apoptosis Decisions in Aged Skeletal Muscle Stem Cells. *Stem Cell Rep.* **2018**, *11*, 425–439. [CrossRef] [PubMed]
3. Tekirdag, K.; Cuervo, A.M. Chaperone-mediated autophagy and endosomal microautophagy: Joint by a chaperone. *J. Biol. Chem.* **2018**, *293*, 5414–5424. [CrossRef]
4. De Duve, C. The lysosome. *Sci. Am.* **1963**, *208*, 64–72. [CrossRef] [PubMed]
5. Takeshige, K.; Baba, M.; Tsuboi, S.; Noda, T.; Ohsumi, Y. Autophagy in yeast demonstrated with proteinase-deficient mutants and conditions for its induction. *J. Cell Biol.* **1992**, *119*, 301–311. [CrossRef] [PubMed]
6. Mortimore, G.E.; Schworer, C.M. Induction of autophagy by amino-acid deprivation in perfused rat liver. *Nature* **1977**, *270*, 174. [CrossRef] [PubMed]
7. Kroemer, G.; Marino, G.; Levine, B. Autophagy and the integrated stress response. *Mol. Cell* **2010**, *40*, 280–293. [CrossRef] [PubMed]
8. Mizushima, N.; Komatsu, M. Autophagy: Renovation of cells and tissues. *Cell* **2011**, *147*, 728–741. [CrossRef] [PubMed]
9. Yang, Z.; Huang, J.; Geng, J.; Nair, U.; Klionsky, D.J.; Brodsky, J. Atg22 Recycles Amino Acids to Link the Degradative and Recycling Functions of Autophagy. *Mol. Biol. Cell* **2006**, *17*, 5094–5104. [CrossRef]
10. Guo, J.Y.; Chen, H.Y.; Mathew, R.; Fan, J.; Strohecker, A.M.; Karsli-Uzunbas, G.; Kamphorst, J.J.; Chen, G.; Lemons, J.M.; Karantza, V.; et al. Activated Ras requires autophagy to maintain oxidative metabolism and tumorigenesis. *Genes Dev.* **2011**, *25*, 460–470. [CrossRef] [PubMed]
11. Singh, R.; Kaushik, S.; Wang, Y.; Xiang, Y.; Novak, I.; Komatsu, M.; Tanaka, K.; Cuervo, A.M.; Czaja, M.J. Autophagy regulates lipid metabolism. *Nature* **2009**, *458*, 1131–1135. [CrossRef] [PubMed]
12. Mizushima, N.; Levine, B. Autophagy in mammalian development and differentiation. *Nat. Cell Biol.* **2010**, *12*, 823–830. [CrossRef] [PubMed]
13. Kroemer, G. Autophagy: A druggable process that is deregulated in aging and human disease. *J. Clin. Investig.* **2015**, *125*, 1–4. [CrossRef] [PubMed]
14. Mehrpour, M.; Esclatine, A.; Beau, I.; Codogno, P. Overview of macroautophagy regulation in mammalian cells. *Cell Res.* **2010**, *20*, 748–762. [CrossRef] [PubMed]
15. Wei, Y.; Pattingre, S.; Sinha, S.; Bassik, M.; Levine, B. JNK1-mediated phosphorylation of Bcl-2 regulates starvation-induced autophagy. *Mol. Cell* **2008**, *30*, 678–688. [CrossRef] [PubMed]
16. Copetti, T.; Bertoli, C.; Dalla, E.; Demarchi, F.; Schneider, C. p65/RelA modulates BECN1 transcription and autophagy. *Mol. Cell. Biol.* **2009**, *29*, 2594–2608. [CrossRef] [PubMed]
17. Bohensky, J.; Shapiro, I.M.; Leshinsky, S.; Terkhorn, S.P.; Adams, C.S.; Srinivas, V. HIF-1 regulation of chondrocyte apoptosis: Induction of the autophagic pathway. *Autophagy* **2007**, *3*, 207–214. [CrossRef] [PubMed]
18. Zhao, J.; Brault, J.J.; Schild, A.; Cao, P.; Sandri, M.; Schiaffino, S.; Lecker, S.H.; Goldberg, A.L. FoxO3 coordinately activates protein degradation by the autophagic/lysosomal and proteasomal pathways in atrophying muscle cells. *Cell Metab.* **2007**, *6*, 472–483. [CrossRef] [PubMed]
19. Kim, D.H.; Sarbassov, D.D.; Ali, S.M.; King, J.E.; Latek, R.R.; Erdjument-Bromage, H.; Tempst, P.; Sabatini, D.M. mTOR interacts with raptor to form a nutrient-sensitive complex that signals to the cell growth machinery. *Cell* **2002**, *110*, 163–175. [CrossRef]
20. Ganley, I.G.; Lam du, H.; Wang, J.; Ding, X.; Chen, S.; Jiang, X. ULK1.ATG13.FIP200 complex mediates mTOR signaling and is essential for autophagy. *J. Biol. Chem.* **2009**, *284*, 12297–12305. [CrossRef]
21. Blagosklonny, M.V. Hypoxia, MTOR and autophagy: Converging on senescence or quiescence. *Autophagy* **2013**, *9*, 260–262. [CrossRef] [PubMed]
22. Choi, A.M.K.; Ryter, S.W.; Levine, B. Autophagy in Human Health and Disease. *N. Engl. J. Med.* **2013**, *368*, 651–662. [CrossRef] [PubMed]

23. Rubinsztein, D.C.; Marino, G.; Kroemer, G. Autophagy and aging. *Cell* **2011**, *146*, 682–695. [CrossRef] [PubMed]

24. Matecic, M.; Smith, D.L., Jr.; Pan, X.; Maqani, N.; Bekiranov, S.; Boeke, J.D.; Smith, J.S. A Microarray-Based Genetic Screen for Yeast Chronological Aging Factors. *PLoS Genet.* **2010**, *6*, e1000921. [CrossRef] [PubMed]

25. Tóth, M.L.; Sigmond, T.; Borsos, É.; Barna, J.; Erdélyi, P.; Takács-Vellai, K.; Orosz, L.; Kovács, A.L.; Csikós, G.; Sass, M.; et al. Longevity pathways converge on autophagy genes to regulate life span in Caenorhabditis elegans. *Autophagy* **2008**, *4*, 330–338. [CrossRef] [PubMed]

26. Simonsen, A.; Cumming, R.C.; Brech, A.; Isakson, P.; Schubert, D.R.; Finley, K.D. Promoting basal levels of autophagy in the nervous system enhances longevity and oxidant resistance in adult Drosophila. *Autophagy* **2008**, *4*, 176–184. [CrossRef] [PubMed]

27. Lipinski, M.M.; Zheng, B.; Lu, T.; Yan, Z.; Py, B.F.; Ng, A.; Xavier, R.J.; Li, C.; Yankner, B.A.; Scherzer, C.R.; et al. Genome-wide analysis reveals mechanisms modulating autophagy in normal brain aging and in Alzheimer's disease. *Proc. Natl. Acad. Sci. USA* **2010**, *107*, 14164–14169. [CrossRef] [PubMed]

28. De Kreutzenberg, S.V.; Ceolotto, G.; Papparella, I.; Bortoluzzi, A.; Semplicini, A.; Man, C.D.; Cobelli, C.; Fadini, G.P.; Avogaro, A. Downregulation of the Longevity-Associated Protein Sirtuin 1 in Insulin Resistance and Metabolic Syndrome: Potential Biochemical Mechanisms. *Diabetes* **2010**, *59*, 1006–1015. [CrossRef] [PubMed]

29. Caramés, B.; Taniguchi, N.; Otsuki, S.; Blanco, F.J.; Lotz, M. Autophagy is a protective mechanism in normal cartilage, and its aging-related loss is linked with cell death and osteoarthritis. *Arthritis Rheum.* **2010**, *62*, 791–801. [CrossRef] [PubMed]

30. Decuypere, J.P.; Monaco, G.; Missiaen, L.; De Smedt, H.; Parys, J.B.; Bultynck, G. IP(3) Receptors, Mitochondria, and Ca Signaling: Implications for Aging. *J. Aging Res.* **2011**, *2011*, 920178. [CrossRef]

31. Xiao, M.; Li, L.; Hu, Q.; Ma, L.; Liu, L.; Chu, W.; Zhang, H. Rapamycin reduces burn wound progression by enhancing autophagy in deep second-degree burn in rats. *Wound Repair Regen.* **2013**, *21*, 852–859. [CrossRef] [PubMed]

32. Masiero, E.; Agatea, L.; Mammucari, C.; Blaauw, B.; Loro, E.; Komatsu, M.; Metzger, D.; Reggiani, C.; Schiaffino, S.; Sandri, M. Autophagy is required to maintain muscle mass. *Cell Metab.* **2009**, *10*, 507–515. [CrossRef] [PubMed]

33. De Palma, C.; Morisi, F.; Cheli, S.; Pambianco, S.; Cappello, V.; Vezzoli, M.; Rovere-Querini, P.; Moggio, M.; Ripolone, M.; Francolini, M.; et al. Autophagy as a new therapeutic target in Duchenne muscular dystrophy. *Cell Death Dis.* **2012**, *3*, e418. [CrossRef] [PubMed]

34. He, C.; Bassik, M.C.; Moresi, V.; Sun, K.; Wei, Y.; Zou, Z.; An, Z.; Loh, J.; Fisher, J.; Sun, Q.; et al. Exercise-induced BCL2-regulated autophagy is required for muscle glucose homeostasis. *Nature* **2012**, *481*, 511–515. [CrossRef] [PubMed]

35. Fan, J.; Kou, X.; Jia, S.; Yang, X.; Yang, Y.; Chen, N. Autophagy as a Potential Target for Sarcopenia. *J. Cell. Physiol.* **2016**, *231*, 1450–1459. [CrossRef] [PubMed]

36. Penna, F.; Costamagna, D.; Pin, F.; Camperi, A.; Fanzani, A.; Chiarpotto, E.M.; Cavallini, G.; Bonelli, G.; Baccino, F.M.; Costelli, P. Autophagic degradation contributes to muscle wasting in cancer cachexia. *Am. J. Pathol.* **2013**, *182*, 1367–1378. [CrossRef] [PubMed]

37. Saera-Vila, A.; Kish, P.E.; Louie, K.W.; Grzegorski, S.J.; Klionsky, D.J.; Kahana, A. Autophagy regulates cytoplasmic remodeling during cell reprogramming in a zebrafish model of muscle regeneration. *Autophagy* **2016**, *12*, 1864–1875. [CrossRef]

38. Brown, J.L.; Lee, D.E.; Rosa-Caldwell, M.E.; Brown, L.A.; Perry, R.A.; Haynie, W.S.; Huseman, K.; Sataranatarajan, K.; Van Remmen, H.; Washington, T.A.; et al. Protein imbalance in the development of skeletal muscle wasting in tumour-bearing mice. *J. CachexiaSarcopenia Muscle* **2018**, *9*, 987–1002. [CrossRef]

39. White, J.P.; Baynes, J.W.; Welle, S.L.; Kostek, M.C.; Matesic, L.E.; Sato, S.; Carson, J.A. The regulation of skeletal muscle protein turnover during the progression of cancer cachexia in the Apc(Min/+) mouse. *PLoS ONE* **2011**, *6*, e24650. [CrossRef]

40. Koga, H.; Kaushik, S.; Cuervo, A.M. Altered lipid content inhibits autophagic vesicular fusion. *FASEB J.* **2010**, *24*, 3052–3065. [CrossRef]

41. Laker, R.C.; Drake, J.C.; Wilson, R.J.; Lira, V.A.; Lewellen, B.M.; Ryall, K.A.; Fisher, C.C.; Zhang, M.; Saucerman, J.J.; Goodyear, L.J.; et al. Ampk phosphorylation of Ulk1 is required for targeting of mitochondria to lysosomes in exercise-induced mitophagy. *Nat. Commun.* **2017**, *8*, 548. [CrossRef] [PubMed]

42. Lira, V.A.; Okutsu, M.; Zhang, M.; Greene, N.P.; Laker, R.C.; Breen, D.S.; Hoehn, K.L.; Yan, Z. Autophagy is required for exercise training-induced skeletal muscle adaptation and improvement of physical performance. *FASEB J.* **2013**, *27*, 4184–4193. [CrossRef] [PubMed]

43. Nichenko, A.S.; Southern, W.M.; Atuan, M.; Luan, J.; Peissig, K.B.; Foltz, S.J.; Beedle, A.M.; Warren, G.L.; Call, J.A. Mitochondrial maintenance via autophagy contributes to functional skeletal muscle regeneration and remodeling. *Am. J. Physiol. Cell Physiol.* **2016**, *311*, C190–C200. [CrossRef] [PubMed]

44. Fiacco, E.; Castagnetti, F.; Bianconi, V.; Madaro, L.; De Bardi, M.; Nazio, F.; D'Amico, A.; Bertini, E.; Cecconi, F.; Puri, P.L.; et al. Autophagy regulates satellite cell ability to regenerate normal and dystrophic muscles. *Cell Death Differ.* **2016**, *23*, 1839–1849. [CrossRef] [PubMed]

45. Paolini, A.; Omairi, S.; Mitchell, R.; Vaughan, D.; Matsakas, A.; Vaiyapuri, S.; Ricketts, T.; Rubinsztein, D.C.; Patel, K. Attenuation of autophagy impacts on muscle fibre development, starvation induced stress and fibre regeneration following acute injury. *Sci. Rep.* **2018**, *8*, 9062. [CrossRef] [PubMed]

46. Call, J.A.; Wilson, R.J.; Laker, R.C.; Zhang, M.; Kundu, M.; Yan, Z. Ulk1-mediated autophagy plays an essential role in mitochondrial remodeling and functional regeneration of skeletal muscle. *Am. J. Physiol. Cell Physiol.* **2017**, *312*, C724–C732. [CrossRef]

47. McMillan, E.M.; Quadrilatero, J. Autophagy is required and protects against apoptosis during myoblast differentiation. *Biochem. J.* **2014**, *462*, 267–277. [CrossRef]

48. Chazaud, B. Inflammation during skeletal muscle regeneration and tissue remodeling: Application to exercise-induced muscle damage management. *Immunol. Cell Biol.* **2016**, *94*, 140–145. [CrossRef]

49. Studitsky, A.N. FREE AUTO- AND HOMOGRAFTS OF MUSCLE TISSUE IN EXPERIMENTS ON ANIMALS. *Ann. N. Y. Acad. Sci.* **1964**, *120*, 789–801. [CrossRef]

50. Clevers, H. STEM CELLS. What is an adult stem cell? *Science* **2015**, *350*, 1319–1320. [CrossRef]

51. Moss, F.P.; Leblond, C.P. Satellite cells as the source of nuclei in muscles of growing rats. *Anat. Rec.* **1971**, *170*, 421–435. [CrossRef] [PubMed]

52. McCarthy, J.J.; Mula, J.; Miyazaki, M.; Erfani, R.; Garrison, K.; Farooqui, A.B.; Srikuea, R.; Lawson, B.A.; Grimes, B.; Keller, C.; et al. Effective fiber hypertrophy in satellite cell-depleted skeletal muscle. *Development* **2011**, *138*, 3657–3666. [CrossRef] [PubMed]

53. Murphy, M.M.; Lawson, J.A.; Mathew, S.J.; Hutcheson, D.A.; Kardon, G. Satellite cells, connective tissue fibroblasts and their interactions are crucial for muscle regeneration. *Development* **2011**, *138*, 3625–3637. [CrossRef] [PubMed]

54. Lepper, C.; Partridge, T.A.; Fan, C.M. An absolute requirement for Pax7-positive satellite cells in acute injury-induced skeletal muscle regeneration. *Development* **2011**, *138*, 3639–3646. [CrossRef] [PubMed]

55. Mauro, A. Satellite cell of skeletal muscle fibers. *J. Biophys. Biochem. Cytol.* **1961**, *9*, 493–495. [CrossRef] [PubMed]

56. Schultz, E.; Lipton, B.H. Skeletal muscle satellite cells: Changes in proliferation potential as a function of age. *Mech. Ageing Dev.* **1982**, *20*, 377–383. [CrossRef]

57. Conboy, I.M.; Conboy, M.J.; Smythe, G.M.; Rando, T.A. Notch-mediated restoration of regenerative potential to aged muscle. *Science* **2003**, *302*, 1575–1577. [CrossRef]

58. Blau, H.M.; Cosgrove, B.D.; Ho, A.T. The central role of muscle stem cells in regenerative failure with aging. *Nat. Med.* **2015**, *21*, 854–862. [CrossRef]

59. Relaix, F.; Zammit, P.S. Satellite cells are essential for skeletal muscle regeneration: The cell on the edge returns centre stage. *Development* **2012**, *139*, 2845–2856. [CrossRef]

60. Rathbone, C.R.; Wenke, J.C.; Warren, G.L.; Armstrong, R.B. Importance of satellite cells in the strength recovery after eccentric contraction-induced muscle injury. *Am. J. Physiol. Regul. Integr. Comp. Physiol.* **2003**, *285*, R1490–R1495. [CrossRef]

61. Lowe, D.A.; Alway, S.E. Stretch-induced myogenin, MyoD, and MRF4 expression and acute hypertrophy in quail slow-tonic muscle are not dependent upon satellite cell proliferation. *Cell Tissue Res.* **1999**, *296*, 531–539. [CrossRef] [PubMed]

62. Fielding, R.A.; Vellas, B.; Evans, W.J.; Bhasin, S.; Morley, J.E.; Newman, A.B.; Abellan van Kan, G.; Andrieu, S.; Bauer, J.; Breuille, D.; et al. Sarcopenia: An undiagnosed condition in older adults. Current consensus definition: Prevalence, etiology, and consequences. International working group on sarcopenia. *J. Am. Med Dir. Assoc.* **2011**, *12*, 249–256. [CrossRef] [PubMed]

63. Fry, C.S.; Lee, J.D.; Mula, J.; Kirby, T.J.; Jackson, J.R.; Liu, F.; Yang, L.; Mendias, C.L.; Dupont-Versteegden, E.E.; McCarthy, J.J.; et al. Inducible depletion of satellite cells in adult, sedentary mice impairs muscle regenerative capacity without affecting sarcopenia. *Nat. Med.* **2015**, *21*, 76–80. [CrossRef] [PubMed]

64. Shefer, G.; Rauner, G.; Yablonka-Reuveni, Z.; Benayahu, D. Reduced satellite cell numbers and myogenic capacity in aging can be alleviated by endurance exercise. *PLoS ONE* **2010**, *5*, e13307. [CrossRef] [PubMed]

65. Collins, C.A.; Zammit, P.S.; Ruiz, A.P.; Morgan, J.E.; Partridge, T.A. A population of myogenic stem cells that survives skeletal muscle aging. *Stem Cells (Dayt. Ohio)* **2007**, *25*, 885–894. [CrossRef] [PubMed]

66. Brooks, N.E.; Schuenke, M.D.; Hikida, R.S. No change in skeletal muscle satellite cells in young and aging rat soleus muscle. *J. Physiol. Sci.* **2009**, *59*, 465–471. [CrossRef] [PubMed]

67. Hikida, R.S. Aging changes in satellite cells and their functions. *Curr. Aging Sci.* **2011**, *4*, 279–297. [CrossRef]

68. Bernet, J.D.; Doles, J.D.; Hall, J.K.; Kelly Tanaka, K.; Carter, T.A.; Olwin, B.B. p38 MAPK signaling underlies a cell-autonomous loss of stem cell self-renewal in skeletal muscle of aged mice. *Nat. Med.* **2014**, *20*, 265–271. [CrossRef]

69. Collins-Hooper, H.; Woolley, T.E.; Dyson, L.; Patel, A.; Potter, P.; Baker, R.E.; Gaffney, E.A.; Maini, P.K.; Dash, P.R.; Patel, K. Age-related changes in speed and mechanism of adult skeletal muscle stem cell migration. *Stem Cells (Dayt. Ohio)* **2012**, *30*, 1182–1195. [CrossRef]

70. Chakkalakal, J.V.; Jones, K.M.; Basson, M.A.; Brack, A.S. The aged niche disrupts muscle stem cell quiescence. *Nature* **2012**, *490*, 355–360. [CrossRef]

71. Cosgrove, B.D.; Gilbert, P.M.; Porpiglia, E.; Mourkioti, F.; Lee, S.P.; Corbel, S.Y.; Llewellyn, M.E.; Delp, S.L.; Blau, H.M. Rejuvenation of the muscle stem cell population restores strength to injured aged muscles. *Nat. Med.* **2014**, *20*, 255–264. [CrossRef]

72. Price, F.D.; von Maltzahn, J.; Bentzinger, C.F.; Dumont, N.A.; Yin, H.; Chang, N.C.; Wilson, D.H.; Frenette, J.; Rudnicki, M.A. Inhibition of JAK-STAT signaling stimulates adult satellite cell function. *Nat. Med.* **2014**, *20*, 1174–1181. [CrossRef]

73. Liu, L.; Charville, G.W.; Cheung, T.H.; Yoo, B.; Santos, P.J.; Schroeder, M.; Rando, T.A. Impaired Notch Signaling Leads to a Decrease in p53 Activity and Mitotic Catastrophe in Aged Muscle Stem Cells. *Cell Stem Cell* **2018**. [CrossRef]

74. Carnio, S.; LoVerso, F.; Baraibar, M.A.; Longa, E.; Khan, M.M.; Maffei, M.; Reischl, M.; Canepari, M.; Loefler, S.; Kern, H.; et al. Autophagy impairment in muscle induces neuromuscular junction degeneration and precocious aging. *Cell Rep.* **2014**, *8*, 1509–1521. [CrossRef]

75. Wen, X.; Klionsky, D.J. Autophagy is a key factor in maintaining the regenerative capacity of muscle stem cells by promoting quiescence and preventing senescence. *Autophagy* **2016**, *12*, 617–618. [CrossRef]

76. Tang, A.H.; Rando, T.A. Induction of autophagy supports the bioenergetic demands of quiescent muscle stem cell activation. *EMBO J.* **2014**, *33*, 2782–2797. [CrossRef]

77. Ryall, J.G. Simultaneous Measurement of Mitochondrial and Glycolytic Activity in Quiescent Muscle Stem Cells. *Methods Mol. Biol. (Clifton N.J.)* **2017**, *1556*, 245–253. [CrossRef]

78. Jejurikar, S.S.; Henkelman, E.A.; Cederna, P.S.; Marcelo, C.L.; Urbanchek, M.G.; Kuzon, W.M., Jr. Aging increases the susceptibility of skeletal muscle derived satellite cells to apoptosis. *Exp. Gerontol.* **2006**, *41*, 828–836. [CrossRef]

79. Godwin, J.W.; Pinto, A.R.; Rosenthal, N.A. Macrophages are required for adult salamander limb regeneration. *Proc. Natl. Acad. Sci. USA* **2013**, *110*, 9415–9420. [CrossRef]

80. Li, L.; Yan, B.; Shi, Y.Q.; Zhang, W.Q.; Wen, Z.L. Live imaging reveals differing roles of macrophages and neutrophils during zebrafish tail fin regeneration. *J. Biol. Chem.* **2012**, *287*, 25353–25360. [CrossRef]

81. Nahrendorf, M.; Swirski, F.K.; Aikawa, E.; Stangenberg, L.; Wurdinger, T.; Figueiredo, J.L.; Libby, P.; Weissleder, R.; Pittet, M.J. The healing myocardium sequentially mobilizes two monocyte subsets with divergent and complementary functions. *J. Exp. Med.* **2007**, *204*, 3037–3047. [CrossRef]

82. van Amerongen, M.J.; Harmsen, M.C.; van Rooijen, N.; Petersen, A.H.; van Luyn, M.J. Macrophage depletion impairs wound healing and increases left ventricular remodeling after myocardial injury in mice. *Am. J. Pathol.* **2007**, *170*, 818–829. [CrossRef]

83. Sieweke, M.H.; Allen, J.E. Beyond stem cells: Self-renewal of differentiated macrophages. *Science* **2013**, *342*, 1242974. [CrossRef]

84. Saclier, M.; Cuvellier, S.; Magnan, M.; Mounier, R.; Chazaud, B. Monocyte/macrophage interactions with myogenic precursor cells during skeletal muscle regeneration. *FEBS J.* **2013**, *280*, 4118–4130. [CrossRef]

85. Cuervo, A.M.; Macian, F. Autophagy and the immune function in aging. *Curr. Opin. Immunol.* **2014**, *29*, 97–104. [CrossRef]

86. Mohyeldin, A.; Garzon-Muvdi, T.; Quinones-Hinojosa, A. Oxygen in stem cell biology: A critical component of the stem cell niche. *Cell Stem Cell* **2010**, *7*, 150–161. [CrossRef]

87. Papandreou, I.; Lim, A.L.; Laderoute, K.; Denko, N.C. Hypoxia signals autophagy in tumor cells via AMPK activity, independent of HIF-1, BNIP3, and BNIP3L. *Cell Death Differ.* **2008**, *15*, 1572–1581. [CrossRef]

88. Guan, J.L.; Simon, A.K.; Prescott, M.; Menendez, J.A.; Liu, F.; Wang, F.; Wang, C.; Wolvetang, E.; Vazquez-Martin, A.; Zhang, J. Autophagy in stem cells. *Autophagy* **2013**, *9*, 830–849. [CrossRef]

89. Salemi, S.; Yousefi, S.; Constantinescu, M.A.; Fey, M.F.; Simon, H.U. Autophagy is required for self-renewal and differentiation of adult human stem cells. *Cell Res.* **2012**, *22*, 432–435. [CrossRef]

90. Moran-Crusio, K.; Reavie, L.B.; Aifantis, I. Regulation of hematopoietic stem cell fate by the ubiquitin proteasome system. *Trends Immunol.* **2012**, *33*, 357–363. [CrossRef]

91. Simsek, T.; Kocabas, F.; Zheng, J.; Deberardinis, R.J.; Mahmoud, A.I.; Olson, E.N.; Schneider, J.W.; Zhang, C.C.; Sadek, H.A. The distinct metabolic profile of hematopoietic stem cells reflects their location in a hypoxic niche. *Cell Stem Cell* **2010**, *7*, 380–390. [CrossRef]

92. Suda, T.; Takubo, K.; Semenza, G.L. Metabolic regulation of hematopoietic stem cells in the hypoxic niche. *Cell Stem Cell* **2011**, *9*, 298–310. [CrossRef]

93. Mortensen, M.; Soilleux, E.J.; Djordjevic, G.; Tripp, R.; Lutteropp, M.; Sadighi-Akha, E.; Stranks, A.J.; Glanville, J.; Knight, S.; Jacobsen, S.E.; et al. The autophagy protein Atg7 is essential for hematopoietic stem cell maintenance. *J. Exp. Med.* **2011**, *208*, 455–467. [CrossRef]

94. Warr, M.R.; Binnewies, M.; Flach, J.; Reynaud, D.; Garg, T.; Malhotra, R.; Debnath, J.; Passegue, E. FOXO3A directs a protective autophagy program in haematopoietic stem cells. *Nature* **2013**, *494*, 323–327. [CrossRef]

95. Phadwal, K.; Alegre-Abarrategui, J.; Watson, A.S.; Pike, L.; Anbalagan, S.; Hammond, E.M.; Wade-Martins, R.; McMichael, A.; Klenerman, P.; Simon, A.K. A novel method for autophagy detection in primary cells: Impaired levels of macroautophagy in immunosenescent T cells. *Autophagy* **2012**, *8*, 677–689. [CrossRef]

96. Chen, C.; Liu, Y.; Liu, Y.; Zheng, P. mTOR regulation and therapeutic rejuvenation of aging hematopoietic stem cells. *Sci. Signal.* **2009**, *2*, ra75. [CrossRef]

97. Chen, C.; Liu, Y.; Liu, R.; Ikenoue, T.; Guan, K.L.; Liu, Y.; Zheng, P. TSC-mTOR maintains quiescence and function of hematopoietic stem cells by repressing mitochondrial biogenesis and reactive oxygen species. *J. Exp. Med.* **2008**, *205*, 2397–2408. [CrossRef]

98. Kharas, M.G.; Okabe, R.; Ganis, J.J.; Gozo, M.; Khandan, T.; Paktinat, M.; Gilliland, D.G.; Gritsman, K. Constitutively active AKT depletes hematopoietic stem cells and induces leukemia in mice. *Blood* **2010**, *115*, 1406–1415. [CrossRef]

99. Zhang, Y.; Morgan, M.J.; Chen, K.; Choksi, S.; Liu, Z.G. Induction of autophagy is essential for monocyte-macrophage differentiation. *Blood* **2012**, *119*, 2895–2905. [CrossRef]

100. Jacquel, A.; Obba, S.; Boyer, L.; Dufies, M.; Robert, G.; Gounon, P.; Lemichez, E.; Luciano, F.; Solary, E.; Auberger, P. Autophagy is required for CSF-1-induced macrophagic differentiation and acquisition of phagocytic functions. *Blood* **2012**, *119*, 4527–4531. [CrossRef]

101. Jacquel, A.; Obba, S.; Solary, E.; Auberger, P. Proper macrophagic differentiation requires both autophagy and caspase activation. *Autophagy* **2012**, *8*, 1141–1143. [CrossRef]

102. Martinez, F.O.; Gordon, S. The M1 and M2 paradigm of macrophage activation: Time for reassessment. *F1000prime Rep.* **2014**, *6*, 13. [CrossRef]

103. Lemos, D.R.; Babaeijandaghi, F.; Low, M.; Chang, C.K.; Lee, S.T.; Fiore, D.; Zhang, R.H.; Natarajan, A.; Nedospasov, S.A.; Rossi, F.M. Nilotinib reduces muscle fibrosis in chronic muscle injury by promoting TNF-mediated apoptosis of fibro/adipogenic progenitors. *Nat. Med.* **2015**, *21*, 786–794. [CrossRef]

104. Varga, T.; Mounier, R.; Horvath, A.; Cuvellier, S.; Dumont, F.; Poliska, S.; Ardjoune, H.; Juban, G.; Nagy, L.; Chazaud, B. Highly Dynamic Transcriptional Signature of Distinct Macrophage Subsets during Sterile Inflammation, Resolution, and Tissue Repair. *J. Immunol.* **2016**, *196*, 4771–4782. [CrossRef]

105. Heredia, J.E.; Mukundan, L.; Chen, F.M.; Mueller, A.A.; Deo, R.C.; Locksley, R.M.; Rando, T.A.; Chawla, A. Type 2 innate signals stimulate fibro/adipogenic progenitors to facilitate muscle regeneration. *Cell* **2013**, *153*, 376–388. [CrossRef]

106. Chang, C.P.; Su, Y.C.; Lee, P.H.; Lei, H.Y. Targeting NFKB by autophagy to polarize hepatoma-associated macrophage differentiation. *Autophagy* **2013**, *9*, 619–621. [CrossRef]

107. Chang, C.P.; Su, Y.C.; Hu, C.W.; Lei, H.Y. TLR2-dependent selective autophagy regulates NF-kappaB lysosomal degradation in hepatoma-derived M2 macrophage differentiation. *Cell Death Differ.* **2013**, *20*, 515–523. [CrossRef]

108. Chen, W.; Ma, T.; Shen, X.N.; Xia, X.F.; Xu, G.D.; Bai, X.L.; Liang, T.B. Macrophage-induced tumor angiogenesis is regulated by the TSC2-mTOR pathway. *Cancer Res.* **2012**, *72*, 1363–1372. [CrossRef]

109. Chen, P.; Cescon, M.; Bonaldo, P. Autophagy-mediated regulation of macrophages and its applications for cancer. *Autophagy* **2014**, *10*, 192–200. [CrossRef]

110. Levine, B.; Mizushima, N.; Virgin, H.W. Autophagy in immunity and inflammation. *Nature* **2011**, *469*, 323–335. [CrossRef]

111. Deretic, V.; Saitoh, T.; Akira, S. Autophagy in infection, inflammation and immunity. *Nat. Rev. Immunol.* **2013**, *13*, 722–737. [CrossRef]

112. Stranks, A.J.; Hansen, A.L.; Panse, I.; Mortensen, M.; Ferguson, D.J.; Puleston, D.J.; Shenderov, K.; Watson, A.S.; Veldhoen, M.; Phadwal, K.; et al. Autophagy Controls Acquisition of Aging Features in Macrophages. *J. Innate Immun.* **2015**, *7*, 375–391. [CrossRef]

113. Martinez, J.; Cunha, L.D.; Park, S.; Yang, M.; Lu, Q.; Orchard, R.; Li, Q.Z.; Yan, M.; Janke, L.; Guy, C.; et al. Noncanonical autophagy inhibits the autoinflammatory, lupus-like response to dying cells. *Nature* **2016**, *533*, 115–119. [CrossRef]

114. Lu, Q.; Yokoyama, C.C.; Williams, J.W.; Baldridge, M.T.; Jin, X.; DesRochers, B.; Bricker, T.; Wilen, C.B.; Bagaitkar, J.; Loginicheva, E.; et al. Homeostatic Control of Innate Lung Inflammation by Vici Syndrome Gene Epg5 and Additional Autophagy Genes Promotes Influenza Pathogenesis. *Cell Host Microbe* **2016**, *19*, 102–113. [CrossRef]

115. Kang, Y.H.; Cho, M.H.; Kim, J.Y.; Kwon, M.S.; Peak, J.J.; Kang, S.W.; Yoon, S.Y.; Song, Y. Impaired macrophage autophagy induces systemic insulin resistance in obesity. *Oncotarget* **2016**, *7*, 35577–35591. [CrossRef]

116. Huang, S.C.; Everts, B.; Ivanova, Y.; O'Sullivan, D.; Nascimento, M.; Smith, A.M.; Beatty, W.; Love-Gregory, L.; Lam, W.Y.; O'Neill, C.M.; et al. Cell-intrinsic lysosomal lipolysis is essential for alternative activation of macrophages. *Nat. Immunol.* **2014**, *15*, 846–855. [CrossRef]

117. Kim, J.; Kundu, M.; Viollet, B.; Guan, K.L. AMPK and mTOR regulate autophagy through direct phosphorylation of Ulk1. *Nat. Cell Biol.* **2011**, *13*, 132–141. [CrossRef]

118. Hallowell, R.W.; Collins, S.L.; Craig, J.M.; Zhang, Y.; Oh, M.; Illei, P.B.; Chan-Li, Y.; Vigeland, C.L.; Mitzner, W.; Scott, A.L.; et al. mTORC2 signalling regulates M2 macrophage differentiation in response to helminth infection and adaptive thermogenesis. *Nat. Commun.* **2017**, *8*, 14208. [CrossRef]

119. Byles, V.; Covarrubias, A.J.; Ben-Sahra, I.; Lamming, D.W.; Sabatini, D.M.; Manning, B.D.; Horng, T. The TSC-mTOR pathway regulates macrophage polarization. *Nat. Commun.* **2013**, *4*, 2834. [CrossRef]

120. Pawelec, G.; Larbi, A.; Derhovanessian, E. Senescence of the human immune system. *J. Comp. Pathol.* **2010**, *142* (Suppl. 1), S39–S44. [CrossRef]

121. Shaw, A.C.; Goldstein, D.R.; Montgomery, R.R. Age-dependent dysregulation of innate immunity. *Nat. Rev. Immunol.* **2013**, *13*, 875–887. [CrossRef]

122. Koike, E.; Kobayashi, T.; Mochitate, K.; Murakami, M. Effect of aging on nitric oxide production by rat alveolar macrophages. *Exp. Gerontol.* **1999**, *34*, 889–894. [CrossRef]

123. Renshaw, M.; Rockwell, J.; Engleman, C.; Gewirtz, A.; Katz, J.; Sambhara, S. Cutting edge: impaired Toll-like receptor expression and function in aging. *J. Immunol.* **2002**, *169*, 4697–4701. [CrossRef]

124. Herrero, C.; Marques, L.; Lloberas, J.; Celada, A. IFN-gamma-dependent transcription of MHC class II IA is impaired in macrophages from aged mice. *J. Clin. Investig.* **2001**, *107*, 485–493. [CrossRef]

125. Henry, C.J.; Huang, Y.; Wynne, A.M.; Godbout, J.P. Peripheral lipopolysaccharide (LPS) challenge promotes microglial hyperactivity in aged mice that is associated with exaggerated induction of both pro-inflammatory IL-1beta and anti-inflammatory IL-10 cytokines. *BrainBehav. Immun.* **2009**, *23*, 309–317. [CrossRef]

126. Franceschi, C.; Bonafe, M.; Valensin, S.; Olivieri, F.; De Luca, M.; Ottaviani, E.; De Benedictis, G. Inflamm-aging. An evolutionary perspective on immunosenescence. *Ann. N. Y. Acad. Sci.* **2000**, *908*, 244–254. [CrossRef]

127. De Martinis, M.; Franceschi, C.; Monti, D.; Ginaldi, L. Inflammation markers predicting frailty and mortality in the elderly. *Exp. Mol. Pathol.* **2006**, *80*, 219–227. [CrossRef]

128. Fulop, T.; Larbi, A.; Witkowski, J.M.; McElhaney, J.; Loeb, M.; Mitnitski, A.; Pawelec, G. Aging, frailty and age-related diseases. *Biogerontology* **2010**, *11*, 547–563. [CrossRef]

129. Effros, R.B.; Svoboda, K.; Walford, R.L. Influence of age and caloric restriction on macrophage IL-6 and TNF production. *Lymphokine Cytokine Res.* **1991**, *10*, 347–351.

130. Mahbub, S.; Deburghgraeve, C.R.; Kovacs, E.J. Advanced Age Impairs Macrophage Polarization. *J. Interferon Cytokine Res.* **2012**, *32*, 18–26. [CrossRef]

131. Sandmand, M.; Bruunsgaard, H.; Kemp, K.; Andersen-Ranberg, K.; Pedersen, A.N.; Skinhøj, P. Is ageing associated with a shift in the balance between Type 1 and Type 2 cytokines in humans? *Clin. Exp. Immunol.* **2002**, *127*, 107–114. [CrossRef]

132. Dethlefsen, M.M.; Kristensen, C.M.; Tondering, A.S.; Lassen, S.B.; Ringholm, S.; Pilegaard, H. Impact of liver PGC-1alpha on exercise and exercise training-induced regulation of hepatic autophagy and mitophagy in mice on HFF. *Physiol. Rep.* **2018**, *6*, e13731. [CrossRef]

133. He, C.; Sumpter, R., Jr.; Levine, B. Exercise induces autophagy in peripheral tissues and in the brain. *Autophagy* **2012**, *8*, 1548–1551. [CrossRef]

134. Yang, L.; Licastro, D.; Cava, E.; Veronese, N.; Spelta, F.; Rizza, W.; Bertozzi, B.; Villareal, D.T.; Hotamisligil, G.S.; Holloszy, J.O.; et al. Long-Term Calorie Restriction Enhances Cellular Quality-Control Processes in Human Skeletal Muscle. *Cell Rep.* **2016**, *14*, 422–428. [CrossRef]

135. Milton-Laskibar, I.; Aguirre, L.; Etxeberria, U.; Milagro, F.I.; Martinez, J.A.; Portillo, M.P. Involvement of autophagy in the beneficial effects of resveratrol in hepatic steatosis treatment. A comparison with energy restriction. *Food Funct.* **2018**, *9*, 4207–4215. [CrossRef]

136. Holloszy, J.O. Mortality rate and longevity of food-restricted exercising male rats: A reevaluation. *J. Appl. Physiol.* **1997**, *82*, 399–403. [CrossRef]

137. McKiernan, S.H.; Colman, R.J.; Lopez, M.; Beasley, T.M.; Aiken, J.M.; Anderson, R.M.; Weindruch, R. Caloric restriction delays aging-induced cellular phenotypes in rhesus monkey skeletal muscle. *Exp. Gerontol.* **2011**, *46*, 23–29. [CrossRef]

138. Zampieri, S.; Pietrangelo, L.; Loefler, S.; Fruhmann, H.; Vogelauer, M.; Burggraf, S.; Pond, A.; Grim-Stieger, M.; Cvecka, J.; Sedliak, M.; et al. Lifelong physical exercise delays age-associated skeletal muscle decline. *J. Gerontol. Ser. ABiol. Sci. Med Sci.* **2015**, *70*, 163–173. [CrossRef]

139. Holloszy, J.O.; Schechtman, K.B. Interaction between exercise and food restriction: effects on longevity of male rats. *J. Appl. Physiol.* **1991**, *70*, 1529–1535. [CrossRef]

140. Goh, J.; Ladiges, W.C. Exercise enhances wound healing and prevents cancer progression during aging by targeting macrophage polarity. *Mech. Ageing Dev.* **2014**, *139*, 41–48. [CrossRef]

141. Shefer, G.; Rauner, G.; Stuelsatz, P.; Benayahu, D.; Yablonka-Reuveni, Z. Moderate-intensity treadmill running promotes expansion of the satellite cell pool in young and old mice. *FEBS J.* **2013**, *280*, 4063–4073. [CrossRef]

142. Fujimaki, S.; Hidaka, R.; Asashima, M.; Takemasa, T.; Kuwabara, T. Wnt protein-mediated satellite cell conversion in adult and aged mice following voluntary wheel running. *J. Biol. Chem.* **2014**, *289*, 7399–7412. [CrossRef]

143. Vanfleteren, J.R.; Braeckman, B.P. Mechanisms of life span determination in Caenorhabditis elegans. *Neurobiol. Aging* **1999**, *20*, 487–502. [CrossRef]

144. Il'yasova, D.; Fontana, L.; Bhapkar, M.; Pieper, C.F.; Spasojevic, I.; Redman, L.M.; Das, S.K.; Huffman, K.M.; Kraus, W.E. Effects of 2 years of caloric restriction on oxidative status assessed by urinary F2-isoprostanes: The CALERIE 2 randomized clinical trial. *Aging Cell* **2018**, *17*. [CrossRef]

145. Mazzoccoli, G.; Tevy, M.F.; Borghesan, M.; Delle Vergini, M.R.; Vinciguerra, M. Caloric restriction and aging stem cells: The stick and the carrot? *Exp. Gerontol.* **2014**, *50*, 137–148. [CrossRef]

146. Cerletti, M.; Jang, Y.C.; Finley, L.W.; Haigis, M.C.; Wagers, A.J. Short-term calorie restriction enhances skeletal muscle stem cell function. *Cell Stem Cell* **2012**, *10*, 515–519. [CrossRef]

147. Pala, F.; Di Girolamo, D.; Mella, S.; Yennek, S.; Chatre, L.; Ricchetti, M.; Tajbakhsh, S. Distinct metabolic states govern skeletal muscle stem cell fates during prenatal and postnatal myogenesis. *J. Cell Sci.* **2018**, *131*. [CrossRef]

148. Fehr, H.-G.; Lötzerich, H.; Michna, H. Human macrophage function and physical exercise: Phagocytic and histochemical studies. *Eur. J. Appl. Physiol. Occup. Physiol.* **1989**, *58*, 613–617. [CrossRef]

149. Bartlett, D.B.; Shepherd, S.O.; Wilson, O.J.; Adlan, A.M.; Wagenmakers, A.J.M.; Shaw, C.S.; Lord, J.M. Neutrophil and Monocyte Bactericidal Responses to 10 Weeks of Low-Volume High-Intensity Interval or Moderate-Intensity Continuous Training in Sedentary Adults. *Oxid. Med. Cell. Longev.* **2017**, *2017*, 8148742. [CrossRef]

150. Bartlett, D.B.; Fox, O.; McNulty, C.L.; Greenwood, H.L.; Murphy, L.; Sapey, E.; Goodman, M.; Crabtree, N.; Thogersen-Ntoumani, C.; Fisher, J.P.; et al. Habitual physical activity is associated with the maintenance of neutrophil migratory dynamics in healthy older adults. *Brain Behav. Immun.* **2016**, *56*, 12–20. [CrossRef]

151. Terra, R.; Alves, P.J.; Goncalves da Silva, S.A.; Salerno, V.P.; Dutra, P.M. Exercise improves the Th1 response by modulating cytokine and NO production in BALB/c mice. *Int. J. Sports Med.* **2013**, *34*, 661–666. [CrossRef]

152. Kawanishi, N.; Yano, H.; Yokogawa, Y.; Suzuki, K. Exercise training inhibits inflammation in adipose tissue via both suppression of macrophage infiltration and acceleration of phenotypic switching from M1 to M2 macrophages in high-fat-diet-induced obese mice. *Exerc. Immunol. Rev.* **2010**, *16*, 105–118.

153. Fabbiano, S.; Suarez-Zamorano, N.; Rigo, D.; Veyrat-Durebex, C.; Stevanovic Dokic, A.; Colin, D.J.; Trajkovski, M. Caloric Restriction Leads to Browning of White Adipose Tissue through Type 2 Immune Signaling. *Cell Metab.* **2016**, *24*, 434–446. [CrossRef]

154. Neff, F.; Flores-Dominguez, D.; Ryan, D.P.; Horsch, M.; Schroder, S.; Adler, T.; Afonso, L.C.; Aguilar-Pimentel, J.A.; Becker, L.; Garrett, L.; et al. Rapamycin extends murine lifespan but has limited effects on aging. *J. Clin. Investig.* **2013**, *123*, 3272–3291. [CrossRef]

155. Eisenberg, T.; Abdellatif, M.; Schroeder, S.; Primessnig, U.; Stekovic, S.; Pendl, T.; Harger, A.; Schipke, J.; Zimmermann, A.; Schmidt, A.; et al. Cardioprotection and lifespan extension by the natural polyamine spermidine. *Nat. Med.* **2016**, *22*, 1428–1438. [CrossRef]

156. Eisenberg, T.; Knauer, H.; Schauer, A.; Buttner, S.; Ruckenstuhl, C.; Carmona-Gutierrez, D.; Ring, J.; Schroeder, S.; Magnes, C.; Antonacci, L.; et al. Induction of autophagy by spermidine promotes longevity. *Nat. Cell Biol.* **2009**, *11*, 1305–1314. [CrossRef]

157. Fan, J.; Yang, X.; Li, J.; Shu, Z.; Dai, J.; Liu, X.; Li, B.; Jia, S.; Kou, X.; Yang, Y.; et al. Spermidine coupled with exercise rescues skeletal muscle atrophy from D-gal-induced aging rats through enhanced autophagy and reduced apoptosis via AMPK-FOXO3a signal pathway. *Oncotarget* **2017**, *8*, 17475–17490. [CrossRef]

158. Chrisam, M.; Pirozzi, M.; Castagnaro, S.; Blaauw, B.; Polishchuck, R.; Cecconi, F.; Grumati, P.; Bonaldo, P. Reactivation of autophagy by spermidine ameliorates the myopathic defects of collagen VI-null mice. *Autophagy* **2015**, *11*, 2142–2152. [CrossRef]

159. Borzi, R.M.; Guidotti, S.; Minguzzi, M.; Facchini, A.; Platano, D.; Trisolino, G.; Filardo, G.; Cetrullo, S.; D'Adamo, S.; Stefanelli, C.; et al. Polyamine delivery as a tool to modulate stem cell differentiation in skeletal tissue engineering. *Amino Acids* **2014**, *46*, 717–728. [CrossRef]

160. Zhang, L.; Gong, H.; Sun, Q.; Zhao, R.; Jia, Y. Spermidine-Activated Satellite Cells Are Associated with Hypoacetylation in ACVR2B and Smad3 Binding to Myogenic Genes in Mice. *J. Agric. Food Chem.* **2018**, *66*, 540–550. [CrossRef]

161. Araki, K.; Turner, A.P.; Shaffer, V.O.; Gangappa, S.; Keller, S.A.; Bachmann, M.F.; Larsen, C.P.; Ahmed, R. mTOR regulates memory CD8 T-cell differentiation. *Nature* **2009**, *460*, 108–112. [CrossRef]

162. Yang, Q.; Zheng, C.; Cao, J.; Cao, G.; Shou, P.; Lin, L.; Velletri, T.; Jiang, M.; Chen, Q.; Han, Y.; et al. Spermidine alleviates experimental autoimmune encephalomyelitis through inducing inhibitory macrophages. *Cell Death Differ.* **2016**, *23*, 1850–1861. [CrossRef]

Review

Cardiac Autophagy in Sepsis

Yuxiao Sun [1], Ying Cai [2] and Qun S. Zang [1],*

[1] Departments of Surgery, University of Texas Southwestern Medical Center, Dallas, TX 75390, USA; yuxiao.sun@utsouthwestern.edu

[2] Department of Developmental Cell Biology, School of Life Sciences, China Medical University, 77 Puhe Road, Shenbei New District, Shenyang 110122, China; ycai27@cmu.edu.cn

* Correspondence: qun.zang@utsouthwestern.edu

Received: 27 December 2018; Accepted: 5 February 2019; Published: 10 February 2019

Abstract: Sepsis is a leading cause of death in intensive care units, and cardiac dysfunction is an identified serious component of the multi-organ failure associated with this critical condition. This review summarized the current discoveries and hypotheses of how autophagy changes in the heart during sepsis and the underlying mechanisms. Recent investigations suggest that specific activation of autophagy initiation factor Beclin-1 has a potential to protect cardiac mitochondria, attenuate inflammation, and improve cardiac function in sepsis. Accordingly, pharmacological interventions targeting this pathway have a potential to become an effective approach to control sepsis outcomes. The role of autophagy during sepsis pathogenesis has been under intensive investigation in recent years. It is expected that developing therapeutic approaches with specificities targeting at autophagy regulatory factors may provide new opportunities to alleviate organ dysfunction caused by maladaptive autophagy during sepsis.

Keywords: Beclin-1; autophagy; mitophagy; cardiac dysfunction; sepsis; endotoxemia

---

1. Introduction

Sepsis is a leading cause of death in intensive care units worldwide [1]. This devastating condition presents a life-threatening organ dysfunction caused by dysfunctional host response to infection [2]. Despite improvements in antibiotic therapies and critical care techniques [3], the reported incidence of sepsis is still increasing, most likely reflecting ageing populations with more comorbidities and greater recognition [4,5]. Further, patients who survive sepsis often bear long term disabilities with significant health care and social implications [6]. Sepsis has become a major public health concern. According to the Centers for Disease Control and Prevention (CDC), sepsis was accounted for over twenty billion dollars (about 5%) of total US hospital costs in 2011. It was named as the most expensive in-patient cost in US hospitals in 2014, averaging more than $18,000 per hospital stay [7]. In 2017, the CDC launched a national educational campaign, "Get Ahead of Sepsis", which aims to raise awareness and knowledge about prevention, early recognition, and timely treatment of sepsis among the public and among healthcare providers. Though sepsis has been a subject of intensive research for decades, current management for sepsis remains to be supportive care, and most attempts of molecule-based treatments have failed clinically [8,9]. Clearly, investigation of the pathological mechanisms and exploration of new therapeutic interventions are urgently needed to advance the treatment of this devastating clinical condition.

Cardiac dysfunction is an identified serious component of the sepsis-induced multi-organ failure, and it is associated with adverse outcomes and higher mortality [10,11]. The mechanisms that underlie sepsis-induced cardiomyopathy are not well-known; exuberated inflammation, comprised metabolism, and impaired beta-adrenergic response are identified potential driving forces [12]. Because mitochondria comprise about 30% of myocardial volume [13], the pathophysiologic mechanisms of sepsis-induced cardiomyopathy via mitochondrial signaling has been a focused area of investigation. In vitro and in vivo studies using preclinical sepsis models demonstrated that sepsis triggers impairments in the structure and function of mitochondria, which abnormality leads to not only a deficiency in energy supply but also an overproduction of mitochondria-derived danger-associated molecular patterns (DAMPs), such as reactive oxygen species (mtROS) [14], fragmented mitochondrial DNA (mtDNA) [15–18], N-formyl peptides [19], cardiolipin [20], ATP [21], mitochondrial transcription factor A [22], and cytochrome c [23]. These harmful molecules exacerbate myocardial inflammation and sequential cardiomyopathy during sepsis [14–17,24].

Inflammation has been center-staged in the field of sepsis research in the past. It is now clear that sepsis is a multifaceted host response to pathogens, involving the early activation of both pro- and anti-inflammatory responses, along with major changes in nonimmunologic pathways [2]. Along this line, the sepsis-associated increase in autophagy, a lysosome-dependent process of removing damaged proteins and organelles [25], was recognized in both preclinical and clinical samples [26–30]. Accumulating evidence indicates that sepsis triggers autophagy in multiple organs including the heart [27–29]. To date, the role of autophagy in the pathogenesis of sepsis is not yet well understood. This short review is focused on a discussion of sepsis-induced changes in cardiac autophagy and the potential of targeting autophagy as a therapeutic intervention to attenuate organ dysfunction in sepsis.

2. Autophagy Changes Dynamically During Sepsis

Autophagy is considered to provide cellular quality control to promote survival, and is therefore adaptive, under physiological responses or mild stress. However, under severe or chronic stress, excessive or inadequate autophagy causes massive self-degradation or accumulation of toxic materials; both are maladaptive and eventually provoke cell death [31,32]. Both adaptive and maladaptive features of cardiac autophagy under the condition of septic challenge were observed in published studies. For example, investigations in vivo using a mouse cecal ligation and puncture (CLP) sepsis model [33] and in vitro using cultured, lipopolysaccharide (LPS)-challenged cardiomyocytes [34] indicated that stimulating autophagy pharmacologically protects the myocardium, thus suggesting that autophagy is an adaptive response. Conversely, reducing autophagy directly via an autophagy inhibitor or indirectly via antioxidants improved cardiac contractility in a mouse model of LPS-induced endotoxemia, and thus supporting the conclusion that autophagy is maladaptive [35]. The discrepancy of these observations may be due to the differences in experimental settings, in which the severity of sepsis, drug specificity, and timing of delivery differed.

A recent investigation suggested a status that cardiac autophagy changes dynamically in response to the severity of sepsis. The study examined the degree of autophagic responses in the heart tissue of mice challenged with LPS-induced endotoxemia and found that LPS triggered a dose-dependent autophagic response [36]. When LPS was given at low doses, modeling mild sepsis, autophagy increased proportionally to the magnitude of the insult. However, under conditions of severe sepsis, this capability declined proportionally to the severity of the insult. Further, it was detected that the failure of autophagy induction at high-dose LPS challenges correlated with the activation of mTOR signaling and the appearance of clinical signs of pathogenesis, manifested as a decline in cardiac function, elevation in inflammation and cardiac tissue injury. These observations of cardiac autophagy are consistent with previous reports in the liver showing increased autophagy in the early phases of sepsis followed by a decline near late-stage organ failure in the mouse CLP sepsis model [28,37]. Thus, these changes documented in the heart may mimic the progression of a systemic multi-organ failure during sepsis. It is speculated that, during the beginning phase of sepsis or mild sepsis, autophagy is adaptive; it provides a level of control to promote survival and sustain normal function of organs. However, with sepsis progresses to severe conditions, the autophagic responses become inadequate and therefore leads to a maladaptive outcome.

The mTOR pathway is a well-known upstream nodal point that acts to inhibit autophagy [38]. In the experimental settings described above, significant decreases in the activation status of mTOR complex were not detectable in the heart of animals challenged by low-dose LPS, compared with shams. However, the attenuation of autophagy in response to high-dose LPS is clearly associated with mTOR activation [36]. These results suggest that mTOR activation inhibits beneficial autophagic activities during severe stages of sepsis. The data also suggests that the activation of autophagy in early sepsis may be independent of mTOR. Though mTOR has long been considered a conventional regulatory switch for turning on and off autophagy, recent studies have discovered a number of autophagy stimulatory pathways whose actions do not involve mTOR. Signals in this category include the intracellular inositol-IP$_3$ pathway [39], Ca^{2+}-calpain pathway [40], cAMP-exchange protein activated by cAMP (Epac)-PLCε-IP$_3$ pathway [40], leucine-rich repeat kinase 2 [41], and trehalose [42], etc. However, whether sepsis utilizes any of these signals or other unknown mechanisms to operate autophagy machinery in the heart as well as in other organs remains to be investigated. Future studies in this area will potentially identify new targets for the development of autophagy-based therapeutic approaches.

3. Beclin-1-Dependent Autophagy Protects the Heart During Sepsis

Beclin-1 is one of the first mammalian autophagy effectors identified [43,44]. This protein is ubiquitously expressed, and homozygous deletion of the *beclin-1* gene results in early embryonic lethality [45]. Beclin-1 functions as an autophagy initiation factor through interaction with PtdIns(3)-kinase (Vps34) [46]. Together, this protein complex initiates the nucleation step of autophagy to begin autophagic flux and also participates in later steps involving the fusion of autophagosomes to lysosomes [47–49].

Genetic mouse models with altered expression of Beclin-1 were applied to determine the role of cardiac autophagy in response to LPS-induced endotoxemia [36]. Transgenic mice with cardiac-specific overexpression of Beclin-1 and heterozygous deficiency were used to increase and decrease Beclin-1 in vivo. Forced overexpression of Beclin-1 attenuated cardiac inflammation and fibrotic injury, preserved mitochondrial quality, and ultimately improved cardiac performance in response to LPS-challenge. Additionally, the activation of mTOR was blunted in the hearts with Beclin-1 overexpression in response to high-dose LPS challenge [36]. Since the activation of mTOR is inversely correlated with autophagic activities, the result suggests that enhancing Beclin-1 signaling can suppress mTOR activation, thereby sustaining autophagy even under conditions of severe sepsis. In parallel, Beclin-1-dependent activation of AMP-activated protein kinase (AMPK) and Unc-51 like-autophagy-activating kinase 1 (ULK1) was also observed. It has been a general understanding that mTOR suppresses autophagy by inhibiting ULK1, a autophagy activating kinase that functions upstream of Beclin-1 [50]. The newly obtained data described above suggest a notion that Beclin-1 may involve a positive feedback regulation of autophagy by enhancing AMPK and ULK1 in the heart in response to the challenge by endotoxemia.

Beclin-1 mediated protection in sepsis was also suggested by a study of carbon monoxide therapy (CO) in the mouse CLP sepsis model [51]. Knockdown Beclin-1 abolished the beneficial effects of CO on attenuation of inflammation and reduction of bacteremia. Beclin-1 is also required for the CO-dependent enhancement of phagocytosis by macrophages. Thus, the protection by Beclin-1 during sepsis does not seem to be restricted to the heart. However, the regulatory function of Beclin-1 in various cell types and tissues under the pathological condition of sepsis remain further investigation.

4. Beclin-1-Dependent Protection of Cardiac Mitochondria

Sepsis induces mitochondrial damage, releasing mitochondrial DAMPs that aggravate myocardial inflammation and cardiac dysfunction [14–18,52]. During endotoxemia, LPS causes a disruption of mitochondrial structure, reduction in metabolic function, and the release of mtDNA fragments to the cytosol in the heart tissue. These manifestations of mitochondrial damage following LPS challenge were attenuated in the heart of mice with transgenic overexpression of Beclin-1, suggesting a critical function of Beclin-1 in the protection of cardiac mitochondria in sepsis [36].

As dysfunctional mitochondria can be segregated and eliminated through autophagy [25,53], a process termed mitophagy, Beclin-1-mediated quality control of cardiac mitochondria during endotoxemia is expected to be a product of an upregulated mitophagy. Indeed, overexpression of Beclin-1 leads to more formation of mitophagosomes/mitolysosomes in the heart tissue [36]. It is known that mitophagy occurs via multiple pathways. One route is regulated by PTEN-induced putative kinase 1 (PINK1) and E3 ubiquitin ligase Parkin, which target mitochondria with lost membrane potential and subsequently bring these mitochondria to autophagosomes for degradation [54,55]. Alternatively, mitophagy can be initiated via outer mitochondrial membranes (OMM)-located receptors, such as BNIP3L/NIX, BNIP3, and FUNDC1, and these receptors connect mitochondria to autophagosomes [56]. Interestingly, not all mitophagy seems to be created equal; and signals to activate mitophagy are selectively utilized in response to distinct stimuli. In the hearts of animals challenged by endotoxemia, Beclin-1 stimulates a striking difference in the spectrum of mitochondria-localized mitophagy factors, indicating a differential regulation of mitophagy pathways [36]. In response to LPS, Beclin-1 stimulates mitophagy, and this action is accompanied by a selective increase in the recruitment of PINK1 and Parkin to mitochondria, while strongly suppressing the receptor proteins BNIP3L and BNIP3. These data suggest that Beclin-1 protects mitochondria via a selective activation of a particular mitophagy pathway, instead of a bulk induction of all types of mitophagy. The data also support that PINK1-Parkin mitophagy is cardiac-protective, an adaptive response, during sepsis. Similar adaptive features of PINK1-Parkin mitophagy in the heart are also supported by previous published results [57,58].

The signal transduction pathway of whether and how Beclin-1 targets PINK1-Parkin mitophagy has not been fully understood. Several lines of investigation suggest that PINK1 recruits Parkin to damaged mitochondria via phosphorylated mitofusin 2 (Mfn2) [59–61]. In the experimental setting of endotoxemia described above [36], phosphorylated form of either Parkin or Mfn2 was not detectable in the heart tissue of mice with Beclin-1 overexpression using the published approach of Phos-tag Western blotting [59,60]. However, it is worthy to note that the detection of phosphorylated Parkin or Mfn2 was accomplished in cultured cells with an overexpression of protein targets [59,60]. The current method may have a limitation in detecting low contents of phosphorylation in in vivo models when PINK1, Parkin and Mfn2 are expressed at endogenous physiological levels. It is also speculated that the stimulation of PINK1-Parkin mitophagy by Beclin-1 may involve mitochondria-associated membranes (MAMs). MAMs are specialized subcellular domains that physically link mitochondria with the endoplasmic reticulum (ER) [62], and they are essential to mitochondrial health [63,64]. Beclin-1 and PINK1 are found to re-localize to MAMs during mitophagy initiation, and via direct interaction, they promote ER-mitochondria tethering and the formation of autophagosome precursors to facilitate mitophagy [65,66]. Beclin-1 was found to interact with Parkin, and this association is required for the progress of PINK1-Parkin mitophagy [67]. Thus, the PINK1-Parkin mitophagy pathway is more accessible for activation when Beclin-1 signaling is upregulated.

In addition to remove damaged mitochondria by mitophagy, Beclin-1 may promote mitochondrial biogenesis via the upregulation of PINK1/Parkin and/or AMPK/ULK1 [68–73]. Recent studies have shown that Parkin can positively regulate mitochondrial biogenesis through proteasomal degradation of its substrate PARIS, a zinc-finger protein [69,70]. In neuroblastoma cells, increases in mitochondrial and lysosomal biogenesis via transcription factor Nrf2 and TFEB were detected following PINK1-Parkin mitophagy [71]. In vivo, a lack of Parkin expression in the ventral midbrain resulted in decreases in mitochondrial size, number, and mitochondrial biogenesis makers, together with declines in mitochondrial respiration, implicating that Parkin is required for the production of new, healthy mitochondria [69]. In cultured human endothelial cells and mouse aortas, AMPK phosphorylates epigenetic factors of DNA methyltransferase DNMT1, histone acetyltransferase HAT1, and retinoblastoma binding protein 7 (RBBP7), which in turn activates the transcription of nuclear DNA encoded genes of mitochondrial biogenesis and energy production [72]. To date, whether similar mechanisms are utilized to regulate mitochondria in septic hearts remains for further investigation.

The mechanism for how Beclin-1 suppresses BNIP3 signaling also remains to be determined. Similar to the due-function of PINK1-Parkin, BNIP3 also functions as a dual regulator in mitochondria. It is regulated transcriptionally via hypoxia-inducible factor 1 [74] and FOXO3a [75] and/or by posttranslational oxidation via ROS [76]. Upon activation, BNIP3 prompts the opening of the mitochondrial permeability transition pore (mPTP), recruits LC3 for autophagosome formation, and initiates mitophagy [77–79]. This protein also causes mitochondrial dysfunction and subsequently induces cell death via the activation of downstream effectors Bax/Bak under stress conditions [80]. Both BINP3-induced mitophagy and mitochondrial damage were observed in the myocardium [77,81]. It was further revealed that transcriptional upregulation of BNIP3 by FOXO3a caused a decrease in mitochondrial membrane potential and an increase in mitochondrial Ca^{2+}, leading to mitochondrial fragmentation and apoptosis of cardiomyocytes [75]. Hence, the effect of BNIP3 accumulation on mitochondria is a result of the balance between its double actions. In the hearts of LPS-challenged mice, the increase in mitochondrial BNIP3 may aggravate detrimental mitochondrial deficiency while the induced mitophagy is not strong enough to clear damaged mitochondria, and Beclin-1 may have a control to mitigate BNIP3 signaling [36]. BNIP3 signaling stimulates pathological responses under conditions of hypoxia [80] and ischemia/reperfusion [76], however, whether BNIP3 is pathological in sepsis-induced cardiac dysfunction and how Beclin-1 interacts with BNIP3 require further investigation.

Taken all together, the improved status of the mitochondria in the hearts by Beclin-1 is likely the result of several folds of signaling regulations. While Beclin-1 selectively facilitate PINK1-Parkin mitophagy for the clearance of damaged mitochondria, Beclin-1 also promotes mitochondrial biogenesis via PINK1/Parkin as well as AMPK/ULK1 [68–73]. These effects act together, leading to a preservation of the mass of functional mitochondria during sepsis when Beclin-1 signal is enhanced. In contrast, under septic challenge, a stronger mitochondrial BNIP3 signal and low levels of AMPK and ULK1 activation, together with the overwhelming inflammatory responses, aggravate the deterioration of cardiac mitochondria when the signal of Beclin-1 is not sufficiently available.

5. Autophagy/Mitophagy and Inflammation in Cardiac Dysfunction During Sepsis

Autophagy presents a control over inflammation by limiting the availability of inflammasome activators and/or components [82], and by reducing mitochondrial DAMPs via mitophagy [52]. On the other hand, an increase in autophagy under certain severe or prolonged stress may exacerbate unwanted outcomes due to deregulated degradation of cellular components, resulting in aggressive inflammation [83,84].

The influence of mitochondria and mitophagy on the regulation of inflammation has received intensive attention in recent years. It is now discovered that cytosolic mtDNA binds to intracellular TLR9 and activates inflammatory factor NF-κB [85]. Cytosolic mtDNA fragments also stimulate the DNA sensor cGAS and promote STING-IRF3-dependent pathway [86]. Furthermore, newly synthesized and oxidized mtDNA activates NLRP3-containing inflammasome by direct binding during innate immune response [87]. Therefore, mitophagy is expected to be an effective tool to remove dysfunctional mitochondria and hence reduce mitochondrial DAMPs such as mtDNA. A strong evidence comes from a recent investigation in animal models lacking mitophagy factor Parkin or PINK1. Under the stress condition of exhaustive excursive, inflammation resulted from accumulation of cytosolic mtDNA was abolished by loss of STING, supporting an important role of PINK1/Parkin mitophagy in restraining innate immunity [88].

Previous research indicates that cardiac inflammation during sepsis and trauma condition such as burn injury is mediated at least by the activation of toll-like receptor 4 (TLR4)/CD14 complex [24] and the increase in mitochondrial DAMPs [14,16]. In the model of LPS-induced endotoxemia, increasing Beclin-1-dependent autophagy improved cardiac outcomes and attenuated the production of cytokines [36]. However, this benefit comes with certain limitations, since in response to high-dose LPS (10 mg/kg), overwhelming inflammation still occurs in Beclin-1 overexpressed mice even when significant autophagic activity was provided. Thus, inflammation remains, at least in part, a major cause of cardiac dysfunction in these mice. Additionally, the possibility that the increase in autophagy itself may contribute to the heart failure can't be excluded. Signaling crosstalk between autophagy and inflammation happens dynamically throughout the development of various disease conditions [84]. How autophagy alters individual inflammation pathways via inflammasomes, caspases, NF-κB and/or MAPKs, etc. at different stages of sepsis remains to be defined.

LPS triggers cytokine production via binding to the TLR4/CD14/MD2 receptor complex on cellular membranes and/or to caspase inside of cells, resulting in the activation of NF-κB and inflammasomes [89,90]. This action sequentially causes the release of DAMPs from activated, injured, or necrotic cells [91,92]. LPS also stimulates mtROS overproduction, leading to mitochondrial damage [93] and a release of mitochondrial DAMPs including mtDNA fragments [18], N-formyl peptides [19], mtROS [14], cardiolipin [20], ATP [21], mitochondrial transcription factor A [22], and cytochrome c [23]. Since combined signals from PAMPs and DAMPs stimulate inflammation in the heart during endotoxemia, it is not a surprise that levels of cytosolic mtDNA measured are not proportional to the production of total cytokines in the heart tissue [36]. As commented in a recent review [94], the investigation of Beclin-1-mediated cardiac protection during endotoxemia suggests that enhancing Beclin-1 signal in cardiomyocytes mitigates inflammation by suppressing the release of mitochondrial DAMPs via PINK1/Parkin mitophagy, which may in turn interrupt local inflammatory circuitries, reduce neutrophil infiltration, and inhibit further cytokine production by leukocytes and non-myocytes such as fibroblasts.

LPS triggers an aggressive accelerated overall mitochondrial deterioration that contributes to the animals' rapid decline in cardiac performance via multiple pathways [36]. In addition to inflammation, other types of consequences of mitochondrial damage such as a deficiency in energy supply and alterations in mitochondrial metabolisms, are considered noninflammatory factors that may significantly impact cardiac dysfunction under septic challenge. Whether Beclin-1 presents regulation in these aspects of mitochondria properties remains to be determined.

6. Autophagy-Based Therapeutic Opportunities for Sepsis

Changes in autophagy are associated with a number of pathological disorders, ranging from inflammatory and autoimmune conditions to neurodegeneration, neuronal injury, cardiovascular diseases, cancer, hepatic and metabolic disorders. Accordingly, pharmacological modulators of autophagy are expected to provide a control over pathogenesis in disease models. Indeed, new interventions are being developed and tested at various stages [95]. However, at the current time, autophagy-based therapies have not yet been available for clinical treatments. Although certain FDA-approved drugs, such as rapamycin, chloroquine, and metformin, have effects to activate or deactivate autophagy, they were not developed for the purpose to adjust autophagy and these drugs have broad-spectrum impacts in vivo. For example, rapamycin is an inhibitor of mTOR, a serine/threonine kinase that negatively regulates autophagy [96]. mTOR is also involved in functions outside of autophagy, such as protein turnover, metabolism, energy balance, and stress responses [96]. Therefore, due to the complexity of mTOR signaling, rapamycin may cause unwanted toxicity, which is likely the reason of inconsistent test results of rapamycin in preclinical sepsis models [33,97–100]. Rapamycin was shown to improved cardiac performance [33], reduced cognitive impairments [97] in a mouse CLP-induced sepsis model. However, adverse effects of rapamycin on the survival of mice subjected to CLP sepsis [101] and on the lung injury of mice upon LPS-induced endotoxemia were also reported [99,100]. Due to the rapamycin's lack of specificity to autophagy, it becomes difficult to draw a conclusion regarding the pathological role of autophagy in sepsis. To date, the pathways of how sepsis incites autophagic responses are not fully understood. Future success in the research of this area will greatly facilitate the development of novel pharmacological interventions that specifically target autophagy factors, which may become a much-improved approach to combat sepsis.

In recent years, emerging drug development effort has been deliciated to regulatory factors of the autophagic machinery but with limited roles in cellular processes other than autophagy. As results, new autophagy inhibitors and activators are identified. Small molecules that inhibit autophagy by targeting autophagy-related 4B cysteine peptidase (ATG4B), UNC-51-like autophagy-activating enzymes (ULK1), and LC3-associated phagocytosis (LAP) have yield promising results in in vitro studies using cultured cancer cells [102–104]. However, their application in specific animal disease models await further investigation. A significant leap in the development of autophagy-inducing therapy is the discovery of a cell-permeable Beclin-1 activating peptide, Tat-Beclin-1 peptide (TB peptide). TB peptide contains 18 amino acids of the BARA domain of Beclin-1, and thus induces autophagy by competitively binding of the endogenous Beclin-1 to its negative regulator, Golgi-associated plant pathogenesis-related protein 1 [105]. This peptide has demonstrated therapeutic benefits in disease models related to reducing viral infection [105], improving cardiac performance during pressure overload [106], and enhancing the effectiveness of chemotherapy [107]. Additionally, three novel small molecules with the feature of autophagy inducer have been identified by a method of high-throughput screen lately [108]. These molecules block the binding of Beclin-1 to its downstream inhibitor Bcl2 and therefore stimulate autophagic flux. Their specificity and capability to induce autophagy was confirmed in cultured cells [108].

The therapeutic potential of TB peptide in sepsis is suggested by a recent preclinical evaluation in the mouse model of LPS-induced endotoxemia [36]. TB peptide was given in mice subjected to LPS challenge. The dose of TB peptide was chosen based on published results [105–107] to find which dose induced sufficient autophagic flux without causing detectable toxicity in both sham and LPS-challenged mice [36]. This treatment significantly improved cardiac function and reduced circulating cytokines, especially TNF-α, IFN-γ, IL-17α, and IL-6, following LPS. Additional data showed that the peptide rescued the phonotypes in mice with heterozygous knockdown of Beclin1, including a significant improvement in survival in response to a lethal dose of LPS. The results further demonstrated that the peptide's mechanism of action is mediated though a directly targeted stimulation of Beclin-1. Future evaluation of TB peptide in other sepsis models, such as CLP-induced sepsis and infection-induced sepsis, will provide essential evidence to estimate the therapeutic potential of this drug in sepsis. In addition, whether the effects of this peptide are tissue- or cell-specific warranties further investigation. Nonetheless, current evidence suggests that autophagy inducers such as TB-peptide, used by itself or in combination with other therapies, may holds an exciting therapeutic potential for the control of sepsis.

7. Summary

Autophagy plays an important role in sepsis-induced pathology of organ dysfunction. Accumulating evidence indicates that autophagy dynamically changes during the progress of sepsis, with insufficient and maladaptive autophagy occurs at the later stage of sepsis. This deficiency is associated with an upregulation of mTOR signaling, and the ineffectiveness of removing dysfunctional organelles and toxic materials intracellularly results in an overwhelming accumulation of DAMPs. Specific targeting autophagy factors offers an opportunity of developing novel therapeutic interventions for sepsis. For example, a newly developed cell permeable peptide, TB peptide that activates Beclin-1, showed therapeutic promise in a mouse model of LPS-induced endotoxemia [36]. Important questions await to be addressed, such as cell type or tissue-specific autophagic responses and their changes during the course of sepsis development. Additionally, evaluation of a potential therapy needs to be further validated in multiple preclinical models. Future investigations to answer these questions and new discoveries of sepsis-associated pathways of autophagy will provide a great potential to identify additional therapeutic targets for sepsis.

Funding: Studies by the authors were supported by National Institute of Health grant 1R01GM111295-01 (to Q.S.Z.).

Conflicts of Interest: The authors declare no conflict of interest.

References

1. Angus, D.C.; Pereira, C.A.; Silva, E. Epidemiology of severe sepsis around the world. *Endocr. Metab. Immune Disord. Drug Targets* **2006**, *6*, 207–212. [CrossRef] [PubMed]
2. Singer, M.; Deutschman, C.S.; Seymour, C.W.; Shankar-Hari, M.; Annane, D.; Bauer, M.; Bellomo, R.; Bernard, G.R.; Chiche, J.D.; Coopersmith, C.M.; et al. The Third International Consensus Definitions for Sepsis and Septic Shock (Sepsis-3). *JAMA* **2016**, *315*, 801–810. [CrossRef] [PubMed]
3. Levy, M.M.; Dellinger, R.P.; Townsend, S.R.; Linde-Zwirble, W.T.; Marshall, J.C.; Bion, J.; Schorr, C.; Artigas, A.; Ramsay, G.; Beale, R.; et al. The Surviving Sepsis Campaign: results of an international guideline-based performance improvement program targeting severe sepsis. *Crit. Care Med.* **2010**, *38*, 367–374. [CrossRef] [PubMed]
4. Iwashyna, T.J.; Ely, E.W.; Smith, D.M.; Langa, K.M. Long-term cognitive impairment and functional disability among survivors of severe sepsis. *JAMA* **2010**, *304*, 1787–1794. [CrossRef] [PubMed]
5. Nasa, P.; Juneja, D.; Singh, O. Severe sepsis and septic shock in the elderly: An overview. *World J. Crit. Care Med.* **2012**, *1*, 23–30. [PubMed]
6. Shankar-Hari, M.; Rubenfeld, G.D. Understanding Long-Term Outcomes Following Sepsis: Implications and Challenges. *Curr. Infect. Dis. Rep.* **2016**, *18*, 37. [CrossRef] [PubMed]
7. Chang, D.W.; Tseng, C.H.; Shapiro, M.F. Rehospitalizations Following Sepsis: Common and Costly. *Crit. Care Med.* **2015**, *43*, 2085–2093. [CrossRef] [PubMed]
8. Venkataraman, R.; Subramanian, S.; Kellum, J.A. Clinical review: extracorporeal blood purification in severe sepsis. *Crit. Care* **2003**, *7*, 139–145. [CrossRef] [PubMed]
9. Lovat, R.; Preiser, J.C. Antioxidant therapy in intensive care. *Curr. Opin. Crit. Care* **2003**, *9*, 266–270. [CrossRef] [PubMed]
10. Zanotti-Cavazzoni, S.L.; Hollenberg, S.M. Cardiac dysfunction in severe sepsis and septic shock. *Curr. Opin. Crit. Care* **2009**, *15*, 392–397. [CrossRef] [PubMed]
11. Landesberg, G.; Gilon, D.; Meroz, Y.; Georgieva, M.; Levin, P.D.; Goodman, S.; Avidan, A.; Beeri, R.; Weissman, C.; Jaffe, A.S.; et al. Diastolic dysfunction and mortality in severe sepsis and septic shock. *Eur. Heart J.* **2012**, *33*, 895–903. [CrossRef] [PubMed]
12. Drosatos, K.; Lymperopoulos, A.; Kennel, P.J.; Pollak, N.; Schulze, P.C.; Goldberg, I.J. Pathophysiology of sepsis-related cardiac dysfunction: driven by inflammation, energy mismanagement, or both? *Curr. Heart Fail. Rep.* **2015**, *12*, 130–140. [CrossRef]
13. Kayar, S.R.; Banchero, N. Volume density and distribution of mitochondria in myocardial growth and hypertrophy. *Respir. Physiol.* **1987**, *70*, 275–286. [CrossRef]
14. Yao, X.; Carlson, D.; Sun, Y.; Ma, L.; Wolf, S.E.; Minei, J.P.; Zang, Q.S. Mitochondrial ROS Induces Cardiac Inflammation via a Pathway through mtDNA Damage in a Pneumonia-Related Sepsis Model. *PLoS ONE* **2015**, *10*, e0139416. [CrossRef] [PubMed]
15. Zang, Q.S.; Martinez, B.; Yao, X.; Maass, D.L.; Ma, L.; Wolf, S.E.; Minei, J.P. Sepsis-induced cardiac mitochondrial dysfunction involves altered mitochondrial-localization of tyrosine kinase Src and tyrosine phosphatase SHP2. *PLoS ONE* **2012**, *7*, e43424. [CrossRef]
16. Zang, Q.S.; Sadek, H.; Maass, D.L.; Martinez, B.; Ma, L.; Kilgore, J.A.; Williams, N.S.; Frantz, D.E.; Wigginton, J.G.; Nwariaku, F.E.; et al. Specific inhibition of mitochondrial oxidative stress suppresses inflammation and improves cardiac function in a rat pneumonia-related sepsis model. *Am. J. Physiol. Heart Circ. Physiol.* **2012**, *302*, H1847–H1859. [CrossRef] [PubMed]
17. Zang, Q.; Maass, D.L.; Tsai, S.J.; Horton, J.W. Cardiac mitochondrial damage and inflammation responses in sepsis. *Surg. Infect. (Larchmt)* **2007**, *8*, 41–54. [CrossRef]
18. Zhang, Q.; Raoof, M.; Chen, Y.; Sumi, Y.; Sursal, T.; Junger, W.; Brohi, K.; Itagaki, K.; Hauser, C.J. Circulating mitochondrial DAMPs cause inflammatory responses to injury. *Nature* **2010**, *464*, 104–107. [CrossRef]
19. Crouser, E.D.; Shao, G.; Julian, M.W.; Macre, J.E.; Shadel, G.S.; Tridandapani, S.; Huang, Q.; Wewers, M.D. Monocyte activation by necrotic cells is promoted by mitochondrial proteins and formyl peptide receptors. *Crit. Care Med.* **2009**, *37*, 2000–2009. [CrossRef]

20. Chakraborty, K.; Raundhal, M.; Chen, B.B.; Morse, C.; Tyurina, Y.Y.; Khare, A.; Oriss, T.B.; Huff, R.; Lee, J.S.; St Croix, C.M.; et al. The mito-DAMP cardiolipin blocks IL-10 production causing persistent inflammation during bacterial pneumonia. *Nat. Commun.* **2017**, *8*, 13944. [CrossRef]

21. Schwiebert, E.M.; Zsembery, A. Extracellular ATP as a signaling molecule for epithelial cells. *Biochim. Biophys. Acta* **2003**, *1615*, 7–32. [CrossRef]

22. Julian, M.W.; Shao, G.; Bao, S.; Knoell, D.L.; Papenfuss, T.L.; VanGundy, Z.C.; Crouser, E.D. Mitochondrial transcription factor A serves as a danger signal by augmenting plasmacytoid dendritic cell responses to DNA. *J. Immunol.* **2012**, *189*, 433–443. [CrossRef] [PubMed]

23. Eleftheriadis, T.; Pissas, G.; Liakopoulos, V.; Stefanidis, I. Cytochrome c as a Potentially Clinical Useful Marker of Mitochondrial and Cellular Damage. *Front. Immunol.* **2016**, *7*, 279. [CrossRef] [PubMed]

24. Zang, Q.S.; Maass, D.L.; Wigginton, J.G.; Barber, R.C.; Martinez, B.; Idris, A.H.; Horton, J.W.; Nwariaku, F.E. Burn serum causes a CD14-dependent mitochondrial damage in primary cardiomyocytes. *Am. J. Physiol. Heart Circ. Physiol.* **2010**, *298*, H1951–H1958. [CrossRef]

25. Mizushima, N.; Levine, B. Autophagy in mammalian development and differentiation. *Nat. Cell Biol.* **2010**, *12*, 823–830. [CrossRef]

26. Mofarrahi, M.; Sigala, I.; Guo, Y.; Godin, R.; Davis, E.C.; Petrof, B.; Sandri, M.; Burelle, Y.; Hussain, S.N. Autophagy and skeletal muscles in sepsis. *PLoS ONE* **2012**, *7*, e47265. [CrossRef]

27. Hsiao, H.W.; Tsai, K.L.; Wang, L.F.; Chen, Y.H.; Chiang, P.C.; Chuang, S.M.; Hsu, C. The decline of autophagy contributes to proximal tubular dysfunction during sepsis. *Shock* **2012**, *37*, 289–296. [CrossRef]

28. Chien, W.S.; Chen, Y.H.; Chiang, P.C.; Hsiao, H.W.; Chuang, S.M.; Lue, S.I.; Hsu, C. Suppression of autophagy in rat liver at late stage of polymicrobial sepsis. *Shock* **2011**, *35*, 506–511. [CrossRef]

29. Watanabe, E.; Muenzer, J.T.; Hawkins, W.G.; Davis, C.G.; Dixon, D.J.; McDunn, J.E.; Brackett, D.J.; Lerner, M.R.; Swanson, P.E.; Hotchkiss, R.S. Sepsis induces extensive autophagic vacuolization in hepatocytes: a clinical and laboratory-based study. *Lab. Investig.* **2009**, *89*, 549–561. [CrossRef]

30. Watts, J.A.; Kline, J.A.; Thornton, L.R.; Grattan, R.M.; Brar, S.S. Metabolic dysfunction and depletion of mitochondria in hearts of septic rats. *J. Mol. Cell. Cardiol.* **2004**, *36*, 141–150. [CrossRef]

31. Ferdous, A.; Battiprolu, P.K.; Ni, Y.G.; Rothermel, B.A.; Hill, J.A. FoxO, autophagy, and cardiac remodeling. *J. Cardiovasc. Transl. Res.* **2010**, *3*, 355–364. [CrossRef] [PubMed]

32. Xie, M.; Morales, C.R.; Lavandero, S.; Hill, J.A. Tuning flux: Autophagy as a target of heart disease therapy. *Curr. Opin. Cardiol.* **2011**, *26*, 216–222. [CrossRef] [PubMed]

33. Hsieh, C.H.; Pai, P.Y.; Hsueh, H.W.; Yuan, S.S.; Hsieh, Y.C. Complete induction of autophagy is essential for cardioprotection in sepsis. *Ann. Surg.* **2011**, *253*, 1190–1200. [CrossRef] [PubMed]

34. Yuan, H.; Perry, C.N.; Huang, C.; Iwai-Kanai, E.; Carreira, R.S.; Glembotski, C.C.; Gottlieb, R.A. LPS-induced autophagy is mediated by oxidative signaling in cardiomyocytes and is associated with cytoprotection. *Am. J. Physiol. Heart Circ. Physiol.* **2009**, *296*, H470–H479. [CrossRef] [PubMed]

35. Turdi, S.; Han, X.; Huff, A.F.; Roe, N.D.; Hu, N.; Gao, F.; Ren, J. Cardiac-specific overexpression of catalase attenuates lipopolysaccharide-induced myocardial contractile dysfunction: role of autophagy. *Free Radic. Biol. Med.* **2012**, *53*, 1327–1338. [CrossRef] [PubMed]

36. Sun, Y.; Yao, X.; Zhang, Q.J.; Zhu, M.; Liu, Z.P.; Ci, B.; Xie, Y.; Carlson, D.; Rothermel, B.A.; Sun, Y.; et al. Beclin-1-Dependent Autophagy Protects the Heart During Sepsis. *Circulation* **2018**, *138*, 2247–2262. [CrossRef] [PubMed]

37. Takahashi, W.; Watanabe, E.; Fujimura, L.; Watanabe-Takano, H.; Yoshidome, H.; Swanson, P.E.; Tokuhisa, T.; Oda, S.; Hatano, M. Kinetics and protective role of autophagy in a mouse cecal ligation and puncture-induced sepsis. *Crit. Care* **2013**, *17*, R160. [CrossRef] [PubMed]

38. Kim, Y.C.; Guan, K.L. mTOR: a pharmacologic target for autophagy regulation. *J. Clin. Investig.* **2015**, *125*, 25–32. [CrossRef]

39. Sarkar, S.; Floto, R.A.; Berger, Z.; Imarisio, S.; Cordenier, A.; Pasco, M.; Cook, L.J.; Rubinsztein, D.C. Lithium induces autophagy by inhibiting inositol monophosphatase. *J. Cell Biol.* **2005**, *170*, 1101–1111. [CrossRef]

40. Williams, A.; Sarkar, S.; Cuddon, P.; Ttofi, E.K.; Saiki, S.; Siddiqi, F.H.; Jahreiss, L.; Fleming, A.; Pask, D.; Goldsmith, P.; et al. Novel targets for Huntington's disease in an mTOR-independent autophagy pathway. *Nat. Chem. Biol.* **2008**, *4*, 295–305. [CrossRef]

41. Manzoni, C.; Mamais, A.; Roosen, D.A.; Dihanich, S.; Soutar, M.P.; Plun-Favreau, H.; Bandopadhyay, R.; Hardy, J.; Tooze, S.A.; Cookson, M.R.; et al. mTOR independent regulation of macroautophagy by Leucine Rich Repeat Kinase 2 via Beclin-1. *Sci. Rep.* **2016**, *6*, 35106. [CrossRef] [PubMed]

42. Sarkar, S.; Davies, J.E.; Huang, Z.; Tunnacliffe, A.; Rubinsztein, D.C. Trehalose, a novel mTOR-independent autophagy enhancer, accelerates the clearance of mutant huntingtin and alpha-synuclein. *J. Biol. Chem.* **2007**, *282*, 5641–5652. [CrossRef] [PubMed]

43. Liang, X.H.; Kleeman, L.K.; Jiang, H.H.; Gordon, G.; Goldman, J.E.; Berry, G.; Herman, B.; Levine, B. Protection against fatal Sindbis virus encephalitis by beclin, a novel Bcl-2-interacting protein. *J. Virol.* **1998**, *72*, 8586–8596. [PubMed]

44. Liang, X.H.; Jackson, S.; Seaman, M.; Brown, K.; Kempkes, B.; Hibshoosh, H.; Levine, B. Induction of autophagy and inhibition of tumorigenesis by beclin 1. *Nature* **1999**, *402*, 672–676. [CrossRef] [PubMed]

45. Yue, Z.; Jin, S.; Yang, C.; Levine, A.J.; Heintz, N. Beclin 1, an autophagy gene essential for early embryonic development, is a haploinsufficient tumor suppressor. *Proc. Natl. Acad. Sci. USA* **2003**, *100*, 15077–15082. [CrossRef] [PubMed]

46. Kihara, A.; Kabeya, Y.; Ohsumi, Y.; Yoshimori, T. Beclin-phosphatidylinositol 3-kinase complex functions at the trans-Golgi network. *EMBO Rep.* **2001**, *2*, 330–335. [CrossRef]

47. Matsunaga, K.; Saitoh, T.; Tabata, K.; Omori, H.; Satoh, T.; Kurotori, N.; Maejima, I.; Shirahama-Noda, K.; Ichimura, T.; Isobe, T.; et al. Two Beclin 1-binding proteins, Atg14L and Rubicon, reciprocally regulate autophagy at different stages. *Nat. Cell Biol.* **2009**, *11*, 385–396. [CrossRef]

48. Itakura, E.; Kishi, C.; Inoue, K.; Mizushima, N. Beclin 1 forms two distinct phosphatidylinositol 3-kinase complexes with mammalian Atg14 and UVRAG. *Mol. Biol. Cell* **2008**, *19*, 5360–5372. [CrossRef]

49. Zhong, Y.; Wang, Q.J.; Li, X.; Yan, Y.; Backer, J.M.; Chait, B.T.; Heintz, N.; Yue, Z. Distinct regulation of autophagic activity by Atg14L and Rubicon associated with Beclin 1-phosphatidylinositol-3-kinase complex. *Nat. Cell Biol.* **2009**, *11*, 468–476. [CrossRef]

50. Cao, Y.; Klionsky, D.J. Physiological functions of Atg6/Beclin 1: a unique autophagy-related protein. *Cell Res.* **2007**, *17*, 839–849. [CrossRef]

51. Lee, S.; Lee, S.J.; Coronata, A.A.; Fredenburgh, L.E.; Chung, S.W.; Perrella, M.A.; Nakahira, K.; Ryter, S.W.; Choi, A.M. Carbon monoxide confers protection in sepsis by enhancing beclin 1-dependent autophagy and phagocytosis. *Antioxid. Redox Signal.* **2014**, *20*, 432–442. [CrossRef] [PubMed]

52. Oka, T.; Hikoso, S.; Yamaguchi, O.; Taneike, M.; Takeda, T.; Tamai, T.; Oyabu, J.; Murakawa, T.; Nakayama, H.; Nishida, K.; et al. Mitochondrial DNA that escapes from autophagy causes inflammation and heart failure. *Nature* **2012**, *485*, 251–255. [CrossRef] [PubMed]

53. Twig, G.; Elorza, A.; Molina, A.J.; Mohamed, H.; Wikstrom, J.D.; Walzer, G.; Stiles, L.; Haigh, S.E.; Katz, S.; Las, G.; et al. Fission and selective fusion govern mitochondrial segregation and elimination by autophagy. *EMBO J.* **2008**, *27*, 433–446. [CrossRef] [PubMed]

54. Narendra, D.P.; Jin, S.M.; Tanaka, A.; Suen, D.F.; Gautier, C.A.; Shen, J.; Cookson, M.R.; Youle, R.J. PINK1 is selectively stabilized on impaired mitochondria to activate Parkin. *PLoS Biol.* **2010**, *8*, e1000298. [CrossRef]

55. Narendra, D.; Tanaka, A.; Suen, D.F.; Youle, R.J. Parkin is recruited selectively to impaired mitochondria and promotes their autophagy. *J. Cell Biol.* **2008**, *183*, 795–803. [CrossRef] [PubMed]

56. Moyzis, A.G.; Sadoshima, J.; Gustafsson, A.B. Mending a broken heart: the role of mitophagy in cardioprotection. *Am. J. Physiol. Heart Circ. Physiol.* **2015**, *308*, H183–H192. [CrossRef]

57. Piquereau, J.; Godin, R.; Deschenes, S.; Bessi, V.L.; Mofarrahi, M.; Hussain, S.N.; Burelle, Y. Protective role of PARK2/Parkin in sepsis-induced cardiac contractile and mitochondrial dysfunction. *Autophagy* **2013**, *9*, 1837–1851. [CrossRef]

58. Kubli, D.A.; Zhang, X.; Lee, Y.; Hanna, R.A.; Quinsay, M.N.; Nguyen, C.K.; Jimenez, R.; Petrosyan, S.; Murphy, A.N.; Gustafsson, A.B. Parkin protein deficiency exacerbates cardiac injury and reduces survival following myocardial infarction. *J. Biol. Chem.* **2013**, *288*, 915–926. [CrossRef]

59. Chen, Y.; Dorn, G.W., 2nd. PINK1-phosphorylated mitofusin 2 is a Parkin receptor for culling damaged mitochondria. *Science* **2013**, *340*, 471–475. [CrossRef]

60. Shiba-Fukushima, K.; Imai, Y.; Yoshida, S.; Ishihama, Y.; Kanao, T.; Sato, S.; Hattori, N. PINK1-mediated phosphorylation of the Parkin ubiquitin-like domain primes mitochondrial translocation of Parkin and regulates mitophagy. *Sci. Rep.* **2012**, *2*, 1002. [CrossRef]

61. Jin, S.M.; Youle, R.J. The accumulation of misfolded proteins in the mitochondrial matrix is sensed by PINK1 to induce PARK2/Parkin-mediated mitophagy of polarized mitochondria. *Autophagy* **2013**, *9*, 1750–1757. [CrossRef] [PubMed]

62. Mannella, C.A.; Buttle, K.; Rath, B.K.; Marko, M. Electron microscopic tomography of rat-liver mitochondria and their interaction with the endoplasmic reticulum. *Biofactors* **1998**, *8*, 225–228. [CrossRef] [PubMed]

63. Raturi, A.; Simmen, T. Where the endoplasmic reticulum and the mitochondrion tie the knot: The mitochondria-associated membrane (MAM). *Biochim. Biophys. Acta* **2013**, *1833*, 213–224. [CrossRef] [PubMed]

64. Giorgi, C.; Missiroli, S.; Patergnani, S.; Duszynski, J.; Wieckowski, M.R.; Pinton, P. Mitochondria-associated membranes: composition, molecular mechanisms, and physiopathological implications. *Antioxid. Redox Signal.* **2015**, *22*, 995–1019. [CrossRef] [PubMed]

65. Gelmetti, V.; De Rosa, P.; Torosantucci, L.; Marini, E.S.; Romagnoli, A.; Di Rienzo, M.; Arena, G.; Vignone, D.; Fimia, G.M.; Valente, E.M. PINK1 and BECN1 relocalize at mitochondria-associated membranes during mitophagy and promote ER-mitochondria tethering and autophagosome formation. *Autophagy* **2017**, *13*, 654–669. [CrossRef]

66. Michiorri, S.; Gelmetti, V.; Giarda, E.; Lombardi, F.; Romano, F.; Marongiu, R.; Nerini-Molteni, S.; Sale, P.; Vago, R.; Arena, G.; et al. The Parkinson-associated protein PINK1 interacts with Beclin1 and promotes autophagy. *Cell Death Differ.* **2010**, *17*, 962–974. [CrossRef] [PubMed]

67. Choubey, V.; Cagalinec, M.; Liiv, J.; Safiulina, D.; Hickey, M.A.; Kuum, M.; Liiv, M.; Anwar, T.; Eskelinen, E.L.; Kaasik, A. BECN1 is involved in the initiation of mitophagy: it facilitates PARK2 translocation to mitochondria. *Autophagy* **2014**, *10*, 1105–1119. [CrossRef] [PubMed]

68. Laker, R.C.; Drake, J.C.; Wilson, R.J.; Lira, V.A.; Lewellen, B.M.; Ryall, K.A.; Fisher, C.C.; Zhang, M.; Saucerman, J.J.; Goodyear, L.J.; et al. Ampk phosphorylation of Ulk1 is required for targeting of mitochondria to lysosomes in exercise-induced mitophagy. *Nat. Commun.* **2017**, *8*, 548. [CrossRef] [PubMed]

69. Stevens, D.A.; Lee, Y.; Kang, H.C.; Lee, B.D.; Lee, Y.I.; Bower, A.; Jiang, H.; Kang, S.U.; Andrabi, S.A.; Dawson, V.L.; et al. Parkin loss leads to PARIS-dependent declines in mitochondrial mass and respiration. *Proc. Natl. Acad. Sci. USA* **2015**, *112*, 11696–11701. [CrossRef]

70. Shin, J.H.; Ko, H.S.; Kang, H.; Lee, Y.; Lee, Y.I.; Pletinkova, O.; Troconso, J.C.; Dawson, V.L.; Dawson, T.M. PARIS (ZNF746) repression of PGC-1alpha contributes to neurodegeneration in Parkinson's disease. *Cell* **2011**, *144*, 689–702. [CrossRef] [PubMed]

71. Ivankovic, D.; Chau, K.Y.; Schapira, A.H.; Gegg, M.E. Mitochondrial and lysosomal biogenesis are activated following PINK1/parkin-mediated mitophagy. *J. Neurochem.* **2016**, *136*, 388–402. [CrossRef] [PubMed]

72. Marin, T.L.; Gongol, B.; Zhang, F.; Martin, M.; Johnson, D.A.; Xiao, H.; Wang, Y.; Subramaniam, S.; Chien, S.; Shyy, J.Y. AMPK promotes mitochondrial biogenesis and function by phosphorylating the epigenetic factors DNMT1, RBBP7, and HAT1. *Sci. Signal.* **2017**, *10*. [CrossRef] [PubMed]

73. Shimizu, Y.; Polavarapu, R.; Eskla, K.L.; Nicholson, C.K.; Koczor, C.A.; Wang, R.; Lewis, W.; Shiva, S.; Lefer, D.J.; Calvert, J.W. Hydrogen sulfide regulates cardiac mitochondrial biogenesis via the activation of AMPK. *J. Mol. Cell. Cardiol.* **2018**, *116*, 29–40. [CrossRef]

74. Bruick, R.K. Expression of the gene encoding the proapoptotic Nip3 protein is induced by hypoxia. *Proc. Natl. Acad. Sci. USA* **2000**, *97*, 9082–9087. [CrossRef] [PubMed]

75. Chaanine, A.H.; Kohlbrenner, E.; Gamb, S.I.; Guenzel, A.J.; Klaus, K.; Fayyaz, A.U.; Nair, K.S.; Hajjar, R.J.; Redfield, M.M. FOXO3a regulates BNIP3 and modulates mitochondrial calcium, dynamics, and function in cardiac stress. *Am. J. Physiol. Heart Circ. Physiol.* **2016**, *311*, H1540–H1559. [CrossRef] [PubMed]

76. Kubli, D.A.; Quinsay, M.N.; Huang, C.; Lee, Y.; Gustafsson, A.B. Bnip3 functions as a mitochondrial sensor of oxidative stress during myocardial ischemia and reperfusion. *Am. J. Physiol. Heart Circ. Physiol.* **2008**, *295*, H2025–H2031. [CrossRef] [PubMed]

77. Hamacher-Brady, A.; Brady, N.R.; Logue, S.E.; Sayen, M.R.; Jinno, M.; Kirshenbaum, L.A.; Gottlieb, R.A.; Gustafsson, A.B. Response to myocardial ischemia/reperfusion injury involves Bnip3 and autophagy. *Cell Death Differ.* **2007**, *14*, 146–157. [CrossRef]

78. Hanna, R.A.; Quinsay, M.N.; Orogo, A.M.; Giang, K.; Rikka, S.; Gustafsson, A.B. Microtubule-associated protein 1 light chain 3 (LC3) interacts with Bnip3 protein to selectively remove endoplasmic reticulum and mitochondria via autophagy. *J. Biol. Chem.* **2012**, *287*, 19094–19104. [CrossRef] [PubMed]

79. Zhang, H.; Bosch-Marce, M.; Shimoda, L.A.; Tan, Y.S.; Baek, J.H.; Wesley, J.B.; Gonzalez, F.J.; Semenza, G.L. Mitochondrial autophagy is an HIF-1-dependent adaptive metabolic response to hypoxia. *J. Biol. Chem.* **2008**, *283*, 10892–10903. [CrossRef]

80. Kubli, D.A.; Ycaza, J.E.; Gustafsson, A.B. Bnip3 mediates mitochondrial dysfunction and cell death through Bax and Bak. *Biochem. J.* **2007**, *405*, 407–415. [CrossRef]

81. Regula, K.M.; Ens, K.; Kirshenbaum, L.A. Inducible expression of BNIP3 provokes mitochondrial defects and hypoxia-mediated cell death of ventricular myocytes. *Circ. Res.* **2002**, *91*, 226–231. [CrossRef]

82. Shi, C.S.; Shenderov, K.; Huang, N.N.; Kabat, J.; Abu-Asab, M.; Fitzgerald, K.A.; Sher, A.; Kehrl, J.H. Activation of autophagy by inflammatory signals limits IL-1beta production by targeting ubiquitinated inflammasomes for destruction. *Nat. Immunol.* **2012**, *13*, 255–263. [CrossRef] [PubMed]

83. Zhu, H.; Tannous, P.; Johnstone, J.L.; Kong, Y.; Shelton, J.M.; Richardson, J.A.; Le, V.; Levine, B.; Rothermel, B.A.; Hill, J.A. Cardiac autophagy is a maladaptive response to hemodynamic stress. *J. Clin. Investig.* **2007**, *117*, 1782–1793. [CrossRef] [PubMed]

84. Levine, B.; Mizushima, N.; Virgin, H.W. Autophagy in immunity and inflammation. *Nature* **2011**, *469*, 323–335. [CrossRef] [PubMed]

85. Rodriguez-Nuevo, A.; Diaz-Ramos, A.; Noguera, E.; Diaz-Saez, F.; Duran, X.; Munoz, J.P.; Romero, M.; Plana, N.; Sebastian, D.; Tezze, C.; et al. Mitochondrial DNA and TLR9 drive muscle inflammation upon Opa1 deficiency. *EMBO J.* **2018**, *37*. [CrossRef] [PubMed]

86. West, A.P.; Khoury-Hanold, W.; Staron, M.; Tal, M.C.; Pineda, C.M.; Lang, S.M.; Bestwick, M.; Duguay, B.A.; Raimundo, N.; MacDuff, D.A.; et al. Mitochondrial DNA stress primes the antiviral innate immune response. *Nature* **2015**, *520*, 553–557. [CrossRef]

87. Zhong, Z.; Liang, S.; Sanchez-Lopez, E.; He, F.; Shalapour, S.; Lin, X.J.; Wong, J.; Ding, S.; Seki, E.; Schnabl, B.; et al. New mitochondrial DNA synthesis enables NLRP3 inflammasome activation. *Nature* **2018**, *560*, 198–203. [CrossRef]

88. Sliter, D.A.; Martinez, J.; Hao, L.; Chen, X.; Sun, N.; Fischer, T.D.; Burman, J.L.; Li, Y.; Zhang, Z.; Narendra, D.P.; et al. Parkin and PINK1 mitigate STING-induced inflammation. *Nature* **2018**, *561*, 258–262. [CrossRef]

89. Kim, H.M.; Park, B.S.; Kim, J.I.; Kim, S.E.; Lee, J.; Oh, S.C.; Enkhbayar, P.; Matsushima, N.; Lee, H.; Yoo, O.J.; et al. Crystal structure of the TLR4-MD-2 complex with bound endotoxin antagonist Eritoran. *Cell* **2007**, *130*, 906–917. [CrossRef]

90. Shi, J.; Zhao, Y.; Wang, Y.; Gao, W.; Ding, J.; Li, P.; Hu, L.; Shao, F. Inflammatory caspases are innate immune receptors for intracellular LPS. *Nature* **2014**, *514*, 187–192. [CrossRef]

91. Chen, G.Y.; Nunez, G. Sterile inflammation: sensing and reacting to damage. *Nat. Rev. Immunol.* **2010**, *10*, 826–837. [CrossRef] [PubMed]

92. Seong, S.Y.; Matzinger, P. Hydrophobicity: an ancient damage-associated molecular pattern that initiates innate immune responses. *Nat. Rev. Immunol.* **2004**, *4*, 469–478. [CrossRef] [PubMed]

93. Brealey, D.; Brand, M.; Hargreaves, I.; Heales, S.; Land, J.; Smolenski, R.; Davies, N.A.; Cooper, C.E.; Singer, M. Association between mitochondrial dysfunction and severity and outcome of septic shock. *Lancet* **2002**, *360*, 219–223. [CrossRef]

94. Abdellatif, M.; Sedej, S.; Madeo, F.; Kroemer, G. Cardioprotective effects of autophagy induction in sepsis. *Ann. Transl. Med.* **2018**, *6*, S61. [CrossRef] [PubMed]

95. Galluzzi, L.; Bravo-San Pedro, J.M.; Levine, B.; Green, D.R.; Kroemer, G. Pharmacological modulation of autophagy: therapeutic potential and persisting obstacles. *Nat. Rev. Drug Discov.* **2017**, *16*, 487–511. [CrossRef]

96. Laplante, M.; Sabatini, D.M. mTOR signaling in growth control and disease. *Cell* **2012**, *149*, 274–293. [CrossRef] [PubMed]

97. Liu, W.; Guo, J.; Mu, J.; Tian, L.; Zhou, D. Rapamycin Protects Sepsis-Induced Cognitive Impairment in Mouse Hippocampus by Enhancing Autophagy. *Cell. Mol. Neurobiol.* **2016**. [CrossRef] [PubMed]

98. Lin, C.W.; Lo, S.; Perng, D.S.; Wu, D.B.; Lee, P.H.; Chang, Y.F.; Kuo, P.L.; Yu, M.L.; Yuan, S.S.; Hsieh, Y.C. Complete activation of autophagic process attenuates liver injury and improves survival in septic mice. *Shock* **2014**, *41*, 241–249. [CrossRef] [PubMed]

99. Fielhaber, J.A.; Carroll, S.F.; Dydensborg, A.B.; Shourian, M.; Triantafillopoulos, A.; Harel, S.; Hussain, S.N.; Bouchard, M.; Qureshi, S.T.; Kristof, A.S. Inhibition of mammalian target of rapamycin augments

lipopolysaccharide-induced lung injury and apoptosis. *J. Immunol.* **2012**, *188*, 4535–4542. [CrossRef] [PubMed]

100. Yan, Z.; Xiaoyu, Z.; Zhixin, S.; Di, Q.; Xinyu, D.; Jing, X.; Jing, H.; Wang, D.; Xi, Z.; Chunrong, Z.; et al. Rapamycin attenuates acute lung injury induced by LPS through inhibition of Th17 cell proliferation in mice. *Sci. Rep.* **2016**, *6*, 20156. [CrossRef] [PubMed]

101. Horwacik, I.; Gaik, M.; Durbas, M.; Boratyn, E.; Zajac, G.; Szychowska, K.; Szczodrak, M.; Koloczek, H.; Rokita, H. Inhibition of autophagy by 3-methyladenine potentiates sulforaphane-induced cell death of BE(2)-C human neuroblastoma cells. *Mol. Med. Rep.* **2015**, *12*, 535–542. [CrossRef] [PubMed]

102. Akin, D.; Wang, S.K.; Habibzadegah-Tari, P.; Law, B.; Ostrov, D.; Li, M.; Yin, X.M.; Kim, J.S.; Horenstein, N.; Dunn, W.A., Jr. A novel ATG4B antagonist inhibits autophagy and has a negative impact on osteosarcoma tumors. *Autophagy* **2014**, *10*, 2021–2035. [CrossRef] [PubMed]

103. Egan, D.F.; Chun, M.G.; Vamos, M.; Zou, H.; Rong, J.; Miller, C.J.; Lou, H.J.; Raveendra-Panickar, D.; Yang, C.C.; Sheffler, D.J.; et al. Small Molecule Inhibition of the Autophagy Kinase ULK1 and Identification of ULK1 Substrates. *Mol. Cell* **2015**, *59*, 285–297. [CrossRef] [PubMed]

104. Petherick, K.J.; Conway, O.J.; Mpamhanga, C.; Osborne, S.A.; Kamal, A.; Saxty, B.; Ganley, I.G. Pharmacological inhibition of ULK1 kinase blocks mammalian target of rapamycin (mTOR)-dependent autophagy. *J. Biol. Chem.* **2015**, *290*, 11376–11383. [CrossRef]

105. Shoji-Kawata, S.; Sumpter, R.; Leveno, M.; Campbell, G.R.; Zou, Z.; Kinch, L.; Wilkins, A.D.; Sun, Q.; Pallauf, K.; MacDuff, D.; et al. Identification of a candidate therapeutic autophagy-inducing peptide. *Nature* **2013**, *494*, 201–206. [CrossRef] [PubMed]

106. Shirakabe, A.; Zhai, P.; Ikeda, Y.; Saito, T.; Maejima, Y.; Hsu, C.P.; Nomura, M.; Egashira, K.; Levine, B.; Sadoshima, J. Drp1-Dependent Mitochondrial Autophagy Plays a Protective Role Against Pressure Overload-Induced Mitochondrial Dysfunction and Heart Failure. *Circulation* **2016**, *133*, 1249–1263. [CrossRef] [PubMed]

107. Pietrocola, F.; Pol, J.; Vacchelli, E.; Rao, S.; Enot, D.P.; Baracco, E.E.; Levesque, S.; Castoldi, F.; Jacquelot, N.; Yamazaki, T.; et al. Caloric Restriction Mimetics Enhance Anticancer Immunosurveillance. *Cancer Cell* **2016**, *30*, 147–160. [CrossRef]

108. Chiang, W.C.; Wei, Y.; Kuo, Y.C.; Wei, S.; Zhou, A.; Zou, Z.; Yehl, J.; Ranaghan, M.J.; Skepner, A.; Bittker, J.A.; et al. High-Throughput Screens To Identify Autophagy Inducers That Function by Disrupting Beclin 1/Bcl-2 Binding. *ACS Chem. Biol.* **2018**, *13*, 2247–2260. [CrossRef]

Review

Protective Features of Autophagy in Pulmonary Infection and Inflammatory Diseases

Kui Wang [1,2,†], Yi Chen [3,†], Pengju Zhang [1], Ping Lin [2], Na Xie [1,4,*] and Min Wu [2,*]

1   West China School of Basic Medical Sciences & Forensic Medicine, and State Key Laboratory of Biotherapy, Sichuan University, and Collaborative Innovation Center for Biotherapy, Chengdu 610041, China; wangkui416@163.com (K.W.); zhangpengju526@163.com (P.Z.)
2   Department of Biomedical Sciences, University of North Dakota, Grand Forks, ND 58203, USA; bio_lp@126.com
3   Department of Gastrointestinal Surgery, State Key Laboratory of Biotherapy, Sichuan University, Chengdu 610041, China; toddychan@163.com
4   Section of Infection and Immunity, Herman Ostrow School of Dentistry, Norris Comprehensive Cancer Center, University of Southern California, Los Angeles, CA 90089-0641, USA
*   Correspondence: xnshina@126.com (N.X.); min.wu@med.und.edu (M.W.); Tel.: +86-158-8455-5293 (N.X.); +1-(701)-777-4875 (M.W.)
†   These authors contributed equally to this work.

Received: 31 December 2018; Accepted: 31 January 2019; Published: 3 February 2019

Abstract: Autophagy is a highly conserved catabolic process involving autolysosomal degradation of cellular components, including protein aggregates, damaged organelles (such as mitochondria, endoplasmic reticulum, and others), as well as various pathogens. Thus, the autophagy pathway represents a major adaptive response for the maintenance of cellular and tissue homeostasis in response to numerous cellular stressors. A growing body of evidence suggests that autophagy is closely associated with diverse human diseases. Specifically, acute lung injury (ALI) and inflammatory responses caused by bacterial infection or xenobiotic inhalation (e.g., chlorine and cigarette smoke) have been reported to involve a spectrum of alterations in autophagy phenotypes. The role of autophagy in pulmonary infection and inflammatory diseases could be protective or harmful dependent on the conditions. In this review, we describe recent advances regarding the protective features of autophagy in pulmonary diseases, with a focus on ALI, idiopathic pulmonary fibrosis (IPF), chronic obstructive pulmonary disease (COPD), tuberculosis, pulmonary arterial hypertension (PAH) and cystic fibrosis.

Keywords: Autophagy; inflammation; acute lung injury; idiopathic pulmonary fibrosis; COPD; tuberculosis; PAH; cystic fibrosis

---

1. Introduction

Macroautophagy (henceforth referred to as autophagy) is an evolutionarily conserved process by which intracellular materials are sequestered by double-membrane autophagosomes and then delivered to lysosomes for degradation and recycling in various physiological and pathological conditions [1]. The degradation substrates include aggregate–prone proteins, lipids, organelles (including mitochondria, endoplasmic reticulum, peroxisomes, etc.), and intracellular pathogens (bacteria and viruses) [2,3]. The digestion of these autophagy cargoes can maintain cellular homeostasis by facilitating the quality control of the cytoplasm, recycling intracellular components (amino acids, fatty acids, and carbohydrates) to fuel anabolic pathways and energy generation, or by enabling pathogen clearance [2,4]. Therefore, the autophagy process appears to serve as a cellular protective mechanism to counter diverse diseases, including cancer, neurodegenerative diseases, and infectious diseases [3,5]. Conversely, dysregulation of autophagy is also known to exacerbate the disease progression under certain conditions, suggesting that the role of autophagy in human diseases is complex [3,5].

The lung is the primary organ for gas exchange, delivering O_2 from the atmosphere to the bloodstream and releasing CO_2 into the atmosphere. During respiration, the lung is continuously exposed to various harmful environmental stimuli, including pathogens (such as viruses and bacteria) and xenobiotics (such as cigarette smoke and particles) [6]. Acute or chronic exposure to these harmful agents can cause damage to the lung, resulting in respiratory dysfunction and pulmonary diseases [6,7]. Both acute lung injury (ALI) and chronic pulmonary diseases are associated with high morbidity and mortality with limited effective therapeutics, thus representing major public health problems worldwide [7,8]. In coping with these outside threats, the lung has evolved various defense mechanisms (such as innate and adaptive immune responses) to maintain its normal function. During the past decade, altered autophagy phenotypes in lung cells have been observed in response to these harmful stimuli [9]. Autophagy is capable of eliminating pathogens, degrading damaged organelles, and regulating inflammatory responses or apoptosis. Thus, autophagy is primarily characterized as a novel defense mechanism for lung injury [10–12]. However, autophagy dysfunction has also been reported to represent a harmful event that promotes the progression of pulmonary diseases [11,12]. This seemingly contradictory role of autophagy in pulmonary diseases underlies the lack of an in-depth understanding of the complex autophagy mechanisms in lung injury and pulmonary diseases. In this review, we will summarize the current knowledge of the protective features of autophagy in pulmonary infection and inflammatory diseases, and discuss the perspective of targeting autophagy for the clinical intervention for lung diseases.

2. Molecular Regulation of the Autophagy Process

The autophagy process involves a sequence of molecular events, including initiation (the formation of phagophore), elongation/closure (the formation of autophagosome), and maturation (the fusion of autophagosome with lysosome) [5] (Figure 1). The initiation of autophagosome biogenesis is triggered by the activation of the UNC51-like kinase (ULK) complex (also called the preinitiation complex), which is composed of ULK1/2, ATG13, FIP200, and ATG101 [4]. The ULK complex can be activated by inactivation of the mammalian target of rapamycin complex 1 (mTORC1), in response to nutrient starvation or the activation of 5′-AMP-activated protein kinase (AMPK) under energy-deprived conditions, to transmit stress signals for autophagosome formation [13]. Meanwhile, in addition to AMPK and mTORC1, the activity of the ULK complex can be regulated by other signals [4]. In turn, the activation of the ULK complex stimulates the class III phosphatidylinositol-3-kinase (class III PI3K) complex (also termed the VPS34 complex or initiation complex), which consists of VPS34, VPS15, Beclin 1, ATG14L, and AMBRA1 [14]. The dissociation of Beclin 1 from Bcl-2/xL anti-apoptotic proteins is a prerequisite for the formation and activation of the class III PI3K complex [14]. This class III PI3K complex enables the conversion of phosphatidylinositol to generate phosphatidylinositol-3-phosphate (PI3P) required for the nucleation of phagophore [15].

The phagophore then elongates and closes up to form the double-membrane autophagosome, which is tightly regulated by PI3P-binding proteins, such as the WD-repeat protein interacting with phosphoinosides (WIPI) family of proteins and two ubiquitin-like (UBL) protein conjugation systems. The completion of the first ubiquitin–like conjugation system leads to the formation of the ATG12/ATG5/ATG16L1 complex, which marks the sites of autophagosome formation and acts as a E3-like ligase for the second conjugation system to generate LC3-II (LC3-PE, the phosphatidylethanolamine-conjugated LC3) from the ATG4–mediated proteolytic cleavage of LC3 [4,16]. The lipidated LC3-II is closely associated with the elongation of the phagophore for autophagosome formation [17]. Following the completion of autophagosome formation, the autophagosome will fuse with a lysosome to form an autolysosome, in which the sequestered contents are degraded by a variety of lysosomal acid hydrolases and released into the cytosol for recycling [18,19].

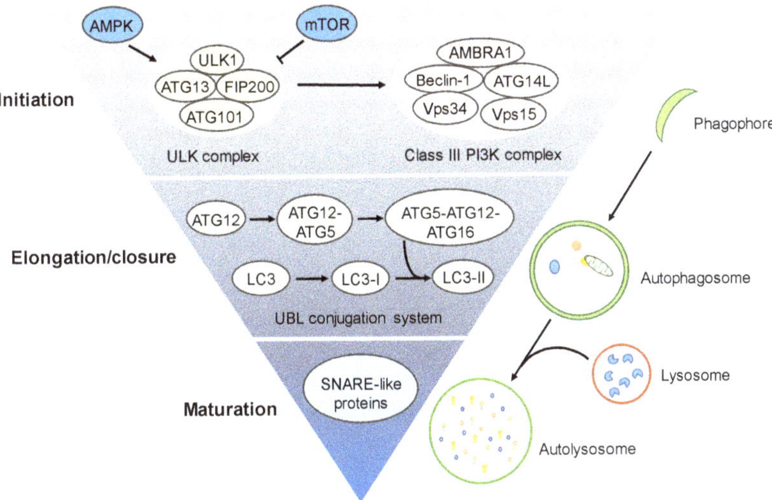

Figure 1. Autophagy machinery. The autophagy process involves initiation, elongation/closure and maturation. The autophagy process is initiated by autophagosome biogenesis to form phagophore, which is regulated by the activation of the preinitiation complex (also known as the ULK complex, containing ULK1/2, ATG13, FIP200, and ATG101) and subsequent activation of the initiation complex (also called the class III PI3K complex, consisting of VPS34, VPS15, Beclin 1, ATG14L, and AMBRA1). The phagophore is then elongated and closed to form a double-membrane autophagosome, which is tightly regulated by the ubiquitin–like (UBL) conjugation systems. The autophagosome will fuse with a lysosome to form an autolysosome for degradation. The SNARE-like proteins may play important roles in autophagosome–lysosome degradation. AMPK—5'-AMP-activated protein kinase; mTOR—the mammalian target of rapamycin; ULK1—UNC51-like kinase 1; class III PI3K—the class III phosphatidylinositol-3-kinase.

Autophagy-mediated degradation was previously recognized as a nonspecific process to remove cellular debris. Recently, increasing evidence suggests that autophagic encapsulation and degradation in some cases could be highly selective for specific substrates (termed 'selective autophagy') [2,3]. For example, autophagy can selectively digest damaged or depolarized mitochondria for the maintenance of mitochondrial homeostasis (mitophagy), remove invading pathogens (i.e., bacteria) to enhance host defense (xenophagy), clear polyubiquitinated protein for protein turnover (aggrephagy), and so on [12,20,21]. These types of selective autophagy act as cell survival mechanisms in most cases and are reported to play protective roles in pulmonary infection and inflammatory diseases [22]. Interestingly, mitophagy might also be cytotoxic if it is excessively induced to degrade even functional mitochondria [23,24]. In addition, emerging studies found that several pathogens, such as hepatitis B virus or hepatitis C virus, can adapt to autophagy induction, or even employ autophagy machinery to facilitate their replication [25–27]. The length of airway epithelial cilia can also be regulated by autophagic degradation (ciliophagy) [12]. Cilia shortening, mediated by ciliophagy, can impair the clearance ability of the airway against invading pathogens, thereby exacerbating pulmonary infection [28,29]. The double-edged sword role of autophagy in pulmonary diseases might be attributed to different cell types and different types of diseases.

3. The Protective Roles of Autophagy in Acute Lung Injury (ALI)

Acute lung injury (ALI) is a common and severe clinical syndrome with high morbidity and mortality [7]. ALI is characterized with increased alveolar–capillary permeability, noncardiogenic pulmonary edema, neutrophil recruitment and diffuse alveolar damage, and represents a major cause of acute respiratory failure [11,30]. The intrapulmonary inflammatory response with the release of proinflammatory cytokines could be observed before and during the process of ALI, and has been intensively investigated recently [30,31]. However, the mechanisms underlying the pathogenesis and resolution of ALI remain largely unclear. Accumulating evidence suggests that autophagy is stimulated in response to diverse stimuli of ALI, including bacterial infection, lipopolysaccharide (LPS), sepsis, hyperoxia, and chlorine, etc. [32]. In addition, the loss of autophagy-related (ATG) genes, such as *Atg7*, *Atg5* and *Atg4b*, significantly aggravates the development of ALI in mice [11,32], suggesting that autophagy may exert protective effects for the initiation and progression of ALI in certain contexts (Figure 2).

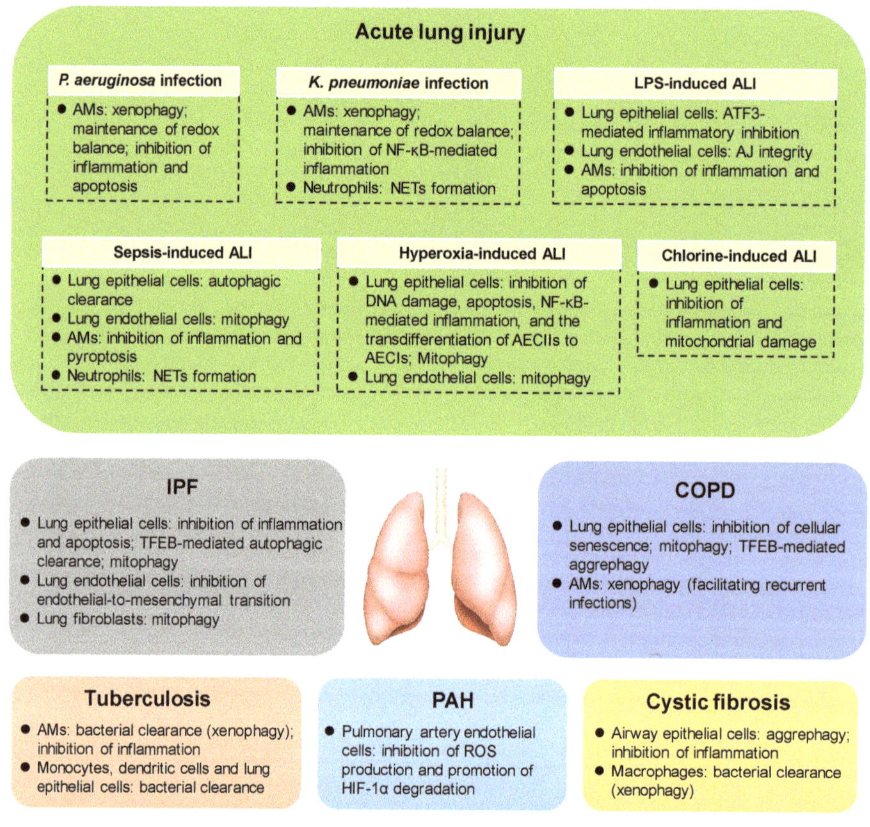

Figure 2. The protective mechanisms of autophagy in lung diseases. Autophagy may provide a protective role in the pathogenesis of various lung diseases (including ALI, IPF, COPD, tuberculosis, PAH, cystic fibrosis, etc.), through regulating diverse biological events, including inflammatory response, redox balance, DNA damage repair, apoptosis, pyroptosis, cellular senescence, NETs formation, mitochondrial homeostasis, pathogen or aggresome clearance, etc. ALI—acute lung injury; IPF—idiopathic pulmonary fibrosis; COPD—chronic obstructive pulmonary disease; PAH—pulmonary arterial hypertension; TFEB—transcription factor EB; AMs—alveolar macrophages; NETs—neutrophil extracellular traps; AJ integrity—adherens junctional integrity; *P. aeruginosa*—*Pseudomonas aeruginosa*; *K. pneumoniae*—*Klebsiella pneumoniae*; LPS—lipopolysaccharide.

3.1. The Protective Roles of Autophagy in Bacteria–Induced ALI

Pseudomonas aeruginosa (*P. aeruginosa*), an opportunistic Gram–negative human pathogen, was reported to induce autophagosome formation and subsequent autolysosomal degradation in alveolar macrophages (AMs), which are known as part of the first line of host defense in the lung [33]. The *P. aeruginosa*-induced autophagy is partially mediated by the Annexin A2 (ANXA2)–Akt1–mTOR–ULK1/2 and Beclin-1–ATG7–ATG5 signaling pathways [33,34]. *Anxa2* knockout mice exhibit elevated inflammatory cytokines, decreased bacterial clearance, increased lung injury and mortality [34]. How autophagy enhances host defense against *P. aeruginosa* remains largely to be investigated. We have recently found that following *P. aeruginosa* infection, toll-like receptor 2 (TLR2) initiates the phagocytic process in AMs and activates the *Src* kinase Lyn, which in turn delivers bacteria to lysosomes for degradation through xenophagy [35]. In addition to Lyn, the Wnt5A–Rac1–Disheveled pathway is also required for inducing xenophagy in AMs [36]. We also reported that regulation of redox balance and inflammatory response is involved in autophagy-mediated eradication of *P. aeruginosa*. *Atg7* deficiency promotes the release of reactive oxygen species (ROS) but limits NO production through inhibiting JAK2/STAT1α/NOS2 signaling, leading to the intracellular redox imbalance, elevated inflammatory cytokines, enhanced apoptosis of AMs, exaggerated lung infection and aggravated lung injury in mice [37]. Interestingly, *P. aeruginosa*-mediated autophagy induction and inflammasome activation can be mutually regulated to subtly orchestrate the host defense. For example, *P. aeruginosa* infection triggers protective autophagy by activating TLR4-TRIP signaling in bone marrow-derived macrophages (BMDMs). Meanwhile, the NLRC4 inflammasome can be activated, leading to caspase-1-mediated TRIF cleavage, and subsequent autophagy inhibition, thereby reducing bacterial clearance [38]. Autophagy, in turn, abrogates the activation of NLRC4 inflammasome by selectively removing damaged mitochondria (mitophagy) in BMDMs, leading to increased bacterial clearance [39]. Thus, autophagy induction and NLRC4 inflammasome activation may constitute a negative feedback loop in BMDMs following *P. aeruginosa* infection, which might facilitate the development of novel therapeutic options for the treatment of *P. aeruginosa* infection. However, whether this negative feedback loop is present in *P. aeruginosa*-infected AMs remains to be further investigated.

Klebsiella pneumoniae (*K. pneumoniae*) is another Gram-negative bacterium that can activate the autophagy process in AMs [40]. It has been reported that *Atg7* deficiency significantly elevates the levels of inflammatory cytokines and superoxide, leading to increased susceptibility to *K. pneumoniae* infection in mice, suggesting that ATG7-mediated autophagy may represent a major resistance mechanism to *K. pneumoniae* infection [40]. Further study found that ATG7 can directly bind phosphorylated IκBα (p-IκBα). In *Atg7*–deficient AMs with *K. pneumoniae* infection, the binding of p-IκBα switches from ATG7 to ubiquitin, leading to the ubiquitin-mediated degradation of IκBα, activation of NF-κB, intensified inflammation, and decreased bacterial clearance [41]. Similar to *P. aeruginosa* infection, the TLR2–Lyn– or Wnt5A–Rac1–Disheveled-mediated xenophagy in AMs also contributes to the degradation and clearance of *K. pneumoniae* [35,36]. In addition to AMs, neutrophils also play important roles in the anti-bacterial host defense in the lung. In response to bacterial infection, the recruited neutrophils can release decondensed chromatin fibrils to form neutrophil extracellular traps (NETs) in a highly oxidative milieu, in order to trap, neutralize, and destroy microbes extracellularly [42]. It has been reported that TRPM2–AMPK–p38– or Mincle–mediated induction of autophagy is required for NETs formation following *K. pneumoniae* infection in a ROS–dependent or independent manner, respectively [43,44]. Future studies are needed for understanding the molecular mechanism underlying autophagy–regulated NETs formation during bacterial infection.

3.2. The Protective Roles of Autophagy in LPS–Induced ALI

The outer membrane of Gram–negative bacteria is composed predominantly of LPS (also known as endotoxin), which is a pathogen-associated molecular pattern (PAMP) that enables the recognition of bacterial invasion and activates innate immune system [45]. It has been reported that LPS stimulation can regulate autophagy in lung epithelial cells, pulmonary endothelial cells and AMs. For example, LPS induces autophagy in mice lung tissues and bronchial epithelial cells. *Atg4b* deficiency significantly increases the susceptibility of the lung to LPS–mediated injury by impairing ATF3 activity, suggesting a protective role of autophagy in LPS–induced lung injury [46]. The LPS–induced protective autophagy may be due to the involvement of endoplasmic reticulum (ER) stress [47]. Interestingly, LPS was also reported to inhibit autophagy through TLR4– or AMPK inactivation–mediated mTOR activation in bronchial or alveolar epithelial cells [48,49]. *MTOR* knockdown, AMPK activation or autophagy stimulation significantly attenuates LPS-induced airway inflammation and injury, suggesting that autophagy functions as a protective mechanism to LPS–induced lung injury [48,49]. The inconsistent effects of LPS on the induction of autophagy may be due to different cell types and different sources of LPS. Despite this inconsistency, it can be concluded that autophagy in general confers a cytoprotective role in LPS–induced lung injury.

In addition to lung epithelial cells, LPS also induces autophagy in pulmonary endothelial cells. The inhibition of autophagy by si*ATG5*, si*ATG7* or chloroquine markedly reduces the permeability of human pulmonary microvascular endothelial cells and attenuates LPS-induced lung injury in mice, in part through restricting the injury of lung microvascular barrier, suggesting a protective role of autophagy in LPS–induced lung injury [50]. Mechanistically, RAB26, a newly identified small GTPase, can induce autophagic degradation of active SRC and the resultant CDH5 dephosphorylation, leading to the maintenance of lung vascular permeability and the protection of adherens junctional integrity in LPS–induced ALI [51]. In contrast, it was reported in another recent study that the inhibition of autophagy by 3-methyladenine (3-MA) significantly disrupts the endothelial barrier in human pulmonary artery endothelial cells and ameliorates lung vascular injury upon LPS treatment, suggesting that autophagy promotes LPS–induced lung injury [52]. This contradictory outcome of autophagy in LPS–induced lung injury might be due to the use of different autophagy inhibitors in different types of endothelial cells.

LPS was also reported to induce autophagy in macrophages during LPS treatment. In response to LPS stimulation, the activated calcium/calmodulin-dependent protein kinase Iα (CaMKIα) can phosphorylate AMPK to form the CaMKIα–AMPK–ATG7 complex that contributes to autophagy induction in an mTOR–independent manner. The CaMKIα–AMPK–ATG7 signaling-mediated autophagy markedly attenuates LPS–induced lung neutrophilic inflammation [53]. Stimulation of autophagy by BML-111, a lipoxin A4 receptor agonist, significantly inhibits apoptosis, reduces the levels of proinflammatory cytokines, and ameliorates the LPS–induced lung injury [54]. These studies suggest that autophagy in macrophages confers the resolution of LPS–induced ALI, and may represent a potential therapeutic target.

3.3. The Protective Roles of Autophagy in Sepsis–Induced ALI

Sepsis is a syndrome of excessive inflammatory response to infection with high morbidity commonly leading to ALI [55]. However, the pathogenesis of sepsis still remains largely unclear. Emerging evidence suggests a critical role of autophagy in preventing sepsis, and the modulation of autophagy may provide novel insights for the treatment of sepsis. For example, in the cecal ligation puncture (CLP)—induced sepsis mice model, the levels of LC3-II, ATG5, and ATG7 are downregulated in the lung of mice with sepsis, suggesting that sepsis may suppress autophagy. Stimulation of autophagy using rapamycin or activated protein C (APC) results in reduced inflammation and attenuated lung injury [56]. Interestingly, another group found that the LC3-II level is markedly increased in the lung of septic mice. The increased LC3-II level is due to autophagosome accumulation caused by the retarded autophagosome–lysosome fusion. Transgenic mice overexpressing the *LC3* gene exhibit accelerated fusion of autophagosome with lysosome, and survive longer after CLP [57]. This study suggests that the role of autophagy in CLP-induced sepsis might depend on the autophagic flux: the preservation of autophagic flux is cytoprotective to sepsis, while autophagosome accumulation due to impaired autophagic flux may contribute to lung injury in the late stage of sepsis. The discrepancy in LC3-II level observed in the same sepsis model in these two studies may be due to the ignorance of the LC3-II/LC3-I ratio, or the different detection time periods.

Mitochondrial dysfunction is recognized as an important mediator of sepsis pathogenesis. It was recently shown that the deficiency of kinase MKK3 ameliorates mitochondrial injury by lowering ROS levels and stimulating mitophagy, and increases mitochondrial biogenesis in pulmonary endothelial cells, leading to reduced septic lung injury [58]. Although the mechanism underlying the upstream signaling for mitophagy initiation remains to be defined, mitophagy may help provide novel therapeutic window for the treatment of sepsis. In addition to mitochondrial quality control, autophagy can also regulate inflammasome during sepsis. In a *P. aeruginosa*-induced sepsis mice model, *Atg7* deficiency significantly intensifies inflammasome activation and provokes pyroptosis in AMs, leading to impaired pathogen clearance and aggravated lung injury [59]. In addition, autophagy was found to be activated in neutrophils from both patients who survived sepsis or septic mice. Interestingly, autophagy augmentation in neutrophils leads to the formation of NETs in order to protect mice from lethal sepsis [60].

Considerable efforts have been made to develop autophagy–modulating strategies for the treatment of sepsis. For example, miR-155 was found to induce autophagy by inhibiting transforming growth factor-β (TGF-β)-activated kinase-1-binding protein 2 (TAB2), resulting in the alleviation of inflammation in septic lung injury [61]. In addition, it has been reported that the clinically approved anthracyclines at low doses can effectively confer disease tolerance to severe sepsis in mice via activation of DNA damage response and the stimulation of autophagy pathways in the lung [62]. Notably, carbon monoxide (CO) administered at low physiologic doses was reported to promote the Beclin 1–dependent autophagy process in lung epithelial cells through mitochondrial ROS generation, thereby increasing the survival of septic mice [63,64]. These studies suggest that CO exhibits a protective effect on sepsis, supporting the potential therapeutic application of CO for sepsis treatment.

3.4. The Protective Roles of Autophagy in Hyperoxia–Induced ALI

Hyperoxia (high levels of oxygen) exposure is commonly used for critically ill patients, including those with acute respiratory distress syndrome and chronic obstructive pulmonary disease (COPD) [65]. However, prolonged hyperoxia treatment induces the generation of excessive ROS, DNA damage and inflammatory response, leading to ALI and even respiratory failure [66]. The injury of pulmonary epithelium and subsequent apoptotic cell death is one of the major effects of hyperoxia [66]. It has been reported that hyperoxia upregulates ATG7, and induces LC3 turnover and autophagosome formation by activating c-Jun N-terminal kinase (JNK). Under hyperoxia, LC3 can interact with Fas by associating with caveolin-1 in lipid rafts to prevent apoptosis facilitating the survival of lung epithelial cells [67]. The hyperoxia–induced increased interaction of LC3 with Fas is due to the dissociation of LC3 with p62, an autophagic adaptor linking ubiquitinated substrates to the autophagy pathway for degradation [68]. Hyperoxia–mediated LC3 activation was also found to promote the accumulation of surfactant protein C (SP-C) in type II alveolar epithelial cells (AECIIs) and inhibit the transdifferentiation of AECIIs to type I alveolar epithelial cells (AECIs) [69,70]. In addition, hyperoxia—induced ROS accumulation causes DNA damage in lung epithelial cells, which could be repaired by 8-oxoguanine-DNA glycosylase (OGG-1). Through regulating *ATG7* promoter, OGG-1 links DNA damage with autophagy in stimulating NF-κB–mediated inflammatory response to protect hyperoxia–induced epithelial injury [71]. Hyperoxia also causes a morphological change in mitochondria accomplished with increased expression of mitophagy–associated markers (PINK1 and PARK2) in lung epithelial cells, implying that mitophagy might play a role in protecting epithelial cells from hyperoxia–induced injury [72]. It is worth noting that the hyperoxia–induced ROS accumulation, mitochondrial damage and autophagy were also observed in pulmonary endothelial cells [73,74]. It has recently been reported that PINK1–mediated mitophagy is required for the ability of pulmonary endothelial cells to resist to hyperoxia [75]. It remains to be investigated whether autophagy functions in other types of lung cells under hyperoxia.

3.5. The Protective Roles of Autophagy in Chlorine–Induced ALI

Chlorine (Cl_2), which is extensively used in industrial applications worldwide, is a common toxic inhalant [76]. Cl_2 inhalation, depending on the dose and duration of exposure, may cause ALI and respiratory failure, and represents a significant public health problem [77]. Cl_2 exposure to lung epithelial cells leads to mitochondrial dysfunction and ROS accumulation, which might be a major cause of lung injury [77]. Interestingly, autophagy can be induced to prevent mitochondrial damage, decrease inflammation, and ameliorate Cl_2 toxicity [78]. This study suggests a protective role of autophagy in Cl_2–induced lung injury, and implies that autophagy might represent a potential therapeutic target for the treatment of toxic Cl_2 exposure. However, it lacks evidence of mitophagy in maintaining mitochondrial homeostasis, which merits further investigation. Moreover, autophagic alterations in Cl_2–challenged pulmonary endothelial cells or AMs and their underlying mechanisms may also be critical to prevent lung injury, and remain poorly defined.

4. The Protective Roles of Autophagy in Idiopathic Pulmonary Fibrosis (IPF)

Idiopathic pulmonary fibrosis (IPF) is a chronic and fatal lung disease of unknown cause characterized by chronic lung inflammation, diffuse alveolar damage, the accumulation of fibroblasts and myofibroblasts, abundant collagen deposition and extracellular matrix proteins [79]. Decreased LC3-II expression and mTOR overactivation were observed in alveolar epithelial cells in bleomycin–induced pulmonary fibrosis mice model, as well as lung tissues from IPF patients compared to normal counterparts, suggesting impaired autophagic activity in IPF [80–83]. The compromised autophagy is due, in part, to the activation of IL-17A in lung epithelial cells during the fibrotic process. IL-17A stimulation activates the PI3K-glycogen synthase kinase 3β (GSK-3β) signaling pathway to inhibit Bcl-2 degradation, leading to the suppression of autophagy. Neutralization of IL-17A effectively induces autophagy, enhances collagen degradation, and decreases bleomycin–induced pulmonary fibrosis [84,85]. Moreover, *Atg4b*–deficient mice display reduced autophagy induction, increased inflammatory response, augmented apoptosis and hyperproliferation of alveolar and bronchiolar epithelial cells, thereby increasing collagen accumulation and exaggerating bleomycin–induced pulmonary fibrosis [86]. In addition, *Atg7* deficiency in endothelial cells impairs autophagic flux, upregulates TGF-β signaling, and promotes the endothelial-to-mesenchymal transition for fibroblast formation, leading to more extensive and severe fibrosis in bleomycin–challenged mice [87]. These studies suggest a protective role of autophagy in IPF.

Indeed, stimulation of autophagy by rapamycin (an mTOR inhibitor promoting autophagic flux) significantly inhibits the fibrotic phenotype in bleomycin-induced pulmonary fibrosis. However, this protective effect of rapamycin can be partially reversed by chloroquine (an inhibitor of autolysosome formation blocking autophagic flux) [80,81,84,88]. Our recent findings suggest that bleomycin can directly bind ANXA2 in lung epithelial cells to prevent the translocation of transcription factor EB (TFEB) into the nucleus, leading to TFEB inactivation and impeded autophagic flux, thereby inducing pulmonary fibrosis. Pharmacological activation of TFEB using Torin 1 accelerates autophagic flux and significantly ameliorates bleomycin–induced pulmonary fibrosis [83]. These studies suggest that the autophagic flux might be inhibited to facilitate fibrotic progression in lung endothelial and epithelial cells. Further studies are required to investigate the upstream mechanisms by which autophagic flux is dysregulated in lung endothelial and epithelial cells in IPF.

Autophagy alteration in fibroblasts has also been reported to be critical in human IPF pathogenesis. Interestingly, human IPF fibroblasts show reduced autophagy induction and decreased autophagic flux, due to mTOR activation or reduced FoxO3a–mediated LC3 transcription [89–91]. The defective autophagy is required for maintaining the cell death-resistant phenotype for the fibroblasts on collagen-rich matrix [90,91]. Considering the profibrotic role of autophagy in IPF fibroblasts, the use of autophagy activators for IPF treatment should be re-evaluated in a context–specific manner.

Emerging evidence reveals the critical roles of deregulated mitochondrial homeostasis in AECIIs, fibroblasts or AMs in the pathogenesis of IPF. For example, it was reported that dysmorphic and dysfunctional mitochondria are accumulated in AECIIs in the lungs of IPF patients [92]. The impaired mitochondria in AECIIs are associated with decreased levels of PINK1 and defective mitophagy in AECIIs. *PINK1*–deficient mice exhibit deregulated mitochondrial homeostasis and development of pulmonary fibrosis [92]. The expression of PARK2, another mitophagy–associated protein, is downregulated in the lung fibroblasts of IPF patients. *PARK2* deficiency aggravates bleomycin–induced pulmonary fibrosis in mice through promoting PDGFR-PI3K-Akt-mediated myofibroblast differentiation and proliferation [93]. Pirfenidone, an FDA–approved agent for IPF treatment, exerts its anti-fibrotic effect partially by inducing PARK2–mediated mitophagy and inhibiting myofibroblast differentiation [94]. Different from the protective role of mitophagy in AECIIs or fibroblasts for IPF, mitophagy is increased in IPF AMs and is required for the development of pulmonary fibrosis. During fibrosis, Akt1 in AMs is activated to induce the generation of mitochondrial ROS, leading to stimulation of PARK2–mediated mitophagy [95]. The Akt1–mediated mitophagy induction contributes to apoptosis resistance of AMs, enables the expression of macrophage–derived TGF-β1, and ultimately promotes fibroblast differentiation and progression of pulmonary fibrosis [95]. Given the contrary effects of mitophagy of different cell types in IPF pathogenesis, the manipulation of cell type–specific mitophagy, rather than global mitophagy, may achieve better therapeutic outcome for IPF treatment.

5. The Protective and Deleterious Roles of Autophagy in COPD

COPD is a pulmonary disorder characterized by excessive inflammation and airway obstruction (i.e., chronic bronchitis and emphysema) [96]. Cigarette smoke (CS) remains the key risk factor for COPD worldwide [96]. The molecular mechanisms underlying COPD pathogenesis remain incompletely understood. It has been shown that the expression of ATG proteins, such as LC3, is increased in lung tissues from COPD patients and mouse lung tissues subjected to CS exposure, suggesting an increase of autophagosome formation in COPD [97,98]. The increased autophagosome formation is correlated with a cumulative increase in autophagic flux, suggesting that the autophagy pathway in lung epithelial cells is activated in COPD [28,99]. The increased activity of autophagy caused by CS exposure is at least partially due to the decreased histone deacetylase (HDAC) –mediated Egr-1 inhibition, elevated PGF–JNK1–p38–TSC2–mediated mTOR inhibition, or upregulation of oxidative stress-induced growth inhibitor 1 (OSGIN1) [98,100–102]. In response to CS exposure, LC3 dissociates from the extrinsic apoptotic factor Fas, leading to apoptotic cell death of lung epithelial cells for emphysema progression [103]. The activation of autophagy is also observed in particulate matter (PM) –induced experimental COPD model, and *Atg7* deficiency protects mice from PM–induced COPD [104]. In addition to lung epithelial cells, increased autophagy was also observed in CS-treated neutrophils. CS exposure induces autophagic cell death of neutrophils by activating PAFR–HMGB1–Beclin-1–Bcl-2 signaling, leading to the development of emphysema [105]. These studies indicate that autophagy stimulation with increased autophagic flux, either in lung epithelial cells or neutrophils, contributes to the development of COPD.

Interestingly, autophagy has been reported to regulate bronchial epithelial cell senescence in CS–induced senescence–associated COPD. CS exposure leads to autophagy inhibition in COPD patients, which might be, in part, due to the activation of the SIRT6–IGF–Akt–mTOR signaling pathway [106,107]. Autophagy inhibition by 3-MA results in increased senescence in human bronchial epithelial cells, whereas autophagy activation by Torin 1 significantly inhibits cell senescence, indicating that the insufficient autophagy accelerates bronchial epithelial cell senescence in COPD [106]. The CS–impaired autophagy is characterized by the enhanced formation of aggresome and resultant insufficient autophagic clearance (impaired aggrephagy) [106,108,109]. A possible mechanism of CS–impaired autophagy is the perinuclear aggresome sequestration of TFEB, the master regulator of autophagy. Activation of TFEB using gemfibrozil significantly decreases CS–induced formation of aggresome, resulting in the mitigation of COPD progression [110]. These studies suggest that CS exposure promotes the accumulation of aggresome bodies and consequent autophagy impairment, which accelerates bronchial epithelial cell senescence and exacerbates the development of COPD.

The pathogenesis of CS–induced COPD is also associated with elevated levels of ROS caused by mitochondrial damage [111]. PARK2 deficiency results in increased mitochondrial damage, enhanced ROS accumulation, and accelerated senescence of lung epithelial cells under CS exposure, suggesting that CS–induced PARK2–mediated mitophagy may attenuate cellular senescence and inhibit the progression of COPD [111,112]. However, a study from another group indicates that PINK1–regulated mitophagy promotes necroptosis and cell death in lung epithelial cells, thereby contributing to COPD development [23]. The different outcomes of mitophagy in regulating senescence or necroptosis probably depend on the injury degree in response to CS [23,111]. In addition to damaged mitochondria, CS–induced autophagy also regulates cilia length by selective consumption of cilia components (ciliophagy) in respiratory epithelial cells in COPD pathogenesis [28,29]. In contrast to mitophagy and ciliophagy, CS exposure leads to autophagy inhibition and xenophagy impairment in AMs. In smokers' AMs, the autophagy degradation is defective as evidenced by the accumulation of both LC3 and p62, which may explain the clinical issue of recurrent infections for smokers [113].

Collectively, it seems that different autophagy machineries are involved in COPD pathogenesis, and the roles of autophagy in COPD pathogenesis vary in different reports. One possibility is that autophagy machineries in different types of lung cells are differentially regulated. In addition, the period of CS exposure in animals or the stages in humans might also be critical to the roles of autophagy in CS–induced COPD. Further studies are needed to decipher the precise roles of autophagy in COPD.

6. The Protective Roles of Autophagy in Tuberculosis

Extensive studies have demonstrated the critical roles of autophagy in the pathogenesis of tuberculosis caused by *Mycobacterium tuberculosis* (Mtb) infection. Mtb could interfere with the fusion of autophagosome with lysosome to prevent autophagosome maturation and subsequent autolysosomal degradation in macrophages [114,115]. Stimulation of autophagy by rapamycin, IFN-γ or vitamin D promotes autophagic flux, enabling autophagy–mediated clearance of Mtb [114,116]. In addition to suppressing Mtb growth, autophagy also contributes to the resolution of damaging inflammation [117]. Interestingly, autophagy in monocytes is also involved in Mtb defense, and induction of autophagy in monocytes could enhance the antimicrobial activity against Mtb [118,119]. Moreover, the Mtb–eradicating role of autophagy was observed in dendritic cells and lung epithelial cells [120–122]. However, a recent study shows that myeloid cell–specific deficiency of *Atg5*, but not other ATG genes (including *Atg3*, *Atg7*, *Atg12*, *Atg14L* and *Atg16L1*), significantly provokes Mtb infection and hampers the survival of infected mice [123]. This study suggests that the canonical autophagy pathway may not play a major role in the pathogenesis of tuberculosis. Instead of autophagy induction, Atg5 functions in a protective manner for Mtb infection by preventing polymorphonuclear cell (PMN)–mediated immunopathology [123]. Therefore, a more in-depth evaluation of the role of autophagy in tuberculosis pathogenesis is needed.

7. The Protective Roles of Autophagy in Cystic Fibrosis (CF)

Cystic fibrosis (CF) is a life–threatening lung disease caused by a loss-of-function mutation of cystic fibrosis transmembrane conductance regulator (CFTR, F508del) [124,125]. It has been reported that CFTR deficiency causes defective autophagic flux in both human airway epithelial cells and nasal biopsies from CF patients, leading to the formation of aggresome through the production of ROS, upregulation of tissue transglutaminase (TG2), sequestration of the class III PI3K complex and subsequent accumulation of p62 [126,127]. This disruption of autophagic clearance also heightens the inflammatory response in CFTR–mutant cells [128]. In addition to the airway epithelial cells, defective autophagic degradation was also observed in macrophages with CFTR mutation. The decreased autophagic clearance subverts the bactericidal function of macrophages, consequently resulting in pathogen infection, such as *Nontuberculous mycobacteria* (NTM) and *Burkholderia cenocepacia* (*B. cepacia*) [129,130]. Induction of autophagy by rapamycin or clearance of aggresome by p62 deletion could markedly enhance the elimination of pathogens and ameliorate the associated inflammation [130,131]. Together, these studies suggest that autophagy is a survival mechanism in the pathogenesis of CF, and pharmacological induction of autophagy might be a promising strategy to delay CF progression.

8. The Protective Roles of Autophagy in Pulmonary Arterial Hypertension (PAH)

Pulmonary arterial hypertension (PAH) is a lethal syndrome characterized by elevated pulmonary arterial pressure with unclear etiology [132]. Hypoxia is known as a common cause of PAH. It has been reported that human lungs with PAH reveal elevated LC3B levels and increased autophagosomes compared to normal lungs. In addition, autophagy induction is promoted following hypoxia treatment in human pulmonary artery endothelial cells (PAECs). In a chronic hypoxia–induced PH model, LC3B knockout mice show apparent PAH phenotypes relative to wild-type mice [133]. These results suggest a protective function of autophagy in PAH pathogenesis. The stimulation of autophagy was also observed in pulmonary artery smooth muscle cells (PASMCs) in a rat PAH model induced by monocrotaline or hypoxia. Paradoxically, the inhibition of autophagy by chloroquine or κ-opioid receptor exerts beneficial effects for PAH [134,135], implying that autophagy may contribute to the pathogenesis of PAH. The various roles of autophagy in PAH pathogenesis might be explained by the different cell types, approaches and models used in these studies.

9. Conclusions and Perspectives

Accumulating evidence demonstrates that autophagy is involved in the regulation of diverse biological functions, such as inflammatory response, redox balance, DNA damage repair, apoptosis, and necroptosis in different cell types in the lung, and thus plays crucial roles in pulmonary infection and inflammatory diseases, including ALI, IPF, COPD, tuberculosis, PAH, CF, etc. (Figure 2). Autophagy is initially known as a protective process in the pathogenesis of most lung diseases. Recent findings also support the notion that autophagy may promote the pathogenesis of lung diseases in certain contexts. The diverse roles of autophagy in lung disease pathogenesis might be due to the different types of lung diseases (ALI, IPF, COPD, tuberculosis, PAH, CF, etc.), the diverse stressors for the etiology (infection, CS exposure, the stimulus intensity, etc.), the various cell types in the lung (epithelial cells, endothelial cells, fibroblasts, neutrophils, AMs, etc.), and the different mechanisms underlying disease initiation and progression (cell death such as apoptosis and necroptosis, cellular senescence, fibroblast differentiation, DNA damage, etc.). In addition, the analysis methods, experimental approaches, reagents, and models with different cells and animals (e.g., age, sex) all contribute to the variations in the laboratories. Furthermore, selective autophagy, such as mitophagy, xenophagy, aggrephagy, and ciliophagy, has recently attracted much attention in the pathogenesis of human lung diseases. It remains unclear how cells orchestrate nonselective autophagy and selective autophagy during disease initiation and progression, and whether nonselective autophagy cross-talks with selective autophagy [22]. Moreover, the lack of autophagy inhibitors to specifically target nonselective autophagy and selective autophagy in a given lung cell type also remains a major challenge for therapeutic intervention. Finally, some of the previous studies (especially those in vivo studies) only examined LC3-II accumulation which might be a result of the activation or inhibition of autophagic flux–mediated degradation. Therefore, the non-unified interpretation of autophagy activation and suppression remains a major problem for the evaluation of the exact roles of autophagy in pathological or therapeutic aspects. Careful consideration of the autophagy activity is needed to achieve a better and deeper understanding of the role of autophagy in lung disease pathogenesis for the development of potential therapeutic strategies.

Author Contributions: K.W., Y.C., P.J.Z., P.L. and M.W. reviewed the literature and co-wrote the manuscript; N.X. and M.W. revised the manuscript.

Funding: This work was supported by the Chinese NSFC (81602194 and 81872277), US National Institute of Health (R01 AI101973-04, R01 AI138203-01 and P20 GM113123 to M.W.), and the Fundamental Research Funds for the central Universities.

Conflicts of Interest: The authors declare no conflict of interest.

References

1. Klionsky, D.J.; Abdelmohsen, K.; Abe, A.; Abedin, M.J.; Abeliovich, H.; Acevedo Arozena, A.; Adachi, H.; Adams, C.M.; Adams, P.D.; Adeli, K.; et al. Guidelines for the use and interpretation of assays for monitoring autophagy (3rdedition). *Autophagy* **2016**, *12*, 1–222. [CrossRef] [PubMed]
2. Gatica, D.; Lahiri, V.; Klionsky, D.J. Cargo recognition and degradation by selective autophagy. *Nat. Cell Biol.* **2018**, *20*, 233–242. [CrossRef] [PubMed]
3. Anding, A.L.; Baehrecke, E.H. Cleaning House: Selective Autophagy of Organelles. *Dev. Cell* **2017**, *41*, 10–22. [CrossRef] [PubMed]
4. Green, D.R.; Levine, B. To be or not to be? How selective autophagy and cell death govern cell fate. *Cell* **2014**, *157*, 65–75. [CrossRef] [PubMed]
5. Morel, E.; Mehrpour, M.; Botti, J.; Dupont, N.; Hamai, A.; Nascimbeni, A.C.; Codogno, P. Autophagy: A Druggable Process. *Annu. Rev. Pharmacol. Toxicol.* **2017**, *57*, 375–398. [CrossRef] [PubMed]
6. Ryter, S.W.; Nakahira, K.; Haspel, J.A.; Choi, A.M. Autophagy in pulmonary diseases. *Annu. Rev. Physiol.* **2012**, *74*, 377–401. [CrossRef] [PubMed]
7. Bhattacharya, J.; Matthay, M.A. Regulation and repair of the alveolar-capillary barrier in acute lung injury. *Annu. Rev. Physiol.* **2013**, *75*, 593–615. [CrossRef]
8. Nakahira, K.; Choi, A.M. Autophagy: A potential therapeutic target in lung diseases. *Am. J. Physiol. Lung Cell. Mol. Physiol.* **2013**, *305*, L93–L107. [CrossRef]
9. Nakahira, K.; Cloonan, S.M.; Mizumura, K.; Choi, A.M.; Ryter, S.W. Autophagy: A crucial moderator of redox balance, inflammation, and apoptosis in lung disease. *Antioxid. Redox Signal.* **2014**, *20*, 474–494. [CrossRef]
10. Haspel, J.A.; Choi, A.M. Autophagy: A core cellular process with emerging links to pulmonary disease. *Am. J. Respir. Crit. Care Med.* **2011**, *184*, 1237–1246. [CrossRef]
11. Aggarwal, S.; Mannam, P.; Zhang, J. Differential regulation of autophagy and mitophagy in pulmonary diseases. *Am. J. Physiol. Lung Cell. Mol. Physiol.* **2016**, *311*, L433–L452. [CrossRef] [PubMed]
12. Nakahira, K.; Pabon Porras, M.A.; Choi, A.M. Autophagy in Pulmonary Diseases. *Am. J. Respir. Crit. Care Med.* **2016**, *194*, 1196–1207. [CrossRef] [PubMed]
13. Antonioli, M.; Di Rienzo, M.; Piacentini, M.; Fimia, G.M. Emerging Mechanisms in Initiating and Terminating Autophagy. *Trends Biochem. Sci.* **2017**, *42*, 28–41. [CrossRef] [PubMed]
14. Marino, G.; Niso-Santano, M.; Baehrecke, E.H.; Kroemer, G. Self-consumption: The interplay of autophagy and apoptosis. *Nat. Rev. Mol. Cell Biol.* **2014**, *15*, 81–94. [CrossRef] [PubMed]
15. Zhang, L.; Wang, K.; Lei, Y.; Li, Q.; Nice, E.C.; Huang, C. Redox signaling: Potential arbitrator of autophagy and apoptosis in therapeutic response. *Free Radic. Biol. Med.* **2015**, *89*, 452–465. [CrossRef] [PubMed]
16. Kwon, Y.T.; Ciechanover, A. The Ubiquitin Code in the Ubiquitin-Proteasome System and Autophagy. *Trends Biochem. Sci.* **2017**, *42*, 873–886. [CrossRef] [PubMed]
17. Ichimura, Y.; Kirisako, T.; Takao, T.; Satomi, Y.; Shimonishi, Y.; Ishihara, N.; Mizushima, N.; Tanida, I.; Kominami, E.; Ohsumi, M.; et al. A ubiquitin-like system mediates protein lipidation. *Nature* **2000**, *408*, 488–492. [CrossRef] [PubMed]
18. Shen, H.M.; Mizushima, N. At the end of the autophagic road: An emerging understanding of lysosomal functions in autophagy. *Trends Biochem. Sci.* **2014**, *39*, 61–71. [CrossRef] [PubMed]
19. Moreau, K.; Renna, M.; Rubinsztein, D.C. Connections between SNAREs and autophagy. *Trends Biochem. Sci.* **2013**, *38*, 57–63. [CrossRef]
20. Pickles, S.; Vigie, P.; Youle, R.J. Mitophagy and Quality Control Mechanisms in Mitochondrial Maintenance. *Curr. Biol.* **2018**, *28*, R170–R185. [CrossRef]
21. Sui, X.; Liang, X.; Chen, L.; Guo, C.; Han, W.; Pan, H.; Li, X. Bacterial xenophagy and its possible role in cancer: A potential antimicrobial strategy for cancer prevention and treatment. *Autophagy* **2017**, *13*, 237–247. [CrossRef] [PubMed]
22. Mizumura, K.; Cloonan, S.; Choi, M.E.; Hashimoto, S.; Nakahira, K.; Ryter, S.W.; Choi, A.M. Autophagy: Friend or Foe in Lung Disease? *Ann. Am. Thorac. Soc.* **2016**, *13*, S40–S47. [PubMed]
23. Mizumura, K.; Cloonan, S.M.; Nakahira, K.; Bhashyam, A.R.; Cervo, M.; Kitada, T.; Glass, K.; Owen, C.A.; Mahmood, A.; Washko, G.R.; et al. Mitophagy-dependent necroptosis contributes to the pathogenesis of COPD. *J. Clin. Investig.* **2014**, *124*, 3987–4003. [CrossRef]

24. Sentelle, R.D.; Senkal, C.E.; Jiang, W.; Ponnusamy, S.; Gencer, S.; Selvam, S.P.; Ramshesh, V.K.; Peterson, Y.K.; Lemasters, J.J.; Szulc, Z.M.; et al. Ceramide targets autophagosomes to mitochondria and induces lethal mitophagy. *Nat. Chem. Biol.* **2012**, *8*, 831–838. [CrossRef] [PubMed]

25. Liu, B.; Fang, M.; Hu, Y.; Huang, B.; Li, N.; Chang, C.; Huang, R.; Xu, X.; Yang, Z.; Chen, Z.; et al. Hepatitis B virus X protein inhibits autophagic degradation by impairing lysosomal maturation. *Autophagy* **2014**, *10*, 416–430. [CrossRef] [PubMed]

26. Sir, D.; Tian, Y.; Chen, W.L.; Ann, D.K.; Yen, T.S.; Ou, J.H. The early autophagic pathway is activated by hepatitis B virus and required for viral DNA replication. *Proc. Natl. Acad. Sci. USA* **2010**, *107*, 4383–4388. [CrossRef] [PubMed]

27. Deretic, V.; Levine, B. Autophagy, immunity, and microbial adaptations. *Cell Host Microbe* **2009**, *5*, 527–549. [CrossRef]

28. Lam, H.C.; Cloonan, S.M.; Bhashyam, A.R.; Haspel, J.A.; Singh, A.; Sathirapongsasuti, J.F.; Cervo, M.; Yao, H.; Chung, A.L.; Mizumura, K.; et al. Histone deacetylase 6-mediated selective autophagy regulates COPD-associated cilia dysfunction. *J. Clin. Investig.* **2013**, *123*, 5212–5230. [CrossRef]

29. Cloonan, S.M.; Lam, H.C.; Ryter, S.W.; Choi, A.M. "Ciliophagy": The consumption of cilia components by autophagy. *Autophagy* **2014**, *10*, 532–534. [CrossRef]

30. Matute-Bello, G.; Frevert, C.W.; Martin, T.R. Animal models of acute lung injury. *Am. J. Physiol. Lung Cell. Mol. Physiol.* **2008**, *295*, L379–L399. [CrossRef]

31. Lang, J.D.; McArdle, P.J.; O'Reilly, P.J.; Matalon, S. Oxidant-antioxidant balance in acute lung injury. *Chest* **2002**, *122*, 314S–320S. [CrossRef] [PubMed]

32. Li, Z.Y.; Wu, Y.F.; Xu, X.C.; Zhou, J.S.; Wang, Y.; Shen, H.H.; Chen, Z.H. Autophagy as a double-edged sword in pulmonary epithelial injury: A review and perspective. *Am. J. Physiol. Lung Cell. Mol. Physiol.* **2017**, *313*, L207–L217. [CrossRef] [PubMed]

33. Yuan, K.; Huang, C.; Fox, J.; Laturnus, D.; Carlson, E.; Zhang, B.; Yin, Q.; Gao, H.; Wu, M. Autophagy plays an essential role in the clearance of Pseudomonas aeruginosa by alveolar macrophages. *J. Cell Sci.* **2012**, *125*, 507–515. [CrossRef] [PubMed]

34. Li, R.; Tan, S.; Yu, M.; Jundt, M.C.; Zhang, S.; Wu, M. Annexin A2 Regulates Autophagy in Pseudomonas aeruginosa Infection through the Akt1-mTOR-ULK1/2 Signaling Pathway. *J. Immunol.* **2015**, *195*, 3901–3911. [CrossRef] [PubMed]

35. Li, X.; He, S.; Zhou, X.; Ye, Y.; Tan, S.; Zhang, S.; Li, R.; Yu, M.; Jundt, M.C.; Hidebrand, A.; et al. Lyn Delivers Bacteria to Lysosomes for Eradication through TLR2-Initiated Autophagy Related Phagocytosis. *PLoS Pathog.* **2016**, *12*, e1005363. [CrossRef] [PubMed]

36. Jati, S.; Kundu, S.; Chakraborty, A.; Mahata, S.K.; Nizet, V.; Sen, M. Wnt5A Signaling Promotes Defense Against Bacterial Pathogens by Activating a Host Autophagy Circuit. *Front. Immunol.* **2018**, *9*, 679. [CrossRef]

37. Li, X.; Ye, Y.; Zhou, X.; Huang, C.; Wu, M. Atg7 enhances host defense against infection via downregulation of superoxide but upregulation of nitric oxide. *J. Immunol.* **2015**, *194*, 1112–1121. [CrossRef] [PubMed]

38. Jabir, M.S.; Ritchie, N.D.; Li, D.; Bayes, H.K.; Tourlomousis, P.; Puleston, D.; Lupton, A.; Hopkins, L.; Simon, A.K.; Bryant, C.; et al. Caspase-1 cleavage of the TLR adaptor TRIF inhibits autophagy and beta-interferon production during Pseudomonas aeruginosa infection. *Cell Host Microbe* **2014**, *15*, 214–227. [CrossRef] [PubMed]

39. Jabir, M.S.; Hopkins, L.; Ritchie, N.D.; Ullah, I.; Bayes, H.K.; Li, D.; Tourlomousis, P.; Lupton, A.; Puleston, D.; Simon, A.K.; et al. Mitochondrial damage contributes to Pseudomonas aeruginosa activation of the inflammasome and is downregulated by autophagy. *Autophagy* **2015**, *11*, 166–182. [CrossRef]

40. Ye, Y.; Li, X.; Wang, W.; Ouedraogo, K.C.; Li, Y.; Gan, C.; Tan, S.; Zhou, X.; Wu, M. Atg7 deficiency impairs host defense against Klebsiella pneumoniae by impacting bacterial clearance, survival and inflammatory responses in mice. *Am. J. Physiol. Lung Cell. Mol. Physiol.* **2014**, *307*, L355–L363. [CrossRef]

41. Ye, Y.; Tan, S.; Zhou, X.; Li, X.; Jundt, M.C.; Lichter, N.; Hidebrand, A.; Dhasarathy, A.; Wu, M. Inhibition of p-IkappaBalpha Ubiquitylation by Autophagy-Related Gene 7 to Regulate Inflammatory Responses to Bacterial Infection. *J. Infect. Dis.* **2015**, *212*, 1816–1826. [CrossRef] [PubMed]

42. Papayannopoulos, V. Neutrophil extracellular traps in immunity and disease. *Nat. Rev. Immunol.* **2018**, *18*, 134–147. [CrossRef] [PubMed]

43. Tripathi, J.K.; Sharma, A.; Sukumaran, P.; Sun, Y.; Mishra, B.B.; Singh, B.B.; Sharma, J. Oxidant sensor cation channel TRPM2 regulates neutrophil extracellular trap formation and protects against pneumoseptic bacterial infection. *FASEB J.* **2018**. [CrossRef] [PubMed]

44. Sharma, A.; Simonson, T.J.; Jondle, C.N.; Mishra, B.B.; Sharma, J. Mincle-Mediated Neutrophil Extracellular Trap Formation by Regulation of Autophagy. *J. Infect. Dis.* **2017**, *215*, 1040–1048. [CrossRef] [PubMed]

45. Tang, D.; Kang, R.; Coyne, C.B.; Zeh, H.J.; Lotze, M.T. PAMPs and DAMPs: Signal 0s that spur autophagy and immunity. *Immunol. Rev.* **2012**, *249*, 158–175. [CrossRef] [PubMed]

46. Aguirre, A.; Lopez-Alonso, I.; Gonzalez-Lopez, A.; Amado-Rodriguez, L.; Batalla-Solis, E.; Astudillo, A.; Blazquez-Prieto, J.; Fernandez, A.F.; Galvan, J.A.; dos Santos, C.C.; et al. Defective autophagy impairs ATF3 activity and worsens lung injury during endotoxemia. *J. Mol. Med.* **2014**, *92*, 665–676. [CrossRef] [PubMed]

47. Zeng, M.; Sang, W.; Chen, S.; Chen, R.; Zhang, H.; Xue, F.; Li, Z.; Liu, Y.; Gong, Y.; Kong, X. 4-PBA inhibits LPS-induced inflammation through regulating ER stress and autophagy in acute lung injury models. *Toxicol. Lett.* **2017**, *271*, 26–37. [CrossRef]

48. Hu, Y.; Lou, J.; Mao, Y.Y.; Lai, T.W.; Liu, L.Y.; Zhu, C.; Zhang, C.; Liu, J.; Li, Y.Y.; Zhang, F.; et al. Activation of MTOR in pulmonary epithelium promotes LPS-induced acute lung injury. *Autophagy* **2016**, *12*, 2286–2299. [CrossRef]

49. Fan, K.; Lin, L.; Ai, Q.; Wan, J.; Dai, J.; Liu, G.; Tang, L.; Yang, Y.; Ge, P.; Jiang, R.; et al. Lipopolysaccharide-Induced Dephosphorylation of AMPK-Activated Protein Kinase Potentiates Inflammatory Injury via Repression of ULK1-Dependent Autophagy. *Front. Immunol.* **2018**, *9*, 1464. [CrossRef]

50. Zhang, D.; Zhou, J.; Ye, L.C.; Li, J.; Wu, Z.; Li, Y.; Li, C. Autophagy maintains the integrity of endothelial barrier in LPS-induced lung injury. *J. Cell. Physiol.* **2018**, *233*, 688–698. [CrossRef]

51. Dong, W.; He, B.; Qian, H.; Liu, Q.; Wang, D.; Li, J.; Wei, Z.; Wang, Z.; Xu, Z.; Wu, G.; et al. RAB26-dependent autophagy protects adherens junctional integrity in acute lung injury. *Autophagy* **2018**, *14*, 1677–1692. [CrossRef] [PubMed]

52. Slavin, S.A.; Leonard, A.; Grose, V.; Fazal, F.; Rahman, A. Autophagy inhibitor 3-methyladenine protects against endothelial cell barrier dysfunction in acute lung injury. *Am. J. Physiol. Lung Cell. Mol. Physiol.* **2018**, *314*, L388–L396. [CrossRef] [PubMed]

53. Guo, L.; Stripay, J.L.; Zhang, X.; Collage, R.D.; Hulver, M.; Carchman, E.H.; Howell, G.M.; Zuckerbraun, B.S.; Lee, J.S.; Rosengart, M.R. CaMKIalpha regulates AMP kinase-dependent, TORC-1-independent autophagy during lipopolysaccharide-induced acute lung neutrophilic inflammation. *J. Immunol.* **2013**, *190*, 3620–3628. [CrossRef] [PubMed]

54. Liu, H.; Zhou, K.; Liao, L.; Zhang, T.; Yang, M.; Sun, C. Lipoxin A4 receptor agonist BML-111 induces autophagy in alveolar macrophages and protects from acute lung injury by activating MAPK signaling. *Respir. Res.* **2018**, *19*, 243. [CrossRef] [PubMed]

55. Rudd, K.E.; Kissoon, N.; Limmathurotsakul, D.; Bory, S.; Mutahunga, B.; Seymour, C.W.; Angus, D.C.; West, T.E. The global burden of sepsis: Barriers and potential solutions. *Crit. Care* **2018**, *22*, 232. [CrossRef]

56. Yen, Y.T.; Yang, H.R.; Lo, H.C.; Hsieh, Y.C.; Tsai, S.C.; Hong, C.W.; Hsieh, C.H. Enhancing autophagy with activated protein C and rapamycin protects against sepsis-induced acute lung injury. *Surgery* **2013**, *153*, 689–698. [CrossRef] [PubMed]

57. Lo, S.; Yuan, S.S.; Hsu, C.; Cheng, Y.J.; Chang, Y.F.; Hsueh, H.W.; Lee, P.H.; Hsieh, Y.C. Lc3 over-expression improves survival and attenuates lung injury through increasing autophagosomal clearance in septic mice. *Ann. Surg.* **2013**, *257*, 352–363. [CrossRef]

58. Mannam, P.; Shinn, A.S.; Srivastava, A.; Neamu, R.F.; Walker, W.E.; Bohanon, M.; Merkel, J.; Kang, M.J.; Dela Cruz, C.S.; Ahasic, A.M.; et al. MKK3 regulates mitochondrial biogenesis and mitophagy in sepsis-induced lung injury. *Am. J. Physiol. Lung Cell. Mol. Physiol.* **2014**, *306*, L604–L619. [CrossRef]

59. Pu, Q.; Gan, C.; Li, R.; Li, Y.; Tan, S.; Li, X.; Wei, Y.; Lan, L.; Deng, X.; Liang, H.; et al. Atg7 Deficiency Intensifies Inflammasome Activation and Pyroptosis in Pseudomonas Sepsis. *J. Immunol.* **2017**, *198*, 3205–3213. [CrossRef]

60. Park, S.Y.; Shrestha, S.; Youn, Y.J.; Kim, J.K.; Kim, S.Y.; Kim, H.J.; Park, S.H.; Ahn, W.G.; Kim, S.; Lee, M.G.; et al. Autophagy Primes Neutrophils for Neutrophil Extracellular Trap Formation during Sepsis. *Am. J. Respir. Crit. Care Med.* **2017**, *196*, 577–589. [CrossRef]

61. Liu, F.; Nie, C.; Zhao, N.; Wang, Y.; Liu, Y.; Li, Y.; Zeng, Z.; Ding, C.; Shao, Q.; Qing, C.; et al. MiR-155 Alleviates Septic Lung Injury by Inducing Autophagy Via Inhibition of Transforming Growth Factor-beta-Activated Binding Protein 2. *Shock* **2017**, *48*, 61–68. [CrossRef] [PubMed]

62. Figueiredo, N.; Chora, A.; Raquel, H.; Pejanovic, N.; Pereira, P.; Hartleben, B.; Neves-Costa, A.; Moita, C.; Pedroso, D.; Pinto, A.; et al. Anthracyclines induce DNA damage response-mediated protection against severe sepsis. *Immunity* **2013**, *39*, 874–884. [CrossRef] [PubMed]

63. Lee, S.J.; Ryter, S.W.; Xu, J.F.; Nakahira, K.; Kim, H.P.; Choi, A.M.; Kim, Y.S. Carbon monoxide activates autophagy via mitochondrial reactive oxygen species formation. *Am. J. Respir. Cell Mol. Biol.* **2011**, *45*, 867–873. [CrossRef] [PubMed]

64. Lee, S.; Lee, S.J.; Coronata, A.A.; Fredenburgh, L.E.; Chung, S.W.; Perrella, M.A.; Nakahira, K.; Ryter, S.W.; Choi, A.M. Carbon monoxide confers protection in sepsis by enhancing beclin 1-dependent autophagy and phagocytosis. *Antioxid. Redox Signal.* **2014**, *20*, 432–442. [CrossRef] [PubMed]

65. Dias-Freitas, F.; Metelo-Coimbra, C.; Roncon-Albuquerque, R., Jr. Molecular mechanisms underlying hyperoxia acute lung injury. *Respir. Med.* **2016**, *119*, 23–28. [CrossRef] [PubMed]

66. Zaher, T.E.; Miller, E.J.; Morrow, D.M.; Javdan, M.; Mantell, L.L. Hyperoxia-induced signal transduction pathways in pulmonary epithelial cells. *Free Radic. Biol. Med.* **2007**, *42*, 897–908. [CrossRef] [PubMed]

67. Tanaka, A.; Jin, Y.; Lee, S.J.; Zhang, M.; Kim, H.P.; Stolz, D.B.; Ryter, S.W.; Choi, A.M. Hyperoxia-induced LC3B interacts with the Fas apoptotic pathway in epithelial cell death. *Am. J. Respir. Cell Mol. Biol.* **2012**, *46*, 507–514. [CrossRef]

68. Liang, X.; Wei, S.Q.; Lee, S.J.; Fung, J.K.; Zhang, M.; Tanaka, A.; Choi, A.M.; Jin, Y. p62 sequestosome 1/light chain 3b complex confers cytoprotection on lung epithelial cells after hyperoxia. *Am. J. Respir. Cell Mol. Biol.* **2013**, *48*, 489–496. [CrossRef]

69. Zhang, L.; Zhao, S.; Yuan, L.J.; Wu, H.M.; Jiang, H.; Zhao, S.M.; Luo, G.; Xue, X.D. Autophagy regulates hyperoxia-induced intracellular accumulation of surfactant protein C in alveolar type II cells. *Mol. Cell. Biochem.* **2015**, *408*, 181–189. [CrossRef]

70. Zhang, L.; Zhao, S.; Yuan, L.; Wu, H.; Jiang, H.; Luo, G. Hyperoxia-mediated LC3B activation contributes to the impaired transdifferentiation of type II alveolar epithelial cells (AECIIs) to type I cells (AECIs). *Clin. Exp. Pharmacol. Physiol.* **2016**, *43*, 834–843. [CrossRef]

71. Ye, Y.; Lin, P.; Zhang, W.; Tan, S.; Zhou, X.; Li, R.; Pu, Q.; Koff, J.L.; Dhasarathy, A.; Ma, F.; et al. DNA Repair Interacts with Autophagy To Regulate Inflammatory Responses to Pulmonary Hyperoxia. *J. Immunol.* **2017**, *198*, 2844–2853. [CrossRef]

72. Narala, V.R.; Fukumoto, J.; Hernandez-Cuervo, H.; Patil, S.S.; Krishnamurthy, S.; Breitzig, M.; Galam, L.; Soundararajan, R.; Lockey, R.F.; Kolliputi, N. Akap1 genetic deletion increases the severity of hyperoxia-induced acute lung injury in mice. *Am. J. Physiol. Lung Cell. Mol. Physiol.* **2018**, *314*, L860–L870. [CrossRef]

73. Ma, C.; Beyer, A.M.; Durand, M.; Clough, A.V.; Zhu, D.; Norwood Toro, L.; Terashvili, M.; Ebben, J.D.; Hill, R.B.; Audi, S.H.; et al. Hyperoxia Causes Mitochondrial Fragmentation in Pulmonary Endothelial Cells by Increasing Expression of Pro-Fission Proteins. *Arterioscler. Thromb. Vasc. Biol.* **2018**, *38*, 622–635. [CrossRef]

74. Zhang, Y.; Jiang, G.; Sauler, M.; Lee, P.J. Lung endothelial HO-1 targeting in vivo using lentiviral miRNA regulates apoptosis and autophagy during oxidant injury. *FASEB J.* **2013**, *27*, 4041–4058. [CrossRef]

75. Zhang, Y.; Sauler, M.; Shinn, A.S.; Gong, H.; Haslip, M.; Shan, P.; Mannam, P.; Lee, P.J. Endothelial PINK1 mediates the protective effects of NLRP3 deficiency during lethal oxidant injury. *J. Immunol.* **2014**, *192*, 5296–5304. [CrossRef]

76. Evans, R.B. Chlorine: State of the art. *Lung* **2005**, *183*, 151–167. [CrossRef]

77. Carlisle, M.; Lam, A.; Svendsen, E.R.; Aggarwal, S.; Matalon, S. Chlorine-induced cardiopulmonary injury. *Ann. N. Y. Acad. Sci.* **2016**, *1374*, 159–167. [CrossRef]

78. Jurkuvenaite, A.; Benavides, G.A.; Komarova, S.; Doran, S.F.; Johnson, M.; Aggarwal, S.; Zhang, J.; Darley-Usmar, V.M.; Matalon, S. Upregulation of autophagy decreases chlorine-induced mitochondrial injury and lung inflammation. *Free Radic. Biol. Med.* **2015**, *85*, 83–94. [CrossRef]

79. Wolters, P.J.; Collard, H.R.; Jones, K.D. Pathogenesis of idiopathic pulmonary fibrosis. *Annu. Rev. Pathol.* **2014**, *9*, 157–179. [CrossRef]

80. Patel, A.S.; Lin, L.; Geyer, A.; Haspel, J.A.; An, C.H.; Cao, J.; Rosas, I.O.; Morse, D. Autophagy in idiopathic pulmonary fibrosis. *PLoS ONE* **2012**, *7*, e41394. [CrossRef]

81. Gui, Y.S.; Wang, L.; Tian, X.; Li, X.; Ma, A.; Zhou, W.; Zeng, N.; Zhang, J.; Cai, B.; Zhang, H.; et al. mTOR Overactivation and Compromised Autophagy in the Pathogenesis of Pulmonary Fibrosis. *PLoS ONE* **2015**, *10*, e0138625. [CrossRef]

82. Araya, J.; Kojima, J.; Takasaka, N.; Ito, S.; Fujii, S.; Hara, H.; Yanagisawa, H.; Kobayashi, K.; Tsurushige, C.; Kawaishi, M.; et al. Insufficient autophagy in idiopathic pulmonary fibrosis. *Am. J. Physiol. Lung Cell. Mol. Physiol.* **2013**, *304*, L56–L69. [CrossRef]

83. Wang, K.; Zhang, T.; Lei, Y.; Li, X.; Jiang, J.; Lan, J.; Liu, Y.; Chen, H.; Gao, W.; Xie, N.; et al. Identification of ANXA2 (annexin A2) as a specific bleomycin target to induce pulmonary fibrosis by impeding TFEB-mediated autophagic flux. *Autophagy* **2018**, *14*, 269–282. [CrossRef]

84. Mi, S.; Li, Z.; Yang, H.Z.; Liu, H.; Wang, J.P.; Ma, Y.G.; Wang, X.X.; Liu, H.Z.; Sun, W.; Hu, Z.W. Blocking IL-17A promotes the resolution of pulmonary inflammation and fibrosis via TGF-beta1-dependent and -independent mechanisms. *J. Immunol.* **2011**, *187*, 3003–3014. [CrossRef]

85. Liu, H.; Mi, S.; Li, Z.; Hua, F.; Hu, Z.W. Interleukin 17A inhibits autophagy through activation of PIK3CA to interrupt the GSK3B-mediated degradation of BCL2 in lung epithelial cells. *Autophagy* **2013**, *9*, 730–742. [CrossRef]

86. Cabrera, S.; Maciel, M.; Herrera, I.; Nava, T.; Vergara, F.; Gaxiola, M.; Lopez-Otin, C.; Selman, M.; Pardo, A. Essential role for the ATG4B protease and autophagy in bleomycin-induced pulmonary fibrosis. *Autophagy* **2015**, *11*, 670–684. [CrossRef]

87. Singh, K.K.; Lovren, F.; Pan, Y.; Quan, A.; Ramadan, A.; Matkar, P.N.; Ehsan, M.; Sandhu, P.; Mantella, L.E.; Gupta, N.; et al. The essential autophagy gene ATG7 modulates organ fibrosis via regulation of endothelial-to-mesenchymal transition. *J. Biol. Chem.* **2015**, *290*, 2547–2559. [CrossRef]

88. Yang, H.Z.; Wang, J.P.; Mi, S.; Liu, H.Z.; Cui, B.; Yan, H.M.; Yan, J.; Li, Z.; Liu, H.; Hua, F.; et al. TLR4 activity is required in the resolution of pulmonary inflammation and fibrosis after acute and chronic lung injury. *Am. J. Pathol.* **2012**, *180*, 275–292. [CrossRef]

89. Ricci, A.; Cherubini, E.; Scozzi, D.; Pietrangeli, V.; Tabbi, L.; Raffa, S.; Leone, L.; Visco, V.; Torrisi, M.R.; Bruno, P.; et al. Decreased expression of autophagic beclin 1 protein in idiopathic pulmonary fibrosis fibroblasts. *J. Cell. Physiol.* **2013**, *228*, 1516–1524. [CrossRef]

90. Romero, Y.; Bueno, M.; Ramirez, R.; Alvarez, D.; Sembrat, J.C.; Goncharova, E.A.; Rojas, M.; Selman, M.; Mora, A.L.; Pardo, A. mTORC1 activation decreases autophagy in aging and idiopathic pulmonary fibrosis and contributes to apoptosis resistance in IPF fibroblasts. *Aging Cell* **2016**, *15*, 1103–1112. [CrossRef]

91. Im, J.; Hergert, P.; Nho, R.S. Reduced FoxO3a expression causes low autophagy in idiopathic pulmonary fibrosis fibroblasts on collagen matrices. *Am. J. Physiol. Lung Cell. Mol. Physiol.* **2015**, *309*, L552–L561. [CrossRef]

92. Bueno, M.; Lai, Y.C.; Romero, Y.; Brands, J.; St Croix, C.M.; Kamga, C.; Corey, C.; Herazo-Maya, J.D.; Sembrat, J.; Lee, J.S.; et al. PINK1 deficiency impairs mitochondrial homeostasis and promotes lung fibrosis. *J. Clin. Investig.* **2015**, *125*, 521–538. [CrossRef]

93. Kobayashi, K.; Araya, J.; Minagawa, S.; Hara, H.; Saito, N.; Kadota, T.; Sato, N.; Yoshida, M.; Tsubouchi, K.; Kurita, Y.; et al. Involvement of PARK2-Mediated Mitophagy in Idiopathic Pulmonary Fibrosis Pathogenesis. *J. Immunol.* **2016**, *197*, 504–516. [CrossRef]

94. Kurita, Y.; Araya, J.; Minagawa, S.; Hara, H.; Ichikawa, A.; Saito, N.; Kadota, T.; Tsubouchi, K.; Sato, N.; Yoshida, M.; et al. Pirfenidone inhibits myofibroblast differentiation and lung fibrosis development during insufficient mitophagy. *Respir. Res.* **2017**, *18*, 114. [CrossRef]

95. Larson-Casey, J.L.; Deshane, J.S.; Ryan, A.J.; Thannickal, V.J.; Carter, A.B. Macrophage Akt1 Kinase-Mediated Mitophagy Modulates Apoptosis Resistance and Pulmonary Fibrosis. *Immunity* **2016**, *44*, 582–596. [CrossRef]

96. Tuder, R.M.; Petrache, I. Pathogenesis of chronic obstructive pulmonary disease. *J. Clin. Investig.* **2012**, *122*, 2749–2755. [CrossRef]

97. Ryter, S.W.; Chen, Z.H.; Kim, H.P.; Choi, A.M. Autophagy in chronic obstructive pulmonary disease: Homeostatic or pathogenic mechanism? *Autophagy* **2009**, *5*, 235–237. [CrossRef]

98. Chen, Z.H.; Kim, H.P.; Sciurba, F.C.; Lee, S.J.; Feghali-Bostwick, C.; Stolz, D.B.; Dhir, R.; Landreneau, R.J.; Schuchert, M.J.; Yousem, S.A.; et al. Egr-1 regulates autophagy in cigarette smoke-induced chronic obstructive pulmonary disease. *PLoS ONE* **2008**, *3*, e3316. [CrossRef]

99. Kim, H.P.; Wang, X.; Chen, Z.H.; Lee, S.J.; Huang, M.H.; Wang, Y.; Ryter, S.W.; Choi, A.M. Autophagic proteins regulate cigarette smoke-induced apoptosis: Protective role of heme oxygenase-1. *Autophagy* **2008**, *4*, 887–895. [CrossRef]

100. Wang, Y.; Liu, J.; Zhou, J.S.; Huang, H.Q.; Li, Z.Y.; Xu, X.C.; Lai, T.W.; Hu, Y.; Zhou, H.B.; Chen, H.P.; et al. MTOR Suppresses Cigarette Smoke-Induced Epithelial Cell Death and Airway Inflammation in Chronic Obstructive Pulmonary Disease. *J. Immunol.* **2018**, *200*, 2571–2580. [CrossRef]

101. Hou, H.H.; Cheng, S.L.; Chung, K.P.; Kuo, M.Y.; Yeh, C.C.; Chang, B.E.; Lu, H.H.; Wang, H.C.; Yu, C.J. Elastase induces lung epithelial cell autophagy through placental growth factor: A new insight of emphysema pathogenesis. *Autophagy* **2014**, *10*, 1509–1521. [CrossRef]

102. Wang, G.; Zhou, H.; Strulovici-Barel, Y.; Al-Hijji, M.; Ou, X.; Salit, J.; Walters, M.S.; Staudt, M.R.; Kaner, R.J.; Crystal, R.G. Role of OSGIN1 in mediating smoking-induced autophagy in the human airway epithelium. *Autophagy* **2017**, *13*, 1205–1220. [CrossRef]

103. Chen, Z.H.; Lam, H.C.; Jin, Y.; Kim, H.P.; Cao, J.; Lee, S.J.; Ifedigbo, E.; Parameswaran, H.; Ryter, S.W.; Choi, A.M. Autophagy protein microtubule-associated protein 1 light chain-3B (LC3B) activates extrinsic apoptosis during cigarette smoke-induced emphysema. *Proc. Natl. Acad. Sci. USA* **2010**, *107*, 18880–18885. [CrossRef]

104. Li, X.; Yang, H.; Sun, H.; Lu, R.; Zhang, C.; Gao, N.; Meng, Q.; Wu, S.; Wang, S.; Aschner, M.; et al. Taurine ameliorates particulate matter-induced emphysema by switching on mitochondrial NADH dehydrogenase genes. *Proc. Natl. Acad. Sci. USA* **2017**, *114*, E9655–E9664. [CrossRef]

105. Lv, X.X.; Liu, S.S.; Li, K.; Cui, B.; Liu, C.; Hu, Z.W. Cigarette smoke promotes COPD by activating platelet-activating factor receptor and inducing neutrophil autophagic death in mice. *Oncotarget* **2017**, *8*, 74720–74735. [CrossRef]

106. Fujii, S.; Hara, H.; Araya, J.; Takasaka, N.; Kojima, J.; Ito, S.; Minagawa, S.; Yumino, Y.; Ishikawa, T.; Numata, T.; et al. Insufficient autophagy promotes bronchial epithelial cell senescence in chronic obstructive pulmonary disease. *Oncoimmunology* **2012**, *1*, 630–641. [CrossRef]

107. Takasaka, N.; Araya, J.; Hara, H.; Ito, S.; Kobayashi, K.; Kurita, Y.; Wakui, H.; Yoshii, Y.; Yumino, Y.; Fujii, S.; et al. Autophagy induction by SIRT6 through attenuation of insulin-like growth factor signaling is involved in the regulation of human bronchial epithelial cell senescence. *J. Immunol.* **2014**, *192*, 958–968. [CrossRef]

108. Tran, I.; Ji, C.; Ni, I.; Min, T.; Tang, D.; Vij, N. Role of Cigarette Smoke-Induced Aggresome Formation in Chronic Obstructive Pulmonary Disease-Emphysema Pathogenesis. *Am. J. Respir. Cell Mol. Biol.* **2015**, *53*, 159–173. [CrossRef]

109. Bodas, M.; Pehote, G.; Silverberg, D.; Gulbins, E.; Vij, N. Autophagy augmentation alleviates cigarette smoke-induced CFTR-dysfunction, ceramide-accumulation and COPD-emphysema pathogenesis. *Free Radic. Biol. Med.* **2018**, *131*, 81–97. [CrossRef]

110. Bodas, M.; Patel, N.; Silverberg, D.; Walworth, K.; Vij, N. Master Autophagy Regulator Transcription Factor EB Regulates Cigarette Smoke-Induced Autophagy Impairment and Chronic Obstructive Pulmonary Disease-Emphysema Pathogenesis. *Antioxid. Redox Signal.* **2017**, *27*, 150–167. [CrossRef]

111. Ito, S.; Araya, J.; Kurita, Y.; Kobayashi, K.; Takasaka, N.; Yoshida, M.; Hara, H.; Minagawa, S.; Wakui, H.; Fujii, S.; et al. PARK2-mediated mitophagy is involved in regulation of HBEC senescence in COPD pathogenesis. *Autophagy* **2015**, *11*, 547–559. [CrossRef]

112. Araya, J.; Tsubouchi, K.; Sato, N.; Ito, S.; Minagawa, S.; Hara, H.; Hosaka, Y.; Ichikawa, A.; Saito, N.; Kadota, T.; et al. PRKN-regulated mitophagy and cellular senescence during COPD pathogenesis. *Autophagy* **2018**. [CrossRef]

113. Monick, M.M.; Powers, L.S.; Walters, K.; Lovan, N.; Zhang, M.; Gerke, A.; Hansdottir, S.; Hunninghake, G.W. Identification of an autophagy defect in smokers' alveolar macrophages. *J. Immunol.* **2010**, *185*, 5425–5435. [CrossRef]

114. Gutierrez, M.G.; Master, S.S.; Singh, S.B.; Taylor, G.A.; Colombo, M.I.; Deretic, V. Autophagy is a defense mechanism inhibiting BCG and Mycobacterium tuberculosis survival in infected macrophages. *Cell* **2004**, *119*, 753–766. [CrossRef]

115. Chandra, P.; Kumar, D. Selective autophagy gets more selective: Uncoupling of autophagy flux and xenophagy flux in Mycobacterium tuberculosis-infected macrophages. *Autophagy* **2016**, *12*, 608–609. [CrossRef]

116. Campbell, G.R.; Spector, S.A. Vitamin D inhibits human immunodeficiency virus type 1 and Mycobacterium tuberculosis infection in macrophages through the induction of autophagy. *PLoS Pathog.* **2012**, *8*, e1002689. [CrossRef]

117. Castillo, E.F.; Dekonenko, A.; Arko-Mensah, J.; Mandell, M.A.; Dupont, N.; Jiang, S.; Delgado-Vargas, M.; Timmins, G.S.; Bhattacharya, D.; Yang, H.; et al. Autophagy protects against active tuberculosis by suppressing bacterial burden and inflammation. *Proc. Natl. Acad. Sci. USA* **2012**, *109*, E3168–E3176. [CrossRef]

118. Kim, J.K.; Lee, H.M.; Park, K.S.; Shin, D.M.; Kim, T.S.; Kim, Y.S.; Suh, H.W.; Kim, S.Y.; Kim, I.S.; Kim, J.M.; et al. MIR144* inhibits antimicrobial responses against Mycobacterium tuberculosis in human monocytes and macrophages by targeting the autophagy protein DRAM2. *Autophagy* **2017**, *13*, 423–441. [CrossRef]

119. Tateosian, N.L.; Pellegrini, J.M.; Amiano, N.O.; Rolandelli, A.; Casco, N.; Palmero, D.J.; Colombo, M.I.; Garcia, V.E. IL17A augments autophagy in Mycobacterium tuberculosis-infected monocytes from patients with active tuberculosis in association with the severity of the disease. *Autophagy* **2017**, *13*, 1191–1204. [CrossRef]

120. Etna, M.P.; Sinigaglia, A.; Grassi, A.; Giacomini, E.; Romagnoli, A.; Pardini, M.; Severa, M.; Cruciani, M.; Rizzo, F.; Anastasiadou, E.; et al. Mycobacterium tuberculosis-induced miR-155 subverts autophagy by targeting ATG3 in human dendritic cells. *PLoS Pathog.* **2018**, *14*, e1006790. [CrossRef]

121. Fine, K.L.; Metcalfe, M.G.; White, E.; Virji, M.; Karls, R.K.; Quinn, F.D. Involvement of the autophagy pathway in trafficking of Mycobacterium tuberculosis bacilli through cultured human type II epithelial cells. *Cell. Microbiol.* **2012**, *14*, 1402–1414. [CrossRef]

122. Romagnoli, A.; Etna, M.P.; Giacomini, E.; Pardini, M.; Remoli, M.E.; Corazzari, M.; Falasca, L.; Goletti, D.; Gafa, V.; Simeone, R.; et al. ESX-1 dependent impairment of autophagic flux by Mycobacterium tuberculosis in human dendritic cells. *Autophagy* **2012**, *8*, 1357–1370. [CrossRef] [PubMed]

123. Kimmey, J.M.; Huynh, J.P.; Weiss, L.A.; Park, S.; Kambal, A.; Debnath, J.; Virgin, H.W.; Stallings, C.L. Unique role for ATG5 in neutrophil-mediated immunopathology during M. tuberculosis infection. *Nature* **2015**, *528*, 565–569. [CrossRef]

124. Villella, V.R.; Esposito, S.; Bruscia, E.M.; Maiuri, M.C.; Raia, V.; Kroemer, G.; Maiuri, L. Targeting the Intracellular Environment in Cystic Fibrosis: Restoring Autophagy as a Novel Strategy to Circumvent the CFTR Defect. *Front. Pharmacol.* **2013**, *4*, 1. [CrossRef] [PubMed]

125. Junkins, R.D.; McCormick, C.; Lin, T.J. The emerging potential of autophagy-based therapies in the treatment of cystic fibrosis lung infections. *Autophagy* **2014**, *10*, 538–547. [CrossRef]

126. Luciani, A.; Villella, V.R.; Esposito, S.; Brunetti-Pierri, N.; Medina, D.; Settembre, C.; Gavina, M.; Pulze, L.; Giardino, I.; Pettoello-Mantovani, M.; et al. Defective CFTR induces aggresome formation and lung inflammation in cystic fibrosis through ROS-mediated autophagy inhibition. *Nat. Cell Biol.* **2010**, *12*, 863–875. [CrossRef] [PubMed]

127. Luciani, A.; Villella, V.R.; Esposito, S.; Gavina, M.; Russo, I.; Silano, M.; Guido, S.; Pettoello-Mantovani, M.; Carnuccio, R.; Scholte, B.; et al. Targeting autophagy as a novel strategy for facilitating the therapeutic action of potentiators on DeltaF508 cystic fibrosis transmembrane conductance regulator. *Autophagy* **2012**, *8*, 1657–1672. [CrossRef]

128. Mayer, M.L.; Blohmke, C.J.; Falsafi, R.; Fjell, C.D.; Madera, L.; Turvey, S.E.; Hancock, R.E. Rescue of dysfunctional autophagy attenuates hyperinflammatory responses from cystic fibrosis cells. *J. Immunol.* **2013**, *190*, 1227–1238. [CrossRef]

129. Renna, M.; Schaffner, C.; Brown, K.; Shang, S.; Tamayo, M.H.; Hegyi, K.; Grimsey, N.J.; Cusens, D.; Coulter, S.; Cooper, J.; et al. Azithromycin blocks autophagy and may predispose cystic fibrosis patients to mycobacterial infection. *J. Clin. Investig.* **2011**, *121*, 3554–3563. [CrossRef]

130. Abdulrahman, B.A.; Khweek, A.A.; Akhter, A.; Caution, K.; Kotrange, S.; Abdelaziz, D.H.; Newland, C.; Rosales-Reyes, R.; Kopp, B.; McCoy, K.; et al. Autophagy stimulation by rapamycin suppresses lung inflammation and infection by Burkholderia cenocepacia in a model of cystic fibrosis. *Autophagy* **2011**, *7*, 1359–1370. [CrossRef]

131. Abdulrahman, B.A.; Khweek, A.A.; Akhter, A.; Caution, K.; Tazi, M.; Hassan, H.; Zhang, Y.; Rowland, P.D.; Malhotra, S.; Aeffner, F.; et al. Depletion of the ubiquitin-binding adaptor molecule SQSTM1/p62 from macrophages harboring cftr DeltaF508 mutation improves the delivery of Burkholderia cenocepacia to the autophagic machinery. *J. Biol. Chem.* **2013**, *288*, 2049–2058. [CrossRef] [PubMed]

132. Lai, Y.C.; Potoka, K.C.; Champion, H.C.; Mora, A.L.; Gladwin, M.T. Pulmonary arterial hypertension: The clinical syndrome. *Circ. Res.* **2014**, *115*, 115–130. [CrossRef] [PubMed]

133. Lee, S.J.; Smith, A.; Guo, L.; Alastalo, T.P.; Li, M.; Sawada, H.; Liu, X.; Chen, Z.H.; Ifedigbo, E.; Jin, Y.; et al. Autophagic protein LC3B confers resistance against hypoxia-induced pulmonary hypertension. *Am. J. Respir. Crit. Care Med.* **2011**, *183*, 649–658. [CrossRef] [PubMed]

134. Long, L.; Yang, X.; Southwood, M.; Lu, J.; Marciniak, S.J.; Dunmore, B.J.; Morrell, N.W. Chloroquine prevents progression of experimental pulmonary hypertension via inhibition of autophagy and lysosomal bone morphogenetic protein type II receptor degradation. *Circ. Res.* **2013**, *112*, 1159–1170. [CrossRef] [PubMed]

135. Zhou, Y.; Wang, Y.; Wang, X.; Tian, X.; Zhang, S.; Yang, F.; Guo, H.; Fan, R.; Feng, N.; Jia, M.; et al. The Protective Effects of Kappa-Opioid Receptor Stimulation in Hypoxic Pulmonary Hypertension Involve Inhibition of Autophagy Through the AMPK-MTOR Pathway. *Cell. Physiol. Biochem.* **2017**, *44*, 1965–1979. [CrossRef] [PubMed]

Review

Relevance of Autophagy in Parenchymal and Non-Parenchymal Liver Cells for Health and Disease

Ralf Weiskirchen [1],* and Frank Tacke [2],*

[1]   Institute of Molecular Pathobiochemistry, Experimental Gene Therapy and Clinical Chemistry, University Hospital RWTH Aachen, D-52074 Aachen, Germany

[2]   Department of Medicine III, University Hospital RWTH Aachen, D-52074 Aachen, Germany

*   Correspondence: rweiskirchen@ukaachen.de (R.W.); frank.tacke@gmx.net (F.T.); Tel.: +49-241-80-88683 (R.W.); +49-241-80-35848 (F.T.)

Received: 13 December 2018; Accepted: 26 December 2018; Published: 1 January 2019

Abstract: Autophagy is a highly conserved intracellular process for the ordered degradation and recycling of cellular components in lysosomes. In the liver, parenchymal cells (i.e., mainly hepatocytes) utilize autophagy to provide amino acids, glucose, and free fatty acids as sources of energy and biosynthesis functions, but also for recycling and controlling organelles such as mitochondria. Non-parenchymal cells of the liver, including endothelial cells, macrophages (Kupffer cells), and hepatic stellate cells (HSC), also employ autophagy, either for maintaining cellular homeostasis (macrophages, endothelium) or for providing energy for their activation (stellate cells). In hepatocytes, autophagy contributes to essential homeostatic functions (e.g., gluconeogenesis, glycogenolysis, fatty acid oxidation), but is also implicated in diseases. For instance, storage disorders (alpha 1 antitrypsin deficiency, Wilson's disease), metabolic (non-alcoholic steatohepatitis, NASH), and toxic (alcohol) liver diseases may benefit from augmenting autophagy in hepatocytes. In hepatic fibrosis, autophagy has been implicated in the fibrogenic activation of HSC to collagen-producing myofibroblasts. In hepatocellular carcinoma (HCC), autophagy may contribute to tumor surveillance as well as invasiveness, indicating a dual and stage-dependent function in cancer. As many drugs directly or indirectly modulate autophagy, it is intriguing to investigate autophagy-targeting, possibly even cell type-directed strategies for the treatment of hereditary liver diseases, NASH, fibrosis, and HCC.

Keywords: hepatocytes; hepatic stellate cells; sinusoidal endothelial cells; macrophages; fibrosis; cirrhosis; hepatocellular carcinoma; biomarkers

---

1. Introduction

The term autophagy summarizes the processes involved in the orderly degradation and recycling of worn, abnormal, or malfunctional cellular components. It is commonly accepted today that the term "autophagy" was first introduced in 1963 by the Belgian cytologist and biochemistry Christian René de Duve, who also coined the terms "endocytosis" and "phagocytosis" to designate pathways bringing substrates for digestion in lysosomes [1]. However, the terms autophagy/autophagy/autophagia were in fact already used a century earlier and published in 1859 in a French journal [2]. The importance of autophagy was prominently acknowledged in 2016, when Yoshinori Ohsumi was awarded the Nobel Prize for Physiology or Medicine for his discoveries of mechanisms for autophagy. Autophagy is nowadays considered as a dynamic recycling system, which is essential for cellular renovation and homeostasis [3]. As such, the resultant degradation products can be used for new protein synthesis, energy production, and gluconeogenesis. There are three classes of autophagy, namely macroautophagy, microautophagy, and chaperone-mediated autophagy, requiring different sets of autophagy-related genes and cellular compounds [3] (Figure 1). Macroautophagy is the most prevalent form of autophagy. It is dependent on the "autophagosome", a spherical vesicle appearing randomly throughout the cytoplasm with the capacity to traffic along microtubules towards the microtubule-organizing center, where lysosomes are concentrated [4]. These ring-shaped structures are majorly formed by the "AuTophaGy" (ATGs) genes that are evolutionarily conserved from yeast to higher eukaryotes. This cellular compartment has the capacity to sequester small portions of cytoplasm enriched in soluble materials and organelles and to fuse with lysosomes forming the autolysosome, in which the material is finally degraded. On the contrary, microautophagy is a more diverse type of autophagy, in which cytoplasmic compounds or spontaneous formed vesicles are directly engulfed by lysosomes. Recent studies demonstrate that this pathway is of particular relevance for cells under amino acid starvation [5]. Based on the finding that vascular membranes and endosomes can also incorporate or capture peroxisomes or lysosome-derived organelles, it was proposed that this autophagy branch should be classified in three distinct subtypes of microautophagy [6]. Chaperone-mediated autophagy is more selective and not associated with membrane reorganization [3]. Instead, chaperone and co-chaperone proteins recognize cytosolic proteins that carry specific peptide recognition sites and are then targeted to receptors on lysosomes, which subsequently internalize these proteins for degradation (Figure 1). This pathway majorly contributes to the maintenance of cellular homeostasis by facilitating degrading of proteins and recycling of amino acids. However, transgenic mouse models have shown that this pathway participates in the regulation of glucose and lipid metabolism, DNA repair, cellular reprogramming, and cellular response to stress [7].

With regards to the liver, there is strong evidence that the process of macroautophagy in particular is the most important for maintaining hepatic homeostasis and suppressing spontaneous tumorigenesis. The systemic mosaic deletion of *Atg5* in mice resulted in multiple benign tumors that developed only in the liver but not in other tissues [8]. On the other side, host-specific deletion of *Atg7* impaired the growth of multiple allografted tumors in mice, most likely by inducing release of arginosuccinate synthase 1 from the liver and degradation of circulating arginine, which is essential for tumor growth [9]. These inverse findings demonstrate that autophagy plays a dual role in cancer cells with potential to both inhibit and promote tumor progression and promotion.

In the present review, we will highlight some principal and cell-type specific functions of autophagy in the liver, its role in hepatic homeostasis, and its impact on the pathogenesis of liver diseases. In addition, we will discuss how the present knowledge in autophagy research might influence future directions in therapy of liver diseases.

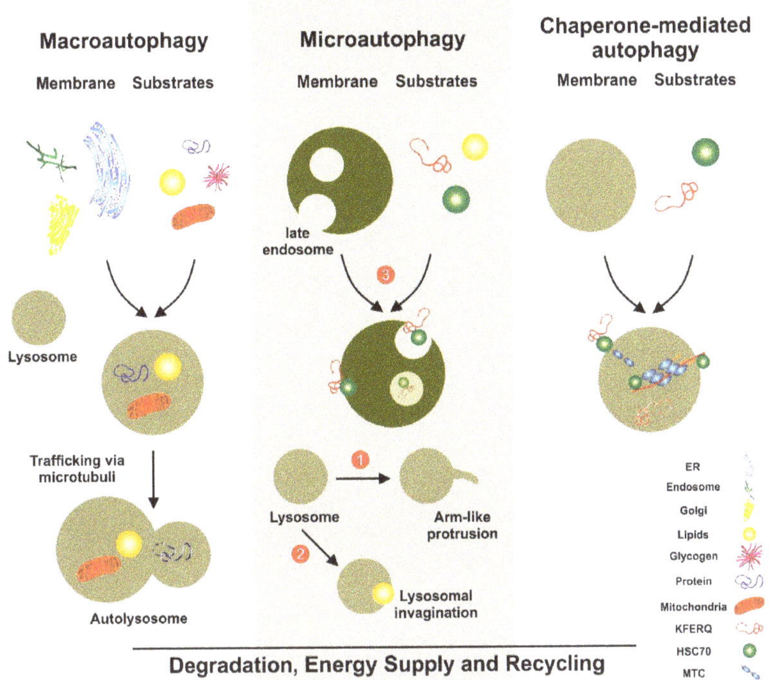

Figure 1. Simplified models of autophagy pathways in the liver. Macroautophagy involves the formation of a double-membrane vesicle, in which the substrates to be degraded are included. This vesicle called the autophagosome is then fused with the lysosome, allowing the degradation of the products. Three distinct types of microautophagy exist. In one type, the lysosome forms arm-like protrusions capable of engulfing substances. In a second branch, the lysosome can form invaginations, in which substrates (e.g., lipids) can be wrapped. The most important pathway in microautophagy involves the late endosome. In this compartment, substrates such as proteins carrying the pentapeptide lysine-phenylalanine-glutamic acid-arginine-glutamine (KFERQ)-like motifs are internalized and degraded. In chaperone-mediated autophagy, substrates with a KFERQ-like motif are first recognized by the cytosolic chaperone. Subsequently, this complex is recognized by chaperone-mediated autophagy associated receptors located at the lysosomal compartment. After internalization, the incorporated substances are degraded. The three autophagy pathways serve as a dynamic recycling system that produces new building blocks and provides energy necessary to guarantee cellular homeostasis. ER: endoplasmic reticulum; HSC70: heat-shock 70-Kd protein; MTC: multimeric translocation complex.

2. Principal Functions and Molecular Mechanisms of Autophagy

Autophagy is an important conserved recycling process necessary to maintain energy balance in the cells. In the liver, the activity of this cellular autophagy activity is enhanced or reduced in response to environmental changes and cellular needs [10]. It is not only essential for replenishing the free pool of amino acids through protein breakdown, but it also contributes to mobilization and hydrolysis of lipid stores and glycogen, thereby significantly contributing to the cellular energetics and energetic flux through different metabolic pathways [10]. The occurrence of three different types of autophagy provides a high functional variety of possible breakdown and recycling processes, which are particularly relevant for the liver, which represents the central organ in the control of organismal energy balance (Figure 1). Consequently, alteration in proper autophagy function can result in severe metabolic disorders such as obesity, fatty liver, diabetes, and other metabolic age-related disorders [11,12]. Recent findings further suggest autophagy as a critical mechanism in regulating the "liver clock" and circadian glucose metabolism by timely degrading core circadian repressor clock proteins such as crytochrome 1 (CRY1), resulting in gluconeogenesis and increased blood glucose levels [13]. Interestingly, high-fat feeding decreased CRY1 protein expression in an autophagy-dependent manner, while restoring hepatic CRY1 reversed obesity-associated hyperglycemia, suggesting that this regulatory network is a potential attractive target for therapy of obesity-associated hyperglycemia [13].

There is also first evidence that autophagy in liver aggravates the oxidative stress response during acute liver injury. In particular, autophagy maintains liver endothelial cell homeostasis and protects against cellular dysfunction, intrahepatic nitric oxide accumulation, and a liver microenvironment that promotes fibrosis [14]. Similarly, the blockade of autophagy by the autophagy inhibitor LY294002 or small interfering RNAs (siRNAs) targeting *Atg5* attenuated drug-induced anti-inflammatory effects in hepatic stellate cells and on liver fibrosis [15].

Mechanistically, there is experimental evidence showing the PI3K/Akt/mTOR pathway to be critically involved in the activation of autophagy, thereby preventing cell death, promoting anticancer effects of therapeutic drugs, and reducing tumor growth [16]. On the contrary, in hepatocellular carcinoma (HCC) cells, the induction of the PI3K/Akt/mTOR pathway by α-fetoprotein (AFP) resulted in reduced cell autophagy and more malignant behavior [17]. These opposite findings demonstrate that the same autophagy-associated pathway are highly dynamic and can have pro-tumor or anti-tumor effects. Hence, the role of autophagy in HCC development is dependent on the context of liver cells, the hepatic microenvironment, stage of tumor development, or many other unrecognized factors. It is most likely that autophagy plays an anti-tumor role in normal liver cells by maintaining cell homeostasis, while it promotes the survival of HCC cells within the tumor microenvironment once the tumor is formed [18].

3. Autophagy in Homeostasis of the Liver—Implications for Hereditary Liver Diseases

The importance of autophagy for the maintenance of liver homeostasis is best exemplified in conditions, in which large quantities of misfolded proteins are formed that lead to an overburden of the proteolytic pathway involved in autophagy. Prototypically, patients suffering from classical α1-antitrypsin (α1AT) deficiency synthesize large quantities of mutant α1AT Z (ATZ) protein in which a point mutation results in a substitution of lysine for glutamate at residue 342 [19]. While the normal α1AT protein (M protein) is rapidly secreted into the blood, the missense mutation results in a polymerized mutant α1AT protein (Z protein) that is retained in the endoplasmic reticulum of hepatocytes rather than secreted in the body fluids where its physiological function is to inhibit neutrophil proteases [19,20]. Hepatocytes deal with the burden of insoluble aggregates by activating endoplasmic reticulum-associated proteasomal degradation pathways and by macroautophagy [21]. However, in most homozygous individuals these countermeasures are insufficient to overcome the overload with insoluble proteins, provoking cell death and chronic liver damage. The clinical manifestation of liver disease associated with α1AT deficiency is highly variable, and there is currently no specific treatment of α1AT-related liver disease [22]. Enhancing cellular degradation pathways, particularly autophagy, for mutant ATZ proteins may therefore represent a realistic option in the near future [23]. Independent experimental studies have shown that the induction of autophagic degradation of mutant polymerized Z protein by hepatic gene transfer of master autophagy regulators or by autophagy-enhancing drugs such as carbamazepine, rapamycin, or 24-norursodeoxycholic acid (norUDCA) can significantly reduce liver injury [21,24–26]. These approaches, along other targets (e.g., blocking mutant ATZ production by siRNA), are currently under clinical evaluation,

Another inherited disorder reflecting the importance of autophagy in liver homeostasis is Wilson's disease, also known as hepatolenticular degeneration or "copper storage disease". It represents a rare autosomal recessive disorder caused by mutation in the ATPase copper transporting protein ATP7B, preventing the body from removing excess copper and leading to accumulation of this trace metal in liver and brain [27]. Recently, it was shown that ATP7B-deficient cells showed significant increased expression of autophagy-associated genes when compared to control cells. Furthermore, hepatocytes derived from patients suffering from Wilson's disease, as well as hepatocytes derived from *Atp7b* null mice and rats, contained elevated quantities of autophagosomes [28]. Interestingly, the pharmacological inhibition of ATG7 and ATG13 accelerated cell death in the hepatoma cell line HepG2 when depleted for ATP7B expression, suggesting that autophagy protects against metal toxicity and copper-induced cell death in the setting of Wilson's disease [28].

Alcohol abuse is a third condition in which the importance of autophagy for liver homeostasis is well documented. Alcoholic liver disease (ALD) is a global healthcare problem associated with fatty liver, alcoholic hepatitis, fibrosis, and cirrhosis. During chronic ethanol consumption, the rates of autophagy are retarded in the liver, because ethanol is thought to cause faulty lysosome biogenesis and slower breakdown of lipid droplets [29]. A recent experimental study found that liver tissue from mice fed with ethanol displayed lower expression levels of total and nuclear transcription factor EB (TFEB) compared with control mice, alongside decreased parenchymal lysosome biogenesis and autophagy [30]. When the hepatic expression of the transcription factor TFEB was increased by administration of torin-1, representing an effective inducer of autophagy, or by administration of an adenoviral vector expressing TFEB, mice showed decreased steatosis and liver injury induced by ethanol, while the knock down of TFEB using an adenovirus small hairpin RNA (shRNA) approach resulted in more severe liver disease [30]. These experiments demonstrate the fundamental protective role of autophagy in formation of ALD.

Collectively, these findings from hereditary and toxic liver diseases corroborate that autophagy as a cellular degradation and clearance pathway is critical for maintaining liver homeostasis, especially in conditions of hepatic insults.

4. Autophagy in Liver Metabolism and Fatty Liver Disease

The most common liver disease worldwide is non-alcoholic fatty liver disease (NAFLD), that is characterized by extrahepatic features of the metabolic syndrome (obesity, type 2 diabetes, dyslipidemia) and distinct hepatic histological features [31]. A fraction of these patients develop non-alcoholic steatohepatitis (NASH), characterized by steatosis, inflammation, and hepatocyte ballooning, and are at a particular risk for progressing towards fibrosis, cirrhosis, and HCC [32]. Autophagy is a central "recycling mechanism" in hepatocytes, evolutionarily evolved to provide energy and to salvage key metabolites for sustaining anabolism [33]. Autophagy is therefore a key mediator of liver metabolism and is dysregulated in NAFLD [10]. For instance, autophagy provides amino acids to cellular processes via protein degradation and recycling of cell organelles [33,34], mobilizes intracellular glycogen storages ("glycophagy") in case of starvation [33], and breaks down lipid droplets ("lipophagy"), which increases intracellular triglyceride and free fatty acid concentrations [35]. High levels of energy substrates (e.g., ATP), insulin, or free fatty acids negatively regulate autophagy, while starvation is one of the strongest physiological activators of autophagy in hepatocytes [10]. Importantly, hepatic autophagy is decreased overall in association with conditions that predispose to NAFLD such as obesity and aging [36]. Although an extensive body of literature suggests that the pharmacological modulation of either autophagy directly or autophagy-related up- or downstream pathways could hold therapeutic potential in obesity, metabolic syndrome, or NAFLD/NASH [37], lifestyle interventions including fasting, dietary changes, and exercise may also be very potent inducers of beneficial autophagy-related changes in metabolism [38,39].

The multidomain adaptor protein p62/SQSTM1 is an important substrate for autophagy in hepatocytes, as it can interact with a large set of ligands, such as arginylated substrates [40]. More recent work indicates that p62/SQSTM1 is phosphorylated and accumulated upon lipotoxic stimuli, aggravating steatohepatitis and autophagy defects [41].

Due to the central role of autophagy for hepatocyte metabolism, relatively fewer data exist on the role of autophagy in non-parenchymal cells during NAFLD. However, autophagy is certainly one contributing factor in the inflammatory and pro-fibrogenic (see below) environment. For instance, fatty acids, particularly palmitic acid, are capable of activating hepatic macrophages via the transcription factor hypoxia-inducible factor 1 alpha (HIF-1α), leading to impaired autophagy and a more inflammatory macrophage phenotype (e.g., interleukin-1β) [42]. Thus, impaired autophagy may not only affect hepatocyte metabolism, but also aggravate inflammation in fatty liver disease.

5. Autophagy in Liver Fibrosis and Cirrhosis

The liver responds to chronic tissue injury by organ scarring, termed fibrosis, which may result in end-stage cirrhosis [43]. Liver fibrosis is characterized by concerted actions of non-parenchymal cells of the liver, particularly hepatic stellate cells, macrophages (including Kupffer cells), and endothelial cells [44]. Autophagy appears to be critically involved in the development of liver fibrosis, but has very different, opposing functions in specific cell types [45] (Figure 2).

The activation of hepatic stellate cells (HSCs) is central for liver fibrogenesis, because these cells transdifferentiate into myofibroblasts and represent the major extracellular matrix producing cells in the liver [46]. Activation of HSC depends on autophagy, because the autophagy-mediated degradation of lipid droplets stored in these cells provides energy supply and promotes fibrogenic cell functions [47]. Some of the molecular mechanisms have now been clarified. For instance, the micro-RNA miR-16 inhibits the expression of guanine nucleotide-binding α-subunit 12 (Gα$_{12}$). During fibrogenesis, Gα$_{12}$ is overexpressed and facilitates autophagy through ATG12-5 formation, thereby activating stellate cells [48]. Similar to hepatocytes, p62 is an autophagy substrate and thus negatively controls HSC activation [49]. Mechanistically, p62 promotes the formation of heterodimers between the vitamin D receptor (VDR) and retinoid X receptor-alpha (RXRα) that suppresses the fibrogenic response in HSC [49].

Autophagy-pathways in stellate cells can be induced via several signals. These include hypoxia-inducible factor-1alpha (Hif-1α) [50] and the potent fibrogenic cytokine transforming growth factor β1 (TGF-β1) [51], as well as the danger-associated pattern molecule high-mobility group box-1 (HMGB-1) [52]. Importantly, stellate cells also induce autophagy-related and fibrogenic genes in response to endoplasmatic reticulum (ER) stress signals [53], suggesting that autophagy indeed represents a central pathway of fibrogenic HSC activation. Consequently, the HSC-specific deletion of *Atg7* in mice attenuated liver fibrosis in chronic injury models [54]. Inhibiting autophagy by bafilomycin A1 decreased the proliferation and activation of primary mouse HSC in vitro, suggesting that autophagy inhibition in HSC could be an interesting therapeutic strategy [47].

While autophagy is profibrogenic in HSCs, autophagy seems to exert the opposite (i.e., antifibrotic) function in hepatic macrophages (Figure 2), the key cellular component of innate immune responses in the liver, during hepatofibrogenesis [55]. In mouse models of fibrosis, the macrophage-specific deletion of *Atg5* attenuated fibrogenesis [56]. Mechanistically, autophagy prevented the release of inflammatory cytokines, particularly interleukin-1, from hepatic macrophages, which subsequently reduced HSC activation [56]. Similarly, suppression of *Atg5* by a siRNA-approach confirmed that autophagy-deficient liver macrophages promote liver inflammation and fibrosis by enhancing mitochondrial ROS/NF-κB/IL-1α/β pathways [57]. Autophagy in hepatic macrophages is counteracted by the enzyme monoacylglycerol lipase that metabolises 2-arachidonoylglycerol into arachidonic acid for inflammatory macrophage activation [58].

Autophagy is also important for liver sinusoidal endothelial cells, which are a highly specialized endothelial cells separating the hepatocytes and hepatic stellate cells from the sinusoidal blood. These endothelial cells maintain the vascular tone, keep the stellate cells in a quiescent state, and promote tolerance in homeostasis [59] (Figure 2). Studies on isolated primary liver endothelial cells from either control or *Atg7*-deficient mice emphasized that autophagy is important for maintaining endothelial homeostasis [14]. In mouse and rat models of fibrosis induction, the selective loss of endothelial autophagy aggravated fibrosis by reduction in intrahepatic nitric oxide (NO) and impairment in handling oxidative stress, suggesting that autophagy is important for endothelial cell functions during chronic liver injury [14].

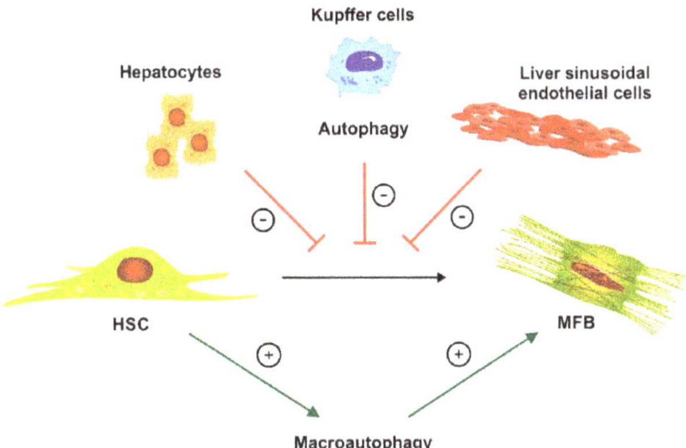

Figure 2. Cell type-specific functions of autophagy in liver fibrosis. Hepatic stellate cells (HSCs) transdifferentiate into collagen-producing myofibroblasts (MFB) in liver fibrosis. This process depends on macroautophagy, which provides energy for the HSC activation. On the contrary, autophagy maintains cellular homeostasis in hepatocytes, Kupffer cells (macrophages), and liver sinusoidal endothelial cells, thereby counteracting fibrogenesis in the liver.

6. Autophagy in Liver Cancer

Autophagy is important for hepatocyte homeostasis, as protein aggregates, lipid droplets, or organelles are eliminated via this pathway [60]. The lack of autophagy is associated with the development of spontaneous liver tumors (Figure 3), as demonstrated in liver- or hepatocyte-specific *Atg5-* and *Atg7*-knock-out mice [8]. These tumors indeed originate from autophagy-deficient hepatocytes and are characterized by aberrant p62 protein aggregation and mitochondrial swelling as well as increased genomic damage and oxidative stress responses [8]. On a molecular level, the elimination of p62 is a well-recognized anti-tumor function of autophagy [61], particularly in HCC [62]. In hepatoma cells, p62 accumulates, resulting in the persistent activation of nuclear factor (erythroid-derived 2)-like 2 (Nrf2) [63], which drives tumorigenesis in the liver in vivo [64]. Functionally, p62 not only activates Nrf2, but also mTORC1 and c-Myc, collectively promoting the survival of HCC-initiating cells [40].

Similarly, the oncogenic cell cycle regulator cyclin D1 is degraded by autophagy; defects in autophagy-dependent cyclin D1 degradation have been found in patients with HCC and confirmed in experimental HCC models in mice [65]. Autophagy also degrades the micro-RNA 224 (miR-224), which is linked to HCC development and poor prognosis in patients with hepatitis B virus (HBV) infections [66]. Moreover, autophagy-deficient hepatocytes release HMGB-1, which drives a proliferative ductular reaction as well as promotes tumorigenesis via the receptor for advanced glycation end product (RAGE) [67]. The exact molecular pathways of autophagy for HCC biology are the subject of many ongoing studies, which are summarized elsewhere [60,68,69].

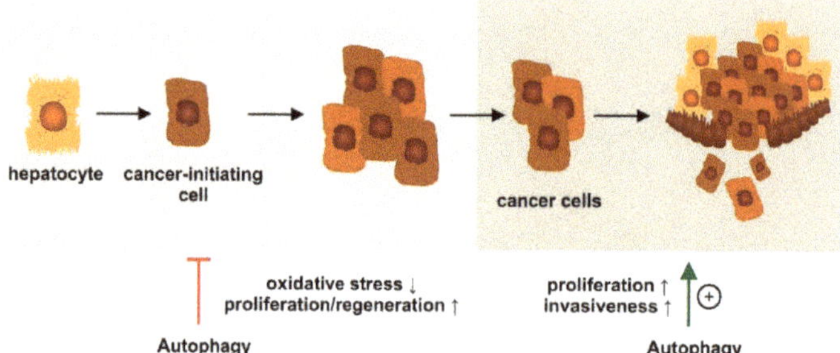

Figure 3. Stage-dependent functions of autophagy in hepatocellular carcinoma (HCC). Experimental data indicate opposing, stage-dependent functions of autophagy in HCC. At early stages, autophagy activation may reduce genotoxic stress and prevent tumor formation. At advanced stages with established tumors, autophagy is related to malignant proliferation and metastatic invasion.

There are controversial reports on the effects of drugs used in HCC regarding autophagy. An early study reported that sorafenib, a tyrosine-kinase inhibitor approved for the treatment of HCC, induced autophagy in HCC cell-lines [70]. However, autophagy has also been linked to sorafenib resistance [71, 72]. Accordingly, the expression of autophagic markers in samples from HCC patients strongly correlate with annexin A3, which confers resistance to sorafenib as well as regorafenib [73]. Importantly, while autophagy apparently suppresses hepatocarcinogenesis, it is a pro-survival factor for cells and can therefore be also linked to tumor progression (Figure 3). This became evident from mouse models of metastatic liver cancer, in which autophagy favored disease progression [74,75]. Tumor cells may gain energy through autophagy, which favors their survival and migratory properties. Moreover, autophagy is associated with changes in the expression of cell adhesion molecules, which may facilitate the migration and invasiveness of malignantly transformed hepatocytes [69].

In addition to specific effects on hepatocarcinogenesis, autophagy in hepatocytes is also important for tumor surveillance in the whole body. However, while autophagy in hepatocytes mainly suppresses tumor formation in the liver [64], hepatocytic autophagy in general supports tumor growth [76]. This became evident in mice with a liver-specific deletion of either *Atg5* or *Atg7* that demonstrated an impaired growth of multiple allografted tumors. This observation was linked to the release of arginosuccinate synthase 1 from the liver and the subsequent degradation of circulating arginine, which is essential for tumor growth [9].

While most studies focused on the roles of autophagy in parenchymal cells for liver cancer, relatively little is known about the contribution of autophagy in non-parenchymal cells for HCC. During the preneoplastic state, autophagy in liver macrophages was found to suppress experimental hepatocarcinogenesis, mainly due to the anti-inflammatory role of autophagy in macrophages [57].

7. Therapeutic Implications and Outlook

Autophagy is a highly conserved process for degradation or recycling of cellular components and mobilization of energy substrates. Many drugs target directly or indirectly such processes, including the autophagy inducers carbamazepine, rapamycin, resveratrol, metformin, amitryptiline, or citalopram as well as inhibitors like choloroquine or hydroxycholoroquine. Many other more specific compounds are currently under development for various disease areas [77]. As described in our review, autophagy has both positive and negative roles in liver diseases, making it attractive but challenging to manipulate autophagy as a therapeutic approach in liver diseases. In this regard, two very exciting areas of research regarding autophagy-modulating therapies are metabolic [37] and malignant diseases [78]. Enhancing autophagy as a physiological process of reducing hepatocytic lipid accumulation and cellular stress signals emerges as an attractive target in NAFLD and NASH [10]. This could potentially include the repurposing of "known drugs" with an excellent safety profile. For instance, the autophagy activators carbamazepine and rapamycin decreased steatosis, dyslipidemia and insulin resistance in NAFLD mouse models [79]. However, enhancing autophagy should, ideally, target specifically parenchymal cells in the liver, muscle, and adipose tissue, to avoid the activation of fibrogenic HSC [54].

For liver fibrosis, many pharmacological approaches are currently being evaluated [80], but none of these approaches directly targets autophagy, likely due to the complex and cell type-specific role of autophagy during liver fibrosis. Based on the solid body of experimental data, the augmentation of autophagy in liver sinusoidal endothelial cells [14] as well as in macrophages [56] should be beneficial for fibrogenesis, particularly in early stages of the disease. On the other hand, autophagy is a key mechanism for the activation of hepatic stellate cells [46]. Thus, the HSC-specific inhibition of autophagy may be a potent antifibrotic strategy [47].

For HCC, it is intriguing to speculate that pharmacological induction of autophagy could limit tumor development. There are indications from mouse models that the pharmacological inducers amiodarone and rapamycin can prevent experimental hepatocarcinogenesis [66]. However, given the concomitant tumor-promoting functions of hepatocytic autophagy, it might be more advisable to target downstream effects, such as inhibiting phosphorylated p62-dependent Nrf2 activation [62]. In patients with metastatic HCC, it might be even advisable to inhibit autophagy, as this would likely increase the susceptibility to chemotherapy [45].

8. Conclusions

The deep mechanistic understanding of autophagy in the liver has uncovered a complex network of related molecular processes and the central role of autophagy for homeostasis and response to threats in the liver. Given the broad range of potential pharmacological and non-pharmacological (e.g., nutritional) interventions to target autophagy, it is intriguing to speculate on how to translate these findings into new therapeutics. Not surprisingly, autophagy is involved in disease-promoting as well as disease-limiting functions in a broad range of hepatological disorders. Cell-type- or disease-stage dependent effects can explain large parts of the dual functionality of autophagy. Thus, any autophagy-modulating intervention needs to be tailored to target the essential parenchymal or non-parenchymal cell type in the liver at the right moment of disease pathogenesis. With this caveat in mind, manifold options targeting autophagy for the treatment of hereditary, metabolic, toxic, fibrotic, or malignant liver disease may be anticipated in the future.

Funding: This research was funded by the German Research Foundation (DFG, SFB/TRR57, Projects P09, P13, and Q3) and the Interdisciplinary Centre for Clinical Research within the Faculty of Medicine at RWTH Aachen University (IZKF Aachen, Projects O3-1 and O3-2).

Acknowledgments: The authors are grateful to Sabine Weiskirchen (Institute of Molecular Pathobiochemistry, Experimental Gene Therapy and Clinical Chemistry, University Hospital RWTH Aachen, Aachen), who prepared figures for this review.

Conflicts of Interest: The authors declare no conflict of interest related to this article. However, work in the laboratory of F.T. has been supported by funding from Allergan, Galapagos, Inventiva, and Bristol Myers Squibb. The laboratory of R.W. cooperates with Silence Therapeutics. The funders or cooperation companies had no role in the design of the study, in the writing of the manuscript, or in the decision to publish this review.

References

1. Sabatini, D.D.; Adesnik, M. Christian de Duve: Explorer of the cell who discovered new organelles by using a centrifuge. *Proc. Natl. Acad. Sci. USA* **2013**, *110*, 13234–13235. [CrossRef]
2. Ktistakis, N.T. In praise of M. Anselmier who first used the term "autophagie" in 1859. *Autophagy* **2017**, *13*, 2015–2017. [CrossRef] [PubMed]
3. Mizushima, N.; Komatsu, M. Autophagy: Renovation of cells and tissues. *Cell* **2011**, *147*, 728–741. [CrossRef]
4. Rubinsztein, D.C.; Shpilka, T.; Elazar, Z. Mechanisms of autophagosome biogenesis. *Curr. Biol.* **2012**, *22*, 29–34. [CrossRef] [PubMed]

5. Olsvik, H.L.; Svenning, S.; Abudu, Y.P.; Brech, A.; Stenmark, H.; Johansen, T.; Mejlvang, J. Endosomal microautophagy is an integrated part of the autophagic response to amino acid starvation. *Autophagy* **2018**, *15*, 182–183. [CrossRef] [PubMed]

6. Oku, M.; Sakai, Y. Three distinct types of microautophagy based on membrane dynamics and molecular machineries. *Bioessays* **2018**, *40*, e1800008. [CrossRef]

7. Kaushik, S.; Cuervo, A.M. The coming of age of chaperone-mediated autophagy. *Nat. Rev. Mol. Cell Biol.* **2018**, *19*, 365–381. [CrossRef]

8. Takamura, A.; Komatsu, M.; Hara, T.; Sakamoto, A.; Kishi, C.; Waguri, S.; Eishi, Y.; Hino, O.; Tanaka, K.; Mizushima, N. Autophagy-deficient mice develop multiple liver tumors. *Genes Dev.* **2011**, *25*, 795–800. [CrossRef]

9. Poillet-Perez, L.; Xie, X.; Zhan, L.; Yang, Y.; Sharp, D.W.; Hu, Z.S.; Su, X.; Maganti, A.; Jiang, C.; Lu, W.; et al. Autophagy maintains tumour growth through circulating arginine. *Nature* **2018**, *563*, 569–573. [CrossRef]

10. Madrigal-Matute, J.; Cuervo, A.M. Regulation of liver metabolism by autophagy. *Gastroenterology* **2016**, *150*, 328–339. [CrossRef]

11. Schneider, J.L.; Cuervo, A.M. Liver autophagy: Much more than just taking out the trash. *Nat. Rev. Gastroenterol. Hepatol.* **2014**, *11*, 187–200. [CrossRef] [PubMed]

12. Moulis, M.; Vindis, C. Autophagy in metabolic age-related human diseases. *Cells* **2018**, *7*, 149. [CrossRef] [PubMed]

13. Toledo, M.; Batista-Gonzalez, A.; Merheb, E.; Aoun, M.L.; Tarabra, E.; Feng, D.; Sarparanta, J.; Merlo, P.; Botrè, F.; Schwartz, G.J.; et al. Autophagy regulates the liver clock and glucose metabolism by degrading CRY1. *Cell Metab.* **2018**, *28*, 268–281. [CrossRef] [PubMed]

14. Ruart, M.; Chavarria, L.; Campreciós, G.; Suárez-Herrera, N.; Montironi, C.; Guixé-Muntet, S.; Bosch, J.; Friedman, S.L.; Garcia-Pagán, J.C.; Hernández-Gea, V. Impaired endothelial autophagy promotes liver fibrosis by aggravating the oxidative stress response during acute liver injury. *J. Hepatol.* **2018**. [CrossRef] [PubMed]

15. Liu, Z.; Zhu, P.; Zhang, L.; Xiong, B.; Tao, J.; Guan, W.; Li, C.; Chen, C.; Gu, J.; Duanmu, J.; et al. Autophagy inhibition attenuates the induction of anti-inflammatory effect of catalpol in liver fibrosis. *Biomed. Pharmacother.* **2018**, *103*, 1262–1271. [CrossRef]

16. Yang, J.; Pi, C.; Wang, G. Inhibition of PI3K/Akt/mTOR pathway by apigenin induces apoptosis and autophagy in hepatocellular carcinoma cells. *Biomed. Pharmacother.* **2018**, *103*, 699–707. [CrossRef]

17. Wang, S.; Zhu, M.; Wang, Q.; Hou, Y.; Li, L.; Weng, H.; Zhao, Y.; Chen, D.; Ding, H.; Guo, J.; et al. Alpha-fetoprotein inhibits autophagy to promote malignant behaviour in hepatocellular carcinoma cells by activating PI3K/AKT/mTOR signalling. *Cell Death Dis.* **2018**, *9*, 1027. [CrossRef]

18. Liu, L.; Liao, J.Z.; He, X.X.; Li, P.Y. The role of autophagy in hepatocellular carcinoma: Friend or foe. *Oncotarget* **2017**, *8*, 57707–57722. [CrossRef]

19. Teckman, J.H.; An, J.K.; Blomenkamp, K.; Schmidt, B.; Perlmutter, D. Mitochondrial autophagy and injury in the liver in alpha 1-antitrypsin deficiency. *Am. J. Physiol. Gastrointest. Liver Physiol.* **2004**, *286*, 851–862. [CrossRef]

20. Teckman, J.H.; Blomenkamp, K.S. Pathophysiology of alpha-1 antitrypsin deficiency liver disease. *Methods Mol. Biol.* **2017**, *1639*, 1–8. [CrossRef]

21. Tang, Y.; Blomenkamp, K.S.; Fickert, P.; Trauner, M.; Teckman, J.H. NorUDCA promotes degradation of α1-antitrypsin mutant Z protein by inducing autophagy through AMPK/ULK1 pathway. *PLoS ONE* **2018**, *13*, e0200897. [CrossRef] [PubMed]

22. Patel, D.; Teckman, J.H. Alpha-1-antitrypsin deficiency liver disease. *Clin. Liver Dis.* **2018**, *22*, 643–655. [CrossRef] [PubMed]

23. Tacke, F.; Trautwein, C. Controlling autophagy: A new concept for clearing liver disease. *Hepatology* **2011**, *53*, 356–358. [CrossRef] [PubMed]

24. Pastore, N.; Blomenkamp, K.; Annunziata, F.; Piccolo, P.; Mithbaokar, P.; Maria Sepe, R.; Vetrini, F.; Palmer, D.; Ng, P.; Polishchuk, E.; et al. Gene transfer of master autophagy regulator TFEB results in clearance of toxic protein and correction of hepatic disease in alpha-1-anti-trypsin deficiency. *EMBO Mol. Med.* **2013**, *5*, 397–412. [CrossRef] [PubMed]

25. Hidvegi, T.; Ewing, M.; Hale, P.; Dippold, C.; Beckett, C.; Kemp, C.; Maurice, N.; Mukherjee, A.; Goldbach, C.; Watkins, S.; et al. An autophagy-enhancing drug promotes degradation of mutant alpha1-antitrypsin Z and reduces hepatic fibrosis. *Science* **2010**, *329*, 229–232. [CrossRef] [PubMed]

26. Kaushal, S.; Annamali, M.; Blomenkamp, K.; Rudnick, D.; Halloran, D.; Brunt, E.M.; Teckman, J.H. Rapamycin reduces intrahepatic alpha-1-antitrypsin mutant Z protein polymers and liver injury in a mouse model. *Exp. Biol. Med.* **2010**, *235*, 700–709. [CrossRef] [PubMed]

27. Weiskirchen, S.; Kim, P.; Weiskirchen, R. Determination of copper poisoning in Wilson's disease using laser ablation inductively coupled plasma spectrometry. *Ann. Transl. Med.* **2018**. [CrossRef]

28. Polishchuk, E.V.; Merolla, A.; Lichtmannegger, J.; Romano, A.; Indrieri, A.; Ilyechova, E.Y.; Concilli, M.; De Cegli, R.; Crispino, R.; Mariniello, M.; et al. Activation of autophagy, observed in liver tissues from patients with Wilson disease and from *Atp7b*-deficient animals, protects hepatocytes from copper-induced apoptosis. *Gastroenterology* **2018**. [CrossRef]

29. Osna, N.A.; Donohue, T.M., Jr.; Kharbanda, K.K. Alcoholic liver disease: Pathogenesis and current management. *Alcohol Res.* **2017**, *38*, 147–161.

30. Chao, X.; Wang, S.; Zhao, K.; Li, Y.; Williams, J.A.; Li, T.; Chavan, H.; Krishnamurthy, P.; He, X.C.; Li, L.; et al. Impaired TFEB-mediated lysosome biogenesis and autophagy promote chronic ethanol-induced liver injury and steatosis in mice. *Gastroenterology* **2018**, *155*, 865–879. [CrossRef]

31. Younossi, Z.; Tacke, F.; Arrese, M.; Sharma, B.C.; Mostafa, I.; Bugianesi, E.; Wong, V.W.; Yilmaz, Y.; George, J.; Fan, J.; et al. Global perspectives on non-alcoholic fatty liver disease and non-alcoholic steatohepatitis. *Hepatology* **2018**. [CrossRef] [PubMed]

32. Diehl, A.M.; Day, C. Cause, pathogenesis, and treatment of nonalcoholic steatohepatitis. *N. Engl. J. Med.* **2017**, *377*, 2063–2072. [CrossRef] [PubMed]

33. Kaur, J.; Debnath, J. Autophagy at the crossroads of catabolism and anabolism. *Nat. Rev. Mol. Cell Biol.* **2015**, *16*, 461–472. [CrossRef] [PubMed]

34. Lamming, D.W.; Bar-Peled, L. Lysosome: The metabolic signaling hub. *Traffic* **2019**, *20*, 27–38. [CrossRef] [PubMed]

35. Schulze, R.J.; Drižytė, K.; Casey, C.A.; McNiven, M.A. Hepatic lipophagy: New insights into autophagic catabolism of lipid droplets in the liver. *Hepatol. Commun.* **2017**, *1*, 359–369. [CrossRef] [PubMed]

36. Czaja, M.J. Function of autophagy in nonalcoholic fatty liver disease. *Dig. Dis. Sci.* **2016**, *61*, 1304–1313. [CrossRef] [PubMed]

37. Zhang, Y.; Sowers, J.R.; Ren, J. Targeting autophagy in obesity: From pathophysiology to management. *Nat. Rev. Endocrinol.* **2018**, *14*, 356–376. [CrossRef] [PubMed]

38. Van Niekerk, G.; du Toit, A.; Loos, B.; Engelbrecht, A.M. Nutrient excess and autophagic deficiency: Explaining metabolic diseases in obesity. *Metabolism* **2018**, *82*, 14–21. [CrossRef] [PubMed]

39. He, C.; Bassik, M.C.; Moresi, V.; Sun, K.; Wei, Y.; Zou, Z.; An, Z.; Loh, J.; Fisher, J.; Sun, Q.; et al. Exercise-induced BCL2-regulated autophagy is required for muscle glucose homeostasis. *Nature* **2012**, *481*, 511–555. [CrossRef]

40. Umemura, A.; He, F.; Taniguchi, K.; Nakagawa, H.; Yamachika, S.; Font-Burgada, J.; Zhong, Z.; Subramaniam, S.; Raghunandan, S.; Duran, A.; et al. p62, upregulated during preneoplasia, induces hepatocellular carcinogenesis by maintaining survival of stressed HCC-initiating cells. *Cancer Cell* **2016**, *29*, 935–948. [CrossRef]

41. Cho, C.S.; Park, H.W.; Ho, A.; Semple, I.A.; Kim, B.; Jang, I.; Park, H.; Reilly, S.; Saltiel, A.R.; Lee, J.H. Lipotoxicity induces hepatic protein inclusions through TANK binding kinase 1-mediated p62/sequestosome 1 phosphorylation. *Hepatology* **2018**, *68*, 1331–1346. [CrossRef] [PubMed]

42. Wang, X.; Ribeiro, M.; Iracheta-Vellve, A.; Lowe, P.; Ambade, A.; Satishchandran, A.; Bukong, T.; Catalano, D.; Kodys, K.; Szabo, G. Macrophage-specific HIF-1α contributes to impaired autophagic flux in non-alcoholic steatohepatitis. *Hepatology* **2018**. [CrossRef] [PubMed]

43. Weiskirchen, R.; Weiskirchen, S.; Tacke, F. Organ and tissue fibrosis: Molecular signals, cellular mechanisms and translational implications. *Mol. Asp. Med.* **2018**. [CrossRef] [PubMed]

44. Weiskirchen, R.; Weiskirchen, S.; Tacke, F. Recent advances in understanding liver fibrosis: Bridging basic science and individualized treatment concepts. *F1000Research* **2018**, *7*. [CrossRef] [PubMed]

45. Gracia-Sancho, J.; Guixé-Muntet, S. The many-faced role of autophagy in liver diseases. *J. Hepatol.* **2018**, *68*, 593–594. [CrossRef] [PubMed]

46. Tsuchida, T.; Friedman, S.L. Mechanisms of hepatic stellate cell activation. *Nat. Rev. Gastroenterol. Hepatol.* **2017**, *14*, 397–411. [CrossRef]

47. Thoen, L.F.; Guimarães, E.L.; Dollé, L.; Mannaerts, I.; Najimi, M.; Sokal, E.; van Grunsven, L.A. A role for autophagy during hepatic stellate cell activation. *J. Hepatol.* **2011**, *55*, 1353–1360. [CrossRef]

48. Kim, K.M.; Han, C.Y.; Kim, J.Y.; Cho, S.S.; Kim, Y.S.; Koo, J.H.; Lee, J.M.; Lim, S.C.; Kang, K.W.; Kim, J.S.; et al. Gα$_{12}$ overexpression induced by miR-16 dysregulation contributes to liver fibrosis by promoting autophagy in hepatic stellate cells. *J. Hepatol.* **2018**, *68*, 493–504. [CrossRef]

49. Duran, A.; Hernandez, E.D.; Reina-Campos, M.; Castilla, E.A.; Subramaniam, S.; Raghunandan, S.; Roberts, L.R.; Kisseleva, T.; Karin, M.; Diaz-Meco, M.T.; et al. p62/SQSTM1 by binding to vitamin D receptor inhibits hepatic stellate cell activity, fibrosis, and liver cancer. *Cancer Cell* **2016**, *30*, 595–609. [CrossRef]

50. Deng, J.; Huang, Q.; Wang, Y.; Shen, P.; Guan, F.; Li, J.; Huang, H.; Shi, C. Hypoxia-inducible factor-1alpha regulates autophagy to activate hepatic stellate cells. *Biochem. Biophys. Res. Commun.* **2014**, *454*, 328–334. [CrossRef]

51. Fu, M.Y.; He, Y.J.; Lv, X.; Liu, Z.H.; Shen, Y.; Ye, G.R.; Deng, Y.M.; Shu, J.C. Transforming growth factor-β1 reduces apoptosis via autophagy activation in hepatic stellate cells. *Mol. Med. Rep.* **2014**, *10*, 1282–1288. [CrossRef] [PubMed]

52. Li, J.; Zeng, C.; Zheng, B.; Liu, C.; Tang, M.; Jiang, Y.; Chang, Y.; Song, W.; Wang, Y.; Yang, C. HMGB1-induced autophagy facilitates hepatic stellate cells activation: A new pathway in liver fibrosis. *Clin. Sci.* **2018**, *132*, 1645–1667. [CrossRef] [PubMed]

53. Hernández-Gea, V.; Hilscher, M.; Rozenfeld, R.; Lim, M.P.; Nieto, N.; Werner, S.; Devi, L.A.; Friedman, S.L. Endoplasmic reticulum stress induces fibrogenic activity in hepatic stellate cells through autophagy. *J Hepatol.* **2013**, *59*, 98–104. [CrossRef] [PubMed]

54. Hernández-Gea, V.; Ghiassi-Nejad, Z.; Rozenfeld, R.; Gordon, R.; Fiel, M.I.; Yue, Z.; Czaja, M.J.; Friedman, S.L. Autophagy releases lipid that promotes fibrogenesis by activated hepatic stellate cells in mice and in human tissues. *Gastroenterology* **2012**, *142*, 938–946. [CrossRef] [PubMed]

55. Krenkel, O.; Tacke, F. Liver macrophages in tissue homeostasis and disease. *Nat. Rev. Immunol.* **2017**, *17*, 306–321. [CrossRef] [PubMed]

56. Lodder, J.; Denaës, T.; Chobert, M.N.; Wan, J.; El-Benna, J.; Pawlotsky, J.M.; Lotersztajn, S.; Teixeira-Clerc, F. Macrophage autophagy protects against liver fibrosis in mice. *Autophagy* **2015**, *11*, 1280–1292. [CrossRef] [PubMed]

57. Sun, K.; Xu, L.; Jing, Y.; Han, Z.; Chen, X.; Cai, C.; Zhao, P.; Zhao, X.; Yang, L.; Wei, L. Autophagy-deficient Kupffer cells promote tumorigenesis by enhancing mtROS-NF-κB-IL1α/β-dependent inflammation and fibrosis during the preneoplastic stage of hepatocarcinogenesis. *Cancer Lett.* **2017**, *388*, 198–207. [CrossRef]

58. Habib, A.; Chokr, D.; Wan, J.; Hegde, P.; Mabire, M.; Siebert, M.; Ribeiro-Parenti, L.; Le Gall, M.; Lettéron, P.; Pilard, N.; et al. Inhibition of monoacylglycerol lipase, an anti-inflammatory and antifibrogenic strategy in the liver. *Gut* **2018**. [CrossRef]

59. Poisson, J.; Lemoinne, S.; Boulanger, C.; Durand, F.; Moreau, R.; Valla, D.; Rautou, P. Liver sinusoidal endothelial cells: Physiology and role in liver diseases. *J. Hepatol.* **2017**, *66*, 212–227. [CrossRef]

60. Ueno, T.; Komatsu, M. Autophagy in the liver: Functions in health and disease. *Nat. Rev. Gastroenterol. Hepatol.* **2017**, *14*, 170–184. [CrossRef]

61. Mathew, R.; Karp, C.M.; Beaudoin, B.; Vuong, N.; Chen, G.; Chen, H.Y.; Bray, K.; Reddy, A.; Bhanot, G.; Gelinas, C.; et al. Autophagy suppresses tumorigenesis through elimination of p62. *Cell* **2009**, *137*, 1062–1075. [CrossRef] [PubMed]

62. Saito, T.; Ichimura, Y.; Taguchi, K.; Suzuki, T.; Mizushima, T.; Takagi, K.; Hirose, Y.; Nagahashi, M.; Iso, T.; Fukutomi, T.; et al. p62/Sqstm1 promotes malignancy of HCV-positive hepatocellular carcinoma through Nrf2-dependent metabolic reprogramming. *Nat. Commun.* **2016**, *7*, 12030. [CrossRef] [PubMed]

63. Inami, Y.; Waguri, S.; Sakamoto, A.; Kouno, T.; Nakada, K.; Hino, O.; Watanabe, S.; Ando, J.; Iwadate, M.; Yamamoto, M.; et al. Persistent activation of Nrf2 through p62 in hepatocellular carcinoma cells. *J. Cell Biol.* **2011**, *193*, 275–284. [CrossRef] [PubMed]

64. Ni, H.M.; Woolbright, B.L.; Williams, J.; Copple, B.; Cui, W.; Luyendyk, J.P.; Jaeschke, H.; Ding, W.X. Nrf2 promotes the development of fibrosis and tumorigenesis in mice with defective hepatic autophagy. *J. Hepatol.* **2014**, *61*, 617–625. [CrossRef] [PubMed]

65. Wu, S.Y.; Lan, S.H.; Wu, S.R.; Chiu, Y.C.; Lin, X.Z.; Su, I.J.; Tsai, T.F.; Yen, C.J.; Lu, T.H.; Liang, F.W.; et al. Hepatocellular carcinoma-related cyclin D1 is selectively regulated by autophagy degradation system. *Hepatology* **2018**, *68*, 141–154. [CrossRef] [PubMed]

66. Lan, S.H.; Wu, S.Y.; Zuchini, R.; Lin, X.Z.; Su, I.J.; Tsai, T.F.; Lin, Y.J.; Wu, C.T.; Liu, H.S. Autophagy suppresses tumorigenesis of hepatitis B virus-associated hepatocellular carcinoma through degradation of microRNA-224. *Hepatology* **2014**, *59*, 505–517. [CrossRef] [PubMed]

67. Khambu, B.; Huda, N.; Chen, X.; Antoine, D.J.; Li, Y.; Dai, G.; Köhler, U.A.; Zong, W.X.; Waguri, S.; Werner, S.; et al. HMGB1 promotes ductular reaction and tumorigenesis in autophagy-deficient livers. *J. Clin. Investig.* **2018**, *128*, 2419–2435. [CrossRef]

68. Di Fazio, P.; Matrood, S. Targeting autophagy in liver cancer. *Transl. Gastroenterol. Hepatol.* **2018**, *3*, 39. [CrossRef]

69. Huang, F.; Wang, B.R.; Wang, Y.G. Role of autophagy in tumorigenesis, metastasis, targeted therapy and drug resistance of hepatocellular carcinoma. *World J. Gastroenterol.* **2018**, *24*, 4643–4651. [CrossRef]

70. Tai, W.T.; Shiau, C.W.; Chen, H.L.; Liu, C.Y.; Lin, C.S.; Cheng, A.L.; Chen, P.J.; Chen, K.F. Mcl-1-dependent activation of Beclin 1 mediates autophagic cell death induced by sorafenib and SC-59 in hepatocellular carcinoma cells. *Cell Death Dis.* **2013**, *4*, e485. [CrossRef]

71. Lu, S.; Yao, Y.; Xu, G.; Zhou, C.; Zhang, Y.; Sun, J.; Jiang, R.; Shao, Q.; Chen, Y. CD24 regulates sorafenib resistance via activating autophagy in hepatocellular carcinoma. *Cell Death Dis.* **2018**, *9*, 646. [CrossRef] [PubMed]

72. Zhang, K.; Chen, J.; Zhou, H.; Chen, Y.; Zhi, Y.; Zhang, B.; Chen, L.; Chu, X.; Wang, R.; Zhang, C. PU.1/microRNA-142-3p targets ATG5/ATG16L1 to inactivate autophagy and sensitize hepatocellular carcinoma cells to sorafenib. *Cell Death Dis.* **2018**, *9*, 312. [CrossRef]

73. Tong, M.; Che, N.; Zhou, L.; Luk, S.T.; Kau, P.W.; Chai, S.; Ngan, E.S.; Lo, C.M.; Man, K.; Ding, J.; et al. Efficacy of annexin A3 blockade in sensitizing hepatocellular carcinoma to sorafenib and regorafenib. *J. Hepatol.* **2018**, *69*, 826–839. [CrossRef] [PubMed]

74. Fu, X.T.; Shi, Y.H.; Zhou, J.; Peng, Y.F.; Liu, W.R.; Shi, G.M.; Gao, Q.; Wang, X.Y.; Song, K.; Fan, J.; et al. MicroRNA-30a suppresses autophagy-mediated anoikis resistance and metastasis in hepatocellular carcinoma. *Cancer Lett.* **2018**, *412*, 108–117. [CrossRef] [PubMed]

75. Peng, Y.F.; Shi, Y.H.; Ding, Z.B.; Ke, A.W.; Gu, C.Y.; Hui, B.; Zhou, J.; Qiu, S.J.; Dai, Z.; Fan, J. Autophagy inhibition suppresses pulmonary metastasis of HCC in mice via impairing anoikis resistance and colonization of HCC cells. *Autophagy* **2013**, *9*, 2056–2068. [CrossRef] [PubMed]

76. Kimmelman, A.C.; White, E. Autophagy and tumor metabolism. *Cell Metab.* **2017**, *25*, 1037–1043. [CrossRef]

77. Towers, C.G.; Thorburn, A. Therapeutic targeting of autophagy. *EBioMedicine* **2016**, *14*, 15–23. [CrossRef]

78. Levy, J.M.M.; Towers, C.G.; Thorburn, A. Targeting autophagy in cancer. *Nat. Rev. Cancer* **2017**, *17*, 528–542. [CrossRef] [PubMed]

79. Lin, C.W.; Zhang, H.; Li, M.; Xiong, X.; Chen, X.; Chen, X.; Dong, X.C.; Yin, X.M. Pharmacological promotion of autophagy alleviates steatosis and injury in alcoholic and non-alcoholic fatty liver conditions in mice. *J. Hepatol.* **2013**, *58*, 993–999. [CrossRef] [PubMed]

80. Tacke, F.; Weiskirchen, R. An update on the recent advances in antifibrotic therapy. *Expert Rev. Gastroenterol. Hepatol.* **2018**, *12*, 1143–1152. [CrossRef]

Review

Autophagy: Dual Response in the Development of Hepatocellular Carcinoma

Hamza O. Yazdani [1], Hai Huang [2] and Allan Tsung [2,*]

[1] Department of Surgery, University of Pittsburgh, Pittsburg, PA 15213-2582, USA; obaidh3@upmc.edu
[2] Division of Surgical Oncology, Department of Surgery, The Ohio State University Wexner Medical Center, N924 Doan Hall, 410 West 10th Ave., Columbus, OH 43210, USA; huang.3900@osu.edu
* Correspondence: Allan.Tsung@osumc.edu; Tel.: +1-614-293-8304; Fax: +1-614-293-3465

Received: 31 December 2018; Accepted: 26 January 2019; Published: 28 January 2019

Abstract: Autophagy is an evolutionary conserved intracellular mechanism which helps eukaryotic cells in maintaining their metabolic state to afford high-efficiency energy requirements. In the physiology of a normal liver and the pathogenesis of liver diseases, autophagy plays a crucial role. Autophagy has been found to be both upregulated and downregulated in different cancers providing the evidence that autophagy plays a dual role in suppressing and promoting cell survival. Hepatocellular carcinoma (HCC) is the most common primary liver cancer and the major leading cause of cancer mortality worldwide. In light of its high complexity and poor prognosis, it is essential to improve our understanding of autophagy's role in HCC. In this review, we summarize the dual mechanism of autophagy in the development of HCC and elucidate the currently used therapeutic strategies for anti-HCC therapy.

Keywords: hepatocellular carcinoma; inflammation; mitophagy; oxidative stress; HCC therapy

---

1. Introduction

Autophagy (macroautophagy) is the fundamental cellular process in maintaining cell homeostasis by targeting damaged intracellular organelles and misfolded proteins to lysosomal degradation [1]. It is a conserved evolutionary process that takes part in all mammalian cells under basal conditions and generates building block molecules to support essential cellular processes [2]. Autophagy is a multistep process including membrane rearrangement in forming a double-membrane bond structure known as autophagosomes. The vesicle fusion of these autophagosomes with lytic compartments generates autolysosomes where lysosomal enzymatic degradation of contents is recycled and releases nucleotides, fatty acids, and amino acids to refuel the cells with energy to maintain necessary molecular synthesis [2].

The role of autophagy is complex and differs from organ to organ. An organ such as muscles and the liver requires autophagy to remove excessive protein aggregation, lipid accumulation, and damaged mitochondria to prevent excessive ROS generation leading to oxidative stress [3,4]. Defects in autophagy have shown to contributes in several pathogeneses of human diseases ranging from neurodegenerative and metabolic diseases to cancers [5]. The dysregulation of autophagy has been increasingly indicated to play a role in liver diseases such as alcoholic liver disease, non-alcoholic fatty liver disease (NAFLD), hepatosteatosis, hepatomegaly, and primary liver malignancies such as hepatocellular carcinoma (HCC) [6,7].

Hepatocellular carcinoma is a serious threat towards human health. It is the sixth most malignant cancer worldwide and the fifth most common malignancy in men [8]. Despite recent advances in treatments and surgical resection, the five-year survival rate remains unsatisfactory [9]. The most common identified risk factors for HCC development are the consequences of unresolved oxidative stress, persistent inflammation, viral infections, metabolic dysfunction, liver alcohol disease, and fatty liver disease. Autophagy may serve as a protective mechanism against the initial and persistent liver injury in these disease states but autophagy may also play a significant role in the development and growth of hepatic tumor cells in this inflammatory environment [10,11]. The link between autophagy and cancer has been long proposed. The underlying mechanisms regulating the autophagic response in HCC requires further understanding to develop effective treatment strategies.

2. Role of Autophagy in Normal Liver Homeostasis

Autophagy is involved in diverse physiology and pathophysiology of the liver. The liver displays a complex metabolism with a variety of functions including protein and lipid synthesis and secretion of bile acid. Increased accumulation of ubiquitin proteins aggregation observed in the liver-specific Atg7 knockout mice suggested a basal function of autophagy in continuous turnover of the cytoplasmic proteins [12,13]. Disturbance in the basal autophagy of the liver can lead to the accumulation of elementary bodies, damaged mitochondria, deformed peroxisomes, and abnormal membrane structures resulting in liver injury. Autophagy can be general and nonselective, involving the degradation of a bulk cytoplasmic portion or organelle-specific degradation. The cell can undergo different forms of autophagy which include xenophagy (degradation of viruses), lipophagy (degradation of lipid droplets), ribophagy (degradation of ribosomes), pexophagy (degradation of peroxisomes), reticulophagy (degradation of ER), and mitophagy (degradation of mitochondria). Of these, mitophagy is one of the most well characterized since hepatocytes contain numerous mitochondria to provide the high energy demand for metabolism. Liver specific autophagy deficient mice provide evidence for swollen mitochondria and increased ROS formation [14]. Liver injury is also associated with mitochondrial membrane permeabilization which can activate a mitochondrial apoptotic pathway regulating BAX and Bad (BCL2 family) mediated cell death [15]. The different forms and role of autophagy in the healthy liver are best described in detail by Takashi U Eno et al. [16].

Hepatocytes are primarily dependent on autophagy degradation due to its intense metabolism and high energy demand to maintain proper functioning. The defect in any of the forms of autophagy can contribute to severe liver functional damage such as hepatitis, fibrosis, cirrhosis, and HCC development [17,18]. One of the most common causes of acute and chronic liver disease is the infection of the liver with hepatotropic viruses. Hepatitis B and C viruses are both linked to the autophagy. It has been shown that the X protein of the HBV (HBx) can induce autophagy due to its ability to bind to the PI3k autophagic molecule. On the other hand, the Hepatitis C virus (HCV) can adapt autophagy content to enhance its replication by inhibiting the maturation of autophagosome into autophagolysosomes. Both these viruses are shown to induce autophagy by transcriptional upregulation of Beclin1 [19].

Autophagy also plays a role in lipid metabolism and thus can influence the development of fatty liver disease, a rapidly increasing cause of chronic liver disease in the world. Hepatocytes are the main source for natural lipids stored in the form of triglycerides (TGs) and lipid droplets (LDs). Interestingly, the first degradation of lipid droplets through lipophagy was observed in mouse liver. It has been shown that ATg7 knockout mice showed significant increase levels of TGs and LDs in the hepatocytes leading to a decrease in the levels of free fatty acids (FFAs), necessary for ATP generation [20]. Another study illustrates the formation of hepatic steatosis in mice due to the consumption of a high-fat diet. This process occurs through autophagy activation in hepatic stellate cells and is due to the suppression of mTOR phosphorylation which increased expression of Sirt1 through the AMPK pathway [21].

3. Role of Autophagy in Hepatocellular Carcinoma

Hepatocellular carcinoma is one of the most common primary cancer and a major leading cause of death worldwide [22]. An estimation of 30,200 deaths is predicted this year [23]. The high proliferative capability of HCC cells has been linked to persistent inflammation and increased oxidative stress. Autophagy has been shown to play a dual role in cancer. Autophagy could be either tumor suppressive or tumor promoting. Here we review both the pro- and anti-tumor mechanism of autophagy that take place during the development and growth of HCC.

3.1. Tumor-Suppressive Role of Autophagy

Inflammation is recognized as a hallmark of cancer in promoting tumor growth and is associated with the poor prognosis of many solid tumors [24]. It is well known that HCC progression is highly correlated with the persistent inflammatory stimulation [25]. Autophagy has been suggested to prevent cancer progression by suppressing inflammation [26–29] while inhibition of autophagy can lead to a sustained and elevated level of inflammation [30,31]. Inflammasomes are the major drivers for chronic inflammation in the liver [32,33]. Interestingly, the capability of cells to suppress inflammation through autophagy was first observed in autophagic inhibited mice. Lack of autophagic responses in ATG16L1 knockout mice undergoing septic shock revealed an elevated level of inflammasome associated IL-1β and IL-18 cytokine production compared to wild-type controls [28]. Further studies showed that depletion of the autophagic proteins, LC3B and Beclin1, enhanced Caspase-1 activation which was NALP3 inflammasomes dependent. Mice lacking LC3B protein were more susceptible to LPS induced mortality [34]. In addition, a recent study showed the effect of chemokine (C-X-C motif) ligand 17 (CXCL17) in suppressing autophagy [35]. In human HCC tissues, elevated expression of CXCL17 has been observed which can also promote cell proliferation and migration when treated invitro. Silencing of this induced autophagy which is due to the enhanced nuclear translocation of liver kinase b1 (LKB1) that phosphorylates and activates AMPK. This lead to decrease in tumor volume and proliferation.

Beclin1, an important autophagic protein, has been shown to be associated with HCC tumors. The decreased Beclin1 expression observed in human HCC tissues correlated with tumor recurrence and disease-free survival [36]. Studies have also shown that knocking out Beclin1 in mice is embryonically lethal whereas heterogeneous Beclin1 mice developed spontaneous HCC [37]. In addition, normal hepatocytes show higher expression and activity of autophagic-associated proteins compared with HCC cell lines providing evidence that autophagy plays a tumor suppressive role [14]. A recent study demonstrated the effect of adrenaline in promoting hepatocarcinogenesis [38]. Treatment of adrenaline in DEN-induced HCC mice showed a remarkable increase in liver injury along with increased tumor number and tumor size. Mechanistically, increase in adrenaline activated the adrenergic receptors ADRB2 which inhibited autophagy activation by disrupting the Beclin1/VPS34/ATg14 complex.

Since autophagy plays a vital role in suppressing cancer inflammation, inhibition of autophagy has also been shown to result in an excessive accumulation of p62 protein [39]. P62 is an autophagic substrate which is used in measuring autophagic activity [40,41]. Transgenic P62 knockout animals displayed irregular cell mitotic activity with an increased expression of insulin-like growth factor 2 (IGF2) in their HCC tumors [42]. It has been reported that p62 is necessary for the HCC initiation by maintaining metabolic homeostasis through the mTOR pathway [43] and ablation of p62 inhibits growth and proliferation [14]. In a study, 90 HCC-resected tumors were analyzed for the accumulation of intracellular hyaline bodies (IHB) which are cytoplasmic inclusions consisting of p62. Patients with increased IHB were shown to be associated with significantly shorter overall survival [44]. Moreover. P62 is also known to interact with tumor necrosis factor receptor-associated factor 6 (TRAF6) that induces nuclear factor (NF-kB) activation [45]. Zhang et al. [46] have shown that DEAD-box protein 5 (DDX5), a tumor suppressor protein in the liver [47], binds to p62 and interferes with P62/TRAF6 interaction. This results in autophagy induction. However, the expression of DDX5 in the human HCC tumor tissues is relatively lower when compared to its non-tumor counterpart. Autophagy has also been shown to contribute to the anti-proliferative activity of interferon gamma (IFN-gamma), a pleiotropic cytokine that facilitates anti-viral and anti-proliferative effects in cancer cells. In HCC cell lines, stimulated autophagosome formation inhibited cell growth. Silencing of autophagy in these cells abolished the inhibitory effect, suggesting an essential anti-tumorigenic activity [48].

Similarly, multiple miRNAs which are found to target autophagic comprised genes for autophagy modulation [49–51] may also play a part in HCC growth and inhibition. miR-7 is a well acknowledged tumor suppressive microRNA in cancers. In HCC tumors, levels of miR-7 are significantly downregulated. It has been shown that upregulation of miR-7 in HCC cell lines increases autophagic activity by targeting the mTOR pathway, leading to a decrease in cancer cell proliferation [52]. miR-85 is an essential component during liver development and has also been linked as a tumor suppressor in HCC. In human HCC cell line HepG2, transfection of miR-85 upregulated autophagic activity which resulted in cell cycle arrest [53]. Our group has also previously shown that miR-375 is downregulated in HCC cell lines and tissues [54]. We found that miR-375 inhibits autophagy by suppressing the conversion of LC3I to LC3II by downregulating ATG7. Inoculating miR-375 overexpressed cells in nude mice showed significantly decreased tumor growth [51].

3.2. Tumor-Promoting Role of Autophagy

Hypoxia-induced oxidative stress is one of the most prominent features in all solid tumors [55,56] due to the inadequate blood supply that tumors experience as they grow. Under oxygen deprivation, cells respond by regulating their metabolic and bioenergetics demands to overcome the hypoxic resistance [57–59]. Hypoxia-induced autophagy in hepatocytes and HCC tumor cells relies upon the stabilization of hypoxia-inducible factor (HIF1α). HIF is the important regulator that maintains oxygen homeostasis. It has been shown that HIF1-α upregulates BNIP3 and BNIP3L proteins which binds to the BCL-2 protein. This process inhibits the disruptive interaction between BCL-2 and Beclin1 [60] to induce autophagy for cellular survival in hypoxic conditions. In addition, hypoxia is also shown to upregulate early growth response gene-1 (Egr-1) expression. Egr-1 is a zinc finger nuclear protein and functions as a transcriptional regulator [61]. Upregulation of hypoxia induced Egr-1 has shown to induce autophagy in HCC cell lines promoting migration. Inhibiting Egr-1 function by Ad-DN-Egr-1 revealed the attenuated autophagosome formation due to inhibited binding of Egr-1 at LC3 promoter region (-233 to -214) [62].

The extensive reactive oxygen species generation during the developing tumor is the primary outcome of hypoxic stress. Increased ROS levels are shown to oxidize cellular components such as DNA, lipids, and proteins [63,64]. ROS can be generated by the NADPH oxidase complexes in the cell membrane, endoplasmic reticulum, peroxisomes, and mitochondria [65,66]. Tumors adapt different mechanisms to eliminates intracellular ROS, one of which is by the upregulation of anti-oxidant proteins NRF2 [67]. NRF2 is a cytoplasmic protein which translocates to the nucleus for the transcription of redox-balancing proteins and β-oxidant enzymes and is upregulated by autophagy. The autophagic protein p62 has been shown to interact with NRF2 [68]. Phosphorylated p62 binds with Keap1 (NRF2 inhibitory protein) allowing NRF2 release and cytosolic stabilization [69,70]. The clinical implication of NRF2 was elucidated in 107 HCC patients where patients that expressed higher levels of pNRF2 were significantly associated with worst disease-free survival and poor overall survival [71]. Thus, p62 induces the antioxidant activation pathway to prevent extreme organelle injury leading to tumor cell death.

Another important mechanism to control excess ROS production is by the removal of damaged organelles from the cell. Injured and non-functional mitochondria are the major source of cellular ROS production and the induction of mitophagy helps clear these damaged mitochondria to maintain cell function and bioenergetics [72,73]. Mitochondrial ROS is eliminated regularly by the superoxide dismutase within the cytosol [74,75] which is also activated by the NRF2 protein [76]. Depolarized mitochondria cleared via mitophagy are regulated by PINK1 and Parkin1 [77]. It is reported that mitophagy can degrade tumor suppressor p53 once localized to mitochondria and inhibit its subcellular localization. Mitophagy impairment results in p53 accumulation and its phosphorylation by PINK1 prevent hepatic cancer cell stemness [78]. However, excessive induction of mitophagy can also inhibit HCC migration. When yes-activated protein (Yap), a highly upregulated protein in HCC, is depleted, mitophagy is overactivated leading to cellular energy deprivation [79]. In contrast, the excessive activation of autophagy may also lead to autophagic cell death [80,81]. This process requires an additional cell death signaling, including the phosphorylation of c-Jun N-terminal kinase (JNK) [82]. Interestingly, the pro-apoptotic (Bax/Bak) deficient cells showed an autophagic cell death when exposed to apoptotic stimuli. This was driven through the increase in the level of JNK phosphorylation. However, treatment with the JNK inhibitor further revealed that a simultaneous activation of autophagy and JNK is required for the autophagic cell death. Numerous other cell death and tumor suppressor-related proteins are shown to trigger autophagic cell death in the literature [83–85].

Autophagy can also regulate inflammatory immune response by the release and degradation of damage associated molecular patterns (DAMPS) including high mobility group box 1 (HMGB1), histones, ATP, mitochondrial (mt)DNA, and mitochondrial transcription factor A (TFAM). HMGB1 is a well-characterized DAMP which can be released from necrotic or apoptotic hepatocytes [86,87]. Interestingly, autophagy-mediated intracellular mobilization of HMGB1 enables tumor growth by inducing cell survival and apoptosis [88,89]. We have previously shown that under hypoxic stress, HMGB1 translocates from nucleus to cytoplasm in HCC cells. Intracellular translocation of HMGB1 facilitates its interaction with mtDNA in the cytosol where together they activate TLR9 signaling pathways to enhance tumor growth [90].

3.3. Autophagy in HCC Metastasis

Autophagy, due to its tumor promoting role, also plays a part in tumor metastasis. Increasing evidence suggests the upregulation of autophagy during the process of tumor metastasis [91,92]. As the primary tumor grows and encounter harsh microenvironment, part of it escapes and intravasates within the circulatory and lymphatic system, localizing at distal organs [93]. Cell detachment from the extracellular matrix (ECM) has demonstrated to trigger autophagy which then protects it from anoikis, a type of cell death induced in response to ECM detachment [94]. In addition, Autophagy can also induce changes in the cell adhesion signaling that facilitates invasion and migration [95].

Autophagy in hepatocellular carcinoma has shown to facilitate metastasis by upregulating the expression of epithelial–mesenchymal transition (EMT). Induction of autophagy in the starved cells inhibited the expression of epithelial markers and induced mesenchymal expression along with cell invasion marker matrix metalloproteinase-9 (MMP9) [96]. These changes were regulated by the activation of TGF-beta and phosphorylation of Smad3 signaling pathway. In another study, inhibition of autophagy via silencing Beclin1 and ATG5 in HCC lung metastasis model markedly decreased distal metastasis to the lungs [97]. This effect is observed due to the impaired anoikis resistance that can suppress the colonization of HCC cells. However, silencing of autophagy mediators showed no effect in the expression of cell migration and invasion regulators.

Autophagy-mediated cancer cell metastasis can be stimulated by numerous stress factors persisting within the tumor microenvironment. One of which is the fluid shear stress (FSS). Wang et al. [98] showed that HCC cells, when exposed to 1.4 dyn/cm^2 of FSS, induce autophagy in a time-dependent manner. Furthermore, inhibition of autophagy attenuated cells to migrate and downregulate the expression of PI3K/FAK/Rho GTPase pathway. This suggests that the activation of autophagy via FSS is a PI3K/FAK/Rho GTPase-dependent pathway.

4. Autophagy in HCC Therapy

As described above, autophagy can be either be pro- or anti-tumorigenic for HCC. Therefore, modulation of autophagy-based HCC therapy is very complex and will vary depending on the setting. Autophagy can suppress liver inflammation and thus decrease the carcinogenic environment in the liver but it can also promote and maintain tumor cell homeostasis by inducing mitophagy in growing HCC tumors. In addition, both the induction and inhibition of autophagy has been investigated to induce tumor cell death [99,100]. Currently, there are a variety of therapeutic agents that are being used either individually or in combination with other agents for anti-HCC therapy. The current agents used to selectively target autophagy to induce HCC cell death are described in Table 1.

4.1. Autophagy Inducers

The autophagy inducer sorafenib is the first-line drug used for the treatment of advanced HCC [101]. Currently, sorafenib is the only drug that has been shown to improve HCC patient survival [102]. In a randomized controlled trial, patients with advanced HCC treated with sorafenib had an improved rate of overall survival compared to patients given placebo. Sorafenib has been shown to promote cell death through the upregulation of autophagy via myeloid cell leukemia-1 (Mcl-1) signaling pathway [103]. In addition, sorafenib can also inhibit tumor growth by targeting the RAF/MEK/ERK pathway to induce cell cycle arrest [104]. Besides Mcl-1 and ERK pathways, sorafenib can also inhibit the activation of PI3K/AKT/mTOR pathways which initiates a signaling cascade for autophagy induction [105,106]. In a recent study, sorafenib is also shown to regulate cell endoplasmic reticulum (ER) stress, JNK, Akt, and AMPK pathway leading to elevated autophagy which later shifts towards apoptosis [107]. At an early time point (3–12 h) sorafenib increases ER stress which is shown to induce the autophagic survival process in HCC cell line by regulating JNK/AMPK signaling pathway. At a later stage (24 h), a significant increase in the ER stress and PERK-CHOP dependent rise of Bim shifted autophagy to apoptosis cell death.

Besides its tumor suppressing function, long term sorafenib treatment has also shown to trigger chemo-resistance in HCC cells [108]. Thus, the combination of sorafenib with SAHA, another autophagy-inducer, has been used to improve responses against HCC compared to treating with sorafenib alone [109]. Sustained treatment of sorafenib has also shown to increase tumor hypoxic environment that leads to decrease treatment efficiency [110]. Combination of melatonin with sorafenib has shown to enhance sorafenib's cytotoxicity against human HCC cells by decreasing hypoxic resistance [111]. Co-administration diminished the expression of BNIP3 and NIX, hypoxia induced mitophagy mediators. Due to the common occurrence of tumor resistance, the combinations of different drugs with sorafenib are currently being studied to increase chemo-sensitivity and decrease tumor growth. A detailed combination of reagents with sorafenib are extensively reviewed elsewhere [112].

4.2. Autophagy Inhibitors

Since autophagy can be utilized by the growing cancer cells for its survival and add resistance towards chemotherapeutic reagents, inhibiting autophagy can also be a promising strategy against cancer therapy. At present chloroquine (CQ), an anti-malarial drug, can be used for the inhibition of autophagy through the suppression of lysosomes. Treatment with CQ neutralizes the pH levels of lysosomes required in the final stages of autophagy for degradation [113]. CQ is being effectively used in patients with the combination of drugs capable of inducing cell apoptosis such as oxaliplatin [114]. It is reported that co-treatment of proliferative HCC cell lines with CQ and sorafenib can lead to a marked suppression of its growth [105]. In a liver xenograft tumor model, nude mice treated with CQ and sorafenib combined achieved a higher level of tumor regression compared to treatment with sorafenib alone. In addition, 3-methyladenine (3-MA) which inhibits the interaction of autophagosomes and lysosomes can enhance anti-HCC therapy when combined with cisplatin, doxorubicin, and sorafenib [115]. Similarly, suppression of autophagy by administration of 3-MA and inactive ATg4B suppresses the proliferation of Huh7 cells [116]. Hence, inhibition of autophagy can promote the death of HCC cells but these treatments with their known side effects highlight a major risk in triggering the neoplasticism within the normal hepatocytes.

Table 1. Therapeutic reagents modulating autophagy in anti-HCC treatment.

Reagents	Autophagy Target	Cells Treated	Result	Ref.
Sirolimus (Rapamycin)	mTOR	HepG2	Upregulation of autophagy-cell death	[117,118]
Temsirolimus (CCI-779)	mTOR	HepG2, Huh7	Upregulation of autophagy-cell death	[119]
Everolimus (RAD001)	mTOR	Hep3B, HepG2, Huh7	Upregulation of autophagy-cell death	[120]
Pemetrexed	mTORC1	HepG2	Upregulation of autophagy-cell death	[121]
SC-59	mTORC1	PLC5, Sk-Hep1, HepG2 and Hep3B	Upregulation of autophagy-cell death	[122,123]
BEZ235	PI3K/mTOR	Hep3B, PLC/PRF/5	Upregulation of autophagy-cell death	[124]
MK-2206	AKT	SNU449, SNU378, SNU475	Upregulation of autophagy-cell death	[125]
SB203580	MAPK	HepG2, Hep3B, PLC/PRF/5, Huh-7	Upregulation of autophagy-cell death	[126]
Regorafenib	Tyrosine-kinase inhibitor	HepG2 and Hep3B	Upregulation of autophagy-cell death	[127]
Sorafenib	Tyrosine-kinase inhibitor	Hep3B, HepG2, Huh7	Upregulation of autophagy-cell death	[105,112]
Nilotinib	Tyrosine kinase inhibitor	PLC5, Huh-7, Hep3B	Upregulation of autophagy-cell death	[128]
ABT-737	JNK pathway	Huh7, HepG2	Upregulation of autophagy-cell death	[129]
OSU-03012	PDK1/AKT	Huh7, Hep3B, and HepG2	Upregulation of autophagy-cell death	[130]
5-FU	Induce ER stress	HepG2, SMMC-7721, Hep3B, BEL-7402	Upregulation of autophagy-cell survival	[114]
Bortezomib	Proteasome inhibitor	Huh7, HepG2, HuH7, human hepatocytes, rat hepatocytes	Upregulation of autophagy-cell death	[131]
Chloroquine	Lysosome	HepG2, Huh7, HA22T/VGH, Mahlavu	Downregulation of autophagy-cell death	[132,133]
3-MA	PI3K III	H22, HepG2, PLC/PRF/5, SMMC7721	Downregulation of autophagy-cell death and cell survival	[134,135]
Bafilomycin A1	Lysosome	BEL7402, HepG2, Huh7, SMMC-7721	Downregulation of autophagy-cell death	[136]

5. Concluding Remarks

Autophagy is the vital response for hepatocytes undergoing stress in the maintenance of cellular homeostasis and quality control. As we outlined in this review, evidence supports a dual role of autophagy in the progression of HCC (Figure 1). Targeting autophagy can be used to treat liver cancer. However, caution should be noted as autophagy can inhibit the development of HCC but also act as a tumor promoter resulting resistance to HCC tumor therapy [137]. Multiple direct and indirect interactions including complex mechanistic overlap between apoptotic and autophagic cell death have been studied [138,139]. Many studies indicate that the apoptotic events alter autophagy. However, the molecular role of autophagy controlling apoptosis requires further investigation. In the developing tumor microenvironment, hypoxia is a common stimulus in many cancers and hepatotropic viruses can induce a hypoxic environment initiating hypoxic oxidative and inflammatory responses [140]. Thus improving tumor oxygenation or suppressing hypoxia-induced autophagy signaling could be a potential future therapeutic pathway to target. We currently have a minimal understanding regarding the stress signaling that takes part in the complex coordination of autophagy to respond during different intracellular and extracellular stimuli in HCC. Additional studies are necessary to further elucidate the mechanisms underlying autophagy's role in HCC.

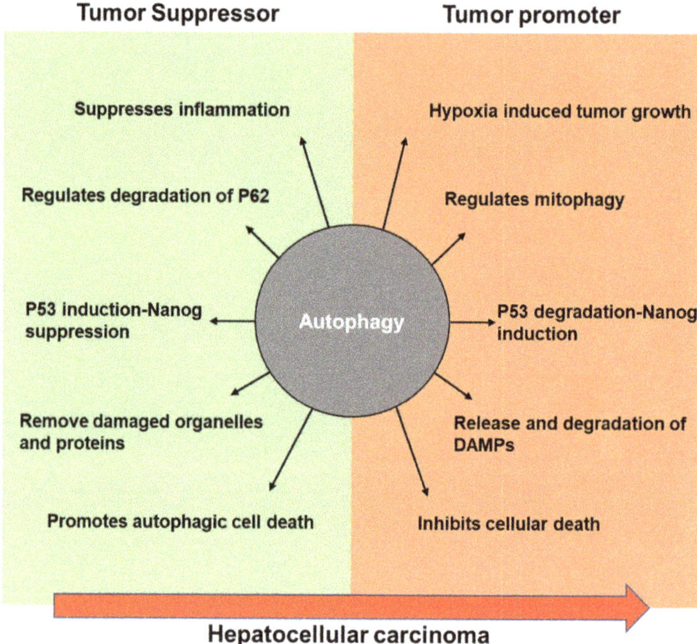

Figure 1. Schematic diagram illustrating the proposed role of autophagy during the development of hepatocellular carcinoma.

Funding: This work is supported by the grants from National Institute of Health, CA214865-01 (AT) and GM095566-06 (AT).

Acknowledgments: We thank Jannat Malik for linguistic revision.

Conflicts of Interest: The authors declared nothing to disclose regarding the conflict of interest concerning this paper.

References

1. Xie, Z.; Klionsky, D.J. Autophagosome formation: Core machinery and adaptations. *Nat. Cell Biol.* **2007**, *9*, 1102–1109. [CrossRef] [PubMed]
2. Devenish, R.J.; Klionsky, D.J. Autophagy: Mechanism and physiological relevance "brewed" from yeast studies. *Front. Biosci.* **2012**, *54*, 1354–1363. [CrossRef]
3. White, E. The role for autophagy in cancer. *J. Clin. Investig.* **2015**, *125*, 42–46. [CrossRef] [PubMed]
4. Mizushima, N.; Komatsu, M. Autophagy: Renovation of Cells and Tissues. *Cell* **2011**, *147*, 728–741. [CrossRef] [PubMed]
5. Huang, J.; Klionsky, D.J. Autophagy and human disease. *Cell Cycle* **2007**, *6*, 1837–1849. [CrossRef] [PubMed]
6. Yorimitsu, T.; Klionsky, D.J. Autophagy: Molecular machinery for self-eating. *Cell Death Differ.* **2005**, *12*, 1542–1552. [CrossRef] [PubMed]
7. Kwanten, W.J.; Martinet, W.; Michielsen, P.P.; Francque, S.M. Role of autophagy in the pathophysiology of nonalcoholic fatty liver disease: A controversial issue. *World J. Gastroenterol.* **2014**, *20*, 7325–7338. [CrossRef]
8. Cui, J.; Gong, Z.; Shen, H.-M. The role of autophagy in liver cancer: Molecular mechanisms and potential therapeutic targets. *Biochim. Biophys. Acta Rev. Cancer* **2013**, *1836*, 15–26. [CrossRef]

9. Portolani, N.; Coniglio, A.; Ghidoni, S.; Giovanelli, M.; Benetti, A.; Tiberio, G.A.M.; Giulini, S.M. Early and Late Recurrence after Liver Resection for Hepatocellular Carcinoma. *Ann. Surg.* **2006**, *243*, 229–235. [CrossRef]

10. White, E. Deconvoluting the context-dependent role for autophagy in cancer. *Nat. Rev. Cancer* **2012**, *12*, 401–410. [CrossRef]

11. Janku, F.; McConkey, D.J.; Hong, D.S.; Kurzrock, R. Autophagy as a target for anticancer therapy. *Nat. Rev. Clin. Oncol.* **2011**, *8*, 528–539. [CrossRef] [PubMed]

12. Komatsu, M.; Waguri, S.; Ueno, T.; Iwata, J.; Murata, S.; Tanida, I.; Ezaki, J.; Mizushima, N.; Ohsumi, Y.; Uchiyama, Y.; et al. Impairment of starvation-induced and constitutive autophagy in Atg7-deficient mice. *J. Cell Biol.* **2005**, *169*, 425–434. [CrossRef] [PubMed]

13. Ding, W.-X. Role of autophagy in liver physiology and pathophysiology. *World J. Biol. Chem.* **2010**, *1*, 3–12. [CrossRef]

14. Takamura, A.; Komatsu, M.; Hara, T.; Sakamoto, A.; Kishi, C.; Waguri, S.; Eishi, Y.; Hino, O.; Tanaka, K.; Mizushima, N. Autophagy-deficient mice develop multiple liver tumors. *Genes Dev.* **2011**, *25*, 795–800. [CrossRef] [PubMed]

15. Malhi, H.; Gores, G.J. Cellular and Molecular Mechanisms of Liver Injury. *Gastroenterology* **2008**, *134*, 1641–1654. [CrossRef] [PubMed]

16. Ueno, T.; Komatsu, M. Autophagy in the liver: Functions in health and disease. *Nat. Rev. Gastroenterol. Hepatol.* **2017**, *14*, 170–184. [CrossRef]

17. Rautou, P.E.; Mansouri, A.; Lebrec, D.; Durand, F.; Valla, D.; Moreau, R. Autophagy in liver diseases. *J. Hepatol.* **2010**, *53*, 1123–1134. [CrossRef] [PubMed]

18. Wang, Z.; Han, W.; Sui, X.; Fang, Y.; Pan, H. Autophagy: A novel therapeutic target for hepatocarcinoma (Review). *Oncol. Lett.* **2014**, *7*, 1345–1351. [CrossRef]

19. Abdoli, A.; Alirezaei, M.; Mehrbod, P.; Forouzanfar, F. Autophagy: The multi-purpose bridge in viral infections and host cells. *Rev. Med. Virol.* **2018**, *28*, e1973. [CrossRef] [PubMed]

20. Singh, R.; Kaushik, S.; Wang, Y.; Xiang, Y.; Novak, I.; Komatsu, M.; Tanaka, K.; Cuervo, A.M.; Czaja, M.J. Autophagy regulates lipid metabolism. *Nature* **2009**, *458*, 1131–1135. [CrossRef] [PubMed]

21. Xu, L.; Kanasaki, M.; He, J.; Kitada, M.; Nagao, K.; Jinzu, H.; Noguchi, Y.; Maegawa, H.; Kanasaki, K.; Koya, D. Ketogenic essential amino acids replacement diet ameliorated hepatosteatosis with altering autophagy-associated molecules. *Biochim. Biophys. Acta Mol. Basis Dis.* **2013**, *1832*, 1605–1612. [CrossRef] [PubMed]

22. Siegel, R.L.; Miller, K.D.; Jemal, A. Cancer statistics, 2017. *CA Cancer J. Clin.* **2017**, *67*, 7–30. [CrossRef] [PubMed]

23. Auld, S.K.J.R.; Scholefield, J.A.; Little, T.J. Genetic variation in the cellular response of Daphnia magna (Crustacea: Cladocera) to its bacterial parasite. *Proc. Biol. Sci.* **2010**, *277*, 3291–3297. [CrossRef] [PubMed]

24. Zhong, J.-H.; Huang, D.-H.; Chen, Z.-Y. Prognostic role of systemic immune-inflammation index in solid tumors: A systematic review and meta-analysis. *Oncotarget* **2017**, *8*, 75381–75388. [CrossRef] [PubMed]

25. Arzumanyan, A.; Reis, H.M.; Feitelson, M.A. Pathogenic mechanisms in HBV- and HCV-associated hepatocellular carcinoma. *Nat. Rev. Cancer* **2013**, *13*, 123–135. [CrossRef] [PubMed]

26. Zhang, L.; Sung, J.J.Y.; Yu, J.; Ng, S.C.; Wong, S.H.; Cho, C.H.; Ng, S.S.M.; Chan, F.K.L.; Wu, W.K.K. Xenophagy in Helicobacter pylori- and Epstein-Barr virus-induced gastric cancer. *J. Pathol.* **2014**, *233*, 103–112. [CrossRef] [PubMed]

27. Shibutani, S.T.; Saitoh, T.; Nowag, H.; Münz, C.; Yoshimori, T. Autophagy and autophagy-related proteins in the immune system. *Nat. Immunol.* **2015**, *16*, 1014–1024. [CrossRef] [PubMed]

28. Saitoh, T.; Fujita, N.; Jang, M.H.; Uematsu, S.; Yang, B.-G.; Satoh, T.; Omori, H.; Noda, T.; Yamamoto, N.; Komatsu, M.; et al. Loss of the autophagy protein Atg16L1 enhances endotoxin-induced IL-1β production. *Nature* **2008**, *456*, 264–268. [CrossRef]

29. Zhou, R.; Yazdi, A.S.; Menu, P.; Tschopp, J. A role for mitochondria in NLRP3 inflammasome activation. *Nature* **2011**, *469*, 221–225. [CrossRef]

30. Bujak, A.L.; Crane, J.D.; Lally, J.S.; Ford, R.J.; Kang, S.J.; Rebalka, I.A.; Green, A.E.; Kemp, B.E.; Hawke, T.J.; Schertzer, J.D.; et al. AMPK activation of muscle autophagy prevents fasting-induced hypoglycemia and myopathy during aging. *Cell Metab.* **2015**, *21*, 883–890. [CrossRef]

31. Zhong, Z.; Sanchez-Lopez, E.; Karin, M. Autophagy, Inflammation, and Immunity: A Troika Governing Cancer and Its Treatment. *Cell* **2016**, *166*, 288–298. [CrossRef] [PubMed]

32. Mridha, A.R.; Wree, A.; Robertson, A.A.B.; Yeh, M.M.; Johnson, C.D.; Van Rooyen, D.M.; Haczeyni, F.; Teoh, N.C.H.; Savard, C.; Ioannou, G.N.; et al. NLRP3 inflammasome blockade reduces liver inflammation and fibrosis in experimental NASH in mice. *J. Hepatol.* **2017**, *66*, 1037–1046. [CrossRef] [PubMed]

33. Petrasek, J.; Bala, S.; Csak, T.; Lippai, D.; Kodys, K.; Menashy, V.; Barrieau, M.; Min, S.-Y.; Kurt-Jones, E.A.; Szabo, G. IL-1 receptor antagonist ameliorates inflammasome-dependent alcoholic steatohepatitis in mice. *J. Clin. Investig.* **2012**, *122*, 3476–3489. [CrossRef] [PubMed]

34. Nakahira, K.; Haspel, J.A.; Rathinam, V.A.K.; Lee, S.-J.; Dolinay, T.; Lam, H.C.; Englert, J.A.; Rabinovitch, M.; Cernadas, M.; Kim, H.P.; et al. Autophagy proteins regulate innate immune responses by inhibiting the release of mitochondrial DNA mediated by the NALP3 inflammasome. *Nat. Immunol.* **2011**, *12*, 222–230. [CrossRef] [PubMed]

35. Wang, L.; Li, H.; Zhen, Z.; Ma, X.; Yu, W.; Zeng, H.; Li, L. CXCL17 promotes cell metastasis and inhibits autophagy via the LKB1-AMPK pathway in hepatocellular carcinoma. *Gene* **2019**, *690*, 129–136. [CrossRef]

36. Kotsafti, A.; Farinati, F.; Cardin, R.; Cillo, U.; Nitti, D.; Bortolami, M. Autophagy and apoptosis-related genes in chronic liver disease and hepatocellular carcinoma. *BMC Gastroenterol.* **2012**, *12*, 118. [CrossRef]

37. Yue, Z.; Jin, S.; Yang, C.; Levine, A.J.; Heintz, N. Beclin 1, an autophagy gene essential for early embryonic development, is a haploinsufficient tumor suppressor. *Proc. Natl. Acad. Sci. USA* **2003**, *100*, 15077–15082. [CrossRef]

38. Wu, F.-Q.; Fang, T.; Yu, L.-X.; Lv, G.-S.; Lv, H.-W.; Liang, D.; Li, T.; Wang, C.-Z.; Tan, Y.-X.; Ding, J.; et al. ADRB2 signaling promotes HCC progression and sorafenib resistance by inhibiting autophagic degradation of HIF1α. *J. Hepatol.* **2016**, *65*, 314–324. [CrossRef]

39. Pursiheimo, J.-P.; Rantanen, K.; Heikkinen, P.T.; Johansen, T.; Jaakkola, P.M. Hypoxia-activated autophagy accelerates degradation of SQSTM1/p62. *Oncogene* **2009**, *28*, 334–344. [CrossRef]

40. Komatsu, M.; Waguri, S.; Koike, M.; Sou, Y.; Ueno, T.; Hara, T.; Mizushima, N.; Iwata, J.; Ezaki, J.; Murata, S.; et al. Homeostatic Levels of p62 Control Cytoplasmic Inclusion Body Formation in Autophagy-Deficient Mice. *Cell* **2007**, *131*, 1149–1163. [CrossRef]

41. Yoshii, S.R.; Mizushima, N. Monitoring and Measuring Autophagy. *Int. J. Mol. Sci.* **2017**, *18*, 1865. [CrossRef] [PubMed]

42. Kessler, S.M.; Laggai, S.; Barghash, A.; Schultheiss, C.S.; Lederer, E.; Artl, M.; Helms, V.; Haybaeck, J.; Kiemer, A.K. IMP2/p62 induces genomic instability and an aggressive hepatocellular carcinoma phenotype. *Cell Death Dis.* **2015**, *6*, e1894. [CrossRef] [PubMed]

43. Umemura, A.; He, F.; Taniguchi, K.; Nakagawa, H.; Yamachika, S.; Font-Burgada, J.; Zhong, Z.; Subramaniam, S.; Raghunandan, S.; Duran, A.; et al. p62, Upregulated during Preneoplasia, Induces Hepatocellular Carcinogenesis by Maintaining Survival of Stressed HCC-Initiating Cells. *Cancer Cell* **2016**, *29*, 935–948. [CrossRef] [PubMed]

44. Aigelsreiter, A.; Neumann, J.; Pichler, M.; Halasz, J.; Zatloukal, K.; Berghold, A.; Douschan, P.; Rainer, F.; Stauber, R.; Haybaeck, J.; et al. Hepatocellular carcinomas with intracellular hyaline bodies have a poor prognosis. *Liver Int.* **2017**, *37*, 600–610. [CrossRef]

45. Moscat, J.; Diaz-Meco, M.T. p62 at the Crossroads of Autophagy, Apoptosis, and Cancer. *Cell* **2009**, *137*, 1001–1004. [CrossRef] [PubMed]

46. Zhang, H.; Zhang, Y.; Zhu, X.; Chen, C.; Zhang, C.; Xia, Y.; Zhao, Y.; Andrisani, O.; Kong, L. DEAD Box Protein 5 Inhibits Liver Tumorigenesis by Stimulating Autophagy via Interaction with p62/SQSTM1. *Hepatology* **2018**. [CrossRef] [PubMed]

47. Nicol, S.M.; Bray, S.E.; Derek Black, H.; Lorimore, S.A.; Wright, E.G.; Lane, D.P.; Meek, D.W.; Coates, P.J.; Fuller-Pace, F.V. The RNA helicase p68 (DDX5) is selectively required for the induction of p53-dependent p21 expression and cell-cycle arrest after DNA damage. *Oncogene* **2013**, *32*, 3461–3469. [CrossRef] [PubMed]

48. Li, P.; Du, Q.; Cao, Z.; Guo, Z.; Evankovich, J.; Yan, W.; Chang, Y.; Shao, L.; Stolz, D.B.; Tsung, A.; et al. Interferon-gamma induces autophagy with growth inhibition and cell death in human hepatocellular carcinoma (HCC) cells through interferon-regulatory factor-1 (IRF-1). *Cancer Lett.* **2012**, *314*, 213–222. [CrossRef] [PubMed]

49. Zhu, H.; Wu, H.; Liu, X.; Li, B.; Chen, Y.; Ren, X.; Liu, C.-G.; Yang, J.-M. Regulation of autophagy by a beclin 1-targeted microRNA, miR-30a, in cancer cells. *Autophagy* **2009**, *5*, 816–823. [CrossRef] [PubMed]

50. Frankel, L.B.; Wen, J.; Lees, M.; Høyer-Hansen, M.; Farkas, T.; Krogh, A.; Jäättelä, M.; Lund, A.H. microRNA-101 is a potent inhibitor of autophagy. *EMBO J.* **2011**, *30*, 4628–4641. [CrossRef]

51. Chang, Y.; Yan, W.; He, X.; Zhang, L.; Li, C.; Huang, H.; Nace, G.; Geller, D.A.; Lin, J.; Tsung, A. MiR-375 inhibits autophagy and reduces viability of hepatocellular carcinoma cells under hypoxic conditions. *Gastroenterology* **2012**, *143*, 177–187. [CrossRef]

52. Wang, Y.; Wang, Q.; Song, J. Inhibition of autophagy potentiates the proliferation inhibition activity of microRNA-7 in human hepatocellular carcinoma cells. *Oncol. Lett.* **2017**, *14*, 3566–3572. [CrossRef] [PubMed]

53. Zhou, L.; Liu, S.; Han, M.; Feng, S.; Liang, J.; Li, Z.; Li, Y.; Lu, H.; Liu, T.; Ma, Y.; et al. MicroRNA-185 induces potent autophagy via AKT signaling in hepatocellular carcinoma. *Tumour Biol.* **2017**, *39*, 1010428317694313. [CrossRef] [PubMed]

54. Chang, Y.; Lin, J.; Tsung, A. Manipulation of autophagy by MIR375 generates antitumor effects in liver cancer. *Autophagy* **2012**, *8*, 1833–1834. [CrossRef] [PubMed]

55. Wong, C.C.-L.; Kai, A.K.-L.; Ng, I.O.-L. The impact of hypoxia in hepatocellular carcinoma metastasis. *Front. Med.* **2014**, *8*, 33–41. [CrossRef] [PubMed]

56. Wilson, G.K.; Tennant, D.A.; McKeating, J.A. Hypoxia inducible factors in liver disease and hepatocellular carcinoma: Current understanding and future directions. *J. Hepatol.* **2014**, *61*, 1397–1406. [CrossRef] [PubMed]

57. Eales, K.L.; Hollinshead, K.E.R.; Tennant, D.A. Hypoxia and metabolic adaptation of cancer cells. *Oncogenesis* **2016**, *61*, 1397–1406. [CrossRef]

58. Tohme, S.; Yazdani, H.O.; Liu, Y.; Loughran, P.; van der Windt, D.J.; Huang, H.; Simmons, R.L.; Shiva, S.; Tai, S.; Tsung, A. Hypoxia mediates mitochondrial biogenesis in hepatocellular carcinoma to promote tumor growth through HMGB1 and TLR9 interaction. *Hepatology* **2017**, *66*, 182–197. [CrossRef]

59. Schito, L.; Rey, S. Cell-Autonomous Metabolic Reprogramming in Hypoxia. *Trends Cell Biol.* **2018**, *28*, 128–142. [CrossRef]

60. Bellot, G.; Garcia-Medina, R.; Gounon, P.; Chiche, J.; Roux, D.; Pouysségur, J.; Mazure, N.M. Hypoxia-Induced Autophagy Is Mediated through Hypoxia-Inducible Factor Induction of BNIP3 and BNIP3L via Their BH3 Domains. *Mol. Cell. Biol.* **2009**, *29*, 2570–2581. [CrossRef]

61. Sijtsema, W.Y. Sport voor mensen met een handicap. *Tijdschrift voor Ziekenverpleging* **1977**, *30*, 115–125. [PubMed]

62. Peng, W.X.; Xiong, E.M.; Ge, L.; Wan, Y.Y.; Zhang, C.L.; Du, F.Y.; Xu, M.; Bhat, R.A.; Jin, J.; Gong, A.H. Egr-1 promotes hypoxia-induced autophagy to enhance chemo-resistance of hepatocellular carcinoma cells. *Exp. Cell Res.* **2016**, *340*, 62–70. [CrossRef] [PubMed]

63. Bjelland, S.; Seeberg, E. Mutagenicity, toxicity and repair of DNA base damage induced by oxidation. *Mutat. Res.* **2003**, *531*, 37–80. [CrossRef]

64. Scherz-Shouval, R.; Elazar, Z. ROS, mitochondria and the regulation of autophagy. *Trends Cell Biol.* **2007**, *17*, 422–427. [CrossRef] [PubMed]

65. Han, D.; Williams, E.; Cadenas, E. Mitochondrial respiratory chain-dependent generation of superoxide anion and its release into the intermembrane space. *Biochem. J.* **2001**, *353*, 411–416. [CrossRef]

66. Muller, F. The nature and mechanism of superoxide production by the electron transport chain: Its relevance to aging. *Age* **2000**, *23*, 227–253. [CrossRef] [PubMed]

67. Jain, A.; Lamark, T.; Sjøttem, E.; Larsen, K.B.; Awuh, J.A.; Øvervatn, A.; McMahon, M.; Hayes, J.D.; Johansen, T. p62/SQSTM1 is a target gene for transcription factor NRF2 and creates a positive feedback loop by inducing antioxidant response element-driven gene transcription. *J. Biol. Chem.* **2010**, *285*, 22576–22591. [CrossRef] [PubMed]

68. Copple, I.M.; Lister, A.; Obeng, A.D.; Kitteringham, N.R.; Jenkins, R.E.; Layfield, R.; Foster, B.J.; Goldring, C.E.; Park, B.K. Physical and functional interaction of sequestosome 1 with Keap1 regulates the Keap1-Nrf2 cell defense pathway. *J. Biol. Chem.* **2010**, *285*, 16782–16788. [CrossRef] [PubMed]

69. Katsuragi, Y.; Ichimura, Y.; Komatsu, M. Regulation of the Keap1–Nrf2 pathway by p62/SQSTM1. *Curr. Opin. Toxicol.* **2016**, *1*, 54–61. [CrossRef]

70. Bartolini, D.; Dallaglio, K.; Torquato, P.; Piroddi, M.; Galli, F. Nrf2-p62 autophagy pathway and its response to oxidative stress in hepatocellular carcinoma. *Transl. Res.* **2018**, *193*, 54–71. [CrossRef] [PubMed]

71. Chen, J.; Yu, Y.; Ji, T.; Ma, R.; Chen, M.; Li, G.; Li, F.; Ding, Q.; Kang, Q.; Huang, D.; et al. Clinical implication of Keap1 and phosphorylated Nrf2 expression in hepatocellular carcinoma. *Cancer Med.* **2016**, *5*, 2678–2687. [CrossRef] [PubMed]

72. Lemasters, J.J. Selective Mitochondrial Autophagy, or Mitophagy, as a Targeted Defense against Oxidative Stress, Mitochondrial Dysfunction, and Aging. *Rejuv. Res.* **2005**, *8*, 3–5. [CrossRef] [PubMed]

73. Wild, P.; Dikic, I. Mitochondria get a Parkin' ticket. *Nat. Cell Biol.* **2010**, *12*, 104–106. [CrossRef] [PubMed]

74. Bedard, K.; Krause, K.-H. The NOX Family of ROS-Generating NADPH Oxidases: Physiology and Pathophysiology. *Physiol. Rev.* **2007**, *87*, 245–313. [CrossRef] [PubMed]

75. Lambeth, J.D. NOX enzymes and the biology of reactive oxygen. *Nat. Rev. Immunol.* **2004**, *4*, 181–189. [CrossRef] [PubMed]

76. Ma, Q. Role of Nrf2 in Oxidative Stress and Toxicity. *Annu. Rev. Pharmacol. Toxicol.* **2013**, *53*, 401–426. [CrossRef] [PubMed]

77. Twig, G.; Elorza, A.; Molina, A.J.A.; Mohamed, H.; Wikstrom, J.D.; Walzer, G.; Stiles, L.; Haigh, S.E.; Katz, S.; Las, G.; et al. Fission and selective fusion govern mitochondrial segregation and elimination by autophagy. *EMBO J.* **2008**, *27*, 433–446. [CrossRef]

78. Liu, K.; Lee, J.; Kim, J.Y.; Wang, L.; Tian, Y.; Chan, S.T.; Cho, C.; Machida, K.; Chen, D.; Ou, J.-H.J. Mitophagy Controls the Activities of Tumor Suppressor p53 to Regulate Hepatic Cancer Stem Cells. *Mol. Cell* **2017**, *68*, 281–292. [CrossRef] [PubMed]

79. Shi, C.; Cai, Y.; Li, Y.; Li, Y.; Hu, N.; Ma, S.; Hu, S.; Zhu, P.; Wang, W.; Zhou, H. Yap promotes hepatocellular carcinoma metastasis and mobilization via governing cofilin/F-actin/lamellipodium axis by regulation of JNK/Bnip3/SERCA/CaMKII pathways. *Redox Biol.* **2018**, *14*, 59–71. [CrossRef]

80. Inbal, B.; Bialik, S.; Sabanay, I.; Shani, G.; Kimchi, A. DAP kinase and DRP-1 mediate membrane blebbing and the formation of autophagic vesicles during programmed cell death. *J. Cell Biol.* **2002**, *157*, 455–468. [CrossRef] [PubMed]

81. Dasari, S.K.; Bialik, S.; Levin-Zaidman, S.; Levin-Salomon, V.; Merrill, A.H.; Futerman, A.H.; Kimchi, A. Signalome-wide RNAi screen identifies GBA1 as a positive mediator of autophagic cell death. *Cell Death Differ.* **2017**, *24*, 1288–1302. [CrossRef] [PubMed]

82. Shimizu, S.; Konishi, A.; Nishida, Y.; Mizuta, T.; Nishina, H.; Yamamoto, A.; Tsujimoto, Y. Involvement of JNK in the regulation of autophagic cell death. *Oncogene* **2010**, *29*, 2070–2082. [CrossRef] [PubMed]

83. Arakawa, S.; Tsujioka, M.; Yoshida, T.; Tajima-Sakurai, H.; Nishida, Y.; Matsuoka, Y.; Yoshino, I.; Tsujimoto, Y.; Shimizu, S. Role of Atg5-dependent cell death in the embryonic development of Bax/Bak double-knockout mice. *Cell Death Differ.* **2017**, *24*, 1598–1608. [CrossRef] [PubMed]

84. Reef, S.; Zalckvar, E.; Shifman, O.; Bialik, S.; Sabanay, H.; Oren, M.; Kimchi, A. A short mitochondrial form of p19ARF induces autophagy and caspase-independent cell death. *Mol. Cell* **2006**, *22*, 463–475. [CrossRef] [PubMed]

85. Yanagisawa, H.; Miyashita, T.; Nakano, Y.; Yamamoto, D. HSpin1, a transmembrane protein interacting with Bcl-2/Bcl-xL, induces a caspase-independent autophagic cell death. *Cell Death Differ.* **2003**, *10*, 798–807. [CrossRef] [PubMed]

86. Chen, M.; Liu, Y.; Varley, P.; Chang, Y.; He, X.X.; Huang, H.; Tang, D.; Lotze, M.T.; Lin, J.; Tsung, A. High-mobility group box 1 promotes hepatocellular carcinoma progression through MIR-21-mediated matrix metalloproteinase activity. *Cancer Res.* **2015**, *75*, 1645–1656. [CrossRef] [PubMed]

87. Huang, H.; Nace, G.W.; McDonald, K.-A.; Tai, S.; Klune, J.R.; Rosborough, B.R.; Ding, Q.; Loughran, P.; Zhu, X.; Beer-Stolz, D.; et al. Hepatocyte-specific high-mobility group box 1 deletion worsens the injury in liver ischemia/reperfusion: A role for intracellular high-mobility group box 1 in cellular protection. *Hepatology* **2014**, *59*, 1984–1997. [CrossRef]

88. Pan, B.; Chen, D.; Huang, J.; Wang, R.; Feng, B.; Song, H.; Chen, L. HMGB1-mediated autophagy promotes docetaxel resistance in human lung adenocarcinoma. *Mol. Cancer* **2014**, *13*, 165. [CrossRef] [PubMed]

89. Zhao, M.; Yang, M.; Yang, L.; Yu, Y.; Xie, M.; Zhu, S.; Kang, R.; Tang, D.; Jiang, Z.; Yuan, W.; et al. HMGB1 regulates autophagy through increasing transcriptional activities of JNK and ERK in human myeloid leukemia cells. *BMB Rep.* **2011**, *44*, 601–606. [CrossRef]

90. Liu, Y.; Yan, W.; Tohme, S.; Chen, M.; Fu, Y.; Tian, D.; Lotze, M.; Tang, D.; Tsung, A. Hypoxia induced HMGB1 and mitochondrial DNA interactions mediate tumor growth in hepatocellular carcinoma through Toll-like receptor 9. *J. Hepatol.* **2015**, *63*, 114–121. [CrossRef] [PubMed]

91. Debnath, J. Detachment-induced autophagy during anoikis and lumen formation in epithelial acini. *Autophagy* **2008**, *4*, 351–353. [CrossRef] [PubMed]

92. Peng, Y.-F.; Shi, Y.-H.; Shen, Y.-H.; Ding, Z.-B.; Ke, A.-W.; Zhou, J.; Qiu, S.-J.; Fan, J. Promoting colonization in metastatic HCC cells by modulation of autophagy. *PLoS ONE* **2013**, *8*, e74407. [CrossRef] [PubMed]

93. Seyfried, T.N.; Huysentruyt, L.C. On the Origin of Cancer Metastasis. *Crit. Rev. Oncog.* **2013**, *18*, 43–73. [CrossRef] [PubMed]

94. Avivar-Valderas, A.; Salas, E.; Bobrovnikova-Marjon, E.; Diehl, J.A.; Nagi, C.; Debnath, J.; Aguirre-Ghiso, J.A. PERK Integrates Autophagy and Oxidative Stress Responses To Promote Survival during Extracellular Matrix Detachment. *Mol. Cell. Biol.* **2011**, *31*, 3616–3629. [CrossRef] [PubMed]

95. Sharifi, M.N.; Mowers, E.E.; Drake, L.E.; Collier, C.; Chen, H.; Zamora, M.; Mui, S.; Macleod, K.F. Autophagy Promotes Focal Adhesion Disassembly and Cell Motility of Metastatic Tumor Cells through the Direct Interaction of Paxillin with LC3. *Cell Rep.* **2016**, *15*, 1660–1672. [CrossRef]

96. Li, J.; Yang, B.; Zhou, Q.; Wu, Y.; Shang, D.; Guo, Y.; Song, Z.; Zheng, Q.; Xiong, J. Autophagy promotes hepatocellular carcinoma cell invasion through activation of epithelial–mesenchymal transition. *Carcinogenesis* **2013**, *34*, 1343–1351. [CrossRef]

97. Peng, Y.F.; Shi, Y.H.; Ding, Z.B; Ke, A.W.; Gu, C.Y.; Hui, B.; Zhou, J.; Qiu, S.J.; Dai, Z.; Fan, J. Autophagy inhibition suppresses pulmonary metastasis of HCC in mice via impairing anoikis resistance and colonization of HCC cells. *Autophagy* **2013**, *9*, 2056–2068. [CrossRef]

98. Wang, X.; Zhang, Y.; Feng, T.; Su, G.; He, J.; Gao, W.; Shen, Y.; Liu, X. Fluid shear stress promotes autophagy in hepatocellular carcinoma cells. *Int. J. Biol. Sci.* **2018**, *14*, 1277–1290. [CrossRef]

99. Shen, H.-M.; Codogno, P. Autophagic cell death: Loch Ness monster or endangered species? *Autophagy* **2011**, *7*, 457–465. [CrossRef]

100. Boya, P.; Gonzalez-Polo, R.-A.; Casares, N.; Perfettini, J.-L.; Dessen, P.; Larochette, N.; Metivier, D.; Meley, D.; Souquere, S.; Yoshimori, T.; et al. Inhibition of Macroautophagy Triggers Apoptosis. *Mol. Cell. Biol.* **2005**, *25*, 1025–1040. [CrossRef]

101. Cheng, A.-L.; Kang, Y.-K.; Chen, Z.; Tsao, C.-J.; Qin, S.; Kim, J.S.; Luo, R.; Feng, J.; Ye, S.; Yang, T.-S.; et al. Efficacy and safety of sorafenib in patients in the Asia-Pacific region with advanced hepatocellular carcinoma: A phase III randomised, double-blind, placebo-controlled trial. *Lancet Oncol.* **2009**, *10*, 25–34. [CrossRef]

102. Abdel-Rahman, O.; Fouad, M. Sorafenib-based combination as a first line treatment for advanced hepatocellular carcinoma: A systematic review of the literature. *Crit. Rev. Oncol. Hematol.* **2014**, *91*, 1–8. [CrossRef] [PubMed]

103. Decaens, T.; Luciani, A.; Itti, E.; Hulin, A.; Roudot-Thoraval, F.; Laurent, A.; Zafrani, E.S.; Mallat, A.; Duvoux, C. Phase II study of sirolimus in treatment-naive patients with advanced hepatocellular carcinoma. *Dig. Liver Dis.* **2012**, *44*, 610–616. [CrossRef]

104. Adnane, L.; Trail, P.A.; Taylor, I.; Wilhelm, S.M. Sorafenib (BAY 43-9006, Nexavar®), a Dual-Action Inhibitor That Targets RAF/MEK/ERK Pathway in Tumor Cells and Tyrosine Kinases VEGFR/PDGFR in Tumor Vasculature. *Methods Enzymol.* **2006**, *407*, 597–612. [PubMed]

105. Shimizu, S.; Takehara, T.; Hikita, H.; Kodama, T.; Tsunematsu, H.; Miyagi, T.; Hosui, A.; Ishida, H.; Tatsumi, T.; Kanto, T.; et al. Inhibition of autophagy potentiates the antitumor effect of the multikinase inhibitor sorafenib in hepatocellular carcinoma. *Int. J. Cancer* **2012**, *131*, 548–557. [CrossRef] [PubMed]

106. Gedaly, R.; Angulo, P.; Hundley, J.; Daily, M.F.; Chen, C.; Evers, B.M. PKI-587 and sorafenib targeting PI3K/AKT/mTOR and Ras/Raf/MAPK pathways synergistically inhibit HCC cell proliferation. *J. Surg. Res.* **2012**, *176*, 542–548. [CrossRef] [PubMed]

107. Rodríguez-Hernández, M.A.; González, R.; de la Rosa, Á.J.; Gallego, P.; Ordóñez, R.; Navarro-Villarán, E.; Contreras, L.; Rodríguez-Arribas, M.; González-Gallego, J.; Álamo-Martínez, J.M.; et al. Molecular characterization of autophagic and apoptotic signaling induced by sorafenib in liver cancer cells. *J. Cell. Physiol.* **2019**, *234*, 692–708. [CrossRef] [PubMed]

108. Nishida, N.; Kitano, M.; Sakurai, T.; Kudo, M. Molecular Mechanism and Prediction of Sorafenib Chemoresistance in Human Hepatocellular Carcinoma. *Dig. Dis.* **2015**, *33*, 771–779. [CrossRef]

109. Lachenmayer, A.; Toffanin, S.; Cabellos, L.; Alsinet, C.; Hoshida, Y.; Villanueva, A.; Minguez, B.; Tsai, H.W.; Ward, S.C.; Thung, S.; et al. Combination therapy for hepatocellular carcinoma: Additive preclinical efficacy of the HDAC inhibitor panobinostat with sorafenib. *J. Hepatol.* **2012**, *56*, 1343–1350. [CrossRef]

110. Liang, Y.; Zheng, T.; Song, R.; Wang, J.; Yin, D.; Wang, L.; Liu, H.; Tian, L.; Fang, X.; Meng, X.; et al. Hypoxia-mediated sorafenib resistance can be overcome by EF24 through Von Hippel-Lindau tumor suppressor-dependent HIF-1α inhibition in hepatocellular carcinoma. *Hepatology* **2013**, *57*, 1847–1857. [CrossRef]

111. Prieto-Domínguez, N.; Méndez-Blanco, C.; Carbajo-Pescador, S.; Fondevila, F.; García-Palomo, A.; González-Gallego, J.; Mauriz, J.L. Melatonin enhances sorafenib actions in human hepatocarcinoma cells by inhibiting mTORC1/p70S6K/HIF-1α and hypoxia-mediated mitophagy. *Oncotarget* **2017**, *8*, 91402–91414. [CrossRef] [PubMed]

112. Prieto-Domínguez, N.; Ordóñez, R.; Fernández, A.; García-Palomo, A.; Muntané, J.; González-Gallego, J.; Mauriz, J.L. Modulation of Autophagy by Sorafenib: Effects on Treatment Response. *Front. Pharmacol.* **2016**, *7*, 151. [CrossRef] [PubMed]

113. Zhi, X.; Zhong, Q. Autophagy in cancer. *F1000Prime Rep.* **2015**, *7*, 18. [CrossRef] [PubMed]

114. Ding, Z.-B.; Hui, B.; Shi, Y.-H.; Zhou, J.; Peng, Y.-F.; Gu, C.-Y.; Yang, H.; Shi, G.-M.; Ke, A.-W.; Wang, X.-Y.; et al. Autophagy Activation in Hepatocellular Carcinoma Contributes to the Tolerance of Oxaliplatin via Reactive Oxygen Species Modulation. *Clin. Cancer Res.* **2011**, *17*, 6229–6238. [CrossRef] [PubMed]

115. Sheng, J.; Qin, H.; Zhang, K.; Li, B.; Zhang, X. Targeting autophagy in chemotherapy-resistant of hepatocellular carcinoma. *Am. J. Cancer Res.* **2018**, *8*, 354–365. [PubMed]

116. Toshima, T.; Shirabe, K.; Matsumoto, Y.; Yoshiya, S.; Ikegami, T.; Yoshizumi, T.; Soejima, Y.; Ikeda, T.; Maehara, Y. Autophagy enhances hepatocellular carcinoma progression by activation of mitochondrial β-oxidation. *J. Gastroenterol.* **2014**, *49*, 907–916. [CrossRef] [PubMed]

117. Hu, P.; Cheng, B.; He, Y.; Wei, Z.; Wu, D.; Meng, Z. Autophagy suppresses proliferation of HepG2 cells via inhibiting glypican-3/wnt/β-catenin signaling. *Oncotargets Ther.* **2018**, *11*, 193–200. [CrossRef]

118. Da Silva, E.F.G.; Krause, G.C.; Lima, K.G.; Haute, G.V.; Pedrazza, L.; Mesquita, F.C.; Basso, B.S.; Velasquez, A.C.; Nunes, F.B.; De Oliveira, J.R. Rapamycin and fructose-1,6-bisphosphate reduce the HEPG2 cell proliferation via increase of free radicals and apoptosis. *Oncol. Rep.* **2016**, *36*, 2647–2652. [CrossRef]

119. Engl, T.; Rutz, J.; Maxeiner, S.; Juengel, E.; Roos, F.; Khoder, W.; Bechstein, W.O.; Nelson, K.; Tsaur, I.; Haferkamp, A.; et al. mTOR inhibition reduces growth and adhesion of hepatocellular carcinoma cells in vitro. *Mol. Med. Rep.* **2017**, *16*, 7064–7071. [CrossRef]

120. Kim, J.-O.; Kim, K.-H.; Song, I.S.; Cheon, K.-S.; Kim, O.-H.; Lee, S.C.; Lee, S.K.; Kim, S.-J. Potentiation of the anticancer effects of everolimus using a dual mTORC1/2 inhibitor in hepatocellular carcinoma cells. *Oncotarget* **2017**, *8*, 2936–2948. [CrossRef]

121. Tong, Y.; Huang, H.; Pan, H. Inhibition of MEK/ERK activation attenuates autophagy and potentiates pemetrexed-induced activity against HepG2 hepatocellular carcinoma cells. *Biochem. Biophys. Res. Commun.* **2015**, *456*, 86–91. [CrossRef] [PubMed]

122. Huang, C.-Y.; Tai, W.-T.; Hsieh, C.-Y.; Hsu, W.-M.; Lai, Y.-J.; Chen, L.-J.; Shiau, C.-W.; Chen, K.-F. A sorafenib derivative and novel SHP-1 agonist, SC-59, acts synergistically with radiotherapy in hepatocellular carcinoma cells through inhibition of STAT3. *Cancer Lett.* **2014**, *349*, 136–143. [CrossRef] [PubMed]

123. Tai, W.-T.; Shiau, C.-W.; Chen, H.-L.; Liu, C.-Y.; Lin, C.-S.; Cheng, A.-L.; Chen, P.-J.; Chen, K.-F. Mcl-1-dependent activation of Beclin 1 mediates autophagic cell death induced by sorafenib and SC-59 in hepatocellular carcinoma cells. *Cell Death Dis.* **2013**, *4*, e485. [CrossRef] [PubMed]

124. Chang, Z.; Shi, G.; Jin, J.; Guo, H.; Guo, X.; Luo, F.; Song, Y.; Jia, X. Dual PI3K/mTOR inhibitor NVP-BEZ235-induced apoptosis of hepatocellular carcinoma cell lines is enhanced by inhibitors of autophagy. *Int. J. Mol. Med.* **2013**, *31*, 1449–1456. [CrossRef] [PubMed]

125. Simioni, C.; Martelli, A.M.; Cani, A.; Cetin-Atalay, R.; McCubrey, J.A.; Capitani, S.; Neri, L.M. The AKT Inhibitor MK-2206 is Cytotoxic in Hepatocarcinoma Cells Displaying Hyperphosphorylated AKT-1 and Synergizes with Conventional Chemotherapy. *Oncotarget* **2013**, *4*, 1496–1506. [CrossRef] [PubMed]

126. Zhang, H.; Chen, G.G.; Zhang, Z.; Chun, S.; Leung, B.C.S.; Lai, P.B.S. Induction of autophagy in hepatocellular carcinoma cells by SB203580 requires activation of AMPK and DAPK but not p38 MAPK. *Apoptosis* **2012**, *17*, 325–334. [CrossRef] [PubMed]

127. D'Alessandro, R.; Refolo, M.G.; Lippolis, C.; Messa, C.; Cavallini, A.; Rossi, R.; Resta, L.; Di Carlo, A.; Carr, B.I. Reversibility of regorafenib effects in hepatocellular carcinoma cells. *Cancer Chemother. Pharmacol.* **2013**, *72*, 869–877. [CrossRef] [PubMed]

128. Yu, H.C.; Lin, C.S.; Tai, W.T.; Liu, C.Y.; Shiau, C.W.; Chen, K.F. Nilotinib induces autophagy in hepatocellular carcinoma through AMPK activation. *J. Biol. Chem.* **2013**, *288*, 18249–18259. [CrossRef]

129. Ni, Z.; Wang, B.; Dai, X.; Ding, W.; Yang, T.; Li, X.; Lewin, S.; Xu, L.; Lian, J.; He, F. HCC cells with high levels of Bcl-2 are resistant to ABT-737 via activation of the ROS-JNK-autophagy pathway. *Free Radic. Biol. Med.* **2014**, *70*, 194–203. [CrossRef]

130. Gao, M.; Yeh, P.Y.; Lu, Y.S.; Hsu, C.H.; Chen, K.F.; Lee, W.C.; Feng, W.C.; Chen, C.S.; Kuo, M.L.; Cheng, A.L. OSU-03012, a novel celecoxib derivative, induces reactive oxygen species-related autophagy in hepatocellular carcinoma. *Cancer Res.* **2008**, *68*, 9348–9357. [CrossRef]

131. Saeki, I.; Terai, S.; Fujisawa, K.; Takami, T.; Yamamoto, N.; Matsumoto, T.; Hirose, Y.; Murata, Y.; Yamasaki, T.; Sakaida, I. Bortezomib induces tumor-specific cell death and growth inhibition in hepatocellular carcinoma and improves liver fibrosis. *J. Gastroenterol.* **2013**, *48*, 738–750. [CrossRef] [PubMed]

132. Du, H.; Yang, W.; Chen, L.; Shi, M.; Seewoo, V.; Wang, J.; Lin, A.; Liu, Z.; Qiu, W. Role of autophagy in resistance to oxaliplatin in hepatocellular carcinoma cells. *Oncol. Rep.* **2012**, *27*, 143–150. [PubMed]

133. Chen, L.H.; Loong, C.C.; Su, T.L.; Lee, Y.J.; Chu, P.M.; Tsai, M.L.; Tsai, P.H.; Tu, P.H.; Chi, C.W.; Lee, H.C.; et al. Autophagy inhibition enhances apoptosis triggered by BO-1051, an N-mustard derivative, and involves the ATM signaling pathway. *Biochem. Pharmacol.* **2011**, *81*, 594–605. [CrossRef] [PubMed]

134. Hou, Y.J.; Dong, L.W.; Tan, Y.X.; Yang, G.Z.; Pan, Y.F.; Li, Z.; Tang, L.; Wang, M.; Wang, Q.; Wang, H.Y. Inhibition of active autophagy induces apoptosis and increases chemosensitivity in cholangiocarcinoma. *Lab. Invest.* **2011**, *91*, 1146–1157. [CrossRef] [PubMed]

135. Rong, L.-W.; Wang, R.-X.; Zheng, X.-L.; Feng, X.-Q.; Zhang, L.; Zhang, L.; Lin, Y.; Li, Z.-P.; Wang, X. Combination of wogonin and sorafenib effectively kills human hepatocellular carcinoma cells through apoptosis potentiation and autophagy inhibition. *Oncol. Lett.* **2017**, *13*, 5028–5034. [CrossRef] [PubMed]

136. Yan, Y.; Jiang, K.; Liu, P.; Zhang, X.; Dong, X.; Gao, J.; Liu, Q.; Barr, M.P.; Zhang, Q.; Hou, X.; et al. Bafilomycin A1 induces caspase-independent cell death in hepatocellular carcinoma cells via targeting of autophagy and MAPK pathways. *Sci. Rep.* **2016**, *6*, 37052. [CrossRef] [PubMed]

137. Thoen, L.F.R.; Guimarães, E.L.M.; Dollé, L.; Mannaerts, I.; Najimi, M.; Sokal, E.; van Grunsven, L.A. A role for autophagy during hepatic stellate cell activation. *J. Hepatol.* **2011**, *55*, 1353–1360. [CrossRef] [PubMed]

138. Eisenberg-Lerner, A.; Bialik, S.; Simon, H.-U.; Kimchi, A. Life and death partners: Apoptosis, autophagy and the cross-talk between them. *Cell Death Differ.* **2009**, *16*, 966–975. [CrossRef]

139. Booth, L.A.; Tavallai, S.; Hamed, H.A.; Cruickshanks, N.; Dent, P. The role of cell signalling in the crosstalk between autophagy and apoptosis. *Cell. Signal.* **2014**, *26*, 549–555. [CrossRef] [PubMed]

140. McFarlane, S.; Nicholl, M.J.; Sutherland, J.S.; Preston, C.M. Interaction of the human cytomegalovirus particle with the host cell induces hypoxia-inducible factor 1 alpha. *Virology* **2011**, *414*, 83–90. [CrossRef]

Review

Impact of Autophagy of Innate Immune Cells on Inflammatory Bowel Disease

Tomoya Iida, Yoshihiro Yokoyama, Kohei Wagatsuma, Daisuke Hirayama and Hiroshi Nakase *

Department of Gastroenterology and Hepatology, Sapporo Medical University School of Medicine, Sapporo 060-8543, Japan; tomoya.iida.0306@gmail.com (T.I.); yoshi_yokoyamaa@yahoo.co.jp (Y.Y.); waga_a05m@yahoo.co.jp (K.W.); hirarin95@yahoo.co.jp (D.H.)
* Correspondence: hiropynakase@gmail.com; Tel.: +81-11-611-2111

Received: 4 December 2018; Accepted: 18 December 2018; Published: 22 December 2018

Abstract: Autophagy, an intracellular degradation mechanism, has many immunological functions and is a constitutive process necessary for maintaining cellular homeostasis and organ structure. One of the functions of autophagy is to control the innate immune response. Many studies conducted in recent years have revealed the contribution of autophagy to the innate immune response, and relationships between this process and various diseases have been reported. Inflammatory bowel disease is an intractable disorder with unknown etiology; however, immunological abnormalities in the intestines are known to be involved in the pathology of inflammatory bowel disease, as is dysfunction of autophagy. In Crohn's disease, many associations with autophagy-related genes, such as *ATG16L1, IRGM, NOD2*, and others, have been reported. Abnormalities in the *ATG16L1* gene, in particular, have been reported to cause autophagic dysfunction, resulting in enhanced production of inflammatory cytokines by macrophages as well as abnormal function of Paneth cells, which are important in intestinal innate immunity. In this review, we provide an overview of the autophagy mechanism in innate immune cells in inflammatory bowel disease.

Keywords: autophagy; innate immunity; immune cell; inflammasome; Paneth cell; inflammatory bowel disease; Crohn's disease

---

1. Introduction

The gastrointestinal tract is continuously involved in regulating the gut flora, modulating immune responses to food antigens and other substances, and maintaining homeostasis. Inflammatory bowel disease (IBD) occurs when this homeostasis is disrupted. The innate immune response is indispensable for maintaining homeostasis, and abnormal innate immune activity is deeply involved in the pathogenesis of IBD; research in this field has made substantial advancements in recent years [1–3]. To date, more than 200 IBD disease susceptibility loci have been identified by genome wide association studies (GWASs) [4,5]. Within these 200 loci, based upon single nucleotide polymorphism frequencies in patients with IBD versus controls, are approximately 1500 potential associated genes [6,7]. Numerous molecules involved in producing innate immune responses are also included among these loci.

Cells closely involved in the innate immune response with respect to IBD include blood cells, macrophages, dendritic cells, Paneth cells, and goblet cells, which are also involved in the pathology of IBD [8–10]. These cells have been found to play important roles in the development of abnormalities, including maintaining homeostasis against stress at the cellular level and modulating autophagy.

In this review, we outline the mechanism of autophagy in innate immune cells in IBD.

2. Pathology and Pathogenesis of IBD

IBD is a chronic inflammatory disease involving idiopathic inflammation, primarily in the gastrointestinal tract; when defined more specifically, this condition encompasses ulcerative colitis

(UC) and Crohn's disease (CD). Both are characterized by onset at a young age and the number of affected patients has risen sharply in recent years in Europe, the United States of America, and Japan [11]. Genetic predisposition (innate and acquired immunity, cytokine, and racial difference) and environmental factors (meal, drug, smoking, and infection) are greatly involved in the onset of IBD, and intestinal immune abnormalities are caused by the involvement of the state of dysbiosis, which is believed to cause IBD [11–15] (Figure 1).

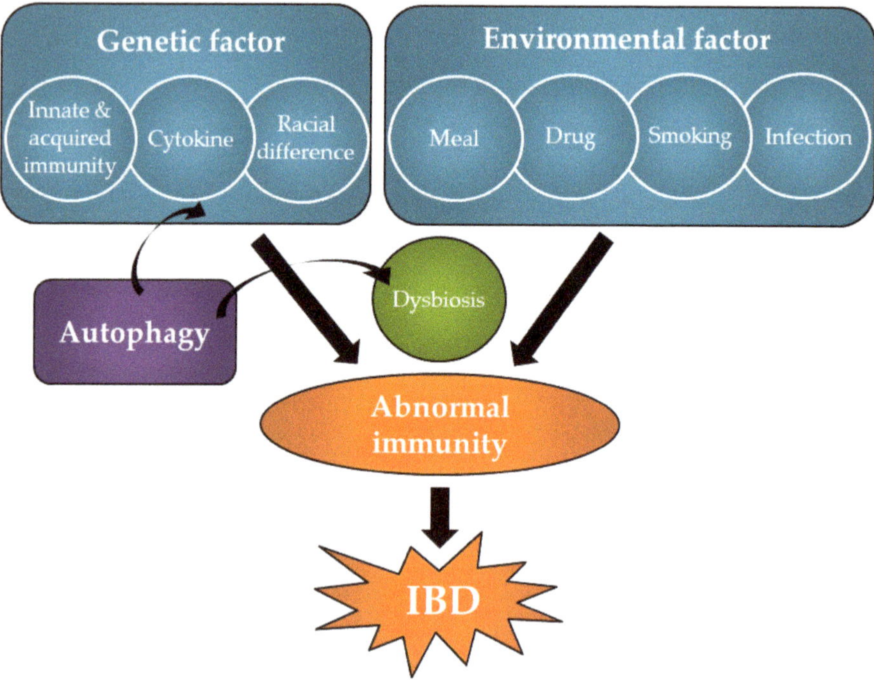

Figure 1. Pathology and pathogenesis of inflammatory bowel disease (IBD). Genetic predisposition and environmental factors are greatly involved in the onset of IBD, and intestinal immune abnormalities are caused by the involvement of the state of dysbiosis, which is believed to cause IBD.

Abnormalities related to genetic predisposition and autophagy are deeply involved in dysbiosis. Representative autophagy-related genes include *nucleotide-binding oligomerization domain containing 2 (NOD2), autophagy-related 16 like 1 (ATG16L1), and immunity-related GTPase family M (IRGM)* [16–18]. Autophagy has been linked to a variety of diseases; however, its link to IBD is currently the subject of much debate.

3. Autophagy

Autophagy is a term derived from a Greek word meaning "self-eating" and is a process that together with the ubiquitin-proteasome system, governs the degradation of intracellular proteins. In addition to immunological functions, such as antigen presentation and protection against infection, autophagy is also involved in the starvation response, carcinogenesis, and quality control of intracellular proteins and is a constitutive process necessary for maintaining proper cell homeostasis and organ health [19–21]. In addition to IBD, autophagy has been shown to be associated with other diseases, such as asthma [22–25], systemic lupus erythematosus [26,27], and Parkinson's disease [28,29].

During the autophagy process, the endoplasmic reticulum or other membranous cellular structures respond to stimuli by generating a double-membrane structure called a phagophore. The

ATG16L1/ATG5/ATG12 complex multimerizes and then lipidates light chain 3 (LC3)-II on this phagophore. Concurrently, the phagophore elongates to envelop the cytoplasm or organelle to be degraded, forming an autophagosome, which is a unique double-membrane organelle. The outer membrane of the autophagosome then integrates with a lysosome and forms an autolysosome. Finally, the inner membrane degrades and absorbs its contents [30] (Figure 2).

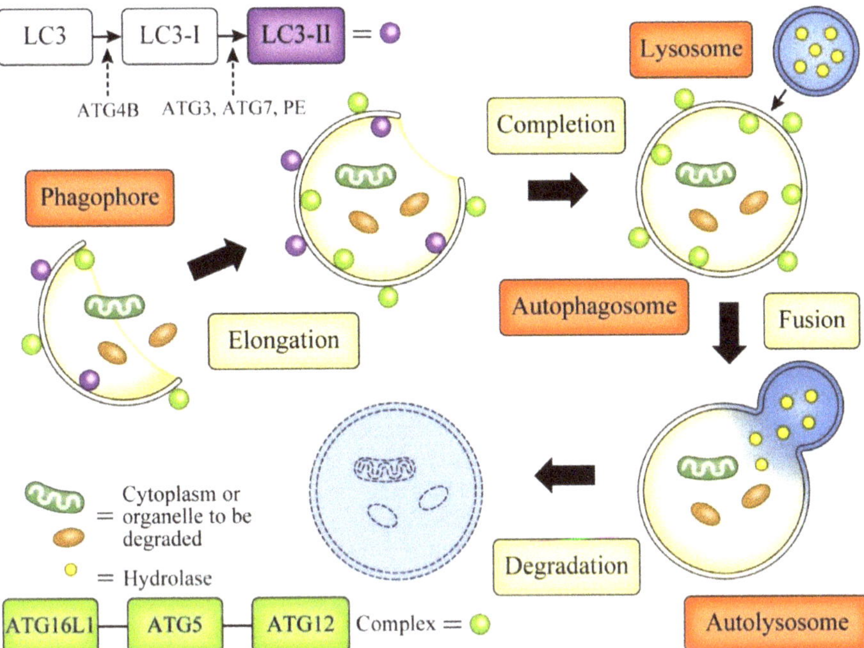

Figure 2. Autophagy mechanism. The endoplasmic reticulum or other membranous cellular structures respond to stimuli by generating a double-membrane structure called a phagophore. ATG16L1-ATG5-ATG12 complex multimerizes and then lipidates light chain 3 (LC3)-II on this phagophore. Concurrently, the phagophore elongates to envelop the cytoplasm or organelle to be degraded, forming an autophagosome. The outer membrane of the autophagosome then integrates with a lysosome and forms an autolysosome. Finally, the inner membrane degrades and absorbs its contents.

4. Role of Autophagy in Innate Immunity

One of the functions of autophagy is control of the innate immune response. Many studies have revealed the involvement of autophagy in innate immune reactions, and extremely precise control mechanisms and pathophysiological roles are becoming more clearly understood and have begun to be elucidated [31,32].

4.1. Xenophagy, Mitophagy

Innate immunity is a mechanism through which almost all multicellular organisms protect themselves from pathogens. This pathway is activated when the constructive patterns of pathogen's components are recognized (i.e., the cell wall components of a bacterial cell or the genome of a virus). Autophagy was initially thought to be a nonspecific mechanism for degrading substances by incorporating them into a membrane structure; however, recent studies have shown that autophagosomes selectively isolate a variety of substrates through sequestosome 1-like receptors, as is observed in autophagy of pathogens (xenophagy) [33–35]. Although the ubiquitin-proteasome system is a well-known selective intracellular degradation system, autophagy can selectively engulf and decompose small substances, such as mitochondria, which are larger than the targets of the ubiquitin-proteasome system, indicating characteristics similar to that of mitophagy [36,37]. The major difference between autophagosomes and other membranous organelles is that autophagosomes have a dynamic structure in which necessary fractions are newly created and disappear with the digestion of contents by fusion with lysosomes; as the necessity increases, as in the starvation state, its production efficiency dramatically increases. These features are convenient for quickly carrying out quantitative control, and even when functioning to control the immune response, autophagy is more suitable than degradation by the proteasome system, and it is believed to be essential for the resolution of quantitative problems. However, when autophagy works in connection with innate immunity, the substrates to be decomposed are rarely clear except in the cases of xenophagy and mitophagy.

4.2. The Role of Autophagy in Inflammasomal and Type I Interferon Response

A controllable receptor tripartite motif (TRIM) protein that facilitates autophagy by recruiting autophagy-regulating factors and recognizing the target of autophagy has recently been reported as a receptor for autophagy in a new process called precision autophagy [38]. Inflammasomal and type I interferon (IFN) responses are representative components of the precision autophagic processes involved in innate immunity.

The Nod-like receptor (NLR) family of proteins, including NLRP1, NLRP3, and NLRC4, together with the apoptosis-associated speck-like protein containing a caspase recruitment domain and the protease caspase-1, functions as downstream innate inflammasomes [39] that are activated in phagocytic cells, such as macrophages, and are induced by caspase-1 via maturation of the inflammatory cytokines interleukin (IL)-1β and IL-18 and their subsequent production [40]. NLRP3 inflammasomes have attracted much attention in recent years with respect to various diseases [41–44], and numerous relationships between the state and severity of *NLRP3* gene polymorphism and IBD presentation have also been reported [45–50].

The type I IFN response plays an essential role in the innate immune response to viral infection, and RNA derived from RNA viruses invading cells can be recognized by the helicase retinoic acid inducible gene 1/melanoma differentiation-associated protein 5 and type I IFN [51]. Because signaling from type I IFN follows the Janus kinase/signal transducer and activator of transcription pathway, this cytokine has also been reported to be associated with IBD [52].

4.2.1. Modulation of NLRP3 Inflammasome Suppression via Autophagy

Gram-negative bacterial lipopolysaccharides (LPSs) stimulate toll-like receptor (TLR) 4 and induce the activation of NLRP3 inflammasomes in a TIR-domain-containing adapter-inducing IFN-β (TRIF)-dependent manner with the information transfer factor. Active oxygen species derived from mitochondria are involved in the activation of NLRP3 inflammasomes. In the TRIF downstream pathway, evolutionarily conserved signaling intermediate in the Toll pathway has been reported as a factor that induces the production of reactive oxygen species (ROS) from mitochondria. This pathway is only slightly activated in wild-type macrophages. In addition, when phagolysosomes are damaged during gram-negative bacterial infection and LPS leaks into cells, NLRP3 inflammasomes are activated via a noncanonical pathway. Activation of the noncanonical pathway is thought to be induced by an unknown LPS sensor present in the cell. In addition, metabolites, such as urate crystals, cholesterol crystals, and free fatty acids, cause damage to phagolysosomes when taken up by macrophages, causing further mitochondrial damage. Adenosine triphosphate, which is known to activate surrounding cells after being released from dead cells, induces mitochondrial damage via the Purinergic 2X7 receptor (P2X7R). Influenza viral infection can cause damage to organelles, such as mitochondria and the Golgi apparatus. When damaged mitochondria produce ROS, NLRP3 inflammasomes become activated. By suppressing this series of pathways, autophagy suppresses the activation of excessive inflammasomes [53–56] (Figure 3).

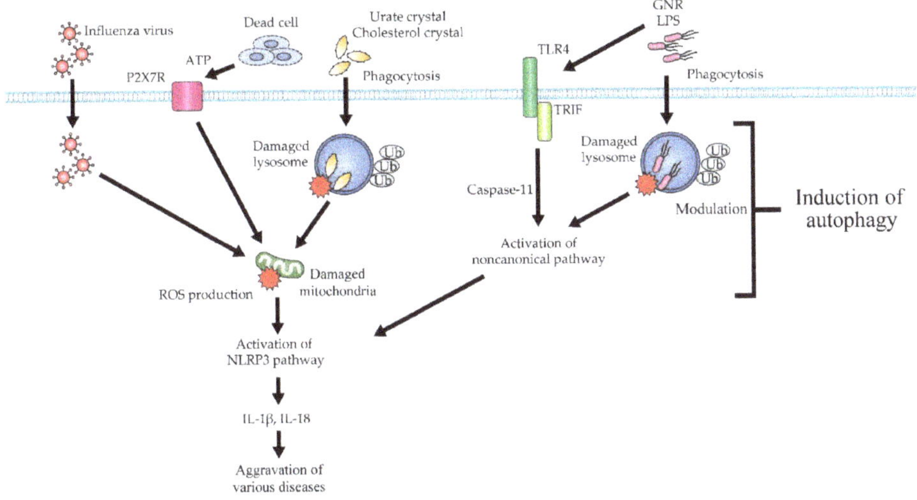

Figure 3. Modulation of NLRP3 inflammasome suppression via autophagy, ATP; adenosine triphosphate, GNR; gram negative rods, IL; interleukin, LPS; lipopolysaccharide, P2X7R; Purinergic 2X7 receptor, ROS; reactive oxygen species, TLR4; Toll-like receptor 4, TRIF; TIR-domain-containing adapter-inducing interferon-β, Ub; ubiquitin.

Autophagy is also believed to cause the decomposition of NLRP3 and AIM2, which are constituent factors of inflammasomes [57,58], and pro-IL-1β has been reported to be degraded by autophagy [59]. Furthermore, as described above, precision autophagy via TRIM protein is also involved in the decomposition of this inflammasome constituent factor by autophagy. TRIM20 binds to NLRP3 and pro-caspase 1, recruits autophagic regulatory factors (e.g., ULK1 and Beclin1), and is degraded by autophagy [38,60,61].

Conversely, autophagy also positively regulates NLRP3 inflammasomes and is involved in both decomposition and secretion. Autophagy is involved in the secretion of cytokines, such as IL-1β, IL-18, and high mobility group box 1 protein, and when inflammasomes become activated [62], folding of IL-1β by heat shock protein 90 is necessary; the IL-1β is then secreted after being transported to the lumen of LC3-II-positive autophagy-related structures [63].

Thus, autophagy plays an important role in the innate immune response by controlling NLRP3 inflammasomes. both positively and negatively.

4.2.2. Modulation of Type I IFN Responses via Autophagy

The TRIM protein regulates type I IFN responses via precision autophagy. TRIM21 binds to the IRF3 dimer, recruits autophagic regulators (e.g., ULK1 and Beclin1), and suppresses type I IFN responses by degrading this dimer via autophagy [61]. Moreover, autophagy also positively controls type I IFN responses. Intracellular viral replication intermediates on endosomes are recognized by TLR7 and cause a type I IFN response, but autophagy promotes type I IFN responses by this TLR7 via viral recognition [64]. As such, autophagy also positively and negatively controls type I IFN responses.

5. Role of Autophagy of Innate Immune Cells in IBD

As discussed above, autophagic abnormalities are deeply involved in the pathology of IBD, particularly CD. Recently, GWASs identified several genetic variants, including variants of *NOD2* [53,65–68], *ATG16L1* [69–77], *IRGM* [78–81], and *XIAP* [82–87] linked to the onset of CD. *NOD2* is the first disease-susceptibility gene discovered for CD [16]. Abnormalities in the *NOD2* gene are found primarily in Westerners and not in Asians. NOD2 is an intracytoplasmic pattern recognition receptor belonging to the NLR family, which recognizes and defends against pathogens and foreign components invading the cytoplasm [88]. NOD2 is strongly expressed by macrophages and dendritic cells (DCs), particularly Paneth cells, and functions through mechanisms involving autophagy, intracellular bacterial sensing, modulation of the antibacterial peptide α-defensin in the Paneth cells of the small intestine, and improvement of immune tolerance by suppressing TLR signals [89]. ATG16L1 is a homolog of ATG16, the existence of which was first reported by Mizushima et al. [69,70]. The *ATG16L1* gene is involved in host immune responses against intracellular parasitic bacteria and viruses via autophagy. In particular, the *ATG16L1* gene is closely associated with Paneth cells and plays an important role in CD pathology. In addition, many genes are associated with various pathologies of IBD in connection with autophagy, and these genes play important roles in immune cells, such as macrophages and DCs, as well as intestinal epithelial cells, including Paneth cells. The relationship between immune cells and autophagy in the IBD state is described below.

5.1. Hematopoietic Cells

5.1.1. Macrophages and DCs

Macrophages and DCs phagocytose foreign substances and bacteria in different tissues, serve as a first line of defense, and act as antigen-presenting cells to exert the functions of the acquired immune system [90,91]. Given the key role of the interactions between host and microbes in the intestine, it is critical to properly regulate pattern recognition receptor (PRR) signals and cytokine secretion. The NLRs in the cytoplasm and TLRs on the cell surface are the two main types of PRRs in innate immune cells [92]. NLRs and TLRs in macrophages are closely associated with autophagy, and macrophage autophagy is highly related to the mediation of innate immune responses in the intestinal wall [16,17]. Additionally, various antigens are degraded by the actions of proteasomes and lysosomes and are then presented by macrophages and DCs via class I and class II MHCs, after which the adaptive immune system is activated. Although it remains unclear as to how intracellular antigens are delivered to lysosomes and decomposed, recent studies have shown that autophagy is deeply involved in this process [93]. In the following section, we describe the relationships among macrophages, DCs, and autophagy in the pathology of IBD with respect to three components: pathogen degradation, suppression of inflammatory cytokine secretion, and antigen presentation.

Pathogen Degradation

NOD2 recruits the autophagy protein ATG16L1 to the plasma membrane at the bacterial entry site; mutant NOD2 fails to recruit ATG16L1 to the plasma membrane, and the wrapping of invading bacteria by the autophagosome is impaired. Thus, patients with CD with *NOD2* variants exhibit autophagy-related disorders [65–68]. Additionally, the capacity for autophagy and the phagocytosis of pathogenic bacteria become impaired in macrophages harboring mutant *NOD2* [94]. Furthermore, autophagy has been reported to be impaired in macrophages transfected with siRNA targeted to ATG16L1 or IRGM, and intracellular adherent-invasive *Escherichia coli* (AIEC) populations increase in the presence of intraperitoneal macrophages in *NOD2*-deficient mice [95]. Moreover, death-receptor activation or starvation-induced metabolic stress in human and murine macrophages increases the degradation of T300A or T316A variants of *ATG16L1*, respectively, resulting in diminished autophagy. In addition, knock-in mice harboring the *ATG16L1* T316A variant show defective clearance of the ileal pathogen *Yersinia enterocolitica* [74]. In an experiment using a cell line originating from macrophages, infection with CD-associated AIEC or administration of LPS or muramyl dipeptide induces IRGM expression [81]. Macrophages and epithelial cells lacking *GPR65* exhibit impaired autophagy for clearance of intracellular bacteria [96].

Suppressing Inflammatory Cytokine Secretion

ATG16L1-deficient macrophages are known to overproduce the inflammatory cytokine IL-1β in response to LPS stimulation, and the importance of ATG16L1 in inflammation has been described based on the finding that intestinal inflammation, induced by dextran sodium sulfate (DSS) intake in bone marrow chimeric mice, results in IL-1β overproduction by hematopoietic cells, leading to increased inflammation and cell fragility [53]. Moreover, in macrophages and DCs, autophagy controls IL-1β secretion by mediating the degradation of pro-IL-1β [59]. Furthermore, macrophages lacking ATG7, another autophagy-related factor, and macrophages that inhibit the activity of Vps34, which is essential for the induction of autophagy, also produce excessive quantities of IL-1β in response to LPS. Macrophages lacking ATG5 have also been reported to produce IL-1β in excess in response to the presence of gram-negative bacteria [97]. These phenomena are caused by the activation of NLRP3 inflammasomes due to autophagic disorders, and in recent years, activation of NLRP3 inflammasomes in response to various stimuli has been found to be controlled by autophagy [54–56] (Figure 3). In another recent report, impairing autophagy using ATG5 siRNA or an autophagy inhibitor (3-MA) was found to induce more robust initiation and activation of the NLRP3 inflammasome combined with increased caspase-1 activation and IL-1β production in peritoneal macrophages treated with LPS/DSS. 3-MA has also been shown to aggravate symptoms of DSS-induced colitis [98].

Loss of the autophagy-related gene *ATG16L1* has been shown to promote accumulation of the adaptor TRIF and enhance production of IFN-β and IL-1β as downstream signaling molecules in macrophages [99]. Macrophages from IBD risk carriers show increased myotubularin-related protein 3 expression and, in turn, decreased autophagy and increased cytokine secretion [100]. DSS and *Saccharomyces cerevisiae* were also inoculated into mice deficient in *ATG16L1*, an autophagy-related gene specific to CD11c+ DCs. Colitis has been reported to be exacerbated by elevated levels of IL-1β and tumor necrosis factor (TNF)-α when exposed to *Salmonella typhimurium* [101].

Antigen Presentation

In DCs, autophagy controls how antigens are processed and presented for antigen presentation [93]. Both *NOD2* 1007fs and *ATG16L1* T300A block muramyl dipeptide induction of autophagy, and this process is associated with defective bacterial handling in DCs and impaired antigen presentation in association with MHC class II at the cell surface [65]. Deletion of *ATG16L1* in a mouse model resulted in increased T-cell stimulation by DCs [102]. Additionally, *ATG7*-deficient mouse DCs are unable to stimulate CD4+ T-cell activation when exposed to *Toxoplasma gondii* antigens [103].

5.1.2. Neutrophils

Neutrophils have strong phagocytic and bacterial killing ability against foreign materials and bacteria, similar to macrophages, and play a central role in innate immunity [104]. Neutrophils react sensitively to stimuli and exhibit various functions. The initial response of neutrophils is quick, and neutrophils are subjected to sophisticated control mechanisms because they are involved in tissue restoration and minimization of injury to surrounding tissues. When this balance is impaired, neutrophils exhibit abnormal activation and are involved in various diseases [105]. Neutrophils are also involved in IBD pathophysiology and have been reported to be associated with cytokines, chemokines, ROS, and elastase [106]. Several reports have described the relationship between neutrophils and autophagy in IBD. For example, impaired *Salmonella typhimurium* clearance and increased ROS production were observed in *ATG16L1*-deficient murine neutrophils [107]. Thus, autophagy-related *ATG16L1* is essential for bacterial clearance and suppression of ROS production by neutrophils. In addition, autophagy receptor optineurin-deficient mice have been shown to be more susceptible to *Citrobacter* colitis and *E. coli* peritonitis and showed reduced levels of TNF-α in serum and diminished neutrophil recruitment to sites of acute inflammation compared with that in wild-type mice [108]. Thus, the autophagy receptor optineurin plays a role in acute inflammation and neutrophil recruitment.

5.1.3. Innate Lymphoid Cells (ILCs)

ILCs are innate immunocompetent cells belonging to the lymphocyte system; some are similar to helper T cells, although cytotoxic natural killer cells (NKs) are also considered ILCs. ILCs are classified into groups 1–3 based on cytokine production. Group I ILCs include ILC1s and NK cells, ILC2s are assigned to group 2 ILCs, and group 3 ILCs include ILC3s. These groups of cells have attracted much attention from researchers interested in IBD pathology and are important for the maintenance of homeostasis and inflammatory immune responses [109]. In addition, autophagy has been shown to be required for ILC development and function. Atg5, an essential component of the autophagy machinery, is required for the development of mature NKs and group 1–3 ILCs [110]. Phosphorylated Forkhead box O (FoxO) 1 is localized in the cytoplasm of immature NKs and interacts with ATG7. FoxO1-mediated autophagy has been shown to be required for NK development and NK-induced innate immunity [111,112].

5.1.4. NKT Cells (NKTs)

NKTs are immunocompetent cells that recognize antigens presented mainly on CDld molecules of antigen-presenting cells and produce cytokines. Because CD1d-restricted NKTs have an invariant T-cell receptor α chain, these cells are expressed as intramucosal NKTs (iNKTs). Mice with oxazolone-induced enteritis are considered a Th2-dominant ulcerative colitis model, and IL-13 produced from iNKTs is an associated cytokine [113]. It has been reported that the number of NKTs is increased in the intestinal mucosa of patients with ulcerative colitis, and IL-13 production is enhanced [114]. Thus, NKTs are thought to be involved in the pathogenesis of IBD, and autophagy is important for the development and differentiation of iNKTs [115,116]. Recent reports have demonstrated that IL-15 induces autophagy of NKTs via TBK-binding protein 1 [117].

5.2. Intestinal Epithelial Cells

5.2.1. Paneth Cells

Paneth cells are found at the base of small intestinal crypts and were first reported in 1888 as epithelial cells with dense coarse granules. Subsequently, α-defensin, an antimicrobial peptide and an innate immune effector, was discovered within Paneth cell granules [118]. Paneth cells play an important role as intestinal epithelial cells responsible for innate immunity [119–121]. In Caucasians, abnormalities in the *NOD2* gene, which was first identified as a CD susceptibility gene, inhibit α-defensin secretion by Paneth cells [122,123]. In addition, in mice with low ATG16L1 expression, significant abnormalities were observed in the secretory pathway of Paneth cell granules, and in patients with CD harboring homozygous *ATG16L1* T300A mutations, abnormal Paneth cells, similar to low ATG16L1 expression mice, were reported to have been found in noninflammatory sites in the ileum [72]. In addition, as described above, autophagic abnormalities are involved in the pathology of CD, and abnormal control of endoplasmic reticulum stress (ERS), ROS, and gut flora by Paneth cells each play important roles.

ER Stress (ERS)

Various intracellular proteins are synthesized in the ER, and these proteins undergo proper folding and are transported to the Golgi apparatus. Unfolded or misfolded proteins accumulate in the ER. The accumulation of proteins with these conformational abnormalities is called ERS, and excessive ERS ultimately induces cell apoptosis. The homeostatic mechanism mediating excessive ERS is known as the unfolded protein response (UPR). The UPR plays an important role in the survival and function of intestinal epithelial cells. In recent studies, the UPR has been shown to control abnormalities involved in the pathogenesis of IBD, and several genes associated with ERS have been reported as disease susceptibility genes by GWASs [12,13,21,89].

As intestinal epithelial cells, Paneth cells are closely related to ERS [12]. ERS results in the induction of autophagy in Paneth cells through three signaling pathways: insulin response element (IRE) 1/c-Jun N-terminal kinase/nuclear factor-κB/X-box binding protein 1 (XBP-1), pancreatic ER kinase/eukaryotic initiation factor (eIF) 2α-activated transcription factor 4, and GRP78-activated transcription factor 6/CCAAT-enhancer-binding protein homologous protein signaling pathways [124–126]. In terms of genetic abnormalities, reports describing the relationships between ERS and autophagy in Paneth cells have focused on the roles of the *NOD2* and *ATG16L1* genes [12,122,127–129]. Secretory autophagy, which is triggered in Paneth cells by bacteria-induced ERS and limited bacterial dissemination, is disrupted in Paneth cells expressing *ATG16L1* T300A [122]. In mice lacking *ATG16L1* specifically in the epithelium, CD-like ileitis occurs spontaneously in an age-dependent manner in Paneth cells, which are ERS sensors and causes changes in IRE1α, which is important for Paneth cell homeostasis [129]. ER stress is induced via deletion of the UPR transcription factor XBP-1 in the intestinal epithelium, resulting in autophagosome formation in Paneth cells via a mechanism involving the eukaryotic translation initiation factor eIF2α [8]. Thus, the involvement of autophagy in ERS may be a new therapeutic target for IBD in the future.

ROS

ROS have been shown to be involved in the pathogenesis of IBD, and many reports have suggested that IBD is associated with an imbalance between ROS and antioxidant activity, causing oxidative stress as a result of either ROS overproduction or decreased antioxidant activity [130–132]. Although many of the details of the relationship between ROS and autophagy have not been elucidated, accumulation of ROS has been reported to be related to induction of autophagy [133]. Notably, mitochondrial dysfunction is known to trigger the accumulation of ROS in Paneth cells, resulting in induction of autophagy through the p53/TP53 induced glycolysis regulatory phosphatase/damage-regulated autophagy modulator, p62-NF-E2-related factor 2, and BCL2/adenovirus E1B 19 kDa protein-interacting protein 3 pathways, thus protecting against cellular damage caused by various stresses [134,135]. Additionally, mutations in Atg promote the production of ROS via mitochondrial insufficiency in Paneth cells [136]. Further studies are needed to fully elucidate the relationship between ROS and autophagy in IBD.

Gut Microbiota

There are in the order of 100 trillion intestinal bacteria present in the human intestinal tract, and these cells play important roles in maintaining host metabolism and immunological homeostasis. Although findings suggesting the involvement of intestinal bacteria in the pathology of IBD are accumulating, it is unclear whether changes in the composition of the gut flora are the cause of IBD. Paneth cells are important factors influencing the gut flora [137], and autophagy abnormalities in Paneth cells are known to be related to alterations in the gut flora [137–139]. Autophagy dysfunction in Paneth cell disrupts the normal intestinal flora and promotes intracellular survival of AIEC and *Salmonella typhimurium* [138]. Vitamin D receptors in the intestinal tract contribute to Paneth cell function, autophagy function, and maintenance of normal intestinal microflora via ATG16L1 [139]. In addition, the microbiota induces basal Paneth cell autophagy by IFN-γ, facilitating the maintenance of intestinal homeostasis [140]. Dysfunction of autophagy by Paneth cells has also been reported to cause not only changes in the gut microbiome, but also improper responses to the altered flora [141]. As described above, the gut flora is closely related to autophagic abnormalities in Paneth cells, and many IBD treatments, particularly those utilizing probiotics, aim to correct intestinal bacterial flora populations [142,143].

5.2.2. Goblet Cells

Goblet cells are intestinal epithelial cells with cytoplasmic granules containing large quantities of mucin, a glycoprotein [144,145]. In the gastrointestinal tract, Goblet cells can be found in both the small intestine and the large intestine, and mucin secreted into the intestinal lumen is thought to contribute to mucosal protection and repair of the intestinal epithelium [146]. Dysfunction in mucin secretion and defects in the mucus layer allow large quantities of bacteria to reach the epithelium and trigger excess host immune responses, which have been shown to be associated with IBD [147].

In recent studies, autophagy has been reported to affect the functions of Goblet cells. Mice or cells lacking autophagy by depletion of autophagy-related proteins, such as ATG5, ATG7, ATG16L1, and LC3, show altered goblet cell morphology and decreased mucin secretion [73,148,149]. In addition, inflammasomes have been shown to be involved in mucin secretion by Goblet cells, and NLRP6 inflammasomes have been reported to promote exccocytosis of mucin by Goblet cells through promotion of autophagy [150]. Sonic hedgehog intestinal epithelial conditional knockout mice showed decreased numbers of ileal mucin-secreting Goblet cells accompanied by a significant reduction in autophagy [151]. Apple polysaccharide has been shown to inhibit dysbiosis-associated gut permeability and chronic inflammation due to the induction of autophagy in Goblet cells [152]. As described above, Goblet cells play important roles in the secretion of mucin via autophagy, act to maintain intestinal microflora, and are attracting attention as new therapeutic targets for IBD [149,153,154].

An overview of the autophagy mechanism of innate immunity cells in IBD is shown in Figure 4.

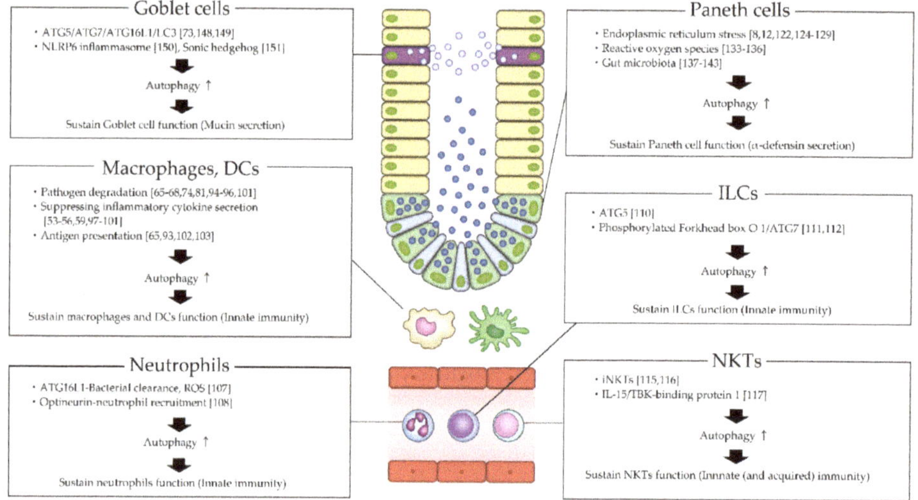

Figure 4. Role of autophagy of innate immune cells on IBD. DCs; dendritic cells, IL; interleukin, ILCs; innate lymphoid cells, NKTs; natural killer T cells, ROS; reactive oxygen species.

6. Conclusions

In this review, we have provided an overview of the autophagy mechanism of innate immune cells in IBD. Numerous studies have revealed that autophagy is an essential key player in controlling inflammatory responses mediated by innate immune cells. We anticipate that in the future, and based on further research, a therapy based on autophagic control will be established for IBD, a condition that does not yet have a curative therapy.

Author Contributions: Conceptualization, T.I. and H.N.; Investigation, T.I., Y.Y., K.W. and D.H.; Writing-Original Draft Preparation, T.I., Y.Y., K.W. and D.H.; Writing-Review & Editing, H.N.; Supervision, H.N.; Funding Acquisition, T.I. and H.N.

Funding: This work was partly supported by Health and Labour Sciences Research Grants for research on intractable diseases from the Ministry of Health, Labour and Welfare of Japan (Investigation and Research for intractable Inflammatory Bowel Disease), and Japan Society for the Promotion of Science (JSPS) Grants-in-Aid for

Scientific Research (KAKENHI) Grant Number JP17J02428 (to T.I.) and JP18H02799 (to H.N.). The funders of the study had no role in the study design, data collection, data analysis, data interpretation, or writing of the report.

Conflicts of Interest: The authors have nothing to declare.

References

1. Ebbo, M.; Crinier, A.; Vély, F.; Vivier, E. Innate lymphoid cells: Major players in inflammatory diseases. *Nat. Rev. Immunol.* **2017**, *17*, 665–678. [CrossRef] [PubMed]

2. Choy, M.C.; Visvanathan, K.; De Cruz, P. An overview of the innate and adaptive immune system in inflammatory bowel disease. *Inflamm. Bowel Dis.* **2017**, *23*, 2–13. [CrossRef] [PubMed]

3. Lee, S.H.; Kwon, J.E.; Cho, M.L. Immunological pathogenesis of inflammatory bowel disease. *Intest. Res.* **2018**, *16*, 26–42. [CrossRef] [PubMed]

4. Jostins, L.M.; Ripke, S.; Weersma, R.K.; Duerr, R.H.; McGovern, D.P.; Hui, K.Y.; Lee, J.C.; Schumm, L.P.; Sharma, Y.; Anderson, C.A.; et al. Host-microbe interactions have shaped the genetic architecture of inflammatory bowel disease. *Nature* **2012**, *491*, 119–124. [CrossRef] [PubMed]

5. Liu, J.Z.; van Sommeren, S.; Huang, H.; Ng, S.C.; Alberts, R.; Takahashi, A.; Ripke, S.; Lee, J.C.; Jostins, L.; Shah, T.; et al. Association analyses identify 38 susceptibility loci for IBD and highlight shared genetic risk across populations. *Nat. Genet.* **2015**, *47*, 979–986. [CrossRef] [PubMed]

6. Cho, J.H.; Brant, S.R. Recent insights into the genetics of inflammatory bowel disease. *Gastroenterology* **2011**, *140*, 1704–1712. [CrossRef] [PubMed]

7. Ek, W.E.; D'Amato, M.; Halfvarson, J. The history of genetics in inflammatory bowel disease. *Ann. Gastroenterol.* **2014**, *27*, 294–303. [PubMed]

8. Adolph, T.E.; Tomczak, M.F.; Niederreiter, L.; Ko, H.J.; Böck, J.; Martinez-Naves, E.; Glickman, J.N.; Tschurtschenthaler, M.; Hartwig, J.; Hosomi, S.; et al. Paneth cells as a site of origin for intestinal inflammation. *Nature* **2013**, *503*, 272–276. [CrossRef] [PubMed]

9. Patman, G. Crohn's disease. TCF1 regulates Paneth cell α-defensins. *Nat. Rev. Gastroenterol. Hepatol.* **2014**, *11*, 517. [CrossRef]

10. Eriguchi, Y.; Nakamura, K.; Yokoi, Y.; Sugimoto, R.; Takahashi, S.; Hashimoto, D.; Teshima, T.; Ayabe, T.; Selsted, M.E.; Ouellette, A.J. Essential role of IFN-γ in T cell-associated intestinal inflammation. *JCI. Insight.* **2018**, *20*, pii:121886. [CrossRef]

11. Molodecky, N.A.; Soon, I.S.; Rabi, D.M.; Ghali, W.A.; Ferris, M.; Chernoff, G.; Benchimol, E.I.; Panaccione, R.; Ghosh, S.; Barkema, H.W.; et al. Increasing incidence and prevalence of the inflammatory bowel diseases with time, based on systematic review. *Gastroenterology* **2012**, *142*, 46–54. [CrossRef] [PubMed]

12. Kaser, A.; Blumberg, R.S. Autophagy, microbial sensing, endoplasmic reticulum stress, and epithelial function in inflammatory bowel disease. *Gastroenterology* **2011**, *140*, 1738–1747. [CrossRef] [PubMed]

13. Kaser, A.; Zeissig, S.; Blumberg, R.S. Inflammatory bowel disease. *Annu. Rev. Immunol.* **2010**, *28*, 573–621. [CrossRef] [PubMed]

14. Khor, B.; Gardet, A.; Xavier, R.J. Genetics and pathogenesis of inflammatory bowel disease. *Nature* **2011**, *474*, 307–317. [CrossRef]

15. Weterman, I.T.; Peña, A.S. Familial incidence of Crohn's disease in the Netherlands and a review of the literature. *Gastroenterology* **1984**, *86*, 449–452.

16. Hugot, J.P.; Chamaillard, M.; Zouali, H.; Lesage, S.; Cézard, J.P.; Belaiche, J.; Almer, S.; Tysk, C.; O'Morain, C.A.; Gassull, M.; et al. Association of NOD2 leucine-rich repeat variants with susceptibility to Crohn's disease. *Nature* **2001**, *411*, 599–603. [CrossRef]

17. Ogura, Y.; Bonen, D.K.; Inohara, N.; Nicolae, D.L.; Chen, F.F.; Ramos, R.; Britton, H.; Moran, T.; Karaliuskas, R.; Duerr, R.H.; et al. A frameshift mutation in NOD2 associated with susceptibility to Crohn's disease. *Nature* **2001**, *411*, 603–606. [CrossRef]

18. Goldstein, D.B. Common genetic variation and human traits. *N. Engl. J. Med.* **2009**, *360*, 1696–1698. [CrossRef]

19. Levine, B.; Mizushima, N.; Virgin, H.W. Autophagy in immunity and inflammation. *Nature* **2011**, *469*, 323–325. [CrossRef]

20. Hooper, K.M.; Barlow, P.G.; Stevens, C.; Henderson, P. Inflammatory bowel disease drugs: A focus on autophagy. *J. Crohn's Colitis* **2017**, *11*, 118–127. [CrossRef]

21. Lassen, K.G.; Xavier, R.J. Mechanisms and function of autophagy in intestinal disease. *Autophagy* **2018**, *14*, 216–220. [CrossRef] [PubMed]
22. Zeki, A.A.; Yeganeh, B.; Kenyon, N.J.; Post, M.; Ghavami, S. Autophagy in airway diseases: A new frontier in human asthma? *Allergy* **2016**, *71*, 5–14. [CrossRef] [PubMed]
23. Poon, A.H.; Choy, D.F.; Chouiali, F.; Ramakrishnan, R.K.; Mahboub, B.; Audusseau, S.; Mogas, A.; Harris, J.M.; Arron, J.R.; Laprise, C.; et al. Increased autophagy-related 5 gene expression is associated with collagen expression in the airways of refractory asthmatics. *Front. Immunol.* **2017**, *8*, 355. [CrossRef] [PubMed]
24. Mabalirajan, U. A possible differential role of autophagy in asthma? *J. Allergy Clin. Immunol.* **2017**, *139*, 712. [CrossRef] [PubMed]
25. Racanelli, A.C.; Kikkers, S.A.; Choi, A.M.K.; Cloonan, S.M. Autophagy and inflammation in chronic respiratory disease. *Autophagy* **2018**, *14*, 221–232. [CrossRef] [PubMed]
26. Allison, S.J. Systemic lupus erythematosus: Defective noncanonical autophagy in SLE-like disease. *Nat. Rev. Rheumatol.* **2016**, *12*, 311. [CrossRef] [PubMed]
27. Mistry, P.; Kaplan, M.J. Cell death in the pathogenesis of systemic lupus erythematosus and lupus nephritis. *Clin. Immunol.* **2017**, *185*, 59–73. [CrossRef]
28. Fujikake, N.; Shin, M.; Shimizu, S. Association between autophagy and neurodegenerative diseases. *Front. Neurosci.* **2018**, *12*, 255. [CrossRef]
29. Harper, J.W.; Ordureau, A.; Heo, J.M. Building and decoding ubiquitin chains for mitophagy. *Nat. Rev. Mol. Cell Biol.* **2018**, *19*, 93–108. [CrossRef]
30. Iida, T.; Onodera, K.; Nakase, H. Role of autophagy in the pathogenesis of inflammatory bowel disease. *World J. Gastroenterol.* **2017**, *23*, 1944–1953. [CrossRef]
31. Rogov, V.; Dötsch, V.; Johansen, T.; Kirkin, V. Interactions between autophagy receptors and ubiquitin-like proteins form the molecular basis for selective autophagy. *Mol. Cell* **2014**, *53*, 167–178. [CrossRef] [PubMed]
32. Kawai, T.; Akira, S. The role of pattern-recognition receptors in innate immunity: Update on Toll-like receptors. *Nat. Immunol.* **2010**, *11*, 373–384. [CrossRef] [PubMed]
33. Mizushima, N.; Yoshimori, T.; Ohsumi, Y. The role of Atg proteins in autophagosome formation. *Annu. Rev. Cell Dev. Biol.* **2011**, *27*, 107–132. [CrossRef] [PubMed]
34. Levine, B. Eating oneself and uninvited guests: Autophagy-related pathways in cellular defense. *Cell* **2005**, *120*, 159–162. [CrossRef] [PubMed]
35. Nozawa, T.; Minowa-Nozawa, A.; Aikawa, C.; Nakagawa, I. The STX6-VTI1B-VAMP3 complex facilitates xenophagy by regulating the fusion between recycling endosomes and autophagosomes. *Autophagy* **2017**, *13*, 57–69. [CrossRef]
36. Hailey, D.W.; Rambold, A.S.; Satpute-Krishnan, P.; Mitra, K.; Sougrat, R.; Kim, P.K.; Lippincott-Schwartz, J. Mitochondria supply membranes for autophagosome biogenesis during starvation. *Cell* **2010**, *141*, 656–667. [CrossRef]
37. Yao, Z.; Klionsky, D.J. An unconventional pathway for mitochondrial protein degradation. *Autophagy* **2016**, *12*, 1971–1972. [CrossRef]
38. Kimura, T.; Mandell, M.; Deretic, V. Precision autophagy directed by receptor regulators-emerging examples within the TRIM family. *J. Cell Sci.* **2016**, *129*, 881–891. [CrossRef]
39. Martinon, F.; Burns, K.; Tschopp, J. The inflammasome: A molecular platform triggering activation of inflammatory caspases and processing of proIL-beta. *Mol. Cell* **2002**, *10*, 417–426. [CrossRef]
40. Rathinam, V.A.; Vanaja, S.K.; Fitzgerald, K.A. Regulation of inflammasome signaling. *Nat. Immunol.* **2012**, *13*, 333–342. [CrossRef]
41. Strowig, T.; Henao-Mejia, J.; Elinav, E.; Flavell, R. Inflammasomes in health and disease. *Nature* **2012**, *481*, 278–286. [CrossRef] [PubMed]
42. Guo, H.; Callaway, J.B.; Ting, J.P. Inflammasomes: Mechanism of action, role in disease, and therapeutics. *Nat. Med.* **2015**, *21*, 677–687. [CrossRef] [PubMed]
43. Mangan, M.S.J.; Olhava, E.J.; Roush, W.R.; Seidel, H.M.; Glick, G.D.; Latz, E. Targeting the NLRP3 inflammasome in inflammatory diseases. *Nat. Rev. Drug Discov.* **2018**, *17*, 588–606. [CrossRef] [PubMed]
44. Rathinam, V.A.K.; Chan, F.K. Inflammasome, Inflammation, and Tissue Homeostasis. *Trends Mol. Med.* **2018**, *24*, 304–318. [CrossRef] [PubMed]
45. Becker, C.; Watson, A.J.; Neurath, M.F. Complex roles of caspases in the pathogenesis of inflammatory bowel disease. *Gastroenterology* **2013**, *144*, 283–293. [CrossRef] [PubMed]

46. Opipari, A.; Franchi, L. Role of inflammasomes in intestinal inflammation and Crohn's disease. *Inflamm. Bowel Dis.* **2015**, *21*, 173–181. [CrossRef]
47. de Souza, H.S.; Fiocchi, C. Immunopathogenesis of IBD: Current state of the art. *Nat. Rev. Gastroenterol. Hepatol.* **2016**, *13*, 13–27. [CrossRef]
48. de Souza, H.S.P. Etiopathogenesis of inflammatory bowel disease: Today and tomorrow. *Curr. Opin. Gastroenterol.* **2017**, *33*, 222–229. [CrossRef]
49. Lazaridis, L.D.; Pistiki, A.; Giamarellos-Bourboulis, E.J.; Georgitsi, M.; Damoraki, G.; Polymeros, D.; Dimitriadis, G.D.; Triantafyllou, K. Activation of NLRP3 inflammasome in inflammatory bowel disease: Differences between Crohn's disease and ulcerative colitis. *Dig. Dis. Sci.* **2017**, *62*, 2348–2356. [CrossRef]
50. Mao, L.; Kitani, A.; Similuk, M.; Oler, A.J.; Albenberg, L.; Kelsen, J.; Aktay, A.; Quezado, M.; Yao, M.; Montgomery-Recht, K.; et al. Loss-of-function CARD8 mutation causes NLRP3 inflammasome activation and Crohn's disease. *J. Clin. Investig.* **2018**, *128*, 1793–1806. [CrossRef]
51. Kawai, T.; Akira, S. The roles of TLRs, RLRs and NLRs in pathogen recognition. *Int. Immunol.* **2009**, *21*, 317–337. [CrossRef] [PubMed]
52. Giles, E.M.; Sanders, T.J.; McCarthy, N.E.; Lung, J.; Pathak, M.; MacDonald, T.T.; Lindsay, J.O.; Stagg, A.J. Regulation of human intestinal T-cell responses by type 1 interferon-STAT1 signaling is disrupted in inflammatory bowel disease. *Mucosal Immunol.* **2017**, *10*, 184–193. [CrossRef] [PubMed]
53. Saitoh, T.; Fujita, N.; Jang, M.H.; Uematsu, S.l.; Yang, B.G.; Satoh, T.; Omori, H.; Noda, T.; Yamamoto, N.; Komatsu, M.; et al. Loss of the autophagy protein Atg16L1 enhances endotoxin-induced IL-1beta production. *Nature* **2008**, *456*, 264–268. [CrossRef] [PubMed]
54. Zhou, R.; Yazdi, A.S.; Menu, P.; Tschopp, J. A role for mitochondria in NLRP3 inflammasome activation. *Nature* **2011**, *469*, 221–225. [CrossRef] [PubMed]
55. Wen, H.; Gris, D.; Lei, Y.; Jha, S.; Zhang, L.; Huang, M.T.; Brickey, W.J.; Ting, J.P. Fatty acid-induced NLRP3-ASC inflammasome activation interferes with insulin signaling. *Nat. Immunol.* **2011**, *12*, 408–415. [CrossRef] [PubMed]
56. Lupfer, C.; Thomas, P.G.; Anand, P.K.; Vogel, P.; Milasta, S.; Martinez, J.; Huang, G.; Green, M.; Kundu, M.; Chi, H.; et al. Receptor interacting protein kinase 2-mediated mitophagy regulates inflammasome activation during virus infection. *Nat. Immunol.* **2013**, *14*, 480–488. [CrossRef] [PubMed]
57. Chuang, S.Y.; Yang, C.H.; Chou, C.C.; Chiang, Y.P.; Chuang, T.H.; Hsu, L.C. TLR-induced PAI-2 expression suppresses IL-1β processing via increasing autophagy and NLRP3 degradation. *Proc. Natl. Acad. Sci. USA* **2013**, *110*, 16079–16084. [CrossRef]
58. Shi, C.S.; Shenderov, K.; Huang, N.N.; Kabat, J.; Abu-Asab, M.; Fitzgerald, K.A.; Sher, A.; Kehrl, J.H. Activation of autophagy by inflammatory signals limits IL-1β production by targeting ubiquitinated inflammasomes for destruction. *Nat. Immunol.* **2012**, *13*, 255–263. [CrossRef]
59. Harris, J.; Hartman, M.; Roche, C.; Zeng, S.G.; O'Shea, A.; Sharp, F.A.; Lambe, E.M.; Creagh, E.M.; Golenbock, D.T.; Tschopp, J.; et al. Autophagy controls IL-1beta secretion by targeting pro-IL-1beta for degradation. *J. Biol. Chem.* **2011**, *286*, 9587–9597. [CrossRef]
60. Deretic, V.; Kimura, T.; Timmins, G.; Moseley, P.; Chauhan, S.; Mandell, M. Immunologic manifestations of autophagy. *J. Clin. Investig.* **2015**, *125*, 75–84. [CrossRef]
61. Kimura, T.; Jain, A.; Choi, S.W.; Mandell, M.A.; Schroder, K.; Johansen, T.; Deretic, V. TRIM-mediated precision autophagy targets cytoplasmic regulators of innate immunity. *J. Cell Biol.* **2015**, *210*, 973–989. [CrossRef] [PubMed]
62. Dupont, N.; Jiang, S.; Pilli, M.; Ornatowski, W.; Bhattacharya, D.; Deretic, V. Autophagy-based unconventional secretory pathway for extracellular delivery of IL-1β. *EMBO J.* **2011**, *30*, 4701–4711. [CrossRef] [PubMed]
63. Zhang, M.; Kenny, S.J.; Ge, L.; Xu, K.; Schekman, R. Translocation of interleukin-1β into a vesicle intermediate in autophagy-mediated secretion. *Elife* **2015**, *4*. [CrossRef]
64. Lee, H.K.; Lund, J.M.; Ramanathan, B.; Mizushima, N.; Iwasaki, A. Autophagy-dependent viral recognition by plasmacytoid dendritic cells. *Science* **2007**, *315*, 1398–1401. [CrossRef] [PubMed]
65. Cooney, R.; Baker, J.; Brain, O.; Danis, B.; Pichulik, T.; Allan, P.; Ferguson, D.J.; Campbell, B.J.; Jewell, D.; Simmons, A. NOD2 stimulation induces autophagy in dendritic cells influencing bacterial handling and antigen presentation. *Nat. Med.* **2010**, *16*, 90–97. [CrossRef] [PubMed]

66. Homer, C.R.; Richmond, A.L.; Rebert, N.A.; Achkar, J.P.; McDonald, C. ATG16L1 and NOD2 interact in an autophagy-dependent antibacterial pathway implicated in Crohn's disease pathogenesis. *Gastroenterology* **2010**, *139*, 1630–1641. [CrossRef] [PubMed]

67. Travassos, L.H.; Carneiro, L.A.; Ramjeet, M.; Hussey, S.; Kim, Y.G.; Magalhães, J.G.; Yuan, L.; Soares, F.; Chea, E.; Le Bourhis, L.; et al. Nod1 and Nod2 direct autophagy by recruiting ATG16L1 to the plasma membrane at the site of bacterial entry. *Nat. Immunol.* **2010**, *11*, 55–62. [CrossRef]

68. Negroni, A.; Colantoni, E.; Vitali, R.; Palone, F.; Pierdomenico, M.; Costanzo, M.; Cesi, V.; Cucchiara, S.; Stronati, L. NOD2 induces autophagy to control AIEC bacteria infectiveness in intestinal epithelial cells. *Inflamm. Res.* **2016**, *65*, 803–813. [CrossRef]

69. Mizushima, N.; Noda, T.; Ohsumi, Y. Apg16p is required for the function of the Apg12p-Apg5p conjugate in the yeast autophagy pathway. *EMBO J.* **1999**, *18*, 3888–3896. [CrossRef] [PubMed]

70. Mizushima, N.; Kuma, A.; Kobayashi, Y.; Yamamoto, A.; Matsubae, M.; Takao, T.; Natsume, T.; Ohsumi, Y.; Yoshimori, T. Mouse Apg16L, a novel WD-repeat protein, targets to the autophagic isolation membrane with the Apg12-Apg5 conjugate. *J. Cell Sci.* **2003**, *116*, 1679–1688. [CrossRef]

71. Prescott, N.J.; Fisher, S.A.; Franke, A.; Hampe, J.; Onnie, C.M.; Soars, D.; Bagnall, R.; Mirza, M.M.; Sanderson, J.; Forbes, A.; et al. A nonsynonymous SNP in ATG16L1 predisposes to ileal Crohn's disease and is independent of CARD15 and IBD5. *Gastroenterology* **2007**, *132*, 1665–1671. [CrossRef] [PubMed]

72. Cadwell, K.; Liu, J.Y.; Brown, S.L.; Miyoshi, H.; Loh, J.; Lennerz, J.K.; Kishi, C.; Kc, W.; Carrero, J.A.; Hunt, S.; et al. A key role for autophagy and the autophagy gene Atg16l1 in mouse and human intestinal Paneth cells. *Nature* **2008**, *456*, 259–263. [CrossRef] [PubMed]

73. Lassen, K.G.; Kuballa, P.; Conway, K.L.; Patel, K.K.; Becker, C.E.; Peloquin, J.M.; Villablanca, E.J.; Norman, J.M.; Liu, T.C.; Heath, R.J.; et al. Atg16L1 T300A variant decreases selective autophagy resulting in altered cytokine signaling and decreased antibacterial defense. *Proc. Natl. Acad. Sci. USA* **2014**, *111*, 7741–7746. [CrossRef] [PubMed]

74. Murthy, A.; Li, Y.; Peng, I.; Reichelt, M.; Katakam, A.K.; Noubade, R.; Roose-Girma, M.; DeVoss, J.; Diehl, L.; Graham, R.R.; et al. A Crohn's disease variant in Atg16l1 enhances its degradation by caspase 3. *Nature* **2014**, *506*, 456–462. [CrossRef] [PubMed]

75. Chu, H.; Khosravi, A.; Kusumawardhani, I.P.; Kwon, A.H.; Vasconcelos, A.C.; Cunha, L.D.; Mayer, A.E.; Shen, Y.; Wu, W.L.; Kambal, A.; et al. Gene-microbiota interactions contribute to the pathogenesis of inflammatory bowel disease. *Science* **2016**, *352*, 1116–1120. [CrossRef] [PubMed]

76. Yue, C.; Yang, X.; Li, J.; Chen, X.; Zhao, X.; Chen, Y.; Wen, Y. Trimethylamine N-oxide prime NLRP3 inflammasome via inhibiting ATG16L1-induced autophagy in colonic epithelial cells. *Biochem. Biophys. Res. Commun.* **2017**, *490*, 541–551. [CrossRef] [PubMed]

77. Pott, J.; Kabat, A.M.; Maloy, K.J. Intestinal epithelial cell autophagy is required to protect against TNF-induced apoptosis during chronic colitis in mice. *Cell Host Microbe* **2018**, *23*, 191–202. [CrossRef] [PubMed]

78. Singh, S.B.; Davis, A.S.; Taylor, G.A.; Deretic, V. Human IRGM induces autophagy to eliminate intracellular mycobacteria. *Science* **2006**, *313*, 1438–1441. [CrossRef] [PubMed]

79. McCarroll, S.A.; Huett, A.; Kuballa, P.; Chilewski, S.D.; Landry, A.; Goyette, P.; Zody, M.C.; Hall, J.L.; Brant, S.R.; Cho, J.H.; et al. Deletion polymorphism upstream of IRGM associated with altered IRGM expression and Crohn's disease. *Nat. Genet.* **2008**, *40*, 1107–1112. [CrossRef]

80. Rufini, S.; Ciccacci, C.; Di Fusco, D.; Ruffa, A.; Pallone, F.; Novelli, G.; Biancone, L.; Borgiani, P. Autophagy and inflammatory bowel disease: Association between variants of the autophagy related IRGM gene and susceptibility to Crohn's disease. *Dig. Liver Dis.* **2015**, *47*, 744–750. [CrossRef]

81. Chauhan, S.; Mandell, M.A.; Deretic, V. IRGM governs the core autophagy machinery to conduct antimicrobial defense. *Mol. Cell* **2015**, *58*, 507–521. [CrossRef] [PubMed]

82. Crook, N.E.; Clem, R.J.; Miller, L.K. An apoptosis-inhibiting baculovirus gene with a zinc finger-like motif. *J. Virol.* **1993**, *67*, 2168–2174. [PubMed]

83. Eckelman, B.P.; Salvesen, G.S.; Scott, F.L. Human inhibitor of apoptosis proteins: Why XIAP is the black sheep of the family. *EMBO Rep.* **2006**, *7*, 988–994. [CrossRef] [PubMed]

84. Mizushima, N.; Levine, B.; Cuervo, A.M.; Klionsky, D.J. Autophagy fights disease through cellular self-digestion. *Nature* **2008**, *451*, 1069–1075. [CrossRef] [PubMed]

85. Huang, X.; Wu, Z.; Mei, Y.; Wu, M. XIAP inhibits autophagy via XIAP-Mdm2-p53 signalling. *EMBO J.* **2013**, *32*, 2204–2216. [CrossRef] [PubMed]

86. Zeissig, Y.; Petersen, B.S.; Milutinovic, S.; Bosse, E.; Mayr, G.; Peuker, K.; Hartwig, J.; Keller, A.; Kohl, M.; Laass, M.W.; et al. XIAP variants in male Crohn's disease. *Gut* **2015**, *64*, 66–76. [CrossRef]

87. Schwerd, T.; Pandey, S.; Yang, H.T.; Bagola, K.; Jameson, E.; Jung, J.; Lachmann, R.H.; Shah, N.; Patel, S.Y.; Booth, C.; et al. Impaired antibacterial autophagy links granulomatous intestinal inflammation in Niemann-Pick disease type C1 and XIAP deficiency with NOD2 variants in Crohn's disease. *Gut* **2017**, *66*, 1060–1073. [CrossRef]

88. Elinav, E.; Strowig, T.; Henao-Mejia, J.; Flavell, R.A. Regulation of the antimicrobial response by NLR proteins. *Immunity* **2011**, *34*, 665–679. [CrossRef]

89. Yano, T.; Kurata, S. Intracellular recognition of pathogens and autophagy as an innate immune host defence. *J. Biochem.* **2011**, *150*, 143–149. [CrossRef]

90. Mazzini, E.; Massimiliano, L.; Penna, G.; Rescigno, M. Oral tolerance can be established via gap junction transfer of fed antigens from CX3CR1$^+$ macrophages to CD103$^+$ dendritic cells. *Immunity* **2014**, *40*, 248–261. [CrossRef]

91. Martin, B.; Hirota, K.; Cua, D.J.; Stockinger, B.; Veldhoen, M. Interleukin-17-producing gamma delta T cells selectively expand in response topathogen products and environmental signals. *Immunity* **2009**, *31*, 321–330. [CrossRef] [PubMed]

92. Talero, E.; Garcia-Maurino, S.; Motilva, V. Melatonin, autophagy and intestinal bowel disease. *Curr. Pharm. Des.* **2014**, *20*, 4816–4827. [CrossRef] [PubMed]

93. Münz, C. Autophagy beyond intracellular MHC class II antigen presentation. *Trends. Immunol.* **2016**, *37*, 755–763. [CrossRef] [PubMed]

94. Strisciuglio, C.; Duijvestein, M.; Verhaar, A.P.; Vos, A.C.; van den Brink, G.R.; Hommes, D.W.; Wildenberg, M.E. Impaired autophagy leads to abnormal dendritic cell-epithelial cell interactions. *J. Crohns. Colitis.* **2013**, *7*, 534–541. [CrossRef]

95. Lapaquette, P.; Bringer, M.A.; Darfeuille-Michaud, A. Defects in autophagy favour adherent-invasive Escherichia coli persistence within macrophages leading to increased pro-inflammatory response. *Cell. Microbiol.* **2012**, *14*, 791–807. [CrossRef] [PubMed]

96. Lassen, K.G.; McKenzie, C.I.; Mari, M.; Murano, T.; Begun, J.; Baxt, L.A.; Goel, G.; Villablanca, E.J.; Kuo, S.Y.; Huang, H.; et al. Genetic coding variant in GPR65 alters lysosomal pH and links lysosomal dysfunction with colitis risk. *Immunity* **2016**, *44*, 1392–1405. [CrossRef] [PubMed]

97. Meunier, E.; Dick, M.S.; Dreier, R.F.; Schürmann, N.; Kenzelmann Broz, D.; Warming, S.; Roose-Girma, M.; Bumann, D.; Kayagaki, N.; Takeda, K.; et al. Caspase-11 activation requires lysis of pathogen-containing vacuoles by IFN-induced GTPases. *Nature* **2014**, *509*, 366–370. [CrossRef]

98. Ke, P.; Shao, B.Z.; Xu, Z.Q.; Wei, W.; Han, B.Z.; Chen, X.W.; Su, D.F.; Liu, C. Activation of cannabinoid receptor 2 ameliorates DSS-induced colitis through inhibiting NLRP3 inflammasome in macrophages. *PLoS ONE* **2016**, *11*, e0155076. [CrossRef]

99. Samie, M.; Lim, J.; Verschueren, E.; Baughman, J.M.; Peng, I.; Wong, A.; Kwon, Y.; Senbabaoglu, Y.; Hackney, J.A.; Keir, M.; et al. Selective autophagy of the adaptor TRIF regulates innate inflammatory signaling. *Nat. Immunol.* **2018**, *19*, 246–254. [CrossRef]

100. Fan, K.; Lin, L.; Ai, Q.; Wan, J.; Dai, J.; Liu, G.; Tang, L.; Yang, Y.; Ge, P.; Jiang, R.; et al. Lipopolysaccharide-induced dephosphorylation of AMPK-activated protein kinase potentiates inflammatory injury via repression of ULK1-dependent autophagy. *Front. Immunol.* **2018**, *9*, 1464. [CrossRef]

101. Zhang, H.; Zheng, L.; Chen, J.; Fukata, M.; Ichikawa, R.; Shih, D.Q.; Zhang, X. The protection role of Atg16l1 in CD11c+dendritic cells in murine colitis. *Immunobiology* **2017**, *222*, 831–841. [CrossRef] [PubMed]

102. Baxt, L.A.; Xavier, R.J. Role of autophagy in the maintenance of intestinal homeostasis. *Gastroenterology* **2015**, *149*, 553–562. [CrossRef] [PubMed]

103. Liu, E.; Van Grol, J.; Subauste, C.S. Atg5 but not Atg7 in dendritic cells enhances IL-2 and IFN-γ production by Toxoplasma gondii-reactive CD4+ T cells. *Microbes Infect.* **2015**, *17*, 275–284. [CrossRef] [PubMed]

104. Kolaczkowska, E.; Kubes, P. Neutrophil recruitment and function in health and inflammation. *Nat. Rev. Immunol.* **2013**, *13*, 159–175. [CrossRef] [PubMed]

105. Mantovani, A.; Cassatella, M.A.; Costantini, C.; Jaillon, S. Neutrophils in the activation and regulation of innate and adaptive immunity. *Nat. Rev. Immunol.* **2011**, *11*, 519–531. [CrossRef]

106. Wéra, O.; Lancellotti, P.; Oury, C. The dual role of neutrophils in inflammatory bowel diseases. *Clin. Med.* **2016**, *5*. [CrossRef]

107. Zhang, H.; Zheng, L.; McGovern, D.P.; Hamill, A.M.; Ichikawa, R.; Kanazawa, Y.; Luu, J.; Kumagai, K.; Cilluffo, M.; Fukata, M.; et al. Myeloid ATG16L1 facilitates host-bacteria interactions in maintaining intestinal homeostasis. *J. Immunol.* **2017**, *198*, 2133–2146. [CrossRef] [PubMed]

108. Chew, T.S.; O'Shea, N.R.; Sewell, G.W.; Oehlers, S.H.; Mulvey, C.M.; Crosier, P.S.; Godovac-Zimmermann, J.; Bloom, S.L.; Smith, A.M.; Segal, A.W. Optineurin deficiency in mice contributes to impaired cytokine secretion and neutrophil recruitment in bacteria-driven colitis. *Dis. Model. Mech.* **2015**, *8*, 817–829. [CrossRef] [PubMed]

109. Goldberg, R.; Prescott, N.; Lord, G.M.; MacDonald, T.T.; Powell, N. The unusual suspects–innate lymphoid cells as novel therapeutic targets in IBD. *Nat. Rev. Gastroenterol. Hepatol.* **2015**, *12*, 271–283. [CrossRef] [PubMed]

110. O'Sullivan, T.E.; Geary, C.D.; Weizman, O.E.; Geiger, T.L.; Rapp, M.; Dorn, G.W., 2nd; Overholtzer, M.; Sun, J.C. Atg5 is essential for the development and survival of innate lymphocytes. *Cell Rep.* **2016**, *15*, 1910–1919. [CrossRef]

111. Wang, S.; Xia, P.; Huang, G.; Zhu, P.; Liu, J.; Ye, B.; Du, Y.; Fan, Z. FoxO1-mediated autophagy is required for NK cell development and innate immunity. *Nat. Commun.* **2016**, *7*, 11023. [CrossRef] [PubMed]

112. López-Soto, A.; Bravo-San Pedro, J.M.; Kroemer, G.; Galluzzi, L.; Gonzalez, S. Involvement of autophagy in NK cell development and function. *Autophagy* **2017**, *13*, 633–636. [CrossRef] [PubMed]

113. Heller, F.; Fuss, I.J.; Nieuwenhuis, E.E.; Blumberg, R.S.; Strober, W. Oxazolone colitis, a Th2 colitis model resembling ulcerative colitis, is mediated by IL-13-producing NK-T cells. *Immunity* **2002**, *17*, 629–638. [CrossRef]

114. Fuss, I.J.; Heller, F.; Boirivant, M.; Leon, F.; Yoshida, M.; Fichtner-Feigl, S.; Yang, Z.; Exley, M.; Kitani, A.; Blumberg, R.S.; et al. Nonclassical CD1d-restricted NK T cells that produce IL-13 characterize an atypical Th2 response in ulcerative colitis. *J. Clin. Investig.* **2004**, *113*, 1490–1497. [CrossRef] [PubMed]

115. Salio, M.; Puleston, D.J.; Mathan, T.S.; Shepherd, D.; Stranks, A.J.; Adamopoulou, E.; Veerapen, N.; Besra, G.S.; Hollander, G.A.; Simon, A.K. Essential role for autophagy during invariant NKT cell development. *Proc. Natl. Acad. Sci. USA* **2014**, *111*, E5678–E5687. [CrossRef] [PubMed]

116. Pei, B.; Zhao, M.; Miller, B.C.; Véla, J.L.; Bruinsma, M.W.; Virgin, H.W.; Kronenberg, M. Invariant NKT cells require autophagy to coordinate proliferation and survival signals during differentiation. *J. Immunol.* **2015**, *194*, 5872–5884. [CrossRef]

117. Zhu, L.; Xie, X.; Zhang, L.; Wang, H.; Jie, Z.; Zhou, X.; Shi, J.; Zhao, S.; Zhang, B.; Cheng, X. TBK-binding protein 1 regulates IL-15-induced autophagy and NKT cell survival. *Nat. Commun.* **2018**, *9*, 2812. [CrossRef]

118. Ouellette, A.J.; Hsieh, M.M.; Nosek, M.T.; Cano-Gauci, D.F.; Huttner, K.M.; Buick, R.N.; Selsted, M.E. Mouse Paneth cell defensins: Primary structures and antibacterial activities of numerous cryptdin isoforms. *Infect. Immun.* **1994**, *62*, 5040–5047.

119. Ayabe, T.; Satchell, D.P.; Wilson, C.L.; Parks, W.C.; Selsted, M.E.; Ouellette, A.J. Secretion of microbicidal alpha-defensins by intestinal Paneth cells in response to bacteria. *Nat. Immunol.* **2000**, *1*, 113–118. [CrossRef]

120. Bar Shira, E.; Friedman, A. Innate immune functions of avian intestinal epithelial cells: Response to bacterial stimuli and localization of responding cells in the developing avian digestive tract. *PLoS ONE* **2018**, *13*, e0200393. [CrossRef]

121. Cobo, E.R.; Holani, R.; Moreau, F.; Nakamura, K.; Ayabe, T.; Mastroianni, J.R.; Ouellette, A.; Chadee, K. Entamoeba histolytica alters ileal Paneth cell functions in intact and Muc2 mucin deficiency. *Infect. Immun.* **2018**. [CrossRef] [PubMed]

122. Bel, S.; Pendse, M.; Wang, Y.; Li, Y.; Ruhn, K.A.; Hassell, B.; Leal, T.; Winter, S.E.; Xavier, R.J.; Hooper, L.V. Paneth cells secrete lysozyme via secretory autophagy during bacterial infection of the intestine. *Science* **2017**, *357*, 1047–1052. [CrossRef]

123. Stappenbeck, T.S.; McGovern, D.P.B. Paneth cell alterations in the development and phenotype of Crohn's disease. *Gastroenterology* **2017**, *152*, 322–326. [CrossRef] [PubMed]

124. Urano, F.; Wang, X.; Bertolotti, A.; Zhang, Y.; Chung, P.; Harding, H.P.; Ron, D. Coupling of stress in the ER to activation of JNK protein kinases by transmembrane protein kinase IRE1. *Science* **2000**, *287*, 664–666. [CrossRef] [PubMed]

125. Oyadomari, S.; Mori, M. Roles of CHOP/GADD153 in endoplasmic reticulum stress. *Cell Death Differ.* **2004**, *11*, 381–389. [CrossRef] [PubMed]

126. Kaneko, M.; Niinuma, Y.; Nomura, Y. Activation signal of nuclear factor-kappa B in response to endoplasmic reticulum stress is transduced via IRE1 and tumor necrosis factor receptor-associated factor 2. *Biol. Pharm. Bull.* **2003**, *26*, 931–935. [CrossRef] [PubMed]

127. Fritz, T.; Niedereiter, L.; Adolph, T.; Blumberg, R.S.; Kaser, A. Crohn's disease: NOD2, autophagy and ER stress converge. *Gut* **2011**, *60*, 1580–1588. [CrossRef]

128. Kaser, A.; Blumberg, R.S. ATG16L1 Crohn's disease risk stresses the endoplasmic reticulum of Paneth cells. *Gut* **2014**, *63*, 1038–1039. [CrossRef] [PubMed]

129. Matsuzawa-Ishimoto, Y.; Shono, Y.; Gomez, L.E.; Hubbard-Lucey, V.M.; Cammer, M.; Neil, J.; Dewan, M.Z.; Lieberman, S.R.; Lazrak, A.; Marinis, J.M.; et al. Autophagy protein ATG16L1 prevents necroptosis in the intestinal epithelium. *J. Exp. Med.* **2017**, *214*, 3687–3705. [CrossRef]

130. Balmus, I.M.; Ciobica, A.; Trifan, A.; Stanciu, C. The implications of oxidative stress and antioxidant therapies in Inflammatory Bowel Disease: Clinical aspects and animal models. *Saudi J. Gastroenterol.* **2016**, *22*, 3–17. [CrossRef]

131. Chen, L.; You, Q.; Hu, L.; Gao, J.; Meng, Q.; Liu, W.; Wu, X.; Xu, Q. The antioxidant procyanidin reduces reactive oxygen species signaling in macrophages and ameliorates experimental colitis in mice. *Front. Immunol.* **2018**, *8*, 1910. [CrossRef] [PubMed]

132. Denson, L.A.; Jurickova, I.; Karns, R.; Shaw, K.A.; Cutler, D.J.; Okou, D.T.; Dodd, A.; Quinn, K.; Mondal, K.; Aronow, B.J.; et al. Clinical and genomic correlates of neutrophil reactive oxygen species production in pediatric patients with Crohn's disease. *Gastroenterology* **2018**, *154*, 2097–2110. [CrossRef] [PubMed]

133. Zhang, C.; Li, P.; Zhang, S.; Lei, R.; Li, B.; Wu, X.; Jiang, C.; Zhang, X.; Ma, R.; Yang, L.; et al. Oxidative stress-elicited autophagosome accumulation contributes to human neuroblastoma SH-SY5Y cell death induced by PBDE-47. *Environ. Toxicol. Pharmacol.* **2017**, *56*, 322–328. [CrossRef] [PubMed]

134. Cheung, E.C.; Ludwig, R.L.; Vousden, K.H. Mitochondrial localization of TIGAR under hypoxia stimulates HK2 and lowers ROS and cell death. *Proc. Natl. Acad. Sci. USA* **2012**, *109*, 20491–20496. [CrossRef] [PubMed]

135. Mahalingaiah, P.K.; Singh, K.P. Chronic oxidative stress increases growth and tumorigenic potential of MCF-7 breast cancer cells. *PLoS ONE* **2014**, *9*, e87371. [CrossRef] [PubMed]

136. Tal, M.C.; Sasai, M.; Lee, H.K.; Yordy, B.; Shadel, G.S.; Iwasaki, A. Absence of autophagy results in reactive oxygen species-dependent amplification of RLR signaling. *Proc. Natl. Acad. Sci. USA* **2009**, *106*, 770–775. [CrossRef]

137. Adolph, T.E.; Mayr, L.; Grabherr, F.; Tilg, H. Paneth cells and their antimicrobials in intestinal immunity. *Curr. Pharm. Des.* **2018**, *24*, 1121–1129. [CrossRef]

138. Kostic, A.D.; Xavier, R.J.; Gevers, D. The microbiome in inflammatory bowel disease: Current status and the future ahead. *Gastroenterology* **2014**, *146*, 1489–1499. [CrossRef]

139. Sun, J. VDR/vitamin D receptor regulates autophagic activity through ATG16L1. *Autophagy* **2016**, *12*, 1057–1058. [CrossRef]

140. Burger, E.; Araujo, A.; López-Yglesias, A.; Rajala, M.W.; Geng, L.; Levine, B.; Hooper, L.V.; Burstein, E.; Yarovinsky, F.; et al. Loss of Paneth cell autophagy causes acute susceptibility to Toxoplasma gondii-mediated Inflammation. *Cell Host Microbe* **2018**, *23*, 177–190. [CrossRef]

141. Garrett, W.S.; Gordon, J.I.; Glimcher, L.H. Homeostasis and inflammation in the intestine. *Cell* **2010**, *140*, 859–870. [CrossRef] [PubMed]

142. Kim, D.H.; Kim, S.; Lee, J.H.; Kim, J.H.; Che, X.; Ma, H.W.; Seo, D.H.; Kim, T.I.; Kim, W.H.; Kim, S.W.; et al. Lactobacillus acidophilus suppresses intestinal inflammation by inhibiting endoplasmic reticulum stress. *J. Gastroenterol. Hepatol.* **2018**. [CrossRef] [PubMed]

143. Ganji-Arjenaki, M.; Rafieian-Kopaei, M. Probiotics are a good choice in remission of inflammatory bowel diseases: A meta analysis and systematic review. *J. Cell. Physiol.* **2018**, *233*, 2091–2103. [CrossRef] [PubMed]

144. Verdugo, P. Goblet cells secretion and mucogenesis. *Annu. Rev. Physiol.* **1990**, *52*, 157–176. [CrossRef] [PubMed]

145. Specian, R.D.; Oliver, M.G. Functional biology of intestinal goblet cells. *Am. J. Physiol.* **1991**, *260*, C183–C193. [CrossRef] [PubMed]

146. Itoh, H.; Beck, P.L.; Inoue, N.; Xavier, R.; Podolsky, D.K. A paradoxical reduction in susceptibility to colonic injury upon targeted transgenic ablation of goblet cells. *J. Clin. Investig.* **1999**, *104*, 1539–1547. [CrossRef] [PubMed]

147. Swidsinski, A.; Loening-Baucke, V.; Herber, A. Mucosal flora in Crohn's disease and ulcerative colitis–An overview. *J. Physiol. Pharmacol.* **2009**, *60*, 61–71. [PubMed]

148. Patel, K.K.; Miyoshi, H.; Beatty, W.L.; Head, R.D.; Malvin, N.P.; Cadwell, K.; Guan, J.L.; Saitoh, T.; Akira, S.; Seglen, P.O.; et al. Autophagy proteins control goblet cell function by potentiating reactive oxygen species production. *EMBO J.* **2013**, *32*, 3130–3144. [CrossRef]

149. Johansson, M.E.; Hansson, G.C. Is the intestinal goblet cell a major immune cell? *Cell Host Microbe* **2014**, *15*, 251–252. [CrossRef] [PubMed]

150. Wlodarska, M.; Thaiss, C.A.; Nowarski, R.; Henao-Mejia, J.; Zhang, J.P.; Brown, E.M.; Frankel, G.; Levy, M.; Katz, M.N.; Philbrick, W.M.; et al. NLRP6 inflammasome orchestrates the colonic host-microbial interface by regulating goblet cell mucus secretion. *Cell* **2014**, *156*, 1045–1059. [CrossRef] [PubMed]

151. Gagné-Sansfaçon, J.; Allaire, J.M.; Jones, C.; Boudreau, F.; Perreault, N. Loss of Sonic hedgehog leads to alterations in intestinal secretory cell maturation and autophagy. *PLoS ONE* **2014**, *9*, e98751. [CrossRef] [PubMed]

152. Wang, S.; Li, Q.; Zang, Y.; Zhao, Y.; Liu, N.; Wang, Y.; Xu, X.; Liu, L.; Mei, Q. Apple Polysaccharide inhibits microbial dysbiosis and chronic inflammation and modulates gut permeability in HFD-fed rats. *Int. J. Biol. Macromol.* **2017**, *99*, 282–292. [CrossRef] [PubMed]

153. El-Khider, F.; McDonald, C. Links of Autophagy Dysfunction to Inflammatory Bowel Disease Onset. *Dig. Dis.* **2016**, *34*, 27–34. [CrossRef] [PubMed]

154. Ke, P.; Shao, B.Z.; Xu, Z.Q.; Chen, X.W.; Liu, C. Intestinal Autophagy and Its Pharmacological Control in Inflammatory Bowel Disease. *Front. Immunol.* **2017**, *7*, 695. [CrossRef] [PubMed]

Review

Roles of Autophagy-Related Genes in the Pathogenesis of Inflammatory Bowel Disease

Sup Kim [1,2,3,4], **Hyuk Soo Eun** [5,6] **and Eun-Kyeong Jo** [1,2,3,*]

[1] Department of Microbiology, Chungnam National University School of Medicine, Daejeon 35015, Korea; mysskks@naver.com
[2] Department of Medical Science, Chungnam National University School of Medicine, Daejeon 35015, Korea
[3] Infection Control Convergence Research Center, Chungnam National University School of Medicine, Daejeon 35015, Korea
[4] Department of Radiation Oncology, Chungnam National University Hospital, 282, Munwha-ro, Jung-gu, Daejeon 34952, Korea
[5] Department of Internal Medicine, Chungnam National University Hospital, 282, Munwha-ro, Jung-gu, Daejeon 34952, Korea; liver@kaist.ac.kr
[6] Department of Internal Medicine, School of Medicine, Chungnam National University, 266, Munwha-ro, Jung-gu, Daejeon 35015, Korea
*   Correspondence: hayoungj@cnu.ac.kr; Tel.: +82-42-580-8243; Fax: +82-42-585-3686

Received: 15 December 2018; Accepted: 11 January 2019; Published: 21 January 2019

Abstract: Autophagy is an intracellular catabolic process that is essential for a variety of cellular responses. Due to its role in the maintenance of biological homeostasis in conditions of stress, dysregulation or disruption of autophagy may be linked to human diseases such as inflammatory bowel disease (IBD). IBD is a complicated inflammatory colitis disorder; Crohn's disease and ulcerative colitis are the principal types. Genetic studies have shown the clinical relevance of several autophagy-related genes (ATGs) in the pathogenesis of IBD. Additionally, recent studies using conditional knockout mice have led to a comprehensive understanding of ATGs that affect intestinal inflammation, Paneth cell abnormality and enteric pathogenic infection during colitis. In this review, we discuss the various ATGs involved in macroautophagy and selective autophagy, including *ATG16L1, IRGM, LRRK2, ATG7, p62, optineurin* and *TFEB* in the maintenance of intestinal homeostasis. Although advances have been made regarding the involvement of ATGs in maintaining intestinal homeostasis, determining the precise contribution of autophagy has remained elusive. Recent efforts based on direct targeting of ATGs and autophagy will further facilitate the development of new therapeutic opportunities for IBD.

Keywords: autophagy; ATGs; intestinal homeostasis; inflammatory bowel diseases

---

1. Introduction

Inflammatory bowel disease (IBD) is a complicated autoimmune disorder with multiple etiologies including genetic predisposition, environmental factors and immune-associated pathogenesis [1]. Both Crohn's disease (CD) and ulcerative colitis (UC), the major clinical phenotypes of IBD, are systemic diseases associated with autoimmune manifestations [2,3]. Although the intestinal host defense is maintained by balancing inflammation and the immune response, excessive inflammation may damage the intestine and its mucosal barrier [1,3]. Although IBD is known to be a polygenic disorder, emerging evidence indicates that genetic susceptibility associated with host autophagy is an important factor in the pathogenesis of IBD [4,5].

Autophagy is a cytosolic process that triggers lysosomal degradation of cytosolic materials to maintain intracellular homeostasis under conditions of stress by recycling metabolic building blocks [6,7]. Intracellular cargos sequestered by autophagosomes include damaged cellular organelles, large protein aggregates and intracellular pathogens [8,9]. It is now clear that activation of autophagy contributes to the amelioration of excessive inflammatory responses [10,11]. Dysfunctional or dysregulated autophagy can lead to diverse inflammatory, immune and metabolic disorders [10,11]. Previous studies have demonstrated the involvement of genetic variations of autophagy genes, including *ATG16L1* and *IRGM*, in the pathogenesis of colitis [12–18]. More recently, it was shown that autophagy-related genes (ATGs), such as optineurin (*OPTN*), transcription factor EB (*TFEB*) and leucine-rich repeat kinase (*LRRK*), are associated with increased susceptibility to colitis, suggesting that these genes are important in colonic immune homeostasis [19–25].

This review will focus on recent progress in elucidating the roles of ATGs in colonic inflammation and their clinical relevance. We will highlight recent findings regarding several ATGs and the mechanisms through which colitis severity is regulated.

2. Overview of Autophagy, Selective Autophagy and ATGs

Macroautophagy (herein referred to as autophagy) is an intracellular catabolic process through which cytoplasmic cargos are sequestered and delivered to lysosomes for degradation [26]. Autophagy plays a critical role in the maintenance of cellular homeostasis during a variety of stress responses, including starvation, hypoxia, toxicity and inflammation [27]. Although it was originally believed that autophagy was a nonspecific process that occurred under starvation conditions, it is now known that autophagy can target specific intracellular organelles or foreign pathogens for timely degradation, which is known as selective autophagy. A detailed discussion of the general aspects of autophagy is beyond the scope of this review; there are numerous excellent reviews dealing in detail about autophagy [28,29]. Here, we briefly review nonselective and selective autophagy, as well as ATGs (Figure 1), before focusing on the relationship of ATGs and autophagy with the pathogenesis of IBD.

2.1. Autophagy

Autophagy plays an important housekeeping function in cells through the removal of superfluous or damaged organelles in lysosomes. The autophagic process consists of multiple stages: initiation and biogenesis of autophagosomes, followed by maturation and fusion with lysosomes (Figure 1A) [30]. Autophagy is initiated by the formation of the phagophore, in which the edges of isolation membranes elongate and engulf cytoplasmic cargos [30]. Once the double-membrane structure contains cytoplasmic cargos, autophagosomes undergo maturation to form a completed autophagosome structure and ultimately are fused with a late endosome and lysosome to initiate degradation of cargos [31,32].

Regulation of autophagy is important to prevent cell death and pathogenic conditions [33]. It is now clear that autophagic activity is tightly regulated by molecular machinery and transcription factors at transcriptional and post-translational levels [33]. Recent studies have identified several nuclear transcription factors that coordinate autophagy via transcriptional activation of ATGs [33]. For example, *TFEB* plays an essential role in lysosomal biogenesis and activity during autophagy (Figure 2) [34]. We also briefly highlight the involvement of *TFEB* in the regulation of colonic inflammation (Figure 2).

(A)

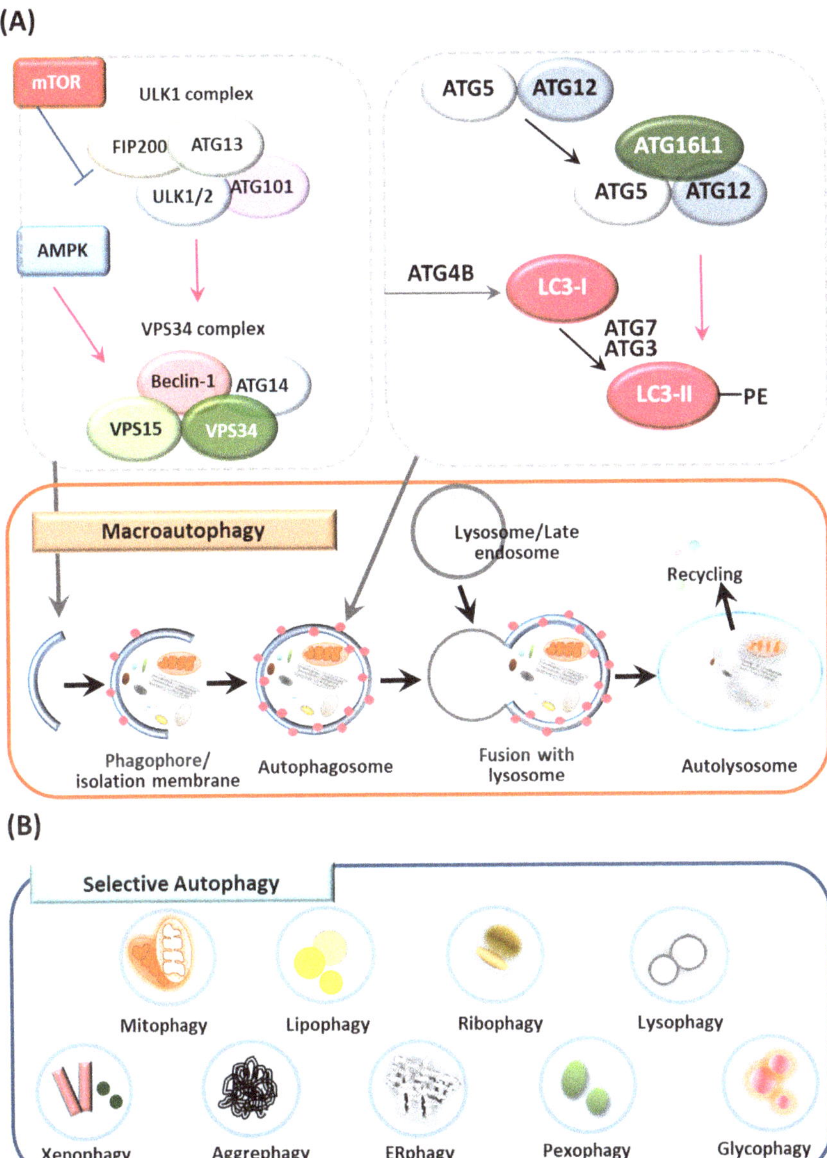

(B)

Figure 1. Overview of autophagy, selective autophagy and ATGs (**A**) Molecular machinery of autophagy process. After mTOR inhibition or AMPK activation, the autophagy process begins with the biogenesis of the phagophore/isolation membrane. The ATG16L1-ATG5-ATG12 and LC3-II-PE conjugates participate in autophagosome formation process. The mature autophagosomes are fused with a late endosome and lysosome to initiate degradation of cargos. Finally, cells recycle the released products in cytosol. (**B**) Selective autophagy clears various targets such as subcellular structure, bacteria, protein and lipid aggregates.

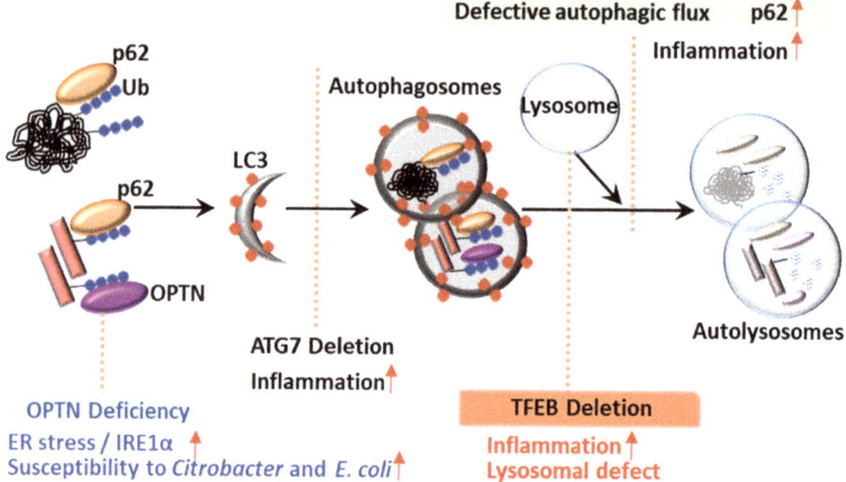

Figure 2. The process of autophagy flux and involved genes. The autophagy flux is depicted. A normal autophagic flux includes the autophagosome formation and maturation step and the autolysosome formation step. The possible conditions associated with involved genes are depicted: (1) *OPTN* deficiency leads to an accumulation of IRE1α and increased susceptibility of *Citrobacter* and *E. coli*. (2) *ATG7* deletion is associated with increased inflammation. (3) *TFEB* deletion results in increased inflammation and lysosomal defect.

2.2. Selective Autophagy

In addition to nonselective degradation, autophagy also plays a role in the targeting and clearance of specific targets/substrates, that is, selective autophagy, which is named depending on its specific targets and includes mitophagy, xenophagy and aggrephagy (Figure 1B) [35–38]. Selective autophagy involves several steps, including a degradation cue, cargo recognition via selective autophagy receptors, ubiquitination and the recruitment of autophagosome machinery but it does not necessarily occur in a stepwise manner [39,40]. Several ubiquitin binding proteins, such as p62, neighbor of breast cancer 1 (NBR1), OPTN and NDP52/CALCOCO2, have been identified as autophagy receptors responsible for the delivery of ubiquitinated cargos to the autophagy system [41–46]. Cargo signals can be classified as ubiquitin-dependent and -independent recognition [40]. Autophagic cargo receptors contain the LC3-interacting region (LIR) motif, which connects cargos to ATG8 family proteins for selective autophagic degradation [45,46]. Despite advances in knowledge of the mechanisms and players involved in canonical and noncanonical autophagy, we still lack a clear understanding of its function in a variety of physiologic and pathologic responses. A few reports have demonstrated the involvement of several autophagic receptors, including p62 and OPTN, in the control of intestinal homeostasis. However, additional autophagic receptors or regulators of autophagic signaling pathways must operate to ameliorate excessive colonic inflammation. Finally, it will be important to investigate the mechanisms by which autophagic receptors or ATGs impact clinical outcomes.

2.3. ATGs and the Control of Autophagy

Each step of the autophagy process is highly orchestrated by numerous ATGs; nearly 40 ATGs have been identified in yeast and orthologs of yeast ATGs have been identified in higher eukaryotes with some exceptions, such as mammalian ATG101 [47–49]. Among these ATGs, certain gene groups are required for autophagosome formation and are shared among various types of autophagy, such as nonselective and selective autophagy. Mammalian ATGs can be divided into several functional clusters including the ULK1-ATG13-FIP200-ATG101 protein kinase complex, the PtdIns3K class

III complex containing VPS34, VPS15 and Beclin 1, the ubiquitin-like ATG5/ATG12 complex and the ubiquitin-like ATG8/LC3 conjugation system [50]. These ATGs participate in different stages of autophagy, such as the induction of autophagosome formation, expansion of phagophores and autophagosome completion [50,51].

Recent studies have identified and reported the roles of numerous cargo receptors including NBR1, multi-domain scaffold/adaptor protein p62/sequestosome-1 (p62/SQSTM-1), nuclear domain 10 protein 52 (NDP52) and OPTN [41,42,44]. These selective autophagic receptors contain the LIR motif, thereby connecting ubiquitin-tagged substrates to ATG8 family members such as microtubule-associated protein 1A/1B-light chain 3/γ-aminobutyric acid receptor-associated protein (LC3/GABARAP) [42,45,52].

The roles of ATGs in autophagy have been described in detail in numerous review articles [26,30]. In this review, we focus on ATGs that play essential roles in IBD pathogenesis in terms of autophagy regulation.

3. Overview of IBD

IBD is a disease in which chronic inflammation of intestinal cells occurs due to unknown causes [53]. CD and UC are classified according to the clinical features and characteristics of the disease. Both diseases have similar clinical symptoms including diarrhea, abdominal pain, hematochezia and weight loss; however, the location of inflammation, infiltration degree and complications differ [54]. In general, CD is known to mediate Th1 cell-mediated inflammatory responses and UC is known to mediate Th2 cells [55]. Recently, loss of the suppressive functions of interleukin (IL)-17A-producing regulatory T cells was reported to cause IBD [56]. In general, both types of IBD are treated with anti-inflammatory drugs, such as 5-aminosalicylic acid and corticosteroids; however, in the absence of clinical improvement following treatment with anti-inflammatory drugs, patients achieved a high remission rate using anti-tumor necrosis factor (TNF)-α drugs [57]. However, more than one-third of IBD patients do not respond to anti-TNF-α drugs [58]. Recently, a new therapeutic target for IBD has emerged and the role of Paneth cells in intestinal homeostasis is discussed.

Crypts, concave structures of granulated cells clustered in the base of the small intestine, contain 5–12 Paneth cells. Unlike ordinary enterocytes, which have an average lifespan of 3–5 days, Paneth cells have a longer life expectancy of 20 days [59]. Paneth cells can differentiate into three different cell lineages: enterocytes, goblet cells and enteroendocrine cells [60]. Paneth cells exhibit antimicrobial effects by secreting secretory granules containing antimicrobial peptides (AMPs) and other peptides including lysozymes, alpha-defensins and secretory phospholipase A1 in response to cell stimuli to crypt lumen [61–63]. Paneth cell secretion of AMPs plays an important role not only in clearing invading pathogens but also in maintaining the diversity and quantity of intestinal microbiota via intestinal antimicrobial function [64]. Although Paneth cells are normally localized to the small intestine, diseases such as chronic inflammation may result in intestinal metaplasia, which is characterized by the localization and function of Paneth cells in aberrant sites, such as the colon [65]. These metaplastic Paneth cells protect the colonic epithelium from bacterial invasion [59]. However, Paneth cell loss may occur in situations with acute inflammation such as Grade II/III graft versus host disease or in CD [66,67]. In this case, Paneth cells are replaced with lysozyme-producing mucus cells, which can be followed by the development of diseases such as IBD in the small intestine [68].

Paneth cells present in the intestinal epithelium are essential for maintaining the homeostasis of normal colonizing microbes of the host. The important pathway in this process is xenophagy, an autophagic pathogen removal process that allows the host to maintain normal metabolic function [69,70]. However, when dysfunction of Paneth cells occurs due to environmental or genetic influences, AMPs are not secreted properly. As a result, dysbiosis, a discrepancy in the composition of normal intestinal microbiota, occurs, which is an important cause of intestinal disorders, especially IBD [71]. For example, in CD patients with impaired xenophagy, adherent-invasive *Escherichia coli* (AIEC) or *Salmonella typhimurium* colonize intestinal epithelial cells (IECs) due to the autophagic dysfunction of Paneth cells [72–74]. Thus, the impairment of autophagy in Paneth cells makes it difficult to treat incoming pathogenic bacteria as well as to respond to alterations in the composition of the intestinal microbiota [75]. Ultimately, the poor xenophagy of Paneth cells makes the intestinal epithelium hypersensitive to infiltrating microbes or their products and promotes bacterial self-proliferation and the onset of IBD [76,77].

4. ATG Involvement in IBD Pathogenesis

The clinical diversity and heterogeneity of the IBD phenotype are likely due to the presence of genetic heterogeneity together with environmental factors. Susceptibility to IBD may be due to an interaction of several genes, identified by genome-wide association studies (GWASs) [78–80]. To date, over 200 loci have been identified as genetically significant loci by a meta-analysis combined with GWAS [81,82]. Earlier independent GWASs showed that autophagy gene variants, including autophagy-related gene 16-like 1 (*ATG16L1*) and immunity-related GTPase M (*IRGM*) are linked to CD susceptibility highlighting the role of autophagy in controlling infection, inflammation and cancer [13,15,83,84]. Furthermore, gene mutation or deletion studies have indicated that the autophagy pathway affects the onset and exacerbation of IBD via several mechanisms including clearance of invading bacteria, secretion of granules from Paneth cells, inflammasome activity, pro-inflammatory cytokine production and endoplasmic reticulum (ER) stress. However, the role of autophagy in the pathogenesis of IBD is still debated. Although many researchers focused on the involvement of ATGs in IBD pathogenesis, little is known about the autophagic role of ATGs and the mechanisms that confer intestinal inflammation. Table 2 summarizes the ATGs and transcription factors described in this review and their functional relationships in intestinal pathogenesis.

Table 1. Genetic models related to autophagy in intestinal pathogenesis.

Knocked-Out Gene	Cell Type	Mechanism	Outcome	Reference
ATG16L1	Intestinal epithelial cells	Abnormality of Paneth cell granule secretion and defect in the granule exocytosis pathway		[76]
	Intestinal epithelial cells	ER stress sensor inositol-requiring enzyme (IRE)-1α accumulated in Paneth cells	Increased intestinal inflammation	[85]
	Intestinal epithelial cells	Elevated pro-inflammatory cytokine secretion and increased IEC apoptosis after *Helicobacter hepaticus* infection	Exacerbated murine model of chronic colitis	[86]
	Myeloid cells	Production high amounts of the inflammatory cytokines IL-1β and IL-18 via Toll/IL-1 receptor domain-containing adaptor inducing interferon (IFN)-β (TRIF)-dependent activation of the inflammasome	Increased susceptibility to dextran sulfate sodium (DSS)-induced colitis	[87]
	Myeloid cells	Increased reactive oxygen species production, impaired mitophagy, reduced microbial killing, impaired processing of MHC class II Ags and altered intracellular trafficking to the lysosomal compartments	Exacerbated murine model of acute and chronic colitis	[88]
	Myeloid cells		No effect on disease severity in murine model of chronic colitis	[86]
IRGM	Intestinal epithelial cells	Marked alterations of Paneth cell location and granule morphology	Hyperinflammation in the colon and ileum following chemical exposure	[85]
LRRK2/ MUC19	Myeloid cells	Activation of the transcription factor NFAT	Increased susceptibility to DSS-induced colitis in mouse models	[23]
ATG7	Intestinal epithelial cells	Higher expression levels of pro-inflammatory cytokine mRNA in the large intestine after infection	Increased susceptibility to *Citrobacter rodentium* infectious colitis in mouse models	[89]
	Intestinal antigen presenting cells	Enhanced immunopathology and inflammatory Th17 responses, as well as abnormal mitochondrial function and oxidative stress	Increased susceptibility to DSS-induced colitis in mouse models	[90]
	Myeloid cells	Increased colonic cytokine expression, T helper 1 skewing and systemic bacterial invasion	Increased susceptibility to DSS-induced colitis in mouse models	[91]

Table 2. Genetic models related to autophagy in intestinal pathogenesis.

Knocked-Out Gene	Cell Type	Mechanism	Outcome	Reference
OPTN	Myeloid cells	Decreased antimicrobial host defense (decreased production of TNFα and IL-6) after infection	Increased susceptibility to *Citrobacter* colitis and *E. coli* peritonitis	[19]
TFEB	Intestinal epithelial cells	Defect in Paneth cell granules, lower expression levels of lipoprotein ApoA1	Exaggerated colitis upon DSS injury	[21]

4.1. ATG16L1

Numerous studies have reported that genetic variation in *ATG16L1* is associated with IBD risk in ethnically diverse populations [13,14,92–96]. Notably, the rs2241880 single nucleotide polymorphism (SNP; T300A) of *ATG16L1* was repeatedly found in several Caucasian cohorts, suggesting a strong association of this variant with the incidence of CD, although it was not frequently found in other populations, particularly in Asian patients [13,84,96].

ATG16L1, a homolog of ATG16, is essential in the formation of autophagosomes, along with the ATG12-ATG5 conjugate [97,98]. Importantly, Cadwell et al. showed that mice with low expression of *ATG16L1* (ATG16L1^{HM} mice) exhibited abnormal Paneth cell granule secretion and that mice with *ATG16L1* deficiency in Paneth cells had a defect in the granule exocytosis pathway [76]. Similarly, patients carrying the *ATG16L1* risk allele (T300A) had pathological features such as disorganized granules or diffuse Paneth cell cytoplasmic lysozyme staining [76]. Using IEC-specific *ATG16L1*-deficient mice and ex vivo IEC organoids, a recent study showed that *ATG16L1* in IECs played an essential role in controlling pathology, intestinal inflammation and TNF-induced apoptosis [86]. Additionally, previous studies showed that the ER stress sensor inositol-requiring enzyme (IRE)-1α accumulated in Paneth cells of *ATG16L1*$^{\Delta IEC}$ mice and CD patients (T300A), suggesting that defective autophagy leads to pathological activation of IRE1α to drive intestinal inflammation [85]. Moreover, loss of IKKα function markedly impaired the secretion of cytoprotective IL-18 and upregulated ER stress responses through decreased ATG16L1 stabilization [99]. These data emphasize the role of ER stress in defective *ATG16L1*-mediated colonic inflammation [85,99]. Indeed, IEC-specific deletion of *ATG16L1* or *ATG7* led to hyper-activated ER stress, which may amplify the severity of intestinal inflammation in autophagy-defective conditions [100].

Although IECs, particularly Paneth cells, are important in defective *ATG16L1*-associated intestinal inflammation, the function of ATG16L1 in myeloid cells has also been demonstrated [87]. Saitoh et al. showed that *ATG16L1*-deficient macrophages exhibited Toll/IL-1 receptor domain-containing adaptor inducing interferon (IFN)-β (TRIF)-dependent activation of the inflammasome, resulting in the production of high amounts of the inflammatory cytokines IL-1β and IL-18 [87]. Deficiency of *ATG16L1* in hematopoietic cells resulted in an increased susceptibility to dextran sulfate sodium (DSS)-induced colitis, suggesting an essential role for ATG16L1 in the control of intestinal inflammation [87]. Another study using mice with myeloid *ATG16L1* deficiency showed exacerbated colitis with upregulated proinflammatory responses as well as increased colitogenic bacteria, indicating that *ATG16L1* deficiency results in alterations in macrophage function that affect the severity of CD [88].

Peripheral blood mononuclear cells (PBMCs) isolated from CD patients with the *ATG16L1* T300A risk variant have been shown to exhibit increased production of the proinflammatory cytokines IL-1β and IL-6, particularly in response to NOD2 ligands [101]. Moreover, the loss of *ATG16L1* increased TRIF and its signaling, resulting in increased production of type I IFN and IL-1β [102]. Interestingly, the genetic variant *ATG16L1* T300A was found to be associated with adalimumab treatment, suggesting that this SNP affects the response to treatment with immunomodulatory drugs [103]. Importantly, the CD risk allele T300A variant (T316A in mice) is associated with accelerated degradation of ATG16L1 due to caspase-3 activation. Upon apoptotic stimuli or metabolic stress, human and murine macrophages harboring T300A or T316A variants of *ATG16L1*, respectively, exhibited accelerated degradation of ATG16L1, leading to decreased autophagy, defective clearance of the pathogen and enhanced inflammation [104]. These data strongly suggest that the functional defect in ATG16L1 is involved in the dysregulation of intestinal homeostasis and CD pathogenesis (Figure 3).

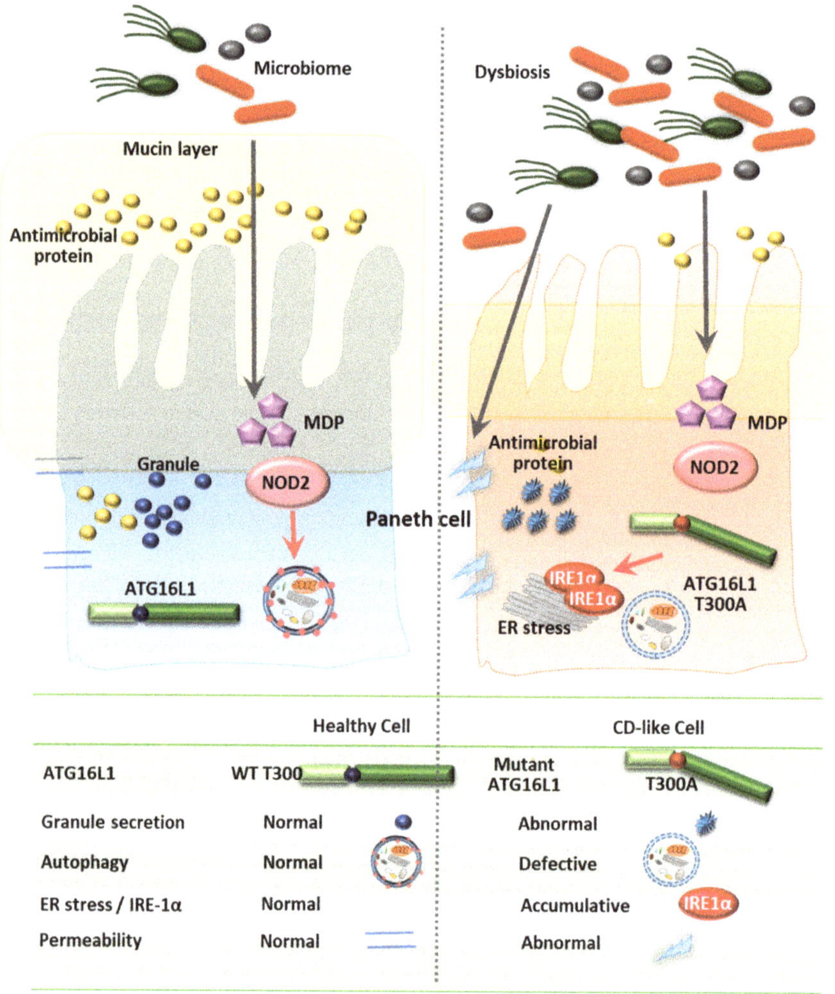

Figure 3. Summary diagram showing the role of ATG16L1 in the Crohn's disease. The left panel demonstrates the normal host defense mechanism against intracellular pathogens. Healthy cells exhibit normal granule secretion, autophagic activity, ER stress response and permeability. The right panel shows the ATG16L1 T300A variant cells defective in granule secretion, autophagy process, IRE1α degradation and tight junction barrier function.

4.2. IRGM

Human immunity-related guanosine triphosphatase (GTPase) family M (IRGM) encodes the only functional immunity-related GTPase (IRG) among IRG family members [105]. Involvement of genetic polymorphisms of *IRGM* in CD and tuberculosis has been previously demonstrated, particularly in GWASs [16,106,107]. A meta-analysis showed that the *IRGM* variants rs13361189 and rs4958847 are associated with both UC and CD in human IBD [12]. However, another study in a Korean population showed that selected SNPs of *IRGM* were associated with CD but not UC susceptibility [17].

Human *IRGM* (syn: *LRG47, IFI1*), which is encoded by the immunity-related GTPase protein family, M gene (*IRGM*; 5q33.1), is thought to be distant from a class of IRGs in mice. There are more than 20 IRG genes (*IRGM1–3, IRGN1–8, IRGB1–10* and *IRGD*) in mice, whereas there is only one *IRGM* gene present in humans and chimpanzees, making the study of the role of IRGs *in vivo* difficult. Earlier studies showed that the murine GTPase IRGM1 (LRG-47) was important for autophagy activation to eliminate intracellular *Mycobacterium tuberculosis* [108–110]. A further study showed that a human IRG protein, the human ortholog IRGM1 (IRGM), contributed to the control of *M. tuberculosis* through autophagy activation [111]. Tiwari et al. reported an essential function of Irgm1 as an innate effector in targeting the mycobacterial phagosome through lipid-mediated binding to enhance phagosome maturation and the antimicrobial response [112]. Furthermore, IRGM has been shown to regulate autophagy by translocating to the mitochondria and influencing mitochondrial fission, which is required for autophagic defense against intracellular mycobacteria [113]. Studies using *IRG*-deficient mice showed that IRGM can be induced by IFN-γ and plays a role in the clearance of intracellular bacteria including *Toxoplasma gondii*, *Listeria monocytogenes* and *Salmonella* spp. as well as mycobacteria (Figure 4) [110,114–118]. Human IRGM and murine IRGM1 contribute to cell-autonomous defense though autophagy activation via the recruitment of both autophagic and SNARE adaptor proteins during infection (Figure 4) [18,110,111,117,119–122]. However, IRGM favors viral replication through autophagy activation. For example, IRGM is translocated to the Golgi apparatus, where it regulates Golgi membrane fragmentation and is involved in virus-triggered autophagy activation during hepatitis C infection [123].

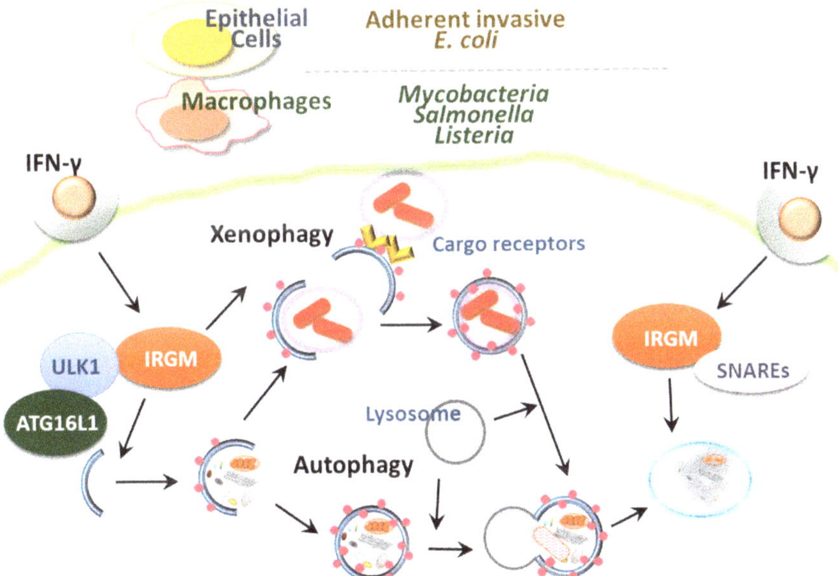

Figure 4. Autophagy targets adherent-invasive *Escherichia coli* (AIEC), Mycobacteria, Salmonella and Listeria by different mechanisms. Stimulation with IFN-γ induce IRGM to clear intracellular bacteria. Furthermore, IRGM can be induced by IFN-γ contribute to cell-autonomous defense though autophagy activation via the recruitment of both autophagic and SNARE adaptor proteins during infection.

Murine and human studies have demonstrated the protective role of IRGM in the maintenance of intestinal homeostasis. *Irgm1*-deficient mice have been shown to exhibit functional defects in intestinal Paneth cells and hyperinflammation in the colon and ileum following chemical exposure [124]. In addition, the IRGM protein contributed to the limitation of CD-associated intracellular AIEC in epithelial cells through autophagy activation and phagosomal maturation [121]. In the intestinal mucosa, greater quantities of pathogenic AIEC, which invade IECs and induce TNF-α, are found in CD patients than in healthy controls [72,125]. These data collectively suggest the importance of IRGM in CD pathogenesis via limitation of pathogenic bacteria through autophagy activation. A recent cohort study revealed the relationship among autophagy-related *IRGM* variants, visceral adipose tissue and nonalcoholic fatty liver disease, which shows an increased morbidity with CD [126]. However, there is still a debate regarding the relevance of autophagy in CD in terms of IRGM, as autophagy activation has been observed in Paneth cells in CD patients, independently of *IRGM* variants associated with CD susceptibility [127]. Moreover, RNA analysis showed that most autophagy gene sets were downregulated by appendectomy, which contributed to protection against UC [128]. Suppression of autophagy may offer cross-reactive immunity between host antigens and microbes through decreased antigen processing, thereby ameliorating symptoms of colitis [128].

4.3. LRRK2/MUC19

LRRK2/MUC19 is a complex protein that contains a RAS of complex proteins (ROC) GTPase domain, a C-terminal ROC domain and a Ser/Thr kinase domain and is involved in NOD2-mediated signaling, of which autophagy is a downstream process [129]. Because *LRRK2* is a well-known gene involved in the pathogenesis of Parkinson's disease (PD), most earlier studies were performed in neuronal cells [130,131]. Later, meta-GWASs identified the links between *LRRK2* and CD and leprosy, suggesting a role for LRRK2 in immune regulation during infection and inflammation [80,132,133]. LRRK2 is highly expressed in myeloid cells and B cells which is induced by IFN-γ and is involved in the production of inflammatory cytokines and antimicrobial responses in macrophages [80,132,133]. In addition, LRRK2 is required for commensal bacteria-driven cargo sorting through recruitment to lysozyme-containing dense core vesicles in Paneth cells, thereby participating in the coordination of the lysozyme-sorting process in the intestine to promote symbiosis [134].

A previous genome-wide linkage analysis suggested that a locus on chromosome 12 (historically known as PARK8) is linked to familial parkinsonism in the Japanese population [135]. Further studies have demonstrated the involvement of *LRRK2* in autosomal-dominant parkinsonism in multiple families [130,131]. In addition, two meta-GWASs reported *LRRK2* as a CD susceptibility gene [79,80]. A genome-wide conjunctional analysis revealed several novel loci, which are potentially involved in the association between PD and autoimmune diseases [136]. For example, known PD loci adjacent to *LRRK2* (rs17467164) were proposed as overlapping susceptibility loci for UC and CD [136]. Accumulating data in conjunction with the development of *in silico* analyses may identify novel genetic variants that affect the risk of several diseases occurring in combinatorial patterns. In a Japanese CD cohort, a defective Paneth cell phenotype was correlated with clinical characteristics and autophagy-associated *LRRK2* (*LRRK2*M2397T) was associated with Paneth cell defects [22]. The majority of *LRRK2* SNPs, which are associated with IBD, are found in non-coding intronic regions [24]. There is speculation that there might be a relationship between the high frequency of non-coding region SNPs in *LRRK2* and the stability/expression levels of LRRK2 [24].

Several studies have investigated the mechanistic aspects of pathogenic LRRK2 in PD models (Figure 5). Pathogenic LRRK2 is involved in protein translation through regulation of microRNA function (let-7 and miR-184*), which results in altered production of E2F1/DP and is critical for cell cycle and survival [137]. The autosomal dominant mutant protein LRRK2 phosphorylates and activates transcription of the forkhead box transcription factor FoxO1, which is crucial in the upregulation of cell death molecules and is associated with LRRK2-mediated cell death [138]. Importantly, *LRRK2* deficiency led to impairment of the autophagy-lysosomal pathway, altered expression of LC3-II and p62 and increased α-synuclein aggregates in the kidney, in an age-dependent manner [139]. Recent studies have shown that mitochondrial RHOT1-dependent mitophagy is delayed with the PD mutant *LRRK2*G2019S, suggesting a critical function of LRRK2 in the regulation of mitophagy [140]. Although LRRK2 is known to be involved in autophagic flux, the exact roles and mechanisms by which LRRK2 controls intestinal homeostasis are not completely understood in terms of autophagy regulation [129,139].

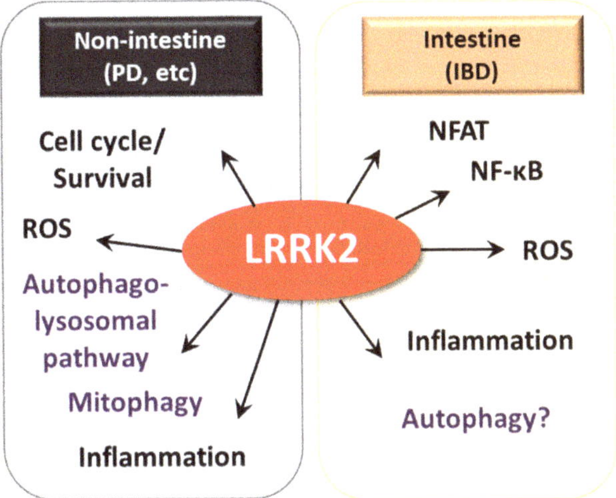

Figure 5. The pathogenic roles of LRRK in non-intestine and intestine diseases. In Parkinson's disease, LRRK2 is involved in cell cycle/survival, ROS generation, autophagolysosomal pathway, mitophagy and inflammation. LRRK2 plays a key role in intestine homeostasis through regulating NFAT, NF-κB, ROS generation, inflammation and autophagy.

The molecular mechanisms underlying how LRRK2 affects the pathogenesis of CD have not been widely examined. An earlier study showed that *LRRK2* deficiency led to increased susceptibility to DSS-induced colitis in mouse models by negatively regulating activation of the transcription factor NFAT [23]. In a recent study, both lymphoblastoid cells from control patients bearing a high-risk allele of *LRRK2* and dendritic cells from CD patients exhibited elevated LRRK2 expression, which resulted in severe colitis with increased Dectin-1-mediated NF-κB activation and proinflammatory cytokine responses [25]. As an IFN-γ target gene, LRRK2 induction and function were investigated in immune cells [133,141]. LRRK2 was previously detected in inflamed intestinal tissues, particularly in macrophages of the lamina propria and was shown to play a role in host defense through regulation of reactive oxygen species generation [133]. These studies collectively suggest that the fine-tuning of LRRK2 is required for the prevention and treatment of colitis and related infections (Figure 5).

4.4. ATG7

ATG7 is an E1-like activating enzyme that facilitates autophagosome formation through two ubiquitin-like conjugation systems, LC3 lipidation and Atg12 conjugation. Availability of ATG conditional deletion mice have improved our understanding of the contribution of different ATGs in specific cells/tissues and provided insight into the role of individual ATGs in intestinal homeostasis during colitis. In intestinal cells, the function of Atg7 has been studied using intestinal epithelium-specific (tamoxifen-inducible) *Atg7* knockout (*ATG7*[IEC-KO]) mice. An earlier study showed that *ATG7*[IEC-KO] mice had a similar pathology in the ileum and Paneth cell abnormality with defective granule exocytosis as those observed in Atg16L1HM and Atg5flox/floxvillin-Cre mice [142]. Consistent with these observations, *ATG7*[IEC-KO] mice exhibited decreased granule size and decreased lysozyme levels in Paneth cells and increased production of TNF-α and IL-1β mRNA in response to lipopolysaccharide in the epithelium of the small intestine when compared to those of control small intestinal tissue [143,144]. A further study showed that the exacerbated experimental colitis in *ATG7*[IEC-KO] mice was associated with abnormal microflora composition and dysregulated expression of antimicrobial or antiparasitic peptides (angiogenin-4, Relmβ, intelectin-1 and intelectin-2), as well as suppressed secretion of colonic mucins [145].

ATG7 conditional knockout mice also exhibited increased susceptibility to and reduced clearance of *Citrobacter rodentium* infection in the intestinal epithelium during *C. rodentium* infectious colitis [89]. A recent study emphasized the role of autophagy in controlling intestinal homeostasis using mice with conditionally deleted *ATG7* in CD11c+ antigen-presenting cells (*ATG7*$^{\Delta APC}$), which enhanced immunopathology and inflammatory Th17 responses, as well as abnormal mitochondrial function and oxidative stress [90]. Another group showed that mice with myeloid cell-specific deletion of *ATG7* exhibited increased susceptibility to experimental colitis accompanied with increased colonic inflammation [91]. Furthermore, *ATG7* deletion in intestinal epithelium-specific *XBP1*-deficient mice synergistically aggravated the intestinal pathology, resulting in the development of extensive submucosal or transmural inflammation and recapitulated the features of human CD, suggesting that autophagy contributes to a compensatory process in the intestinal epithelium during sustained ER stress [100]. These data strongly indicate that *ATG7* is crucial for controlling intestinal inflammatory responses and defense against the virulence of enteric pathogens to maintain intestinal homeostasis (Figure 2). However, there is little evidence that ATG7 is clinically relevant in IBD.

5. Selective Autophagic Receptors and IBD

The involvement of the autophagic receptors p62 and TFEB in IBD pathogenesis has been reported [21,146]. Several studies have also identified SNPs of *NDP52* and *OPTN* in individuals with IBD [20,147,148]. Here, we discuss the current evidence regarding the role of these cargo receptors in terms of IBD.

5.1. p62

The ubiquitin-binding protein sequestosome 1 (SQSTM1/p62) is a well-known autophagy adaptor and was initially identified as a p56lck binding protein [149]. Mutations of *p62* are known to be associated with Paget's disease of bone [150]. An earlier study showed that a direct interaction between p62 and LC3/GABARAP family members led to autophagy-mediated destruction of p62-positive, polyubiquitin-containing bodies [151]. In addition, Komatsu et al. showed the function of p62 in selective autophagy activation via the binding of ubiquitinylated protein aggregates for delivery to LC3 autophagosomes [152]. In canonical autophagy, accumulation of p62 in the cytoplasm is generally regarded as a sign of reduced autophagic activity and the impaired autophagy, because increased autophagic flux degrades p62 (Figure 2) [153]. Overall, p62 is an essential scaffold protein that can bind a variety of partner proteins, participating in diverse biological signaling that affects innate immunity, apoptosis, inflammatory responses and tumorigenesis [154].

Although there are a few reports on the involvement of p62 in the pathogenesis of colitis, defective autophagy with decreased turnover of p62 levels has been observed in intestinal inflammation [155,156]. In a study performed in an epithelial cell line, the intracellular survival of AIEC LF82 bacteria, which promote the gastrointestinal inflammatory response, was higher in cells silenced for *p62* than in cells transduced with empty vector (ShCTR) [157]. In animal and human studies, defective autophagic flux with elevated p62 was observed in IBD tissues and models [156]. Furthermore, immunohistochemical expression of p62 was higher in epithelial cells of damaged mucosa than in those of non-damaged mucosa [146]. Understanding how p62 regulates intestinal homeostasis will enable the development of more effective therapeutic strategies against IBD.

5.2. Optineurin (OPTN)

OPTN is a selective autophagy adaptor protein that plays an important role in mitophagy and xenophagy. OPTN is involved in various biological responses including vesicular trafficking, anti-bacterial and antiviral responses and autophagy and interacts with numerous cellular proteins including myosin VI, Rab8 and Tank-binding kinase 1 [158–160]. The clinical relevance of OPTN has been indicated by the genetic variants/mutations of OPTN linked to glaucoma, Paget's disease of bone and amyotrophic lateral sclerosis [161–163]. OPTN plays an essential role in mitophagy and is involved in several neurodegenerative diseases, including PD [160,164]. OPTN is also required for the clearance of pathogens, such as *Salmonella* and *Listeria*, to promote activation of xenophagy [43,165].

A few studies have identified *OPTN* deficiency in CD patients [19,20]. The function of OPTN in the regulation of intestinal homeostasis was suggested in IRE1α-driven colitis as an IRE1α-interacting protein [85]. *OPTN* deficiency led to an accumulation of IRE1α, which enhanced colitis pathology during ER stress (Figure 2) [85]. Indeed, a subgroup of CD patients with low OPTN expression has been identified [20]. The same study showed that *OPTN* deficiency led to decreased production of TNFα and IL-6 and increased susceptibility to Citrobacter colitis and *E. coli* peritonitis (Figure 2) [19]. Thus, these data suggest the importance of OPTN in macrophage inflammation and bactericidal function to promote the antimicrobial host defense and may explain the link between *OPTN* deficiency and increased CD pathogenesis [19]. These insights indicate that selective autophagy and cargo receptors may play important roles in the regulation of colonic homeostasis (Figure 2). A better understanding of the players and mechanisms underlying selective autophagy in intestinal inflammation will aid in the discovery of new therapeutic targets for IBD.

6. Transcription Factor *TFEB*

TFEB, a member of the microphthalmia-associated transcription factor (MITF)/transcriptional factor E (TFE) family, has been identified as a key regulator of autophagy maturation and lysosome biogenesis [166–169]. TFEB activation is required for clearance of pathogenic molecular aggregates in neurodegenerative diseases, such as α-synuclein and aberrant tau protein, to promote therapeutic effects in PD and Alzheimer's disease, respectively [170–172].

Our understanding of the effects of TFEB in IBD is currently in its infancy. A recent study showed that mice with a conditional deletion of *TFEB* in the intestinal epithelium ($TFEB^{\Delta IEC}$) had a defect in Paneth cell granules, lower expression levels of lipoprotein ApoA1 and exaggerated colitis upon DSS injury [21]. Further studies evaluating the function of TFEB and its clinical relevance in IBD pathogenesis are needed, given the essential role of TFEB in regulating the autophagy lysosome pathway [168]. Elucidation of the involvement of TFEB and other transcription factors in colitis will improve our understanding of the mechanism of autophagic regulation in the complicated pathogenesis of IBD.

7. Conclusions

Studies over the last decade have suggested that genetic variants of several ATGs are highly associated with IBD susceptibility. Although the distinct genetic variations or manipulations provide strong support for the causative role of ATGs in the pathogenesis of IBD, they also raise two important questions: whether defective autophagy is a major trigger for pathogenic inflammation in IBD and what signaling pathways control canonical and noncanonical autophagy in intestinal epithelial cells/tissues. We focused our review on ATGs, selective autophagy receptors and transcription factors involved in maintaining intestinal homeostasis in human and mouse studies.

Both ATG16L1 and IRGM, two important ATGs in IBD, have principally been investigated in human and murine intestinal epithelial cells, particularly in Paneth cells, the major secretory cells of the small intestine. Recent studies have suggested that defective ATG16L1-mediated inflammation is due to aberrant ER stress, as upregulated IRE1α was observed in Paneth cells from $ATG16L1^{\Delta IEC}$ mice and CD patients (T300A). The interactions between ATGs and other biological systems such as the ER stress response may have a significant impact on the pathogenesis of IBD as well as other inflammatory diseases. Furthermore, genetic association studies have suggested that *LRRK2/MUC19* and *ATG7* deficiency aggravate intestinal inflammation in a mouse model of colitis.

Selective autophagy receptors, p62 and OPTN and the transcription factor TFEB have been suggested to play key roles in controlling intestinal inflammation and homeostasis. Future studies to further define the mechanisms by which cargo receptors contribute to specific types of autophagy will enhance our understanding of intestinal homeostasis in terms of autophagy regulation. This knowledge will ultimately aid in the development of novel therapeutic strategies and drug targets for combating intractable chronic inflammatory diseases such as IBD.

Funding: This work was supported by the National Research Foundation of Korea (NRF) Grant funded by the Korean Government (MSIP) (No. 2017R1A5A2015385), by the National Research Foundation of Korea (NRF) grant funded by the Korea government (MSIP) (No. NRF-2015M3C9A2054326) and by research fund of Chungnam National University.

Acknowledgments: We thank Y.S.K. and P. Silwal for critical discussion and reading of the paper.

Conflicts of Interest: The authors declare no conflict of interest.

References

1. Ke, P.; Shao, B.Z.; Xu, Z.Q.; Chen, X.W.; Liu, C. Intestinal Autophagy and Its Pharmacological Control in Inflammatory Bowel Disease. *Front. Immunol.* **2016**, *7*, 695. [CrossRef]
2. Podolsky, D.K. Inflammatory bowel disease. *N. Engl. J. Med.* **2002**, *347*, 417–429. [CrossRef]
3. Xavier, R.J.; Podolsky, D.K. Unravelling the pathogenesis of inflammatory bowel disease. *Nature* **2007**, *448*, 427–434. [CrossRef]
4. Muzes, G.; Tulassay, Z.; Sipos, F. Interplay of autophagy and innate immunity in Crohn's disease: A key immunobiologic feature. *World J. Gastroenterol.* **2013**, *19*, 4447–4454. [CrossRef]
5. Fritz, T.; Niederreiter, L.; Adolph, T.; Blumberg, R.S.; Kaser, A. Crohn's disease: NOD2, autophagy and ER stress converge. *Gut* **2011**, *60*, 1580–1588. [CrossRef]
6. Ma, Y.; Galluzzi, L.; Zitvogel, L.; Kroemer, G. Autophagy and cellular immune responses. *Immunity* **2013**, *39*, 211–227. [CrossRef]
7. Ryter, S.W.; Cloonan, S.M.; Choi, A.M. Autophagy: A critical regulator of cellular metabolism and homeostasis. *Mol. Cells* **2013**, *36*, 7–16. [CrossRef]
8. Pareja, M.E.; Colombo, M.I. Autophagic clearance of bacterial pathogens: Molecular recognition of intracellular microorganisms. *Front. Cell. Infect. Microbiol.* **2013**, *3*, 54. [CrossRef]
9. Bah, A.; Vergne, I. Macrophage Autophagy and Bacterial Infections. *Front. Immunol.* **2017**, *8*, 1483. [CrossRef]
10. Fesus, L.; Demeny, M.A.; Petrovski, G. Autophagy shapes inflammation. *Antioxid. Redox Signal.* **2011**, *14*, 2233–2243. [CrossRef]
11. Netea-Maier, R.T.; Plantinga, T.S.; van de Veerdonk, F.L.; Smit, J.W.; Netea, M.G. Modulation of inflammation by autophagy: Consequences for human disease. *Autophagy* **2016**, *12*, 245–260. [CrossRef]
12. Palomino-Morales, R.J.; Oliver, J.; Gomez-Garcia, M.; Lopez-Nevot, M.A.; Rodrigo, L.; Nieto, A.; Alizadeh, B.Z.; Martin, J. Association of *ATG16L1* and IRGM genes polymorphisms with inflammatory bowel disease: A meta-analysis approach. *Genes Immun.* **2009**, *10*, 356–364. [CrossRef]
13. Hampe, J.; Franke, A.; Rosenstiel, P.; Till, A.; Teuber, M.; Huse, K.; Albrecht, M.; Mayr, G.; De La Vega, F.M.; Briggs, J.; et al. A genome-wide association scan of nonsynonymous SNPs identifies a susceptibility variant for Crohn disease in ATG16L1. *Nat. Genet.* **2007**, *39*, 207–211. [CrossRef]
14. Lakatos, P.L.; Szamosi, T.; Szilvasi, A.; Molnar, E.; Lakatos, L.; Kovacs, A.; Molnar, T.; Altorjay, I.; Papp, M.; Tulassay, Z.; et al. *ATG16L1* and IL23 receptor (IL23R) genes are associated with disease susceptibility in Hungarian CD patients. *Dig. Liver Dis.* **2008**, *40*, 867–873. [CrossRef]
15. Salem, M.; Ammitzboell, M.; Nys, K.; Seidelin, J.B.; Nielsen, O.H. ATG16L1: A multifunctional susceptibility factor in Crohn disease. *Autophagy* **2015**, *11*, 585–594. [CrossRef]
16. Parkes, M.; Barrett, J.C.; Prescott, N.J.; Tremelling, M.; Anderson, C.A.; Fisher, S.A.; Roberts, R.G.; Nimmo, E.R.; Cummings, F.R.; Soars, D.; et al. Sequence variants in the autophagy gene IRGM and multiple other replicating loci contribute to Crohn's disease susceptibility. *Nat. Genet.* **2007**, *39*, 830–832. [CrossRef]
17. Moon, C.M.; Shin, D.J.; Kim, S.W.; Son, N.H.; Park, A.; Park, B.; Jung, E.S.; Kim, E.S.; Hong, S.P.; Kim, T.I.; et al. Associations between genetic variants in the IRGM gene and inflammatory bowel diseases in the Korean population. *Inflamm. Bowel Dis.* **2013**, *19*, 106–114. [CrossRef]
18. McCarroll, S.A.; Huett, A.; Kuballa, P.; Chilewski, S.D.; Landry, A.; Goyette, P.; Zody, M.C.; Hall, J.L.; Brant, S.R.; Cho, J.H.; et al. Deletion polymorphism upstream of IRGM associated with altered IRGM expression and Crohn's disease. *Nat. Genet.* **2008**, *40*, 1107–1112. [CrossRef]

19. Chew, T.S.; O'Shea, N.R.; Sewell, G.W.; Oehlers, S.H.; Mulvey, C.M.; Crosier, P.S.; Godovac-Zimmermann, J.; Bloom, S.L.; Smith, A.M.; Segal, A.W. Optineurin deficiency in mice contributes to impaired cytokine secretion and neutrophil recruitment in bacteria-driven colitis. *Dis. Models Mech.* **2015**, *8*, 817–829. [CrossRef]

20. Smith, A.M.; Sewell, G.W.; Levine, A.P.; Chew, T.S.; Dunne, J.; O'Shea, N.R.; Smith, P.J.; Harrison, P.J.; Macdonald, C.M.; Bloom, S.L.; et al. Disruption of macrophage pro-inflammatory cytokine release in Crohn's disease is associated with reduced optineurin expression in a subset of patients. *Immunology* **2015**, *144*, 45–55. [CrossRef]

21. Murano, T.; Najibi, M.; Paulus, G.L.C.; Adiliaghdam, F.; Valencia-Guerrero, A.; Selig, M.; Wang, X.; Jeffrey, K.; Xavier, R.J.; Lassen, K.G.; et al. Transcription factor TFEB cell-autonomously modulates susceptibility to intestinal epithelial cell injury in vivo. *Sci. Rep.* **2017**, *7*, 13938. [CrossRef]

22. Liu, T.C.; Naito, T.; Liu, Z. *LRRK2* but not *ATG16L1* is associated with Paneth cell defect in Japanese Crohn's disease patients. *JCI Insight* **2017**, *2*, e91917. [CrossRef]

23. Liu, Z.; Lee, J.; Krummey, S.; Lu, W.; Cai, H.; Lenardo, M.J. The kinase *LRRK2* is a regulator of the transcription factor NFAT that modulates the severity of inflammatory bowel disease. *Nat. Immunol.* **2011**, *12*, 1063–1070. [CrossRef]

24. Liu, Z.; Lenardo, M.J. The role of *LRRK2* in inflammatory bowel disease. *Cell Res.* **2012**, *22*, 1092–1094. [CrossRef]

25. Takagawa, T.; Kitani, A. An increase in *LRRK2* suppresses autophagy and enhances Dectin-1-induced immunity in a mouse model of colitis. *Sci. Transl. Med.* **2018**, *10*. [CrossRef]

26. Xie, Z.; Klionsky, D.J. Autophagosome formation: Core machinery and adaptations. *Nat. Cell Biol.* **2007**, *9*, 1102–1109. [CrossRef]

27. Kuballa, P.; Nolte, W.M.; Castoreno, A.B.; Xavier, R.J. Autophagy and the immune system. *Annu. Rev. Immunol.* **2012**, *30*, 611–646. [CrossRef]

28. Glick, D.; Barth, S.; Macleod, K.F. Autophagy: Cellular and molecular mechanisms. *J. Pathol.* **2010**, *221*, 3–12. [CrossRef]

29. Levine, B.; Kroemer, G. Autophagy in the pathogenesis of disease. *Cell* **2008**, *132*, 27–42. [CrossRef]

30. Mizushima, N. Autophagy: Process and function. *Genes Dev.* **2007**, *21*, 2861–2873. [CrossRef]

31. Nakamura, S.; Yoshimori, T. New insights into autophagosome-lysosome fusion. *J. Cell Sci.* **2017**, *130*, 1209–1216. [CrossRef] [PubMed]

32. Yin, Z.; Pascual, C.; Klionsky, D.J. Autophagy: Machinery and regulation. *Microb. Cell* **2016**, *3*, 588–596. [CrossRef] [PubMed]

33. Jin, M.; Klionsky, D.J. Regulation of autophagy: Modulation of the size and number of autophagosomes. *FEBS Lett.* **2014**, *588*, 2457–2463. [CrossRef] [PubMed]

34. Puertollano, R.; Ferguson, S.M. The complex relationship between TFEB transcription factor phosphorylation and subcellular localization. *EMBO J.* **2018**, *37*. [CrossRef] [PubMed]

35. Levine, B.; Mizushima, N.; Virgin, H.W. Autophagy in immunity and inflammation. *Nature* **2011**, *469*, 323–335. [CrossRef] [PubMed]

36. Mizumura, K.; Choi, A.M.; Ryter, S.W. Emerging role of selective autophagy in human diseases. *Front. Pharmacol.* **2014**, *5*, 244. [CrossRef] [PubMed]

37. Youle, R.J.; Narendra, D.P. Mechanisms of mitophagy. *Nat. Rev. Mol. Cell Biol.* **2011**, *12*, 9–14. [CrossRef]

38. Yamamoto, A.; Simonsen, A. The elimination of accumulated and aggregated proteins: A role for aggrephagy in neurodegeneration. *Neurobiol. Dis.* **2011**, *43*, 17–28. [CrossRef]

39. Shaid, S.; Brandts, C.H.; Serve, H.; Dikic, I. Ubiquitination and selective autophagy. *Cell Death Differ.* **2013**, *20*, 21–30. [CrossRef]

40. Mancias, J.D.; Kimmelman, A.C. Mechanisms of Selective Autophagy in Normal Physiology and Cancer. *J. Mol. Biol.* **2016**, *428*, 1659–1680. [CrossRef]

41. Bjorkoy, G.; Lamark, T.; Brech, A.; Outzen, H.; Perander, M.; Overvatn, A.; Stenmark, H.; Johansen, T. p62/SQSTM1 forms protein aggregates degraded by autophagy and has a protective effect on huntingtin-induced cell death. *J. Cell Biol.* **2005**, *171*, 603–614. [CrossRef] [PubMed]

42. Kirkin, V.; Lamark, T.; Sou, Y.S.; Bjorkoy, G.; Nunn, J.L.; Bruun, J.A.; Shvets, E.; McEwan, D.G.; Clausen, T.H.; Wild, P.; et al. A role for NBR1 in autophagosomal degradation of ubiquitinated substrates. *Mol. Cell* **2009**, *33*, 505–516. [CrossRef] [PubMed]

43. Wild, P.; Farhan, H.; McEwan, D.G.; Wagner, S.; Rogov, V.V.; Brady, N.R.; Richter, B.; Korac, J.; Waidmann, O.; Choudhary, C.; et al. Phosphorylation of the autophagy receptor optineurin restricts Salmonella growth. *Science* **2011**, *333*, 228–233. [CrossRef] [PubMed]

44. Thurston, T.L.; Ryzhakov, G.; Bloor, S.; von Muhlinen, N.; Randow, F. The TBK1 adaptor and autophagy receptor NDP52 restricts the proliferation of ubiquitin-coated bacteria. *Nat. Immunol.* **2009**, *10*, 1215–1221. [CrossRef] [PubMed]

45. Zaffagnini, G.; Martens, S. Mechanisms of Selective Autophagy. *J. Mol. Biol.* **2016**, *428*, 1714–1724. [CrossRef]

46. Rogov, V.; Dotsch, V.; Johansen, T.; Kirkin, V. Interactions between autophagy receptors and ubiquitin-like proteins form the molecular basis for selective autophagy. *Mol. Cell* **2014**, *53*, 167–178. [CrossRef] [PubMed]

47. Feng, Y.; Yao, Z.; Klionsky, D.J. How to control self-digestion: Transcriptional, post-transcriptional, and post-translational regulation of autophagy. *Trends Cell Biol.* **2015**, *25*, 354–363. [CrossRef]

48. Hosokawa, N.; Sasaki, T.; Iemura, S.; Natsume, T.; Hara, T.; Mizushima, N. Atg101, a novel mammalian autophagy protein interacting with Atg13. *Autophagy* **2009**, *5*, 973–979. [CrossRef]

49. Mercer, C.A.; Kaliappan, A.; Dennis, P.B. A novel, human Atg13 binding protein, Atg101, interacts with ULK1 and is essential for macroautophagy. *Autophagy* **2009**, *5*, 649–662. [CrossRef]

50. Wesselborg, S.; Stork, B. Autophagy signal transduction by ATG proteins: From hierarchies to networks. *Cell. Mol. Life Sci.* **2015**, *72*, 4721–4757. [CrossRef]

51. Kuma, A.; Komatsu, M.; Mizushima, N. Autophagy-monitoring and autophagy-deficient mice. *Autophagy* **2017**, *13*, 1619–1628. [CrossRef] [PubMed]

52. Birgisdottir, A.B.; Lamark, T.; Johansen, T. The LIR motif—Crucial for selective autophagy. *J. Cell Sci.* **2013**, *126*, 3237–3247. [CrossRef] [PubMed]

53. Podolsky, D.K. Inflammatory bowel disease (1). *N. Engl. J. Med.* **1991**, *325*, 928–937. [CrossRef] [PubMed]

54. Rubin, D.C.; Shaker, A.; Levin, M.S. Chronic intestinal inflammation: Inflammatory bowel disease and colitis-associated colon cancer. *Front. Immunol.* **2012**, *3*, 107. [CrossRef] [PubMed]

55. Abraham, C.; Cho, J.H. Inflammatory bowel disease. *N. Engl. J. Med.* **2009**, *361*, 2066–2078. [CrossRef] [PubMed]

56. Jung, M.K.; Kwak, J.E.; Shin, E.C. IL-17A-Producing Foxp3(+) Regulatory T Cells and Human Diseases. *Immune Netw.* **2017**, *17*, 276–286. [CrossRef] [PubMed]

57. Mowat, C.; Cole, A.; Windsor, A.; Ahmad, T.; Arnott, I.; Driscoll, R.; Mitton, S.; Orchard, T.; Rutter, M.; Younge, L.; et al. Guidelines for the management of inflammatory bowel disease in adults. *Gut* **2011**, *60*, 571–607. [CrossRef]

58. Kim, D.H.; Cheon, J.H. Pathogenesis of Inflammatory Bowel Disease and Recent Advances in Biologic Therapies. *Immune Netw.* **2017**, *17*, 25–40. [CrossRef]

59. Elphick, D.A.; Mahida, Y.R. Paneth cells: Their role in innate immunity and inflammatory disease. *Gut* **2005**, *54*, 1802–1809. [CrossRef]

60. Noah, T.K.; Donahue, B.; Shroyer, N.F. Intestinal development and differentiation. *Exp. Cell Res.* **2011**, *317*, 2702–2710. [CrossRef]

61. Bry, L.; Falk, P.; Huttner, K.; Ouellette, A.; Midtvedt, T.; Gordon, J.I. Paneth cell differentiation in the developing intestine of normal and transgenic mice. *Proc. Natl. Acad. Sci. USA* **1994**, *91*, 10335–10339. [CrossRef] [PubMed]

62. Cheng, H.; Leblond, C.P. Origin, differentiation and renewal of the four main epithelial cell types in the mouse small intestine. V. Unitarian Theory of the origin of the four epithelial cell types. *Am. J. Anat.* **1974**, *141*, 537–561. [CrossRef] [PubMed]

63. Ouellette, A.J. Paneth cells and innate mucosal immunity. *Curr. Opin. Gastroenterol.* **2010**, *26*, 547–553. [CrossRef] [PubMed]

64. Cederlund, A.; Gudmundsson, G.H.; Agerberth, B. Antimicrobial peptides important in innate immunity. *FEBS J.* **2011**, *278*, 3942–3951. [CrossRef] [PubMed]

65. Wong, W.M.; Stamp, G.W.; Elia, G.; Poulsom, R.; Wright, N.A. Proliferative populations in intestinal metaplasia: Evidence of deregulation in Paneth and goblet cells, but not endocrine cells. *J. Pathol.* **2000**, *190*, 107–113. [CrossRef]

66. Gunther, C.; Martini, E.; Wittkopf, N.; Amann, K.; Weigmann, B.; Neumann, H.; Waldner, M.J.; Hedrick, S.M.; Tenzer, S.; Neurath, M.F.; et al. Caspase-8 regulates TNF-alpha-induced epithelial necroptosis and terminal ileitis. *Nature* **2011**, *477*, 335–339. [CrossRef] [PubMed]

67. Grootjans, J.; Hodin, C.M.; de Haan, J.J.; Derikx, J.P.; Rouschop, K.M.; Verheyen, F.K.; van Dam, R.M.; Dejong, C.H.; Buurman, W.A.; Lenaerts, K. Level of activation of the unfolded protein response correlates with Paneth cell apoptosis in human small intestine exposed to ischemia/reperfusion. *Gastroenterology* **2011**, *140*, 529–539.e523. [CrossRef]

68. Rubio, C.A. Lysozyme-rich mucus metaplasia in duodenal crypts supersedes Paneth cells in celiac disease. *Virchows Arch.* **2011**, *459*, 339–346. [CrossRef]

69. Paulus, G.L.; Xavier, R.J. Autophagy and checkpoints for intracellular pathogen defense. *Curr. Opin. Gastroenterol.* **2015**, *31*, 14–23. [CrossRef]

70. Gardet, A.; Xavier, R.J. Common alleles that influence autophagy and the risk for inflammatory bowel disease. *Curr. Opin. Immunol.* **2012**, *24*, 522–529. [CrossRef]

71. Salzman, N.H.; Bevins, C.L. Dysbiosis–a consequence of Paneth cell dysfunction. *Semin. Immunol.* **2013**, *25*, 334–341. [CrossRef] [PubMed]

72. Darfeuille-Michaud, A.; Boudeau, J.; Bulois, P.; Neut, C.; Glasser, A.L.; Barnich, N.; Bringer, M.A.; Swidsinski, A.; Beaugerie, L.; Colombel, J.F. High prevalence of adherent-invasive Escherichia coli associated with ileal mucosa in Crohn's disease. *Gastroenterology* **2004**, *127*, 412–421. [CrossRef] [PubMed]

73. Darfeuille-Michaud, A.; Neut, C.; Barnich, N.; Lederman, E.; Di Martino, P.; Desreumaux, P.; Gambiez, L.; Joly, B.; Cortot, A.; Colombel, J.F. Presence of adherent Escherichia coli strains in ileal mucosa of patients with Crohn's disease. *Gastroenterology* **1998**, *115*, 1405–1413. [CrossRef]

74. Kostic, A.D.; Xavier, R.J.; Gevers, D. The microbiome in inflammatory bowel disease: Current status and the future ahead. *Gastroenterology* **2014**, *146*, 1489–1499. [CrossRef] [PubMed]

75. Garrett, W.S.; Gordon, J.I.; Glimcher, L.H. Homeostasis and inflammation in the intestine. *Cell* **2010**, *140*, 859–870. [CrossRef]

76. Cadwell, K.; Liu, J.Y.; Brown, S.L.; Miyoshi, H.; Loh, J.; Lennerz, J.K.; Kishi, C.; Kc, W.; Carrero, J.A.; Hunt, S.; et al. A key role for autophagy and the autophagy gene Atg16l1 in mouse and human intestinal Paneth cells. *Nature* **2008**, *456*, 259–263. [CrossRef]

77. Kobayashi, K.S.; Chamaillard, M.; Ogura, Y.; Henegariu, O.; Inohara, N.; Nunez, G.; Flavell, R.A. Nod2-dependent regulation of innate and adaptive immunity in the intestinal tract. *Science* **2005**, *307*, 731–734. [CrossRef]

78. Barrett, J.C.; Hansoul, S.; Nicolae, D.L.; Cho, J.H.; Duerr, R.H.; Rioux, J.D.; Brant, S.R.; Silverberg, M.S.; Taylor, K.D.; Barmada, M.M.; et al. Genome-wide association defines more than 30 distinct susceptibility loci for Crohn's disease. *Nat. Genet.* **2008**, *40*, 955–962. [CrossRef]

79. Anderson, C.A.; Boucher, G.; Lees, C.W.; Franke, A.; D'Amato, M.; Taylor, K.D.; Lee, J.C.; Goyette, P.; Imielinski, M.; Latiano, A.; et al. Meta-analysis identifies 29 additional ulcerative colitis risk loci, increasing the number of confirmed associations to 47. *Nat. Genet.* **2011**, *43*, 246–252. [CrossRef]

80. Franke, A.; McGovern, D.P.; Barrett, J.C.; Wang, K.; Radford-Smith, G.L.; Ahmad, T.; Lees, C.W.; Balschun, T.; Lee, J.; Roberts, R.; et al. Genome-wide meta-analysis increases to 71 the number of confirmed Crohn's disease susceptibility loci. *Nat. Genet.* **2010**, *42*, 1118–1125. [CrossRef]

81. de Lange, K.M.; Barrett, J.C. Understanding inflammatory bowel disease via immunogenetics. *J. Autoimmun.* **2015**, *64*, 91–100. [CrossRef] [PubMed]

82. Liu, J.Z.; van Sommeren, S.; Huang, H.; Ng, S.C.; Alberts, R.; Takahashi, A.; Ripke, S.; Lee, J.C.; Jostins, L.; Shah, T.; et al. Association analyses identify 38 susceptibility loci for inflammatory bowel disease and highlight shared genetic risk across populations. *Nat. Genet.* **2015**, *47*, 979–986. [CrossRef] [PubMed]

83. Rioux, J.D.; Xavier, R.J.; Taylor, K.D.; Silverberg, M.S.; Goyette, P.; Huett, A.; Green, T.; Kuballa, P.; Barmada, M.M.; Datta, L.W.; et al. Genome-wide association study identifies new susceptibility loci for Crohn disease and implicates autophagy in disease pathogenesis. *Nat. Genet.* **2007**, *39*, 596–604. [CrossRef]

84. Brest, P.; Corcelle, E.A.; Cesaro, A.; Chargui, A.; Belaid, A.; Klionsky, D.J.; Vouret-Craviari, V.; Hebuterne, X.; Hofman, P.; Mograbi, B. Autophagy and Crohn's disease: At the crossroads of infection, inflammation, immunity, and cancer. *Curr. Mol. Med.* **2010**, *10*, 486–502. [CrossRef] [PubMed]

85. Tschurtschenthaler, M.; Adolph, T.E.; Ashcroft, J.W. Defective ATG16L1-mediated removal of IRE1alpha drives Crohn's disease-like ileitis. *J. Exp. Med.* **2017**, *214*, 401–422. [CrossRef] [PubMed]

86. Pott, J.; Kabat, A.M.; Maloy, K.J. Intestinal Epithelial Cell Autophagy Is Required to Protect against TNF-Induced Apoptosis during Chronic Colitis in Mice. *Cell Host Microbe* **2018**, *23*, 191–202.e194. [CrossRef] [PubMed]

87. Saitoh, T.; Fujita, N.; Jang, M.H.; Uematsu, S.; Yang, B.G.; Satoh, T.; Omori, H.; Noda, T.; Yamamoto, N.; Komatsu, M.; et al. Loss of the autophagy protein Atg16L1 enhances endotoxin-induced IL-1beta production. *Nature* **2008**, *456*, 264–268. [CrossRef]

88. Zhang, H.; Zheng, L.; McGovern, D.P.; Hamill, A.M. Myeloid *ATG16L1* Facilitates Host-Bacteria Interactions in Maintaining Intestinal Homeostasis. *J. Immunol.* **2017**, *198*, 2133–2146. [CrossRef]

89. Inoue, J.; Nishiumi, S.; Fujishima, Y.; Masuda, A.; Shiomi, H.; Yamamoto, K.; Nishida, M.; Azuma, T.; Yoshida, M. Autophagy in the intestinal epithelium regulates Citrobacter rodentium infection. *Arch. Biochem. Biophys.* **2012**, *521*, 95–101. [CrossRef]

90. Ravindran, R.; Loebbermann, J.; Nakaya, H.I.; Khan, N.; Ma, H.; Gama, L.; Machiah, D.K.; Lawson, B.; Hakimpour, P.; Wang, Y.C.; et al. The amino acid sensor GCN2 controls gut inflammation by inhibiting inflammasome activation. *Nature* **2016**, *531*, 523–527. [CrossRef]

91. Lee, H.Y.; Kim, J.; Quan, W.; Lee, J.C.; Kim, M.S.; Kim, S.H.; Bae, J.W.; Hur, K.Y.; Lee, M.S. Autophagy deficiency in myeloid cells increases susceptibility to obesity-induced diabetes and experimental colitis. *Autophagy* **2016**, *12*, 1390–1403. [CrossRef] [PubMed]

92. Cummings, J.R.; Cooney, R.; Pathan, S.; Anderson, C.A.; Barrett, J.C.; Beckly, J.; Geremia, A.; Hancock, L.; Guo, C.; Ahmad, T.; et al. Confirmation of the role of *ATG16L1* as a Crohn's disease susceptibility gene. *Inflamm. Bowel Dis.* **2007**, *13*, 941–946. [CrossRef] [PubMed]

93. Prescott, N.J.; Fisher, S.A.; Franke, A.; Hampe, J.; Onnie, C.M.; Soars, D.; Bagnall, R.; Mirza, M.M.; Sanderson, J.; Forbes, A.; et al. A nonsynonymous SNP in *ATG16L1* predisposes to ileal Crohn's disease and is independent of CARD15 and IBD5. *Gastroenterology* **2007**, *132*, 1665–1671. [CrossRef] [PubMed]

94. Yamazaki, K.; Onouchi, Y.; Takazoe, M.; Kubo, M.; Nakamura, Y.; Hata, A. Association analysis of genetic variants in IL23R, *ATG16L1* and 5p13.1 loci with Crohn's disease in Japanese patients. *J. Hum. Genet.* **2007**, *52*, 575–583. [CrossRef] [PubMed]

95. Roberts, R.L.; Gearry, R.B.; Hollis-Moffatt, J.E.; Miller, A.L.; Reid, J.; Abkevich, V.; Timms, K.M.; Gutin, A.; Lanchbury, J.S.; Merriman, T.R.; et al. IL23R R381Q and *ATG16L1* T300A are strongly associated with Crohn's disease in a study of New Zealand Caucasians with inflammatory bowel disease. *Am. J. Gastroenterol.* **2007**, *102*, 2754–2761. [CrossRef]

96. Girardelli, M.; Basaldella, F.; Paolera, S.D.; Vuch, J.; Tommasini, A.; Martelossi, S.; Crovella, S.; Bianco, A.M. Genetic profile of patients with early onset inflammatory bowel disease. *Gene* **2018**, *645*, 18–29. [CrossRef] [PubMed]

97. Mizushima, N.; Noda, T.; Ohsumi, Y. Apg16p is required for the function of the Apg12p-Apg5p conjugate in the yeast autophagy pathway. *EMBO J.* **1999**, *18*, 3888–3896. [CrossRef] [PubMed]

98. Mizushima, N.; Kuma, A.; Kobayashi, Y.; Yamamoto, A.; Matsubae, M.; Takao, T.; Natsume, T.; Ohsumi, Y.; Yoshimori, T. Mouse Apg16L, a novel WD-repeat protein, targets to the autophagic isolation membrane with the Apg12-Apg5 conjugate. *J. Cell Sci.* **2003**, *116*, 1679–1688. [CrossRef]

99. Diamanti, M.A.; Gupta, J. IKKalpha controls *ATG16L1* degradation to prevent ER stress during inflammation. *J. Exp. Med.* **2017**, *214*, 423–437. [CrossRef]

100. Adolph, T.E.; Tomczak, M.F.; Niederreiter, L.; Ko, H.J.; Bock, J.; Martinez-Naves, E.; Glickman, J.N.; Tschurtschenthaler, M.; Hartwig, J.; Hosomi, S.; et al. Paneth cells as a site of origin for intestinal inflammation. *Nature* **2013**, *503*, 272–276. [CrossRef]

101. Plantinga, T.S.; Crisan, T.O.; Oosting, M.; van de Veerdonk, F.L.; de Jong, D.J.; Philpott, D.J.; van der Meer, J.W.; Girardin, S.E.; Joosten, L.A.; Netea, M.G. Crohn's disease-associated *ATG16L1* polymorphism modulates pro-inflammatory cytokine responses selectively upon activation of NOD2. *Gut* **2011**, *60*, 1229–1235. [CrossRef]

102. Samie, M.; Lim, J.; Verschueren, E.; Baughman, J.M.; Peng, I.; Wong, A.; Kwon, Y.; Senbabaoglu, Y.; Hackney, J.A. Selective autophagy of the adaptor TRIF regulates innate inflammatory signaling. *Nat. Immunol.* **2018**, *19*, 246–254. [CrossRef] [PubMed]

103. Nuij, V.; Peppelenbosch, M.P.; van der Woude, C.J.; Fuhler, G.M. Genetic polymorphism in *ATG16L1* gene is associated with adalimumab use in inflammatory bowel disease. *J. Transl. Med.* **2017**, *15*, 248. [CrossRef] [PubMed]

104. Murthy, A.; Li, Y.; Peng, I.; Reichelt, M.; Katakam, A.K.; Noubade, R.; Roose-Girma, M.; DeVoss, J.; Diehl, L.; Graham, R.R.; et al. A Crohn's disease variant in Atg16l1 enhances its degradation by caspase 3. *Nature* **2014**, *506*, 456–462. [CrossRef] [PubMed]

105. Deretic, V. Autophagy in infection. *Curr. Opin. Cell Biol.* **2010**, *22*, 252–262. [CrossRef]
106. Chauhan, S.; Mandell, M.A.; Deretic, V. Mechanism of action of the tuberculosis and Crohn disease risk factor IRGM in autophagy. *Autophagy* **2016**, *12*, 429–431. [CrossRef]
107. Fisher, S.A.; Tremelling, M.; Anderson, C.A.; Gwilliam, R.; Bumpstead, S.; Prescott, N.J.; Nimmo, E.R.; Massey, D.; Berzuini, C.; Johnson, C.; et al. Genetic determinants of ulcerative colitis include the ECM1 locus and five loci implicated in Crohn's disease. *Nat. Genet.* **2008**, *40*, 710–712. [CrossRef]
108. Hunn, J.P.; Feng, C.G.; Sher, A.; Howard, J.C. The immunity-related GTPases in mammals: A fast-evolving cell-autonomous resistance system against intracellular pathogens. *Mamm. Genome* **2011**, *22*, 43–54. [CrossRef]
109. Bekpen, C.; Marques-Bonet, T.; Alkan, C.; Antonacci, F.; Leogrande, M.B.; Ventura, M.; Kidd, J.M.; Siswara, P.; Howard, J.C.; Eichler, E.E. Death and resurrection of the human IRGM gene. *PLoS Genet.* **2009**, *5*, e1000403. [CrossRef]
110. Gutierrez, M.G.; Master, S.S.; Singh, S.B.; Taylor, G.A.; Colombo, M.I.; Deretic, V. Autophagy is a defense mechanism inhibiting BCG and Mycobacterium tuberculosis survival in infected macrophages. *Cell* **2004**, *119*, 753–766. [CrossRef]
111. Singh, S.B.; Davis, A.S.; Taylor, G.A.; Deretic, V. Human IRGM induces autophagy to eliminate intracellular mycobacteria. *Science* **2006**, *313*, 1438–1441. [CrossRef] [PubMed]
112. Tiwari, S.; Choi, H.P.; Matsuzawa, T.; Pypaert, M.; MacMicking, J.D. Targeting of the GTPase Irgm1 to the phagosomal membrane via PtdIns(3,4)P(2) and PtdIns(3,4,5)P(3) promotes immunity to mycobacteria. *Nat. Immunol.* **2009**, *10*, 907–917. [CrossRef] [PubMed]
113. Singh, S.B.; Ornatowski, W.; Vergne, I.; Naylor, J.; Delgado, M.; Roberts, E.; Ponpuak, M.; Master, S.; Pilli, M.; White, E.; et al. Human IRGM regulates autophagy and cell-autonomous immunity functions through mitochondria. *Nat. Cell Biol.* **2010**, *12*, 1154–1165. [CrossRef] [PubMed]
114. Taylor, G.A.; Feng, C.G.; Sher, A. p47 GTPases: Regulators of immunity to intracellular pathogens. *Nat. Rev. Immunol.* **2004**, *4*, 100–109. [CrossRef] [PubMed]
115. Henry, S.C.; Daniell, X.; Indaram, M.; Whitesides, J.F.; Sempowski, G.D.; Howell, D.; Oliver, T.; Taylor, G.A. Impaired macrophage function underscores susceptibility to Salmonella in mice lacking Irgm1 (LRG-47). *J. Immunol.* **2007**, *179*, 6963–6972. [CrossRef] [PubMed]
116. Collazo, C.M.; Yap, G.S.; Sempowski, G.D.; Lusby, K.C.; Tessarollo, L.; Vande Woude, G.F.; Sher, A.; Taylor, G.A. Inactivation of LRG-47 and IRG-47 reveals a family of interferon gamma-inducible genes with essential, pathogen-specific roles in resistance to infection. *J. Exp. Med.* **2001**, *194*, 181–188. [CrossRef] [PubMed]
117. Kim, B.H.; Shenoy, A.R.; Kumar, P.; Bradfield, C.J.; MacMicking, J.D. IFN-inducible GTPases in host cell defense. *Cell Host Microbe* **2012**, *12*, 432–444. [CrossRef]
118. Kim, B.H.; Shenoy, A.R.; Kumar, P.; Das, R.; Tiwari, S.; MacMicking, J.D. A family of IFN-gamma-inducible 65-kD GTPases protects against bacterial infection. *Science* **2011**, *332*, 717–721. [CrossRef]
119. Traver, M.K.; Henry, S.C.; Cantillana, V.; Oliver, T.; Hunn, J.P.; Howard, J.C.; Beer, S.; Pfeffer, K.; Coers, J.; Taylor, G.A. Immunity-related GTPase M (IRGM) proteins influence the localization of guanylate-binding protein 2 (GBP2) by modulating macroautophagy. *J. Biol. Chem.* **2011**, *286*, 30471–30480. [CrossRef]
120. Brest, P.; Lapaquette, P.; Souidi, M.; Lebrigand, K.; Cesaro, A.; Vouret-Craviari, V.; Mari, B.; Barbry, P.; Mosnier, J.F.; Hebuterne, X.; et al. A synonymous variant in IRGM alters a binding site for miR-196 and causes deregulation of IRGM-dependent xenophagy in Crohn's disease. *Nat. Genet.* **2011**, *43*, 242–245. [CrossRef]
121. Lapaquette, P.; Glasser, A.L.; Huett, A.; Xavier, R.J.; Darfeuille-Michaud, A. Crohn's disease-associated adherent-invasive E. coli are selectively favoured by impaired autophagy to replicate intracellularly. *Cell Microbiol.* **2010**, *12*, 99–113. [CrossRef]
122. Kumar, S.; Jain, A. Mechanism of Stx17 recruitment to autophagosomes via IRGM and mammalian Atg8 proteins. *J. Cell Biol.* **2018**, *217*, 997–1013. [CrossRef]
123. Hansen, M.D.; Johnsen, I.B.; Stiberg, K.A.; Sherstova, T.; Wakita, T.; Richard, G.M.; Kandasamy, R.K.; Meurs, E.F.; Anthonsen, M.W. Hepatitis C virus triggers Golgi fragmentation and autophagy through the immunity-related GTPase M. *Proc. Natl. Acad. Sci. USA* **2017**, *114*, E3462–E3471. [CrossRef]

124. Liu, B.; Gulati, A.S.; Cantillana, V.; Henry, S.C.; Schmidt, E.A.; Daniell, X.; Grossniklaus, E.; Schoenborn, A.A.; Sartor, R.B.; Taylor, G.A. Irgm1-deficient mice exhibit Paneth cell abnormalities and increased susceptibility to acute intestinal inflammation. *Am. J. Physiol. Gastrointest. Liver Physiol.* **2013**, *305*, G573–G584. [CrossRef]

125. Rolhion, N.; Darfeuille-Michaud, A. Adherent-invasive Escherichia coli in inflammatory bowel disease. *Inflamm. Bowel Dis.* **2007**, *13*, 1277–1283. [CrossRef]

126. Simon, T.G.; Van Der Sloot, K.W.J.; Chin, S.B.; Joshi, A.D.; Lochhead, P.; Ananthakrishnan, A.N.; Xavier, R.; Chung, R.T.; Khalili, H. IRGM Gene Variants Modify the Relationship Between Visceral Adipose Tissue and NAFLD in Patients With Crohn's Disease. *Inflamm. Bowel Dis.* **2018**, *24*, 2247–2257. [CrossRef]

127. Thachil, E.; Hugot, J.P.; Arbeille, B.; Paris, R.; Grodet, A.; Peuchmaur, M.; Codogno, P.; Barreau, F.; Ogier-Denis, E.; Berrebi, D.; et al. Abnormal activation of autophagy-induced crinophagy in Paneth cells from patients with Crohn's disease. *Gastroenterology* **2012**, *142*, 1097–1099.e1094. [CrossRef]

128. Cheluvappa, R.; Luo, A.S.; Grimm, M.C. Autophagy suppression by appendicitis and appendectomy protects against colitis. *Inflamm. Bowel Dis.* **2014**, *20*, 847–855. [CrossRef]

129. Toledo Pinto, T.G.; Batista-Silva, L.R.; Medeiros, R.C.A.; Lara, F.A.; Moraes, M.O. Type I Interferons, Autophagy and Host Metabolism in Leprosy. *Front. Immunol.* **2018**, *9*, 806. [CrossRef]

130. Zimprich, A.; Biskup, S.; Leitner, P.; Lichtner, P.; Farrer, M.; Lincoln, S.; Kachergus, J.; Hulihan, M.; Uitti, R.J.; Calne, D.B.; et al. Mutations in *LRRK2* cause autosomal-dominant parkinsonism with pleomorphic pathology. *Neuron* **2004**, *44*, 601–607. [CrossRef]

131. Paisan-Ruiz, C.; Jain, S.; Evans, E.W.; Gilks, W.P.; Simon, J.; van der Brug, M.; Lopez de Munain, A.; Aparicio, S.; Gil, A.M.; Khan, N.; et al. Cloning of the gene containing mutations that cause PARK8-linked Parkinson's disease. *Neuron* **2004**, *44*, 595–600. [CrossRef]

132. Zhang, F.R.; Huang, W.; Chen, S.M.; Sun, L.D.; Liu, H.; Li, Y.; Cui, Y.; Yan, X.X.; Yang, H.T.; Yang, R.D.; et al. Genomewide association study of leprosy. *N. Engl. J. Med.* **2009**, *361*, 2609–2618. [CrossRef]

133. Gardet, A.; Benita, Y.; Li, C.; Sands, B.E.; Ballester, I.; Stevens, C.; Korzenik, J.R.; Rioux, J.D.; Daly, M.J.; Xavier, R.J.; et al. *LRRK2* is involved in the IFN-gamma response and host response to pathogens. *J. Immunol.* **2010**, *185*, 5577–5585. [CrossRef]

134. Zhang, Q.; Pan, Y.; Yan, R.; Zeng, B.; Wang, H.; Zhang, X.; Li, W.; Wei, H.; Liu, Z. Commensal bacteria direct selective cargo sorting to promote symbiosis. *Nat. Immunol.* **2015**, *16*, 918–926. [CrossRef]

135. Funayama, M.; Hasegawa, K.; Kowa, H.; Saito, M.; Tsuji, S.; Obata, F. A new locus for Parkinson's disease (PARK8) maps to chromosome 12p11.2-q13.1. *Ann. Neurol.* **2002**, *51*, 296–301. [CrossRef]

136. Witoelar, A.; Jansen, I.E.; Wang, Y.; Desikan, R.S.; Gibbs, J.R.; Blauwendraat, C.; Thompson, W.K.; Hernandez, D.G.; Djurovic, S.; Schork, A.J.; et al. Genome-wide Pleiotropy Between Parkinson Disease and Autoimmune Diseases. *JAMA Neurol.* **2017**, *74*, 780–792. [CrossRef]

137. Gehrke, S.; Imai, Y.; Sokol, N.; Lu, B. Pathogenic *LRRK2* negatively regulates microRNA-mediated translational repression. *Nature* **2010**, *466*, 637–641. [CrossRef]

138. Chuang, C.L.; Lu, Y.N.; Wang, H.C.; Chang, H.Y. Genetic dissection reveals that Akt is the critical kinase downstream of LRRK2 to phosphorylate and inhibit FOXO1, and promotes neuron survival. *Hum. Mol. Genet.* **2014**, *23*, 5649–5658. [CrossRef]

139. Tong, Y.; Yamaguchi, H.; Giaime, E.; Boyle, S.; Kopan, R.; Kelleher, R.J., 3rd; Shen, J. Loss of leucine-rich repeat kinase 2 causes impairment of protein degradation pathways, accumulation of alpha-synuclein, and apoptotic cell death in aged mice. *Proc. Natl. Acad. Sci. USA* **2010**, *107*, 9879–9884. [CrossRef]

140. Wang, X. Destructive cellular paths underlying familial and sporadic Parkinson disease converge on mitophagy. *Autophagy* **2017**, *13*, 1998–1999. [CrossRef]

141. Kuss, M.; Adamopoulou, E.; Kahle, P.J. Interferon-gamma induces leucine-rich repeat kinase *LRRK2* via extracellular signal-regulated kinase ERK5 in macrophages. *J. Neurochem.* **2014**, *129*, 980–987. [CrossRef]

142. Cadwell, K.; Patel, K.K.; Komatsu, M.; Virgin, H.W.t.; Stappenbeck, T.S. A common role for Atg16L1, Atg5 and Atg7 in small intestinal Paneth cells and Crohn disease. *Autophagy* **2009**, *5*, 250–252. [CrossRef]

143. Wittkopf, N.; Gunther, C.; Martini, E.; Waldner, M.; Amann, K.U.; Neurath, M.F.; Becker, C. Lack of intestinal epithelial atg7 affects paneth cell granule formation but does not compromise immune homeostasis in the gut. *Clin. Dev. Immunol.* **2012**, *2012*, 278059. [CrossRef]

144. Fujishima, Y.; Nishiumi, S.; Masuda, A.; Inoue, J.; Nguyen, N.M.; Irino, Y.; Komatsu, M.; Tanaka, K.; Kutsumi, H.; Azuma, T.; et al. Autophagy in the intestinal epithelium reduces endotoxin-induced inflammatory responses by inhibiting NF-kappaB activation. *Arch. Biochem. Biophys.* **2011**, *506*, 223–235. [CrossRef]

145. Tsuboi, K.; Nishitani, M.; Takakura, A.; Imai, Y.; Komatsu, M.; Kawashima, H. Autophagy Protects against Colitis by the Maintenance of Normal Gut Microflora and Secretion of Mucus. *J. Biol. Chem.* **2015**, *290*, 20511–20526. [CrossRef]

146. Ortiz-Masia, D.; Cosin-Roger, J.; Calatayud, S.; Hernandez, C.; Alos, R.; Hinojosa, J.; Apostolova, N.; Alvarez, A.; Barrachina, M.D. Hypoxic macrophages impair autophagy in epithelial cells through Wnt1: Relevance in IBD. *Mucosal Immunol.* **2014**, *7*, 929–938. [CrossRef]

147. Till, A.; Lipinski, S.; Ellinghaus, D.; Mayr, G.; Subramani, S.; Rosenstiel, P.; Franke, A. Autophagy receptor CALCOCO2/NDP52 takes center stage in Crohn disease. *Autophagy* **2013**, *9*, 1256–1257. [CrossRef]

148. Ellinghaus, D.; Zhang, H.; Zeissig, S.; Lipinski, S.; Till, A.; Jiang, T.; Stade, B.; Bromberg, Y.; Ellinghaus, E.; Keller, A.; et al. Association between variants of PRDM1 and NDP52 and Crohn's disease, based on exome sequencing and functional studies. *Gastroenterology* **2013**, *145*, 339–347. [CrossRef]

149. Joung, I.; Strominger, J.L.; Shin, J. Molecular cloning of a phosphotyrosine-independent ligand of the p56lck SH2 domain. *Proc. Natl. Acad. Sci. USA* **1996**, *93*, 5991–5995. [CrossRef]

150. Laurin, N.; Brown, J.P.; Morissette, J.; Raymond, V. Recurrent mutation of the gene encoding sequestosome 1 (SQSTM1/p62) in Paget disease of bone. *Am. J. Hum. Genet.* **2002**, *70*, 1582–1588. [CrossRef]

151. Pankiv, S.; Clausen, T.H.; Lamark, T.; Brech, A.; Bruun, J.A.; Outzen, H.; Overvatn, A.; Bjorkoy, G.; Johansen, T. p62/SQSTM1 binds directly to Atg8/LC3 to facilitate degradation of ubiquitinated protein aggregates by autophagy. *J. Biol. Chem.* **2007**, *282*, 24131–24145. [CrossRef]

152. Komatsu, M.; Waguri, S.; Koike, M.; Sou, Y.S.; Ueno, T.; Hara, T.; Mizushima, N.; Iwata, J.; Ezaki, J.; Murata, S.; et al. Homeostatic levels of p62 control cytoplasmic inclusion body formation in autophagy-deficient mice. *Cell* **2007**, *131*, 1149–1163. [CrossRef]

153. Klionsky, D.J.; Abdelmohsen, K.; Abe, A.; Abedin, M.J.; Abeliovich, H.; Acevedo Arozena, A.; Adachi, H.; Adams, C.M.; Adams, P.D.; Adeli, K.; et al. Guidelines for the use and interpretation of assays for monitoring autophagy (3rd edition). *Autophagy* **2016**, *12*, 1–222. [CrossRef]

154. Lippai, M.; Low, P. The role of the selective adaptor p62 and ubiquitin-like proteins in autophagy. *BioMed Res. Int.* **2014**, *2014*, 832704. [CrossRef]

155. Cosin-Roger, J.; Simmen, S.; Melhem, H.; Atrott, K.; Frey-Wagner, I.; Hausmann, M.; de Valliere, C.; Spalinger, M.R.; Spielmann, P.; Wenger, R.H.; et al. Hypoxia ameliorates intestinal inflammation through NLRP3/mTOR downregulation and autophagy activation. *Nat. Commun.* **2017**, *8*, 98. [CrossRef]

156. Paiva, N.M.; Pascoal, L.B.; Negreiros, L.M.V.; Portovedo, M.; Coope, A.; Ayrizono, M.L.S.; Coy, C.S.R.; Milanski, M.; Leal, R.F. Ileal pouch of ulcerative colitis and familial adenomatous polyposis patients exhibit modulation of autophagy markers. *Sci. Rep.* **2018**, *8*, 2619. [CrossRef]

157. Mimouna, S.; Bazin, M.; Mograbi, B.; Darfeuille-Michaud, A.; Brest, P.; Hofman, P.; Vouret-Craviari, V. HIF1A regulates xenophagic degradation of adherent and invasive Escherichia coli (AIEC). *Autophagy* **2014**, *10*, 2333–2345. [CrossRef]

158. Sundaramoorthy, V.; Walker, A.K.; Tan, V.; Fifita, J.A.; McCann, E.P.; Williams, K.L.; Blair, I.P.; Guillemin, G.J.; Farg, M.A.; Atkin, J.D. Defects in optineurin- and myosin VI-mediated cellular trafficking in amyotrophic lateral sclerosis. *Hum. Mol. Genet.* **2017**, *26*, 3452. [CrossRef]

159. Ying, H.; Yue, B.Y. Optineurin: The autophagy connection. *Exp. Eye Res.* **2016**, *144*, 73–80. [CrossRef]

160. Ryan, T.A.; Tumbarello, D.A. Optineurin: A Coordinator of Membrane-Associated Cargo Trafficking and Autophagy. *Front. Immunol.* **2018**, *9*, 1024. [CrossRef]

161. Albagha, O.M.; Visconti, M.R.; Alonso, N.; Langston, A.L.; Cundy, T.; Dargie, R.; Dunlop, M.G.; Fraser, W.D.; Hooper, M.J.; Isaia, G.; et al. Genome-wide association study identifies variants at CSF1, OPTN and TNFRSF11A as genetic risk factors for Paget's disease of bone. *Nat. Genet.* **2010**, *42*, 520–524. [CrossRef] [PubMed]

162. Chung, P.Y.; Beyens, G.; Boonen, S.; Papapoulos, S.; Geusens, P.; Karperien, M.; Vanhoenacker, F.; Verbruggen, L.; Fransen, E.; Van Offel, J.; et al. The majority of the genetic risk for Paget's disease of bone is explained by genetic variants close to the CSF1, OPTN, TM7SF4, and TNFRSF11A genes. *Hum. Genet.* **2010**, *128*, 615–626. [CrossRef] [PubMed]

163. Maruyama, H.; Morino, H.; Ito, H.; Izumi, Y.; Kato, H.; Watanabe, Y.; Kinoshita, Y.; Kamada, M.; Nodera, H.; Suzuki, H.; et al. Mutations of optineurin in amyotrophic lateral sclerosis. *Nature* **2010**, *465*, 223–226. [CrossRef] [PubMed]

164. Whitworth, A.J.; Pallanck, L.J. PINK1/Parkin mitophagy and neurodegeneration-what do we really know in vivo? *Curr. Opin. Genet. Dev.* **2017**, *44*, 47–53. [CrossRef] [PubMed]

165. Puri, M.; La Pietra, L.; Mraheil, M.A.; Lucas, R.; Chakraborty, T.; Pillich, H. Listeriolysin O Regulates the Expression of Optineurin, an Autophagy Adaptor That Inhibits the Growth of Listeria monocytogenes. *Toxins (Basel)* **2017**, *9*, 273. [CrossRef] [PubMed]

166. Settembre, C.; Di Malta, C.; Polito, V.A.; Garcia Arencibia, M.; Vetrini, F.; Erdin, S.; Erdin, S.U.; Huynh, T.; Medina, D.; Colella, P.; et al. TFEB links autophagy to lysosomal biogenesis. *Science* **2011**, *332*, 1429–1433. [CrossRef] [PubMed]

167. Sardiello, M.; Palmieri, M.; di Ronza, A.; Medina, D.L.; Valenza, M.; Gennarino, V.A.; Di Malta, C.; Donaudy, F.; Embrione, V.; Polishchuk, R.S.; et al. A gene network regulating lysosomal biogenesis and function. *Science* **2009**, *325*, 473–477. [CrossRef]

168. Napolitano, G.; Ballabio, A. TFEB at a glance. *J. Cell Sci.* **2016**, *129*, 2475–2481. [CrossRef] [PubMed]

169. Palmieri, M.; Impey, S.; Kang, H.; di Ronza, A.; Pelz, C.; Sardiello, M.; Ballabio, A. Characterization of the CLEAR network reveals an integrated control of cellular clearance pathways. *Hum. Mol. Genet.* **2011**, *20*, 3852–3866. [CrossRef] [PubMed]

170. Decressac, M.; Mattsson, B.; Weikop, P.; Lundblad, M.; Jakobsson, J.; Bjorklund, A. TFEB-mediated autophagy rescues midbrain dopamine neurons from alpha-synuclein toxicity. *Proc. Natl. Acad. Sci. USA* **2013**, *110*, E1817–E1826. [CrossRef] [PubMed]

171. Martini-Stoica, H.; Xu, Y.; Ballabio, A.; Zheng, H. The Autophagy-Lysosomal Pathway in Neurodegeneration: A TFEB Perspective. *Trends Neurosci.* **2016**, *39*, 221–234. [CrossRef] [PubMed]

172. Polito, V.A.; Li, H.; Martini-Stoica, H.; Wang, B.; Yang, L.; Xu, Y.; Swartzlander, D.B.; Palmieri, M.; di Ronza, A.; Lee, V.M.; et al. Selective clearance of aberrant tau proteins and rescue of neurotoxicity by transcription factor EB. *EMBO Mol. Med.* **2014**, *6*, 1142–1160. [CrossRef] [PubMed]

MDPI

St. Alban-Anlage 66

4052 Basel

Switzerland

Tel. +41 61 683 77 34

Fax +41 61 302 89 18

www.mdpi.com

Cells Editorial Office

E-mail: cells@mdpi.com

www.mdpi.com/journal/cells